UPGRADING AND REPAIRING MICROSOFT WINDOWS

Scott Mueller
Brian Knittel

Contents at a Glance

800 East 96th Street,
Indianapolis, Indiana 46240

Upgrading and Repairing Microsoft Windows

International Standard Book Number: 0-7897-3403-6

Library of Congress Catalog Card Number: 2005924994

Printed in the United States of America

First Printing: December 2005

08   07   06   05   4   3   2   1

Trademarks

All terms mentioned in this book that are known to be trademarks or service marks have been appropriately capitalized. Que cannot attest to the accuracy of this information. Use of a term in this book should not be regarded as affecting the validity of any trademark or service mark.

Warning and Disclaimer

Every effort has been made to make this book as complete and as accurate as possible, but no warranty or fitness is implied. The information provided is on an "as is" basis. The authors and the publisher shall have neither liability nor responsibility to any person or entity with respect to any loss or damages arising from the information contained in this book or from the use of the DVD or programs accompanying it.

Bulk Sales

Que offers excellent discounts on this book when ordered in quantity for bulk purchases or special sales. For more information, please contact

U.S. Corporate and Government Sales
1-800-382-3419
corpsales@pearsontechgroup.com

For sales outside of the U.S., please contact

International Sales
international@pearsoned.com

Associate Publisher
Greg Wiegand

Acquisitions Editor
Todd Green

Development Editor
Todd Brakke

Managing Editor
Charlotte Clapp

Project Editor
Andy Beaster

Copy Editor
Kate Givens

Indexer
Aaron Black

Proofreader
Paula Lowell

Technical Editors
Mark Reddin
David Eytchison

Publishing Coordinator
Sharry Lee Gregory

Multimedia Developer
Dan Scherf

Book Designer
Anne Jones

Page Layout
Julie Parks

DVD Production
Lynn Mueller

Contents

To Lynn:

Your artistry, skill, tenacity, and intelligence still blow me away, even after all these years!

—Scott Mueller

About the Authors and Contributors

Scott Mueller is president of Mueller Technical Research (MTR), an international research and corporate training firm. Since 1982, MTR has produced the industry's most in-depth, accurate, and effective seminars, books, articles, videos, and FAQs covering PC hardware and data recovery. MTR maintains a client list that includes Fortune 500 companies, the U.S. and foreign governments, major software and hardware corporations, as well as PC enthusiasts and entrepreneurs. His seminars have been presented to several thousands of PC support professionals throughout the world.

Scott is best known as the author of the longest running, most popular, and most comprehensive PC hardware book in the world, *Upgrading and Repairing PCs*, which has not only been produced in more than 16 editions, but has also become the core of an entire series of books.

Scott has authored many books over the last 20+ years, including *Upgrading and Repairing PCs*, 1st through 16th and Academic editions; *Upgrading and Repairing Laptops*, 1st and 2nd editions; *Upgrading and Repairing PCs: A+ Certification Study Guide*, 1st and 2nd editions; *Upgrading and Repairing PCs Field Guide*; *Killer PC Utilities*; *The IBM PS/2 Handbook*; and *Que's Guide to Data Recovery*.

Contact MTR directly if you have a unique book, article, or video project in mind, or if you want Scott to conduct a custom PC troubleshooting, repair, maintenance, upgrade, or data-recovery seminar tailored for your organization:

> Mueller Technical Research
> 3700 Grayhawk Drive
> Algonquin, IL 60102-6325
> 847-854-6794
> 847-854-6795 Fax
> Email: scottmueller@compuserve.com
> Web: http://www.upgradingandrepairingpcs.com

Scott's premiere work, *Upgrading and Repairing PCs*, has sold well over 2 million copies, making it by far the most popular and longest-running PC hardware book on the market today. Scott has been featured in *Forbes* magazine and has written several articles for *Maximum PC* magazine, several newsletters, and the Upgrading and Repairing PCs website.

If you have suggestions for the next edition of this book, any comments about the book in general, or new book or article topics you would like to see covered, send them to Scott via email at scottmueller@compuserve.com or visit www.upgradingandrepairingpcs.com.

When he is not working on PC-related books or on the road teaching seminars, Scott can usually be found in the garage working on several vehicular projects, currently including a 1999 Harley-Davidson FLHRCI Road King Classic and a 1989 Pontiac 20th Anniversary Turbo Trans Am (www.89tta.com).

Brian Knittel has been a software developer for nearly 30 years. After doing graduate work in medical imaging technologies, he began a career as an independent consultant. An eclectic mix of clients has led to long-term projects in medical documentation, workflow management, real-time industrial system control, and most importantly, more than 15 years of real-world experience with MS-DOS, Windows, and computer networking in the business world. He is the author of *Windows XP Under the Hood: Hardcore Scripting and Command Line Power*, and is co-author of several other Que books including *Special Edition Using Microsoft Windows* editions covering XP Home, XP Professional, and Windows 2000 Professional. Brian lives in Albany, California, halfway between the tidal wave zone and the earthquake fault. He spends his free time snowboarding, restoring antique computers (check out www.ibm1130.org), and trying to perfect his wood-fired pizza recipes.

Robert Cowart has written or co-written more than 40 books on computer programming and applications, with more than a dozen on Windows. His titles include *Windows NT Unleashed*, *Mastering Windows* (3.0, 3.1, 95, 98, and Me), *Windows NT Server Administrator's Bible*, *Windows NT Server 4.0: No Experience Required*, and *Special Edition Using Microsoft Windows* editions covering XP Home, XP Professional, and Windows 2000 Professional. Several of his books have been bestsellers in their categories, and have been translated into more than 20 languages. He has written on a wide range of computer-related topics for such magazines as *PC Week, PC World, PC Magazine, PC Tech Journal, Mac World*, and *Microsoft Systems Journal*. He has taught programming classes at the University of California Extension in San Francisco and has appeared as a special guest on the PBS TV series *Computer Chronicles*, CNN's *Headline News*, TechTV's *The Screen Savers*, and ABC's *World News Tonight with Peter Jennings*. He is president and co-founder of Brainsville.com, a company specializing in the production of multimedia training courses. Robert resides in Berkeley, California. In his spare time, he is involved in the music world, presenting chamber-music concerts and playing classical piano. He also is a teacher of the Transcendental Meditation technique.

Mark Reddin is a Microsoft Certified Systems Engineer (MCSE) and A+ Certified PC technician. In his younger days he enjoyed tinkering with computers during the time of the early Commodore and Atari systems (with all those wonderful games). Mark delved more seriously into computer technology during his undergraduate studies at Ball State University and has since been involved in the industry in various capacities. His experience with computers and networks has ranged from consulting to owning and operating a sales and repair shop. Additionally, he has been involved as both a technical and development editor with numerous Que publications over the last few years, including *Upgrading and Repairing PCs* and *How Computers Work*.

Don Poulton has been involved with computers since the days of 80-column punch cards. After a career of more than 20 years in environmental science, Don switched careers and trained as a Windows NT 4.0 MCSE. He has been involved in consulting with a couple of small training providers as a technical writer, during which time he wrote training and exam prep materials for Windows NT 4.0, Windows 2000, and Windows XP. He has worked on programming projects, both in his days as an environmental scientist, and more recently with Visual Basic to update an older statistical package used for multivariate analysis of sediment contaminants.

In the past two years, Don has authored or co-authored *MCSE Windows Server 2003 Active Directory Infrastructure* (70-294), *Exam Cram 2 Implementing and Administering Security in a Windows Server 2003 Network* (Exam 70-299), *Exam Cram 2 Security+ Lab Manual* (Exam SYO-101), and *MCSE/MCSA Exam Prep Installing, Configuring, and Administering Microsoft Windows XP Professional* (Exam 70-270). When not working on computers, Don is an avid amateur photographer who has had his photos displayed in international competitions and published in magazines like *Michigan Natural Resources Magazine* and *National Geographic Traveler*. Don also enjoys traveling and keeping fit. He lives in Burlington, Ontario with his wife Terry.

Aaron Axline is a communications expert, technical writer/editor, and IT project manager specializing in knowledge management and electronic documentation. A professional writer since 1991, Aaron has had more than 800 articles and columns published in print and online. Aaron's last assignment for Que Publishing was as technical editor on the *IT Certification Success Exam Cram 2* title. His laptop is a Dell Inspiron 8100, but he secretly yearns for an Apple PowerBook G4. Aaron makes his home in Edmonton, Alberta, Canada.

Steve Sinchak is a bestselling author, Microsoft MVP, and President of Steve Sinchak Media, LLC. His primary claim to fame was his website, www.TweakXP.com, which provides visitors information on tweaking and customizing every aspect of Microsoft Windows XP as well as free help and advice for all types of Windows problems. Since then, his company has started similar websites for Microsoft Windows Media Center Edition (www.TweakMCE.com) and Microsoft Windows Vista (www.TweakVista.com). Aside from running tech-related websites, Steve used his expertise in tweaking and customizing all aspects of Windows to write the bestselling book *Hacking Windows XP*.

Acknowledgments

Several people have helped me with both the research and production of this book. I would like to thank the following people: First, a very special thanks to my wife and partner, Lynn. A few years ago she returned to school full time, in addition to helping to run our business. She recently graduated with full honors (congratulations!), receiving a degree in Multimedia and Web Design. I'm extremely proud of her, as well as all I've seen her accomplish in the past few years. The dedication she has shown to her schoolwork has been inspiring.

Thanks to Lisa Carlson of Mueller Technical Research for helping with product research and office management. She has fantastic organizational skills that have been a tremendous help in managing all the information that comes into and goes out of this office.

I'd like to thank both Todd Green for his drive to publish this book and the work he did keeping me on task and Todd Brakke for doing the development editing for this project. His excellent tips and suggestions really help to keep the material concise and up to date. I'd also like to thank Andy Beaster and Kate Givens, who also worked on the editing for this book, as well as all the illustrators, designers, and technicians at Que who worked so hard to complete the finished product and get this book out the door! The people at Que are a wonderful team that produce clearly the best computer books on the market. I am happy and proud to be closely associated with Que.

I would like to say thanks also to my publisher Greg Wiegand, who has stood behind all the *Upgrading and Repairing* book and video projects and is willing to take the risks in developing new versions, such as this *Windows* and upcoming *Server* editions.

Greg, the Todds, and the rest all make me feel as if we are on the same team, and they are just as dedicated as I am to producing the best books possible.

Thanks to all the readers who have emailed me with suggestions; I welcome all your comments and even your criticisms. I take them seriously and apply them to the continuous improvement of my books. I especially enjoy answering the many questions you send me; your questions help me to understand areas that might need to be clarified, as well as to point out additional coverage that should be added.

Finally, I would like to thank the thousands of people who have attended my seminars; you might not realize how much I learn from each of you and all your questions!

—Scott Mueller

We Want to Hear from You!

As the reader of this book, *you* are our most important critic and commentator. We value your opinion and want to know what we're doing right, what we could do better, what areas you would like to see us publish in, and any other words of wisdom you're willing to pass our way.

As an associate publisher for Que, I welcome your comments. You can email or write me directly to let me know what you did or didn't like about this book—as well as what we can do to make our books better.

Please note that I cannot help you with technical problems related to the topic of this book. We do have a User Services group, however, where I will forward specific technical questions related to the book.

When you write, please be sure to include this book's title and author as well as your name, email address, and phone number. I will carefully review your comments and share them with the author and editors who worked on the book.

Email: feedback@quepublishing.com

Mail: Greg Wiegand
            Associate Publisher
            Que Publishing
            800 East 96th Street
            Indianapolis, IN 46240 USA

For more information about this book or another Que title, visit our website at www.quepublishing.com. Type the ISBN (excluding hyphens) or the title of a book in the Search field to find the page you're looking for.

Introduction

Welcome to *Upgrading and Repairing Microsoft Windows*. This is the book for people who want to know more about how to use and support Microsoft Windows than most other books dare to detail. Whether you want to install, manage, or troubleshoot the Windows operating system this book goes far deeper than just the basics. Whether you support a large network of Windows machines, a few Windows PCs in a small office/home office environment, or just a single at-home system, this book can quickly turn you into an advanced Windows power user.

Is This Book for You?

Upgrading and Repairing Microsoft Windows is designed for people who want a thorough understanding of Windows and how it works without wasting time and pages on endless handholding through basic, everyday tasks. Each section fully explains management and troubleshooting issues related to Windows, including user management, networking, and security issues. Over the course of this book you'll develop a feel for what goes on behind the stylish graphical user interface so you can rely on your own judgment and observations and not some table of canned troubleshooting steps.

Upgrading and Repairing Microsoft Windows is written for people who will install, configure, maintain, and repair systems they use personally or in a corporate environment. To accomplish these tasks, you need a level of knowledge much higher than that of an average system user. You must know exactly which tool to use for a task and how to use the tool correctly. This book can help you achieve this level of knowledge.

Chapter-by-Chapter Breakdown

Chapter 1, "Windows Version History," examines the very beginnings of PC operating systems from DOS all the way through Windows XP Service Pack 2. Microsoft operating systems have had quite a wild ride over the years and it's amazing to see how the operating system most of us use every day has become what it is.

Chapter 2, "Installing Windows," explains procedures and issues regarding the preparation and installation of Windows XP. It includes detailed steps for baseline installations for single desktops as well as in a more complex networked environment.

Chapter 3, "Upgrading Windows," discusses how to perform an upgrade Windows XP installation from an older version of Windows. You look at paths for upgrading Windows 98 and Windows NT/2000 to Windows XP as well as upgrading Windows XP Home to Windows XP Pro, including two methods for migrating user settings and documents to new Windows XP computers.

Chapter 4, "Windows Startup," details the Windows startup process, including what takes place between power-up and the appearance of the Welcome screen. In addition, it includes detailed information about Windows Services, which are processes that run in the "background" to provide support for Windows networking, searching, authentication, and management.

In Chapter 5, "Managing Windows," we cover the most important Windows management functions: adding and managing user accounts, hardware, device drivers, and hard disks. In addition, Chapter 5 gets down and dirty with Windows Backup, showing you how make essential backups of your precious data and how to restore those backups should the data on your hard drive be lost or corrupted.

Chapter 6, "Tweaking and Tuning Windows," shows you how to configure Windows for peak performance and usability, using the Windows configuration dialogs and special-purpose tools like TweakUI and the Registry Editor. In addition, we'll give you a checklist you can use to identify and fix the most common Windows performance bottlenecks.

Chapter 7, "Networking Windows," tells you how to configure Windows XP to run a reliable and secure network at home or at the office. Whether you have two computers or two hundred, a network can immediately pay for itself—many times over—by letting you share printers, giving you access to files from any computer, and letting you share a single Internet connection among several computers. This chapter also shows you how to set up Windows XP Professional's Remote Desktop feature so that you can access your computer from anywhere in the world.

Chapter 8, "Protecting and Securing Windows," covers the steps you can take to ensure your Windows XP PC is well protected from outside intrusion. Have you lost your administrator account password? Would you like some help protecting your computer from spyware and viruses? We'll help you learn how to recover lost passwords, use firewalls to block intruders, and protect your computer from viruses, spyware, and trojans. Learn how to take an active approach to security and harden your existing security to stop attacks before they start.

In Chapter 9, "Windows Commands and Scripting," we cover Windows scripting essentials and the oft-forgotten-but-highly-useful world of the command prompt. The command prompt environment not only runs old MS-DOS programs, but also gives you access to a large number of efficient, concise, and powerful Windows management and operating tools. The chapter covers the general principles of command-line programs, configuration settings, and several important commands, as well as scripting and batch file procedures that you can use to automate complex jobs.

Chapter 10, "Windows File Systems," covers file systems. If you're a Windows XP user deciding whether to switch to NTFS, or if you just want to know everything there is to know about the FAT file system, this is the place to look.

Chapter 11, "Windows Data Recovery," covers data recovery procedures. If you can't access your drive because of a corrupted master boot record (MBR) or volume boot record (VBR), you'll find information you can use to recover these sectors and regain access to your valuable data.

Chapter 12, "Windows Troubleshooting," looks at some of the more common problems encountered with Windows. Troubleshooting software is one part skill, one part craft, and one part knowing where to look for information. In this chapter, you'll look at how to identify Windows problems, and what tools and methods you should use to solve them. This chapter includes an extensive look at how to deal with a system that cannot stably boot, and how to use both the System Restore feature and the arcane but powerful Recovery Console when you can't even log into your user account.

Appendix A, "Windows Tool Reference," describes several useful categories of Windows management, maintenance, configuration, monitoring, and data processing tools that you may not be familiar with. Many of them are not installed by Windows Setup but instead are hidden away in obscure folders on your Windows Setup CD-ROM. Several more are available from Microsoft via free download over the Internet, and some others must be purchased. In any case, we think you should know about them.

Appendix B, "Windows Command Reference," lists all the executable programs provided with Windows 95, 98, Me, 2000, and the various versions of XP, including application programs, services, system components, built-in commands, control panel applets, MMC Management snap-ins, and screen savers. You can browse this listing to find useful programs you might not be familiar with, or to help identify the many obscure programs that are run automatically by Windows.

Getting the Most From This Book

Upgrading and Repairing Microsoft Windows is not a book that you read through once and never touch again. In fact, this is not a book that needs to be read straight through at all, although any Windows user will learn a great deal from doing just that.

This book is, in fact, a detailed and valuable reference that should be kept next to your PC (and your copy of the latest edition of *Upgrading and Repairing PCs*) at all times. The information shoehorned into every line of every page of this tome will help you put Windows to work the way it was meant to and keep it running for the long term.

Scott's Website— www.upgradingandrepairingpcs.com

Don't miss my book web site at www.upgradingandrepairingpcs.com! Here, you'll find a cache of helpful material to go along with the book you're holding. I've loaded this site with tons of material, from video clips to monthly book updates. I use this spot to keep you updated throughout the year on major changes in both the PC hardware industry and the evolution of Windows. Each month, I write new articles covering new technologies released after this book was printed. These articles are archived so you can refer to them anytime.

I also use this site to post your reader questions and my answers. The Frequently Asked Questions (FAQ) is a tremendous resource because you benefit from the hundreds of reader emails I answer each month. Log on and post a question. I endeavor to answer each and every email personally.

You'll also find exclusive video clips available nowhere else!

I also use this site to tell you about some of the other fantastic *Upgrading and Repairing PCs* products, including

- *Upgrading and Repairing PCs*
- *Upgrading and Repairing Laptops*
- *Upgrading and Repairing Servers*
- *Upgrading and Repairing Networks*

Laptops have become the largest growing segment of PCs, and my new book *Upgrading and Repairing Laptops, 2nd Edition* covers these systems in great detail. Meanwhile, *Upgrading and Repairing Servers* (available by Q2 2006) promises to be the only book of its kind that will help you understand the complex world of server computing and just how much these computers differ from your average desktop. Be sure to check the upgradingandrepairingpcs.com website for more information on all my latest books, videos, articles, FAQs, and more!

CHAPTER 1

Windows Version History

A Brief History of PC Operating Systems

Microsoft Windows has evolved considerably since it was first introduced in 1985. As is typical for evolutionary processes, its progress has been uneven and not always in the forward direction (Windows Me comes to mind). Still, despite the occasional misstep and an antitrust suit or two along the way, Windows today is mostly reliable, reasonably easy to use, and completely ubiquitous.

To give you a picture of where we are now, today's typical computer owner has a machine that scarcely 15 years ago would have been near the top of the list of the world's most powerful computers. And while the original PCs were able to fit an operating system, application software, and user data onto a 160KB single-sided floppy disk, a default Windows XP installation occupies approximately 2GB of disk space even before any user data or application software is added. This is a staggering amount of software! In fact, it's more than a typical IBM mainframe computer has, and mainframe software maintenance is a career in itself, requiring months if not years of training.

The fact that it is possible for anyone but a career computer engineer to use, manage, maintain, upgrade and repair a Windows PC is something of a minor miracle, mostly the result of two decades of effort by hardware manufacturers, software vendors and Microsoft to incorporate a lot of that career engineer's knowledge into software that—to a large extent—can take care of itself. Still, there is a lot left for the user to take care of—that's why you purchased this book.

To get a clearer picture what Windows is now, it's useful to see how it evolved. In this chapter, we'll go through its history and examine its roots, which reach back well before the introduction of the PC as we know it today.

DOS History

A discussion of the different versions of Windows cannot be complete without also talking about DOS. This is because early Windows versions were an add-on or extension to DOS, and actually required DOS to be preinstalled on a system in order to run. Later Windows versions included DOS internally, which was gradually minimized until virtually all of the legacy 16-bit DOS and Windows code was replaced by entirely new 32-bit and 64-bit code in Windows NT, Windows 2000, and later.

Before Windows existed, MS-DOS was the most popular operating system for PCs, and DOS continued to be the most popular OS from 1981 when the PC was introduced until well after 1995 and the appearance of Windows 95. All versions of Windows before Windows 95 actually required MS-DOS to be preinstalled on the system because many of those earlier versions of Windows were more of a DOS graphical user interface extension than a complete standalone operating system. And although Windows 95, 98, and Me were sold as standalone operating systems (no prior DOS required), they actually included MS-DOS and used portions of 16-bit DOS code. Windows 95 included MS-DOS 7.0, Windows 95B and 98 included MS-DOS 7.1, and Windows Me included MS-DOS 8.0.

Windows NT was the first truly standalone fully 32-bit version of Windows that wasn't based on MS-DOS. Because Windows 2000 and XP are the successors of Windows NT, they are also not based on MS-DOS or 16-bit code in any way.

Even though later versions of Windows aren't based on MS-DOS or include 16-bit code in the internal workings, in many ways DOS still plays a role in running certain diagnostic or utility programs, or especially when partitioning and formatting certain types of disks and drives. For example, when you format a floppy disk as a bootable "system" disk in Windows XP by checking the Create an MS-DOS Startup Disk option, Windows XP automatically copies the MS-DOS 8.0 system files to the disk at the completion of the formatting process.

Evolution of DOS

When the IBM PC was announced on August 12, 1981, IBM indicated that three operating systems would be available for their new PC. They were

- IBM Personal Computer Disk Operating System ($40)
- Digital Research CP/M-86 ($240)
- SofTech USCD p-System w/Pascal ($695)

Of those three operating systems, only the IBM Personal Computer Disk Operating System (normally abbreviated as PC DOS, or just DOS) was immediately available. The other two operating systems weren't available until several months later, and were priced significantly higher as well. As you can imagine, due to both availability and price, it was pretty clear that the PC DOS operating system would be the one used by most people on their new PCs.

Although PC DOS was marketed and sold by IBM as an IBM product, most people know that Microsoft actually supplied the core code of PC DOS to IBM in the form of MS-DOS. What many people don't know is that Microsoft first licensed, and then purchased MS-DOS from another company called Seattle Computer Products. One could say that Seattle Computer, Microsoft, and IBM were all intimately involved in the early development and evolution of DOS; however, when you go back far enough, PC DOS owes its existence primarily to one man.

From 1978 through 1980 Tim Paterson worked for a small company called Seattle Computer Products (SCP) developing computer hardware and software products. In June of 1978 Intel introduced the 8086 processor, and shortly thereafter Paterson designed an S-100 bus computer system using the 8086 for SCP. The hardware consisted of three S-100 cards; a CPU card, CPU support card, and a memory card. These cards were designed to be installed in an S-100 chassis, and would then operate together as a complete 8086 computer system.

At that time Microsoft's BASIC-80 (Beginners All-purpose Symbolic Instruction Code for the 8080 processor) was one of the most popular programming languages for microcomputers, so it was only natural to port that language to the new 8086 processor. In May 1979 Paterson spent a week at Microsoft working with a programmer named Bob O'Rear to port Microsoft BASIC-80 to the new SCP 8086 system. The result was Microsoft BASIC-86, one of the first software packages available for the 8086 processor. BASIC-80 and BASIC-86 were unique at the time in that they included a built-in File Allocation Table (FAT) file system originally written by Bill Gates. This meant that they could run standalone; that is, with no operating system or other software required. Both the 8086 computer system and Microsoft BASIC-86 were completed and sold by Seattle Computer starting in November 1979.

While BASIC-86 would run standalone on the new 8086 computer, other languages would require an operating system in order to run. At the time Microsoft had been selling FORTRAN and COBOL for CP/M systems using the Intel 8080 processor, and it wanted to port those operating systems to run in the 8086 like BASIC. Unfortunately that would not be possible without an operating system.

At the time, Digital Research's CP/M (Control Program for Microcomputers) was by far the most popular operating system for microcomputers, and everybody including Microsoft and SCP expected Digital Research to port CP/M over to the new 8086 processor. Unfortunately Digital Research was taking too long, so in April of 1980 Paterson got tired of waiting, and decided to write his own DOS for the 8086, calling it QDOS for Quick and Dirty Operating System. QDOS 0.11 was first released by Seattle Computer Products in August 1980. Paterson continued improving and refining QDOS, which SCP renamed 86-DOS and released in December 1980 as 86-DOS 0.33.

During the summer of 1980 IBM began working on Project Chess, which was the codename for the top-secret IBM PC project. Needing software for its new machine, IBM approached Microsoft to provide BASIC (Beginners All-purpose Symbolic Instruction Code), FORTRAN (FORmula TRANslation), and COBOL (COmmon Business Oriented Language) for the PC. However, before IBM would divulge the details about the secret project, it required that Microsoft sign a very strict non-disclosure agreement. Once the agreement was signed, IBM discussed details about the new system. Original plans apparently called for an 8-bit processor; however, Bill Gates pushed for IBM to use the new 16-bit Intel 8086 instead, which would allow access to up to 1GB of RAM instead of the 64KB limit imposed by 8-bit processors. IBM ended up settling on the Intel 8088, which was essentially a lower-cost version of the 8086 that ran 8086 software.

Then the discussions turned to an operating system. Microsoft knew that BASIC-86 could run stand-alone on the new system, but Microsoft's other languages were designed to run under Digital Research's CP/M-80 operating system. IBM asked Microsoft if it could provide an OS as well, but that was a major undertaking, and Microsoft knew that Digital Research had already been working on CP/M-86. If DR could provide CP/M-86, then Microsoft could port its languages over and meet the tight IBM deadlines. So Microsoft told IBM to visit Digital Research and talk to them about CP/M-86 for the new PC.

Legend has it that when IBM went to visit Digital Research, Gary Kildall (the author of CP/M and principal of the company) stood them up and was out flying his plane. The truth is that Kildall was more of a programmer than a businessman, and he usually left his wife Dorothy McEwen in charge of any business dealings at DR, and the IBM meeting was no exception. The problem wasn't Kildall's presence so much as it was the restrictive non-disclosure agreement. When IBM presented DR with the same non-disclosure agreement that Microsoft had already signed, McEwen and the DR attorneys thought that the terms of the agreement were too strict and they refused to sign. Without a signed agreement, IBM could not divulge any information about their secret PC, so the deal with DR for CP/M-86 was essentially dead in the water.

At this point Microsoft realized that any delays in IBM finding an operating system for the new PC could give IBM reason to cancel the entire project, and consequently Microsoft's deal to provide the languages. In late September of 1980 Microsoft principals Bill Gates, Paul Allen, Steve Ballmer, and Kay Nishi met and decided that they should take the risk and try to provide not only the languages that IBM wanted for the new PC, but also the operating system as well. The problem was that they didn't have the time or manpower to develop a completely new operating system from scratch along with porting over their languages. Microsoft knew it needed a ready-made 8086 operating system, and from their past dealings with Tim Paterson at Seattle Computer Products, they knew just where to get one.

Microsoft made a call to SCP and quickly licensed 86-DOS for unlimited use by a "secret customer" for a one-time fee of $25,000, and in turn licensed the DOS to IBM for a one-time unlimited use fee of $80,000. Although this made a profit for Microsoft, to IBM this was quite a bargain, and would allow IBM to charge a relatively low fee for the operating system to its customers. In consideration of the low license fee, Microsoft bargained to retain the rights to license the operating system to other manufacturers as well. Microsoft believed it could make MS-DOS the industry standard for all PCs based on the 8086 or 8088 processor, and this type of deal would allow Microsoft to retain control over DOS. IBM and Microsoft signed what would probably become the most important deal in computer history on November 6, 1980.

Paterson continued work on 86-DOS at SCP, while at Microsoft Robert O'Rear took the code from Paterson and began modifying it to work on the prototype PC they had been sent. In April 1981 SCP released 86-DOS 1.0, and the very next month Paterson left SCP and was hired by Microsoft to work full time getting 86-DOS ready for Microsoft's still-secret customer. Although there were suspicions, it wasn't until Paterson arrived for work at Microsoft that he knew for sure the secret customer was IBM. Now at Microsoft, Paterson worked once again with Bob O'Rear, cleaning up the code and fulfilling IBM's demands for quality and features. They worked closely with several people at IBM, including David Bradley who was responsible for writing the ROM BIOS code used in the PC. Paterson and O'Rear finished the core of what IBM would call the Personal Computer DOS (also called PC DOS) 1.0 in July 1980. IBM also wrote several additional utility programs to go with DOS 1.0, including the MODE, COMP, DISKCOMP, and DISKCOPY commands, as well as several demo programs in BASIC.

On July 27, 1981 (just over 2 weeks before the IBM PC and the new DOS would be officially introduced) Microsoft decided it would be best if it closed up any loose ends by purchasing 86-DOS outright from SCP for $50,000, thus giving Microsoft full ownership. One condition of the sale was that SCP could retain a perpetual royalty-free license to MS-DOS for themselves. This license would later result in a legal battle that was eventually settled in 1986, with Microsoft paying SCP another $975,000 to purchase that license back. This meant that Microsoft essentially paid SCP just over $1 million dollars total for full ownership of MS-DOS, a very wise investment when you consider that in June of 1986 Microsoft estimated that half of their $61 million annual revenue came from MS-DOS licensing. MS-DOS licensing eventually turned into a multi-billion dollar cash cow for Microsoft.

The IBM PC and PC DOS 1.0 were officially introduced on August 12, 1981, kicking off a family of personal computers that today we simply call PCs. Meanwhile, Paterson continued working at Microsoft on PC DOS 1.1 (which was called MS-DOS 1.25 by Microsoft). PC DOS 1.1 was released in June 1982 along with double-sided floppy drives for the PC. DOS 1.1 was also the first version licensed by Microsoft to other PC OEMs (Original Equipment Manufacturers) as MS-DOS 1.25. One of the first PC-compatible systems with MS-DOS was the Columbia Dataproducts Computer in July 1982, but many others soon followed.

Microsoft licensed MS-DOS to any OEM who wanted to make a system compatible with IBM, which eventually made Microsoft the largest software company in the world. While Windows is by far the most popular OS for PCs today, it wasn't until Windows 95 came out in 1995 that Windows went from being a loss-leader to becoming a huge hit. You could say that up until the release of Windows 95, MS-DOS paid all the bills.

After finishing PC DOS 1.1 (also known as MS-DOS 1.25) and doing initial planning on PC DOS 2.0, Paterson left Microsoft on April 1, 1982 and went back to work at Seattle Computer Products, while Mark Zbikowski took over the development of DOS at Microsoft. DOS 2.0 was virtually a complete rewrite of DOS and introduced many new features including hard disk support, hierarchical directories, and installable device drivers. Zbikowski also designed the executable (*.EXE) file format used in MS-DOS, and used his own initials as the two-byte signature "MZ" (4D5Ah) which can be found at the start of all *.EXE files. IBM wrote and added several utilities of its own including FDISK, TREE, BACKUP/RESTORE, COMP, DISKCOMP, DISKCOPY, MODE, and GRAPHICS, and the final product was eventually released by IBM as PC DOS 2.0 on March 8, 1983.

Paterson eventually left SCP again and went back to work at Microsoft; in fact, he worked for Microsoft at least three times: '81–'82, '86–'88, and '90–'98. Besides his initial work on DOS, Paterson worked on other projects such as Visual Basic and Java. Today Paterson runs his own company called Paterson Technology (www.patersontech.com). In 2001 Paterson gained additional fame as he built the "Hexidecimator" robot, which competed on the *BattleBots* TV show.

MS-DOS Versus PC DOS

With modern PCs having a very high level of standardization and compatibility, today it is easy to see how Microsoft can market complete packaged operating systems that will install and work unmodified on practically any PC you can purchase or build. Without the standardization and compatibility we have come to depend on, different specific "flavors" of a given operating system would be required for specific different hardware.

That is exactly how things were back in the early '80s when the IBM PC was introduced. Many of the Intel x86 processor based PCs in the early '80s were not fully compatible with the IBM PC, and IBM's PC DOS would not run on those systems right out of the box. If a given system would not run PC DOS, the manufacturer could license MS-DOS from Microsoft and produce a custom version for their computer that would run.

For DOS versions up through 3.1 there were only private-labeled OEM (Original Equipment Manufacturer) versions such as PC DOS, Compaq DOS, Zenith-DOS, and so on. Private labeled DOS names and version numbers could vary, even for releases based on the same set of Microsoft code. For example, the code base that Microsoft internally called MS-DOS 1.25 was called IBM PC DOS 1.1 by IBM, and Columbia DOS 2.0 by Columbia Data Products.

In the early to mid-'80s there were many systems that were partially compatible with the IBM PC, but which also differed from the PC in many ways. For example, the Texas Instruments Professional Computer used an 8088 processor, had the same 5.25-inch 360KB floppy drives as an IBM PC (and could read and write the same 360KB disks); however, it also had a different ROM BIOS, an internally different hardware and software interrupt structure, and a higher resolution graphics processor. Because of the differences in system design, IBM's PC DOS would not boot and run on the TI PC.

As you learned in the previous section, the development of PC DOS was a cooperative project between Microsoft and IBM. Microsoft was responsible for producing the core system code, while IBM helped specify the functionality, did testing, and added several additional utility programs to the system to both enhance functionality as well as to work specifically with IBM's hardware. The development agreement between Microsoft and IBM allowed Microsoft to license the Microsoft-developed portions of the PC DOS product (essentially the core system code) to other OEM's, which Microsoft called MS-DOS. As such, MS-DOS was not a complete (finished) product; rather, it was only a core set of code that could be licensed by a computer manufacturer to run on its systems.

To actually have a finished version of MS-DOS for end users, a given computer manufacturer such as Texas Instruments would have to license the core MS-DOS code from Microsoft, test and if necessary modify that code to work properly on its hardware, write their own versions of any or all of the utility programs that IBM had written for PC DOS (as well as possibly write any additional utilities they wanted), and finally write and print the manuals, copy the disks, and package it all together into a finished retail product. If the manufacturer was Texas Instruments, the finished MS-DOS product might be called Texas Instruments DOS, and would only be guaranteed to run on the Texas Instruments computers for which it was designed.

As an end user, once you had the TI version of MS-DOS running on a TI PC, any program strictly written to interface with MS-DOS would work on the system. Unfortunately many programs at the time were designed to go around the operating system and talk directly to the hardware for certain functions in order to improve performance. For example, the popular Lotus 1-2-3 spreadsheet program accessed the IBM graphics hardware directly and would not work on the TI PC. For Lotus 1-2-3 to run on the TI PC, TI had to work with Lotus to produce a special version of the program rewritten to work with the modified graphics on their system.

Besides TI, many other manufacturers at the time were also producing systems that were not 100% compatible with the IBM PC, and therefore also had to license and then produce custom versions of MS-DOS specifically designed for those systems. Owners of those few systems that were 100% compatible with the IBM PC could simply purchase PC DOS from IBM and run that. For example, I used a Compaq Portable PC for a short time, and although Compaq did produce its own custom version of MS-DOS, I ran IBM's PC DOS instead, and it worked perfectly.

As time progressed, most computer manufacturers realized that producing systems that were 100% compatible with the IBM PC was necessary in order to run all of the software that was becoming available for the IBM PC, which in turn became critical for success in the marketplace. Also, PC components such as motherboards became available, enabling smaller computer dealers or even individuals to build their own systems. Although an individual who built a 100% IBM compatible system could simply go to the IBM dealer and purchase a copy of PC DOS, most of the smaller computer manufacturers (who were really just system builders or assemblers) did not want to bundle IBM DOS with their systems, nor did they have the capability to license MS-DOS from Microsoft, write the additional utilities, or produce the manuals and packaging to create a finished product.

What was needed was a generic but complete shrink-wrapped packaged product that a smaller computer manufacturer or assembler could buy from Microsoft and sell with its computers. To oblige, Microsoft wrote its own versions of the utilities provided by IBM in PC DOS, and in August 1986 released Microsoft MS-DOS 3.2, the first Microsoft labeled "shrink-wrapped" packaged version of DOS for smaller OEMs or system builders. This became known as the Microsoft OEM version. On the box, the labeling stated that it was "For Personal Computers Compatible with IBM Personal Computers." This version was technically not sold retail, but was sold through what became known as the Microsoft OEM System Builder program. In fact, later versions of the packaged MS-DOS product contained the statement "Not for retail sale except with a computer system" right on the box. Microsoft was afraid to sell MS-DOS retail because then it would have to support it on the myriad of different systems out there. Instead Microsoft sold it only to system builders, who were responsible for testing the DOS to work properly on their systems, and then provide any and all necessary support to the end user.

IBM and Microsoft had signed a JDA (Joint Development Agreement) in June of 1985 to collaborate on what was originally called Advanced DOS, but which would later be known as OS/2. Although the JDA was centered around OS/2, it also brought on a major change in DOS development. Starting with DOS 3.3, IBM became the main development center for DOS (both the core and the utilities) while Microsoft focused mainly on OS/2. As a result of the JDA, Microsoft gained the right to redistribute the PC DOS utilities written by IBM. This meant that PC DOS 3.3 and the Microsoft MS-DOS 3.3 OEM packaged product version that followed were now almost identical code, with only a few minor exceptions.

Note that many of the larger computer manufacturers continued to license MS-DOS and produce their own custom versions. For example, after the IBM and Microsoft versions of DOS 3.3 were released, Compaq released Compaq DOS 3.31, which included the implementation of support for larger than 32MiB hard disk partitions that would officially appear in DOS 4.0.

As with 3.3, DOS 4.0 was also initially developed at IBM and subsequently released by Microsoft. There were several bugs in the first release, and by the time the Microsoft OEM packaged version came out it had been updated to version 4.01.

During 1991 the joint development agreement between IBM and Microsoft fell apart, which resulted in IBM taking over full responsibility and development for OS/2, and primary development of DOS 5.0 became Microsoft's responsibility. The MS-DOS 5.0 OEM packaged version was released on June 6, 1991, five days before IBM released PC DOS 5.0. This was somewhat significant as up until DOS 5, PC DOS had always been on the market first, and in some cases with a fairly long lead over the same relative version of MS-DOS. For the first time Microsoft also began selling MS-DOS as a retail product in the form of a lower cost upgrade version.

The growing rift forming between IBM and Microsoft after the dissolution of their joint development agreement caused several different and somewhat confusing releases of DOS 6.x. For example, Microsoft developed MS-DOS 6.0 and released its OEM and upgrade versions first. Rather than merely introducing the same thing later, IBM made some changes and subsequently released PC DOS 6.1, skipping a version number in the process (there was no PC DOS 6.0). Microsoft then developed its next version and also skipped a number, calling it MS-DOS 6.2 to eliminate confusion with the IBM product (there was no MS-DOS 6.1). IBM followed suit and called their subsequent release PC DOS 6.3 (there was no PC DOS 6.2).

The last official standalone MS-DOS release from Microsoft was 6.22, while IBM subsequently released PC DOS 7.0 and finally PC DOS 2000 (7.1). IBM's PC DOS 2000 was the last official release of any standalone version of MS-DOS. Later versions of MS-DOS 7.0, 7.1, and 8.0 came with Windows 95, Windows 98, and Windows Me respectively; however, those DOS versions were never released separately as standalone products.

DOS Versions

Now that I have outlined a history of DOS from a market perspective, let's take a look at the actual nuts and bolts that constituted each version of DOS.

DOS 1.x

PC DOS 1.0 was introduced along with the IBM PC on August 12, 1981, and supported only single-sided 5.25-inch drives. Floppy disks were formatted using 8 sectors per track (one side, 40 tracks) resulting in a capacity of only 160KB when formatted. There was no support for hard disks at all, which were generally quite rare for personal computers at the time. DOS was a text-based operating system, hence there was no graphical interface. Unlike CP/M, 8-bit ASCII characters were supported because the PC came with IBM 8-bit ASCII in ROM. This allowed the use of line drawing and other special characters to draw boxes and such on the screen.

For anyone who used the CP/M (Control Program for Microcomputers) operating system, DOS seemed pretty familiar. The "user interface," consisting of a prompt that indicated the logged drive, was very similar to CP/M. This similarity helped many people, including myself, make the transition from older CP/M systems to PC DOS a painless one.

When DOS 1.0 was introduced, it contained several commands and limited batch-processing facilities. About half of the commands were internally part of DOS, while the disk utilities were external assembly language programs. The commands in DOS at that time were:

CHKDSK	DIR	FORMAT	RENAME
COMP	DISKCOMP	MODE	SYS
COPY	DISKCOPY	PAUSE	TIME
DATE	ERASE	REM	TYPE

DOS also came with interpretive BASIC, a text editor called EDLIN, a LINKer, a DEBUGger, and a series of BASIC programs. All of these programs were sold on one single-sided floppy diskette.

People immediately noticed that the IBM-PC and PC DOS could handle only single-sided diskettes. This was seen as a disadvantage at the time, and was an indication of the conservative nature of IBM. But everybody knew that a version supporting double-sided drives was coming. In reality very few PCs ended up being sold with DOS 1.0 as the PC was in pretty short supply for the first few months of its existence. It was really not until the early part of 1982 that just anybody could get one, and by then DOS 1.1 was available.

PC DOS 1.1 was introduced in May 1982. It was called 1.25 internally by Microsoft, and was later released by a number of OEMs under a variety of names and version numbers. DOS 1.1 supported double-sided drives with 8 sectors per track, resulting in a formatted capacity of 320KB. PC DOS 1.1 used 12KB of RAM, and was the last DOS written by Tim Paterson, based on the original Seattle Computer Products 86-DOS.

The major difference between DOS 1.0 and 1.1 is that the latter can operate double-sided drives. All of the external, and most of the internal commands, were rewritten to accommodate double-sided drives. There was still no support for hard disks explicitly, but several manufacturers supplied kits with software patches to DOS that allowed a large disk to be used. Actually many different companies offering expansion products for the PC emerged at this time, and many of these products came with software that patched DOS directly. I remember being concerned about this because the compatibility problems were enormous. I was getting the feeling that PC DOS was to go the route of Apple DOS at the time in that it would become so patched and hacked up by the aftermarket as to cease to be any kind of standard. Anyone who remembers the old Apple DOS for the Apple II series can tell you the problems with this methodology. Fortunately IBM and Microsoft came to the rescue with a new version (DOS 2.0) that was so changed and improved that it brought all of this patching to an abrupt halt. There was no need to patch it if it could already do what you wanted, or be easily adapted with extensions rather than patches.

DOS 2.x

PC DOS 2.0 was introduced on March 8, 1983 (along with the IBM PC XT), and was virtually a complete rewrite over the previous versions. DOS 2.0 added many new features and functions (mostly derived from UNIX), including a tree-structured (hierarchical) file system, support for hard disk drives up to 16.76MB (15.98 MiB) using FAT12, 5.25-inch 9-sector per track floppy formats resulting in 180KB/360KB for single/double sided drives, I/O redirection and piping, and background printing. Many new commands were added as well. PC DOS 2.0 used 24KB of RAM.

In achieving its objectives Microsoft tripled the size of DOS, and added 17 new commands. The major feature of DOS 2.0 was support for the use of a hard disk and a hierarchical file structure in order to support the new IBM PC-XT, which included a 10MB hard disk as a standard feature.

DOS 2.0 also increased the storage capacity of single-sided floppies from 160KB to 180KB, and double-sided floppies from 320KB to 360KB. This was achieved by increasing the number of sectors on each track of the disk from 8 sectors to 9. DOS 2.0 could also read and write any of the older formats, ensuring backwards compatibility.

Another major feature of DOS 2.0 was support for device drivers. This meant that there was a provision for new software routines that supported various hardware and software to be installed into DOS directly. I like to think of this as software "slots" for adding components to DOS, without patching DOS directly.

IBM introduced PC DOS 2.1 on November 1, 1983 (along with the IBM PCjr). It added no new commands or functions, but fixed bugs and altered timing parameters for the half-height floppy drives used in the PCjr and IBM Portable PC. PC DOS 2.1 used 24KB of RAM, same as the previous version. For the most part, DOS 2.1 was considered a maintenance release from 2.0, with no new functionality added.

DOS 3.x

PC DOS 3.0 and 3.1 were both introduced on August 14, 1984 (along with the 286 processor based IBM PC AT). Although both were introduced at the same time, only version 3.0 was available immediately while version 3.1 became available a few months later, in October 1984.

DOS 3.0 was basically an unfinished version of 3.1, designed to get the necessary support in place for the PC AT. DOS 3.0 added support for a virtual disk (VDISK) using memory greater than 1MB, and added FAT16 support for hard drives supporting a single partition of up to 32 MiB (33.55 MB). DOS 2.x and earlier only supported FAT12, even on hard disks. Support was also added for high-density 1.2MB 5.25-inch floppy drives using 15 sectors per track. PC DOS 3.0 used 36KB of RAM.

PC DOS 3.1 was introduced on August 14, 1984 (same as 3.0), but wasn't made available to the public until October 1984. Because 3.0 was really an unfinished 3.1, IBM offered the first DOS upgrade (from 3.0 to 3.1) for $30. International keyboard support was added to 3.1, but the main additions were network printer and file redirection as well as file sharing support. This was designed to support the new IBM PC Network hardware and software that was also released at the same time. PC DOS 3.1 used 36KB of RAM.

PC DOS 3.2 was released on March 18, 1986 (along with the Token Ring Network interconnect program). DOS 3.2 supported the Token Ring Network, and added support for 3.5-inch double-density (720KB) floppy drives. The first 3.5-inch drives for PCs were coming in the PC Convertible, also the first IBM laptop computer (which was introduced less than a month later on April 2, 1986). DOS 3.2 also added the XCOPY and REPLACE commands. PC DOS 3.2 was the first DOS available on both 3.5-inch and 5.25-inch diskettes, and used 44KB of RAM.

After the release of PC DOS 3.2, Microsoft made the first non-specific OEM (generic) packaged version of MS-DOS available. The packaged version of MS-DOS 3.2 was designed for smaller system builders who did not have the ability to produce a finished product from the raw code supplied with the large-scale OEM licenses. As such, the OEM-packaged MS-DOS 3.2 was essentially the first release of MS-DOS available in Microsoft packaging from MS directly. This was also the beginning of Microsoft's OEM program for small system builders, and OEM versions of its software were only sold to OEMs, who then could only resell the software with a system.

Both IBM and Microsoft issued a minor release update to DOS 3.2 called 3.21. This new version was available free of charge if you had 3.2, and corrected problems with BASIC and the keyboard of the IBM Convertible PC, as well as some other minor bugs.

PC DOS 3.3 was released on April 2, 1987, along with IBM's line of PS/2 systems, more than a year after DOS 3.2. DOS 3.3 introduced the extended partition, which could internally support up to 23 sub-partitions (logical drives) of up to 32 MiB (33.55 MB) each. Combined with the primary partition on a disk, this allowed for a total of 24 partitions of up to 32 MiB each, which would be seen by the operating system as logical drives C through Z. Support was also added for 1.44MB high-density 3.5-inch floppy drives.

DOS 3.3 also added support for nested batch file commands (using the new CALL command), and the DATE and TIME commands would finally update the CMOS RTC chip directly. Foreign language support was enhanced with support for Code Pages (alternate international character sets), and the FASTOPEN and APPEND commands were added as well. 128KB of RAM was advertised as the minimum memory required for DOS 3.3.

DOS 4.x

In order to take full advantage of FAT16 and allow for much larger drives and partition sizes, Microsoft collaborated with Compaq, and Compaq introduced Compaq DOS 3.31 in November 1987. Compaq DOS 3.31 was the first DOS to use 32-bit sector addressing internally and in the BPB (BIOS Parameter Block), which when combined with the 16-bit File Allocation Table (FAT16) file system, allowed for a single partition to be supported up to 2GiB in size.

The rest of the PC world followed suit on July 19, 1988, when IBM and Microsoft released PC/MS-DOS 4.0. The use of 32-bit sector addressing meant that FAT16 could now handle partition sizes up to 2 GiB (2.15GB) using 64 sectors per cluster. DOS 4.0 also added support for Lotus, Intel, Microsoft (LIM) Expanded Memory Support (EMS), as well as an optional graphical user interface shell. The MEM command was added. 256KB of RAM was advertised as the minimum memory required for DOS 4.0.

After the initial 4.0 release, IBM followed up with six sets of CSDs (Corrective Service Diskettes), each of them reporting 4.01 as the version. MS followed the IBM CSDs with some (but not all) of the 4.01 corrections and enhancements in the following MS-DOS 4.01 release.

DOS 5.x

After switching initial DOS development back to Microsoft, MS-DOS 5.0 was introduced by Microsoft on June 6, 1991, and PC DOS 5.0 was introduced by IBM on June 11, 1991.

MS-DOS 5.0 was a significant release in that for the first time Microsoft was feeling some competitive heat from Digital Research Corporation, which sold an alternative operating system called DR-DOS. Microsoft was compelled to add several additional useful features to MS-DOS 5.0, including a full-screen editor, significantly improved memory management, and an improved BASIC language interpreter.

By this point, too, it could be assumed that most PCs had an Intel 80286 or better processor, so DOS could take advantage of this processor's ability to "map" extended memory into unused parts of the upper 384KB address range visible to DOS. These memory segments were called *upper memory blocks*. In addition, programmers had by now figured out how to use a programming trick to gain access to the first 64KB of extended memory (called the *high memory block*) from real mode without using the mapping features. These two techniques let MS-DOS locate parts of itself, device drivers and "terminate and stay resident" accessory programs outside the lower 640KB address range, leaving more of the precious lower 640KB memory range available to application programs. MS-DOS 5.0 thus introduced the DOS=HIGH,UMB configuration option and the loadhigh command.

Many commands were added, including: HELP (online help), DOSKEY, SMARTDRV (disk cache), EDIT (full-screen editor), EXPAND (file extractor), FC (file compare), LOADHIGH/DEVICEHIGH (load resident programs or drivers into UMBs—Upper Memory Blocks), MIRROR (backup FAT and directory structures for later UNDELETE or UNFORMAT), QBASIC (a version of BASIC that works on all IBM and IBM-compatible hardware, without the requirement of an IBM ROM as with BASICA), RAMDRIVE (replaces VDISK), SETVER (report different DOS versions to "fool" older programs that check versions before running), UNDELETE (undelete files), and UNFORMAT (unformat disks/partitions). A full-screen editor called EDIT was added to DOS 5.0 in addition to the EDLIN line editor.

DOS 5.0 also added support for 2.88MB ED 3.5-inch floppies, and the FORMAT command used the media sense capability present in most 3.5-inch drives to automatically format 720KB, 1.44MB, or 2.88MB media to the correct capacity. 512KB of RAM was listed as the minimum memory requirement for DOS 5.0.

On November 11, 1991, Microsoft released DOS 5.0a to address data-corrupting bugs in the original DOS 5 CHKDSK and UNDELETE commands. IBM on the other hand was much more diligent in finding and reporting bugs, and released five sets of CSDs (Corrective Service Diskettes) and two sets of IFDs (Interim Fix Diskettes) between July 1991 and September 1992, fixing not only the CHKDSK and UNDELETE problems, but more than 50 other individual problems in DOS 5.

PC DOS 5.00.1 was introduced on April 28, 1992, and is the first IBM version specifically supported on non-IBM hardware (although previous versions ran on all PC-compatible systems). One change was that QBASIC was now included, which no longer depended on the ROM BASIC as with previous DOS versions.

Version 5.00.1 also added refreshed code that included the latest CSD fixes, as well as a new SETUP module that installed over all IBM and IBM-compatible PC/MS-DOS Versions 2.1 and higher, and even across a LAN.

PC DOS 5.02 was introduced on October 20, 1992. It incorporated all of the previous DOS 5 fixes, as well as added APM (Advanced Power Management) support for laptops via the new POWER command. Also added were the INTERLNK and INTERSVR commands supporting file transfer between systems over a parallel or serial cable. Version 5.02 also added support for electrically ejectable/lockable drives and ISO screen fonts. IBM also released various retail bundles with 386Max & Stacker using the 5.00.1 package.

MS-DOS 6.x

Microsoft introduced MS-DOS 6.0 (codename Astro) on March 30, 1993. Again, in response to competitive pressure, Microsoft copied disk data compression technology created by Stac Corporation as the new DoubleSpace feature.

How DoubleSpace Worked

Essentially, the physical hard drive was given a high drive letter; G, for example. The compression driver created a "virtual" C: drive, and intercepted all activity directed at drive C. Data that applications wrote to files on drive C was compressed, and the compressed files were stored on the actual drive G. Likewise, when an application program attempted to read from drive C, the compression software would open the actual file on the physical drive G, uncompress the data as needed, and give it to the application program.

Microsoft introduced MS-DOS 6.2 (codenamed Elroy) in November 1993. It included bug fixes to the DoubleSpace (Stacker) disk compression as well as upgrades to the SCANDISK, DISKCOPY, and Smartdrive (disk cache) programs.

Later it was ruled that Microsoft illegally used the Stac Electronics Stacker disk compression, which they were forced to remove in a 6.21 release. Finally in 1994 Microsoft released MS-DOS 6.22, with disk compression added back in, but using different (noninfringing code) and renamed as DriveSpace. 6.22 was the last standalone version of MS-DOS released by Microsoft.

PC DOS 6.x

IBM introduced PC DOS 6.1 on June 19, 1993 as its version of MS-DOS 6.0, but with some improvements. IBM skipped the 6.0 release number to avoid confusion with Microsoft's 6.0 release, and to indicate to the public that IBM's version included more.

PC DOS Version 6.1 included a library of integrated DOS utilities from other software vendors and IBM Research. The utilities included the following:

- Disk compression (licensed from Stac Electronics)
- Antivirus
- Full-screen backup
- New full-screen editor (called "E")
- Program scheduler

DOS 6.1 also included support for Pen-based systems as well as PCMCIA (PC Card) slots in laptop systems, plus an automatic memory configuration program called RAMBoost.

IBM then released PC DOS 6.3 on April 27, 1994, and included the MSCDEX program for CD-ROM support, plus many minor updates to the various utility programs.

IBM continued to improve DOS, and released PC DOS 7.0. This was followed by PC DOS 2000, which was really 7.0 with updates added to fix certain Y2K issues. PC DOS 2000 was the last standalone version of DOS ever released, and can still be purchased from IBM today.

Windows 9x/Me DOS

Windows 95, 98, and Me all include subsets of MS-DOS as their base, and those versions offer enhancements over the standalone releases from both Microsoft and IBM.

The DOS included with Windows 95 is internally coded as MS-DOS 7.0, and includes support for long filenames. MS-DOS 7.1 was included with Windows 95B (OEM Service Release 2), Windows 98, and Windows 98SE (Second Edition), which added support for FAT32. Windows Me included MS-DOS 8.0, which had some bug fixes for supporting larger drives.

MS-DOS Alternatives

We mentioned earlier that IBM and several other PC manufacturers all sold customized versions of Microsoft's MS-DOS, and that there was a competitor called DR-DOS.

Gary Kildall, whom we left several pages ago spurning IBM's offer to create the operating system for the PC, went on to finish his 16-bit operating system, called CP/M-86. Kildall sued IBM and Microsoft for copying CP/M, and eventually reached a settlement whereby IBM agreed to offer CP/M-86 in addition to PC-DOS. And IBM did offer CP/M-86, for $240 a copy, versus $40 for PC-DOS. It didn't sell well.

By 1987, Kildall had abandoned the idea of promoting CP/M in the 16-bit world. Killdall's company Digital Research eventually produced an MS-DOS clone called DR-DOS, which never, as they say, made the big bucks, but did force Microsoft to significantly lower its prices and make enhancements to MS-DOS that otherwise might never have been made. Anyone who's used edit to edit a text file has Digital Research to thank. Digital Research also produced GEM, a graphical operating system that predated and competed with Windows—more on that shortly. DR-DOS ultimately did not survive, although various legal battles continued. In 2000, Microsoft paid Digital Research's successor company a reputed $150–$200 million to settle suits over the licensing and marketing practices that drove DR-DOS under.

Besides DR-DOS, other operating systems came and went, or came and stayed, including these more popular ones:

- **OS/2**—IBM and Microsoft initially collaborated to create OS/2, a 32-bit protected-mode advanced operating system that was intended to eventually replace DOS. Later versions sported a user interface that served as the inspiration for Windows 95. It was incredibly reliable and seemed to be the future of PC operating systems, but in 1991 Microsoft and IBM parted ways. Microsoft went on to develop Windows NT, which begat Windows 2000 and XP (more on that in the next section). IBM doggedly tried keep OS/2 alive and didn't give up until mid-2005. It eventually found a niche as a network server operating system and as a host for industrial control systems. You may never have seen a computer running it, but you've probably been in buildings whose air conditioning systems were controlled by it. It's sad really—had the Microsoft/IBM partnership survived, we'd all be using OS/2 today, and we would probably have had Windows XP's reliability 10 years earlier.

- **Novell NetWare**—Novell Corporation's NetWare operating system is a platform for file and print servers used in corporate environments. It reigned supreme in this market for many years, was exceedingly reliable and fast, and it commanded a premium price until it was displaced by Microsoft Windows NT, which significantly undercut it in price, while never matching NetWare's reliability or performance. It's still widely used in large corporate environments, primarily for its excellent directory system, and is the competitive target at which Microsoft's Active Directory is aimed. Novell is now moving its corporate network service software away from the proprietary operating system and into Linux.

- **Banyan Vines**—Vines was another high-end network server operating system. It had user directory features that were advanced for its time, but it eventually lost its market share to Novell and withered on the (sorry for this) vine.

- **UNIX**—Many versions of the UNIX operating system were developed for the PC architecture. UNIX was originally created as a "programmer's workbench" by computer scientists at AT&T's Bell Laboratories, and was given away free to universities during the 1970s and 1980s. The result was a generation of programmers (including your author) who were trained in this elegant but somewhat cryptic environment. PC flavors of UNIX include AT&T licensees Xenix and SCO UNIX, and clones XINU, NetBSD, FreeBSD, Linux, and several others.

- **Pick**—Pick was a database system that in some cases was packaged as a standalone operating system. It was one of the earliest multiuser systems for the PC architecture.

Other operating systems were developed, including a multiuser dBASE-like system that I remember seeing once, but they've faded to total obscurity.

The Evolution of Microsoft Windows

Well before Windows first appeared, the graphical user interface (GUI) revolution began in California's Silicon Valley. In 1968, computer pioneer Douglas Engelbart demonstrated a computer system created at Stanford Research Institute that incorporated a mouse, video display, hypertext links, word processing tools, and online help—all things that we'd insist upon on any computer today, but which were radical innovations at the time. For videos of the original 1968 demonstration, see http://sloan.stanford.edu/MouseSite/1968Demo.html. (You'll need RealPlayer to view them.) Engelbert's spectacular lecture established—and delivered—the vision of the computer as a constant companion, "always available, and immediately responsive."

Researchers at Xerox Corporation's nearby Palo Alto Research Center (Xerox PARC) incorporated these concepts to create the MAXC computer in 1972, which included a high-speed bitmapped graphical display, a mouse, overlapping windows, and cut and paste capability. In 1973, Xerox created the more refined Alto, adding a laser printer and an early version of the Ethernet network (also PARC inventions). The Alto had a page-sized display, pull-down menus, icons, disk storage, WYSIWYG editing, email, typeset-quality printing, and network file sharing. Virtually all of the technical elements of today's desktop computing paradigm were present.

If the Alto was such a magnificent invention, why have most people never heard of it? The reasons are threefold. First, Xerox corporate management didn't foresee that computers would eventually become as common as indoor plumbing, and decided that a computer meant for use by just one person was unmarketable. Second, the necessary processing and display hardware required for such a computer was *very* expensive at that time, so the Alto was far too expensive to become a viable mass-market product*. And finally, software was not yet considered patentable, so Xerox did not attempt to protect the Alto concept from being copied by others. So, the Alto was used internally at PARC, but never made it out the front door.

---

* *In 1981, Xerox finally did release a commercial version of the Alto called the Star, but at nearly $17,000, its cost was three to four times that of a PC or CP/M-based computer. The Star sold only about 30,000 units, mostly in the technical documentation publishing market, where its graphical capabilities were unmatched by any other technology available at the time.*

Although the Alto was never sold commercially, it profoundly influenced computer history. Most importantly, it caught the attention of Steve Jobs of Apple Computer. Jobs saw the Alto in 1979, and directed his staff to incorporate its concepts in the Lisa and Macintosh computers that were already under development. The result was the Apple Lisa, released in 1983 to no great fanfare, and the Apple Macintosh in 1984, which was a sensation. An irritatingly slow and clunky sensation to be sure, but it brought the Alto's amazingly intuitive interface to the public at an affordable price for the first time. The Mac smiled at you when you turned it on, and the public smiled back.

The impact and utility of the graphical interface wasn't lost on developers in the PC world. Knowing that Apple was working on the Macintosh, Microsoft and its primary operating systems competitor Digital Research both began projects to develop a graphical operating system for the PC. Digital Research's GEM interface came to market first, in 1983. With GEM on the market, and a VisiCorp competitor named VisiOn and the Apple Macintosh soon to appear, Microsoft responded with a premature demonstration of Windows 1.0 at the Comdex computer industry trade show in November, 1983. This became infamous as the "smoke and mirrors demo," because Windows 1.0 did not actually run at the time; the demo was rigged. But it had its intended effect, and both developers and customers waited for Microsoft's GUI project rather than jumping on the GEM or VisiOn bandwagons. They waited, and waited, until November 1985, when Windows 1.0 was finally released.

While GEM and its early applications were far superior in look, feel, and performance to Windows 1.0 and 2.0 and the early Windows applications, market forces (and business practices that have kept Microsoft in hot water to this day) eventually pushed GEM into obscurity.

16-Bit Windows

Although its initial release was an iffy affair, technical progress and strong-armed marketing have made Windows the world's dominant operating system. Let's take a look how Windows has evolved since it was released in 1985.

Windows 1

Development of a graphical user interface for the IBM PC began in 1981. The goals were: multitasking ability, a graphical user interface, and device-independent screen and printer graphics; that is, application programs would not be required to know the details of how graphics were to be transmitted to each and every supported model of printer and display adapter. The original concept placed the menus at bottom of screen, but this was abandoned for drop-down menus and dialog boxes as seen on Xerox Alto and Macintosh.

Announced in 1983, Windows version 1.01 was not actually released until November 1985, and even then it did not realize its intended potential. In version 1, windows could not be positioned so that they overlapped, but could only be placed side-by-side. Its release really served just as a placeholder, to affirm to the marketplace that Microsoft did intend to release a graphical environment along the likes of Macintosh, GEM, and VisiOn.

While limited in performance and appearance, version 1.0 did include Windows Write and Windows Paint, Notepad, and smaller applications such as Clock, Calculator, Reversi (a game), CardFile, and Terminal, a serial data communications program. It required 256KB of memory, and could run from two double-sided double-density (360KB) floppy disks, or a hard disk. A program called the MS-DOS Executive served as a sort of file manager, and served as the program's shell. It ran entirely in real mode, and could not address memory past the 640KB limit imposed by the initial C architecture. Minor versions 1.03 and 1.04 were released between August 1986 and April 1987 with additional support for national languages, MS-DOS 3.2, more fonts and printers, and additional PC models.

Windows 2

Windows 2 was released in November 1987, and addressed many of the shortcomings of version 1. This release added icons to the interface metaphor, and supported overlapped windows. Version 2 required at least 512KB of memory, but could still be run from floppy disks. Version 2.1, released later, was the first to require a hard disk. Version 2 introduced the Smartdrive disk cache and Dynamic Data Exhange (DDE) support, which allowed a level of automatic interaction between applications.

All program code still ran in "real mode," with a limit of 640KB of RAM directly addressable. However, on computers with enhanced memory, multiple applications whose total memory require-ments exceeded 640KB could still be run. As Windows switched between applications it swapped pro-gram code and data modules between the lower 640KB and enhanced memory. When memory usage was pushed to the limit, program code modules were discarded from memory and reloaded from the hard disk when needed again. This caused a massive slowdown and the familiar sound of disk "thrashing," but it did work.

Windows 2.10, released in May 1988, permitted the use of mice from other manufacturers, and was the first version to require the use of a hard disk. A new version of the himem.sys driver learned the trick of using the first 64K of extended memory for system code, freeing up memory for applications.

As with Digital Research's GEM windowing system, Windows was available as a "runtime-only" ver-sion that software vendors could bundle with application software. Windows version 2.11 was the last to be made available in this bundled format.

Windows 386

Windows 386 was released in 1987 as a specialized version of Windows 2 that required the use of an Intel 80386 processor. The 386 provided hardware support for virtual memory paging, more total sys-tem memory, and used the CPU's protected mode to gain direct access to extended memory. The processor also provided a "virtual 86" CPU mode that let Windows run several DOS applications at once, with preemptive multitasking between DOS applications and Windows. Preemptive multitask-ing gave each DOS application time to run, in round-robin fashion. The memory management and preemptive-multitasking of DOS applications that appeared in Windows 386 were carried forward into the "386 enhanced mode" of Windows 3.0.

Windows 3

Windows version 3.0 was a significant rewrite of Windows, and was released in May 1990. At this time there was a still a significant installed base of 80286-based computers, but 80386 and 80486 processors were found in virtually all newer computers, and it was time for Windows to start to take advantage of these processors' significant memory access improvements.

The 8088 processor used in the original IBM PC and its clones was capable of addressing at most 1MB of memory, due to the processor's design. Programs specified memory locations using two compo-nents: a 16-bit address value, and a 16-bit segment register. 16-bit values alone can specify at most 65,535 distinct addresses, but the segment register increased this many fold. When a program makes reference to a memory location, the processor automatically takes the value from a segment register, multiplies it by 10 (in hexadecimal, which is 16 in decimal), and adds the 16-bit address value to get a physical memory address.

Figure 1.1 shows an example. When fetching program instructions in real mode, the CPU uses the address stored in the Program Counter (PC) register, along with the value in the Code Segment (CS) register.

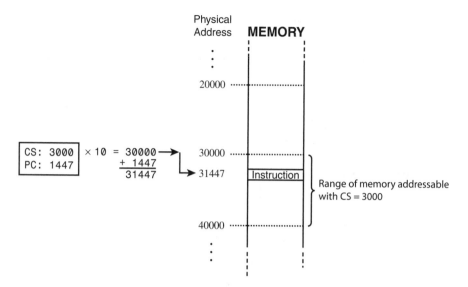

Figure 1.1 Instruction fetching in Real mode.

In this example, the programmer has loaded the CS register with 3000 (hexadecimal). With the PC register holding address 1447, the processor will retrieve the next instruction from physical address 31447. This scheme allows the processor to access at most 1MB of memory.

Note

Using a large segment value and a large address value so that the result is larger than $OFFFFF_{16}$, the 1MB memory access limit could be raised by about 64KB. This is what the HIMEM.SYS driver did for DOS and Windows. Today, it seems odd that programmers went to such trouble to gain access to just 64KB of memory, but it really did matter back then.

Intel 80286 and later processors could use a more flexible memory access scheme called *protected mode*. In protected mode, the value of segment register was not used directly, but was instead used to select an entry from a table that contained 24-bit (80286 processors) or 32-bit (80386 or better) base address values, as shown in Figure 1.2. With the ability to add larger segment values, the protected mode scheme lets 16-bit programs access up to 4GB of physical memory.

Because 16-bit versions of Windows rely upon DOS and the computer's BIOS code to perform input/output operations, and DOS and the BIOS are real-mode programs, Windows needs to be able to rapidly switch the processor back and forth between protected and real mode. The 80286 could not be easily returned to real mode from protected mode. This is why Windows 1 and 2 were forced to rely solely on real mode.

The 80386 and later processors, however, could instantly be switched back and forth between real and protected mode, so with the advent of these processors, Windows 3 was completely redesigned to take advantage of protected mode's vastly larger potential memory space.

Real mode (DOS, Windows 1-2)

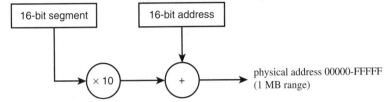

physical address 00000-FFFFF
(1 MB range)

16-bit Protected mode (Windows 3)

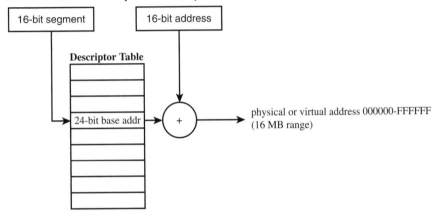

physical or virtual address 000000-FFFFFF
(16 MB range)

32-bit Protected mode (Windows 9x, NT)

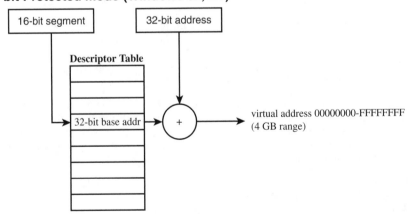

virtual address 00000000-FFFFFFFF
(4 GB range)

Figure 1.2   Intel CPU modes and memory access.

For compatibility with older computers, Windows 3.0 could be run in any of three modes:

- Real mode, with access to at most 1 MB of memory
- Standard mode, which put the CPU into protected mode, and increased the maximum directly usable memory to 16 MB
- 386 Enhanced mode, which let the CPU use the 386 processor's hardware support for running multiple DOS programs at once. This mode had been developed and tested in Windows 386. The DOS multitasking came at a slight decrease in performance, so both Standard and 386 Enhanced modes were made available as options.

Windows 3.0 required 640K of main memory plus at least 256K of extended memory, and required MS-DOS 3.1 or better.

The Windows user interface was also significantly revamped. The MS-DOS Executive was replaced with Program Manager, which used icons to represent program groups, and File Manager, which was a graphical file system browser comparable to today's My Computer. VGA graphics adapters were much more common by this point, and Windows graphical code was enhanced to support the use of more than the 16 primitive colors available in Windows 1 and 2. This made it possible for Windows to display photographic images for the first time.

While Windows 3's access to more memory was a huge improvement over Windows 1 and 2, protected mode introduced a new and soon to become annoying occurrence: the General Protection Fault. In real mode, buggy programs (or hardware drivers, or Windows components) that read from or wrote to incorrect memory addresses would often proceed as if nothing had happened, and only later might the system freeze up due to overwritten program code. Protected mode gave Windows the ability to detect when a program tried to access memory it wasn't supposed to (hence the word *protected*). Because there was nothing that Windows could really do to remedy the situation, it would just display the protection fault warning and terminate the program.

Unfortunately, when Windows 3.0 was first released, most application programs and drivers contained bugs that had never before been detected. Many were benign, but the protection mechanism couldn't know that. And, with much of Windows freshly rewritten, Windows itself contained countless bugs, too. Windows 3.0 quickly gained a reputation as being a phenomenally improved, but barely usable, operating system.

Windows 3.1

Microsoft released Windows 3.1 in April 1992, and for the first time, really got 16-bit Windows right. Most of the bugs were fixed, and developers had gotten their applications cleaned up. Even the General Protection Fault mechanism itself was improved, and was less often encountered. Some technical advances were made: Real mode support was dropped (for Windows itself; DOS applications were run in Real or Virtual 86 mode). Truetype scalable font support was added, as were extensions for multimedia support. Object Linking and Embedding (OLE) technology was released, which made it possible for applications to cooperate without knowing details about each other's internal operations. Windows 3.1 also included client-side networking support as a standard feature.

By this time, the market was way past ready for a reliable multitasking operating system, and Windows 3.1 sold one million copies in two months. Development of character-mode DOS applications virtually ceased, with WordPerfect Corporation being a notably—and fatally—late exception. The software industry focused almost entirely on Windows, and to a lesser extent on Macintosh.

Windows for Workgroups

Windows for Workgroups (WFWG) was a product line based on Windows 3.1 that included file- and printer- sharing support built in at a small additional cost. This made it possible to build peer-to-peer networks with no additional software, and directly targeted Novell's NetWare and Artisoft's LanTastic products, which up until this point had the small office network market to themselves.

WFWG version 3.1 (based on Windows 3.1) was released in October 1992, and version 3.11 in November, 1993.

Windows 3.11

Windows 3.11 was a bug-fix version, distributed as a free upgrade and installed on new computers, released in December 1993. This was the last issue in the 16-bit Windows product line.

For more details on each of the 16-bit Windows versions, see support.microsoft.com/kb/q32905.

The Windows 9x Family

By the mid-1990s, processor power had increased and memory prices had decreased dramatically since Windows' original release. The Internet had also sprung onto the world stage, from an academic tool to an instrument of global communication and commerce. (You may recall that Windows 3.1 did not even include support for the TCP/IP network protocol used on the Internet—you had to purchase it from a third-party vendor.) Users' expectations likewise had grown with computers' capabilities, and desktop publishing, graphics editing, and multimedia applications had reached the point that 16-bit protected mode's 16MB memory was an obstacle.

The 32-bit Windows NT product line had become successful in the business market (more on this shortly), but it was not yet considered a viable product for the consumer market. The primary reason for this is that Windows NT did not include DOS, and provided no means for user programs to run in real mode. This meant that a huge number of games, multimedia programs, and other consumer and business applications would not run correctly under NT. It would be some time before those products faded away, so Microsoft created a new 32-bit Windows version based on DOS, rather than on the NT kernel. This would let developers write Windows programs that took advantage of the NT 32-bit Windows programming model, while DOS was still underneath to support so-called legacy applications.

Windows 95

Windows 95 was released in August, 1995, as a consumer version of 32-bit Windows, meant to bring 32-bit architecture to the consumer market and hold its place while the Windows NT product line ripened to consumer readiness. Windows 95 was wildly successful, and its user interface is still the reigning interface paradigm today.

Windows 95 used Windows NT's 32-bit programming model, but most of the code was freshly written, not based on NT. Windows 95 uses the 32-bit protected mode made available by Intel 80386 and later processors, illustrated in Figure 1.2. Physically, the segment registers are still present and are still used by Windows itself, but with 32-bit addresses used throughout, application programs can access a 4GB memory address range without having to change the segment registers, and within a given program they can be ignored—they can use what is termed a "flat memory space." And because Windows 95 and its successors presume an Intel 80386 or later microprocessor, programs could take full advantage of several more efficient instructions that had been added to the Intel platform's instruction set since the original 8086 was released. It also required 4MB of memory as a minimum.

Perhaps the biggest improvement was the introduction of long filename support. The 8.3 filename structure (eight character filenames with a three character extension), which derived from the 1970s TOPS-10 operating system and was copied by CP/M and then MS-DOS, was finally left behind, and files could be named something like "My research notes on the history of DOS and Windows.doc" rather than DOSWHIST.DOC.

Windows 95 also included a significantly improved user interface. The Start button and taskbar appeared, and pop-up context menus (right-click menus) were introduced as a standard feature. DOS applications could be run inside of a window on the desktop and no longer needed to take over the entire screen as they did with Windows 3.1. Built-in networking support included TCP/IP connectivity, dial-up networking, and Internet Explorer and the entire operating system exhibited faster performance, due to the use of 32-bit drivers throughout.

Additional significant improvements included the following:

- 16-bit (Windows 3.1) applications could still be used, thanks to a "Windows-on-Windows" system that let the older application believe that they were running under the old operating system.

- Preemptive multitasking was implemented throughout, so that all Windows applications remained at least somewhat responsive even if one application attempted to use all available processing time.

- Windows 95 had the ability to terminate runaway applications without having to restart Windows to recover lost resources (limited memory space used by Windows to track a program's disk and graphics requirements).

- Support for Plug and Play meant that Windows could automatically recognize newly added hardware devices and either automatically install the appropriate drivers, or walk the user through the process of locating drivers, through the Add Hardware wizard.

- The Windows Registry, a single database, was used to store system and application configuration information, rather than multiple text (.ini) files.

- Per-user settings. As an option, Windows 95 could be configured with separate logon names, passwords, desktops, and document folders for more than one user.

As yet, however, Windows did not support USB peripherals.

Windows 95 OSR2

In October 1996, Microsoft released an updated version of Windows 95 called OEM Service Release 2, or OSR2. The OEM part stands for Original Equipment Manufacturer, and indeed, OSR2 was made available only to computer manufacturers for sale with a new computer—it wasn't made available as an upgrade, although some parts could be downloaded as hotfixes.

OSR2 included several significant improvements:

- Supported the FAT32 file system, which permits the use of hard drives up to 2TB in size, and can break large disks into clusters of smaller size than FAT16 for more efficient use of space

- Enhanced DriveSpace support for compression on volumes up to 2 GB in size

- Supported Zip drives, removable disk drives, "floptical" media, and detection of CD-ROM disc insertion and removal

- Included Internet Explorer 3, Internet Mail and News reader, NetMeeting, and Personal Web Server. (Internet Explorer 4 was released as a later, separate update.)

- Support for the Intel MMX multimedia processor extensions
- Support for Novell NetWare 4.0 networking software
- Support for newer PCMCIA (PC Card) peripherals

There was also a host of bug fixes in the release as well.

Subsequent OSR releases 2.1 in August 1997 and 2.5 in November 1997 added support for USB peripherals. USB support was not available as a download or update to Windows 95 or Windows 95 OSR 2.

Windows 98

Windows 98 was released in June 1998. It didn't introduce a radical change in the look and feel of Windows, as Windows 95 did. It was an incremental improvement, with the following major enhancements:

- Incorporated all of the enhancements and fixes made to Windows 95 since its original release, including the FAT32 file system and 32-bit PC Card support.
- Improved USB support gave the ability to use USB keyboards and mice without specific drivers, as well as improved support for video devices and scanners. Firewire (IEEE 1394) support was added as well.
- Advanced Configuration and Power Interface (ACPI) support provided software control over system startup, shutdown, pause and suspend, and power consumption.
- Multiple monitor support gave users with more than one graphics adapter (or an adapter designed for multiple monitors) the ability to extend the Windows desktop across several monitors.
- Windows Update provided a web-based utility for downloading important security and bug fixes.
- Utilities included a disk defragmenter, the Task Scheduler, Internet Explorer 4, and improved accessibility tools.
- Improved dial-up networking support included logon scripting, Remote Access Server (dial-in) support, and PPTP Virtual Private Networking.
- The Win32 Driver Model (WDM) made it easier for manufacturers to develop 32-bit device drivers for Windows 98 and subsequent versions.
- Windows Scripting Host provided a means of writing powerful application automation and data processing scripts in VBScript, JavaScript, and other languages.

In addition, subtle user-interface changes like the ability to right-click and drag a shortcut to the QuickLaunch bar or the Start menu made life easier for power users.

Windows 98 Second Edition (SE)

Windows 98 Second Edition was released in May 1999 on new computers, and was available as an upgrade as well. It included the following significant improvements:

- Hardware support included DVD-ROMs.
- Internet Connection Sharing (ICS) permitted a Windows 98 SE computer to share a single dial-up or broadband connection with other computers over a network.
- Internet Explorer 5.0 was included.

- Windows Media Player was provided to play not only MP3 music files but also Apple music and video formats.

- DirectX 6.1 was included to provide driver support for high-performance games and graphics adapters.

- Y2K fixes were included as well.

Windows Me

The end of the road for the Windows 9x product line is the difficult to explain Windows Me. Does Me stand for me, or for Millennium Edition? If it stands for Millennium Edition, shouldn't it be Windows *ME*? And if it's Me they mean, is Windows a verb? Neither me nor I nor Microsoft can give you an answer to these questions, and perhaps that's for the best.

Part of the problem is that Microsoft had promised that a true 32-bit operating system would succeed Windows 98, but a consumer-friendly (that is, game-friendly) version of Windows 2000 could not be created in time, and Windows XP was far off in the future. We can only surmise that Windows Me was produced as way to fish for income from upgrade sales, without having a real product to use as bait.

The marketing campaign stated Windows Me wasn't based on MS-DOS. Actually, it was. Windows Me started up with the assistance of MS-DOS just as its predecessors had. It was really just Windows 98 with the Exit to MS-DOS option removed from the Start menu and better-looking icons. The sys command was also deleted, so that bootable MS-DOS floppy disks could not be created.

Released in September 2000, Windows Me did include some improvements:

- The Home Networking Wizard was added to simplify the task of joining several computers into a small local area network.

- Internet Explorer 5.5 was included.

- A code-signing system brought non-certified drivers to the user's attention during installation, to encourage the use of Microsoft-tested drivers, and hopefully minimize the number of problems caused by poor drivers.

- Windows Movie Maker encouraged home editing of digital video (although, at the time, disk space was still too expensive and processor power too limited for this to be practical).

- System Restore let Windows automatically back up system files before significant configuration changes, so that the changes could be rolled back if problems ensued.

- The Scanner and Camera Wizard greatly simplified the task of copying digital pictures from cameras to the hard disk.

The Windows 9x product line thus ended. Although it was visually slick, it never reached a level of reliability that made it truly acceptable to the business world. You just can't do business with a computer that crashes a couple of times a day (although some tried). But, Windows 2000 and XP were just around the corner. To get to that story we have to back up to the origin of Windows NT.

The Windows NT Family

In April 1987, Microsoft and IBM announced a new operating system initiative, called Microsoft Operating System 2, or OS/2. This was to be the platform to replace DOS, and would be fully 32-bit, memory-protected, preemptively multitasked operating system, written from the ground up. Microsoft and IBM worked on the project jointly, but shortly after the release of Windows 3.0, the relationship soured, and eventually ended.

IBM and Microsoft each continued to work with the project independently. IBM continued to develop OS/2 version 2 on its own, as we mentioned earlier. Microsoft took its initial work on what was to have become OS/2 version 3, and took it in a different direction. In 1988, a team led by Dave Cutler, who was the architect of the RSX-11 and VAX/VMS operating systems for Digital Equipment Corporation, rechristened the project Windows NT, and redesigned and rewrote the "kernel" or mini-operating system on which Windows NT was to be built.

▶▶ To learn more about the kernel and the internal structure of Windows, see "The Windows NT Kernel," p. 126.

Version 3.1

The first release of NT was given version number 3.1 to match the contemporary 16-bit version of Windows. (Magazines of that era claimed the number was also chosen to make it seem more likely to be reliable, as anyone knew that a ".0" release of anything was bound to be buggy.)

Its user interface was visually that of Windows 3.1 but the entire system had been written from scratch; no MS-DOS or Windows 3.1 code was used. From a programming standpoint, as we mentioned earlier in our discussion of Window 9x, a "flat" 32-bit address space freed applications from having to manage 16-bit memory segment registers and their 64KB boundaries. The Windows Application Programming Interface (API) was modified to use 32-bit values in all communication between Windows and applications. This required Windows programmers to make some minor modification to their code in the process of developing applications for the new environment, but the effort required was surprisingly small. Device drivers were completely redesigned, and application programs were totally isolated from each other; it was not possible for an errant application to mangle information stored in memory used by other applications or by Windows itself. And, internally, Windows was made much more robust. For example, an errant application could be terminated, and all of the memory, graphics, files, and other resources it had been using were automatically released and made available for reuse by other programs. These were, of course, not new features for operating systems in general, but it was huge improvement over MS-DOS and Windows 3.1.

Windows NT could still run MS-DOS applications, but MS-DOS itself was not present at all. A clever program called the Windows NT Virtual DOS Machine (NTVDM), using technology Microsoft licensed from Insignia Solutions Inc. that had originally been created to run MS-DOS applications on the Macintosh, provided DOS applications a "fake" DOS environment. NTVDM intercepted the DOS application's attempts to interact with DOS, the display adapter, and other hardware, and issued Windows NT requests to perform the desired functions. A similar (although less complicated) mechanism let Windows NT run 16-bit Windows applications without modification.

Version 3.1 was released August, 1993 in two versions: Workstation, for use by an individual, and Advanced Server, which was basically the same operating system but with a different licensing scheme that allowed it to be used as a file server for larger organizations. Windows NT had taken five years to build, from the point that David Cutler signed on until its release.

Note

During Windows NT's development Microsoft had recognized that it would not be feasible to sell NT to the consumer market for some time…there were simply too many graphics-intensive games and strange, poorly written applications on the market, and NT's emulation system wasn't going to work with them. Thus, the Windows 95 project was initiated independently, to develop a version of 32-bit Windows that was still based on MS-DOS.

The intent was to build a highly reliable system by keeping the NT kernel small, and moving as much code as possible outside of the kernel so that bugs and crashes could cause only limited damage.

Sticking to this concept has made the Novell NetWare, UNIX, and Linux operating systems exceedingly robust, and it might have done so for Windows NT as well. However, this initial version was unacceptably slow, and in subsequent versions, Microsoft moved more and more of the graphical interface program code into the kernel. There, it could run faster, but this brought increased risks that a bug in an errant driver or Windows module could take Windows down with it.

Windows NT 3.5

In April 1994, Microsoft released Windows NT 3.5, in both Workstation and Server versions. This version showed improved performance and reduced memory requirements. This was the first really usable version. Version 3.51 was released in June 1995 and included modifications to make it able to run applications designed for Windows 95.

Windows NT 3.5 servers could not only be licensed to provide shared file service to more than 10 simultaneous users, but could also act as domain controllers, offering authentication (password verification) services for corporate networks. This meant that user accounts could be managed in one place (the server) rather than on each individual workstation.

Windows NT 4.0 Workstation

By the time Windows NT 4.0 was released in August 1996, Microsoft had had time to not only significantly improve NT's performance and reliability, but also to incorporate the Windows 95 user interface, including the Start menu, so the Windows 3.1 program manager was finally left behind.

However, the most significant improvement was the addition of the NTFS file system. Up until this time, all versions of Windows used hard disks formatted with the FAT file system, which Microsoft acknowledges was written in a hurry with only floppy disks in mind. It turned out that FAT-formatted disks were quite vulnerable to data loss due to crashes and power outages. FAT also provided no means of restricting access to files based on usernames, passwords, or other credentials.

Microsoft had worked with IBM to develop the High Performance File System (HPFS) for OS/2, and was able to apply lessons learned there to NTFS. Its goals were:

- **Reliability**—Protection of changes to directory entries and file sizes against loss due to crashes or power outages, by encapsulating them as "transactions."
- **Security**—Fine-grained control of who is allowed to create, read, modify, delete, or manage files and folders. An auditing system makes it possible to track who has succeeded or failed to make changes as well.
- **Capacity**—The ability to handle terabytes of disk capacity.
- **Efficiency**—Better use of disk space, smaller allocation units, and less I/O needed to read and modify disk structures.
- **Long filenames**—The ability to store filenames up to 255 characters.
- **Data spaces**—The ability to store parallel, separate sets of data for a given file. This is used, for example, to accommodate alternative filenames and extended directory information used by different operating systems served by an NT-based file server, or the Macintosh's data and resource forks.

Windows NT 4.0 Workstation was meant as a highly reliable operating system for corporate systems, workstations, and servers.

Windows NT 4.0's Server version included additional networking services such as Windows Internet Naming Service (WINS), Dynamic Host Configuration Protocol (DHCP), Domain Name Service (DNS), Remote Access Service (RAS, a dial-up networking service), and others.

Windows 2000 Professional

Windows 2000 was to have been named Windows NT 5.0, but at this point Microsoft had officially gone berserk with its naming schemes. Windows Me was in the works, and Microsoft would now decide to rearrange their naming schemes for every successive version of Windows. Released in February 2000 after many delays, Windows 2000 was a significant advance in both functionality and reliability. It provided many advantages over Windows NT 4.0, just a few of which are listed here:

- FAT32 support (up to 32GB per partition) in addition to NTFS and FAT16
- Windows 98 user interface
- Microsoft Management Console (MMC) for many maintenance functions (although the split of functions between the Control Panel and the Computer Management MMC tools was somewhat arbitrary and confusing)
- Support for up to 4GB of RAM
- A unified driver model, shared with Windows Me, so that hardware vendors could supply a single driver that could be used on either operating system
- Greatly improved reliability
- NTFS improvements including reparse points, which give Windows 2000 the ability to redirect file accesses to alternative drives or servers, a UNIX-like mountable file system, and UNIX-like links (multiple directory entries for a single file)
- Dynamic disk support, which permits on-the-fly partition resizing
- Improved setup and software installation—fewer reboots required, and the Windows Installer service makes it easier to correctly uninstall or repair applications.
- Plug and Play hardware support, multiple monitors, USB, and FireWire support
- Safe mode and Recovery Console boot options, to maintain and repair unbootable systems
- Active Directory, an enterprise management and security tool that allows very fine-grained delegation of management and security policy settings, automatic application deployment, and other services
- ACPI power management including suspend and hibernate modes, to make it possible to use on laptops.

Windows 2000 was released in several licensing versions:

- Windows 2000 Professional, for individual users. Dual-processor systems were supported under the Professional license. Windows 2000 Professional became the desktop operating system of choice for business users, luring the last of the Windows 3.1 holdouts into upgrading.
- Windows 2000 Server, for file server use. Up to four processors supported on the computer's motherboard.
- Windows 2000 Advanced Server, supporting up to eight processors in a single system and 64GB of RAM (recall that segment registers are still present in 32-bit Protected Mode. At most 4GB of RAM is visible to any one application but if the motherboard is designed for it, Windows can juggle the segment registers to give more applications that much RAM without paging).
- Windows 2000 Datacenter Server, supporting up to 32 processors in a single system, and clustering, which links redundant servers to permit continuous operation should one fail.

Support for all of the early RISC processors was dropped and Windows 2000 was provided only in versions for the standard Intel x86 (IA-32) architecture.

Windows XP

Released in October 2001, Windows XP officially ended the Windows 9x product line and brought Windows NT to the masses, er, to the consumer. With XP, Microsoft finally managed to make the NT product reasonably compatible with the pool of remaining DOS games and applications (it helped that this pool had been dwindling over the years). Microsoft also made it simple enough to manage, and attractive enough to appeal to end consumers. It also didn't hurt that Microsoft could finally promise and actually deliver a truly reliable operating system. This in itself is remarkable given how much Windows had grown. The original version of Windows fit on two floppy disks. Windows XP required 2GB of disk space just to *install*. The massive amount of code can be seen in the number of lines of source code—the raw programming text typed by Microsoft's programmers—estimates of which are listed in Table 1.1.

Table 1.1   Lines of Code in Windows

Version	Million Lines of Code*
Windows NT	10
Windows 95	15
Windows NT 4.0	16
Windows 98	18
Windows 2000	30
Windows XP	40 to 45

Estimated

This is really a staggering amount of code, given that it's estimated that a typical programmer can produce about 100 lines of quality program code per day. If that's true, Windows XP is the product of 1,800 person-years of effort (assuming those persons get weekends off, and two weeks of vacation a year).

Windows XP introduced several enhancements over Windows 2000:

- Improved graphical design. Derided by some as "cartoony" at first, it has sort of grown on us.

- Simple File Sharing makes it easier for consumers and small offices to manage file security on a network and on a given computer when NTFS is used.

- System Restore, which performs automatic backups of system programs, components, and the Registry at regular intervals and before installing new applications.

- Fast User Switching makes it possible for several users to be logged on simultaneously, although only one person can use the computer at a time.

- Remote Desktop allows a user to view and control a Windows XP Professional computer over the Internet.

XP was released in two versions in both Home and Professional versions. XP Professional is the everything-but-the-kitchen-sink desktop operating system and has a licensing allowance for two processors on the motherboard. XP Home Edition, which permits only one processor, had several features that were either restricted or removed. For example, Simple File Sharing cannot be disabled; the Power Users management group cannot be used; and File Encryption, Offline Files, Remote Desktop hosting and domain membership are not available.

Note

Microsoft does not count multicore or hyperthreading CPUs as multiple CPUs for licensing purposes. A dual-core CPU with hyperthreading looks like 4 CPUs to Windows but Windows XP Home Edition will still run on it.

Windows XP Service Pack 2 introduced several additional features and significant security fixes. The three most important additions were

- An improved Windows firewall, which helps prevent damage and abuse to the system from over the Internet
- Windows Security Center, which detects and notifies the user of out-of-date antivirus protection and less-than-optimal security configurations
- Improvements to Internet Explorer to prevent its being hijacked by malicious websites
- Improvements to Outlook Express—finally!—to prevent its automatically displaying graphic and script content, which can notify spammers that their email has been read

Note

In this book, earlier versions of Windows are occassionally discussed, but for the most part, we assume that you are using Windows XP Home Edition or Professional with Service Pack 2 installed. If you are using Windows XP *without* Service Pack 2, we strongly encourage you to install it.

...and beyond

Windows XP was not released in server versions. Instead, Microsoft released the successor to Windows 2000 Server with the name Windows Server 2003 (remember, we said they'd gone berserk).

We won't discuss Windows Server versions in any detail here because our focus is maintenance of Windows XP, and to a lesser extent, earlier single-user versions of Windows.

At this point, Microsoft has decided to call the successor to Windows XP "Windows Vista." Due in the second half of 2006, Vista promises to offer greatly improved graphics and file-searching capabilities.

Alternative CPU Versions: Intel, Alpha, MIPS, and Motorola

Windows NT was designed from the beginning not to be tied exclusively to the Intel CPU architecture used in most PCs. Windows NT's design put the processor's unique setup and control instructions into the Hardware Abstraction Layer (HAL) software component. Most of the rest of Windows is written in high-level languages that have no explicit processor dependence. To run on a new processor, Microsoft or a hardware manufacturer merely had to write a new Hardware Abstraction Layer module and a compiler to convert the rest of the Windows code into machine instructions for the new architecture.

When NT was originally released, Microsoft supported four microprocessors:

- Intel IA-32 (also known as x86), which is the processor architecture in most PCs. x86-compatible CPUs are made by Intel, Advanced Micro Devices (AMD), Winbond, and others.
- Alpha AXP, a Reduced Instruction Set Computer (RISC) chip manufactured by Digital Equipment Corporation.
- MIPS R4000, a RISC processor manufactured by MIPS Computer Systems, Inc.
- PowerPC, yet another RISC processor design, made by IBM.

In addition, some manufacturers developed their own versions of NT for still other architectures under licensing agreements from Microsoft.

Support for alternative architectures was short-lived. One reason for this is that Windows applications had to be compiled and tested for each CPU platform. MS-DOS applications could run thanks to an emulator program that was built into the Virtual DOS environment, but third-party Windows applications were in short supply. This was probably not the largest obstacle, though, as the alternative platforms were usually used primarily to run special-purpose applications.

The main problem facing the RISC chips is that the speed advantage they enjoyed over Intel chips eventually disappeared. While the RISC chips were originally worth the extra expense to get high performance for graphics workstations and servers, once Intel and graphics chip vendors caught up, the commodity PC became as powerful as the workstation at a vastly lower price. Political pressure from Intel and Microsoft also very likely factored into the decisions. Whatever the reasons were, the MIPS and Alpha processors eventually succumbed to decreasing support and demand. Alpha chips are no longer manufactured, nor are MIPS processors, as such; the technology is still available and licensable to chip designers for inclusion in larger designs. IBM still makes PowerPC chips (they are used in Apple Macintosh computers, although Apple plans to switch to Intel), but Windows support for the PowerPC ended after NT 4.0.

Windows XP 64-bit Editions

The CPU story is not over, however. The need for processors capable of handling far more than 4GB of memory has led to development of two competing 64-bit architectures. Intel developed and promoted a 64-bit architecture called IA-64 or Itanium, intended primarily for database and network server computers. Advanced Micro Devices also produced a 64-bit architecture, called x64 or AMD-64. Intel is now manufacturing chips that use the x64 instruction set. x64 processors typically yield better performance than Itanium running 32-bit Windows applications, and thus are better performers in desktop computers. Both new architectures are supported by Microsoft.

Thus, at the time this was written, Windows is available for three architectures:

- IA-32 (x86) for all versions of Windows
- IA-64 (Itanium) for Windows Server 2003
- x64 for Windows XP and Windows Server 2003

The 64-bit versions of Windows are not covered in this book to any great extent. Usage of the x64 version of Windows XP should be very similar to the 32-bit versions with the following exceptions:

- 64-bit versions of Windows will run 32-bit Windows applications, but will not run 16-bit (Windows 3.1) applications, nor can they use 32-bit drivers that is, drivers written for the standard version of Windows XP. This means that hardware support may be limited until vendors produce 64-bit driver versions.
- MS-DOS applications cannot be run.
- DirectX graphics support does not take advantage of hardware graphics acceleration, so gaming performance will likely be less than satisfactory.

DirectX support may be improved in a future Windows version or in a future service pack.

Service Packs, Hotfixes, and Rollups

It's a given that operating systems and large software suites have bugs, and Windows is definitely a member of both categories. The Microsoft method of dealing with bugs in Windows has varied depending on the product line in question.

In the consumer Windows 9x product line, users were largely left on their own. Only the most severe security bugs were addressed, and even then, for the most part, computer owners had to take the initiative to visit Windows Update to download "Critical Updates." It took many years—and tens of millions of virus-infected computers—for Microsoft to develop an automated method of delivering security updates to Windows 9x users, and even then they had to download this updating mechanism themselves. Bugs that affected Windows functionality but not security were largely left unfixed, with the result that a typical Windows 9x could be expected to crash once a day, in heavy use. Patches called *hotfixes* were available as downloads from support.microsoft.com for some problems, but finding these was a job that required a high level of training and technological savvy.

However, Microsoft recognized from the start that operating system products sold to business customers had to have a level of support that rivaled that of other enterprise software vendors, so the Windows NT product line has enjoyed a much higher level of support. This is not a trivial or inexpensive undertaking, as proper software quality management is expensive, time-consuming, and involves interactions with customers on several levels:

- Communicating known bugs to customers.

- Development and announcement of any possible short-term workarounds, and estimated delivery dates for complete fixes.

- Thorough testing of all software changes for possible negative interactions with existing hardware, software, and all previous updates (regression testing). If done properly, this involves testing installation and operation of all fixes on every possible combination of supported hardware and software, with and without every combination of other optional software components, versions, patches, updates, and fixes. Testing a single software change against all of these permutations takes an enormous effort.

- Timely release of individual fixes to customers who are encountering a given problem.

- Periodic bulk updates that combine all known and tested fixes, to simplify the maintenance job for the majority of customers who are not directly affected by each identified problem. This can be accomplished by releasing new operating system versions, or through an updating mechanism.

To meet these needs, Microsoft has established a system for delivering updates for the Windows NT product line that includes Windows 2000 and XP, with five mechanisms:

- The Microsoft *Knowledge Base* contains reports on known problems and solutions, at support.microsoft.com.

- *Hotfixes*, interim patches that address known problems, which are made available for download at support.microsoft.com. Hotfixes are intended for use only by customers directly experiencing a given problem (due to, for example, a particular combination of hardware and software that exposes a given bug). They are not necessarily tested with every possible combination of hardware and software. Several hotfixes are typically posted every week.

- *Service Packs* are cumulative updates of all hotfixes released since the operating system was original released. When Microsoft constructs a Service Pack, hotfixes are tested much more extensively. In addition, new functionality might be included, as we saw with the inclusion of Windows Firewall in Windows XP Service Pack 2, although Microsoft has stated that they expect this to be a rare occurrence.

  Service Packs are generally tested internally by Microsoft, and then by major computer vendors, and then by large corporate clients and possibly the public, through a beta program, and may go through two or more beta versions before being finalized. Service Packs have typically been released six months to two years apart.

Note

On Windows NT 4.0 and earlier, service pack installers copied only files for features in use, and the service pack had to be reapplied if an optional feature was subsequently installed. On Windows 2000 and Windows XP, installing a service pack installs updated files for all Windows features, whether they are in use or not. This ensures that if an optional Windows component is installed later, the updated version will be used.

Windows service packs include all fixes made since the product's initial release, so it's not necessary to install older Windows service packs before installing a newer Windows service pack. *This may not necessarily be true for service packs for other Microsoft products.*

- *Rollups*, which contain a significant set of hotfixes released since the last service pack. Rollups include only the most important hotfixes, ones likely to affect a large number of customers, and are tested for proper installation and correct operation together as a package. Testing is less extensive than for a service pack. Rollups are designed to make installation of important hotfixes easier, and to make them available in a timely fashion without the burden and expense of a full-scale Service Pack. Rollups are produced only on rare occasion.

- *Critical Updates* are patches that address a security risk to the average user. Critical Updates are typically given extensive testing, as they're considered mandatory for all customers. They are distributed through Windows Update, and now through the new Automatic Updates system so that all users will get them in a timely fashion. Critical Updates are typically released once a month on a Tuesday, unless they are considered urgent enough to be released immediately after testing.

- *Optional Updates* are updates to Windows components, new versions of Windows applications, or new functions that have no direct security or usability impact, but which for some reason Microsoft feels it is important to distribute. They're made available through the Windows Update tool.

Now that Windows XP Home Edition has brought NT to the consumer Windows product line, this level of support is available to the average consumer as well.

It's a matter of speculation what will happen to the frequency of issuance of Service Packs for Windows XP, as its increased reliability coupled with a regular stream of bug fixes may prove to be a disincentive for purchasing upgrades to later operating systems.

Service packs can be obtained in several ways:

- On CDs and DVDs, downloaded from Microsoft. These versions contain all of the files needed by any installation of Windows, and typically covers all flavors of the operating system. For example, updates for Windows XP Home Edition, Professional, Media Center Edition, and Tablet PC Edition, are all in the CD version of a Windows XP service pack. At the time this was written, it was not certain that a service pack for Windows XP 64-bit versions would be packaged on the same CD as the 32-bit version, but it is likely that it would be.

- Via download from Windows Update. The update process first downloads a small tool that analyzes the user's Windows installation and determines which updated files are required. Just the files needed by the user's flavor for Windows are retrieved and installed. This is the easiest download format for users with just one or two computers.

- Via download from support.microsoft.com. For sites that must update several Windows computers, the entire Service Pack distribution can be downloaded and stored on a shared network folder. This format is preferred by sites that have many computers to update.

In addition, service packs can be merged into the Windows installation setup files in an operation called *slipstreaming*. Organizations and vendors that install many copies of Windows can use this technique to construct updated Windows installation media. (In addition, a Windows Deployment Toolkit can be obtained from microsoft.com, which lets organizations pre-install applications and customizations onto new computers.)

CHAPTER 2

Installing Windows

Preinstallation Considerations

There is a little-known rule called the five P's that goes like this: Proper Preparation Prevents Poor Performance. Keep this rule in mind as you read this chapter. Before undertaking the installation of Windows XP Professional, there are several factors that you need to consider regardless of the scope and size of the deployment. Whether you are rolling out 5,000 copies of Windows XP Professional to an entire organization using sophisticated deployment methods such as ghosting or Remote Installation, or simply installing it on your home computer, the same issues still require your attention *before* the installation process begins.

In this chapter, you look at each of the following items in more depth, and get a feel for how they affect an installation of Windows XP Professional and how they will impact the computer, both now and into the future:

- System requirements
- Hardware and software compatibility
- Transferring files and settings
- Network configuration
- File system considerations
- Type of installation to perform

When working through this chapter, it might be helpful to build a checklist. For an example, see Figure 2.1.

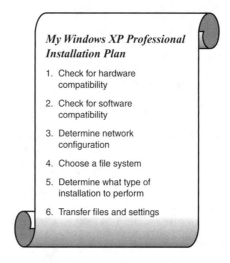

My Windows XP Professional Installation Plan

1. Check for hardware compatibility

2. Check for software compatibility

3. Determine network configuration

4. Choose a file system

5. Determine what type of installation to perform

6. Transfer files and settings

Figure 2.1   My Windows XP Professional installation notes page.

Without any further ado, let's get right into the meat of this chapter and start off by looking at the system requirements for installing Windows XP Professional.

System Requirements

Windows XP Professional combines the best and worst parts of Windows 2000 Professional and Windows Millennium Edition (Me). On the good side, Windows XP Professional has the robust security, stability, and manageability of the Windows 2000 code-base, as well as the robust built-in multimedia and graphics support that Windows Millennium Edition touted. On the bad side, Windows XP Professional is very demanding of system resources, especially so on older or underpowered systems. You wouldn't dare run Windows 2000 Professional or Windows Millennium Edition in a production environment on less than 64MB of RAM, and so you shouldn't try it with Windows XP Professional.

The official system requirements to support installation of Windows XP Professional are presented in Table 2.1. Although Windows XP Home is not quite as demanding as Professional, these minimums still apply.

Table 2.1   Hardware Requirements to Install Windows XP Professional

Minimum Requirements	Recommended Requirements
Pentium (or compatible) 233MHz or higher processor	Pentium II (or compatible) 300MHz or higher processor
64 megabytes (MB) of RAM	128MB (4GB maximum) of RAM
2 gigabyte (GB) hard disk with 650MB of free disk space	1.5GB of free disk space
Video graphics adapter (VGA) or higher display adapter	Super VGA (SVGA) display adapter and Plug and Play monitor
Keyboard, mouse, or other pointing device	Keyboard, mouse, or other pointing device
CD-ROM or DVD-ROM drive (required for CD installations)	CD-ROM or DVD-ROM drive (12× or faster)
Network adapter (required for network installation)	Network adapter (required for network installation)

One or Two Processors

Windows XP Professional, like its predecessor Windows 2000 Professional, is capable of handling up to two CPUs and provides support for symmetric multiprocessing. In addition, dual-core CPUs and Intel processors that feature hyperthreading are seen as two physical CPUs with XP Pro.

Of course, knowing the hardware requirements to support a successful installation (and later operation) of Windows XP is just one small part of the battle. Sticking to your plan of action, as outlined in the list in the first section of this chapter, you need to look at hardware and software compatibility issues, both of which can cause you some annoyance and lack of functionality or, at worst, bring your installation of Windows XP to a screeching halt.

Checking Hardware and Software Compatibility

Verifying that your current hardware will support an installation of Windows XP is critical to getting Windows XP correctly installed and running smoothly. Verifying the existing software installed on your computer when performing an upgrade installation is just as vital—Windows XP can get pretty particular when it comes to dealing with previously installed software.

There are a couple of means at your disposal when it comes to verifying hardware and software compatibility for the installation of Windows XP. The first of these is the Windows Catalog.

Note

Microsoft once provided a Hardware Compatibility List (HCL) for each OS version, but in an attempt to be all inclusive and perhaps capitalistic, it has created a one-stop website. As evidenced in Figure 2.2, the HCLs are not maintained any longer and have been replaced by the Windows Catalog for current OS versions. When the selection "See the Windows Catalog" is clicked, your browser is directed to http://testedproducts.windowsmarketplace.com/ where you will find the Tested Products List section of the new Windows Marketplace.

For more information on the Windows Catalog and the Windows Upgrade Advisor, refer to Chapter 3, "Upgrading Windows."

Known Compatibility Issues

When it comes time to install Windows XP, there are some known issues that you will want to pay attention to; however, there are two main issues that occur most often and will be examined here. These issues deal with CD recording software, such as Roxio Easy CD Creator, and the NetBIOS Extended User Interface (NetBEUI) network protocol on pre–service pack 2 installations.

Easy CD Creator

If you upgrade a computer to Windows XP from Windows NT 4.0, Windows 98, Windows 98 Second Edition, Windows Millennium Edition (Me), or Windows 2000, you may receive the following error message when you first attempt to run Easy CD Creator:

> Easy CD Creator 4 has a known compatibility issue with this version of Windows. For an update that is compatible with this version of Windows, contact Roxio, Inc.

You may also receive this error message when attempting to run Direct CD:

> A driver is installed that causes stability problems with your system.

> This driver will be disabled, please contact the driver manufacturer for an update that is compatible with this version of Windows.

> To run the program, click Continue. For more information, click Details.

This issue is caused by a program incompatibility between Easy CD 5.0 and earlier and Windows XP due to Windows XP's native CD-RW burning support in Windows Media Player 7 and later. To correct this issue, upgrade Easy CD Creator to at least version 5.02d or later by downloading the required updates from the Roxio website, located at http://www.roxio.com/en/support/ecdc/software_updatesv5_2.jhtml.

Easy CD Creator Dangers

The types of errors that you can receive may be even more serious than the ones detailed here. On occasion, computers have suffered STOP errors (Blue Screen of Death) and random rebooting problems—directly as a result of mixing Easy CD 5.0 and Windows XP. Remove any version of Easy CD Creator before installing Windows XP Professional to avoid these problems.

NetBEUI

Should you attempt to upgrade your computer to Windows XP and NetBEUI is installed, you will receive the following message from the Compatibility Wizard:

The currently installed driver for the NETBEUI Transport Protocol is not compatible with Microsoft Windows XP and will be uninstalled during the upgrade. This protocol is removed from this new version of Windows.

For more information about this driver, visit the manufacturer's website at http://www.microsoft.com. Web addresses can change, so you may be unable to connect to this website.

For a list of protocols supported by Windows XP, see the Microsoft Windows Whistler protocols Compatibility List at the Microsoft website.

The venerable NetBEUI protocol has been effectively put out to pasture with the introduction of Windows XP. Microsoft has moved away from a NetBIOS environment with all of its operating systems and recommends a purely TCP/IP environment. This change first appeared with Windows 2000 and the introduction of Active Directory. Active Directory is based on the DNS domain model, and thus NetBIOS (and WINS) had to go. Although Windows 2000 still provides NetBEUI support natively, Windows XP does not. The best option is to move away from NetBIOS on your network.

Should you, for some reason, still need the NetBEUI protocol, it is still available on the Windows XP Professional Setup CD-ROM. You can find it located in the Valueadd\MSFT\Net\NetBEUI folder. MSKB# 301041, located at http://support.microsoft.com/default.aspx?scid=kb;en-us;301041, has more information on installing NetBEUI onto a Windows XP computer.

Other Known Issues

Of course, there are more than two compatibility issues that you may experience with an upgrade to Windows XP, as is the case with every version of Windows. To this end, Microsoft periodically releases packages it calls Application Compatibility Updates, which are available for download from the Windows Update website located at http://windowsupdate.microsoft.com/. The three major Application Compatibility Updates issued for Windows XP were as follows:

- Windows XP Application Compatibility Update (October 25, 2001) deals with issues that arose between the release to manufacture of Windows and the release date of October 25, 2001. Among its various fixes is the fix for the infamous incompatibility issue of the Snow White and Seven Dwarfs DVD. Read more about this Update in MSKB# 308381, located at http://support.microsoft.com/default.aspx?scid=kb;en-us;308381.

- Windows XP Application Compatibility Update (December 17, 2001) dealt with many issues, including issues with several well-known applications such as ZoneAlarm, PCAnywhere, and Norton AntiVirus. Read more about this Update in MSKB# 313484, located at http://support.microsoft.com/default.aspx?scid=kb;en-us;313484.

- Windows XP Application Compatibility Update (April 10, 2002) addresses issues with dozens of games and Works 2001. Read more about this Update in MSKB# 319580, located at http:// support.microsoft.com/default.aspx?scid=kb;en-us;319580.

The latest compatibility issues, as of this writing, involve post service pack 2 installations. Refer to the article MSKB# 884130 at http://support.microsoft.com/default.aspx?scid=kb;en-us;884130 for more information. And it's no surprise that the best place to keep on top of new updates for Windows is the Windows Update website.

With issues of system requirements and compatibility out of the way, you'll next take a look at the methods Windows XP provides for migrating crucial information to a new Windows XP installation.

Migrating Files and Settings to New Installations

In the days of old, if you wanted to transfer files and settings from an existing installation of Windows, you had two choices: You could either perform an upgrade installation (as detailed in Chapter 3) and take your chances with compatibility issues and other problems, or you could procure a third-party utility to perform this task for you. Although both of these options are still available, there are some other options available to you as well. The Files and Settings Transfer Wizard (FSTW) and the User State Migration Tool (USMT) are two migration tools that are provided with Windows XP that can be used to make your operating system migration a more enjoyable experience.

Note

These sections are only intended to introduce the capabilities of these two tools. For specific instructions on using the File and Settings Transfer Wizard, see "Files and Settings Transfer Wizard" p. 104. For a step-by-step guide to using the User State Migration Tool, see "User State Migration Tool (USMT)" p. 104.

The Files and Settings Transfer Wizard

The Files and Settings Transfer Wizard (FSTW) is a fantastic utility new to Windows XP that is provided on the setup CD-ROM. This allows you to run the Files and Settings Transfer Wizard on any computer, or create a Files and Settings Transfer Wizard floppy disk if you want and use that instead. The Files and Settings Transfer Wizard can migrate a user's files and settings from any Windows OS from Windows 95 and Windows NT 4.0 and newer to Windows XP.

By design, the Files and Settings Transfer Wizard is built to transfer settings for Microsoft applications, such as Internet Explorer, Outlook, Outlook Express, and the Office suite. The settings that are migrated fall into these four major groups:

- *Appearance*—Items such as wallpaper, colors, sounds, and the location of the taskbar.
- *Action*—Items such as the keyboard key repeat rate, double-click settings, and so on.
- *Internet*—Settings that control how your browser behaves, including home page, favorites or bookmarks, cookies, security settings, proxy settings, and dial-up settings.
- *Mail*—Settings for Outlook or Outlook Express, such as mail servers, accounts, signature file, views, mail rules, contacts, and your local mail file.

Files can be selected for movement by type, such as .DOC or .XLS; by folder; or specifically by name. The Files and Settings Transfer Wizard automatically moves many of the most common file types for you during the process; however, you can add or remove folders, file types, or specific files from the transfer should you want to.

The Files and Settings Transfer Wizard can also transfer settings for selected third-party applications. The Files and Settings Transfer Wizard only transfers the user's settings; it will not transfer or install the applications themselves. In order for these settings to be successfully transferred, the applications must be installed on the target computer *before* the settings are migrated to it using the Files and Settings Transfer Wizard. For more information on using this wizard, see Chapter 3.

The User State Migration Tool

The User State Migration tool (USMT) is the IT Administrator's version of the File and Settings Transfer Wizard. USMT can perform all the functions of the File and Settings Transfer Wizard, but USMT is made to run from the command line, in environments where you will be migrating a number of users. In contrast, the File and Settings Transfer Wizard runs with a graphical wizard interface, and is only intended for one-off, user-driven migrations.

Because this tool is more useful when performing multiple installations in a networked environment than it is for standalone installations (although it can be used for this purpose if you prefer), full detail on using this tool is covered as part of performing automated installations in the section "Using the User State Migration Tool," p. 85.

Now, as you work your way down the preinstallation preparation path, your next stop is network configuration information—you will look at this in the next section.

Getting the Network Configuration

After you've determined what your hardware and software compatibility picture looks like, you are well on your way to being ready to install Windows XP on your computer. Of the major factors to consider before installing Windows XP, knowing the proper configuration of a networked PC is essential.

If the computer on which Windows XP will be installed is not connected to a network, you can skip this section. By network, I mean a formal (managed) network consisting of servers and client workstations that has a common naming system, uses an IP address assignment system, and uses network user accounts for access to resources. If this sounds exactly like your Windows NT 4.0 or Windows 2000/Server 2003 domain–based network, well then, that's because it is.

As you have likely guessed from this description, this scenario does not apply to a typical peer-to-peer small office or home network that does not employ servers or systems that just connect to the Internet.

If your network uses a peer-to-peer arrangement without using a centralized database for the storage of user accounts and permissions, you are operating in what is called a workgroup. The first piece of network information you need is either the workgroup name (for example, dontpanic) or the domain name (such as netserverworld.com or netserverworld.local). You can always install Windows XP initially in a workgroup arrangement and then join a client/server domain after installation.

If you are upgrading a computer that is already participating in a network environment, the following list of items should be recorded on your checklist *before* starting the upgrade process:

- The computer name.
- The domain or workgroup name, as previously mentioned.
- Many networks use dynamic configuration for TCP/IP address information. However, if these are assigned manually for your network, you'll need this information.
- The username and password of an account with permissions to add or create computer accounts.
- If you are using connection-specific DNS suffixes in addition to a primary DNS suffix, you should record all DNS suffixes. For example, if your primary DNS suffix is netserverworld.com and you ping a computer by machine name server01, your computer will look for server01.netserverworld.com. If you are also using connection-specific DNS suffixes, such as newportnews on a connection, the computer will look for server01.netserverworld.com and server01.newportnews.netserverworld.com. This can affect how your computers locate other computers in the network, so pay close attention to these settings. Figure 2.2 shows this information.

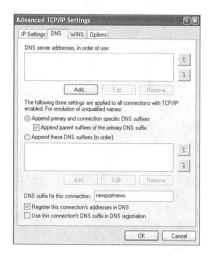

Figure 2.2 The connection-specific DNS suffix affects how your computer searches out other computers on the network.

Of course, you will need all of the appropriate hardware and cabling, too...but that's kind of a given here! When you have all of the network configuration information you need, be sure to write it down in a safe place so it will be available during the installation process.

Note

If you're looking for more detailed information on Windows networking concepts and configuration, see Chapter 7, "Networking Windows."

Now that you've gotten the network configuration information you need for the installation, let's take some time to look in depth at choosing your file system, including the pros and cons of each file system.

Choosing a File System

The choice of a file system is not one to be taken lightly. Unlike most other configurable items in your Windows XP installation, the file system is one that can only be changed one time after installation, and only in one direction.

▶▶ Okay, every rule has to have an exception, so of course the rule about file system conversion has one. To learn more about file systems in general and converting file systems, see Chapter 10, "Windows File Systems."

For a clean installation of Windows XP, you will have to make a choice between using the FAT32 or NTFS. On an upgrade installation from Windows 98, you could possibly even face an existing FAT16-formatted partition, as Windows 98 supported the FAT32 file system but did not automatically invoke it—you had to convert to FAT32 after the fact.

Table 2.2 provides a quick comparison of the FAT16, FAT32, and NTFS file systems.

Table 2.2 File System Comparison

	FAT16	FAT32	NTFS
Supported operating systems	All versions of Windows, MS-DOS, and OS/2.	Windows 95 OSR2, Windows 98, Windows Millennium Edition, Windows 2000, and Windows XP.	Windows NT 4.0 SP4 or later can access files and folders. Windows 2000 and Windows XP can take full advantage of NTFS 5.0.
Volume sizes	Maximum size is limited to 4GB. In MS-DOS, Windows 95, Windows 98 and Windows Me the maximum size is 2GB due to the smallest "largest cluster" size being 32KB.	Minimum size is 512MB, maximum size is 2TB. In Windows XP Professional (and Windows 2000), the maximum size a FAT32 volume can be is 32GB.	Minimum volume size (recommended) is 10MB. Maximum volume size (recommended) is 2TB, although much larger sizes are possible.
Floppy disk usage?	No	No	No
Removable storage usage?	Yes	Yes	Yes, but not recommended.
Maximum file size	Maximum file size is 4GB minus 1 byte.	Maximum file size is 4GB.	Maximum file size 16TB minus 64KB.
Files per volume	65,536 (2^{16} files).	Approximately 4,177,920.	4,294,967,295 (2^{32} minus 1 files).
Supports NTFS 5.0 features?	No	No	Windows 2000 and Windows XP fully support the advanced features of NTFS 5.0. Windows NT 4.0 SP4 supports access only, but not the advanced features.

During the installation process, you may be asked to make a file system selection from the menu shown in Figure 2.3.

You will only be given this choice when dealing with an unformatted volume. If you have a volume that is currently formatted with FAT16 or FAT32, you will be given the opportunity to convert or format it to the NTFS file system. Converting an existing file system is part of performing an upgrade installation of Windows XP, as covered in Chapter 3.

Take the Easy Road

If you are concerned about system stability, you can always make use of the FAT file system during installation of Windows XP. After you've verified that the installation has taken without any stability problems, you can then convert the file system to NTFS.

By installing Windows XP in this way, you can still make use of a variety of DOS boot disks and utilities. On a new installation using new hardware certified for Windows XP, this is probably not going to be a required step.

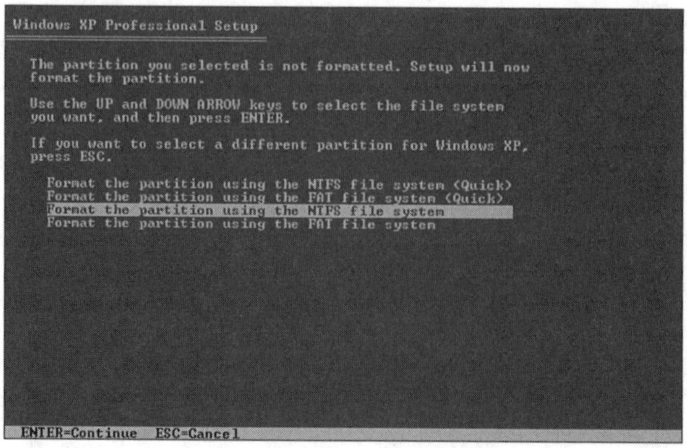

Figure 2.3   Selecting a file system during setup; you can convert FAT to NTFS later if you want.

You cannot change your file system after Windows XP Professional has been installed unless you are converting from FAT16 or FAT32 to NTFS. You cannot (within Windows capabilities at least) revert the file system back to FAT32, although this is possible using a third-party application such as Norton PartitionMagic (http://www.symantec.com/partitionmagic/). The real question you must answer when making the decision about which file system to use is this: Will this computer be used to multiboot another operating system that requires the FAT file system? If your answer is yes then you need to keep at least the System partition (the partition that holds the system files needed to start the computer) formatted as FAT16 or FAT32, depending on what other operating system you will have installed on the computer. You can format your Boot partition that will hold Windows XP Professional with NTFS if you like, but any data on it will be inaccessible to the other operating systems installed on the computer.

File System Misconception

A common misconception that people have about using the NTFS file system is that their files will not be available for access over the network when using a client operating system such as Windows 95 or Windows 98. The only time files on an NTFS volume are inaccessible to a legacy client is when the files reside in a different volume on the same computer in a multiboot arrangement and the legacy operating system is running. When files are accessed across the network, File and Printer sharing for Microsoft networks performs the magic in the background that allows FAT16- and FAT32-based operating systems access to files located on an NTFS volume.

It's always preferred to use the NTFS file system as often as possible, except where you must make the Windows XP Professional volume available to other operating systems installed on the same computer. Should you decide against using NTFS, you will miss the following features, just to name a few:

- *NTFS file and folder permissions*—Using NTFS permissions you can control access to every file on an NTFS volume. You can configure permissions at each level of the directory structure to meet your needs for allowing and/or preventing access to files and folders. However, don't get NTFS permissions confused with share permissions—they are two entirely different items, each requiring consideration both individually and as a pair.

- *The Encrypting File System*—Using a public/private key pair, EFS provides strong cryptographic encryption of files and folders that is extremely resistant to attack and compromise. EFS is completely transparent to the user, and in Windows XP supports multiple user access to an encrypted file. The only down side to using EFS is that its usage is mutually exclusive with NTFS compression.

■ *File compression*—The NTFS file system supports encryption on both files and folders. NTFS uses a *lossless compression* algorithm, which ensures that no data is lost when compressing and decompressing data. *Lossy compression*, such as that used in many video and audio file formats, cannot be used with files that require exact data, such as spreadsheets or document files where data losses due to compression will render the file corrupt and unusable. As previously mentioned, compression is mutually exclusive with EFS encryption.

■ *Disk space quota management*—Using disk quotas enables you to control the amount of data that users can store on your NTFS volumes. Quota control is on a per-volume basis and can be configured with custom quotas for select users as desired. The disk quota system enables you to determine when users are nearing their limits and automatically prevent usage after a user has reached his defined quota limitation.

■ *Volume mount points*—You can finally escape the 26 volume limit on a computer by using volume mount points. Think of it as mapping a path to a hard drive or CD-ROM to a folder on an NTFS volume; thus a new hard drive you've installed to hold user data can be mounted as C:\UserDocs or whatever name you choose.

When you've made your file system choice, you are ready to move onto the next item of consideration: the decision about what type of installation to perform.

Installation Types

Deciding on the type of installation to perform is dictated by many factors, such as the following:

■ Is there an operating system currently installed? If so, do you want to preserve settings and configurations, or start from scratch?

■ Will the installation be performed interactively or remotely?

■ How many computers are to be installed at a single time?

■ Is your network arranged in a domain model using Active Directory?

These are many of the questions that lead to the answer for the larger question: What type of installation will you be performing? There are three distinct possibilities and each of them is explored in the following sections.

Upgrade Installations

Windows XP Professional supports direct upgrades from Windows 98, Windows Millennium Edition, Windows NT 4.0 Workstation, Windows 2000 Professional, and Windows XP Home Edition. If you are currently running any other operating system, including Windows NT 3.x Workstation, Windows 95, or Windows 3.x, you will need to perform a clean installation as upgrading is not supported.

Note

Although we assume most readers of this book are using Windows XP Professional, you might want to note that you can also upgrade Windows 98 and Me (but not Win2K Pro or NT4) to XP Home Edition.

An upgrade installation is most useful in cases where you have customized user settings that you want to preserve. This option, however, does not always work flawlessly, especially if you are upgrading from an operating system other than Windows 2000 Professional or Windows XP Home Edition due to the differences in the Registry structure and the startup process.

Should you decide to upgrade an existing Windows 98 or Windows Millennium Edition installation to Windows XP (and you allow a backup to be made during installation), you will be able to later uninstall Windows XP and effectively revert your computer back to the state it was in immediately preceding the Windows XP upgrade. The ability to uninstall is contingent on the following factors, however:

- The volume on which Windows XP is installed cannot be converted from the FAT32 file system to the NTFS file system.

- You cannot create or delete any volumes on the computer.

- You must not delete the backup files that are created during Windows XP installation. Thirty days after installation, you will be prompted to delete these files. If you do not intend to revert back to your old OS, there's no reason not to delete them.

The easiest process is to upgrade from an installation of Windows 2000 Professional or Windows NT 4.0 Workstation to Windows XP Professional. Windows XP Professional shares a common operating system structure and core with these two operating systems, including device driver requirements and Registry structures. If you upgrade a Windows NT 4.0 Workstation installation that is installed on an NTFS formatted volume, the file system will be automatically upgraded from NTFS 4.0 to NTFS 5.0 as part of the installation process. If the file system is FAT, you will be presented with the option to upgrade to NTFS during the installation.

When upgrading from older Microsoft operating systems, there are a few gotchas to be aware of. The following list details some items of concern when upgrading from Windows 98 or Windows Millennium Edition to Windows XP:

- System tools such as ScanDisk and DriveSpace will not be upgraded in Windows XP. Windows XP brings along its own version of ScanDisk, and NTFS compression replaces legacy compression utilities such as DriveSpace.

- Client software for other network types cannot be upgraded during an upgrade to Windows XP. The only exception to this rule is that if Novell Client32 is installed, the setup routine will detect it and replace it with a newer version of Client32 from the Windows XP Setup CD-ROM.

- Some applications might not run properly under Windows XP due to the fact that the Windows XP Registry is arranged differently than the Windows 98 or Windows Millennium Edition Registry. In some cases, *migration packs* can alleviate this problem. A migration pack (or upgrade pack) is simply a set of new application and library files for a specific application that enables it to run in a newer, more advanced environment than it was originally designed for.

- Some applications might not run properly under Windows XP if they attempt to make calls to APIs that don't exist in Windows XP. In some cases, migration packs can alleviate this problem. In other cases, you will need to remove the application from your computer. The Windows Upgrade Advisor typically identifies these applications for you.

- Some applications might not run properly under Windows XP if they install different files under different operating systems. In this case, you reinstall the application following the upgrade to attempt a fix.

- Applications that directly access hardware or use custom file filters will most likely not run correctly under Windows XP. The most common cases of these types of problems are related to CD-ROM–burning software and antivirus software. You will need to obtain updated versions of these types of applications for use with Windows XP.

All that said, there are some things to watch out for when upgrading from Windows NT 4.0 Workstation as well:

- File system filters written for Windows NT 4.0 will not work with Windows XP due to the upgrade in NTFS. This is commonly seen in antivirus software.

- Networking software written for Windows NT 4.0 will not run on Windows XP if it attempts to use the Windows NT 4.0 TCP/IP or IPX/SPX protocol stacks.

- Custom power management solutions written for Windows NT 4.0 are not compatible with Windows XP and are not required due to Windows XP's native support for ACPI (Advanced Power Configuration Interface) and APM (Advanced Power Management).

- Custom Plug-and-Play solutions written for Windows NT 4.0 are not compatible with Windows XP and are not required, as Windows XP provides full Plug and Play support natively.

- Fault-tolerant disk arrangements, such as disk mirrors, are not supported in Windows XP. Windows 2000 Server and Windows .NET Server support disk mirroring and striping.

Should you have an unsupported upgrade path or decide that you would rather perform a clean installation, but do not want to lose all of your personalized settings, don't despair. You can transfer a large majority of your personalized settings (and even your document files) by using either the Files and Settings Transfer Wizard (FSTW) or the User State Migration Tool (USMT). Full details on performing an upgrade installation of Windows XP and use of these tools can be found in Chapter 3.

One last point about upgrade installations before you move on to clean installations: You cannot perform upgrade installations over the network using Remote Installation Services—RIS only supports clean installations.

Clean Installations

Clean installations are the easiest to perform and should result in the least amount of work at installation time. A clean installation is required in any of the following situations:

- You have an unsupported upgrade path, such as from Windows 95.

- There is no operating system currently installed on the computer.

- The computer has more than one partition, and you want to configure the computer to support multibooting.

- You are performing installations across the network using Remote Installation Services.

- You prefer to perform a clean installation—so as to "start over with a clean slate," rather than risk encountering some of the issues that can crop up from performing an upgrade installation.

When performing a clean installation, there are really no problem areas to watch for in general. The most common problem that people run into is trying to install Windows XP Professional onto a computer in which the CD-ROM is not El Torito–compliant (it does not support booting from the CD-ROM drive). In this case you will need to acquire the Windows XP Setup Boot Disk creation utility (makebt32.exe) by visiting MSKB# 310994, at http://support.microsoft.com/default.aspx?scid=kb;en-us;310994. The makebt32.exe utility will enable you to create a set of setup boot floppy disks; however you will need to have six disks in Windows XP instead of the four disks you needed for Windows 2000 Professional.

You'll find a step-by-step guide through the process of performing a clean installation of Windows XP later in this chapter.

Note

At the time this was written, service pack 2 was the latest update for Windows XP. If Microsoft has released service packs past the one integrated into your Windows XP installation disc, or if you are using a Windows XP installation disc produced before service pack 1 was released, you should install the most recent service pack after completing your initial installation. You can do that before or after using the Settings Transfer Wizard described previously in this chapter and further detailed in Chapter 3.

Multibooting with Other Operating Systems

Your last installation option is to install Windows XP Professional in a multiboot situation with one or more other operating systems, including other instances of Windows XP. Installing in a multiboot situation encompasses either an upgrade installation or clean installation as well—the same rules and caveats apply. The chief difference is in the formatting of the System partition—the place where the files required to start up the computer are loaded. If you are planning on multibooting with an older operating system that does not recognize the NTFS file system, such as Windows 98, you will need to ensure that the System partition is never formatted or converted to the NTFS file system.

The only real trick to successfully installing Windows XP Professional into a multiboot arrangement is that it must be the last operating system installed. As a rule, you should always install Microsoft operating systems from oldest to newest, so if you had a new computer, for example, and you wanted to install Windows XP Professional, Windows 2000 Professional, and Windows 98 on it, you would first install Windows 98, then next install Windows 2000 Professional, and lastly install Windows XP Professional. Of course, you must place each operating system instance in its own separate hard disk partition and you cannot set up a multiboot system using dynamic disks, as only one operating system can own a dynamic disk or dynamic disk set. Lastly, do not install Windows XP Professional on a disk that is compressed using a third-party compression utility—it is not supported and the installation will most likely fail.

▶▶ For more information on partitioning a hard disk, see "Disks, Partitions, and Volumes," p. 446.

Of course, there is one big exception to the rule concerning the order in which you must install the operating systems (remember, oldest to newest). If you are using some sort of third-party boot loader, such as BootMagic from Symantec, its files will create and control the boot menu and operating system selection process. You also gain the capability to install more than one instance of a Windows *9x* operating system when using a third-party boot loader.

One such third-party boot loader is BootMagic, which is part of the Norton PartitionMagic application. BootMagic provides an enhanced boot menu. Read more about PartitionMagic on the Symantec website, located at http://www.symantec.com/partitionmagic/.

Note

You can only install one instance total of Windows 3.x, Windows 95, Windows 98, or Windows Millennium Edition on a computer without using a third-party boot menu application.

Now that you've done all of your homework, you should be ready to deploy Windows XP, at least in the most common scenarios. If your installation is a normal one (by normal, I mean not using exotic procedures such as Remote Installation or disk imaging), you should be ready to move on to the installation phase as discussed in the next section. If you are planning on using Remote Installation or disk imaging, you will find that information beginning with the section "Automated Deployments," on page 73, later in this chapter.

Clean Install Procedure

With Windows XP, Microsoft has made the installation process fairly simple and foolproof, but it will be a bit of a difference to those who have never installed Windows NT or Windows 2000 before. Windows XP may act like Windows 2000 on the inside, as it is built on the ever-stable Windows 2000 code-base, but it is considerably friendlier and easier to get along with on the outside. With the exception of the activation process (which some folks find invasive or at best annoying) the installation procedure and related options benefit from Microsoft's friendly XP approach.

Note

This section documents a clean installation of Windows XP Professional. Windows XP Home install procedures are very similar, but you may encounter some variance based on the options you choose and the environment for which the system is intended.

In this section, you'll be looking at four major areas concerning installation:

- *Installing Windows XP Professional*—Possible installation scenarios include clean installations, upgrade installations, and multiboot installations. Upgrade installations are covered in the next chapter; multiboot installs beyond what was detailed previously are beyond the scope of this book.

- *Uninstalling Windows XP Professional*—A great feature previously unheard of in Windows—but it has limitations. You will look at uninstalling Windows XP Professional in depth.

- *Understanding Microsoft Product Activation*—A not-too-welcome addition to the Windows world, Product Activation has caused quite a stir. You will be taking an in-depth look into Product Activation, including how it works, what it does, and how it affects you.

- *Setup switches*—Powerful ways exist in which to modify and customize the behavior of the Windows XP Professional Setup routine. By using various switches and combinations of switches with the setup commands, winnt32.exe and winnt.exe, you truly can have it your way.

- *Automated System Recovery*—Although not properly part of installing and setting up a Windows XP Professional installation, ASR is a valuable and important part of Windows XP that should not be overlooked—the sooner you understand it the sooner you can make it work for you.

▶▶ To learn more about installing Windows XP Professional by using unattended installation methods, see "Automated Deployments," p. 73.

Installing the OS

Performing a clean installation of Windows XP Professional is easy to carry out and will take about 30–90 minutes, depending on your particular hardware. The setup process consists of several steps, which fall into two phases: the text-mode phase and the GUI-mode phase.

To perform a clean installation of Windows XP Professional, follow the process outlined here:

▶▶ For more information on customizing an installation using Setup switches, see "Using Installation Switches," p. 66.

1. Power on your computer and insert the Windows XP Professional Setup CD-ROM into the CD drive. If your computer is not capable of booting from the CD drive, you will need to create and use the Windows XP Professional Setup floppy disks, as detailed previously in the section, "Installation Types."

2. When prompted onscreen, press any key (or the specific key required) to boot the computer from the CD-ROM.

3. After Setup briefly examines your computer's hardware, you will be prompted to press F6 if you have any third-party drivers that require loading, such as RAID device drivers.

4. At the next screen, you will be prompted to press F2 if you are performing an Automated System Recovery (ASR). Just sit on your hands and let Setup do its thing here.

5. For the next few minutes, Setup will load the files required to perform the installation. If you have an older, slower computer, this is a good time to grab a cup of coffee!

6. When you are presented with the Welcome to Setup screen shown in Figure 2.4, press Enter to continue on with the setup process.

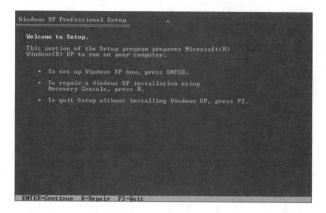

Figure 2.4   Welcome to Setup.

7. Before you can install Windows XP, you must accept the End-User License Agreement. Press F8 to accept this agreement and continue forward with the installation process.

8. From the screen shown in Figure 2.5, you can create and delete partitions on your hard drives. Additionally, you will need to select the partition on which you will install Windows XP. After selecting the partition to install Windows XP on, press Enter to continue.

9. On the screen shown in Figure 2.6, you will need to select what file system to format the selected partition with. If you are installing on a partition that was previously formatted with FAT16 or FAT32, options to convert the file system will also be present. In most clean installations, the NTFS file system is preferable, so consider using it. After making your file system selection, press Enter to continue.

◄◄ For more guidance on choosing a file system, see "Choosing a File System," p. 44, earlier in this chapter.

MBR Versus GPT

MBR (Master Boot Record) and GPT (Globally Unique Identifier Partition Table) refer to types of hard disk arrangement. The MBR method is the old standby...it has been around since the days of old. The GPT method is new to Windows with the 64-bit edition of Windows XP Professional. The TechNet article located at http://www.microsoft.com/technet/prodtechnol/winxppro/reskit/prkb_cnc_ywwc.asp discusses GPT disks at length.

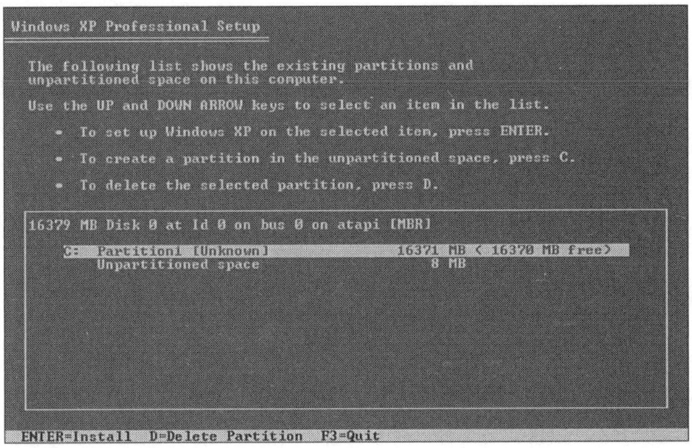

Figure 2.5   Selecting the installation partition.

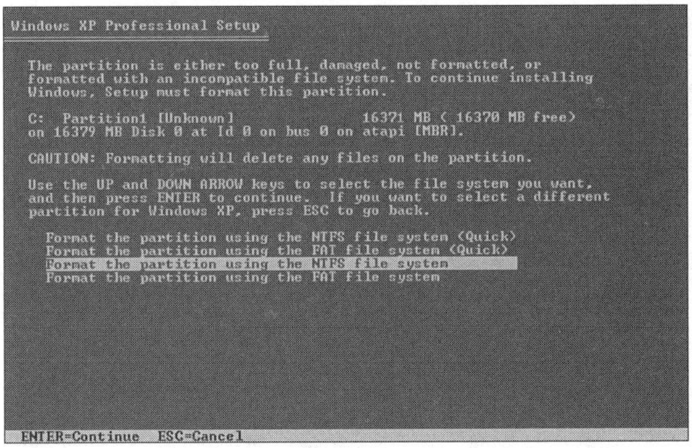

Figure 2.6   Selecting a file system.

10. After the formatting process is complete (see Figure 2.7), Setup will examine your hard drives and then progress to copying the required installation files.

11. After the files have been copied from the installation source to their correct locations on the hard drive, the installation must be initialized.

12. After initialization has completed, the computer will prompt you for a restart. This is the last step of the text-mode phase. If you are prompted to "hit any key" to boot from your CD-ROM on the subsequent startup, *do not* do so; your installation will continue from the hard drive.

13. After the computer restarts, you will be presented with the GUI phase of Setup, as shown in Figure 2.8. Your screen may flash or go blank several times during the GUI phase—this is normal.

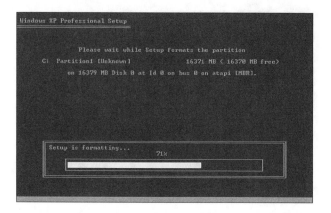

Figure 2.7 Formatting the partition.

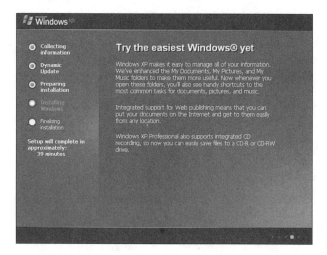

Figure 2.8 The GUI phase of Setup begins.

14. After some time (and after the small progress bar at the bottom-left side of the screen moves to 100%), you will be presented with your first configuration opportunity: the Regional and Language Options page. In most cases, you will want to simply click Next to accept the default values. Should you need to perform a custom configuration, you can change many settings, such as numbers, dates, and currencies, as shown in Figure 2.9, or Text Input Languages and keyboard layouts. When you have finished with your selections, click Next to continue.

15. From the Personalize Your Software page, you can enter your name and organization. At a minimum, you must enter a name. You cannot use the name "Guest" or "Administrator." You do not have to enter an organization. After entering your information, click Next to continue.

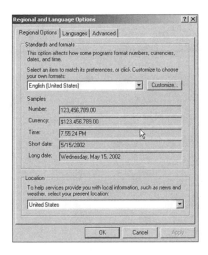

Figure 2.9 Configuring standards and formats.

16. From the Your Product Key page, enter your 25-digit CD key. Click Next to continue after entering your CD key.

17. From the Computer Name and Administrator Password page, shown in Figure 2.10, you will need to enter a unique computer name (that is, no other device on the network should have the same name) and the Administrator password. After entering this information, click Next to move ahead.

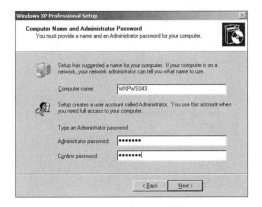

Figure 2.10 Configuring the computer name and administrative password.

18. From the Date and Time Settings page, configure the appropriate date, time, and time zone settings. If you are in a Daylight Savings area, be sure to place a check in the Automatically Adjust Clock for Daylight Savings Changes box. Click Next to continue.

19. After Windows XP Setup performs some more work, you will be presented with the Networking Settings page, as shown in Figure 2.11. If this computer is participating in a domain-based network with DNS servers, DHCP servers, and/or WINS servers, you will want to select the Custom

Settings radio button. If you are setting up this computer to participate in a workgroup or as a standalone computer, you can pretty much rest safely with the default selection of Typical settings. Either way, click Next to move on.

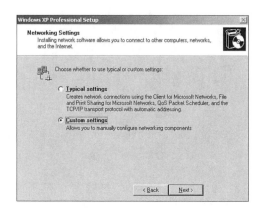

Figure 2.11   Configuring the networking settings.

20. If you selected the Custom Settings option in step 19, you will be presented with the Networking Components page. From here you can install, uninstall, and configure protocols, services, and clients. Because most configuration centers around the TCP/IP protocol, you will look at that. Selecting Internet Protocol (TCP/IP) and clicking Configure will open the Internet Protocol (TCP/IP) Properties page shown in Figure 2.12. Clicking the Advanced button opens the Advanced TCP/IP Settings page, shown in Figure 2.13, which lets you specify many TCP/IP-related settings, including DNS servers, DNS suffixes, WINS servers, NetBIOS over TCP/IP, and TCP/IP filtering among other settings. After you've made your advanced configuration, click OK to close the Advanced TCP/IP Settings page. Click OK to close the Internet Protocol (TCP/IP) Properties page and then click Next after making all configuration entries. (You can change network properties at any time after installation completes, should you need to, so don't worry about it now.)

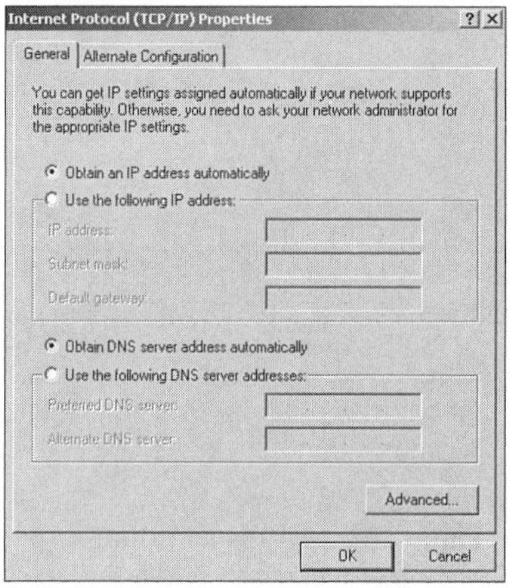

Figure 2.12   The Internet Protocol (TCP/IP) Properties page.

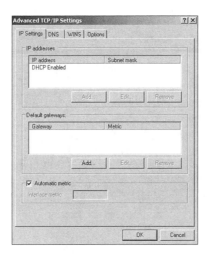

Figure 2.13   The Advanced TCP/IP Settings page.

Alternate Configuration

New in Windows XP, the Alternate Configuration tab of the Internet Protocol (TCP/IP) Properties page enables you to configure an alternate (secondary) TCP/IP setup for those times when a DHCP server is not found. This is a great benefit to portable computer users who would like their portable computer to default to a second set of preconfigured TCP/IP settings when not connected to the corporate network.

21. From the Workgroup or Computer Domain page (see Figure 2.14), you will need to supply either the workgroup name or domain name you will be placing this computer into. If you are installing a standalone computer, you can pick any name you want for the workgroup. If you are installing a computer in a workgroup, ensure you enter the correct workgroup name. Either way, you will want to select the No option. If you want to join the computer to a domain at this time, you will need to supply the username and password of a user who has privileges to add computers to the domain. You can also add the computer to a domain after installation is complete (which is what we will do later). Whatever your selection is, click Next to continue.

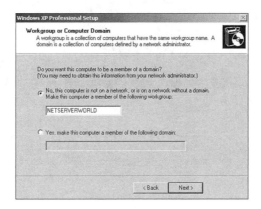

Figure 2.14   The Workgroup or Computer Domain page.

22. Windows Setup performs more configuring and file copying at this point, including installing the Start menu, registering components, saving settings, and lastly, removing temporary files. After Setup completes this phase, the computer restarts once again.

23. After the restart, the Windows XP Professional splash screen appears while Setup completes the installation process.

24. On the Welcome to Microsoft Windows page, click Next to get down to the last stages of Setup.

25. After Windows quickly checks your Internet connectivity status, it progresses to the Will This Computer Connect to the Internet Directly or Through a Network page. If you are using a modem for a dial-up Internet connection, you will most likely want to select the No, This Computer Will Connect Directly to the Internet option. If you are part of a network, you should select the Yes, This Computer Will Connect Through a Local Area Network or Home Network option. Click Next after making your selection to continue. (Here, you will select the Yes option.)

26. From the Ready to Activate Windows? page, shown in Figure 2.15, you will need to decide whether or not you are going to activate your installation at this time via the Internet. This is the easiest option by far, and thus the option we will use here. For more information on Product Activation, see the "Product Activation" section later in this chapter. After making your selection, click Next to continue. If you will not be activating at this time, skip to step 28.

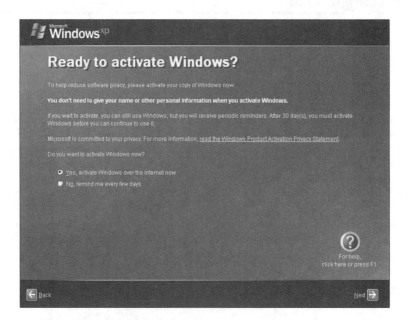

Figure 2.15   Preparing to activate Windows XP.

27. From the Ready to Register with Microsoft page, select either to register or not register your Windows XP Professional software. You do not have to register your software to perform Product Activation. After making your selection, click Next to continue.

28. After activation completes, you will be presented with the Who Will Use This Computer? page. Enter at least one user account, as shown in Figure 2.16, and click Next to continue.

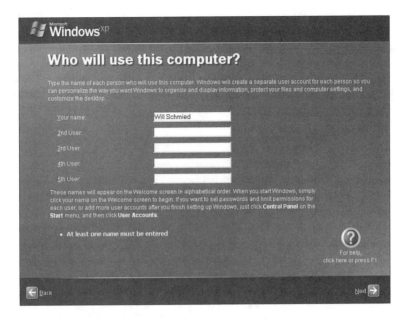

Figure 2.16   Configuring a user account.

29. When all is said and done you will receive a Thank You! page informing you of what has been accomplished, such as installing Windows XP Professional, activating it, and so on. You've just completed the installation of Windows XP Professional! Click Finish to complete the process.

30. After a few moments of disk activity, the first user you configured in step 28 will be logged in to the computer. At this time, you *must* configure a strong password for this user account because the password box is empty. Do this before doing anything else. The password can most easily be changed by using the User Accounts applet located in the Control Panel. To change the password from the User Accounts applet, simply select the user and choose Create a Password.

What Makes a Strong Password?

According to Microsoft, a strong password is one that has the following characteristics:

■ Is at least seven characters long. The most secure passwords are those that are between seven and fourteen characters long.

■ Contains characters from each of the following three groups: letters (A, B, C...a, b, c), numbers (0, 1 ,2), and symbols (!, #, %, and so on).

■ Has at least one symbol character in the second through sixth positions.

■ Is significantly different from prior passwords.

■ Does not contain your name or username.

■ Is not a common word or name, such as family or pet names.

■ Does not contain your address, phone number, license plate number, or any other common knowledge item.

31. At this point, you are done. You can go on to add the computer to a domain, as detailed in step 32, or stop here...the choice is up to you.

32. From the System applet in the Control Panel, switch to the Computer Name tab. Click the Change button to open the Computer Name Changes page, as shown in Figure 2.17. From here you can change the computer name and workgroup or domain membership. Enter the domain name information and click OK. You will need to supply the username and password for an account that is authorized to add computers to the domain. The username should be in the user@domain.com format. After you have joined the domain, a restart will be required to complete the process.

Figure 2.17 Joining a domain.

Product Activation

Product Activation, or Microsoft Product Activation (MPA) as it has become known, was not exactly a welcome addition in Windows XP. However, it was not introduced in Windows XP, as it existed in late versions of Office 2000, all versions of Office XP, and Visio 2002. MPA works to stop casual copying of software by tying the hardware profile of a computer to software installation.

In the next sections, you are going to take an in-depth look at Product Activation, including the different activation scenarios that exist, how Product Activation works and what information it transmits to Microsoft, and how Product Activation will affect you.

When dealing with Product Activation, there are three scenarios that can occur. Without exception, you should fall into one of these three scenarios:

- Retail box purchases
- OEM installations
- Volume licensing

Retail Box Purchases

Retail box purchases of Windows XP present the most complex and confusing situation when it comes to dealing with Product Activation. Product Activation depends on submission of the Installation ID to Microsoft. The *Installation ID* is a unique number generated from two different pieces of information about a computer: the Product ID number and a hardware hash. The Installation ID has been designed to ensure anonymity in that no personally identifying information is ever transmitted to Microsoft. Instead, the Installation ID serves to deter and prevent software piracy by preventing installations of Windows XP Professional that violate its license.

The Product ID uniquely identifies one and only one copy of Windows XP, and is created from the Product Key used during the installation of Windows XP. Each retail copy of Windows XP has a unique Product Key, and thus every Product ID generated from a valid Product Key is also unique. Additionally, as in the past, the Product ID is used by Microsoft for support calls. You can view your Product ID by looking at the General tab of the System applet in the Control Panel (alternatively, you can access this applet by right-clicking on My Computer and selecting Properties from the context menu).

Product Keys and Product IDs

The practice of using Product Keys and Product IDs is not new to Windows XP. Microsoft, like many other software vendors, has been using Product Keys for many years to license software. Likewise, the practice of using a Product ID to validate an installed product has been around for a while as well.

The hardware hash is an eight-byte value that is created by taking information from 10 different components inside the computer and running this information through a mathematical calculation. The hash process is one-way and thus this information cannot be reverse-engineered to yield any specific details about the computer from which it was obtained. The hardware hash also only uses a portion of each individual component hash value, thus further increasing user anonymity and preventing Microsoft from collecting any personally identifying information during the process of implementing Product Activation. Hardware hashes will be discussed at greater length in the "How Product Activation Works" section later in this chapter.

OEM Installations

A large majority of users acquire Windows XP in the process of purchasing a new computer. For these customers, no activation will be required by the consumer because Windows XP Professional is preloaded onto the new computer already. OEMs can preactivate Windows XP as part of the setup and configuration process before the new computer ever leaves the manufacturer. The overwhelming majority of new computers that feature Windows XP will be preactivated by the OEM before shipping. The chief difference between how OEMs license Windows XP comes in how they choose to implement Product Activation.

System Locked Preinstallation

Many OEM computers come with a system restore CD-ROM that allows the user to perform a complete reinstallation or repair of the installed software components, including the operating system. In this way a specific CD-ROM can be tied to a specific system BIOS, thus preventing the CD from being used to install Windows on any other computer. Although OEM CD BIOS locking is not new, it has been expanded and now features integrated Product Activation. This method of protecting the software product is called *System Locked Preinstallation*, or *SLP*.

When SLP is implemented, the information stored in the BIOS is what protects against casual piracy such as installing the product on another computer. No communication is required with the Microsoft activation center, and thus the hardware hash value is required to be calculated. This form of Product Activation relies entirely on the BIOS information matching the SLP information at boot time. Because no hardware hash is calculated, you could thus change out every piece of hardware in the OEM computer without the need for reactivation of Windows XP Professional. In cases where the motherboard must be replaced, this could also be done without reactivation as long as the replacement motherboard was from the same OEM and contained the proper BIOS. Should a different motherboard be installed in the OEM computer that has non-matching BIOS information, the Windows XP installation would then require reactivation within 30 days via the Internet or telephone call.

Using Standard Product Activation

If desired, an OEM can also activate a Windows XP installation in the same way that retail purchase versions are activated. OEM computer installations activated using the standard Product Activation methods have all of the same restrictions that retail purchase versions of Windows XP Professional do.

No OEM Product Activation

Some OEMs may choose to not activate Windows XP at all. Newly purchased OEM computers that fall under this category will require Product Activation by the consumer using the standard Product Activation methods, either via the Internet or by telephone call to Microsoft.

Volume Licensing

The simplest of all scenarios occurs when dealing with Windows XP Professional licenses acquired through one of the Microsoft volume licensing agreements, such as Microsoft Open License, Enterprise Agreement, or Select License. Such installations will not require activation.

Windows XP Professional installations that are performed using volume licensing media and volume licensing keys (VLK) have no Product Activation, hardware checking, or limitations on product installation or disk imaging.

Licensing Lingo

For more information on Microsoft volume licensing and the various programs, see the article "Microsoft Licensing Madness" located at http://infocenter.cramsession.com/techlibrary/gethtml.asp?ID=1409 and also the Microsoft Licensing home page located at http://microsoft.com/licensing/.

How Product Activation Works

As mentioned previously, the hardware hash and the Product ID are the two parts that make up the Installation ID. The Product ID is directly tied to the Product Key that is supplied with the Windows XP retail product. OEMs will usually supply the Product Key with media they ship with new computers. Of the Product ID and the hardware hash, only the hardware hash truly identifies a particular computer enough for Product Activation's purposes. Thus, the hardware hash is of some concern to you, as it ultimately controls how Product Activation functions and whether or not activation is required on an installation.

Table 2.3 lists the hardware components that are used in calculating the hardware hash and the length of the data (in bits) that makes up the hardware hash. The hardware hash value is comprised of two 32-bit double words, for a total of 64 bits (or 8 bytes) worth of data.

Table 2.3 Hardware Hash Components

Component	Length of Hash Value (in Bits)
Volume serial number	10
Network adapter MAC address	10
CD-ROM/DVD-ROM/CD-RW identifier	7
Graphics display adapter	5
Amount of installed RAM (various ranges)	3
CPU type	3
CPU serial number	6

Table 2.3   Continued

Component	Length of Hash Value (in Bits)
Hard drive serial number	7
SCSI controller serial number	5
IDE controller serial number	4
Docking capability	1
Hardware hash version (version of algorithm used)	3

The first four components make up the first double-word value, with the rest of the list making up the second double-word value. With the exception of amount of installed RAM and the hardware hash version, all other values are calculated using selected bits of an MD5 hash.

The value for a docking-capable computer also includes PCMCIA cards because using either a docking station or PCMCIA cards can cause hardware appearing and disappearing. This can lead to the appearance of devices being changed when they are simply not present at that time—such as when a portable computer is undocked.

The possible values for the installed RAM value are listed in Table 2.4. As of the time of this writing, the hardware hash value is always set to a value of 001 decimal, which is a hex value of 0x01. If a component is not installed, such as a SCSI host adapter, the value returned in the hardware hash will be a zero value.

Hex, Huh?

Hexadecimal, or more commonly hex, uses the numbers 0–9 and the letters A–F to form a base-16 numbering system. The 0x in front of a hex value simply notates it as a hexadecimal value.

For a great primer on hexadecimal numbering, see the Intuitor Hexadecimal Headquarters located at http://www.intuitor.com/hex/.

Table 2.4   RAM Amounts and Corresponding Hash Values

Amount of RAM installed	Value
Less than 32MB	1
32MB–63MB	2
64MB–127MB	3
128MB–255MB	4
256MB–511MB	5
512MB–1023MB	6
More than 1023MB	7

As an example, the processor serial number is 96 bits in length. When Product Activation performs the hash calculation on that 96-bit value, it returns a 128-bit long value. Of these 128 bits in the hash value, only 6 bits of data are actually used in the hardware hash value that forms part of the Installation ID.

Six bits provides 64 different combinations (2^6); thus for the millions of computers in existence, only 64 possible processor hash values are possible. As only a fraction of the original data is used in the Product Activation calculation, the data cannot be reverse-engineered, as previously mentioned. The processor serial number can never be determined from these six bits of data; the same holds true for all the other components that Product Activation performs hashes on. In this way, the hardware hash has purposely been designed by Microsoft to ensure the user's privacy is respected at all times.

Perfect Privacy?

Although Microsoft has gone to great lengths to ensure that your private information stays private at all times, no process is perfect, and Product Activation is no exception. For more alternative views on the security of Product Activation, see the Fully Licensed FAQ on Product Activation at http://www.licenturion.com/xp/fully-licensed-faq.txt.

During the installation of Windows XP, the hardware hash is calculated. These eight bytes of data, when combined with the Product ID (nine bytes) make up the Installation ID. When Product Activation is conducted via the Internet, these 17 bytes of data are sent to the Microsoft activation servers in binary format, along with header information, over a secure sockets (SSL) connection.

The activation process requires three steps when completed over the Internet:

1. A handshake request, which establishes the connection between the Windows XP Professional computer and the Microsoft activation servers.

2. A license request, in which the Windows XP Professional computer asks for a PKCS10 digital certificate from the Microsoft activation servers.

3. An acknowledgement request, in which the Microsoft activation servers transmit a signed digital certificate activating the installation.

If the Internet activation succeeds then Product Activation is complete and will not again become an issue unless you exceed the maximum number of allowed changes, as detailed in the "Number of Changeable Items" section.

Should Internet activation not be feasible or desirable, telephone activation is possible as outlined in the following process.

1. Locate the appropriate telephone number by selecting the country from which you are calling.

2. Provide the 50 decimal digit Installation ID to the Microsoft representative.

3. Enter in the corresponding 42 decimal digit Confirmation ID as supplied by the Microsoft representative.

For More Information...

For more information on Product Activation, including how the hardware hash values are calculated for each hardware component, see the Fully Licensed website at http://www.licenturion.com/xp/.

Number of Changeable Items

After Windows XP has been activated, the hardware hash is rechecked at every user logon event. This serves to reduce another prevalent form of software piracy—that of disk cloning. *Disk cloning* is an asset to administrators looking to quickly deploy multiple copies of Windows XP, but is illegal without having the required Product Keys. In most legal cases, disk cloning is done using a volume license copy of Windows XP Professional using a Volume License Key, which does not require Product Activation in the first place.

When Windows XP performs its hardware check, it is looking for changes in the hardware configuration of the computer. If a substantially different configuration is detected then reactivation is required. The actual number of components that will result in a reactivation scenario is discussed shortly. The hardware check at login is done after the SLP BIOS check should the SLP BIOS check fail. As long as an OEM computer is using a genuine replacement motherboard from the OEM containing the correct BIOS data, all other components in an OEM computer activated using the SLP BIOS method can be changed out without requiring reactivation of Windows XP.

The number of hardware items that it takes to achieve "substantially different" configuration (in Microsoft speak) is dependent upon two things: whether the computer has a network adapter at the time of Windows XP activation, and whether the computer is dockable (this also includes the presence of PCMCIA slots), as outlined in Table 2.5.

Table 2.5   Number of Changed Components to Require Reactivation

Network Adapter Status	Docking Capability	Number of Changed Components to Require Reactivation
None installed at the time of Windows XP activation	No	4 or more
Installed at the time of Windows XP activation and subsequently changed	No	4 or more
Installed at the time of Windows XP activation and not changed	No	6 or more
None installed at the time of Windows XP activation	Yes	7 or more
Installed at the time of Windows XP activation and subsequently changed	Yes	7 or more
Installed at the time of Windows XP activation and not changed	Yes	9 or more

To help explain Table 2.5, two scenarios might be helpful.

1. A computer has a network adapter installed at the time of Windows XP activation. You later change the motherboard, CPU, video adapter, and CD-ROM drive. Additionally, you add more memory and a second hard drive.

   Reactivation is not required in this instance because only five components have been changed: motherboard, CPU, video adapter, CD-ROM, and RAM (amount). The addition of a second hard drive is not of significance to Product Activation. If you were to change six or more hardware components, reactivation would be required.

2. A computer has no network adapter installed at the time of Windows XP Professional activation. You later change the motherboard, CPU, video adapter, and CD-ROM drive. Additionally, you add more memory and a second hard drive.

   Reactivation is required in this instance because five components have been changed: motherboard, CPU, video adapter, CD-ROM, and RAM (amount). When you change four or more hardware components, reactivation is required.

If a single device is changed repeatedly, such as a video adapter that is changed from the original one to new adapter A and later to new adapter B, this is evaluated only as one change. Either the current hardware is the same as when activation was completed or it's not. Windows XP doesn't care how many changes have been made in the interim. Adding components after activation that were not present at the time of activation also has no impact on the hardware hash and is ignored by Windows XP during its check to determine whether reactivation is necessary. Microsoft has also built two additional loopholes into Product Activation for power users who frequently reinstall Windows XP or who frequently change the hardware configuration of their computers. Windows XP can be reinstalled and subsequently reactivated on the same computer an infinite number of times. In cases where the hardware configuration has changed enough to require reactivation, Microsoft allows a maximum of four reactivations per year on "substantially different" hardware—this should be enough to keep most power users happy as they continually tweak their systems. Both of these reactivation events can occur over the Internet instead of requiring a phone call.

Using Installation Switches

Depending on your needs and the type of installation you are performing, you can modify the behaviors and actions of the Windows XP Setup routing by using various switches. Depending on how you are installing Windows XP, there are two methods you can use to call the Setup routine: by using the `winnt.exe` command or by using the `winnt32.exe` command. Some typical reasons to use switches include unattended installations, using Dynamic Update, installing the Recovery Console, and changing the location for the installation source files, to name a few.

Winnt32.exe

Let's look first at the more useful, and likely, `winnt32.exe` command. The `winnt32.exe` command can be used to perform a clean installation or an upgrade installation of Windows XP. You can run the `winnt32.exe` command at the command prompt from any computer running one of the following operating systems:

- Windows 95
- Windows 98
- Windows 98 Second Edition
- Windows Millennium Edition
- Windows NT 4.0
- Windows 2000
- Windows XP

Using winnt32.exe *from Windows 95*

You cannot upgrade from Windows 95 to Windows XP. An installation started from Windows 95 using the `winnt32.exe` command can only be a clean installation.

For more information about supported upgrade paths, see the "Upgrade Installations" section earlier in this chapter.

The `winnt32.exe` command has the following syntax and switches as detailed in Table 2.6.

```
winnt32 [/checkupgradeonly] [/cmd:command_line] [/cmdcons]
[/copydir:{i386|ia64}\FolderName] [/copysource:FolderName]
[/debug[Level]:[FileName]] [/dudisable]
[/duprepare:pathname] [/dushare:pathname] [/m:FolderName]
[/makelocalsource] [/noreboot] [/s:SourcePath]
[/syspart:DriveLetter] [/tempdrive:DriveLetter]
[/udf:id [,UDB_file]] [/unattend[num]:[answer_file]]
```

Table 2.6   Winnt32.exe Switches

Switch	Description
/checkupgradeonly	Checks your computer for upgrade compatibility with Windows XP. When used with the /unattend switch, no user input is required. If used without the /unattend switch, the results are displayed on the screen and you can save them as desired. The default location is a file named upgrade.txt located in the %systemroot% folder.
/cmd:command_line	Instructs Setup to carry out a specific command before the final phase of Setup.
/cmdcons	Installs the Recovery Console as a startup option on a functioning x86-based computer. You can only use the /cmdcons option after normal Setup is finished.
/copydir:{i386|ia64}\FolderName	Creates an additional folder within the folder in which the Windows XP files are installed. You can use /copydir to create as many additional folders as you want.
/copysource:FolderName	Creates a temporary additional folder within the folder in which the Windows XP files are installed. Unlike the folders /copydir creates, /copysource folders are deleted after Setup completes.
/debug[Level]:[FileName]	Creates a debug log at the level specified. The default log file is C:\systemroot\Winnt32.log, and the default debug level is 2. The log levels are as follows: 0 represents severe errors, 1 represents errors, 2 represents warnings, 3 represents information, and 4 represents detailed information for debugging. Each level includes the levels below it.
/dudisable	Prevents Dynamic Update from running. This option will disable Dynamic Update even if you use an answer file and specify Dynamic Update options in that file.
/duprepare:pathname	Carries out preparations on an installation share so that it can be used with Dynamic Update files that you downloaded from the Windows Update website.
/dushare:pathname	Specifies a share on which you previously downloaded Dynamic Update files (updated files for use with Setup) from the Windows Update website.
/m:FolderName	Specifies that Setup copies replacement files from an alternate location. Instructs Setup to look in the alternate location first, and if files are present, to use them instead of the files from the default location.
/makelocalsource	Instructs Setup to copy all installation source files to your local hard disk. Use /makelocalsource when installing from a CD to provide installation files when the CD is not available later in the installation.
/noreboot	Instructs Setup to not restart the computer after the file copy phase of Setup is completed so that you can run another command.
/s:SourcePath	Specifies the source location of the Windows XP files. To simultaneously copy files from multiple servers, type the /s:SourcePath option multiple times (up to a maximum of eight). If you type the option multiple times, the first server specified must be available, or Setup will fail.

(continues)

Table 2.6   Continued

Switch	Description
`/syspart:DriveLetter`	On an x86-based computer, specifies that you can copy Setup startup files to a hard disk, mark the disk as active, and then install the disk into another computer. When you start that computer, it automatically starts with the next phase of Setup. You must always use the `/tem drive` parameter with the `/syspart` parameter.
`/tempdrive:DriveLetter`	Directs Setup to place temporary files on the specified partition. For a new installation, Windows XP will also be installed on the specified partition.
`/udf:id [,UDB_file]`	Indicates an identifier (ID) that Setup uses to specify how a Uniqueness Database (UDB) file modifies an answer file (see the `/unattend` entry). If no UDB file is specified, Setup prompts the user to insert a disk that contains the `$Unique$.udb` file.
`/unattend`	Upgrades your previous version of Windows 98, Windows Millennium Edition, Windows NT 4.0, or Windows 2000 in unattended Setup mode. All user settings are taken from the previous installation, so no user intervention is required during Setup.
`/unattend[num]:[answer_file]`	Performs a fresh installation in unattended Setup mode. The specified `answer_file` provides Setup with your custom specifications. *num* is the number of seconds between the time that Setup finishes copying the files and when it restarts your computer.

◄◄ To learn more about using the Windows Upgrade Advisor, see "Checking Hardware and Software Compatibility," p. 39.

Winnt32 on Itanium-based Computers

If you run the `winnt32.exe` command on an Itanium-based computer, the command must be run from the Extensible Firmware Interface (EFI) or from Windows XP. Also, the `/cmdcons` and `/syspart` switches are not available, and options relating to upgrades are also not available.

For more information on EFI, see the TechNet article "Managing GPT Disks in Itanium-based Computers," located at http://www.microsoft.com/technet/prodtechnol/winxppro/reskit/prkb_cnc_ywwc.asp.

Winnt.exe

The second, and less often used, way to invoke startup is by using the `winnt.exe` command. The `winnt.exe` command can be used from the command prompt of even the oldest operating systems, such as Windows 95, Windows 3.x, and MS-DOS. These operating systems are not upgradeable to Windows XP Professional.

The `winnt.exe` command has the following syntax and switches as detailed in Table 2.7.

```
winnt [/s:SourcePath] [/t:TempDrive] [/u:answer file]
[/udf:ID [,UDB_file]] [/r:folder][/rx:folder][/e:command]
[/a]
```

Table 2.7 *Winnt.exe* **Switches**

Switch	Description
/s:SourcePath	Specifies the source location of the Windows XP files. The location must be a full path and can use UNC locations.
/t:TempDrive	Directs Setup to place temporary files on the specified drive and to install Windows XP on that drive.
/u:answer file	Performs an unattended Setup using an answer file. If you use /u, you must also use /s.
/udf:ID [,UDB_file]	Indicates an identifier (ID) that Setup uses to specify how a Uniqueness Database (UDB) file modifies an answer file (see /u). If no UDB_file is specified, Setup prompts you to insert a disk that contains the $Unique$.udb file.
/r:folder	Specifies an optional folder to be installed. The folder remains after Setup finishes.
/rx:folder	Specifies an optional folder to be copied. The folder is deleted after Setup finishes.
/e:command	Specifies a command to be carried out just before the final phase of Setup.
/a	Enables accessibility options.

Clean Install Summary

As you can surely tell from the previous sections, installing Windows XP is a much improved process over previous versions of Windows, although not necessarily a faster one. In most cases, a clean installation using the NTFS file system is the preferred path for installation, but Windows XP is flexible and allows for easy upgrades of existing installations.

The User State Migration Tool and Files and Settings Transfer Wizard, discussed in the next chapter, can also aid you in migrating your settings and files from an old computer to a new computer. Should you decide later that you want to take advantage of the NTFS file system on an upgrade installation, you can easily convert the file system without losing a single file.

Although about 99% of all installations should go smoothly, problems can and do happen. Some of the more common issues that you may see during an installation of Windows XP include the following:

- You see Stop 0x0000000A irql_not_less_or_equal appear on the screen. This error is usually due to hardware or hardware drivers that are not compatible with Windows XP. Ensure that all your hardware is listed on the Hardware Compatibility List and that you have the most up-to-date drivers for your installed hardware. MSKB# 311564, located at http://support.microsoft.com/default.aspx?scid=kb;en-us;311564, has more information on this error.

- You get an error such as Setup cannot copy the file file_name. Press X to retry, Y to abort when attempting to perform the installation. This error can be caused by many problems such as a dirty CD-ROM, a damaged CD-ROM, viruses, or damaged RAM installed on your computer. If possible, attempt to perform the installation using a different CD-ROM, and verify that all installed hardware in your computer is working properly, and that you do not have any viruses. Also, certain third-party applications that may be installed (if performing an upgrade installation) can cause this error to appear. MSKB# 310064, located at http://support.microsoft.com/default.aspx?id=kb;en-us;310064, has more information on this type of error.

- You receive this error: NTLDR is missing. Press any key to restart. This error is usually caused by upgrading over a Windows 9x installation that resides on a FAT32 hard drive with an incorrect geometry configuration. To fix this error, you will need to correct the hard drive geometry configuration. MSKB# 314057, located at http://support.microsoft.com/default.aspx?scid=kb;en-us;314057, has more information on this error.

Should you encounter problems during your installation of Windows XP Professional, a quick search on the Microsoft website will usually turn up the required information. To perform advanced searches, visit the Microsoft Advanced Search page at http://search.microsoft.com/advanced_search.asp.

Automated System Recovery

Automated System Recovery is a new feature in Windows XP that adds another way to perform a system recovery should things go bad during a Windows installation. ASR, shown in Figure 2.18, replaces an older tool from Windows 2000 and Windows NT 4.0: the Emergency Repair Disk.

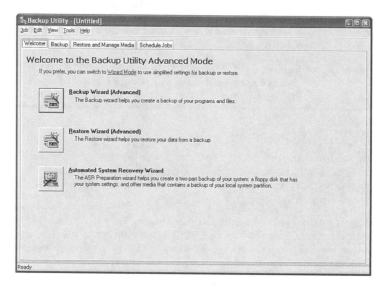

Figure 2.18 Locating ASR in Windows XP.

Automated System Recovery (ASR) uses the Windows XP Backup utility and consists of two parts: a backup of critical files that is made to a local (recommended) or remote storage device, and a floppy disk containing three files critical to the restoration phase.

The files that are backed up include the system state data and all files stored on the system volume. *System state* refers to all of the components that determine the current state of the operating system (hence the clever name) and includes user accounts, hard drive configuration, network configuration, video settings, hardware configuration, software settings, and various other critical files that are required to run Windows XP Professional properly. Additionally, the system state includes files that are required to start the operating system properly, including those that are found in the %systemroot% directory and boot files such as ntldr and ntdetect.

The floppy disk contains three files: asr.sif, asrpnp.sif, and setup.log. If you're thinking that the .SIF extension sounds familiar, you're right. .SIF files are used for answer files to customize unattended installations of Windows XP Professional. The functions of these three files are outlined as follows:

■ Asr.sif contains information about your computer's storage devices including hard drives, partitions, volumes, and removable storage devices. A portion of the asr.sif file is shown in Figure 2.19.

- `Asrpnp.sif` contains information about the Plug and Play information installed in your computer.

- `Setup.log` contains a listing of all system state and critical files that were backed up. It aids in the restoration of these files when you invoke ASR recovery.

▶▶ To learn more about Answer Files, see "Using Interactive Answer Files for Installation," p. 76.

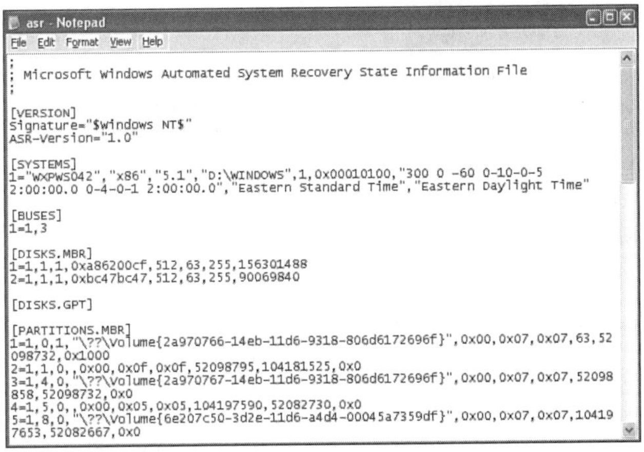

Figure 2.19 `asr.sif` contains information about hard drives and removable storage.

Using asr.sif *and* asrpnp.sif

Although not the intended purpose of **asr.sif** and **asrpnp.sif**, they provide a great wealth of information about installed devices and configurations for exploration into Microsoft Product Activation.

The Automated System Recovery process is one that is not to be taken lightly. You should not consider using ASR until you have unsuccessfully tried to use other recovery methods, such as Driver Rollback, System Restore, Parallel installations, Last Known Good Configuration, Recovery Console, Safe Mode, or restoration using Windows XP Professional Backup. ASR will restore the system state and other critical files that were backed up at the time of its creation.

Backup Frequency

The frequency at which you make your ASR backups is critical to having a good experience when using ASR for recovery. Make them regularly, at least weekly—more often if you make frequent changes to the computer.

The process to create an Automated System Recovery set is outlined here.

1. Start the Windows XP Backup utility by clicking Start, All Programs, Accessories, System Tools, Backup. (If you use Windows XP Home you may need to install Backup from the Windows XP CD-ROM, as it is not installed by default.)

2. If the Wizard view appears, as shown in Figure 2.20, click Advanced Mode.

Figure 2.20   The Windows XP Professional Backup utility in Wizard mode.

3. Click the Automated System Recovery Wizard button.

4. Click Next to dismiss the opening page of the ASR Wizard.

5. From the Backup Destination page, shown in Figure 2.21, configure the location for the backed up files to be placed. For best results, a local storage location is preferred over a network location that may not be available later. After configuring your location, click Next to continue.

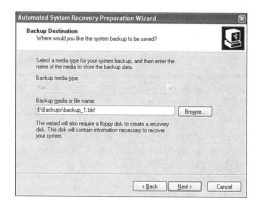

Figure 2.21   Configuring the backup destination.

6. On the Completing the Automated System Recovery Preparation Wizard page, click Finish to initiate the ASR creation process.

7. When prompted, insert a blank 3-1/2 inch 1.44MB floppy disk in the A: drive of your computer. Click OK to create the floppy disk portion of the ASR set.

8. Label and store the floppy disk in a safe, secure location for future use.

Should the day come when you need to use ASR to recover your computer, proceed as outlined here:

1. Start your computer with the Windows XP Professional Setup CD-ROM.

2. When prompted to press a key to boot from the CD-ROM, do so. If your computer does not support booting from a CD-ROM, you will need to use Setup floppy disks to start the process.

3. When prompted to press F2 to start Automated System Recovery, as shown in Figure 2.22, do so. You will be prompted to supply your ASR floppy disk.

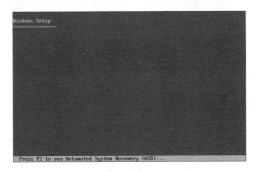

Windows Setup

Press F2 to run Automated System Recovery (ASR)...

Figure 2.22   Starting ASR.

4. Follow the onscreen prompts to complete the Automated System Recovery process.

Automated Deployments

If you're planning to deploy Windows XP to a number of systems, you're probably considering automating the installation process. And if you're not, you should be. Automating a deployment may take a bit of development time up front, but it saves time in the long run when compared to manually installing a large number of systems. Automation ensures consistency by removing most of the opportunities for human error.

So who should use automated deployment? Well, if you're a home user, and you're only planning on installing Windows XP Home Edition on that old machine your kid uses to surf the Web, you probably just want to run with the standard out-of-the-box install process. But if you happen to have 50 such kids, if you need to frequently install the same base configuration on a system or two for testing purposes, if you configure Windows XP systems for resale, or if you're developing a deployment scenario for an organization's IT department, you'll definitely want to consider automating.

A number of options are available when automating the installation of Windows XP, which are listed as follows and illustrated in Figure 2.23:

- *Scripted install from CD or Distribution Share*—This is the most basic type of automated install. Setup runs using the usual `winnt.exe` or `winnt32.exe` installer, and a preconfigured answer file is passed in from a command-line switch. The answer file supplies the information that would normally have to be entered manually.

- *Scripted install using boot CD*—In this process, the system boots from the install CD, and Windows XP Setup reads an answer file from the A: drive.

- *System image prepared with Sysprep*—With this scheme, you install and configure one system to your exact specifications, use a *disk image* (an exact duplicate of a system drive) to deploy identical copies to a large number of systems.

- *Remote Installation Services (RIS)*—This more sophisticated method for deploying Windows XP over the network involves booting from a network interface card (NIC), ROM, or ROM emulator disk.

Scripted Install from CD or Distribution Share

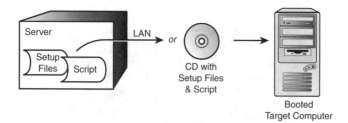

Scripted Install Using Boot CD

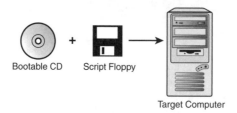

Scripted Install prepared with Sysprep

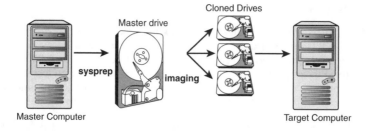

Remote Installation Services (RIS)

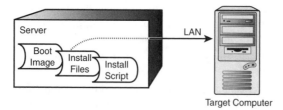

Figure 2.23 Four scenarios for automatic deployment of Windows XP.

Licensing Issues

Whether you choose to automate using the bootable Windows XP CD with an answer file, using a disk image, or using a scripted install over the network, the first thing you'll want to do is make sure you're properly licensed. If I had a dollar for every time I'd created an image using the wrong media for my licensing, I'd have exactly one dollar...because after the first time I screwed it up, I've always remembered to double-check my media before starting development on a new automated install.

Note

Microsoft revises its licensing policies almost as often as it releases service packs. For the latest twists and turns, check out http://www.microsoft.com/licensing.

Under Microsoft's current licensing model, retail Windows XP media cannot be used for multiple installations. Using a scripted install with a separate retail CD for each system is still an option, as long as you aren't trying to fully automate the install. To script installs from retail media, though, you'd need one retail CD with a retail product key for each system, and you'd still need to prompt for the unique retail product key on each machine. Additionally, you'd need to run through the product activation wizard on each system. This method wouldn't be practical for most organizations, but if you're only worried about a handful of systems—in a very small office or in your home, perhaps—it is a valid option. Using an answer file to simplify individual installations is exactly like using an answer file for large-scale installations, except you won't need to spend nearly as much time on development and testing. I prefer the scripted install using the bootable Windows XP installation CD when developing a setup process for a small-scale environment.

◀◀ For more details on product activation, refer back to "Product Activation," p. 60.

If you're planning to install Windows XP on five or more systems, you're eligible for one of Microsoft's Volume Licensing programs. There are four basic programs available for Windows XP volume licensing, listed in Table 2.8. Machines loaded with Windows XP using media acquired through one of these programs and using a valid volume license product key are not required to run the product activation wizard.

Table 2.8   Windows XP Volume Licensing

Program	Description
Open License	For academic institutions, charities, corporations, or government organizations needing licenses for five or more systems.
Select License	For academic institutions, charities, corporations, or government organizations with decentralized purchasing needing licenses for 250 or more systems.
Enterprise Agreement	Software *purchasing* agreement for corporate customers with centralized purchasing, needing licenses for 250 systems or more. In this type of agreement, the company pays for the licenses needed, after which it can use those licenses as long as it wants.
Enterprise Subscription Agreement	Software leasing agreement for corporate customers with centralized purchasing, needing licenses for 250 systems or more. In the leasing agreement, companies pay less for the OS licenses up front, but they pay additional fees to renew their subscriptions yearly to continue using the operating system. This type of agreement usually includes future OS upgrades as part of the deal.

If you've ever used the Select or MSDN media to install a previous version of a Microsoft operating system, you might have noticed that the product key was preconfigured on the CD. With XP, this feature is no longer there. Additionally, the Worldwide Fulfillment media no longer includes a product key on the CD packaging. For these media, you must use the unique Volume License Product Key assigned to your organization.

Adding and Using the Deployment Tools

As with Windows 2000, the deployment tools are in the DEPLOY.CAB file under the \SUPPORT\TOOLS directory of the installation CD. Extract these files to a directory of your choice. For the sake of future reference, we'll assume the files have been extracted to C:\DEPLOYTOOLS

Note

While in this directory, it wouldn't hurt to install the Support Tools by running **SETUP.EXE**. Select Complete Installation for the full toolset. The Support Tools are unsupported utilities included to provide support personnel and experienced users with handy tools for diagnosing and resolving computer problems. About 70 executables and half a dozen script files are documented in the supporting files included with the install.

Not all the included support tools are listed in the Support Tools Help (this Help file shows under the Support Tools program group after installing the tools). For a full list, be sure to read **\SUPPORT\TOOLS\README.HTM**.

Let's look at some of the key files you have under C:\DEPLOYTOOLS:

- DEPLOY.CHM—Windows Help file for the Microsoft Windows XP Corporate Deployment Tools User's Guide. This Help file contains a great deal of useful information. To view it, double-click its icon, or type **start deploy.chm** at the command prompt.

- SYSPREP.EXE—Executable used to prepare a system for disk imaging.

- SETUPCL.EXE—When preparing a system for disk imaging, this executable must be included in the SYSPREP folder with the SYSPREP.EXE and SYSPREP.INF files.

- SETUPMGR.EXE—This is the Windows Setup Manager Wizard. It will run through a series of questions, resulting in a properly formatted answer file suitable for framing.

- REF.CHM—This Windows Help file provides full documentation for all sections used in answer files. In addition, you can find a couple of sample answer files under both the Unattend.txt and the Sysprep.inf sections. Many of the sections listed in this Help file are not exposed by the Windows Setup Manager Wizard.

Using Interactive Answer Files for Installation

The answer file is the cornerstone of any automated installation routine. If you used answer files under Windows 2000, the concept and purpose haven't changed: The answer file provides the answers for both the text mode setup and GUI mode setup portions of the install, relieving end users or technicians from manually completing this repetitive task. Naturally, this speeds up the install process, increases the accuracy over manual data entry, and serves as a form of documentation. The basic structure of the file is the same for a CD-based unattended install, an over-the-network scripted install, an RIS-based install, or an OS image using SYSPREP.

Note

The procedure in the next section can vary if you have a Windows CD slipstreamed with Service Pack 2.

Creating an Answer File

Creating an answer file can be as easy as running a wizard or as complex as manually creating the entire file in Notepad. Personally, I prefer the wizard to create the initial file and Notepad for post-wizard tweaking. To start the Windows Setup Manager Wizard, go to the C:\DEPLOYTOOLS directory and run SETUPMGR.EXE.

Note

You do not have to run the Setup Manager Wizard under Windows XP. It will run on Windows 2000, allowing you to create distribution share points and answer files for Windows XP without having XP installed.

Let's walk through using the wizard to create a complete answer file for a fully automated CD-based installation of Windows XP Professional. If you're following along in the wizard, this should take about 30 minutes to complete. I'm not going to take up space with screen shots, but I will identify and explain all the screens you should expect to see:

1. The first screen is the welcome screen for the wizard. Click Next.

2. The second screen, New or Existing Answer File, lets you select between creating a new file or modifying an existing file. Select Create a New Answer File and click Next.

Note

The Help button becomes active after you reach the second screen of the Setup Manager Wizard. The Help files in the Windows XP Setup Manager are very well developed and provide excellent on-the-spot information if you find yourself questioning the intricacies between multiple options. Be aware that there are different versions of the wizard that may display variations in the options explained here. If you are using a CD that is slipstreamed with SP2, there will be no help button and some of the options will vary.

3. Next is the Product to Install screen. On this screen, select whether to create a file to use with a Windows Unattended Installation, a Sysprep Install, or an install using Remote Installation Services. For our purposes, select Windows Unattended Installation and click Next.

4. The fourth screen, Platform, is where you select between Windows XP Home Edition, Windows XP Professional, and Windows 2002 Server versions. Note that the wizard was released before the server family officially changed names to Windows .NET Server (unless you have a CD with SP2). Select Windows XP Professional and click Next.

5. On the screen titled User Interaction Level, decide how automated the automated install process should be. Table 2.9 details the different options for this screen. After reviewing the table, select Fully Automated and click Next. If using retail media, you actually need to select Hide Pages or Read Only for the user interaction level, which I'll explain further in Step 11.

Table 2.9 Automated Install Interaction Levels

Interaction Level	Description
Provide defaults	Questions posed by Windows Setup are filled in with defaults provided by the answer file, but the user is able to review or change any answers you have supplied.
Fully automated	If you select this option, you must supply all required answers in the answer file. Windows Setup will not prompt the user for any answers, and setup will complete with no action required from the user. If you select this option, the wizard will require you to answer all necessary questions.

(continues)

Table 2.9   Continued

Interaction Level	Description
Hide pages	Any page for which all answers are provided by the answer file will not be displayed. If an answer is missing, the page will be displayed and the user will be prompted to fill in the blanks.
Read only	If you provided answers for questions posed by Windows Setup, the page will still be displayed, but the end user cannot change the answers you have provided. The user will be prompted for any answers left out of the answer file.
GUI attended	The text mode portion of install is automated, but the user must manually complete the graphical portion of Windows Setup.

6. On the sixth screen, select whether to create a distribution folder or run the installation from a CD. If you select the option to create a distribution folder, the Setup Manager Wizard will prompt you to insert a Windows XP CD from which it can copy the required files. For now, select No, This Answer File Will Be Used to Install from a CD.

7. On the License Agreement screen, check the box to accept the EULA. Click Next.

8. The remainder of the screens will prompt for answers to the questions normally presented by the graphical portion of setup. The first of these asks for a name and organization. Enter your name and organization, and click Next.

Note

If you plan to use the option for automatic computer naming (see step 12), you must enter an organization name at this screen.

9. You should see the Display Settings panel. Here, configure the default colors, screen area, and refresh frequency. Sticking with the Windows default for all three options is the safe bet, but if you want different options and know your target hardware will support the exact configuration you select, feel free to adjust accordingly. When done, click Next.

10. Select your time zone and click Next.

11. The next screen is Providing the Product Key. If you're using retail media, you won't really get much use out of this screen; leave it blank and manually enter the product key at this point in each installation. In addition, you'll probably need to go back and select Hide Pages or Read Only for the user interaction level on step 5. If you have your volume license media and volume license product key (refer to the first section of this chapter), this is where you enter it. Enter a product key, and click Next.

12. In the Computer Names screen, click the check mark next to Automatically Generate Computer Names Based on Organization Name at the bottom of the screen. This lets you use the same answer file for any number of systems without naming conflicts. Automatically generated computer names are composed of the first word of the organization name, followed by a hyphen and a randomly generated alphanumeric string.

13. The next screen prompts you for the Administrator password. Unlike previous versions of Windows, you have the option of encrypting the password in the answer file. In Windows 2000 and earlier, the password was stored as clear text, which meant that anyone who found your answer file could compromise your local administrator passwords. Enter your password in both boxes, select the option to encrypt, and click Next.

Note

When using with a disk image, you must clear the Administrator account's password on the system used to make the master image. If you do not, setting the password in the answer file (**SYSPREP.INF**, in this case) will have no effect, and the target systems will retain the same local administrator password as on the master system.

---

14. In the Networking Components screen, select Typical Settings to configure your machine for standard settings (TCP/IP using DHCP for addressing, File and Print sharing for Microsoft Networks, and the Client for Microsoft Networks). Click Next.

Note

If you are in a small office or home office environment, rather than setting up a server just to use as a DHCP server, I recommend the Etherfast Cable/DSL Router from Linksys (www.linksys.com). It offers one-port, four-port, and eight-port versions, all of which can uplink into a hub. Not only do these devices provide full DHCP services for up to 253 clients, but also they act as both an Internet gateway to a broadband connection and as a hardware-based firewall to protect your internal network from outside influences.

---

15. On the Workgroup or Domain screen, select the option for Windows Server Domain. During mass-production installations, you probably won't want to manually set up domain computer accounts in advance, so enter your domain name in the requisite blank, and select the option to create a computer account in the domain during installation. Enter a username and password with rights to add a computer to the domain. If you do not have an accessible domain to use for this, are setting up standalone workstations, or use workgroups instead of domains in your organization, you can select the option for Workgroup and provide a workgroup name.

Note

Strangely enough, even though you can use encryption for the local administrator account password, it is not an option for this area. That means the account information you enter here will be stored in the answer file in clear text. For this reason, it is recommended that you do *not* use a domain administrator's account to join computers to the domain. You might want to create a special domain account that does not have permission to log on as an interactive user but does have permission to create computer accounts in the domain, and enter the account information in these spaces.

---

16. On the Telephone screen, fill in your country, area code, and the number to access an outside line. Select whether your phone system uses pulse or touch-tone, and enter any number sequence required to access an outside line. When you've filled out all the boxes, click Next.

17. On the Regional Settings screen, select Use the Default Regional Settings for the Windows Version You Are Installing. Click Next.

18. The Languages screen provides an opportunity to install additional default language groups. For now, stick with the defaults and click Next.

19. On the Browser and Shell Settings screen select Use Default Internet Explorer Settings and click Next.

20. On the Installation Folder screen, specify where to install Windows XP. By default, Windows XP uses Windows as the folder name. If you want Windows to install to the same location as Windows NT 4.0 or Windows 2000, select the option labeled This Folder and enter **Winnt**. For now, let's stick with the default, a folder named Windows, and click Next.

21. If you want, you can automatically install network printers after the first user logon. You'll con-figure the default printers at this screen, the Install Printers screen. To use this feature, enter a network printer UNC in the form *servername**printername*, and click Next. If you don't have any network printers, leave this blank. It is not required for a successful fully automated setup.

22. The next screen, Run Once, lists commands to run after the user logs in for the first time. Any printers you added on the previous screen will show up here as AddPrinter \\server\share. Do not change anything on this screen; click Next. Any additional commands can be manually added to the script later.

23. After installation, the final screen in this section, Additional Commands, allows you to run commands that do not require a user to be logged on. Commands entered here will execute before the Windows Logon screen shows up the first time. For the purposes of this walk-through, do not add anything at this screen; click Finish.

24. Windows Setup Manager prompts you for the location and filename under which to save your answer file. Save your file somewhere you can find it, with the filename Winnt.sif.

25. In the final window, Setup Manager Complete, if the Next button is not available, click the X in the upper right to close the dialog.

You should now have a complete answer file named Winnt.sif. If you open the file in a text editor, it should look a little like the following:

Note

If you copy the following example file for your own use, I strongly recommend changing the product key I've used to a valid product key for the media you are planning to use. The listing shows a Microsoft-provided generic product key that's suitable for testing purposes only. Refer to http://www.microsoft.com/technet/prodtechnol/winxppro/deploy/default.mspx for a full list of generic Windows XP product keys. These keys are blocked from activation at the Microsoft clearinghouse. If you use one of the generic keys, you will have approximately 14 days to experiment with and test your system before Windows will require activation.

```
;SetupMgrTag
[Data]
    AutoPartition=1
    MsDosInitiated="0"
    UnattendedInstall="Yes"

[Unattended]
    UnattendMode=FullUnattended
    OemSkipEula=Yes
    OemPreinstall=No
    TargetPath=\WINDOWS

[GuiUnattended]
    AdminPassword=eadb1736119939abdd99a9b993edc9a87a44c42236119ae1893bd142a2bbaead
    EncryptedAdminPassword=Yes
    OEMSkipRegional=1
    TimeZone=20
    OemSkipWelcome=1

[UserData]
    ProductID=DR8GV-C8V6J-BYXHG-7PYJR-DB66Y
    FullName="Jeff Ferris"
    OrgName="Ferris Technology Networks"
    ComputerName=*
```

```
[TapiLocation]
    CountryCode=1
    Dialing=Tone
    AreaCode=512

[GuiRunOnce]
    Command0="rundll32 printui.dll,PrintUIEntry /in /n \\printserver01\laser"

[Identification]
    JoinDomain=FERRISTECH
    DomainAdmin=ComputerAddAccount
    DomainAdminPassword=ferristechCA

[Networking]
    InstallDefaultComponents=Yes
```

Customizing the Answer File

To modify an existing answer file, you have two options: First, you can take the easy way out by rerunning the Setup Manager Wizard. After starting the wizard, select Modify an Existing Answer File on the second wizard screen. The rest of the process is the same as in the walk-through under the "Creating an Answer File" section in this chapter. Answers already provided by the existing answer file will show up in the proper locations as you go through the wizard. Change what needs changing, resave the file, and you're good to go. You'd probably want to use the wizard when making major changes to your answer file, such as when changing from a domain to a workgroup model.

Your second option is to modify the answer file using a text editor. Most of the answer file options are fairly self-explanatory, and the REF.CHM file from the DEPLOY.CAB contains full documentation for all sections, keys, and options in case you need additional guidance. I'd document everything for you here, but it would translate to about 150 pages of text that wouldn't be indexed and couldn't be searched (unlike the Help file), and you'd probably fall asleep reading through it all anyway. You'd probably prefer using a text editor to modify an answer file when changing things like the username (FullName=<answer>), the organization name (OrgName=<answer>), or the username and password used to join a computer account to the domain (DomainAdmin=<answer> and DomainAdminPassword= <answer>).

If you are going to use the answer file installation method with standard retail Windows XP licenses, you will need to either edit the product ID in the answer file each time you use it, or you must delete the product ID line from the answer file so that the setup program will prompt for a unique product ID for each installation.

Changing the Answers in a SYSPREP.INF *File*

After you've created a **SYSPREP.INF** file, saved it in the **SYSPREP** directory, executed Sysprep, and created your image, the **SYSPREP.INF** file becomes a permanent part of that image. So, if you need to make changes to something in the answer file, you must create a new image, update the **SYSPREP.INF** file, and rerun Sysprep.

Suppose you only need to change the answer file for a couple of systems. You wouldn't want to go through the whole reimaging process just to change some of the options in the answer file. Fortunately, there's a rarely documented out. Simply make the changes to your **SYSPREP.INF** file, and save **SYSPREP.INF** to the root of a floppy disk. Apply your image to a target system and boot the target system. As soon as the system starts to boot, insert the floppy disk containing the updated **SYSPREP.INF** in the A: drive. The Windows XP Setup Wizard will use the answer file on the floppy disk to override the settings specified in the Sysprep file stored with the image.

Putting an Answer File to Use

Four main types of installations can be performed using an answer file. The name of your answer file will be different depending on the type of install you intend to use it for. Table 2.10 lists the four standard filenames for answer files, as well as their purpose and location.

Table 2.10   Types of Answer Files

Filename	Purpose
RISETUP.SIF	Automate the setup wizard for RIS-based installs. You'll put this file in the \I386\ Templates subdirectory of the folder created for any RIS image.
SYSPREP.INF	Provides answers for the SYSPREP Mini-Setup Wizard. SYSPREP.INF should be placed in the C:\SYSPREP directory before running SYSPREP.EXE to prepare a drive for imaging.
UNATTEND.TXT	Provides responses for the installation process when running an install using WINNT or WINNT32 from a network share or from a command-line–initiated installation from the CD. This file can actually have any name and can be saved in any location that you will be able to access while running the install.
WINNT.SIF	Provides answers for the setup wizard when installing by booting to the Windows XP CD. Save this file to the root of a floppy, and insert the disk right after the installation starts from the bootable Windows XP CD.

Local and Network-Based Unattended Installation

With the answer file created in the "Creating an Answer File" section earlier in this chapter, you might have noticed that the Setup Manager Wizard created a batch file in the same directory as your answer file. This batch file can kick off a Windows XP install from a machine that is already running Windows 95, Windows 98, Windows Me, Windows NT, Windows 2000, or Windows XP. The install will take advantage of the answer file as long as you leave both the batch file and the answer file in the same directory. By default, answer files created to install from the Windows XP CD expect to find your Windows XP CD in the D: drive. If your CD-ROM uses a different drive letter, you must edit the batch file using Notepad to reflect the correct drive letter.

You may remember a point in the walk-through under "Creating an Answer File" (step 6) where the Setup Manager Wizard asked whether to create an answer file to install from CD, or to create or modify a distribution folder. You selected the option to install from CD. Had you selected the distribution folder option, the batch file would point to the UNC to which the install files were copied. Additionally, from within Windows 95/98/Me/NT/2000/XP, you could manually run the installation using the answer file with the WINNT32.EXE command and the optional /unattend switch, using the following syntax:

```
<path_to_install_files>\winnt32 /unattend:filename
```

If you want to complete an over-the-network installation from a system without an operating system, you need to create a DOS-bootable disk capable of connecting to the network and map a drive to the location of the shared Windows XP install files. Instead of running WINNT32.EXE as when running a local or network install from Windows 95/98/Me/NT/2000/XP, use the WINNT.EXE command. To use the answer file, the full command will be

```
Winnt /s:install_source_directory /u:answerfile_name
```

Unattended Install from the Bootable Windows XP CD

Caution

The following paragraph starts a fresh unattended install of Windows XP Professional. This *will* wipe your drive clean. And after you've started, you can't go back. *Do not* attempt to run the bootable CD setup process unless you are willing to clear the primary drive on the target machine.

In the walk-through in the "Creating an Answer File" section of this chapter, the answer file was named WINNT.SIF, allowing it to be used to run a fully automated installation simply by booting from the Windows XP Professional install CD. To make this work, you don't need to worry about the batch file. Just copy WINNT.SIF to the root of a floppy disk. Go to your target system, insert the Windows XP Professional CD in the CD-ROM drive, and boot to the CD.

As discussed in the "Licensing Issues" section earlier in this chapter, you must use volume license media and a volume license product key to use the same product key on multiple systems. If you're not using volume license media with a volume license product key, you must either update the Product ID line in the WINNT.SIF file before loading each different system or leave the Product ID line out of the WINNT.SIF so the system will prompt for the key during the mini-setup wizard.

Note

If setup isn't starting when you attempt to boot to the CD, check two things: First, ensure that your system boot order is configured with the CD-ROM as the first boot device under your system BIOS. Second, pay close attention while booting your system. If you have no operating system, Windows Setup will start on its own. If, however, an active partition with a bootable OS exists, at one point booting to the CD will prompt you with "Press any key to continue booting from CD." Press the Any key at this point. Look closely, the label for the Any key—usually the long key at the bottom center—frequently falls off before a keyboard leaves the factory.

As soon as your system starts to read the CD and recognizes it as bootable, insert the floppy disk containing the answer file into the A: drive. After a few minutes, setup will prompt you to partition and format the drive. This is a safety mechanism to give you one last chance to back out of the install before wiping out your system. After partitioning the disk, you should be able to sit back and relax for about 45 minutes while Windows XP Professional completes installation to your system without prompting you to answer any additional questions.

Now, I know what some of you may be thinking: Hey! If this is automated why is setup asking for my input before it partitions and formats the disk?

Although you selected Fully Automated in the Setup Manager Wizard, the partitioning and formatting of the disk does not complete without user interaction unless you know about this rarely documented trick: Open your WINNT.SIF file in Notepad, and add the following two lines under the (Unattended) section header:

```
FileSystem = ConvertNTFS
Repartition = Yes
```

If you find that this isn't working for you and booting from the Windows XP CD still runs a normal setup, make sure you've named your answer file WINNT.SIF and saved it to the root of the A: drive. Windows Setup will not check for any other filename, and it will not check in any other location. In addition, double-check that you're getting the disk inserted as soon as the system starts to boot from the CD, or Windows Setup will not read the answer file.

If you're having difficulty getting the disk inserted at the right time, you could go into your system BIOS and disable booting from floppy, or move the floppy drive to the end of your boot order. You should then be able to leave the floppy disk containing the `WINNT.SIF` file in your drive from the beginning of the boot process.

Remote Installation Services

If you are familiar with using RIS under Windows 2000, not much has changed with the upgrade to Windows XP. RIS is an optional server-side service provided with Windows 2000 Server and Windows Server 2003 that enables you to deploy Windows XP to a new system by booting to the NIC using an NIC with a Preboot Execution Environment (PXE) boot ROM enabled.

Other than booting client systems using a PXE boot ROM rather than a network boot disk, installing Windows XP using RIS is similar to installing over the network from a network share point. All files are copied over the network to the client station, and Windows XP runs a full install.

From an infrastructure perspective, RIS requires a TCP/IP-based network that uses a DHCP server, a Windows 2000-compliant DNS service conforming with both RFC 2052 and RFC 2136, and Active Directory to provide client authorization and configuration information to the RIS server during the client install process. If you are still using Windows NT 4.0 Server DNS, it does *not* support the required protocols. If using Unix BIND, versions 8.1.2 and later support the required protocols.

To add a Windows XP Professional installation to your RIS server, follow the same procedure as adding a Windows 2000 Professional image, but using the source files and answer file for Windows XP. Remember, you can create the `RISETUP.SIF` answer file by using the Setup Manager Wizard and selecting the option to create an install for RIS on the third screen of the wizard.

Note

For full details on setting up and configuring RIS under Windows 2000, see the Remote Installation Services chapter excerpt from the New Riders title, *Windows 2000 Deployment and Desktop Management,* available online at http://www.microsoft.com/technet/prodtechnol/windows2000serv/deploy/depopt/remoteos.mspx.

Systems Management Server

If so inclined, you can use Microsoft Systems Management Server (SMS) to deploy a Windows XP upgrade. The question is, should you? To be honest, I've tried it, and I don't like it. Part of the problem is that you can only deploy Windows XP via SMS if doing an upgrade. You cannot use SMS to deploy a clean installation of Windows XP. So rather than telling you *how* to use SMS to deploy a Windows XP upgrade, I'm going to tell you why you probably *shouldn't*.

Note

If, after reading the rest of this section, you still want to attempt an upgrade to Windows XP using Microsoft SMS, refer to the Microsoft-provided documentation at http://www.microsoft.com/technet/prodtechnol/winxppro/deploy/default.mspx.

When planning for a mass-scale operating system upgrade, I usually opt to develop a single clean install process to use for all systems in an environment, rather than developing one install process for people who need a clean install and an additional upgrade process for systems that can handle the upgrade. Upgrading an operating system tends to result in a number of difficult-to-diagnose technical inconsistencies; a clean install does away with any questions. I'm sure if you've been working with any Microsoft operating system for very long, you've eventually reinstalled just to improve system performance, get rid of unneeded files, and start with a clean slate. Major operating system upgrades provide an excellent opportunity for a wide-scale cleanup of all systems in an organization.

Using the User State Migration Tool

Unless you're lucky enough to be running in a fully managed environment with roaming user profiles and all unique user data stored on the network, you need to find a way to migrate the settings and documents from the old systems to the new. The User State Migration tool (USMT) helps with this endeavor.

If the Files and Settings Transfer Wizard is like a shiny new Porsche 911 sitting in your driveway, the User State Migration Wizard (USMT) would be a HUMMV. The Files and Settings Transfer Wizard is sleek, easy to get along with, and can be used by end users. The User State Migration Tool is powerful, complex, and intended for administrators and advanced support personnel. The same thing that makes the User State Migration Tool so powerful is what makes it so complicated to most people: its arcane command-line interface that relies on .INF files to control the migration process.

The User State Migration Tool can be found on the Windows XP Setup CD-ROM in the \VALUEACC\ MSFT\USMT folder. In addition to various .DLL files, there are two executable files in this folder: SCANSTATE.EXE and LOADSTATE.EXE as well as four predefined .INF files that you can use to perform a default migration. That said, the whole point of the USMT is to have granular control over what gets migrated and how the migration is applied to the target computer, so you may well want to modify the files to suit your needs.

Table 2.11 explains the primary files and their purposes in more detail.

Table 2.11 The Core USMT Files Explained

File	Description
ScanState.exe	Collects user data and settings based on the information contained in Migapp.inf, Migsys.inf, Miguser.inf, and Sysfiles.inf.
LoadState.exe	Applies the collected user state data on a computer that has a clean installation of Windows XP Professional.
Migapp.inf	Used to collect application settings; can be modified to customize a migration.
Migsys.inf	Used to collect system settings, such as fonts, accessibility settings, and Internet Explorer settings, among others; can be modified to customize a migration.
Miguser.inf	Used to collect personal settings and files from the My Pictures, My Documents, and other user-specific folders; can be modified to customize a migration.
Sysfiles.inf	Used to specify files specific to each version of Windows that USMT can migrate settings from; not normally modified unless the version of Windows that you are migrating settings from is not supported.

USMT and Upgrade Installations

The User State Migration Tool does not support the application of collected settings to computers that have been upgraded from a previous operating system. Install Windows XP in a clean installation before attempting to use the USMT.

Out of the box, USMT migrates the following files and settings:

- Accessibility
- Classic desktop
- Cookies folder
- Dial-up connections
- Folder options
- Fonts
- Internet Explorer settings
- Mouse and keyboard settings
- My Documents folder
- My Pictures folder

- Network drives and printers
- Office settings
- Outlook Express settings and store
- Outlook settings and store
- Phone and modem options
- Regional options
- Screen saver selection
- Sounds settings
- Taskbar settings

As mentioned previously, the User State Migration Tool's .INF files are highly customizable. By modifying the .INF files in the USMT directory, you can change the files and settings that USMT will migrate in order to fit your specific needs.

Customizing the .INF Files

For information on customizing the .INF files that control the migration process in the USMT, see "User State Migration in Windows XP: Modifying the Migration Rule INF File," located at http://www.microsoft.com/technet/prodtechnol/winxppro/deploy/usermigr.asp.

For complete online documentation for the USMT on Microsoft's website, go to http://www.microsoft.com/technet/prodtechnol/winxppro/deploy/default.mspx.

As mentioned previously, the User State Migration Tool consists of two executable files, four migration .INF files, and several supporting .DLL files. The migration process takes place in just four major steps, just the same as when using the Files and Settings Transfer Wizard. Additionally, the information provided for the Files and Settings Transfer Wizard in the "Before Starting the Transfer" section as detailed in the next chapter apply to using the USMT as well.

Let's run through a quick data and settings migration using the default .INF files. To accomplish this task, you need a "used" system with a configured user profile directory, a server (or a workstation on which you can create a data share), and a clean system to which to copy the user state.

1. On the server, create a shared directory called USMT, and copy the entire USMT directory from the \VALUEADD\MSFT\ directory of the Windows XP Installation CD into this directory. Create a subdirectory named DATA.

2. Log on to the "used" system and map the U: drive to the USMT share on your server.

3. Open the command prompt. Switch to the U:\USMT directory, and type the command **SCANSTATE U:\DATA**.

4. You will see the line ScanState is running.... Wait. When ScanState finishes, you will see the line The tool completed successfully.

5. Move to the clean system and map the U: drive to the USMT share on your server.

6. Open the command prompt. Switch to the U:\USMT directory, and type the command **LOADSTATE U:\DATA**.

7. You will see the line LoadState is running.... Wait. When LoadState finishes, you'll be back at the command prompt, and you should have the same data and settings as on the system from which SaveState was run.

Using USMT for a Single System Transfer

You don't have to use USMT in a client/server environment. If you just want to migrate data between a handful of systems, use the following steps instead:

1. On the source computer, logged on as the user in question, run the ScanState file to copy the settings to an intermediate storage location. This can be done via script, shortcut, or manually.

2. Prepare the target computer with a clean installation of Windows XP Professional. There are no restrictions on performing Remote Installations or other automated deployment methods.

3. On the target computer, logged on as the *local* administrator, run the LoadState file to apply the user's settings. This, again, can be done using a script, a shortcut or a scheduled task using the local administrator's credentials.

4. The user logs on to their account and the process is completed.

Using the default settings, that's really all there is to it. Of course, there are any number of switches you can use with the executable files to further modify how USMT works. The ScanState file has the following syntax, which is explained in Table 2.12.

```
scanstate [/c /i input.inf]* [/l scanstate.log]
[/v verbosity_level] [/f] [/u] [/x] migration_path
```

Table 2.12   ScanState Switches

Switch	Description
/c	Instructs ScanState not to stop on filename_too_long errors. These errors will be logged in the Longfile.log log file for later analysis.
/f	A troubleshooting switch that specifies that files will be migrated; not normally used.
/i	Specifies the .INF file (or multiple .INF files) that is to be used with ScanState to define the settings that are to be collected for transfer.
/l	Specifies the file to log errors that may occur during the collection process.
/u	A troubleshooting switch that specifies that user settings will be migrated; not normally used.
/v	Enables verbose output. Use the format: /v #, substituting 1 (least verbose) to 7 (most verbose) for the # symbol.
/x	A troubleshooting switch that specifies that no files or settings will be migrated; not normally used.
migration_path	Specifies the path to the location where files should be written to. You must have the appropriate NTFS and share permissions to this location.

The LoadState file has the following syntax, which is explained in Table 2.13.

```
loadstate [/i input.inf]* [/l loadstate.log] [/v #]
[/f] [/u] [/x] migration_path
```

Table 2.13   LoadState Switches

Switch	Description
/i	Specifies the `.INF` file (or multiple `.INF` files) that are to be used with LoadState to define the settings that are to be migrated.
/f	Specifies that files will be migrated. This is a switch for troubleshooting only.
/l	Specifies the file to log errors that may occur during the collection process.
/u	A troubleshooting switch that specifies that user settings will be migrated; not normally used.
/v	Enables verbose output. Use the format: `/v #`, substituting 1 (least verbose) to 7 (most verbose) for the # symbol.
/x	A troubleshooting switch that specifies that no files or settings will be migrated; not normally used.
migration_path	Specifies the path to the location where files should be read from. You must have the appropriate NTFS and share permissions to this location, as appropriate.

Change and Configuration Management

See the "Change and Configuration Management Deployment Guide" at http://www.microsoft.com/windows2000/techinfo/reskit/deploy/CCM/ for more information on migration user's settings.

The next chapter discusses performing an installation of Windows XP as an upgrade to a system with a previous version of Windows already installed. It may be tempting to skip over this chapter should you not intend to perform an upgrade installation; however, this chapter also includes crucial information on how to migrate key user data and applications from an existing installation to a new one as well as information on installing Windows XP Service Pack 2.

CHAPTER 3

Upgrading Windows

Windows XP Upgrade Installations

Chapter 1, "Windows Version History," introduced you to the various versions of Windows, past and present, and briefly mentioned the features of Windows XP. Large numbers of individuals and companies still have older versions of Windows running on their computers. And even with Windows Vista on the horizon, compared to these older versions, Windows XP still offers a user-friendly experience and security functions that go far beyond its predecessors, including Windows 2000.

In Chapter 2, "Installing Windows," we talked about baseline Windows XP installation concepts and features as well as how to perform clean and professional installations of the XP operating system. In this chapter I cover how to perform an upgrade Windows XP installation, in which Windows XP replaces a previous Windows OS without first removing all data from the system drive and starting from scratch.

An upgrade installation is most useful in cases where you have customized user settings that you want to preserve. This option, however, does not always work flawlessly, especially if you are upgrading from an operating system other than Windows 2000 Professional or Windows XP Home Edition (to XP Pro) due to the differences in the Registry structure and the startup process.

Stability issues aside, if you allow Windows XP to back up the existing operating system during the upgrade you can later uninstall Windows XP and effectively revert your computer back to the state it was in immediately preceding the Windows XP upgrade. The ability to uninstall is contingent on the disk volume being FAT32 and not NTFS, that you have not created or deleted any disk volumes on the system, and that you do not delete any backup files created during the upgrade installation process.

Deciding Whether an Upgrade is Worthwhile

Most individuals and companies acquire Windows XP installed on a new computer. However, a large established base of existing computers running older versions of Windows is present in nearly all organizations. Although nearly everyone would like to take advantage of the new capabilities of Windows XP, upgrades are not always feasible. First and foremost, there is the significant cost of new software and its licenses. In addition, you need to take into account the following:

- Many older computers lack the hardware resources required to run Windows XP.
- You cannot upgrade all operating systems directly to Windows XP.
- Upgrading a large number of computers on a network involves a considerable investment in time and money.
- Applications running on existing computers may not be compatible with Windows XP.

Available Upgrade Paths

Possible upgrade paths for computers running older Windows operating systems depend on the operating system currently installed as well as the version of Windows XP you plan to install. Table 3.1 outlines the available upgrade paths.

Table 3.1   Available Windows XP Upgrade Paths

Operating System	Upgrading to Windows XP Home Edition	Upgrading to Windows XP Professional
Windows 98/Me	Can upgrade directly.	Can upgrade directly.
Windows NT 4.0 Workstation or Windows 2000 Professional	Cannot upgrade. You must perform a clean installation.	Can upgrade directly.

Table 3.1   Continued

Operating System	Upgrading to Windows XP Home Edition	Upgrading to Windows XP Professional
Windows XP Home Edition	–	Can upgrade directly.
Windows 3.1x/95	Upgrade to Windows 98, and then upgrade to Windows XP.	Upgrade to Windows 98, and then upgrade to Windows XP.
Windows NT 3.x Workstation	Cannot upgrade. You must perform a clean installation.	Upgrade to Windows NT 4.0, and then upgrade to Windows XP.
Windows NT/2000 Server	Cannot upgrade. You must perform a clean installation.	Cannot upgrade. You must perform a clean installation.

You should note that while dual upgrade paths described in Table 3.1 for Windows 3.1x/95/NT 3.x computers are theoretically possible, most computers running these older operating systems do not have the required hardware for running Windows XP. Should you need to upgrade such an older computer to Windows XP, it is preferable to perform a clean installation of Windows XP as described in Chapter 2 after you have upgraded the hardware to an appropriate level.

In addition, it is not possible to upgrade any non-Windows computers (Linux, UNIX, MS-DOS, OS/2, and so on) to Windows XP. You must perform a clean installation of Windows XP on these computers.

Verifying System Compatibility

The Windows XP compatibility tool enables you to create a compatibility report that identifies any problems with hardware or software on a computer that is to be upgraded to Windows XP. You can run this compatibility tool from the Windows XP CD-ROM by following these steps:

1. Insert the Windows XP (Home Edition or Professional) CD-ROM.
2. From the Welcome to Microsoft Windows XP screen, select the Check System Compatibility link.
3. Select the Check My System Automatically link.

Tip

You can also test your computer's Windows XP compatibility by opening a command prompt or the Run dialog box and typing the following: **d:\i386\WINNT32 /CHECKUPGRADEONLY** (where d: is the drive containing the Windows XP CD-ROM).

4. The Microsoft Windows Upgrade Advisor dialog box enables you to download updated Setup files from the Microsoft website. If you have an Internet connection, you should choose the Yes, Download the Updated Setup Files option and click Next. Otherwise, select the No, Skip This Step and Continue Installing Windows option and then click Next.
5. If selected, the Microsoft Windows Upgrade Advisor downloads updated Setup files and displays a Restart option. Click this option and then select the Yes, Download the Updated Setup Files option again to proceed.
6. The Microsoft Windows Upgrade Advisor dialog box tracks the construction of the upgrade compatibility report. This will take a minute or two.

7. When this action is completed, the Microsoft Windows Upgrade Advisor displays a list of items that may not be compatible with Windows XP, as shown in Figure 3.1. If no incompatible items are found, it informs you of this fact.

8. To obtain additional information on any item, select it and click More Details. To save a copy of the compatibility report, click Save As, type the name of the file to be saved in the dialog box that appears, and then click Save. Click Finish to close the Microsoft Windows Upgrade Advisor.

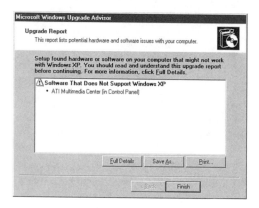

Figure 3.1   The report produced by the Microsoft Windows Upgrade Advisor notifies you of any hardware or software that may not work properly on Windows XP.

Items that may be included in the upgrade report shown in Figure 3.1 include the following:

- Incompatible software that may require upgrade packs, or applications that are not compatible with the Control Panel in Windows XP. If you cannot obtain upgrades, you may need to remove the application using Control Panel Add/Remove Programs before upgrading to Windows XP. If you do not remove these applications, you may receive an error message when upgrading to Windows XP. See Knowledge Base article 891891 (http://support.microsoft.com/default.aspx?scid=kb;en-us;891891) for more information.

- Incompatible entries in MS-DOS files such as `Autoexec.bat` and `Config.sys`.

- Plug and Play hardware devices that are incompatible with Windows XP Professional or require additional files.

Note

When run on Windows NT 4.0, the Microsoft Windows Upgrade Advisor may not provide the option to download upgraded Setup files. If this happens, simply continue the earlier procedure from step 6.

Note that if you have not yet purchased Windows XP and are wondering whether your computer will support an upgrade, the Windows XP Upgrade Advisor is available from Microsoft at http://www.microsoft.com/windowsxp/pro/upgrading/advisor.mspx.

Upgrade Scenarios

After you have run the Microsoft Windows Upgrade Advisor and ascertained that you want to perform an upgrade installation of Windows XP, you are ready to proceed. The following sections look at upgrading computers running Windows 98 and Windows 2000 to Windows XP; upgrading of a Windows NT 4.0 computer is similar.

Before Upgrading to Windows XP

After you are satisfied that an upgrade is worthwhile, you should perform several additional preliminary tasks. The following tasks are suggested, and depend on the current operating system on the computer:

■ Back up your data before upgrading, in case something goes wrong during the upgrade. The easiest way to perform the backup is to simply copy the data folders to another disk or computer because the Windows 98/Me backup and restore utilities are not compatible with those in Windows XP.

■ Check the availability of BIOS upgrades from the BIOS manufacturer's website. If upgrades are available, you should install them before upgrading your computer. Otherwise, machines with older BIOS versions may not shut down or restart properly. Furthermore, if the computer is not Advanced Configuration and Power Interface (ACPI)-compatible, you may need a BIOS upgrade.

■ Turn off power management features so that they do not activate during upgrade. You can do this from the Power Options applet in Control Panel.

■ Use an antivirus program that has been updated with the most recent antivirus signatures to scan the computer to ensure that the computer is free of viruses. In addition, use another program such as the Microsoft AntiSpyware Program (http://www.microsoft.com/athome/security/spyware/software/default.mspx; this utility requires Windows 2000 or later) or a third-party tool to scan for and remove malicious software such as spyware, adware, and rootkits. After you have completed this task, remove or disable these programs because antivirus programs can interfere with the upgrade process.

■ Ensure that all hardware is listed in the Windows Catalog. You can use Device Manager on a Windows 98/Me/2000 computer or Windows NT Diagnostics on a Windows NT 4.0 computer to print out a list of all hardware components. Also check with hardware manufacturer websites for updated device drivers.

■ If you have used programs such as DriveSpace or DoubleSpace to compress partitions on computers running Windows 98 or Windows Me, you should decompress these partitions before upgrading to Windows XP, and then remove the compression utilities. On the other hand, it is not necessary to decompress files or folders on Windows NT or Windows 2000 computers that have been compressed using Windows NT/2000 NTFS compression.

■ If the Microsoft Windows Upgrade Advisor tool has identified software applications as being incompatible with Windows XP, upgrade or remove these programs. Software manufacturers may have released upgrade packs or newer versions that enable older programs to work properly with Windows XP, and with Windows XP SP2 in particular. You should note the following items in particular:

  • Older applications that depend on file system filters such as disk tools, disk-quota applications, and certain older antivirus programs should be removed because they cannot work properly on Windows XP.

  • Some older applications may contain drivers that overwrite Windows XP system files. Windows XP forbids such activity because it would damage the Windows installation. You may need to obtain and install migration dynamic link libraries (DLLs) for such software. Contact the software distributor for upgrade packs containing these DLLs.

  • Network client software for other networks cannot be upgraded for use with Windows XP. You need to obtain new versions for this software. An upgrade for Novell's Client32 is included on the Windows XP Professional CD-ROM.

  • Custom power-management tools have been supplanted in Windows XP by Advanced Power Management (APM) and ACPI. You should remove these tools.

- Custom solutions for PnP-usage with Windows NT should be removed because Windows XP supports full PnP functionality.

- Other third-party software items such as fault-tolerant disk options, uninterruptible power supply software, and certain network clients and services should be upgraded or removed.

- It may be possible to run certain older applications in compatibility mode after you have upgraded to Windows XP; see Chapter 12, "Windows Troubleshooting," for further details.

■ Ensure that the latest service pack is installed on your computer. In particular, Windows NT 4.0 computers must be running at least SP5 and preferably SP6a.

■ Ensure that no unnecessary programs are running when you are ready to begin the upgrade. Access the Task Manager or the Windows 98/Me Close Program dialog box, and close any programs that should not be running.

■ Windows XP does not support volume sets or stripe sets created on basic disk volumes in Windows NT 4.0 or Windows 2000. If you are upgrading a Windows NT 4.0 computer that contains volume sets or stripe sets, you should back up their contents and delete them before upgrading. If you are upgrading a Windows 2000 computer, convert the disks containing these volumes to dynamic storage. For more information on disk volumes in Windows XP, refer to Chapter 5, "Managing Windows."

Note

Because Windows XP is more architecturally similar to Windows NT/2000 than to Windows 98/Me, you generally have fewer application compatibility problems when upgrading a Windows NT or 2000 computer to Windows XP, relative to Windows 98/Me.

Tip

Keyboards, mice, and legacy PnP devices are especially prone to hardware compatibility problems. Some keyboards and mice do not work after an upgrade. One way to prevent this kind of trouble is to check with the vendor for the latest drivers or try installing generic device drivers before upgrading. If Windows XP drivers are not available, Windows 2000 drivers may work.

Upgrading a Windows NT 4.0 or 2000 Computer

After you have ensured that your computer meets all hardware requirements for Windows XP Professional and that you have performed all required preliminary tasks, you are ready to perform the actual upgrade. Remember that you cannot upgrade a computer running Windows NT 4.0 or 2000 to Windows XP Home Edition; you must upgrade to Windows XP Professional. In addition, you cannot upgrade a computer running a server version; you must perform a fresh install.

Note

Microsoft also makes an upgrade version of the Windows XP CD-ROM. Use of this version is nearly identical to the procedure displayed here, except that the option for New Installation (Advanced) is not present.

To upgrade a Windows 2000 Professional computer to Windows XP Professional with SP2, follow this procedure. Note that an upgrade from Windows NT 4.0 Workstation proceeds in a similar manner:

1. Insert the slipstreamed Windows XP/SP2 CD-ROM.

2. If the Welcome to Microsoft Windows XP screen does not appear, double-click the CD-ROM drive in Windows Explorer and then double-click the Setup icon.

Note

You can also upgrade by accessing the installation files from a distribution share located on a server on the network. To do so, use My Network Places (or Network Neighborhood in Windows NT 4.0) to map a drive to the distribution share. Then open the Run dialog box and type **x:\i386\winnt32.exe**, where x is the drive letter you used when mapping to the distribution share.

3. On the Welcome to Microsoft Windows XP screen, click Install Windows XP.

4. The Welcome to Windows Setup dialog box (see Figure 3.2) provides a choice of installation type. Select Upgrade (Recommended) to begin the upgrade, and then click Next. You would select New Installation (Advanced) to completely replace your current version of Windows or to create a dual-boot system.

5. The License Agreement screen appears. Read the license agreement, click I Accept This Agreement, and then click Next.

6. The Your Product Key screen appears. Type the 25-character alphanumeric product key and then click Next.

Figure 3.2   The Welcome to Windows Setup screen provides a choice between upgrading to Windows XP and performing a new installation.

7. The Get Updated Setup Files dialog box appears and enables you to use Dynamic Update to obtain updated Setup files. If you have an Internet connection, you should select Yes, Download the Updated Setup Files. Otherwise, select No, Skip This Step and Continue Installing Windows. Click Next to continue.

8. Installation files are copied and the computer restarts. This takes up to a minute, and involves copying of files to a separate folder on the computer's hard drive. At this point, no change has been made to the old operating system.

9. Press Enter to accept the default of Windows XP Professional Setup from the boot menu.

10. If prompted, insert the Windows XP Professional CD-ROM and press Enter. Then insert the Windows XP Professional Service Pack 2 CD-ROM and press Enter again. This may happen more

than once. If informed that Setup cannot copy a file while the Windows XP Professional CD-ROM is in the drive, switch to the Windows XP Professional Service Pack 2 CD-ROM and press Enter.

11. Setup examines the computer's disks, and text-mode file copying proceeds for 5 to 10 minutes, and then the computer reboots again.

12. Windows XP Setup obtains its additional setup parameters from the previous Windows NT/2000 installation. This can take up to 40 minutes. You are asked for additional information only if Setup cannot obtain a required piece of information. You may be prompted for the original CD-ROM as described in step 10.

13. When installation has completed, the computer reboots and displays the Welcome to Microsoft Windows screen. Click Next.

14. The Help Protect Your PC screen (see Figure 3.3) enables you to turn on Automatic Updates, which enables the operating system to check for updates on a regular basis. You should select the Help Protect My PC by turning on Automatic Updates Now option. Then click Next.

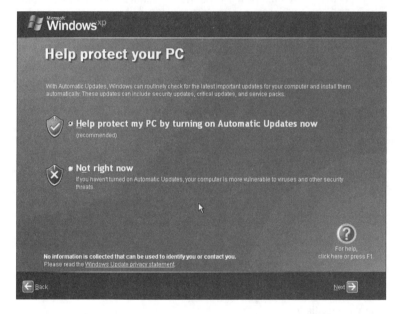

Figure 3.3 The Help protect your PC screen enables you to turn on Automatic Updates.

15. The Let's Activate Windows page appears and prompts you to perform Windows Product Activation (WPA). The options available and the procedure for performing WPA were discussed in Chapter 2.

16. Similar to the option presented during an original installation, enter your name and the names of any other users in the Who Will Use This Computer? page. You might not see this page when upgrading from Windows 2000 Professional. Click Next and then click Finish.

17. The logon page appears. Click your username to begin.

Note

When you upgrade from Windows NT 4.0 to Windows XP, user files and documents are stored in the `C:\WINNT\Profiles\%username%` folder for each user, rather than in the Windows XP default of `C:\Documents and Settings\%username%`. Unlike a new installation of Windows XP, the default desktop contains icons for My Documents, My Computer, and My Network Places.

Upgrading a Windows 98 Computer

As with a Windows NT 4.0 or 2000 computer, once you have performed all preliminary steps, you are ready to proceed with upgrading to Windows XP, either Home Edition or Professional. Upgrading a computer running Windows Me is similar. Perform the following steps:

1. Insert the slipstreamed Windows XP/SP2 CD-ROM (or access a distribution share as described previously).
2. If the Welcome to Microsoft Windows XP screen does not appear, double-click the CD-ROM drive in Windows Explorer and then double-click the Setup icon.
3. On the Welcome to Microsoft Windows XP screen, click Install Windows XP.
4. As with Windows NT or 2000, the Welcome to Windows Setup page (refer to Figure 3.2) offers a choice of upgrading or performing a new installation. To upgrade your computer, select Upgrade (Recommended) and then click Next.
5. Accept the license agreement, and then click Next.
6. Type the Windows product key in the spaces provided, and then click Next.
7. Setup displays an Upgrade Report screen that informs you of possible compatibility issues with your computer (see Figure 3.4). If you have performed a proper assessment of system compatibility issues as described earlier in this chapter, you should not receive any additional warnings. Select the default of Show Me Hardware Issues and a Limited Set of Software Issues, and then click Next.

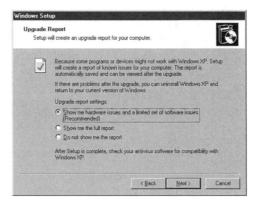

Figure 3.4 When upgrading from Windows 98/Me, Windows XP Setup enables you to create an upgrade report.

8. The Get Updated Setup Files (see Figure 3.5) enables you to download the updated Setup files from the Microsoft website. If you have an Internet connection, you should select this option. Otherwise select the No option. Then click Next.

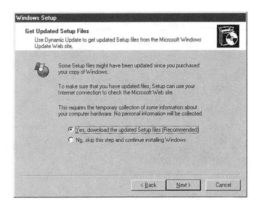

Figure 3.5 The Get Updated Setup Files screen enables you to download updates to the Windows XP Setup files.

9. Setup copies the installation files and restarts the computer. Select the default of Windows XP Professional (or Home Edition) Setup from the boot menu that is displayed. File copying continues and the computer reboots again. Installation proceeds with the Setup program gathering information from the previous Windows installation.

10. The computer reboots and displays the Welcome to Microsoft Windows screen. Click Next and follow the same instructions as provided in steps 13 to 15 of the procedure for upgrading Windows NT.

11. After you have entered the names of users, the Password Creation dialog box asks for passwords for new Windows XP accounts. Type and confirm a password for these accounts, and then click OK. Each of the listed accounts receives the same password, which you can later change from the Control Panel User Accounts applet.

12. Log on to Windows with the username and password supplied in step 11.

Similar to an upgrade from Windows NT, the upgraded desktop contains icons for My Documents, My Computer, and My Network Places. Windows creates a Documents and Settings folder with subfolders for each user who has logged on to the computer. However, documents stored in the `C:\My Documents` folder remain in this folder and are not moved to the new location of My Documents (`C:\Documents and Settings\%username%\My Documents`).

Troubleshooting a Failed Upgrade

Many problems that occur during upgrading an older Windows installation are similar to those you might encounter when installing Windows XP for the first time, as discussed in Chapter 2. You may also encounter one of the following problems:

- Programs or services that are running may interfere with the upgrade process. As mentioned earlier in this chapter, use the Windows NT/2000 Task Manager or the Windows 98/Me Close Program dialog box to close unnecessary programs. You can also use the `Msconfig.exe` utility to choose Selective Startup, clear the check boxes associated with programs that start automatically, and then restart the computer. This procedure is also known as clean booting. Knowledge Base article 192926 (http://support.microsoft.com/kb/192926/) provides additional information.

- If Selective Startup does not work, you may need to start your computer in Safe mode (Windows 98/Me/2000). You can then run the `Winnt32.exe` command to begin upgrade. If your CD-ROM does not function in Safe mode, refer to Knowledge Base article 194846 (http://support.microsoft.com/kb/194846/) for assistance.

■ You may receive messages informing you that Setup cannot copy a file. This may be the result of hardware problems such as an over-clocked processor or damaged memory. Try copying the contents of the Windows XP CD-ROM to a folder on the hard drive and installing from this location.

■ Incompatible hardware may result in the setup program failing to respond ("hanging"), or a Stop message (blue screen error) appearing. Refer to the suggestions presented earlier in this chapter for checking system compatibility. Also refer to Knowledge Base article 310064 and other articles referenced therein.

■ An upgrade error related to the setup catalog may appear when you are attempting to upgrade Windows 98, Me, or XP Home Edition to Windows XP Professional. This problem may occur if the Setup routine fails to delete all files in the `Windows\System32\Catroot2` folder. You can overcome this problem by starting a command prompt and renaming the Catroot2 subfolder. For additional information, refer to Knowledge Base article 307153 at http://support.microsoft.com/kb/307153.

Uninstalling Windows XP

When you upgrade a computer running Windows 98/Me to Windows XP Home Edition or Professional, the Setup routine automatically saves a copy of the Windows XP removal files to the Windows folder. These files enable you to later revert to the previous operating system if desired. The Add or Remove Programs applet in Control Panel contains a Windows XP Uninstall option that restores the previous operating system without changing any data you have created since upgrading to Windows XP. However, you may need to reinstall any applications that were installed or modified since you upgraded to Windows XP because these applications will not have the correct Registry entries for Windows 98/Me. Likewise, if you have removed any applications while running Windows XP, Start menu shortcuts will be present after you revert to Windows 98/Me. Simply delete these shortcuts if this happens.

Caution

If you have upgraded from Windows 98 or Windows Me and think you may want to revert to your previous operating system, do not convert your hard disk to the NTFS file system, or upgrade the disk to dynamic storage. If you do, the option to uninstall Windows XP is no longer available. Refer to Chapter 10, "Windows File Systems," for more information on file systems in Windows XP.

Follow these steps to uninstall Windows XP:

1. Click Start, Control Panel, Add or Remove Programs.

2. As shown in Figure 3.6, the Add or Remove Programs applet will contain a Windows XP Uninstall entry. Select this entry and click Change/Remove.

3. Select Uninstall Windows XP from the options in the Uninstall Windows XP dialog box that appears, and then click Continue. Note that if the removal files are not present or have been deleted, it will not be possible to uninstall Windows XP. In this case, the Uninstall Windows XP option will not appear.

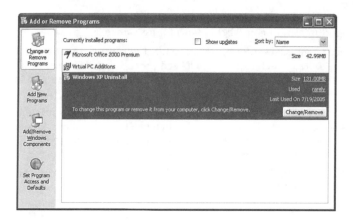

Figure 3.6   If you have upgraded from Windows 98/Me, you can uninstall Windows XP from the Add or Remove Programs applet in Control Panel.

4. The Windows XP Uninstall dialog box (see Figure 3.7) informs you of the programs that have been installed or modified since you installed Windows XP. You will need to reinstall these programs after you complete uninstalling Windows XP. Click Continue to uninstall Windows XP or Quit to cancel.

Tip

To delete the older OS files, follow the first three steps of this procedure, and then select the Remove the Backup of My Previous Operating System option, and click Continue.

Figure 3.7   You are informed of programs that have been installed or modified since installing Windows XP.

5. Click Yes in the confirmation message box that appears.
6. An Uninstall message box appears and Windows XP shuts down.

7. The computer reboots and Windows uninstallation proceeds. When the computer reboots a second time, the previous Windows operating system will start. Note that the Documents and Settings folder created by Windows XP is still present and may contain documents created while Windows XP was running.

Tip

If you are unable to start Windows XP properly after upgrading from Windows 98/Me, you may be able to uninstall Windows XP from the Safe Mode with Command Prompt advanced startup option. See Knowledge Base article 308233 (http://support.microsoft.com/kb/308233/) for more information.

Migrating Existing Installations

Existing networks often contain an entire series of computers running older operating systems that need to be upgraded to Windows XP. Often these computers are replaced by newer ones containing a factory installation of Windows XP. You may need to migrate user settings, applications, and documents to new computers so that users can continue working as they would have on the old computers. We look at these issues in this section.

Moving to a New Drive

As storage costs decrease and space requirements increase, it makes sense to migrate to the newer, high-capacity hard disks. You can upgrade an older Windows operating system at the same time you install a new hard disk by any of several means: You can use a third-party tool such as Norton Partition Magic to move your data to a new drive before upgrading; you can upgrade your operating system on the existing drive and add a new hard disk that holds your data after the upgrade is completed; you can add a new hard disk before upgrading and perform a clean installation of Windows XP on the new disk.

Installing a New Hard Disk

If you install a new hard disk, modern Windows versions will automatically recognize the disk when you restart your computer. To move or copy Windows system files to the new disk, you need to use a third-party tool such as Norton Partition Magic described later in this section. Alternatively, you can use a DOS boot disk to boot your computer and perform a manual copy, provided that partitions are not formatted with the NTFS file system.

Note

It may seem easier to use the Windows Advanced Boot Options menu (accessed by pressing F8 during bootup) to boot to a command prompt. However, starting up your PC this way still uses a few Windows XP system files on the hard disk to bring up the command prompt. To copy or move these files you need to boot your computer without referencing *any* files on the system disk.

You can also install Windows XP on the new hard disk from the Windows version on the first disk. This creates a *dual-boot* system, in which you can start either version of Windows. To install Windows XP with SP2 on the new disk, proceed as follows:

1. Insert the slipstreamed Windows XP/SP2 CD-ROM (or access a distribution share as described previously).

2. If the Welcome to Microsoft Windows XP screen does not appear, open My Computer, navigate to the CD-ROM drive, and double-click the Setup icon.

3. Click Install Windows XP.

4. In the Welcome to Windows Setup dialog box (refer to Figure 3.3), select New Installation (Advanced), and then click Next.

5. Click I Accept This Agreement, and then click Next.

6. On the Your Product Key page, type the product key and then click Next.

7. If necessary, modify any of the options provided in the Setup Options page, and then click Next.

8. On the Get Updated Setup Files, leave the default of Yes, Download the Updated Setup Files (Recommended) selected, and then click Next. If you are not connected to the Internet, select No, Skip This Step and continue installing Windows.

9. Setup copies files to your hard disk. This takes several minutes, after which your computer shuts down and restarts.

10. After the computer restarts, it displays the text-based Welcome to Setup page. Press Enter to proceed with installing the dual-boot system.

11. Setup displays information similar to that shown in Figure 3.8, from which you can select the partition on which you want to install Windows XP and the file system with which you want to format it. Use the arrow keys to make a selection, and then press Enter.

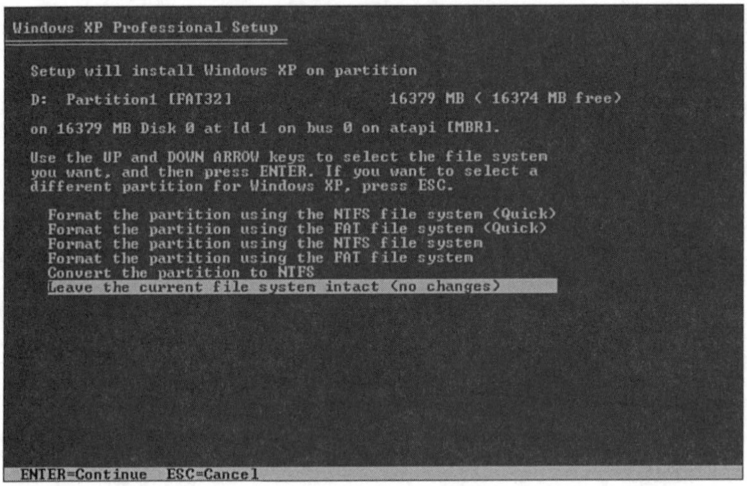

Figure 3.8 When creating a dual-boot system, Setup provides a choice of partitions and formatting options.

12. Setup copies files to the Windows installation folders, and restarts into GUI-mode Setup.

13. The remainder of the installation proceeds in a fashion similar to that of a clean Windows installation described in Chapter 2. You are asked for the same information as described in that chapter.

After installation completes, you can boot your computer into either operating system. On startup, the computer displays a menu called the *boot loader* (see Figure 3.9), which enables you to select either operating system.

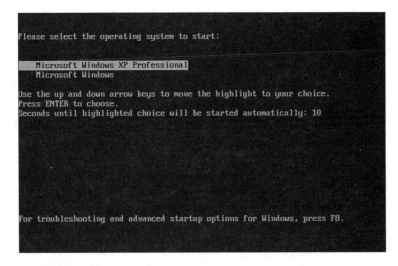

Figure 3.9 On a dual-boot system, the boot loader menu enables you to select which operating system you want to run.

Using Norton Partition Magic

Norton Partition Magic enables you to organize and modify partitions on multiple hard disks. You can add a new hard disk to a computer running any Windows operating system and move the contents of your old hard disk to a partition on the new one. You can also create, move, split, merge, and convert disk partitions including those formatted with NTFS rapidly. You can even recover deleted partitions and the data they contain. Norton Partition Magic 8.0 enables you to perform the following tasks, among others:

- *Move operating system, program, and data files to another hard disk*—From the Pick a Task pane in the main Norton Partition Magic window, select Resize/Move Partition, and then follow the instructions provided. If you are moving operating system files, the computer will shut down and the move will take place as the computer restarts.

- *Separate operating system, program, and data files into separate disk partitions*—This helps protect your data in the event of operating system failure. You can perform these tasks from the Resize/Move Partition option already mentioned.

- *Install Windows XP on a separate partition*—Select Install Another Operating System. This starts the Install Another Operating System Wizard, which enables you to install a second operating system on the new disk. The wizard guides you through the procedure of creating a new partition that meets the requirements of Windows XP. Select the Windows XP option and confirm the changes that are presented to you. Click Finish to proceed, or Back to modify your changes. The Boot Magic tool enables you to select the operating system that the computer will start at the next startup.

- *Create rescue floppy disks*—During the software installation process, you can create a set of floppies that enable you to boot your computer should you happen to make inappropriate changes and be unable to start normally.

Moving Data to a New System

New computers are getting more economical all the time. Rather than taking the time and expense to upgrade an existing computer to Windows XP, it often makes sense to simply purchase a new computer with Windows XP (either Home Edition or Professional) already loaded. You can continue to use the old computer as a backup, recycle it, or donate it to a charitable organization. Organizations exist that will refurbish donated computers for schools, for example.

Windows XP includes two tools for migrating user data, applications, and settings to new computers:

- *User State Migration Tool (USMT)*—Enables network administrators to migrate settings on a large number of old computers to new Windows XP computers in a corporate setting.

- *Files and Settings Transfer Wizard*—Provides a simple means of migrating data and settings on one computer in a home or small office environment. We discuss the Files and Settings Transfer Wizard in a later section.

User State Migration Tool (USMT)

Using the USMT, you can rapidly and easily transfer user documents and settings at the time of deploying new Windows XP Professional computers in a corporate setting. This tool enables you to migrate files and settings from source computers running Windows 95, Windows 98, Windows Me, Windows NT 4.0, or Windows 2000 to new Windows XP Professional computers. The following are several advantages of USMT:

- Technicians spend less time in migrating files and settings for users.

- It improves employee productivity by preventing help desk calls and reducing the amount of time wasted searching for missing files or reconfiguring the new desktop.

- Administrators can provide customized settings such as unique Registry modifications.

- Users become productive more rapidly because they can become familiar with the new operating system faster.

- Users express an improved overall sense of satisfaction with migrating to the new operating system.

◄◄ For more information on the use of this tool, see "Using the User State Migration Tool," p. 85.

Files and Settings Transfer Wizard

Microsoft provides the Files and Settings Transfer Wizard (FSTW) for transferring user settings, files, and folders to a new computer or to a clean Windows XP installation on an existing computer. It is the simplest means of transferring this information when only a few computers are affected, or when individual users are migrating information on their computer. It is automatically installed when you install or upgrade to Windows XP.

Before you go to start the transfer process using the Files and Settings Transfer Wizard, you should pay particular attention to the following list of potential trouble spots:

- Before attempting to transfer files to the target computer, ensure that the appropriate user account has been created and configured with the required NTFS permissions to allow access to the location where the transfer image will be located. If the transfer image is to be located on a network share, ensure that the share permissions are also correctly configured to support access.

- Before attempting to transfer files to the target computer, ensure that any special or specific folder paths that exist in the user's profile on the old computer are created on the new computer. This will help to alleviate problems with orphaned folders and files during the transfer process. Make sure that these folders have the required NTFS and share permissions applied to them as well.

- When performing the transfer process, ensure that you are logged as the user whose files and settings you are transferring. Although this is a minor annoyance on the source computer, it can be a great catastrophe on the target computer if you are logged in under the wrong user account.

- Ensure that the location where the transfer image file will be located has enough available space to support the operation. You will need between 50MB and 600MB per user that you migrate using the Files and Settings Transfer Wizard. Table 3.2 provides some recommended guidelines for space availability.

- After the transfer process is complete, you will have to manually delete the transfer image file and folders.

Space Race

The estimates given in Table 3.2 are fairly realistic. I used more than 700MB to transfer my primary user profile and about 6MB to transfer a new (and unused) user profile. Plan ahead and ensure you have plenty of empty disk space before starting to use the Files and Settings Transfer Wizard!

Table 3.2   Estimated Space Requirements When Using the Files and Settings Transfer Wizard

Type of User	Space Required
Desktop user storing email on server	50–75MB
Desktop user with local email storage	150–400MB
Laptop user	150–300MB

The best practice is to pad these values somewhat as well, just for safety, by adding 25%–50% to them depending on the average user type in your organization.

The process to use the Files and Settings Transfer Wizard is broken down into two separate phases, as you might expect. You will need to first gather the files and settings from the source computer and then apply them to the target computer.

Musical Windows

It is possible to use the Files and Settings Transfer Wizard to transfer a user's files and settings from a Windows XP computer and then apply these settings back to the same computer, either following a new installation of Windows XP or into a new user account.

Collecting Files and Settings from the Source PC

To transfer files and settings from the source computer, follow this procedure:

1. Log in to the source computer using the user account that you want to transfer files and settings from. If this computer is not a Windows XP computer, insert the Windows XP Professional Setup CD-ROM and proceed to step 2. If this computer is a Windows XP computer, you can launch the Files and Settings Transfer Wizard by clicking Start, All Programs, Accessories, System Tools, Files and Settings Transfer Wizard, and then jump to step 4 of this procedure.

2. If this computer is not a Windows XP Professional machine, click Perform Additional Tasks on the Welcome To Microsoft Windows XP screen.

3. From the screen shown in Figure 3.10, select Transfer Files and Settings. Alternatively, you can navigate to the Support\Tools folder on the Windows XP Professional Setup CD-ROM and double-click the FASTWIZ.EXE file.

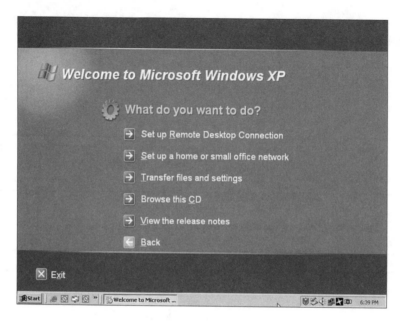

Figure 3.10   Starting the FSTW from the Windows XP Professional Setup CD-ROM.

4. After making your selection, the Files and Settings Transfer Wizard will open, as shown in Figure 3.11.

Figure 3.11   The Files and Settings Transfer Wizard introductory screen.

5. Click Next to dismiss the opening screen of the Files and Settings Transfer Wizard.

6. If prompted, select Old Computer and click Next.

7. On the Select a Transfer Method page, shown in Figure 3.12, configure the transfer method you want to use, and click Next to continue. In most cases, you will want to use a network location for your transfer image, as the size can quickly grow past the capability of most removable storage media. Should you desire to use the direct cable connection, you will need to connect a null modem serial cable between the old computer (source) and the new computer (target) and follow through the prompts given in the wizard.

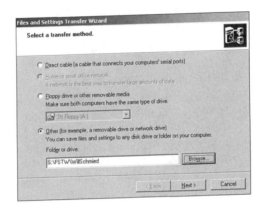

Figure 3.12 Selecting a location to place the transfer image.

8. On the What Do You Want to Transfer? page, shown in Figure 3.13, select to transfer Settings Only, Files Only, or Both Files and Settings. If you want to configure additional transfer settings, place a check in the Let Me Select a Custom List of Files and Settings When I Click Next check box. Click Next to continue. If you are not custom-configuring your transfer settings, skip to step 10 of this procedure.

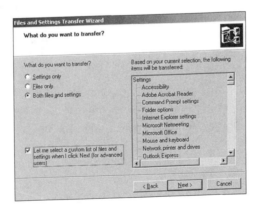

Figure 3.13 Selecting the transferred items: files, settings, or both.

9. If you are custom-configuring your transfer settings, you can use the buttons shown in Figure 3.14 to modify the transfer settings. After you have customized the transfer settings, click Next to continue.

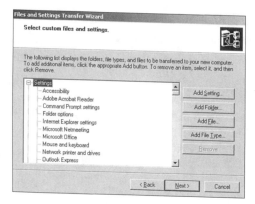

Figure 3.14   Customizing the transfer process ensures you get exactly what you want.

10. The Install programs on your new computer will show you a listing of what the Files and Settings Transfer Wizard thinks you need to install on the target computer before applying the transfer image. Click Next to continue.

11. The Files and Settings Transfer Wizard will now collect data and write it to the transfer image file. While this occurs, you can monitor the progress on the Collection in Progress page.

12. After the Files and Settings Transfer Wizard has completed, a summary page will appear telling you to now move to the new computer and apply the transfer image. Click Finish to close the Files and Settings Transfer Wizard.

Applying Files and Settings to the Target Computer

After you have successfully completed the installation of Windows XP Professional onto your new computer, you can then apply the transfer image to regain your files and settings. However, before you jump back into the Files and Settings Transfer Wizard, you *must* install all of your applications that you transferred settings for—FSTW only transfers files and settings, not applications. If you transfer your settings and then install the application, you stand a good chance of having your settings overwritten during the install process.

To apply your files and settings to the target computer, follow this procedure:

1. Log in to the target computer using the user account that you want to restore the files and settings for.

2. If you've placed your transfer image on a network drive, map the network drive to the local computer and ensure that the user account has the required NTFS and share permissions.

3. Launch the Files and Settings Transfer Wizard either from the Start menu or from the Windows XP Professional Setup CD-ROM.

4. The Files and Transfer Settings Wizard opening page will be displayed, as shown previously in Figure 3.11. Click Next to continue.

5. On the Which Computer Is This? page, shown in Figure 3.15, select New Computer and click Next to continue.

6. Because you have already collected your transfer files and settings, select I Don't Need the Wizard Disk on the Do You Have a Windows XP CD? page, shown in Figure 3.16. Click Next to continue.

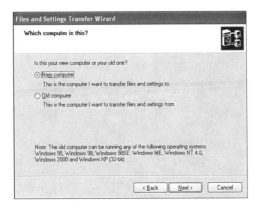

Figure 3.15 Selecting the computer: This time around you are working with the New computer.

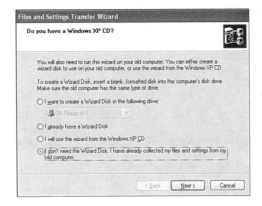

Figure 3.16 Telling the Files and Settings Transfer Wizard how to do its job!

7. On the Where Are the Files and Settings? page, shown in Figure 3.17, select the location where you placed your transfer image in the previous procedure. Click Next to continue.

8. The Files and Settings Transfer Wizard will now transfer and apply the files and settings to the target computer. You can monitor the progress on the Transfer in Progress page.

9. After the Files and Settings Transfer Wizard has completed, a summary page will inform you of any errors or orphaned files that have been created during the process. Click Finish to close the Files and Settings Transfer Wizard.

10. You will receive the following message: You need to log off for the changes to take effect. Do you want to log off now? Select Yes and log back on to the account to see whether the transferred files and settings have taken effect.

If you have only one user or a small number of users to migrate settings for, the Files and Settings Transfer Wizard is the best way to go. However, should you need to migrate settings for a large number of users, or need extreme granular control over what gets transferred, the User State Migration Tool is for you.

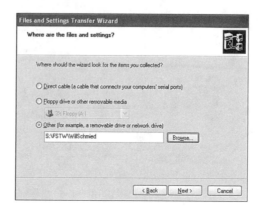

Figure 3.17   Locating the Files and Settings Transfer Wizard image.

Moving Applications

When migrating user documents and settings to new Windows XP computers, an important segment of the task is that of migrating applications. When more than a few users are involved, the manual task of reinstalling applications on every new computer becomes extremely time-consuming and labor-intensive. Fortunately, there are ways to automate this process.

Including Applications with New Installations

Microsoft makes available several methods of performing bulk installations of Windows XP on new computers that include applications. Two methods of automated installation that enable you to include applications are the System Preparation Tool (Sysprep) and Remote Installation Services (RIS).

Sysprep

The *System Preparation Tool*, *Sysprep*, enables you to create an image of a typical installation of Windows XP Professional, including SP2 and a standard set of applications that can be deployed to multiple destination computers. This tool, found in the `Deploy.cab` file in the `Support\Tools` folder of the Windows XP Professional CD-ROM, prepares a reference computer for imaging using a cloning application such as Norton Ghost or Symantec Drive Image.

To use Sysprep, you first install and configure a reference computer with Windows XP Professional, SP2, and the required set of applications including standard application settings. You then run `Sysprep.exe` on this computer to remove computer-specific information such as security identifiers (SIDs). As shown in Figure 3.18, the computer will shut down automatically. Finally, you reboot the computer with a floppy and run the cloning application. You can store the image thus created on a shared folder, from which the target computers can connect and install the Windows XP image.

RIS

Remote Installation Services, or *RIS*, enables you to deploy Windows XP Professional images containing applications and other configuration parameters on an Active Directory–based network that includes Dynamic Host Configuration Protocol (DHCP) and Domain Name System (DNS). Images can contain items such as applications and desktop settings, and users can install these images themselves from any computer equipped with a Preboot Execution Environment (PXE)-compatible network interface card (NIC).

Figure 3.18   When you run Sysprep on a reference computer, you receive a message informing you that the security parameters will be modified and the computer will shut down.

RIS is available as a component on servers running Windows 2000 Server or Windows Server 2003. You set up a series of remote installation shared folders on the server, and then create images of Windows XP Professional installations containing the required settings and applications. RIS includes a Remote Installation Preparation Wizard that you run on the Windows XP computer, which performs a series of copy steps (see Figure 3.19) that places the image on the appropriate subfolder on the server.

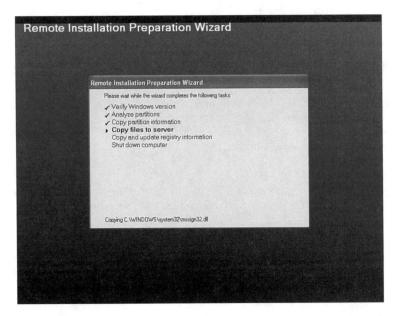

Figure 3.19   The Remote Installation Preparation Wizard prepares the image of the reference computer and copies it to the server.

A remote user who needs to install Windows XP can use the Client Installation Wizard, which is a text-based wizard that guides the user through the process of installing Windows XP. A computer with a PXE-compatible NIC automatically connects to the RIS server and downloads the wizard. The user then logs on to the domain and follows the steps presented by the wizard to install Windows XP Professional, complete with all service packs, hot fixes, and applications, without further involvement by the user.

Tip

If you need to use RIS to install Windows XP on computers that are not equipped with a PXE-compatible NIC, you can create a remote boot floppy disk at the RIS server. This disk enables a client computer to boot and access the RIS server.

Using Group Policy

On a Windows 2000 or Windows Server 2003 domain, you can use Group Policy to distribute software to all computers, both new and existing. This provides a means to push required software out to users and computers at the next reboot or logon. A user receiving a new computer merely needs to start the computer and log on to the domain to receive a complete set of software. You can create policies that apply to the entire domain or to an organizational unit (OU) containing a subset of computers or users requiring specific applications, such as line-of-business applications required by a specific department. Besides installation of software on new computers, you can use software installation policies to automatically update software or remove outdated software from all computers affected by the policy.

Group Policy enables you to deploy software by any of three methods:

- *Assigned to computers*—Software is installed on all computers affected by the policy the next time the users restart their computers.

- *Assigned to users*—Software intended for a specific set of users is installed on the users' computers the next time they log on.

- *Published to users*—Optional software is advertised to users the next time they log on, and a user can install it from the Control Panel Add or Remove Programs applet.

Use of Group Policy for software deployment involves creating one or more shared folders on a software distribution server, copying the software installation files, and creating a Group Policy object (GPO) that specifies the software packages to be installed (see Figure 3.20). Software installation files should include Windows Installer package (.msi) files.

Third-Party Tools

Several third-party tools are available that assist you in moving applications from computers running older operating systems to new Windows XP computers. The following describes a few of the available tools:

- CellarStone Inc. markets StepUpPro, which is a PC migration tool that transfers user settings, data, and applications from a source computer running Windows 95/98/Me/2000 to a new Windows 2000 or Windows XP computer. It provides a wizard-based interface that guides you through the process of a direct migration from the source computer to the destination computer.

- KBOX by Kace Software is an enterprise software management tool. Although KBOX does not migrate applications *per se*, it enables you to view the software installed on all machines on the network, and distribute software to a new or upgraded computer. Users can fix certain problems with the software on their computers without administrator assistance.

- Altiris Migration Suite is a comprehensive product designed for migrating computers to Windows XP, including software migration. It works on networks of all sizes and offers services such as inventorying, upgrade assessment, computer backup, cloning, network configuration, and post-migration reporting.

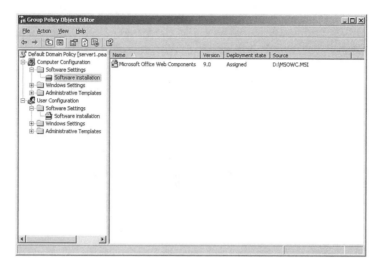

Figure 3.20   Using Group Policy in Windows Server 2003 to deploy a software package.

- IntelliMover by Detto Technologies enables you to migrate data, settings, and applications from an old computer to a new one without overwriting important files such as drivers. It also transfers data and settings from an old application on the source computer to an upgraded application on the new one. Both personal and business versions are available.

- Client Migration 3.0 by Symantec migrates data and application settings to a new computer. It enables you to create application packages for the purpose of updating or installing applications on the new computer, including transferring of application settings to an upgraded version of the application.

Installing Service Packs

When performing either a clean or upgrade installation it is, under most circumstances, vital that one of your first actions is to go to the Windows Update website and install any available service packs for the XP operating system. This section explains several methods you can use to upgrade a system to be SP2-compliant. Several methods are available for installing SP2 on existing Windows XP computers:

- Manual installation of SP2 and additional updates
- Use of Automatic Updates or Windows Update
- Using Group Policy to deploy SP2 to computers in a domain or OU
- Use of Windows Server Update Services (WSUS) to deploy SP2 to network computers

Note

If Microsoft introduces any additional service packs for Windows XP, the procedures described here should be applicable to their installation. Microsoft will publish any changes on its website.

Manual Installation of SP2

You can download SP2 from the Microsoft website or order it on CD-ROM. The download is in the form of an ISO image (an image file representing a one-to-one copy of the files or folders, which can be burned to a CD-ROM using commercial CD burning software). The CD is available for free and upgrades any version of Windows XP. Its use is a simple means of upgrading computers when only a small number of computers are involved.

Perform the following procedure to manually install SP2:

1. Insert the Windows XP SP2 CD-ROM, and then click Continue when the welcome page appears.

2. As shown in Figure 3.21, SP2 displays a page that introduces its new features and provides a link to further information about installation. To proceed with installation, click Install Now.

Figure 3.21 It is easy to install SP2 from the CD-ROM supplied by Microsoft.

3. Files are extracted from the CD-ROM. This takes several minutes.

4. The Windows XP Service Pack 2 Setup Wizard appears. Follow the instructions presented. The installation procedure also takes several minutes.

5. When the completion page appears, click Finish to restart your computer.

Using Automatic Updates or Windows Update to Download SP2

You can configure your computer to automatically download updates from the Automatic Updates tab of the System Properties dialog box (right-click My Computer and choose Properties). After you have done this, your computer will download SP2 automatically, including only those files required for your specific installation. You will receive a notification that SP2 is ready to install; the installation procedure is similar to that described for manual installation from the CD-ROM.

You can also download and install SP2 from the Microsoft Windows Update web page (http://windowsupdate.microsoft.com). This page checks the version of Windows running on your computer and provides a list of available updates that will include SP2. As with Automatic Updates, only the required components of SP2 will be downloaded. Again the installation procedure is similar to that already described.

Using Group Policy to Deploy SP2

Group Policy is an efficient means of deploying SP2 to a large number of Windows XP Professional computers in an Active Directory domain. You can deploy SP2 to all computers in the domain or an OU by creating a software installation policy that assigns SP2 to the required computers.

Use the following procedure to prepare an installation share and create a GPO for SP2 deployment:

1. While logged on to a server running Windows 2000 Server or Windows Server 2003 as an administrator, create and share a folder named XPSP2.

2. Copy all files in the Windows XP SP2 CD-ROM to this share.

3. From a command prompt, navigate to this folder and type **XPSP2 -X** to extract the service pack files.

4. Click OK to create a subfolder named I386 in the XPSP2 shared folder and extract the service pack files to this subfolder.

5. Access the Active Directory Users and Computers console, right-click the domain or OU containing the computers on which SP2 will be installed, and click Properties.

6. On the Group Policy tab of the Properties dialog box that opens, select an appropriate GPO and click Edit. Alternatively, you can click New to create a new GPO and then click Edit.

7. In the Group Policy Object Editor console, expand the Software Settings node under Computer Configuration, right-click the Software Installation subnode, and choose New, Package.

8. In the Open dialog box that appears, select My Network Places and navigate to the I386\Update subfolder of the XPSP2 share, select Update.msi, and then click Open.

9. Click OK to accept the deployment method of Assigned. As shown in Figure 3.22, the Group Policy Object Editor console displays the service pack with the path to its installation files.

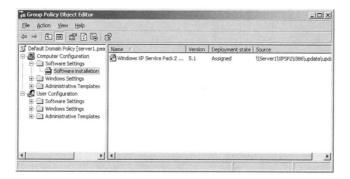

Figure 3.22   Deploying SP2 by means of Group Policy.

After you have completed this procedure, users merely need to shut down and restart their computers to install SP2. The SP2 installation process takes several minutes on each client computer, after which the computer automatically shuts down and restarts.

For detailed information on the use of Group Policy to deploy SP2, refer to the article "Managing Windows XP Service Pack 2 Features using Group Policy" at http://www.microsoft.com/technet/prodtechnol/winxppro/maintain/mangxpsp2/mngintro.mspx.

Using WSUS to Deploy SP2

WSUS is the successor to Software Update Services (SUS), which is installed on a server running Windows 2000 Server SP4 or Windows Server 2003 and provides patches and other software updates to client computers on the network. You can either download the SP2 files from the Microsoft website or copy them from the SP2 CD-ROM to make them available to all client computers that have been configured to obtain their updates from the network SUS or WSUS server.

For detailed information on the use of SUS or WSUS to deploy SP2, refer to the article "Deploying Windows XP Service Pack 2 Using Software Update Services" at http://www.microsoft.com/technet/prodtechnol/winxppro/deploy/xpsp2sus.mspx.

Uninstalling SP2

Should you find that some component or application fails to work properly after installing SP2, you can remove it from Control Panel Add or Remove Programs. Perform the following procedure:

1. In the Control Panel Add or Remove programs applet, select the Windows XP Service Pack 2 entry and click Remove.

2. The Windows XP Service Pack 2 Removal Wizard opens and warns you about actions you should perform to protect your computer. Click Next to proceed.

3. The wizard performs a series of cleanup actions that include inspecting the current configuration, stopping and restarting processes, deleting files, and updating the Registry. These actions take several minutes. To stop the removal, click Cancel.

4. The wizard informs you when these actions have been completed. Click Finish to restart your computer.

CHAPTER 4

Windows Startup

System Layers

Startup—also known as *bootstrapping*—is the process that occurs in the period between turning a computer on and being able to use it. In previous versions of Windows, you probably didn't stick around to observe this process directly, as you felt it best to spend the time more productively—doing the crossword puzzle, weeding the front yard, knitting a new sweater. With Windows XP, the process has been sped up to the point that you can barely fetch the newspaper before the Welcome screen is up. It would be nice to be able to just appreciate the improvement and stop there. At some point, though, you may have to take a deeper look at the startup process—this might happen when you've installed a new hardware device that causes Windows to crash upon startup, or upon finding that your computer has become infected with a virus or adware, or in order to make permanent some change that you have gotten tired of making every time you log on. When this happens, you'll need to know where to start. A lot goes on in the 30-seconds-or-less between the power switch and the Welcome Screen.

When you investigate computer hardware and software you'll repeatedly encounter the concept of *layers*. Computers and their operating systems are amazingly complex constructions, but they have a very definite structure. When you use an application program like Microsoft Word, the application doesn't actually "know" how to read and write data from the hard disk, or how to draw letters on the screen. It relies on the graphics and file system support layers of the operating system to do these jobs for it; the operating system layers in turn rely on device driver software to handle the particular hardware devices in your computer, and the device drivers rely on the hardware to get the job done, as illustrated in Figure 4.1. The figure shows a vastly simplified picture of the software layers in Windows.

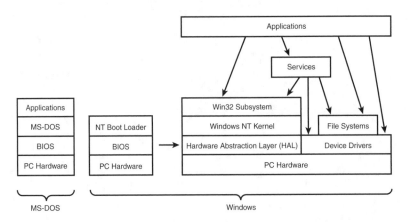

Figure 4.1   Windows has many "layers" of software between your application and the PC's hardware.

Hardware Layers

Ultimately, all the work your computer does is performed by hardware. The CPU or CPUs in it shuffle data around; calculate where to draw the letters, images, and lines on your display; interpret the data stored on your disks; and so on. Ancillary processors also do a considerable amount of work. Every hard disk, for example, has its own dedicated CPU that is responsible for not only moving the magnetic recording head back and forth across the disk surface and generating and interpreting the recorded signals, but also for caching and optimizing the flow of data between the disk and the CPU. Graphic display adapters (video cards) have processor chips that can be *far* more powerful than the main CPU, although their architecture limits them to special purpose processing tasks. Of course, image generation is their intended purpose, but their talents are now being harnessed for digital signal processing, DNA sequence analysis, and other non-graphical tasks as well.

These independent devices must be controlled, coordinated, and managed by software. For the last 30 years or so, the first bit of software that runs when a microcomputer is turned on is called the BIOS.

BIOS

Basic Input Output System (BIOS) is a term that first appeared around 1976 as a component of Gary Kildall's CP/M operating system for the eight-bit Intel 8080 CPU. In early microcomputers, hardware devices were not well standardized, and the interface hardware for each computer's keyboard, display, and floppy disk drives required custom software. Loadable device drivers were not yet widely used, so to make it easier to produce a version of the operating system for a new computer model, the software drivers for the floppy drive, and serial interface or keyboard and display were stored in a separate software module; this way, the majority of the operating system and all application software could be left as is. Once the BIOS was loaded, the routine to read a character from the terminal was stored at one fixed, predetermined address, the routine to send a character to the terminal at another, and so on. CP/M and application programs could thus rely on these BIOS routines, and didn't have to directly deal with differences in hardware from one make of computer to another.

When IBM hired Microsoft to develop an operating system for the original IBM PC in 1980, CP/M quite literally served as the model, and BIOS came along with it, in both name and function. On the IBM PC, the BIOS was stored in a read-only memory chip so that it didn't need to be loaded from disk. Its first task on startup was to perform an extensive test of the computer's hardware, called the Power On Self Test, or POST. If a hardware failure was detected, the BIOS would display a code number that indicated which device had failed. If the POST was successful, the BIOS program used the computer's floppy disk drive to load in MS-DOS. As with CP/M, the PC's BIOS chip contained subroutines to display characters on the screen, read characters from the keyboard, and read and write blocks of data to and from blocks or sectors on the disk. MS-DOS, once loaded, added additional functions to manage the FAT file system, which gave programs access to directories and files.

As the PC evolved into today's version, the BIOS evolved as well. Today's BIOS is stored not in a permanently programmed Read Only Memory (ROM) chip, but in a reprogrammable FLASH chip, so that the BIOS code can be updated. The original PC had only floppy disks for storage, and about three other interface options. Today's BIOS faces hard disks with IDE, SATA, and SCSI interfaces; CD and DVD drives, ISA, PCI, PCI-Express and AGP busses; various types of memory chips with different timing requirements; USB keyboard and mice; and a huge variety of graphics adapters. The BIOS must be able to detect, initialize, and use (in at least a primitive way) all these devices in order to boot whatever operating system is being used. In addition, most hardware devices no longer use fixed assignments for interfaces addresses and interrupts, but rely on the BIOS to enumerate (detect) the installed devices and assign them addresses and interrupts, using the Plug and Play mechanism.

Tip

If the Power On Self Test fails, most BIOSs make the PC speaker beep out a code that tells you what was wrong: memory error, missing display adapter, and so on. I've seen newer BIOSs that literally *tell* you what's wrong, in English, through the sound system—very nice. But BIOSs also write code numbers that denote the particular tests being performed to a specific hardware address. You can purchase a plug-in card called a *POST card* for ISA or PCI-bus computers that display these codes. If the POST fails, the last displayed code tells you what failed. This type of unit can be helpful if the problem can't be displayed on the monitor or spoken aloud.

Today's BIOSs still contain routines to read the keyboard and manage the graphics adapter in a 25-line by 80-column text-only display mode, so you can still run MS-DOS on any of today's PCs, and programs that rely solely on the BIOS and MS-DOS routines to interact with hardware still work. (They may be faster than their authors ever expected, though, so you may find that a game written for an old CPU is over a few milliseconds after you start it).

BIOS support routines are designed only to be run with the CPU in *real mode*, where the CPU acts like an Intel 8086 16-bit processor, there is a limit of 1MB of addressable memory, and, due to the design of the PC, only 640KB of the address range is actually usable. (The BIOS actually does briefly switch the CPU to protected mode during startup in order to test and initialize memory and some hardware, but the CPU is returned to real mode before the BIOS begins the process of loading an operating system). Modern operating systems such as Linux and the 32-bit versions of Windows use the BIOS only to get the CPU started, and once their initial bits are loaded from the selected hard disk, the operating system switches the CPU to 32-bit protected mode and takes over direct control of the hardware. These operating systems use discrete, interchangeable software modules called *device drivers*.

Device Drivers

Device drivers are operating system components written to manage specific hardware devices. Although the driver is concerned with the intimate details of the particular make and model of hardware it's designed to control, it also shields the operating system from having to know these specific details. As far as Windows is concerned, the various categories of device drivers are just interchangeable parts, each doing the same job in exactly the same way.

For example, device drivers for graphic display adapters come in versions for each model of display adapter made, and there are dozens if not hundreds of these. Each one uses memory differently, has different mechanisms for setting resolution and update frequency, and so on. But as far as Windows is concerned, these hardware details are irrelevant; Windows can instruct the driver to shade a particular pixel on the screen a certain color, and the display adapter driver does whatever it has to do to make the hardware display that pixel. Likewise, the drivers for IDE and SCSI hard disk interfaces shield Windows itself from the details of managing those devices; Windows can, for example, simply request data block number 47 from hard disk number 2, and the disk driver will fetch it.

Part of the job of the operating system is to protect each of the system layers and user applications from interference by each other; this increases both security and reliability. On Windows NT-based operating systems like Windows 2000 and XP, user-level programs are not allowed to directly access *any* system hardware; the processor instructions that initiate input/output activity are blocked (or in some cases are intercepted, and the action they would have performed is simulated by the operating system using calls to the appropriate device driver). The memory ranges that correspond to device hardware interfaces are not accessible.

The reason for these restrictions is primarily to give the operating system absolute control over the hardware in an environment where several applications could attempt to perform the same action at the same time. For example, with several applications running, it might happen that two of them would attempt to write data to the disk at the same time. If allowed to access the disk hardware directly, one application might instruct the disk to move its read/write head to a certain position and then to write data at that position. Another application could decide to do the same thing, and could move the disk head to a different location, while the first was still writing. The result would be a scrambled disk.

Device drivers themselves, however, must have unfettered access to the device hardware that they manage. The majority of them run in the context of the Windows kernel, where they are permitted to execute Input/Output instructions and hardware devices. And while each application program is allowed to access only a limited amount of memory dedicated for its use, device drivers have direct access to all of the PC's memory.

This total access carries some risk: a bug in a device driver can cause it to execute inappropriate instructions or memory accesses, leading Windows to conclude that its code *could* have become corrupted, and as discretion is the better part of valor, this causes an immediate halt: Windows displays the infamous Blue Screen of Death (BSOD), so named because the screen is blue with white error message text. The system halts dead in its tracks and the only remedy is to cycle its power. Usually the BSOD indicates that a device driver caused the shutdown, but occasionally the bug corrupts some *other* driver or component, and...well, it's a nasty situation in any case.

But the advantage of a kernel driver is its faster performance. When the device driver is copying data between a hardware device and an application program, kernel mode makes it possible to copy the data in a single step. A user-mode driver would require a copy from the device to the driver's address space, then another copy from the driver to the application.

File Systems and Filters

For storage devices such as hard disks, floppy disks, CDs, and DVDs, device drivers are used to manage the disk's physical controller hardware and to read and write data. However, the data on these devices is structured into files and folders, using any of several different schemes. For example, floppy disk data is organized using a structure called the FAT-12 file system. Most Windows PC hard disks are formatted with a structure called FAT-16, FAT-32, or NTFS, and other PC operating systems such as OS/2 and Linux can use these and other file system organizations. CDs, CD-Rs, CD-RWs, and DVDs use still other formats, and then there are FLASH cards, smart cards, and other devices.

In order to maintain independence between the software that operates the hardware and the software that interprets the data stored on it, there is an additional layer of software called File System drivers.

Here's how these layers work: an application program that wants to read a file from the disk passes its request to the Win32 subsystem. If the desired file is on a disk formatted with the NTFS file system, the NTFS file system driver works out exactly where on the disk the data is located. It asks the disk drive's driver to get it, the driver instructs the disk's hardware to move to a particular location and read it, and the data is passed back up through the same chain.

Now, added to this picture are other drivers called *filters* that position themselves in between any of the layers we've described so far. Filters can let requests move down through the layers and their results come back up, or they can intercept the flow of data and take some other action.

One use of the filter mechanism is to allow a developer to add support for some new feature, file system, or device that hasn't been conceived yet.

Another use of the filter mechanism is to add a security feature. For example, antivirus programs add filter drivers just above the file system drivers, where they intercept requests for reading data from your drives. When the data has been read, they can examine it all *before* any other program has a chance to see it, and can take appropriate action if they decide the data contains a virus program.

Services

Device drivers have unhindered, unprotected access to hardware. A great many of the internal functions of Windows don't need to have the kernel's unrestricted access, but they *do* need to run all the time, whether you're logged in or not, and they *may* need high privileges. Examples of these functions are the Automatic Update service, which downloads and installs critical Windows security patches, the Windows Firewall, which monitors all network activity and blocks attempts by outsiders to hack into your system, and the Print Spooler, which manages the flow of data to your printers.

Most operating systems provide a means of having programs run independently of any logged-on user. On UNIX and Linux, they're called *daemons*, and on Windows, they're called *services*. A Windows service is a program that can be started automatically when Windows starts up, and which provides some essential function. In most cases, services do their jobs without interacting with the keyboard, mouse or display at all. It's possible, though uncommon, for a service for display a message on the screen. The Print Spooler is one service that does this—when a printer jams, the Print Spooler service pops up a message. But most do their job silently, and in the event of a problem usually just record an error message in the Windows Event Log.

We'll discuss services in greater detail later in the chapter.

The Startup Process

When a computer is powered up, all the various layers between the hardware and the visible interface have to be prepared, or *initialized*, from the bottom up. The hardware is initialized first. A circuit on the computer's motherboard sends a reset signal to each chip, module, and external hardware device, to set the hardware to a known state. The reset signal places the Intel or Intel-compatible processors used in Windows PCs in what is called *real mode*, in which the processor addresses memory by physical hardware addresses and in which there are no restrictions on memory or hardware access. The CPU then begins retrieving instructions from a fixed memory address, FFFFFFF0 in hexadecimal. PC motherboards are constructed with a built-in read-only memory chip (ROM) or electrically erasable and reprogrammable memory (FLASH) at that address. This chip contains a set of programs called the Basic Input Output System (BIOS) and its instructions initialize the computer, test its hardware, and load an operating system.

BIOS Startup

A handful of companies produce the BIOS code used in most PCs, and the goings-on inside the BIOS are proprietary. Even the mechanism by which the BIOS is updated in FLASH is secret. However, although the specifics are not public, the boot process goes something like this:

1. A hardware reset puts the CPU in Real mode, and it begins executing instructions starting at the Real-mode segmented address FFFF:0000 hex, which is presented on the address bus as the 32-bit physical address FFFFFFF0.

2. The BIOS chip responds to addresses at the highest end of the memory range. It usually contains a jump instruction at FFFFFFF0 that points to the BIOS cold-start initialization routines.

3. The initialization routine disables interrupts and any known hardware devices, so that any pending hardware operations initiated before reset will not disrupt the startup process, and sets the CPU's memory segment registers to access low memory. A stack is created for interrupt and subroutine data storage. Interrupt vectors (pointers to subroutines used to handle hardware service requests) are set in low memory for hardware and software interrupts.

4. The CPU's memory management registers are set and the CPU is switched to 32-bit protected mode so that it can detect, configure, test, and initialize memory beyond the 1MB Real mode limit. Although early motherboards required you to manually enter memory timing settings, modern DIMM memory contains setup information that is read from the memory modules during startup.

5. The BIOS constructs in memory a list of all known hardware devices and their required interrupt, DMA, and I/O port requirements. Settings for non-Plug and Play ISA bus devices should have been entered into the BIOS setup screens by the user. Plug and Play devices are detected through a complex and peculiar mechanism: bits on the computer's external bus are used to slowly pulse out serial data in a manner not unlike an old time Morse code telegraph system.

6. Some hardware devices respond not only to the CPU's Input/Output (I/O) instructions but also have ROMs, hardware registers, and display buffer memory that is mapped into the standard memory range, and which is readable and perhaps writable as if it were regular system memory. The BIOS scans memory at every 2,048 byte boundary for special "signature" values that mark the presence of a BIOS ROM. These are commonly found on SCSI disk adapters and network adapters so that the BIOS can boot from these nonstandard disks or from the network.

   If found, the routines in these ROMS are called and allowed to initialize their corresponding hardware, and if the user chooses, are used instead of the standard motherboard BIOS program to load the operating system at step 6.

7. If the BIOS is configured for a non–Plug and Play operating system, the BIOS assigns and configures interrupt, DMA, and I/O port addresses for all Plug and Play devices. For a Plug and Play operating system, resource allocation and initialization is left to the operating system.

8. Standard mass storage devices and any detected adapter option ROMs (disk or network) are searched in the user-configured order ("boot order"). The devices are initialized and scanned to find the first device that is online and contains a recognized file system with a valid bootstrap program. The bootstrap program is read from the device and control passes to that program to continue the initialization process.

Note

To read about Plug and Play and other hardware specifications, check out www.microsoft.com/whdc/resources/respec/specs.

When the BIOS or user selects the bootstrap device, a bootstrap loader is used to bring in the actual operating system.

Bootstrap Loaders

As the previous section discussed, the BIOS program stored on the motherboard contains the instructions your PC needs to start up, test itself, and access the keyboard, display, and mass storage devices. Because the BIOS can't know in advance what operating system you're going to use, or how or where that operating system is stored on your disks, or how it's to be read from disk and started up, an intermediate startup program is used, called a *bootstrap loader* or *OS loader*. This is a *very* small operating system-specific program that the BIOS can find and read into memory; the loader is then responsible for actually starting up your operating system. All bootable media use a standard layout so that the BIOS can find the loader.

Note

Disk organization and bootstrap structures are described in detail in Chapter 10, "Windows File Systems."

The BIOS begins the bootstrap process by reading the first 512 bytes stored on whatever startup disk is used, whether it's a floppy disk, hard disk, CD, DVD, Zip disk, Jazz disk, or other removable disk. This block of data is called the *boot sector* and it begins with the bootstrap loader specific to your operating system; it's placed there when you install the OS. It must end with the bytes 55 and AA (hexadecimal), so only 510 bytes are available for the boot program itself. The block is stored starting at address 0000:7C00 and executed there.

Note

You can replace a missing or damaged boot sector loader using the Windows Recovery Console's `fixboot` command, discussed in Chapter 12, "Windows Troubleshooting."

The boot sector loader contains whatever instructions are necessary to

- Identify what file system is used on the disk media.

- Locate and read into memory a secondary, larger, more comprehensive loader program called the *secondary loader*, which is stored elsewhere on the disk.

- Transfer control to the secondary loader, which then continues the operating system's bootstrap process

Because the secondary loader program is not limited to 510 bytes in size, it can do the more sophisticated job of examining the disk's file system and directory structures. The process of locating the secondary loader depends on the medium and operating system in use:

- *Floppy disks*—The bootstrap loader in the first block of a bootable MS-DOS floppy disk contains a small program that interprets the disk's FAT-12 file system to locate files MSDOS.SYS and IO.SYS, which are stored as the first files on the disk (or IBMBIO.SYS and IBMDOS.SYS, in the early DOS versions distributed by IBM). These files are read into memory and contain the code needed to complete MS-DOS's initialization.

- *Hard disks*—The disk's first block contains, in addition to the bootstrap loader code, a table that indicates the location of one or more partitions on the disk. One partition is marked as the *active* partition. The first 512-byte block of the active partition is called the *Master Boot Record* (MBR), and it begins with the code for the secondary loader, followed by the disk's partition table. The primary boot loader relocates itself in memory, calculates the disk location of the MBR, reads it into memory at address 0000:7C00, and runs it.

  When a disk is configured for booting by MS-DOS, Windows 9x, or Windows Me (using the format/s or sys commands), the secondary boot loader locates and reads in files MSDOS.SYS and IO.SYS. Early versions of MS-DOS required these files to be stored at fixed locations on the disk, but later versions are able to examine the FAT file system tables and root directory to locate these files wherever they were physically placed on the disk. (They can move if, for example, the system files are updated after other files have been stored on the disk.)

  For Windows XP, 2000, and NT, the secondary boot program determines whether the disk is formatted with the FAT or NTFS file system, and then locates and reads into memory the file ntldr, which is stored as a hidden file in the drive's root directory. Ntldr—which, as you might guess if you've been keeping count, is a *tertiary loader*—continues the startup process. We'll discuss the NT startup procedure shortly.

Note

You can replace a missing or damaged Windows XP or 2000 Master Boot Record using the Windows Recovery Console and the fixmbr command, discussed in Chapter 12.

- *CDs and DVDs*—Bootable CDs and DVDs contain a data block called the Booting Catalog, which lists one or more bootable operating systems. For each bootable operating system, there is a corresponding block-by-block copy or *image* of an entire (and probably small) bootable hard drive partition. A BIOS that is capable of booting from CD or DVD drives makes it temporarily appear (to itself!) during a boot from CD that an additional hard drive had been detected during startup. Attempts to read data blocks from this virtual hard drive are turned into reads of the corresponding block in the recorded disk image. The standard first-sector boot program is read in from this disk image, and the normal hard disk boot process continues as described in the previous paragraph. The secondary and subsequent bootstrap programs don't actually need to "know" that a CD is being used. As long as they rely on the BIOS to read data from what they think is a regular disk drive, the BIOS can perform the necessary sleight-of-hand to get the data from the CD. This method is used on the Windows Setup CD and on bootable Linux distribution discs.

■ *Networks*—Some network adapters contain BIOS extension ROMS (described earlier) that permit the computer to be booted over a LAN. Typically these ROM-based bootstrap programs broadcast to the network to locate a boot server. The boot server responds by selecting an appropriate boot disk image file, which it transmits to the booting computer. The network BIOS ROM stores this data in memory, and as with the CD boot process, modifies BIOS's data tables to add a virtual hard or floppy disk. The normal boot process continues from there. The first sector of the image contains a bootstrap loader that uses standard BIOS calls to read subsequent data, which is retrieved from the disk image stored in memory. (And, not surprisingly, if the operating system that is being loaded overwrites the section of memory that contains the disk image before the bootstrap process is complete, it crashes.) Network booting can be used to perform Windows Setup on a corporate network, or to load a "thin client" terminal program on a diskless computer. It's also commonly used on network-based computers such as Sun workstations.

The next few sections discuss how the Windows boot-up process continues.

Windows XP/2000/NT Startup

Although Windows 9x and Me computers actually boot up MS-DOS and then start up Windows, Windows NT and its descendents—Windows 2000 and XP—have a completely different startup mechanism.

For Windows NT and relatives, the bootstrap process begins as described previously. However, the active partition's secondary loader takes things in a different direction. The secondary loader determines whether the disk is formatted with the FAT or NTFS file system, and then locates and reads file ntldr from the root directory of the boot partition, and ntldr continues the boot process.

Ntldr locates file boot.ini, also stored in the root folder of the boot partition. Boot.ini contains a list of operating system choices, and optionally, multiple entries for Windows, each with different startup options specified, which can be used to recover from failures and for debugging purposes. If you install your operating systems carefully and in the right order, boot.ini can also contain entries that allow you to select between MS-DOS, Windows 9x, Windows 2000, XP, Linux, and possibly other operating systems. The section "Boot Options," later in this chapter discusses boot.ini further.

For each operating system choice, boot.ini contains a file path that points to a Windows folder or to a folder that contains a file that contains an alternate secondary-boot sector. If there is more than one choice, ntldr displays a menu. If you make a selection, or if a timeout period elapses, ntldr starts the highlighted operating system. You can also press F8 during a very small time window during the startup process, which makes ntldr display the built-in Windows Advanced Options menu. This menu includes the option to boot in Safe mode, with a minimal set of drivers, along with several other startup options.

If MS-DOS, Windows 9x, or Windows Me is selected from the boot menu, ntldr reads a saved copy of the boot sector installed by the older OS (for example, bootsect.dos). The standard DOS or Windows 9x boot process continues from there.

For Windows NT, 2000, and XP, ntldr runs the program ntdetect.com, which collects information about the installed hardware. It performs some hardware detection itself and collects other information from tables left in memory by the BIOS. If multiple hardware profiles are loaded, at this point ntldr may also stop and display the Hardware Profiles/Configuration Recovery menu.

Ntldr then locates files `ntoskrnl.exe` and `hal.dll` in the system32 folder under the selected Windows folder. These two files form the Windows *kernel*, the foundation on which the operating system is based.

The Windows NT Kernel

Windows NT, 2000, and XP are all based on a *kernel* layer that provides basic, fundamental services to mediate access to hardware, start and stop processes, control the CPU's hardware, manage multiple CPUs if present, manage memory, and so on. Differences between motherboard and CPU designs are handled by the kernel's Hardware Abstraction Layer (HAL), which performs CPU hardware management functions for the kernel and higher levels of Windows, without requiring them to know the details of the particular hardware implementation. The standard HAL versions provided with Windows XP are listed in Table 4.1.

Table 4.1   Standard Windows XP HAL versions

HAL Name	Original Filename	Used For
Advanced Configuration and Power Interface (ACPI) PC	`halacpi.dll`	A single-processor motherboard that complies with the ACPI configuration and power management specification.
ACPI Multiprocessor PC	`halmacpi.dll`	An ACPI-compliant multiprocessor motheboard with two or more CPUs installed (or with one or more dual-core or hyperthreading CPUs).
ACPI Uniprocessor PC	`halaapci.dll`	An ACPI-compliant multiprocessor motherboard with one single core, nonhyperthreading CPU installed.
Compaq SystemPro Multiprocessor or 100% Compatible	`Halsp.dll`	A Compaq SystemPro or compatible server motherboard.
MPS Uniprocessor PC	`halapic.dll`	A non-ACPI compliant multiprocessor motherboard with a single processor installed.
MPS Multiprocessor PC	`halmps.dll`	A non-ACPI compliant multiprocessor motheboard with two or more processors installed.
Standard PC	`hal.dll`	A non-ACPI compliant single-processor motherboard.
Other		Custom HALs may be written and provided by computer manufacturers.

Note

Windows Setup detects your CPU and motherboard type during setup, and automatically selects the appropriate HAL version. The HAL module is copied to your `\windows\system32 folder` with the name `hal.dll` no matter which version was selected. If you need to force Setup to make another choice, visit support.microsoft.com and search for Knowledge Base Article 299340. This article describes a procedure that lets you manually choose a HAL version.

On Windows XP, Windows automatically switches between multiprocessor and uniprocessor HALs and kernels; you no longer need to reinstall Windows or use the Device Manager if you change the number of processors, for example, by enabling Hyperthreading or installing a dual-core CPU.

The "NT Kernel" is actually not "Windows." The Windows that you are familiar with, the graphical interface, is actually implemented in layers *above* the kernel, by the 32-bit Windows (Win32) subsystem. And in fact other operating system environments (subsystems) such as UNIX and OS/2 can also take advantage of the NT Kernel. Microsoft provided an OS/2 subsystem that made it possible to run character-mode OS/2 programs on Windows NT and 2000, although it's not provided with Windows XP. The UNIX (actually, POSIX) subsystem provided with Windows NT and 2000 is now called Interix, and it's available as a free download for Windows XP Professional—see Appendix A for more information.

In addition to loading the kernel and HAL into memory, ntldr locates and loads the Registry's component files. It examines the Registry for value HKEY_LOCAL_MACHINE\System\Select\Current or HKEY_LOCAL_MACHINE\System\Select\LastKnownGood, depending on the selected boot mode, and creates key HKEY_LOCAL_MACHINE\System\CurrentControlSet, which is an "alias" to HKEY_LOCAL_MACHINE\System\ControlSet*nnn*, where *nnn* is the value retrieved from Select.

It then examines key HKEY_LOCAL_MACHINE\System\CurrentControlSet\Hardware Profiles to see whether there multiple profiles are defined. If more than one profile is defined and is feasible to load, ntldr displays another menu on the console, and again, if the user does not make a selection, a default setting is used.

With the desired Hardware Profile determined, ntldr scans Registry key HKEY_LOCAL_MACHINE\System\CurrentControlSet\Services for entries with a Type value of 1, which indicates a kernel-level device driver. Drivers that are marked for Boot time startup are loaded by ntldr. At this point, the Windows kernel takes over.

The kernel performs two initialization phases. In the first phase, a minimum of services are initialized: the HAL, the Memory Manager, the Object Manager, the Security Reference manager (which is ultimately responsible for all access control under Windows, including files, Registry keys, synchronization objects, and internal data structures), and the Process Manager. The display is now switched for the first time from the text mode set up by the BIOS to a graphics mode and the small Windows startup progress bar is displayed.

Now, all systems are reinitialized and the startup process starts in earnest. Device drivers and filter drivers are loaded, in the order specified by the Load Ordering list show in Table 4.2, and the Session Manager Subsystem (SMSS) starts. It loads the Win32 subsystem (win32k.sys). At this point, it's fair to say that Windows itself, rather than just the generic kernel, is running. The second Windows graphical startup screen is displayed. The Windows Service Controller (services.exe) is started, and services are started, as described later in the chapter under Windows Services.

Table 4.2 Windows XP Driver, Filter, and Service Load Ordering

1. System Reserved	6. Primary Disk
2. Boot Bus Extender	7. SCSI Class
3. System Bus Extender	8. SCSI CDROM Class
4. SCSI miniport	9. FSFilter Infrastructure
5. Port	10. FSFilter System

(continues)

Table 4.2   Continued

11. FSFilter Bottom	37. Video
12. FSFilter Copy Protection	38. Video Save
13. FSFilter Security Enhancer	39. File System
14. FSFilter Open File	40. Event Log
15. FSFilter Physical Quota Management	41. Streams Drivers
16. FSFilter Encryption	42. NDIS Wrapper
17. FSFilter Compression	43. COM Infrastructure
18. FSFilter HSM	44. UIGroup
19. FSFilter Cluster File System	45. LocalValidation
20. FSFilter System Recovery	46. PlugPlay
21. FSFilter Quota Management	47. PNP_TDI
22. FSFilter Content Screener	48. NDIS
23. FSFilter Continuous Backup	49. TDI
24. FSFilter Replication	50. NetBIOSGroup
25. FSFilter Anti-Virus	51. ShellSvcGroup
26. FSFilter Undelete	52. SchedulerGroup
27. FSFilter Activity Monitor	53. SpoolerGroup
28. FSFilter Top	54. AudioGroup
29. Filter	55. SmartCardGroup
30. Boot File System	56. NetworkProvider
31. Base	57. RemoteValidation
32. Pointer Port	58. NetDDEGroup
33. Keyboard Port	59. Parallel arbitrator
34. Pointer Class	60. Extended Base
35. Keyboard Class	61. PCI Configuration
36. Video Init	

Finally, the Windows logon process, `winlogon.exe`, is started. `Winlogon.exe` displays the Welcome screen or logon dialog. At this point, a user can log on, although for a short time, Windows services not essential for logon such as the IIS web server are still loading.

The Logon Process

When you log on using the Welcome Screen or logon dialog (the only option on corporate networks), Windows checks the logon name and password against the local account database, or in the case of a domain logon, forwards the logon request to a domain controller for verification. Successful domain logons may be cached on the local computer to speed future logons.

Note

For more detailed information about the domain logon process, search microsoft.com for the Microsoft Technet article "How Interactive Logon Works."

The User Profile

When a user has successfully authenticated him- or herself, the user profile is loaded. The profile is a folder stored under Documents and Settings, and it contains several significant files and folders:

- The `ntuser.dat` and `ntuser.dat.log` files, the user's Registry hive file and its transaction file (a file that helps protect against corruption should the system crash while the Registry is being updated). The user's Registry hive is loaded under `HKEY_USERS`, and an alias key named `HKEY_CURRENT_USER` is created that points to this data.

- The `Desktop` folder, which contains the user's personal desktop items. The contents of this folder and the Desktop folder under the All Users profile folder are combined and displayed on the user's desktop.

- The `Start Menu` folder, which contains the user's personal start menu items. The contents of the folder and the `Start Menu` under the All Users profile folder are combined and displayed on the user's Start menu.

- The `My Documents` folder contains the user's personal files. (Windows Explorer displays this folder's name as "My Documents" for the logged-on user, but as "*xxx*'s Documents," where *xxx* is another user's logon name, when displaying other users' profile folders—but the folder is actually still named My Documents, unless the name has been changed in the Registry.)

- Cookies, Favorites, Local Settings, Application Data, My Recent Documents, NetHood, PrintHood, and other folders contain data for specific applications including history lists, bookmarks, email files, and so on. These files may be moved to alternate locations in some cases.

The first time a user logs on to a given computer, a new profile folder is created. For local users, the new profile is a copy of the Default User profile folder. (A simple copy will not work, as Registry key and file permissions must be modified to match the user to whom the profile belongs. This is why user profiles must be managed from the System Properties dialog, using the User Profile management dialog.)

For users on a corporate domain network whose account is set up as a Roaming User Profile, the profile folder must be copied from a server. At logoff, changes will be copied back to the server, and on the next logon, only changes made to the network profile since the last local logon must be copied down again. The Windows File Replication Service manages this process. In this way, the user's settings and My Documents folder "follow" her on the network and are available at any computer. (On such networks, email is typically not stored locally on the computer, but is kept in a central mailbox repository and accessed over the network using IMAP or Exchange services.)

Policy

Group or Local Computer policy is applied next. Group Policy is a function of the Windows Server Active Directory system, and it is constructed from one or more sources, depending on the policy groups and/or containers to which the user and the computer itself are assigned. The resulting set of policy (RSOP) is transmitted to the computer from a domain server.

Policy is actually a set of Registry entries that add to, or supercede when overlapping regular Registry entries, and cannot be modified by the user using the Registry editor. Windows components and applications look at this combined set of Registry data for settings that restrict or enforce certain behavior. This feature is used not only to tighten security by limiting users' ability to make configuration changes, but also to ensure consistent and appropriate configuration for all users of an organization.

The User Environment

The environment variable list is created from the following sources, in the following order:

1. Automatic definitions created by the system, including USERPROFILE, USERNAME and so on.

2. Set commands in `autoexec.bat` in the `%systemroot%` drive (usually C:\).

3. The system environment list, configured from the System properties dialog Advanced tab, and stored in the Registry under key `HKEY_LOCAL_MACHINE\SYSTEM\CurrentControlSet\Control\Session Manager\Environment`. Environment variables within definitions, such as `%USERPROFILE%`, are substituted if possible.

4. The user's personal environment list, configured from the System properties dialog Advanced tab, and stored in the Registry under key `HKEY_CURRENT_USER\Environment`.

If more than one source defines the same environment variable, the last definition is the one that is kept, with the exception of the PATH variable. If there are multiple definitions of PATH, the first definition is kept, a semicolon is added, and the additional definition is appended. This way, PATH accumulates all paths defined in the various sources. Changes to the first two sources only take effect after a reboot or on your next logon. Changes to the third and fourth sources take effect the next time you start a program; for example, on opening a new command prompt window.

Startup Programs

When the user profile has been loaded, `winlogon` starts the user's shell program, which is by default `explorer.exe`, the standard Windows Explorer program. When it recognizes that it is being run as the user's first application, however, it knows that it's being asked to act as the user's desktop shell, so it displays the desktop, taskbar, and Start menu.

Tip

If `explorer.exe` is terminated or crashes, winlogon *should* automatically start another copy. If your desktop icons and taskbar disappear and don't start coming back within a few seconds, you can help the process along by pressing Ctrl+Alt+Del, viewing the Applications tab, clicking New Task, and entering **explorer** as the program name.

Explorer.exe is the default shell, but another program could be used just as well, such as `cmd.exe`—which would give you a command prompt window with no Start menu—or perhaps a custom program of your own devising. The shell program is specified in the registry by the value `Shell` under the key `HKEY_CURRENT_USER\SOFTWARE\Microsoft\Windows NT\CurrentVersion\Winlogon`. If this value is present, it is used to determine the user's shell program; otherwise, the same key and value under `HKEY_LOCAL_MACHINE` is read, which specifies the systemwide default. Be very careful if you decide to change the systemwide setting as you could render your system unusable if you specify an improper program.

Tip

I have seen spyware programs that exploit this Registry entry by adding a program name after **explorer.exe**. This leaves Explorer as the shell but also runs the spyware as soon as anyone logs on. To fix this, press F8 when Windows boots (see the discussion of Safe mode later in this chapter) and select Safe Mode with Command Prompt. Log on, run **regedit**, and repair the **Shell** Registry value. Remove the program from any other startup program entries in which it appears (see the discussion that follows), and delete the program's **.Exe** file(s). Then, restart Windows.

While the desktop icons are being collected and displayed, startup scripts and startup programs are run from the following sources:

- Scripts specified by Group Policy (or Local Computer Policy) under User Configuration, Windows Settings, Scripts (Logon/Logoff), Logon

- Logon script specified by the user profile (configurable, for example, under Computer Management, Local Users and Groups, Users, *username* Properties, Profile tab).

- Shortcuts, files, or programs in the All Users profile subfolder `Start Menu\Programs\Startup`. Shortcuts and programs are executed. Files are opened using the associated application.

- Shortcuts, files or programs in the user's profile, subfolder `Start Menu\Programs\Startup`.

- 16-bit Windows programs listed in `\windows\win.ini` under the `[windows]` section in `run=` entries and `load=` entries.

- Programs listed in Registry key `HKEY_LOCAL_MACHINE\Software\Microsoft\Windows\CurrentVersion\Run`.

- Programs listed in Registry key `HKEY_LOCAL_MACHINE\Software\Microsoft\Windows\CurrentVersion\RunOnce`.

- Programs listed in Registry key `HKEY_LOCAL_MACHINE\Software\Microsoft\Windows\CurrentVersion\RunOnceEx`.

- Programs listed in Registry key `HKEY_CURRENT_USER\Software\Microsoft\Windows\CurrentVersion\Run`.

- Programs listed in Registry key `HKEY_CURRENT_USER\Software\Microsoft\Windows\CurrentVersion\RunOnce`.

- Programs listed in Registry key `HKEY_CURRENT_USER\Software\Microsoft\Windows\CurrentVersion\RunOnceEx`.

At this point, the user is completely logged on and ready to work.

Note

Besides the `Shell` Registry entry and the list of startup program sources listed previously, there is one other method that I've seen spyware authors use to install and run programs in a sneaky manner: creating a bogus print monitor. Print monitors are DLLs (program library modules) loaded by the Windows printing system, and they run in the context of the currently logged on user. If a program appears in the Task Manager's Processes under your username, and you can't find it listed in any other startup location (the Winlogon\Shell value, the Run Registry entries and Startup folder under All Users and your own user account, and the `win.ini` file), look for a bogus print monitor entry under `HKEY_LOCAL_MACHINE\System\CurrentControlSet\Control\Print\Monitors`. Spyware can install a DLL here, Windows will load it, and it then starts the spyware application that you see in the Processes list. If you find such an entry, boot Windows in Safe Mode with Command Prompt, log on, run `regedit`, and delete the bogus key under `Monitors`. There will most likely be several start techniques in use, so you'll need to check carefully—see the "Shell" tip mentioned previously.

Windows Boot Options

As discussed in the previous sections, as Windows XP, 2000, or NT begins its startup process, it runs program `ntldr`, which examines the root folder of the boot drive for a file named `boot.ini`. This file can contain entries for one or more different installations of Windows, and different versions of Windows and even different operating systems such as MS-DOS or Linux. In addition, a special set of disaster-recovery boot options is available called the Windows Advanced Options menu; this menu is your first recourse if some driver or other disaster prevents Windows from starting, and it's discussed later in this chapter. We'll discuss the various startup options in this section.

Note

If the **boot.ini** file is missing, **ntldr** will load the first Windows installation it can find, and if you use SCSI disks it may not be able to find any. If you see a message that **boot.ini** is missing, you should try to restore it from a backup. The Recovery Console can also help you re-create **boot.ini**, as discussed later in the chapter.

Boot.ini and the Boot Menu

When ntldr is starting Windows, it examines the root folder of the boot drive for a file named boot.ini. The file contains a list of one or more operating system choices. If there is just one choice, ntldr proceeds to load the operating system. When you have multiple operating system choices, or if you install the Recovery Console on your hard disk, you will run into the boot menu, an example of which appears in Figure 4.2. This section discusses the boot menu and boot.ini.

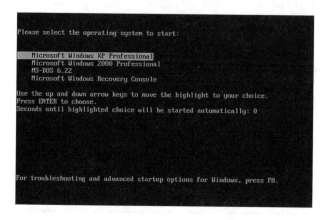

Figure 4.2 The Windows Boot menu lets you select from various operating systems and/or Windows installations.

Just to get us started, a boot.ini file for a system with several boot choices might look like this:

```
[boot loader]
timeout=5
default=multi(0)disk(0)rdisk(1)partition(2)\WINDOWS
[operating systems]
multi(0)disk(0)rdisk(1)partition(1)\WINDOWS="Microsoft Windows XP Professional"
➥    /fastdetect /NoExecute=OptIn
multi(0)disk(0)rdisk(1)partition(2)\WINDOWS="Microsoft Windows 2000 Professional"
➥    /fastdetect
C:\BOOTSECT.DOS="MS-DOS 6.22"
C:\CMDCONS\BOOTSECT.DAT="Microsoft Windows Recovery Console" /cmdcons
```

The [boot loader] section contains entries that control the behavior of the boot menu. The [operating systems] section contains entries for each bootable operating system, one line per entry. (The format of this book isn't wide enough to permit the lines to be printed as they appear in boot.ini; the symbol ➥ indicates that a line had to be split up to be printed. In the real boot.ini file, the text from /fastdetect on appears right after Professional").

Boot Loader Options

The Boot Loader section can contain any of the entries listed in Table 4.3.

Table 4.3   ***Boot.ini* Boot Loader Section Options**

Entry	Description
`timeout=n`	Sets the time that `ntldr` waits for you to press a key while the boot menu is displayed to *n* seconds. If you don't press a key, the default operating system is booted. If you press any key, the countdown stops and `ntldr` waits for you to highlight an entry and press Enter.
	If timeout is set to 0, `ntldr` boots the default operating system without displaying the boot menu. If you set timeout to -1, `ntldr` always waits until you make a selection.
`default=location`	Sets the default operating system. The *location* text must match one of the location paths in the `[operating systems]` section. The location paths are the parts that appear to the left of the equal sign.

On Windows XP, you can change these settings most conveniently from the System Properties dialog, as discussed shortly.

Operating System Options

The `[operating systems]` section of `boot.ini` lists operating system boot choices, one per line, each with the format

```
location="description" options
```

The *description* text on the right-hand side of the equal sign is placed between quotation marks. This is the text displayed as the boot menu choice when Windows starts, and it should be a descriptive name of the operating system and any special startup options that are attached.

The *options* are optional arguments placed after the description text, separated by single spaces, which can be used to control how the operating system starts. Options can be used, for example, to turn on startup logging, enable Safe mode, or let a software developer debug a device driver. The available options for Windows XP are listed in Table 4.4.

Table 4.4   Windows XP (32-bit) *boot.ini* Options

Option	Description
`/basevideo`	Disables your selected video adapter, and instructs Windows to use a plain VGA adapter set to 640×480 resolution.
`/bootlog`	Creates a file named `ntbtlog.txt` in the root folder of the boot drive, listing all device drivers loaded, to help diagnose driver problems. The file may not be created if the kernel crashes before it can load the file system.
`/burnmemory:n`	Decreases the amount of memory available to Windows by *n* MB. Can be used to test Windows or application performance in impoverished circumstances. See also the `\maxmem` option.
`/fastdetect`	Prevents Windows from scanning your COM ports for a serial mouse. This option can speed up the boot process if you use a USB or PS2 mouse.
`/fastdetect:n`	Instructs Windows that you have a serial mouse connected to COM port number *n*. This option can speed up the boot process if you use a serial port mouse.
`/maxmem=n`	Specifies the maximum amount of RAM that Windows is allowed to use, where n is the number of MB. (See `/burnmemory` as well.)

Table 4.4   Continued

Option	Description
/noguiboot	Suppresses the graphical startup and progress bar that appears while Windows is booting. This is said to speed the boot process somewhat, but it results in a troublingly empty black screen during startup, unless you also specify /SOS.
/numproc=n	Limits the number of processors that Windows is to use to n; effective only on multiprocessor (or multicore) systems.
/safeboot:minimal	Starts Windows in Safe mode, with a minimal set of known "safe" drivers and services. See the later section on the Windows Advanced Options menu for more information about Safe mode.
/safeboot:minimal (alternateshell)	Starts Windows in Safe mode with a Command Prompt window instead of the usual desktop.
/safeboot:network	Starts Windows in Safe mode with networking support.
/safeboot:dsrepair	On a Windows domain controller server, starts Directory Services repair mode.
/SOS	Instructs ntldr to display the name of each driver it loads; this can help you identify which driver is crashing and preventing Windows from booting. Use with /basevideo for increased reliability.
	Less Commonly Used Options
/HAL=filename.dll	Specifies a specific HAL module to load, rather than the one selected by Windows Setup. The file must be stored in \windows\system32. Specifying an alternative HAL may not work; see Microsoft Knowledge base article 309283. See also the /kernel option. It also may not be necessary: Windows XP automatically chooses between uni- and multiprocessor HALs and kernels.
/kernel=filename	Specifies the kernel version to load, rather than the one specified by Windows Setup. The file must be stored in the \windows\system32 folder. This option is used primarily by device developers to select a "checked" debugging kernel.
/debug	Enables remote debugging of the Windows kernel or device drivers through a serial port or IEEE-1394 (Firewire) interface connected to a second computer (*remote debugging*). The debugger is activated immediately upon startup.
/crashdebug	Like /debug, but the debugger is not activated until a STOP (blue screen) occurs.
/debugport=n	Used with /debug or /crashdebug, specifies the COM port number to be used for debug communication.
/baudrate=n	Used with /debugport, sets the baud rate of the COM port used for kernel debugging to n, usually 9600 or greater.
/channel=n	Used with /debug, enables kernel debugging over an IEEE-1394 (Firewire) channel.
/nodebug	Disables kernel debugging; needed only when the installed Windows kernel has debugging enabled by default.
/redirect	The /redirect option applies to Windows Server 2003 only and is used to configure boot monitoring over a serial port for servers with no display adapters.
/3GB	Instructs the kernel to allow each application 3GB of *virtual* address space, with the kernel and kernel services mapped into 1GB, rather than the usual 2/2 split. Used primarily in Exchange Server installations.

Table 4.4   Continued

Option	Description
/userva=*n*	Used in conjunction with /3GB; sets the amount of application virtual memory space to *n* MB rather than the default value of 3072 set by /3GB. Applies to Windows Server 2003 only.
/PAE	Instructs ntldr to load a Windows kernel that supports Physical Address Extension (an increased memory architecture) on Server computers. This option is ignored in Safe mode.
/pcilock	Prevents Windows from managing interrupt addresses, IO ports, and memory configuration for PCI devices, leaving the original BIOS settings in place. Using this option may make Windows fail to boot.

The *location* part of each [operating systems] line is a path to the Windows folder, or a specification for the boot sector of an alternative operating system.

For MS-DOS, Windows 95, 98, and Me, and the Recovery Console, the *location* is specified using a standard *drive*:*path**filename* syntax specifying the name of a file that contains a copy of the boot loader originally stored in the first block of the boot partition by the alternative operating system. These original boot loaders are saved in a file by Windows Setup when it replaces an older operating system during installation. (For more information on performing upgrade installations of Windows XP, see Chapter 3, "Upgrading Windows.")

For Windows XP, 2000, and NT entries on Intel and Intel-compatible processors, the location path uses the unusual Advanced RISC Computing (ARC) path syntax rather than the expected *drive*:*path* format used elsewhere in Windows. This is the tricky part.

Tip

To see the correct ARC path names for all of your hard drives, run the Recovery Console as described in Chapter 12, and type the **map** command.

In *most* cases, your Windows folder is c:\windows on an IDE or SATA disk drive. In this case, the ARC path is

multi(0)disk(0)rdisk(0)partition(1)\windows

But, ARC paths can take one of three forms. For drives that can be accessed through standard BIOS INT 13 calls, which includes IDE disks, SATA disks, and SCSI disks on controllers with modern BIOS extensions, thus the majority of drives on home/office computers, the format is

multi(*c*)disk(0)rdisk(*n*)partition(*p*)*foldername*

where: *c* is the disk controller number, counted from 0 up.

n identifies the physical disk drive attached to this controller. For IDE drives this is 0 (master) or 1 (slave); for SATA drives this is a number from 0 to 3; and for SCSI drives this number can be between 0 and 15.

p indicates the partition number on this physical drive, counted from 1 up.

foldername is the name of the %systemroot% folder on this partition, usually windows or winnt.

For SCSI disks that the BIOS cannot access using INT 13 calls, and that require a separate driver (ntbootdd.sys, installed by Windows Setup), the syntax is

scsi(c)disk(n)rdisk(u)partition(p)\foldername

where: c is the disk controller number, counted from 0 up.

n specifies the physical disk drive attached to this controller. For SCSI drives this number can be between 0 and 15.

u indicates the SCSI logical unit number (LUN) of the disk that contains the boot partition, typically 0.

p indicates the desired partition number, counted from 1 up.

foldername is the name of the %systemroot% folder on this partition, usually windows or winnt.

A third syntax is used when either of the following conditions is encountered:

■ Windows is installed on a partition greater than 7.8GB in size or the ending disk cylinder number for the partition is greater than 1024, and, the system BIOS does not support extended INT 13 calls or they are disabled.

■ The disk controller requires BIOS extensions, but they do not support extended INT 13 calls or they are disabled.

(In other words, the Windows partition is too large or too far into the disk to be reachable by non-extended BIOS functions.)

In this case, Windows setup will have installed a driver named ntbootdd.sys in the boot drive's root folder, and the following syntax will be used in boot.ini:

signature(s)disk(n)rdisk(0)partition(p)\foldername

where: s is an 8-digit hexadecimal number that matches a special identifying number written to the hard disk's Master Boot Record during Windows setup.

n specifies the disk's physical drive number, counted from 0 on up.

p indicates the partition number on the this physical drive, counted from 1 up.

foldername is the name of the %systemroot% folder on this partition, usually windows or winnt.

During startup, ntldr must scan the nth disk on each controller until it finds the disk with the indicated signature value.

For more information about basic ARC syntax, see support.microsoft.com/kb/102873. For more information about the signature() syntax, see support.microsoft.com/kb/227704.

Selecting a Default Operating System

You could edit the boot.ini file manually to select the default operating system choice displayed on the boot menu, and the time that the boot loader waits if you make no selection, but there's an easier way. To set these options using a dialog box, follow these steps:

1. Log on as a Computer Administrator.

2. Click Start, and right-click My Computer. Select Properties.

3. Select the Advanced tab, and under Startup and Recovery click the Settings button.

4. The Startup and Recovery dialog will appear, as shown in Figure 4.3.

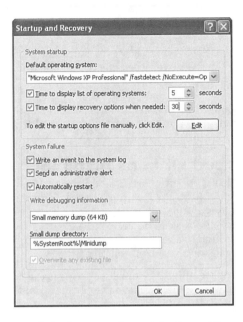

Figure 4.3 The Startup and Recovery dialog lets you select a default operating system and edit `boot.ini`.

5. Select a default operating system from the drop-down list.

6. To speed up the Windows boot process when you're not attending to the screen, set Time To Display List of Operating Systems to a small number like 5 seconds.

7. Alternatively to make Windows wait for you to make a selection no matter how much time passes, uncheck the box next to both of the Time to Display entries.

8. Click OK to save the changes.

Editing boot.ini Manually

If you want to delete boot menu choices or add options to one of the selections, on Windows XP you can use the `bootcfg` command line program (this is distinct from the `bootcfg` Recovery Console command). Its use is described in Microsoft Knowledge Base article number 289022, at support.microsoft.com/kb/289022.

However, it's just about as easy to edit `boot.ini` directly. On Windows XP, open the Startup and Recovery dialog as described in steps 1 through 4 in the previous section. Then, click the Edit button. This will temporarily remove protections from `boot.ini` and will let you edit the file with Notepad. It would be prudent to save a copy of the contents of `boot.ini` before you make any changes. When you have made your changes, save the file and exit Notepad. The file protections will put be back in place automatically.

On Windows 2000 and NT, you must edit `boot.ini` from the command prompt. You must be logged on as a Computer Administrator. Open a Command Prompt window and type the following commands:

```
c:
cd \
attrib -s -h -r boot.ini
copy boot.ini boot.ini.bak
notepad boot.ini
attrib +s +h +r boot.ini
```

This procedure leaves a backup copy of boot.ini named boot.ini.bak. If you have to undo your changes, simply repeat the steps but reverse the copy command:

```
copy boot.ini.bak boot.ini
```

If you can't boot Windows at all, you can use the Recovery Console to repair boot.ini using the bootcfg /rebuild command, or you can create a boot.ini file on another computer and transfer it to your computer on a floppy disk.

Windows Advanced Options Menu (Safe Mode)

If you experience problems after installing a new driver or hardware, or if you are plagued by virus or spyware software that can't be deleted while Windows is running, you can often boot Windows in a special Safe mode that uses a very limited set of known-good device drivers, and very few additional services. In many cases Windows can be started in a degraded but functional mode in which you can then perform repairs. Windows also has boot options that keep a record of all drivers loaded to help you find which one is causing a problem.

The option to boot Windows this way can be set up in special boot.ini entries as described in the previous section, but that would require advance planning, and it's not necessary.

You can access the special Windows Advanced Options menu by pressing F8 while Windows starts up. There are two ways to get to it this menu:

- If your system doesn't pause at the boot menu, you'll have to plan your attack. Start Windows, and as soon as the screen indicates that the BIOS startup is finished, start pressing F8 rapidly and repeatedly. If this doesn't work, restart the computer again (you may need to power it off and back on, if Windows won't start or if you can't shut it down), and this time start pressing F8 as soon as something appears on the screen.

- If your system has multiple boot options, it will pause at the boot menu when Windows starts. You can press F8 while this menu is displayed. (This is a much calmer procedure, and makes another good reason to install the Recovery Console on your hard disk.)

The Windows Advanced Options menu will appear as shown in Figure 4.4.

The most common choices and their uses are as follows:

- If you have set your display adapter to a resolution or refresh rate that your monitor doesn't support, select VGA Mode. This uses your normal graphics adapter driver but sets the resolution to 640×480 at a 60Hz refresh rate.

- If a virus or spyware is causing trouble and you can't delete it, or you can't install an antivirus or antispyware utility because of it, use Safe Mode.

- If you have made a device driver configuration change and Windows no longer works, try Last Known Good Configuration before trying System Restore.

- If you have installed a new driver and Windows no longer works, use Safe mode, and try to update, replace, or disable the driver. If this fails, use Safe mode and use System Restore to roll back your driver change. System Restore data is not saved in Safe mode, so you can't use System Restore to undo changes you've made in Safe mode).

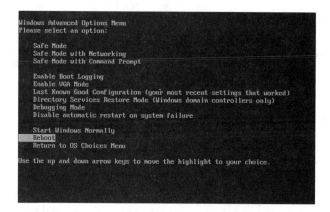

Figure 4.4 Press F8 during startup to display the Windows Advanced Options menu, which includes Safe mode.

- If a device driver is making Windows crash but you don't know which driver is causing it, select Enable Boot Logging. Then, after Windows crashes, restart in Safe mode. Use Notepad to examine the file ntbtlog.txt in your \windows folder, which will display a list of drivers that were loaded. There will be two boots' worth of drivers listed. The first part begins with the operating system version and file ntoskrnl.exe, and ends (hopefully) with the driver that crashed Windows. The second part of the listing starts with the operating system version and ntoskrnl.exe again. This second part was added when you rebooted in Safe mode, so your troublesome driver *should* be the one just above the second part. (You can also examine ntbtlog.txt by booting up the Recovery Console.)

   Delete ntoskrnl.txt after viewing it; otherwise it will just continue to grow and will be difficult to interpret.

- If your display adapter driver is crashing Windows, the previous technique won't help—the crash will probably occur before Windows starts writing the log file. In this case select Safe Mode, which uses a "plain vanilla" VGA display driver, and either update your display driver or use System Restore to roll back a previous one.

All the selections in the Windows Advanced Options menu are described in the following sections.

Safe Mode

Safe mode boots Windows with a limited set of display and disk drivers, and minimal services. The display driver used is for the original IBM PC VGA color adapter, which all current adapters can emulate, set to 640×480 resolution, which all current monitors can display.

Safe mode will often let you start Windows when viruses or adware keep it from starting, or prevent you from loading antivirus or antispyware software. It also usually works when you have a problematic driver or service that is crashing Windows. Start in Safe mode and use Driver Rollback or System Restore to repair the problem.

Selecting Safe mode is the same as adding options /safeboot:minimal /sos /bootlog / noguiboot to whatever standard options are specified in boot.ini, such as /fastdetect.

Safe Mode with Networking

Like Safe mode, Safe mode with Networking uses a small set of very basic drivers and minimal services. In addition, your network adapter driver is loaded and Windows networking services are started. Use this mode when you need to perform a Safe mode repair but you need files that are stored on a network server.

Selecting this mode is the same as adding options `safeboot:network` `/sos` `/bootlog` `/noguiboot` to your `boot.ini` entry.

Safe Mode with Command Prompt

Safe mode with Command Prompt is the same as Safe mode, except that when you have logged on, instead of running `explorer.exe` to display the standard Desktop, a Command Prompt window is opened. This can help circumvent problems that prevent Explorer from starting correctly.

Selecting this mode is the same as adding `/safeboot:minimal(alternateshell)` `/sos` `/bootlog` `/noguiboot` to your `boot.ini` entry.

Enable Boot Logging

This option adds the `/bootlog` option to your standard boot selection. This creates file `\windows\ntbtlog.txt` (or, rather, file `ntbtlog.txt` in whatever folder your copy of Windows is installed in), and this log file lists every driver loaded during startup. See the discussion of boot logging earlier in this section.

Enable VGA Mode

The Enable VGA Mode selection performs a standard startup, but your existing video driver is reset to 640×480 resolution and a 60Hz refresh rate. This should fix things if you've selected an inappropriate video mode. It will *not* help if you have a bad or incorrect video driver installed. In that case, use Safe mode.

Enable VGA Mode adds the `/basevideo` option to the default `boot.ini` options.

Last Known Good Configuration

Last Known Good Configuration starts Windows using the Last Known Good section in the Registry. This is a copy of the service and device driver selections and settings that were in effect the last time Windows was able to start up normally. These settings are recorded when Windows starts, and are marked "Last Known Good" when Windows is then shut down normally.

Directory Services Restore Mode

This optione is used only on a Windows Server Domain controller. It initiates a repair procedure.

Debugging Mode

The Debugging Mode option is used by device driver software developers to let a second computer monitor Windows kernel activity through a serial or IEEE-1394 port. Selecting this option is the same as adding `/debug` to the selected `boot.ini` entry. You should have added the `/channel` or `/debugport` and `/baudrate` options to the `boot.ini` entry before using this selection.

Disable Automatic Restart on System Failure

This option is available on Windows XP Service Pack 2 and later. It disables the Windows automatic restart-after-crash feature so that you can then restart Windows and see what the blue screen says when Windows crashes. It's a very welcome addition.

Start Windows Normally

This selection starts your default or selected operating system with no extra recovery options.

Reboot

This selection restarts the computer.

Return to OS Choices Menu

This selection returns to the boot menu, if it was displayed prior to your pressing F8.

Installing a Multibooting System

Windows makes it reasonably easy to choose between several different operating systems or versions of Windows when you start up your computer. This process is called *multibooting*. There's not room in this book to go into multiboot setup in great detail. I will give you this bit of advice, however: to create a system that lets you choose between different Windows versions and older Windows versions, use the following guidelines:

■ If you want to be able to boot to MS-DOS, set up multiple disk partitions, or multiple disks. Format the first drive, or the first partition, with the FAT file system, using the MS-DOS setup floppy disk. This partition can be small—a few dozen to a few hundred megabytes should be sufficient.

Install MS-DOS first. Then, install later versions of Windows.

■ If you want to boot Windows 95, 98, or Me, set up multiple disk partitions or multiple disks. For Windows 98 or Me, format a partition with the FAT32 file system to get more efficient disk utilization. Install these operating systems after MS-DOS and before Windows XP, 2000, or NT.

■ If you want to install multiple versions of Windows XP, 2000, or NT, install NT first, and then 2000, and then XP. Install each of these onto *separate disk partitions*. Don't succumb to the temptation to install them in differently named folders on the same partition, as the Program Files folders name is fixed, and you will end up with mismatched versions of system utilities.

Install the latest Service Pack for Windows NT before installing Windows 2000, and the latest service pack for Windows 2000 before installing XP. This is necessary because each later version of Windows may upgrade your disks' NTFS version, and the service packs are necessary so that the older operating system can read the newer versions.

■ MS-DOS can't read FAT32 or NTFS partitions, and Windows 95, 98, and Me can't read NTFS partitions. Older operating systems will skip over any partitions they can't read when assigning drive letters, so the disk drive letter assigned to a given partition may vary from one operating system to another.

■ If you want to be able to boot Linux, your best bet is to install Linux last and use a Linux boot loader. Be careful to use the proper procedure to save a copy of the XP boot loader.

For more detailed information on setting up multibooting Windows installations, see *Special Edition Using Windows XP Professional*, published by Que. Also, view Microsoft Knowledge Base article number 306559 at support.microsoft.com/kb/306559.

Windows Services

As mentioned earlier, services are programs that are run by Windows without the need for an interactive logon. They are not part of the Windows kernel, but are applications that nevertheless provide essential system functions.

Services can be configured to start automatically as soon as Windows starts up (this includes services like Remote Desktop and the Event Logging system); to start up manually, either by you, when you want it or more often, when requested by another service or application (this includes the CD Burning service); and a "disabled" setting that prevents the service from running at all.

Most Windows service programs are packaged as dynamic link libraries (.DLLs) rather than as stand-alone executable (.EXE) files. These are loaded and called by svchost.exe. Svchost is a small program that contains the code a service needs to interact with the Windows Service Controller, but none of the code to actually implement a service. Svchost calls functions in the service's dynamic link library to do whatever job the service requires. One running copy of svchost can load and manage any number of services. This reduces the amount of memory each service consumes: the DLL method requires a minimum of about 150KB of memory per added service, versus a minimum of about 800KB for each service contained in a separate .EXE file.

On a typical Windows XP Professional installation, five to seven copies of svchost are started up (you can see them if you type Ctrl+Alt+Del and view the Processes tab), and collectively they manage about 40 services.

Many services rely on other services to do their job. These dependencies are tracked by Windows, and the relied-upon services are automatically started before their dependents. When Windows starts, the Service Controller program services.exe is started, and it uses the following procedure to start device drivers and services in an orderly fashion.

1. The Service Controller (services.exe) scans the Registry subkeys under HKEY_LOCAL_MACHINE\ System\CurrentControlSet\Services. Each subkey lists the service name for each device driver, filter, and service. Entries with a Type value of 10 or 20 (hex) are services. The Service Manager creates a list of all items that have a start mode of System, Boot, or Automatic. All of these are started when Windows boots up.

   Although the Service Controller starts many device drivers as well as services, we'll focus on services here.

2. Under each service's subkey are optional values named Group, DependOnGroup, and DependOnService. The Service Controller starts up services in the following order

   - Services with a Group value are considered first, with groups started in the order specified by the Registry value HKLM\SYSTEM\CurrentControlSet\Control\ServiceGroupOrder\List, which is listed in Table 4.4.

   - Within each group, services with no dependencies are started first. Services with names listed in their DependOnGroup or DependOnService values are started only after, and only if, the named groups or services have successfully started.

   - Services with no group name are started last. Again, services with no dependencies are started first. Services with dependencies are started only after, and only if, the named groups or services have successfully started.

3. When the Service Controller is to start a given service, it examines the Registry value HKLM\ SYSTEM\CurrentControlSet\Services\Alerter\ImagePath, which contains the name of the executable file to start and any additional command-line parameters to pass to it. The Service Controller starts the specified program using the designated account credentials (LOCAL_ SYSTEM, LOCAL_SERVICE, NETWORK_SERVICE, or a specified user account).

4. When the service executable program starts up, it communicates to the Service Controller the name or names of any services it is designed to provide. In the future, if the Service Controller needs to start any other services that this executable program says it supports, it will not start a new copy of the program but will simply notify the existing process to start operating the

additional service. This minimizes the number of separate processes required. (Presumably the Service Controller checks the definitions for any additional services to be sure that they point to the same executable; otherwise, a process could hijack other services and compromise the system.)

5. The Service Controller signals the service process to start operating the designated service. The service process communicates its progress back to the Service Controller, indicating that the service status is "Starting," and then "Started." If the service process fails to report its status within a limited amount of time (30 seconds by default, or more if the service has indicated that it may need more time), or if the service process crashes, the Service Controller considers it to have failed.

`Services.exe`, besides acting as the Service Controller for all services, implements two services by itself: the Event Log service, and the Plug and Play service, presumably because these are required during Windows startup before any other services are started.

For services packaged as DLLs run by `svchost.exe`, the `-k` parameter passed to an instance of svchost tells it what set of services the particular svchost instance is to support. The names are recorded in Registry key `HKLM\Software\Microsoft\WindowsNT\CurrentVersion\Svchost`. For example, when the first service whose `ImagePath` value has the command line `%SystemRoot%\System32\svchost.exe -k LocalService` is started, svchost examines value `HKLM\Software\Microsoft\WindowsNT\ CurrentVersion\Svchost\LocalService`, which contains the `REG_MULTI_SZ` string

```
Alerter
WebClient
LmHosts
RemoteRegistry
upnphost
SSDPSRV
```

This instance of `svchost.exe` will inform the Service Controller that it manages these six services. When the time comes to start one of the other five services, the Service Controller will not run an additional copy of `svchost.exe`, but will instruct the appropriate already-running instance to start the additional service.

For each service that `svchost.exe` is instructed to start, it examines Registry key `HKLM\System\ CurrentControlSet\Services\`*servicename*`\Parameters` value `ServiceDll` for the name of a DLL file to load. It loads the designated DLL and calls routines within it that actually perform the service functions. Table 4.5 lists the services implemented by the five or six instances of `svchost.exe` started when Windows XP starts. (The same DLL might contain more than one service; each would have a different entry point function in the DLL.) The services themselves are listed in detail in the next section.

Table 4.5   Svchost Service Groups

Svchost Group	Logon Account	Service Name
DcomLaunch	LocalSystem	DcomLaunch
HTTPFilter	LocalSystem	HTTPFilter
imgsvc	LocalSystem	StiSvc
LocalService	LocalService	Alerter LmHosts, RemoteRegistry, SSDPSRV, unphost, WebClient

(continues)

Table 4.5   Continued

Svchost Group	Logon Account	Service Name
netsvcs	LocalSystem	6to4, AppMgmt, AudioSrv, BITS, Browser, CryptSvc, DHCP, DMServer, ERSvc, EventSystem, FastUserSwitchingCompatibility, helpsvc, HidServ, Ias, Iprip, Irmon, LanmanServer, LanmanWorkstation, Messenger, Netman, Nla, Ntmssvc, NWCWorkstation, Nwsapagent, asauto, Rasman, Remoteaccess, Schedule, Seclogon, SENS, Sharedaccess, ShellHWDetection, SRService, Tapisrv, TermService, Themes, TrkWks, W32Time, winmgmt, WmdmPmSp, Wmi, wscsvc, wuauserv, WZCSVC, xmlprov
NetworkService	NetworkService	DnsCache
rpcss	NetworkService	RpcSs

Services often have to have wide-ranging privileges. For example, services that catalog (index) or back up the hard disk must be able to read any file on the disk, regardless of permission settings. (They, of course, must take responsibility for the data they collect, and only release it to authorized users.) Yet, one of the basic principles of computer and network security is to never give a program more than the minimum level of privilege it needs to get its job done. Therefore Windows runs services in the context of a user logon account, and the service gains only the privileges of its associated account. There are several "built-in" accounts provided with Windows that are never used for interactive logon, but solely to run services.

Most services are run under the LocalSystem account. This account can access any file or other secured object, and has *all* possible system privileges. It's the service's version of the Administrator account, and lets the service do whatever it needs, but it also is a problem if the service is compromised by a hacker, who could obtain full access to the entire system. When services are written correctly, they can usually be run under lower-privilege user accounts. Windows predefines two accounts for use by services:

LocalService—This account has a reduced privilege level. Its file access rights can be controlled on NTFS file systems. When services under this account access the network, they do not present user credentials to other computers; they use anonymous access methods.

NetworkService—This account is like LocalService but when it accesses the network, it uses the local machine account rather than anonymous access. On a domain network, this lets services run under NetworkService perform domain operations on behalf of another computer, such as replication.

Custom services may be installed with different user credentials.

Caution

Do not attempt to change the logon user account for a standard Windows service without explicit instructions to do so from Microsoft; changing a service's account or privileges may make it fail or may prevent Windows from starting.

List of Windows Services

This section lists the standard services provided with Windows XP. Not all of these services may be installed on a given system, depending on the optional software and hardware installed. The first line in each table row contains the service name in boldface, followed by the service's display name. Where DLL files are listed, the service is run from `svchost.exe`. These details are discussed in more detail later in the section.

Services with a Start mode of "Auto" are started when Windows boots, but may shut themselves down if they have no work to do. Services with a Start mode of "Manual" are usually started automatically by other services or applications when they are needed.

The list of Windows XP services includes:

- **6to4**—IPv6 Helper Service. Provides DDNS name registration and automatic IPv6 connectivity over an IPv4 network. (Installed with the IPV6 optional network protocol. The Tcpip6 item listed in the dependency list is a network protocol driver, not a service.)

Start mode:	Auto
Login account:	LocalSystem
DLL file:	`6to4svc.dll`
Dependencies:	RpcSs, Tcpip6, winmgmt

- **Alerter**—Notifies selected users and computers of administrative alerts.

Start mode:	Auto
Login account:	LocalService
DLL file:	`alrsvc.dll`
Dependencies:	lanmanworkstation

- **ALG**—Application Layer Gateway Service. Provides support for third-party protocol plug-ins for Internet Connection Sharing and the Windows Firewall.

Start mode:	Manual
Login account:	LocalService
EXE file:	`alg.exe`

- **AppMgmt**—Application Management. Provides software installation services such as Assign, Publish, and Remove.

Start mode:	Manual
Login account:	LocalSystem
DLL file:	`appmgmts.dll`

- **aspnet_state**—ASP.NET State Service. Provides support for out-of-process session states for ASP.NET.

Start mode:	Manual
Login account:	NetworkService
EXE file:	`aspnet_state.exe`

- **AudioSrv**—Windows Audio. Manages audio devices for Windows-based programs.

Start mode:	Auto
Login account:	LocalSystem
DLL file:	`audiosrv.dll`
Load group:	AudioGroup
Dependencies:	PlugPlay, RpcSs

- **BITS**—Background Intelligent Transfer Service. Transfers files in the background using idle network bandwidth. Features such as Windows Update, Automatic Updates, and MSN Explorer depend on this service.

Start mode:	Manual
Login account:	LocalSystem
DLL file:	`qmgr.dll`
Dependencies:	RpcSs
Failure action:	Restart service after 60 seconds

- **Browser**—Computer Browser. Maintains an updated list of computers on the network and supplies this list to computers designated as browsers.

Start mode:	Auto
Login account:	LocalSystem
DLL file:	`browser.dll`
Dependencies:	lanmanworkstation, lanmanserver

- **cisvc**—Indexing Service. Indexes contents and properties of files on local and remote computers; used for desktop search and Internet Information Services Server Extensions searching.

Start mode:	Manual
Login account:	LocalSystem
EXE file:	`cisvc.exe`
Dependencies:	RpcSs

- **ClipSrv**—ClipBook. Enables ClipBook Viewer to store information and share it with remote computers. If the service is stopped, ClipBook Viewer will not be able to share information with remote computers.

Start Mode:	Disabled
Login account:	LocalSystem
DLL files:	`catsrv.dll` and `comsvcs.dll`, via COM+ and `dllhost.exe`
Dependencies:	NetDDE

- **COMSysApp**—COM+ System Application. Manages the configuration and tracking of Component Object Model COM+ components. Most COM+-based components depend on this service.

Start mode:	Manual
Login account:	LocalSystem
EXE file:	`dllhost.exe`
Dependencies:	RpcSs
Failure action:	Restart service after 1 second, 5 seconds

- **CryptSvc**—Cryptographic Services. Provides three management services: Catalog Database Service, which confirms the signatures of Windows files; Protected Root Service, which adds and removes Trusted Root Certification Authority certificates from this computer; and Key Service, which helps enroll the computer for certificates.

Start mode:	Auto
Login account:	LocalSystem
DLL file:	`cryptsvc.dll`
Dependencies:	RpcSs

- **DcomLaunch**—DCOM Server Process Launcher. Provides launch functionality for DCOM services.

Start mode:	Auto
Login account:	LocalSystem
DLL file:	`rpcss.dll`
Load group:	Event Log
Failure action:	REBOOT after 60 seconds

- **Dhcp**—DHCP Client. Manages network configuration by registering and updating IP addresses and DNS names.

Start mode:	Auto
Login account:	LocalSystem
DLL file:	`dhcpcsvc.dll`
Load group:	TDI
Dependencies:	Tcpip, AFD, NetBT

- **dmadmin**—Logical Disk Manager Administrative Service. Configures hard disk drives and volumes. The service only runs for configuration processes and then stops.

Start mode:	Manual
Login account:	LocalSystem
EXE file:	`dmadmin.exe`
Dependencies:	RpcSs, PlugPlay, dmserver

- **dmserver**—Logical Disk Manager. Detects and monitors new hard disk drives and sends disk volume information to Logical Disk Manager Administrative Service for configuration. Maintains configuration information for dynamic disks.

Start mode:	Auto
Login account:	LocalSystem
DLL file:	`dmserver.dll`
Dependencies:	RpcSs, PlugPlay

- **Dnscache**—DNS Client. Resolves and caches Domain Name System (DNS) names for this computer.

Start mode:	Auto
Login account:	NetworkService
DLL file:	`dnsrslvr.dll`
Load group:	TDI
Dependencies:	Tcpip

- **ERSvc**—Error Reporting Service. Allows error reporting for services and applications running in nonstandard environments.

Start mode:	Auto
Login account:	LocalSystem
DLL file:	`ersvc.dll`
Dependencies:	RpcSs

- **Eventlog**—Event Log. Enables event log messages issued by Windows-based programs and components to be viewed in Event Viewer. This service cannot be stopped. This service is provided directly by the Service Controller process.

Start mode:	Auto
Login account:	LocalSystem
EXE file:	`services.exe`
Load group:	Event log

- **EventSystem**—COM+ Event System. Supports System Event Notification Service (SENS), which provides automatic distribution of events to subscribing Component Object Model (COM) components.

Start mode:	Manual
Login account:	LocalSystem
DLL file:	`es.dll`
Load group:	Network
Dependencies:	RpcSs

- **FastUserSwitchingCompatibility**—Fast User Switching Compatibility. Provides management for applications that require assistance in a multiple user environment.

Start mode:	Manual
Login account:	LocalSystem
DLL file:	`shsvcs.dll`
Dependencies:	TermService

- **Fax**—Enables you to send and receive faxes, using fax resources available on this computer or on the network.

Start mode:	Auto
Login account:	LocalSystem
EXE file:	`fxssvc.exe`
Dependencies:	TapiSrv, RpcSs, PlugPlay, Spooler

- **helpsvc**—Help and Support. Enables Help and Support Center to run on this computer.

Start mode:	Auto
Login account:	LocalSystem
DLL file:	`pchsvc.dll`
Dependencies:	RpcSs
Failure action:	Restart service after 100 milliseconds

- **HidServ**—HID Input Service. Enables generic input access to Human Interface Devices (HID), which activates and maintains the use of predefined hot buttons on keyboards, remote controls, and other multimedia devices.

Start mode:	Auto
Login account:	LocalSystem
DLL file:	`hidserv.dll`
Dependencies:	RpcSs

- **HTTPFilter**—HTTP SSL. This service implements the secure hypertext transfer protocol (HTTPS) for the HTTP service, using the Secure Socket Layer (SSL).

Start mode:	Manual
Login account:	LocalSystem
DLL file:	`w3ssl.dll`
Dependencies:	HTTP

- **IISADMIN**—IIS Admin. Allows administration of web and FTP services through the Internet Information Services snap-in. Installed with IIS; not available on Windows XP Home Edition.

Start mode:	Auto
Login account:	LocalSystem
EXE file:	`inetinfo.exe`
Dependencies:	RpcSs, SamSs
Failure action:	Run repair program after 1 millisecond

- **ImapiService**—IMAPI CD-Burning COM Service. Manages CD recording using Image Mastering Applications Programming Interface (IMAPI).

Start mode:	Manual
Login account:	LocalSystem
EXE file:	`imapi.exe`

- **Iprip**—RIP Listener. Listens for route updates sent by routers that use the Routing Information Protocol version 1 (RIPv1).

Start mode:	Auto, when RIP network support is installed
Login account:	LocalSystem
DLL file:	`iprip.dll`
Dependencies:	RpcSs

- **irmon**—Infrared Monitor Service. Monitors an infrared (IrDA) interface for connections to other computers and devices; primarily used on laptops, PDAs, and printers.

Startup mode:	Auto
Login account:	LocalSystem
DLL file:	`irmon.dll`

- **lanmanserver**—Server. Supports file, print, and named-pipe sharing over the network for this computer. This service lets you share your folders and printers with other computers.

Start mode:	Auto
Login account:	LocalSystem
DLL file:	srvsvc.dll

- **lanmanworkstation**—Workstation. Creates and maintains client network connections to remote servers. This service lets you use folders and printers shared by other computers.

Start mode:	Auto
Login account:	LocalSystem
DLL file:	wkssvc.dll
Load group:	NetworkProvider

- **LmHosts**—TCP/IP NetBIOS Helper. Enables support for NetBIOS over TCP/IP (NetBT) service and NetBIOS name resolution.

Start mode:	Auto
Login account:	LocalService
DLL file:	lmhsvc.dll
Load group:	TDI
Dependencies:	NetBT, AFD

- **LPDSVC**—TCP/IP Print Server. Provides a TCP/IP-based printing service that uses the Line Printer protocol. Installed as part of Print Services for UNIX.

Start mode:	Manual
Login account:	LocalSystem
EXE file:	tcpsvcs.exe
Dependencies:	Tcpip, Spooler

- **Messenger**—Transmits "net send" and Alerter service messages between clients and servers. This service is used primarily for network administrators to notify users of system outages, or for the Performance Logs and Alerts service to notify system managers of system problems. It is not related to the Windows Messenger chat program. Starting with Windows XP Service Pack 2, this service is disabled by default, as it was abused by spammers to post pop-up ads.

Start mode:	Disabled
Login account:	LocalSystem
DLL file:	msgsvc.dll
Dependencies:	lanmanworkstation, NetBIOS, PlugPlay, RpcSs

- **mnmsrvc**—NetMeeting Remote Desktop Sharing. Enables an authorized user to access this computer remotely by using NetMeeting over a corporate intranet.

Start mode:	Manual
Login account:	LocalSystem
EXE file:	mnmsrvc.exe

  Note: This service can interact with the desktop.

- **MSDTC**—Distributed Transaction Coordinator. Coordinates transactions that span multiple resource managers, such as databases, message queues, and file systems.

Start mode:	Manual
Login account:	NetworkService
EXE file:	msdtc.exe
Load group:	MS Transactions
Dependencies:	RpcSs, SamSs

- **MSFtpsvc**—FTP Publishing. Provides FTP connectivity and administration through the Internet Information Services snap-in. Installed with IIS; not available on Windows XP Home Edition.

Start mode:	Auto
Login account:	LocalSystem
EXE file:	`inetinfo.exe`
Dependencies:	IISADMIN

- **MSIServer**—Windows Installer. The Windows installer service coordinates installation and removal of applications.

Start mode:	Manual
Login account:	LocalSystem
EXE file:	`msiexec.exe`
Dependencies:	RpcSs

- **MSMQ**—Message Queuing. Provides a communications infrastructure for distributed, asynchronous messaging applications. Installed with optional Microsoft Message Queuing network component.

Start mode:	Auto
Login account:	LocalSystem
EXE file:	`mqsvc.exe`
Dependencies:	MQAC, RMCAST, lanmanserver, NtLmSsp, RpcSs, MSDTC

- **MSMQTriggers**—Message Queuing Triggers. Associates the arrival of incoming messages at a queue with functionality in a COM component or a standalone executable program. Installed with optional Microsoft Message Queuing network component.

Start mode:	Auto
Login account:	LocalSystem
EXE file:	`mqtgsvc.exe`
Dependencies:	MSMQ

- **NetDDE**—Network DDE. Provides network transport and security for Dynamic Data Exchange (DDE) for programs running on the same computer or on different computers.

Start mode:	Disabled
Login account:	LocalSystem
EXE file:	`netdde.exe`
Load group:	NetDDEGroup
Dependencies:	NetDDEdsdm

- **NetDDEdsdm**—Network DDE DSDM. Manages Dynamic Data Exchange (DDE) network shares.

Start mode:	Disabled
Login account:	LocalSystem
EXE file:	`netdde.exe`

- **Netlogon**—Net Logon. Supports pass-through authentication of account logon events for computers in a domain.

Start mode:	Manual
Login account:	LocalSystem
EXE file:	`lsass.exe`
Load group:	RemoteValidation
Dependencies:	lanmanworkstation

- **Netman**—Network Connections. Manages objects in the Network and Dial-Up Connections folder, in which you can view both local area network and remote connections.

Start mode:	Manual
Login account:	LocalSystem
DLL file:	`netman.dll`
Dependencies:	RpcSs

  Note: This service can interact with the desktop.

- **Nla**—Network Location Awareness (NLA). Collects and stores network configuration and location information, and notifies applications when this information changes.

Start mode:	Manual
Login account:	LocalSystem
DLL file:	`mswsock.dll`
Dependencies:	Tcpip, AFD

- **NtLmSsp**—NT LM Security Support Provider. Provides security to remote procedure call (RPC) programs that use transports other than named pipes.

Start mode:	Manual
Login account:	LocalSystem
EXE file:	`lsass.exe`

- **NtmsSvc**—Removable Storage. The Removable Storage service tracks and manages removable media such as tapes used for backups and archiving.

Start mode:	Manual
Login account:	LocalSystem
DLL file:	`ntmssvc.dll`
Dependencies:	RpcSs

- **ose**—Office Source Engine. Saves installation files used for Microsoft Office updates and repairs and is required for the downloading of Setup updates and Watson error reports. (Installed as part of Microsoft Office.)

Start mode:	Manual
Login account:	LocalSystem
EXE file:	`ose.exe`

- **p2pgasvc**—Peer Networking Group Authentication. Provides Network Authentication for Peer Group Members. Installed with optional Peer-to-Peer networking support.

Start mode:	Manual
Login account:	LocalService
DLL file:	`p2pgasvc.dll`
Dependencies:	p2pimsvc

- **p2pimsvc**—Peer Networking Identity Manager. Provides Identity service for Peer Networking. Installed with optional Peer-to-Peer networking support.

Start mode:	Manual
Login account:	LocalService
DLL file:	`p2psvc.dll`

- **p2psvc**—Peer Networking. Provides Peer Networking services. Installed with optional Peer-to-Peer networking support.

Start mode:	Manual
Login account:	LocalService
DLL file:	`p2psvc.dll`
Dependencies:	PNRPSvc, p2pgasvc

- **PlugPlay**—Plug and Play. Enables a computer to recognize and adapt to hardware changes with little or no user input. Stopping or disabling this service will result in system instability. This service is provided directly by the Service Controller process.

Start mode:	Auto
Login account:	LocalSystem
EXE file:	`services.exe`
Load group:	PlugPlay

- **PNRPSvc**—Peer Name Resolution Protocol. Enables Serverless Peer Name Resolution over the Internet. Installed with optional Peer-to-Peer networking support.

Start mode:	Manual
Login account:	LocalService
DLL file:	**p2psvc.dll**
Dependencies:	Tcpip6, p2pimsvc

- **PolicyAgent**—IPSEC Services. Manages IP security policy and starts the ISAKMP/Oakley (IKE) and the IP security driver.

Start mode:	Auto
Login account:	LocalSystem
EXE file:	**lsass.exe**
Dependencies:	RpcSs, Tcpip, IPSec

- **ProtectedStorage**—Protected Storage. Provides protected storage for sensitive data, such as private keys, to prevent access by unauthorized services, processes, or users.

Start mode:	Auto
Login account:	LocalSystem
EXE file:	**lsass.exe**
Dependencies:	RpcSs

  Note: This service can interact with the desktop.

- **RasAuto**—Remote Access Auto Connection Manager. Creates a connection to a remote network whenever a program references a remote DNS or NetBIOS name or address.

Start mode:	Manual
Login account:	LocalSystem
DLL file:	**rasauto.dll**
Dependencies:	RasMan, TapiSrv

- **RasMan**—Remote Access Connection Manager. Makes and manages temporary network connections including modem dialup and PPPoE.

Start mode:	Manual
Login account:	LocalSystem
DLL file:	**rasmans.dll**
Dependencies:	TapiSrv

- **RDSessMgr**—Remote Desktop Help Session Manager. Manages and controls Remote Assistance.

Start mode:	Manual
Login account:	LocalSystem
EXE file:	**sessmgr.exe**
Dependencies:	RpcSs

- **RemoteAccess**—Routing and Remote Access. Offers routing services to businesses in local area and wide area network environments.

Start mode:	Auto
Login account:	LocalSystem
DLL file:	**mprdim.dll**
Dependencies:	RpcSs

- **RemoteRegistry**—Remote Registry. Enables remote users to modify Registry settings on this computer. If this service is stopped, the Registry can be modified only by users on this computer.

Start mode:	Auto
Login account:	LocalService
DLL file:	**regsvc.dll**
Dependencies:	RpcSs
Failure action:	Restart service after 1 second

- **RpcLocator**—Remote Procedure Call (RPC) Locator. Manages the RPC name service database.

Start mode:	Manual
Login account:	NetworkService
EXE file:	`locator.exe`
Dependencies:	lanmanworkstation

- **RpcSs**—Remote Procedure Call (RPC). Provides the endpoint mapper and other miscellaneous RPC services.

Start mode:	Auto
Login account:	NetworkService
DLL file:	`rpcss.dll`
Load group:	COM Infrastructure
Failure action:	REBOOT after 60 seconds

- **RSVP**—QoS RSVP. Provides network signaling and local traffic control setup functionality for QoS-aware programs and control applets.

Start mode:	Manual
Login account:	LocalSystem
EXE file:	`rsvp.exe`
Dependencies:	Tcpip, AFD, RpcSs

- **SamSs**—Security Accounts Manager. Stores security information for local user accounts.

Start mode:	Auto
Login account:	LocalSystem
EXE file:	`lsass.exe`
Load group:	LocalValidation
Dependencies:	RpcSs

- **SCardSvr**—Smart Card. Manages access to smart cards read by this computer.

Start mode:	Manual
Login account:	LocalService
EXE file:	`scardsvr.exe`
Load group:	SmartCardGroup
Dependencies:	PlugPlay

- **Schedule**—Task Scheduler. Enables a user to configure and schedule automated tasks on this computer.

Start mode:	Auto
Login account:	LocalSystem
DLL file:	`schedsvc.dll`
Load group:	SchedulerGroup
Dependencies:	RpcSs

  Note: This service can interact with the desktop.

- **seclogon**—Secondary Logon. Enables starting processes under alternative credentials.

Start mode:	Auto
Login account:	LocalSystem
DLL file:	`seclogon.dll`

  Note: This service can interact with the desktop.

- **SENS**—System Event Notification. Tracks system events such as Windows logon, network, and power events. Notifies COM+ Event System subscribers of these events.

Start mode:	Auto
Login account:	LocalSystem
DLL file:	`sens.dll`
Load group:	Network
Dependencies:	EventSystem

- **SharedAccess**—Windows Firewall/Internet Connection Sharing (ICS). Provides network address translation, addressing, name resolution, and/or intrusion prevention services for a home or small office network.

Start mode:	Auto
Login account:	LocalSystem
DLL file:	`ipnathlp.dll`
Dependencies:	Netman, winmgmt

- **ShellHWDetection**—Shell Hardware Detection. Provides notifications for AutoPlay hardware events.

Start mode:	Auto
Login account:	LocalSystem
DLL file:	`shsvcs.dll`
Load group:	ShellSvcGroup
Dependencies:	RpcSs

- **SimpTcp**—Simple TCP/IP Services. Supports the following TCP/IP services: Character Generator, Daytime, Discard, Echo, and Quote of the Day. Installed with Simple TCP/IP Services optional networking component.

Start mode:	Auto
Login account:	LocalSystem
EXE file:	`tcpsvcs.exe`
Dependencies:	AFD

- **SMTPSVC**—Simple Mail Transfer Protocol (SMTP). Transports electronic mail across the network. Installed with IIS; not available on Windows XP Home Edition.

Start mode:	Auto
Login account:	LocalSystem
EXE file:	`inetinfo.exe`
Dependencies:	IISADMIN, Eventlog

- **SNMP**—SNMP Service. Includes agents that monitor the activity in network devices and report to the network console workstation. Installed with the SNMP optional networking component.

Start mode:	Auto
Login account:	LocalSystem
EXE file:	`snmp.exe`
Dependencies:	Eventlog

- **SNMPTRAP**—SNMP Trap Service. Receives trap messages generated by local or remote SNMP agents and forwards the messages to SNMP management programs running on this computer. Installed with the SNMP optional networking component.

Start mode:	Manual
Login account:	LocalService
EXE file:	`snmptrap.exe`
Dependencies:	Eventlog

- **Spooler**—Print Spooler. Loads files to memory for later printing.

Start mode:	Auto
Login account:	LocalSystem
EXE file:	`spoolsv.exe`
Load group:	SpoolerGroup
Dependencies:	RpcSs
Failure action:	Restart service after 60 seconds

Note: This service can interact with the desktop.

- **srservice**—System Restore Service. Performs system restore functions. To stop service, turn off System Restore from the System Restore tab in My Computer, Properties

      Start mode: Auto
      Login account: LocalSystem
      DLL file: `srsvc.dll`
      Dependencies: RpcSs

- **SSDPSRV**—SSDP Discovery Service. Enables discovery of UPnP devices on your home network.

      Start mode: Manual
      Login account: LocalService
      DLL file: `ssdpsrv.dll`
      Dependencies: HTTP

- **SSDPSRV**—SSDP Discovery Service. Enables discovery of UPnP devices on your home network. Installed with the Internet Gateway Device Discovery and Control Client optional networking component.

      Start mode: Manual
      Login account: LocalService
      DLL file: `ssdpsrv.dll`
      Dependencies: HTTP

- **stisvc**—Windows Image Acquisition (WIA). Provides image acquisition services for scanners and cameras.

      Start mode: Auto
      Login account: LocalSystem
      DLL file: `wiaservc.dll`
      Dependencies: RpcSs

- **SwPrv**—MS Software Shadow Copy Provider. Manages software-based volume shadow copies taken by the Volume Shadow Copy service. This service provides crucial support required by backup programs.

      Start mode: Manual
      Login account: LocalSystem
      DLL file: `swprv.dll`, via COM+ and `dllhost.exe`
      Dependencies: RpcSs

- **SysmonLog**—Performance Logs and Alerts. Collects performance data from local or remote computers based on preconfigured schedule parameters; then writes the data to a log or triggers an alert.

      Start mode: Manual
      Login account: NetworkService
      EXE file: `smlogsvc.exe`

- **TapiSrv**—Telephony. Provides Telephony API (TAPI) support for programs that control telephony devices and IP-based voice connections on the local computer and, through the LAN, on servers that are also running the service.

      Start mode: Manual
      Login account: LocalSystem
      DLL file: `tapisrv.dll`
      Dependencies: PlugPlay, RpcSs

- **TermService**—Terminal Services. Allows multiple users to be connected interactively to a machine as well as the display of desktops and applications to remote computers. The service provides the underpinning of Remote Desktop (including RD for Administrators), Fast User Switching, Remote Assistance, and Terminal Server.

```
Start mode:      Manual
Login account:   LocalSystem
DLL file:        termsrv.dll
Dependencies:    RpcSs
```

- **Themes**—Provides user experience theme management.

```
Start mode:      Auto
Login account:   LocalSystem
DLL file:        shsvcs.dll
Load group:      UIGroup
Failure action:  Restart service after 60 seconds
```

- **TlntSvr**—Telnet. Enables a remote user to log on to this computer and run programs, and supports various TCP/IP Telnet clients, including UNIX-based and Windows-based computers.

```
Start mode:      Manual
Login account:   LocalSystem
EXE file:        tlntsvr.exe
```

- **TrkWks**—Distributed Link Tracking Client. Maintains links between NTFS files within a computer or across computers in a network domain.

```
Start mode:      Auto
Login account:   LocalSystem
DLL file:        trkwks.dll
Dependencies:    RpcSs
```

- **UMWdf**—Windows User Mode Driver Framework. Enables Windows user mode drivers.

```
Start mode:      Auto
Login account:   LocalService
EXE file:        wdfmgr.exe
Dependencies:    RpcSs
```

- **upnphost**—Universal Plug and Play Device Host. Provides support to host Universal Plug and Play devices.

```
Start mode:      Manual
Login account:   LocalService
DLL file:        upnphost.dll
Dependencies:    SSDPSRV, HTTP
Failure action:  Restart the service immediately
```

- **UPS**—Uninterruptible Power Supply. Manages an uninterruptible power supply (UPS) connected to the computer.

```
Start mode:      Manual, or Auto if a UPS is installed
Login account:   LocalSystem
EXE file:        ups.exe
```

- **VSS**—Volume Shadow Copy. Manages and implements Volume Shadow Copies used for backup and other purposes. This service provides crucial support required by backup programs.

```
Start mode:      Manual
Login account:   LocalSystem
EXE file:        vssvc.exe
Dependencies:    RpcSs
```

- **W32Time**—Windows Time. Maintains date and time synchronization on all clients and servers in the network.

```
Start mode:      Auto
Login account:   LocalSystem
DLL file:        w32time.dll
Failure action:  Restart service after 60 seconds
```

- **W3SVC**—World Wide Web Publishing. Provides web connectivity and administration through the Internet Information Services snap-in. Installed with IIS; not available on Windows XP Home Edition.

Start mode:	Manual
Login account:	LocalSystem
EXE file:	`inetinfo.exe`
Dependencies:	IISADMIN

- **WebClient**—Enables Windows-based programs to create, access, and modify Internet-based files.

Start mode:	Auto
Login account:	LocalService
DLL file:	`webclnt.dll`
Load group:	NetworkProvider
Dependencies:	MRxDAV

- **winmgmt**—Windows Management Instrumentation. Provides a common interface and object model to access management information about operating system, devices, applications, and services. Most Windows management tools require this service.

Start mode:	Auto
Login account:	LocalSystem
DLL file:	`wmisvc.dll`
Dependencies:	RpcSs, Eventlog
Failure action:	Restart service after 60 seconds

- **WmcCds**—Windows Media Connect (WMC). Serves shared multimedia content to Universal Plug and Play devices. Installed as an optional downloadable extension to Windows Media Player.

Start mode:	Manual
Login account:	NetworkService
EXE file:	`mswmccds.exe`
Dependencies:	RpcSs, upnphost, WmcCdsLs

- **WmcCdsLs**—Windows Media Connect (WMC) Helper. Monitors the network for new UPnP Media Renderer devices.

Start mode:	Manual
Login account:	LocalSystem
EXE file:	`mswmcls.exe`
Dependencies:	RpcSs

- **WmdmPmSN**—Portable Media Serial Number Service. Retrieves the serial number of any portable media player connected to this computer. If this service is stopped, protected content might not be downloaded to the device.

Start mode:	Manual
Login account:	LocalSystem
DLL file:	`mspmsnsv.dll`

- **Wmi**—Windows Management Instrumentation Driver Extensions. Provides systems management information to and from drivers.

Start mode:	Manual
Login account:	LocalSystem
DLL file:	`advapi32.dll`

- **WmiApSrv**—WMI Performance Adapter. Provides performance library information from WMI "HiPerf" providers.

Start mode:	Manual
Login account:	LocalSystem
EXE file:	`wmiapsrv.exe`
Dependencies:	RpcSs

- **wscsvc**—Security Center. Monitors system security settings and configurations. (Windows XP Service Pack 2 and later.)

Start mode:	Auto
Login account:	LocalSystem
DLL file:	`wscsvc.dll`
Dependencies:	RpcSs, winmgmt

- **wuauserv**—Automatic Updates. Enables the download and installation of critical Windows updates. If the service is disabled, the operating system must be manually updated at the Windows Update website.

Start mode:	Auto
Login account:	LocalSystem
DLL file:	`wuauserv.dll`

- **WZCSVC**—Wireless Zero Configuration. Provides automatic configuration for the 802.11 adapters.

Start mode:	Auto
Login account:	LocalSystem
DLL file:	`wzcsvc.dll`
Load group:	TDI
Dependencies:	RpcSs, Ndisuio

- **xmlprov**—Network Provisioning Service. Manages XML configuration files on a domain basis for automatic network provisioning.

Start mode:	Manual
Login account:	LocalSystem
DLL file:	`xmlprov.dll`
Dependencies:	RpcSs

Your computer may have services not listed in this table, as third-party drivers and application software may install additional services. They seem to add up quickly. For instance, I just checked my computer and it has 10 non-standard services installed:

ATI Hotkey Poller and **ATI Smart**—Installed with my ATI graphics adapter driver; monitors the keyboard for function keys set to change screen resolution or orientation.

Cisco Systems, Inc. VPN Service—A Virtual Private Network client that I use to securely connect to other networks over the Internet.

Inadyn Dynamic DNS Update Client—Updates the dyndns.org Domain Name Service when my network connection's IP address changes, as discussed in Chapter 7, "Networking Windows."

iPod Service—Installed with Apple's iTunes program; manages data synchronization between the computer and iPods.

pcAnywhere Host Service—Provides remote access, similar to Remote Desktop Connection, via the Symantec PCAnywhere program.

PDEngine and **PDScheduler**—Installed with the PerfectDisk disk defragmenting utility that I purchased.

POP3Proxy—A Perl script running as a Windows Service, which lets me filter my email through the SpamAssassin spam filter.

SETI@Home controller—Runs the SETI@Home data processing application (setiathome.ssl.berkeley.edu) as a Windows service, so that it runs 24×7 instead of just when I'm logged on.

In addition, other services may be installed as part of Windows in order to support nonstandard hardware.

Tip

If you don't recognize a service installed on your system, check www.sysinfo.org, which has an extensive database of programs and services found on Windows computers, including third-party applications, spyware, adware, and virus programs. It also might help to perform a Google search on the name of the unrecognized executable file.

Using the Services Manager

You can start, stop, configure, and monitor the status of services using the Services management snap-in, which appears in the Computer Management console. To open it, right-click My Computer and select Manage. In the left-hand pane, open Services and Applications, and then select Services. The management console is shown in Figure 4.5.

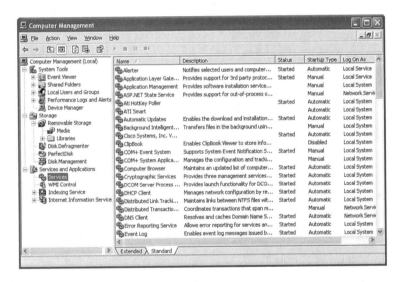

Figure 4.5 The Services management console lets you start, stop, and configure services.

Note

If you are using Windows 2000 or XP Professional, you can start, stop, and restart services using a Power Users account.

To change a service's configuration, you must be logged on as a Computer Administrator. Alternatively, open the Control Panel, select Performance and Maintenance, open Administrative Tools, right-click Computer Management, and select Run As. Select The Following User, and enter an Administrator account and password.

By default, services are listed in alphabetical order by their display name, although as usual for this type of display you can click on a column heading to sort by other column values, such as Status or Startup Type.

To start, stop, or restart (stop and then start) a given service, you can right-click it and select one of these actions from the pop-up menu.

To configure a service, double-click it, or highlight it and right-click Properties. The Service Properties dialog appears as shown in Figure 4.6.

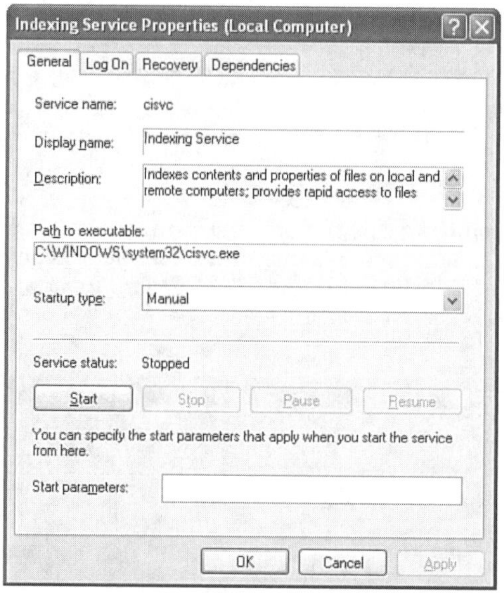

Figure 4.6   The Service Properties dialog lets you configure service startup options.

The dialog has four tabs, from which you can perform the following maintenance tasks:

- *General*—View the path to the service's executable file; set the startup type to Disabled, Manual, or Automatic; Start, Stop, Pause, or Resume the service; add additional command-line parameters used when the service is started.

- *Log On*—Set the user account used to run the service; enable or disable the service in each defined Hardware Profile.

- *Recovery*—Specify actions to be taken if the service fails (crashes or quits unexpectedly), which range from taking no action, restarting the service, rebooting the computer, or running a specified program.

- *Dependencies*—On this display-only tab you can see the services that depend on the selected service (its dependents), and the services on which the selected service depends (its antecedents).

In practice, you will almost never need to manage a service in any way other than to disable services that you do not want to use. Most Windows services are required for normal day-to-day use and should not be disabled. The one exception is the Indexing service. If the following holds:

- You are not running Internet Information Services on your computer, or you are not using any search functions provided by the Server Extensions on your website

  and

- You use an alternative desktop search program like Google Desktop Search, or you rarely perform keyword searches in the Windows Search window then you can safely disable the Indexing service, which will eliminate its annoying tendency to perform massive amounts of disk activity when you're trying to get real work done. To do this, right-click Indexing Service in the list, select the General tab, and set Startup Type to Manual.

Managing Services from the Command Line

On Windows NT, 2000, and XP, you can use the net command to start and stop services from the command line. The command

```
net start servicename
```

starts a service, while

```
net stop servicename
```

stops it. The *servicename* must be one of the service names listed in boldface in the "List of Windows Services" section (earlier in this section), or a service's long Display name, enclosed in quotation marks if it contains spaces.

Windows XP has a more powerful command-line service management tool called sc, which can start, stop, report on, install, delete, or reconfigure services. To get a list of active services, type

```
sc query
```

For a list of all installed services, type

```
sc query type=service state=all
```

For information about a single service, type

```
sc queryex servicename
```

If you are logged on as a Computer Administrator, sc can also manage services on another computer. For example, to view the status of services on a computer named \\bobspc, you could type

```
sc \\bobspc query
```

For a list of all sc commands, type the command sc with no arguments.

Device Drivers and the *sc* Command

Windows Device Drivers are actually very similar to services in that they are executable programs run by the system with no direct connection to the keyboard or display. In fact, the configuration settings for both types of system components are stored in the same part of the Registry under HKEY_LOCAL_MACHINE\System\CurrentControlSet\Services, and only the type and start values serve to distinguish one from the other. The primary difference between the two component types is that drivers are run within the Windows NT kernel and have hardware access, whereas services are "user"-level programs.

The similarity between them is especially notable when you investigate the sc command. Sc can list information about device drivers as well as services, and can change their startup options as well. Surprisingly, it's much easier to see a list of the device drivers that are loaded by your system using sc than it is using the Device Manager GUI program. For example, to display a list of device drivers, type the command

```
sc query type=driver
```

CHAPTER 5

Managing Windows

Managing Users

Modern versions of Windows, the branch of the family tree that includes Windows NT, Windows 2000, and Windows XP, incorporate the distinct concept of a "user." Given your username and password, besides applying your preferences for the desktop and applications, Windows can track which of several dozen privileges you should be allowed to exercise, including the right to install new software, change other users' passwords, access the computer remotely via a network, or—when your disk is formatted appropriately—access any given file. Here are the elements of the Windows environment that are or can be user-specific:

- Your User Profile, a folder under \Documents and Settings in which your personal files are stored. This includes your My Documents folder, your Desktop folder, personal Start menu additions, the Outlook or Outlook Express mailbox and address book files, Favorites (bookmarks), temporary files, and the files that contain personal Registry entries

- Registry entries under the HKEY_CURRENT_USER branch and custom additions to HKEY_CLASSES_ROOT, which are used to store your software preferences

- Environment variables such as PATH and TEMP, which control the behavior of many programs (the information for these are stored in the Registry, but are set through the System Properties control panel; Chapter 9, "Windows Commands and Scripting," discusses environment variables in more detail.)

- File and folder access permissions, for files stored on disks with NTFS formatting

- Shared network printer, file, and folder access permissions

- Windows management and configuration permissions, such as the ability to change the clock, install hardware, or back up the hard disk

- On a corporate network with Active Directory, automatic installation of application software

This is a huge improvement over Windows 9x, where anyone could use the computer with or without a password, and do anything he wanted with it. And, although you certainly can configure Windows 2000/XP to be just as indiscriminate, it's in your own best interest to take full advantage of Windows' security features. In this section I'll give you a bit of background on the Windows security system, and then we'll go over how to set up and manage user accounts. If you want to get right to it, skip ahead to "Adding and Deleting User Accounts from the Control Panel" later in this chapter.

Note

The use of the word *account* in computers goes back to the days of mainframe and time-shared computers that were so expensive that you were charged by the hour—or maybe even the second—of computer use. Your username told the company or university whom to charge. In Windows, an account is a collection of files and security settings identified by a username and optionally secured a password.

Domain and Workgroup Environments

Windows was designed to work in both the home/small office environment and the corporate environment, and these two worlds have distinctly different security needs and management techniques. For home and small office use, convenience and minimal cost are the key parameters. In the corporate world, centralized management, delegation, and fine-grained control are the key concerns. I'll briefly describe how Windows addresses these two distinctly different sets of needs.

Windows uses two different security models, called the Workgroup model and the Domain model, respectively. The difference is illustrated in Figure 5.1.

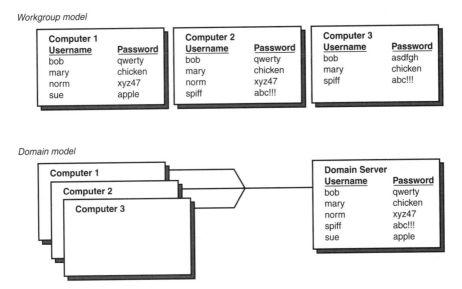

Figure 5.1 In the Workgroup model, user accounts are maintained separately on each computer. In the Domain model, user accounts are centralized.

In the *Workgroup model*, each computer maintains its own list of user accounts. You can see in the figure that user Mary has accounts on all three computers. Spiff has accounts on just two. Norm has accounts on all three, but on one computer, the password is different. This illustrates the important features of Workgroup security:

- User accounts and passwords, called *local accounts* in this model, have to be entered on each computer separately. This is fine if you have only a few computers, or if each person uses just one computer. If you want any person to be able to use any of your computers, though, you have to create a user account on each one.

- If a user changes her password, the change has to be made at each computer separately. (This is discussed further in Chapter 7, "Networking Windows.")

- Although this form of security is a bit more difficult to administer, it's less expensive because you don't need an additional central server or expensive Server operating system.

- Anyone knowing the password to a "Computer Administrator" account on a given computer can do anything at that computer: change user accounts, view files, or reconfigure anything.

- Additional entries, called *local groups*, can be created (although on XP Home Edition, it's not easy). These consist of lists of users, and you can grant file privileges to groups as well as users. If you're protecting sensitive files, for example, it's easier to make one group for, say, all managers, and use that to control access to folders, than to have to add each manager's name to each folder.

With the *Domain model*, each computer is connected to a network, and when a user attempts to sign on, the computer refers to a computer running Windows NT Server, Windows 2000 Server, or Windows Server 2003 to see whether the name and password are recognized. The important points are as follows:

- The centralized list of usernames and passwords ensures that nobody has to visit each and every computer to add or remove user accounts.

- A user has only one password to remember; it's recognized at every computer in the organization.

- In a large organization, the added cost of a central server (or servers) and the more expensive Server operating system is more than offset by the savings in maintenance and the increased security.

- With Microsoft's Active Directory software, assignment of security privileges and delegation of management rights can be extremely well controlled. Although a master network manager can indeed "do anything," the ability to add users and computers, control file security, or access files and folders can be delegated along the company's organizational lines at any level of detail; for instance, department managers might be given the ability to change just their direct subordinates' passwords, and not to make any changes in network configuration at all.

- Large organizations usually have more than one domain server, as insurance against failure and for speedier access at distant worksites. Management updates (like password changes) entered into any one server automatically propagate to the others.

- Accounts created in the domain server are called *global accounts* because they're recognized by every computer, and computers on the network are called *domain members*. Likewise, *global groups* can be created and used to manage security on files and folders.

- Computers on a domain network can also have local accounts and groups, which apply just to the one individual computer. There is usually a local Administrator account that can be used, for example, to install hardware drivers, but this local Administrator logon can't manage the domain server.

What this boils down to is this: If you use your computer on a corporate domain network, you probably can't make any changes to the computer's security setup—not if your organization's network manager did his job correctly. You can skim this section, though, to get an idea of what is going on behind the scenes. However, if you are setting up your own computer for your personal use, or for a small office, read on. You'll see how to use the workgroup model to create individual local accounts, and how to take best advantage of the limited but important security features available to you.

Tip

How do you tell whether your computer is set up for domain or workgroup-type security? Click Start, right-click My Computer, select Properties, and select the Computer Name tab. Under Full Computer Name, the dialog will have the word Workgroup or Domain.

Note

Windows XP Home Edition, by the way, can't be part of a domain network; it uses the Workgroup model only.

Account Types

When you log on, Windows consults a database that it keeps hidden away on your hard disk (for local accounts), or on a networked domain server (for domain accounts). Along with your password, this database contains settings that determine exactly what you are allowed to do to with the computer, such as change other users' passwords. Some of these permission settings are associated directly with your account, but most are inherited through a system called *User Groups*, which contain lists of one or more usernames. Permissions to read files and change Windows settings are usually assigned to groups, and you inherit any privileges assigned to the groups of which you're a member.

User accounts can be customized to some extent, but basically fall into one of four categories, which are, in increasing order of privilege,

- Guests
- Limited Users
- Power Users
- Computer Administrators

I'll briefly discuss each of these in turn.

Guest Accounts

Guest accounts have minimal access rights; they can run programs but generally cannot make any changes to the system, nor save any files in shared folders. In addition, the account's User Profile (a folder created under \Documents and Settings that contains the Registry settings, preferences, application-specific files, and the My Documents folder) is automatically deleted after the user logs out, and created afresh when the next person uses the account.

Guest accounts are fine for public settings, but probably are *not* a good idea for a houseguest who'll be staying for a few days, and who might be irked if she creates a document that disappears as soon as she logs off.

By default, a single Guest-type account is set up when you install Windows XP. The account name is (big surprise) *Guest*. It has no password assigned, and it is also disabled by default, so that it can't be used unless you take steps to enable it. We'll talk more about that later in this chapter.

Computer Administrators

With a *Computer Administrator account* you can make any change, read or write any file, or, well, do anything that a Windows user can do. In addition, while logged on with a Computer Administrator account, any software you run has full access to the computer. This is, of course, a good thing when you're installing a new device or a new application, but it's a terrible risk for day-to-day use, as any virus or other bad software that you might run inadvertently will also have full access to your computer.

Note

You might be tempted to configure a file's permissions to prevent even Computer Administrator users from reading it. You can do this. But, Computer Administrators have a privilege that lets them take ownership of any file, and as owner, they can change the file's read/write permissions so that they can read the file. So, don't assume that you can outsmart the Administrator!

Power Users

A *Power User* can change some settings, for instance, screensaver and Power Management, and can install minor application programs as long as they don't replace any Windows components. Serious changes to Windows, such as networking configuration, Windows configuration, and device driver management, are not allowed. This is the type of account to create for yourself for day-to-day use of the computer. However, for reasons that I can't fathom, the Power User category is available only in Windows 2000 Professional and Windows XP Professional, and is not available on Windows XP Home Edition.

Limited Users

Limited Users can log on, save files, and run most programs, but cannot install software, configure Windows, change security settings, or do much else that doesn't involve the user's own personal data. Limited User accounts are ideal for home systems, and are meant for kids, houseguests, and relatives—in general, anyone whom you want to let use your computer, but whom you're worried might accidentally cause a problem.

Limited User accounts can also be annoying for this same reason, as users can't even change the screensaver or the fonts Windows uses.

Windows XP Home Edition offers only two choices, Limited or Computer Administrator accounts, which I find problematic—Limited accounts are too limited, and for day-to-day use, Computer Administrator accounts are too powerful. Personally, I prefer to use Windows XP Professional so that I can have a Power User-type account. I use the Administrator logon only when I need to make a serious change or install an application (and then, I usually use runas rather than logging off and back on. We'll discuss runas later in this chapter).

Default Accounts and Groups

When you install Windows 2000 or XP, several standard local user accounts and user groups are created as part of the installation process. Some of these are used for maintenance, and some Windows uses internally. You can, and should, add additional personal accounts for your own use. We'll cover that shortly. Here, though, are the default entries that you'll encounter when you go to add your own.

Table 5.1 lists the local user accounts installed with Windows XP. Some additional user accounts are created if you install Internet Information Services on Windows XP Professional. In addition, several local groups are created, as listed in Table 5.2.

Table 5.1   Default Local Users

Username	Description
Administrator	System Administrator, primary member of Administrators group, can make any change via the account's membership in the Administrators group.
ASPNET*	Account under which ASP.NET web server applications are run; it has just enough privilege and file access rights to perform the job but is restricted from accessing the rest of the computer.
Guest	Account that can be used to let unknown users log on with no password. Can be disabled for logon, but is used as the account whose permissions are checked for file access over the network when Simple File Sharing is enabled.
HelpAssistant†	This account is created when you issue a Remote Assistance request. It is the account used to control access by the person from whom you've requested assistance.
IUSR_*xxx**	This account is used for anonymous access via the IIS web server; *xxx* is the name of your computer. In other words, the general public will only be able to view web pages that are readable by IUSR_*xxx* (or Everyone).
IWAM_*xxx**	This account is used as the user associated with "out-of-process" (CGI and ASP) web applications run by the IIS web server.
SUPPORT_*nnnnnnnn*	This is the logon account used by the Remote Assistance system; *nnnnnnnn* is an eight-digit hexadecimal number.

Only on Windows 2000 Professional and Windows XP Professional with Internet Information Services installed.
†*Windows XP only*

Table 5.2   Default Local Groups

Group	Description
Administrators	Members of this group have Computer Administrator privileges, by virtue of the long list of User Rights Assignments granted to this group by default (see Table 5.5).
Backup Operators	Members of this group have permission to back up and restore any file on the computer. This group is generally created also as a Domain group and used for access by remote network-based backup services.
Guests	By default, contains only the Guest user account, which is disabled by default, and which has an absolute minimum of privileges. Guest accounts were discussed earlier in the chapter.
HelpServicesGroup	This group is used for special accounts associated with support applications such as Remote Assistance, and is not meant for normal user accounts. The group exists so that permissions and privileges can be assigned for all support applications collectively.
Network Configuration Operators	Members of this group can change network TCP/IP settings, and force the release and renewal (repair) of DHCP addresses.
Power Users*	Power Users have limited management ability; for example, they can configure the screensaver and install some software, but not modify Windows itself. Power Users can share printers and folders, but not install new hardware.
Remote Desktop Users†	Members of this group are allowed to log on via Remote Desktop. Membership can be edited directly or via the Remote tab on the System Properties dialog. (In addition, accounts must have a password set in order to connect via Remote Desktop.)
Replicator	The Replicator account is used on domain networks to copy files from a domain server to the local computer, automatically. This group should not be modified in any way.
TelnetClients*	Members of this group are allowed to log on via the Telnet service.
Users	By default, all local user accounts are listed in this group; it's meant to assign basic access rights for anyone who has a valid, normal logon account.

Windows 2000 Professional and Windows XP Professional only
†*Windows XP Professional Only*

Security Principals

User and group names can be used when you're assigning permissions to files and folders. There is an additional set of names called *security principals* that are like groups in that you can specify them as having access to files, folders, or other objects. However, their "membership" is contextual. When Windows encounters one of these names in an access control list, it evaluates whether the current user or program has a designated characteristic. For example, if I designate that the "SERVICE" entity is to be granted access to a certain folder, any Windows Service will be able to access the folder, no matter what user account the service is using. These entities can also be used to deny access; for example, a Deny entry for entity NETWORK would mean that a user could access a file while logged on locally, but would not be able to access the file over the network. Table 5.3 lists the built-in security principals.

Table 5.3   **Built-in Security Principals**

Name	Associated With...
ANONYMOUS LOGON	Network access with no username or password supplied (used, for instance, to confirm that Windows can let an unknown network user see the list of shared folders, but not have access to any files).
Authenticated Users	Any user using a recognized account name and if required, password. Exception: The Guest account is never considered an Authenticated User.
BATCH	A program that is not attached to the keyboard and mouse; for example, a program run by the Task Scheduler.
CREATOR GROUP	In an access control list, represents the primary group of the owner.
CREATOR OWNER	The user who created and thus owns the object (for example, file or folder).
DIALUP	Users who are attempting file access via a dial-up modem or Virtual Private Network (VPN) connection.
Everyone	Any user using any means of connection, including Guests but not anonymous network connections.
Enterprise Domain Controllers	Access by a computer that is a domain controller.
INTERACTIVE	A user who is logged in via the keyboard and video display.
LOCAL SERVICE	A program that is running as a Windows Service without authenticated access to the network.
NETWORK	A user who is accessing the computer over the network via file sharing.
NETWORK SERVICE	A program that is running as a Windows Service with access to the network; this service *cannot* interact with the desktop.
REMOTE INTERACTIVE LOGON	A user who has logged in via Remote Desktop.
Restricted	A program that is running in a domain-member computer under a restricted security context.
Self	The user, security, or computer object in which this entry appears (in Active Directory only); used, for instance, in permission lists to let users change their own passwords.
SERVICE	Any program that is running as a Windows Service.
SYSTEM	A part of the Windows operating system itself.
TERMINAL SERVER USER	A user who has logged in via Remote Desktop or, on Windows Server versions, a Terminal Services session.

Account Permissions

Computer Administrator users gain most of their powers by virtue of membership in the Administrators group, which is created by Windows, cannot be deleted, and is recognized by Windows as a special entity. Windows management software and the operating system itself check to see whether you are a member of the Administrators group before deciding whether to let you make certain changes; and at deeper levels, Windows knows to let Administrators bypass the normal security mechanisms that protect files and folders.

There are a number of *User Rights*, such as the ability to change the system clock, that can be individually assigned to users or groups. They serve as the means by which Windows restricts or grants the ability for users or programs to change the way Windows works and, when necessary, to circumvent security features. Not surprisingly, the Administrators group is listed for nearly all of them. On Windows XP Home Edition, these permission settings cannot be changed. However, on Windows XP Professional, Windows 2000, and earlier versions of Windows NT, other accounts can be given these permissions as well.

For example, if you've set up Remote Desktop access to your computer, you know that you have to list the users who are able to log on remotely, using the Remote tab on the System Properties dialog. That dialog actually makes the listed user a member of the Remote Desktop Users group. That group has the "Allow logon through Terminal Services" user right. Thus, the listed users can log on through Remote Desktop.

Although you probably don't want to change their assignment, the settings can be seen in the Local Security Policy management tool, from the Administrative Tools menu or control panel icon. (You must be logged on as a Computer Administrator, or you can right-click the entry and select Run As, and then follow the dialog to run the program as an Administrator.) In the left pane, select Local Policies, User Rights Assignment. The Policy column lists the various user rights, and the Security Setting column lists the users and groups that are granted the rights, as shown in Figure 5.2.

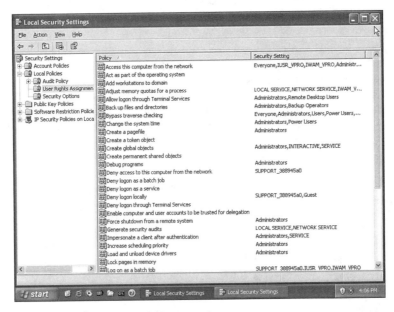

Figure 5.2 User Rights Assignments lists the accounts and security principals that are to be granted each privilege.

Table 5.4 lists the standard User Rights used by Windows XP and Windows Server 2003. In the description column, most entries refer to "users." Here, "users" means any user who is either explicitly listed in the policy entry, is a member of a group that is listed, or has an associated security principal that is granted the associated right. When the description refers to the rights of programs, remember that programs are associated with a specific user, so the program's privileges are the same as the associated user's privileges.

Table 5.4 User Rights

Policy	Description
Access this computer from the network	Allows user to access the computer via file and printer sharing.
Act as part of the operating system	Allows a program to impersonate any user, thus having access to any user's resources.
Add workstations to domain	Allows user to add a computer to the domain (Domain controller only).
Adjust memory quotas for a process	Allows user to increase memory usage limits on another running program.
Allow logon through Terminal Services	Allows user to log on via Terminal Services or Remote Desktop Connection.
Back up files and directories	Allows user to read any file, folder, or Registry entry in the context of performing a system backup.
Bypass traverse checking	Allows user to use a subdirectory (folder) to which he or she has permission, even though he or she does not have permission to read the parent folder. This is normally granted to Everyone and should not be disabled.
Change the system time	Allows user to set the clock and date
Create a pagefile	Allows user to modify the virtual memory Page File settings.
Create a token object	Allows a program to create a Security Token, which could be given to other programs to grant them special access rights.
Create global objects	Allows a program running under a Terminal Service session to create Windows software objects such as semaphores and mutexes that are visible by other sessions.
Create permanent shared objects	Allows a program to create an Active Directory object, or a kernel-mode name object inside Windows.
Debug programs	Allows a program to halt, start, breakpoint, or read the contents of other programs.
Deny access to this computer from the network	Any user who ends up with this policy, by virtue of direct listing, group membership, or security principals, is prohibited from accessing shared files and printers on the computer, as well as other network resources such as Remote Procedure Calls. This policy supercedes and negates "Access This Computer from the Network."
Deny logon as a batch job	In a similar fashion, this policy invalidates "Log On as a Batch Job."
Deny logon as a service	Invalidates "Log On as a Service."
Deny logon locally	Invalidates "Log On Locally."
Deny logon through Terminal Services	Invalidates "Allow Logon through Terminal Services."
Enable computer and user accounts to be trusted for delegation	Allows user to set the Trusted For Delegation setting on a user or computer Group Policy object.
Force shutdown from a remote system	Allows user to shut down or restart Windows remotely through network services.
Generate security audits	Allows a program to write audit entries to the Security log.
Impersonate a client after authentication	Allows a program to impersonate a client using a token received from Windows, usually via networking, without explicitly having provided the username and password. Component Object Model (COM) servers often require this privilege and gain it by virtue of being assigned the SERVICE security principal, which is listed for this policy.

Table 5.4   Continued

Policy	Description
Increase scheduling priority	Allows a program to increase another program's execution priority. If a user has this right, for example, he can modify program permissions using the Task Manager.
Load and unload device drivers	Allows user to force Windows to load or unload device drivers.
Lock pages in memory	Allows program to force Windows to keep specific blocks of memory fixed in place; used by some device drivers.
Log on as a batch job	Allows a user to have programs started by the Task Scheduler, or, in some cases, by certain services.
Log on as a service	Allows user account to be used to run Windows Services.
Log on locally	Allows user to log on directly using the keyboard and display. On domain servers, generally only Administrators are given this privilege.
Manage auditing and security log	Allows user to enable auditing on specific files, folders, and other objects. Auditing as a whole must be enabled separately.
Modify firmware environment values	Allows user to set systemwide Environment variables.
Perform volume maintenance tasks	Allows user to perform disk cleanup and defragmentation.
Profile single process	Allows user to use system tools to measure detailed behavior and performance of application programs.
Profile system performance	Allows user to use system tools to measure detailed behavior and performance of Windows itself.
Remove computer from docking station	Allows user to undock a laptop computer. (The policy can be disabled entirely to let anyone undock the computer without having to log on).
Replace a process-level token	Allows a program to replace the default token (user identity) of another program that it has started itself.
Restore files and directories	Allows user to write to and change security settings of any file, folder, or Registry entry in the context of performing a system restore.
Shut down the system	Allows user to shut down or restart Windows. On a domain controller, generally only Administrators are granted this privilege.
Synchronize directory service data	Allows user to perform Active Directory synchronization.
Take ownership of files or other objects	Allows user to take over ownership of any file, folder, or other system object. Having taken ownership, the user can then change the object's access permissions at will.

In the Local Security Settings tool, each policy is listed along with the groups or principals that are granted the associated privilege. Table 5.5 lists the default assignments for Windows XP Professional in a different way, showing all the privileges granted to each group and security principal. Remember that a given user will likely be a member of several of these groups or principals, so that user gains the combined privileges from each. To maintain tighter security, on a server fewer rights are usually granted to interactive users. Usually only the Administrator logs on directly, and regular users access the computer only over the network.

Table 5.5 Default User Rights Assignments

User, Group, or Principal	Privilege
Administrators	Access this computer from the network
	Adjust memory quotas for a process
	Allow logon through Terminal Services
	Back up files and directories
	Bypass traverse checking
	Change the system time
	Create a pagefile
	Create global objects
	Debug programs
	Force shutdown from a remote system
	Impersonate a client after authentication
	Increase scheduling priority
	Load and unload device drivers
	Log on locally
	Manage auditing and security log
	Modify firmware environment values
	Perform volume maintenance tasks
	Profile single process
	Profile system performance
	Remove computer from docking station
	Restore files and directories
	Shut down the system
	Take ownership of files or other objects
ASPNET	Access this computer from the network
	Deny logon locally
	Deny logon through Terminal Services
	Impersonate a client after authentication
	Log on as a batch job
	Log on as a service
Backup Operators	Access this computer from the network
	Back up files and directories
	Bypass traverse checking
	Log on locally
	Restore files and directories
	Shut down the system
Everyone	Access this computer from the network
	Bypass traverse checking
Guest	Deny access to this computer from the network
	Deny logon locally *(when Guest is disabled from the Users control panel)*
	Log on locally
INTERACTIVE	Create global objects
IUSR_*xxx*	Access this computer from the network
	Log on as a batch job
	Log on locally
IWAM_*xxx*	Access this computer from the network
	Adjust memory quotas for a process
	Log on as a batch job
	Replace a process-level token

Table 5.5 Continued

User, Group, or Principal	Privilege
LOCAL SERVICE	Adjust memory quotas for a process Generate security audits Replace a process-level token
NETWORK SERVICE	Adjust memory quotas for a process Generate security audits Log on as a service Replace a process-level token
Power Users	Access this computer from the network Bypass traverse checking Change the system time Log on locally Profile single process Remove computer from docking station Shut down the system
Remote Desktop Users	Allow logon through Terminal Services
SERVICE	Adjust memory quotas for a process Create global objects Generate security audits Impersonate a client after authentication Log on as a service Replace a process-level token
SUPPORT_*nnnnnnnn*	Deny access to this computer from the network Deny logon locally Log on as a batch job
Users	Access this computer from the network Allow logon through Terminal Services Bypass traverse checking Change the system time Log on locally Profile single process Remove computer from docking station Shut down the system

Although you can change these assignments, it's somewhat risky (you might find that you can no longer log on, use, or manage your own computer), so you should have a very good reason for doing so. One need for adding additional privileges occurs when you install and run a Windows Service using a special user account. You will need to add that account to the Log On as a Service policy entry.

As another example, I use an email system that requires recipients to have a user account, and the accounts must have the Log On as a Batch Job privilege. I don't want most of these email users to have access to the server computer, so I've rounded up the mail users into a group called "Email Users," and have added that group to Log On as a Batch Job. I also deleted most of them from the Users group, because they *only* need to pick up mail, and never log on.

Adding and Deleting User Accounts from the Control Panel

Unless your computer is a member of a domain network, the most straightforward way to create and manage user accounts on Windows XP is with the User Accounts applet in the Control Panel. Here, you can create user accounts, change passwords (your own, or if you are a Computer Administrator, other peoples'), change the Welcome Screen picture associated with the account, and make a "password reset" disk to have on hand in case you forget your password.

Note

If you are using Windows XP Professional, one thing the Control Panel tool won't let you do is to put user accounts into the Power Users category. What I suggest is that when you create new user accounts, create them as Limited Users, and then use the Management Console tool that I'll describe under "Managing Users from the Management Console" to turn them into Power User accounts. You only have to do that once, after creating the account. If you have to make changes in the future, you can still use the Control Panel tool to change the password, picture, and so on.

Select Start, Control Panel, User Accounts to open the User Management applet. You should see something similar to Figure 5.3.

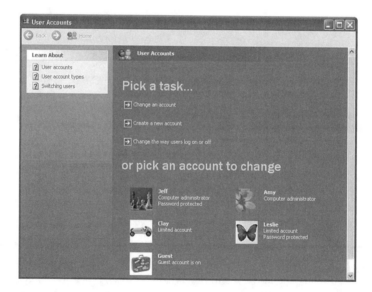

Figure 5.3   The Windows XP User Accounts control panel applet lets you create and manage user accounts.

The links on the left side under Learn About open help documentation for the listed tasks. On the top of the main panel is a list of basic tasks. I'll explain how to create new user accounts shortly.

The bottom section of the main panel lists the local user accounts on this system. You can see details about each of the user accounts, including whether the user has administrative rights and whether the account is password protected. You might also notice that the guest account in Figure 5.3 is enabled. By clicking on it here, you can change the enabled or disabled status of the account. Holding the mouse pointer over one of the accounts opens a pop-up with additional information about what you can change by going into the account. You must be a Computer Administrator to create or modify another user's account.

Tip

To run the User Accounts control panel as a Computer Administrator when you're not currently logged on as one, open a Command Prompt window and type

```
runas /user:Administrator "control nusrmgr.cpl"
```

On XP Home Edition, substitute the name of a Computer Administrator account instead of "Administrator."

If you click on a user account to manage it, the screen like the one shown in Figure 5.4 will appear.

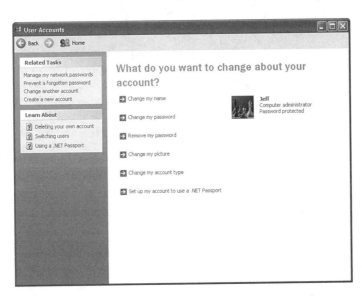

Figure 5.4 Modifying a user account with the User Accounts control panel applet.

In the User Accounts Control Panel applet, there are quick-click actions to do the following:

- *Change the Name*—This option changes the user's "display" name that appears on the Welcome Screen and Start menu. (It does *not* change the actual account logon name; for that, you have to use the Management Console, described under "Managing Users from the Management Console.")

- *[Create* or *Change] a Password*—This option changes depending on whether an account already has an assigned password. If the password is blank, you have the option to create a password. If the password is not blank, you have the option to change it.

- *Remove the Password*—This option only shows up if a password is currently assigned to the account. If the account has no password, this action is not displayed.

- *Change the Picture*—This option changes the 48×48 pixel graphic associated with the user's account. You can select from a variety of included icons or browse to any other graphic. If the selected graphic is too large to fit in the 48×48 pixels, it will be scaled down to fit. Full-sized, full-color, high-detail photos are, therefore, not recommended. I thought this business with the little pictures was silly at first, but it grew on me, and now I have a favorite cartoon character that I scanned in and have copied to every computer I use. Go figure. By the way, Windows stores these images in folder \Documents and Settings\All Users.WINDOWS\Application Data\Microsoft\User Account Pictures.

- *Change the Account Type*—This option allows you to change the account from a Limited account to an Administrative account or vice versa. This is equivalent to adding or removing the user account from the local Administrators group. To assign a user to other groups (Power Users, for instance), use the method that I'll describe under "Managing Users from the Management Console."

  If you've customized an account's group membership, its type will display as "Unknown account type" in the User Accounts window.

- *Delete the Account*—This option deletes the account, including the user's profile folder. Don't delete an account unless you're sure you don't need the associated settings. It is safer to *disable* an account until you're sure you don't need it, using the management console interface described shortly.

In Figure 5.4, I am modifying the account that I am logged in with. This not only modifies the voice of the quick-click actions to the first person (for example, "Change *my* password" rather than "change the password"), but an additional action also appears:

- *Set Up My Account to Use a .NET Passport*—This option associates a Microsoft .NET Passport account to your local user account, relieving you from manually entering the Passport username and password for .NET services that require authentication through the Passport service. Clicking this option starts a wizard. If you do not currently have a passport, the wizard allows you to create one on the spot, though you must have an active connection to the Internet for this wizard to complete successfully.

Note

Carefully consider the privacy implications before you configure your account to use the Passport feature. If you do, then anyone using your account will automatically have access to any websites or services that use Passport as the logon mechanism. Essentially, you're giving Windows and Microsoft permission to validate web transactions in your name.

Adding Users to Your Computer

Here is my recommendation for the best way to add new user accounts to your computer:

1. Make a list of the accounts you want to create, and the passwords you want to assign to each.

2. Log on as a Computer Administrator and open the User Accounts control panel.

3. Click Create a New Account. Enter a logon name for this user. I have a habit of using the person's first initial and last name, but you can choose any sort of names you want to use.

4. Select the account type, Computer Administrator or Limited User. If you are using Windows XP Professional, for regular day-to-day user accounts, I recommend that you create Limited Users here, and then turn them into Power Users by following the instructions in under "Managing Users from the Management Console" or "The Windows 2000 User Manager, for XP, Too." On Windows XP Home Edition, you must have at least one Computer Administrator account (in addition to the main "Administrator" account that remains hidden until you log on in Safe mode).

5. Click on the icon for the new account below the Pick an Account to Change option.

6. Click Create a Password, and enter the password twice as indicated. We recommend that you do create passwords for all of your user accounts, even if just you or your family uses the computer. This helps limit access to any personal information on your computer should it get stolen or should someone come snooping. It's only a small help but it's worthwhile.

You can also add a password hint, but remember that anyone can see this hint, so if security is an issue, it's best to leave this blank.

7. If you want, change the user's picture.

8. If you need to create other new accounts, click Change Another Account under Related Tasks and repeat steps 3 through 7.

If you are using Windows XP Professional, you can then use the Local Users and Groups tool to turn the new user accounts into Power User accounts, as described under "Managing Users from the Management Console." There, you can also create new security groups to simplify the job of file security. (On XP Home Edition, you cannot create or use security groups.)

Before any of these users log on for the first time, you might also want to prepare a customized Default User Profile, as described later in this chapter in the section "Managing User Profiles."

Setting Local Security Policy

In a business setting, you might also want to set your computer's local security policy to require good passwords. To do this, log on as a Computer Administrator and open the Administrative Tools control panel applet, which you'll find in the Control Panel's Performance and Maintenance category. Open the Local Security Policy item, or, if you're not logged on as a Computer Administrator, right-click Local Security Policy and select Run As.

In the left-hand pane, select Account Lockout Policy. In the right-hand pane, double-click the following entries and make the following settings, in this order, as illustrated in Figure 5.5:

1. Account lockout threshold: 5 invalid logon attempts

2. Account lockout duration: 5 minutes

3. Reset account lockout counter after: 5 minutes

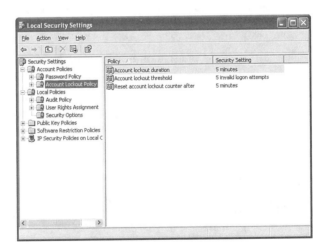

Figure 5.5 Account Lockout Policy lets you block attempts to guess your password.

Then, in the left-hand pane, select Password Policies, and make the following settings:

Minimum password length: 8 characters

Password must meet complexity requirements: enabled

You may also want to enable the settings that require employees to change passwords every so many days.

Local Accounts and Password Reset Disks

Administrators can reset the password for any user account, meaning they could potentially change a password, log on as a user, and see all the user's preferences and files. In addition, before Windows XP, resetting a password would give a user carte blanche access to everything in the user's profile, including stored passwords, encrypted files, and more. Windows XP changes things a bit. If a local administrator forces a password change of a local user account, Windows XP erases all other passwords associated with the user account, including the security key required to decrypt files encrypted using the included Encrypting File System (EFS). This means that a local administrator can't see your encrypted files, but if you lose your password and need to have your password reset, you'll lose your encrypted files, too.

For local accounts, Windows XP provides a mechanism so that you can protect yourself from this consequence of a forgotten password by creating a *password reset disk*. This floppy disk lets you log on to your user account without the password and without losing any other associated passwords or EFS keys. Think of it as a physical "key" to your computer account.

You can only create a password disk for your own account, by following these steps:

1. Insert a blank, formatted floppy into your A: drive.
2. Click Start, Control Panel, User Accounts.
3. Select your user account and click Prevent a Forgotten Password from the Related Tasks list.
4. Follow along with the wizard.
5. Store the completed password reset disk in a secure location.

Remember: Someone who gets hold of this disk has access to your account, so keep it somewhere safe and secure. Each user must create her own password reset disk. However, you will *not* need to re-create this disk if you change your password.

If you have forgotten your password, you can sign on from the Windows XP Welcome screen using these steps:

1. Attempt to sign on using the Windows XP Welcome Screen.
2. After the unsuccessful attempt, click the link marked Did You Forget Your Password?
3. Click Use Your Password Reset Disk.
4. Follow the wizard to reset your password.

Then, put reset disk away in case you need it again in the future.

If you are a domain network user, you still contact a domain user administrator to reset your password or unlock your account. On domain accounts, EFS keys are not destroyed when the account is reset, so the password reset disk mechanism is not needed.

Managing Users from the Management Console

On Windows XP Professional and on Windows 2000, there is an additional tool for user maintenance called the Local Users and Groups Management Console. You can get there in any of four ways:

- Click Start, All Programs, Administrative Tools, if you've enabled Administrative Tools on your Start menu.

- Open Control Panel, Performance and Maintenance, Administrative Tools, Local Users and Groups.

- Right-click My Computer, select Manage, and then select Local Users and Groups.

- At the Command Prompt, type **start lusrmgr.msc**.

Do you think four ways are enough? There are actually more, but let's let it pass for now.

Note

If Administrative Tools doesn't show up under your Start menu, you can add the link. Right-click on Start, and then select Properties, Start Menus, Customize, Advanced, Display.

However you get there, the display will look something like that shown in Figure 5.6.

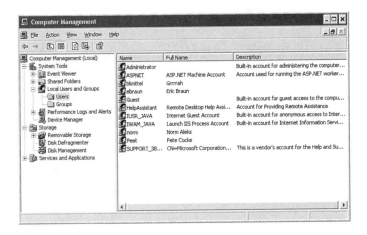

Figure 5.6   The Local Users and Groups Management Console gives you fine-grained control over security group membership.

When you're in the MMC, you can right-click on either the Users or Groups folders in the left-hand pane to create new users and groups. You can double-click an individual user or group to manage properties related to that object, and you can right-click a user or group to rename or delete the object.

For instance, in a home or small office environment, you might find it easiest to create most of your local user accounts as Limited Users with the Control Panel user management tool, and then assign most of your users to the Power Users group. There are two ways to do this. One method is described shortly under "The Windows 2000 User Manager, for XP, Too." The other method uses the Local Users and Groups tool. You must be logged on as a Computer Administrator user. Follow these steps:

1. Open the Groups list and double-click the Power Users entry.

2. Click Add, and under Enter the Object Names to Select, enter the desired usernames separated by semicolons.

Alternatively, you can click Advanced and Find Now to get a list of names. Right-click any you want to add, and then click OK.

3. Click OK, and then click OK again to save the changes.

4. Open the Administrators group, and ensure that the accounts you selected are not also in the Administrators group. If any are there, you can select them and click Remove to remove them. Be *absolutely* sure that the Administrator account remains a member!

5. Open the Users group, and ensure that all of your regular user accounts are listed. If any are missing, add them.

You can also use this tool to create new local security groups. If, for instance, you want only certain employees to have access to your accounting files, you might create a group named Accounting. Add the appropriate users to this new group. Then, edit the file security settings for the folders that hold your accounting files and other sensitive financial files, and be sure that only groups Accounting and Administrators have access.

This will be easier to maintain than adding each individual user to several folders' access lists. In the future, you need only add or remove users from the Accounting group, rather than needing to add or remove names from several different folders.

Managing Users on Another Computer

If you want to connect to a different computer to manage local users and groups, simply right-click Computer Management on the screen depicted in Figure 5.6, select Connect to Another Computer, and enter the computer name. Now all options in the Computer Management MMC reflect the configuration of the remote system, and you can manage the users and groups in the same way as on the local system; however, to do this, your Computer Administrator login name and password must be valid on the other computer.

The Windows 2000 User Manager, for XP, Too

If you are using Windows 2000 Professional, your Users control panel dialog looks like the one shown in Figure 5.7.

It's also available on Windows XP, though you have to perform the trick that brings it up. It has two very important uses: You can use it to make Windows log on automatically, and on XP Professional, you can use it to easily create Power User accounts. To start it up, open a command prompt window with Start, All Programs, Accessories, Command Prompt, and type

```
control userpasswords2
```

If you are not currently logged on as a Computer Administrator, you will be prompted to enter an Administrator account name and password.

This small user manager program can do two very useful things: It can make Windows log on automatically on startup, and it can create Power User accounts.

Power User accounts are very useful, but are only available on Windows 2000 and Windows XP Professional. To change an existing account, select the name from the user list and click Properties. Select the Group Membership tab, and select one of the following categories:

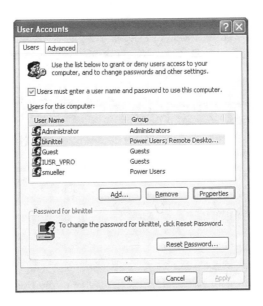

Figure 5.7 The Windows 2000 User Manager control panel applet.

- Standard User—Select this category to make the account a Power User account. This is the best account type for day-to-day use.

- Restricted User—This is what Windows XP calls a Limited User. Select this account type for guests, kids, or other people whom you want to let use your computer, but not make configuration changes.

- Other—You can select this item and select a group from the list to create alternative account types. Administrators is the only useful selection here.

Click OK to save your settings. If you modify your own account, the change won't take effect until you log off and back on again.

On Windows XP Professional, you can create new accounts from this dialog; just click Add and enter the account name, and then select Group Membership and assign the desired account type.

You can also use this tool to assign a password to the Administrator account on Windows XP Home Edition. On Home Edition, there is an account with the name Administrator, which is only available when you boot Windows in Safe mode. By default, it has no password.

Microsoft did this so that even if you forget the password of the Computer Administrator account(s) you've set up yourself, you can still get into your computer. The downside is that *anyone* can boot your computer in Safe mode, select this Administrator account, and gain access to every file on your computer. If this concerns you, you can use the Windows 2000 User Manager to assign a password to the Administrator account: Select Administrator from the list of users, and click Reset Password.

Remember that if you forget the password to this account as well, you will not be able to log on to Windows. To be safe, you should create password reset disks for your other accounts, as discussed earlier.

Another important use for this dialog is to instruct Windows to log on automatically when it's turned on and started up. This works on Windows XP Home Edition, XP Professional, and 2000 Professional. To set this up, uncheck Users Must Enter a User Name and Password to Use This Computer. Click Apply, and Windows will prompt you for a username and password. This account will sign on automatically when Windows starts up.

Managing Users from the Command Prompt

You can manage user accounts from the Command Prompt as well as from the GUI. I tend to use this method when doing quick, simple changes to user accounts, or when creating a large number of accounts for, say, a classroom computer. Here are some commands that you might find handy:

To list all local users:

```
net user
```

To list all local security groups:

```
net localgroup
```

To show all members of a local group:

```
net localgroup groupname
```

To create a local user account (it's automatically added to the Users local group):

```
net user userid password /add
```

To add a local user to a local group:

```
net localgroup groupname userid /add
```

To modify an existing local user's password:

```
net user userid newpassword
```

To delete a local user account (but not the profile folder):

```
net user userid /del
```

Of course, you have to be logged on as a Computer Administrator to create or modify other users' accounts.

Putting them together, you might use these commands to create a new Power User account:

```
net user bknittel secretpassword /add
net localgroup "Power Users" bknittel /add
```

Or use these commands to delete one:

```
net user bknittel /del
rd "c:\Documents and Settings\bknittel*" /s
```

That last command is "iffy"—if a folder with your username already exists in the Documents and Settings folder when you create your account, or if you log on to a Windows domain network, Windows sometimes adds .XXX to the user profile folder name, where XXX is the computer or domain name; you can't always be sure what the exact folder name will be.

Automating User Management

When you have many user accounts to create or modify, you should look to Windows automation tools to help simplify the job and minimize errors due to typing mistakes. You can use the command-line tools I mentioned previously inside batch files as an excellent means of getting the job done. You can also use Windows Script Host (WSH). WSH is by far the more flexible of the two options. By tying in to the Active Directory Service Interfaces (ADSI), you can create, read, or modify any information or configuration options available for a user account.

Here's an example. A common task that help desk personnel often require is the ability to easily unlock user accounts after a user has entered too many incorrect passwords. The following script file named unlock.vbs prompts for an account name and unlocks the account. From the command line, unlock runs the script. The user who is running the script must have the rights to unlock the target account.

```
Set WshNetwork = WScript.CreateObject("Wscript.Network")

CurDomName  = WshNetwork.UserDomain
DomainName = InputBox("Enter the Domain Name", "Domain", CurDomName)
UserName   = InputBox("Enter the account name to unlock", "User ID")

on error resume next

Set myUser = GetObject("WinNT://" & DomainName & "/" & UserName & "")

If myUser is Nothing Then
    msgbox "Unable to find user account " & DomainName & "\" & UserName
ElseIf myUser.IsAccountLocked Then
    myUser.IsAccountLocked = 0
    myUser.SetInfo
    If Err.Number then
        msgbox "Unable to unlock account, you may not have permission"
    Else
        msgbox UserName & " is now unlocked"
    End If
Else
    msgbox UserName & " is already unlocked"
End if
```

For more on this topic, you might consider some of these excellent references:

Windows XP Under the Hood by Brian Knittel; ISBN 0789727331 (our favorite, of course!)

Windows NT/2000 ADSI Scripting for System Administrators by Thomas Eck; ISBN 1578702194

Windows 2000 Script Host by Tim Hill; ISBN 1578701392

You'll also find some downloadable examples of administrative scripts at InformIT.com (www.informit.com) and the Microsoft Development Network (msdn.microsoft.com/scripting). I also recommend taking a look at Andrew Clinick's administrative scripts from the Microsoft TechEd 2000 conference. The article and source code are available for download at http://msdn.microsoft.com/library/en-us/dnclinic/html/scripting06122000.asp.

Managing User Profiles

A *user profile* is a folder that contains all of a user's personalized information: the Registry file that contains his customized settings, his Desktop and My Documents folders, and application data such as the Outlook Express address list and email database. By default, profiles are stored under C:\Documents and Settings, in folders with the same name as the user account.

When you create a new user account, the user's profile folder is *not* created at that time. Instead, it's created when the user logs on for the first time, and it's copied from the default user profile stored in \Documents and Settings\Default User. I'll talk more about this in a moment.

You'll find an interface for simple local user profile management by right-clicking My Computer, selecting Properties, Advanced, and then clicking the Settings button in the User Profiles box. You should see something similar to Figure 5.8.

Figure 5.8   The User Profile Management dialog.

Notice the three buttons:

- Change Type—This configures whether the selected user will use the network-stored roaming profile folder (for domain networks only) or a locally stored profile folder.

- Delete—This permanently deletes the selected profile (but not the account. If the user should log back on, a new profile folder will be created).

- Copy To—This copies the selected profile to another profile directory, overwriting the files and settings in the destination profile with those in the selected users' profile.

One important reason to know about User Profiles is that you can customize the Default profile used for new accounts on your computer.

Configuring a Default User Profile

If you aren't happy with the initial desktop and other settings created for each user at the time of logon, you can configure a profile and copy it into the Default User profile. Subsequently, new users who log on to the system for the first time will get your desired settings, rather than the default profile provided out of the box. Here's how to do it:

1. Create a new user account (someone without an existing personal profile on the system) and log on to that account.

2. Make all the changes you want included in the default profile. For example, you can set a default screensaver configuration, add some default favorites, drop some shortcuts on the desktop, reorganize the shortcuts on the Start bar, and set the background. You can also delete the sample files in My Documents and My Pictures or create new files and folders.

3. Log off as this user and log back in as with a Computer Administrator account. Note that you *must* log off from the new account in order to free the associated Registry files; doing a fast user switch does not work.

4. Under My Computer, click Tools, Folder Options, and go to the View tab. Check Show Hidden Files and Folders and click OK. Otherwise, you will not be able to see the Default User folder.

5. Right-click My Computer, select Properties, Advanced, and click the Settings button in the User Profiles box.

6. Select the profile of the user you just configured, and click the Copy To button.

7. Click Browse, and browse to \Documents and Settings\Default User (usually on the C: drive). Click OK.

8. Click the Change button under Permitted to Use, and type **Everyone**. Click OK. This ensures that all new users have permission to read the default profile. Now, click OK to close the Copy To dialog. You will have to confirm overwriting the default profile.

9. Log out.

Now, when you log on as a user who has not previously logged on to this computer, the initial settings will come from the prepared default profile.

Roaming User Profiles

Roaming profiles are available on domain networks only. A roaming profile is a profile folder created by a domain administrator and stored on a network server. When you log on using a domain account that is configured with a roaming user profile, the profile folders are copied from the network to the computer you are using. When you log out, any changes to your documents or profile settings are copied back to the domain server, so those changes will be available on subsequent logins from different systems. It's a nifty idea—your preferences, desktop, and documents can literally follow you anywhere in the world.

Note

Some relatively unimportant folders are *not* copied back and forth between the domain server and a local computer to save time and network traffic. By default, these folders include Local Settings, Temp, Temporary Internet Files, and the History folder. The list of ignored folders is stored in the Registry under **HKEY_CURRENT_USER\Software\ Microsoft\Windows NT\CurrentVersion\Winlogon\ExcludeProfileDirs**, which can be configured per user.

Controlling How Users Log On and Off

Although Windows 9x treated user authentication (logging on) as an option, user tracking is deeply ingrained in the Windows NT product line and that includes Windows XP. In Windows XP a user must always log on before the Windows desktop can appear. There are three ways to log on: The Welcome Screen, the Logon dialog, or an optional automatic logon upon startup.

The Welcome Screen Versus the Logon Dialog

Windows XP provides a stylish graphical logon screen that lists all available user accounts*. It's convenient, but in some cases it can be seen as a security risk; it displays usernames, and thus provides half of the information needed for an intruder to log on.

* Well, almost all available accounts. On Windows XP Home Edition, Administrator isn't shown, as it's only available in Safe mode. On XP Pro, Administrator isn't shown if any other Computer Administrator accounts exist. If you want, you can control which accounts appear and which don't; we'll discuss that shortly.

An older logon system called the Logon Dialog is also available (and it's the only one available if your computer is a member of a corporate domain network), shown in Figure 5.9. With this system, you must enter your logon name and password, and then click OK.

Figure 5.9   The classic Windows logon dialog.

The Options button hides or displays additional buttons, such as Shut Down. These options may be disabled by the network policy on some corporate systems.

Note

For domain logons, the most obvious method is to enter your username and password in the spaces provided, and then select your domain from the Log on To drop-down box. But you can also specify your username as *username@domain*. For example, if my username in the MyCompany.com domain were bknittel, I could enter my username as bknittel@mycompany.com.

You can also use this method to log on to a local account by entering *accountname@computername*. For example, you can log on to computer JAVA's local Administrator account with administrator@java.

To choose which method is used, go into the User Accounts applet under the Control Panel, and click Change the Way Users Log On Or Off. To use the Logon Dialog, clear the options to Use Fast User Switching and the Welcome Screen. To use the Welcome screen, check both options.

Logging on as Administrator from the Welcome Screen

The Windows XP Welcome screen does not normally list the local Administrator account as an available account unless no other Computer Administrator users are defined (and then, only on XP Professional, not Home Edition). If you don't know the passwords to any of the accounts displayed on the Welcome screen, or if none of the displayed accounts have administrative privileges but you need to perform some administrative function, you can bypass the Welcome screen to log on with the "standard" logon dialog, using any valid local account, by pressing Ctrl+Alt+Del twice.

Then, simply enter the local administrator username and password, make whatever changes to the system you need to make, and log out. You'll be back at the Welcome screen.

Note

On Windows XP Home Edition, the Administrator account is only available when you boot Windows in Safe mode, and by default, a password is not set for the Administrator account.

Remember that you can often save yourself the trouble of logging on as Administrator; you can also right-click a shortcut and select Run As, or use the runas command at the Command Prompt, to run programs with Administrator privileges.

▶▶ For more information about the runas command, see "runas," p. 409.

Showing and Hiding Accounts on the Welcome Screen

By default, the Administrator account and several system service accounts are not shown on the Welcome screen, although Administrator does appear if no other Computer Administrator accounts are defined. You can instruct Windows to display the Administrator account or to remove specific user accounts by editing the Registry key HKEY_LOCAL_MACHINE\SOFTWARE\Microsoft\Windows NT\ CurrentVersion\Winlogon\SpecialAccounts\UserList. (The Registry is discussed in Chapter 6, "Tweaking and Tuning Windows.") This key holds values that determine which accounts are omitted from the Welcome screen.

The UserList key contains values that name the accounts to be hidden, such as Administrator, HelpAssistant, and NetShowServices. The associated values determine how the account is displayed:

Value	Result
0	Account will not be shown.
1	Account will be shown.
0x00010000	Any account whose name starts with the same letters as the value name will not be shown.

To add the Administrator account to the Welcome screen, log on as Administrator and run regedit. Open the key indicated earlier and change the Administrator value from 0 to 1. To hide a user account, add a new DWORD value with the same name as the user's logon name, and enter the numeric value 0.

You can log on to a hidden account by pressing Ctrl+Alt+Del twice at the Welcome screen to display the Logon dialog.

Fast User Switching

Windows XP has a feature called Fast User Switching that lets you log on to alternate accounts without logging off from the first. You might compare this to having a big Lazy Susan on your desk—instead of cleaning it off so someone else can work at it, you just turn it around, leaving your original workspace intact, although out of reach. This is almost exactly what Fast User Switching does. When you switch users, you remain logged in and your programs even keep running; they're just not visible while someone else's desktop is displayed. Several different people can trade off use of the computer using this technique.

Fast User Switching is useful in several different scenarios:

- You can use it to temporarily log on as a Computer Administrator to install software, without having to log off from your primary account.
- You can let someone else use your computer while your own applications run uninterrupted.
- You can leave your computer in a "locked" state, at the Welcome screen, while your applications continue to run. You can then come back later, or even connect from another location using Remote Desktop Connection, and in either case pick up exactly where you left off.

To switch users, click Start, Log Off, Switch Users (or use the Window+L keyboard shortcut). This brings you back to the Welcome Screen. From here, you can log back on to your original account to reconnect with your original session, or you can log on as another user.

Note

By default, you'll also get kicked back to the Welcome screen if your screensaver has time to activate. If you don't like having to sign back on after clearing the screensaver, right-click the desktop, select Properties, view the Screen Saver tab, and uncheck On Resume, Display the Welcome Screen.

I recommend saving any open documents before switching users. If another user shuts Windows down or manages to crash the system, your data could be lost if you have not saved it.

And keep this in mind: You already know that running multiple applications requires more system resources. Running multiple applications for multiple users takes even more. Things will run more smoothly if you have a fast processor and a lot of RAM. Also, some applications may not work correctly in this new multi-user environment. If the application you are using was written to the Microsoft Windows XP Logo standards (see www.microsoft.com/winlogo for details), it should behave properly.

If Fast User Switching doesn't seem to be available on your computer, you may have to make a trade-off. Several Windows XP features are mutually exclusive with Fast User Switching:

- *Domain Networks*—If your computer is a member of a corporate domain network, Fast User Switching is not available, period. Bummer!

- *Login Dialog*—If you have disabled the Welcome Screen and use the Login Dialog to log on, Fast User Switching is not available. You can get Fast User Switching by re-enabling the Welcome Screen, as discussed previously.

- *Offline Files*—If you have enabled Offline File access (network caching), Fast User Switching is not available. You must choose between one and the other. To disable Offline Files, open Windows Explorer and select Tools, Folder Options. Use the Offline Files tab to make the change, and then enable Fast User Switching.

- *Serial Keys*—This accessibility feature is not useable with Fast User Switching and vice versa. Serial Keys provides support for alternative input devices such as puff and sip devices, switch-driven input devices, and other serial-based keyboard or mouse alternatives.

To enable Fast User Switching, log on as a Computer Administrator. Disable any competing features, and then open the User Accounts Control Panel applet. Select the task Change The Way Users Log On Or Off, and then check Use Fast User Switching. If you want to disable it, follow the same steps but uncheck the option. Yours must be the only account currently logged on.

Enabling Automatic Logon

You can't make Windows give up on the concept of user accounts, but you *can* tell Windows to log on to one account automatically when it boots up. You might want to do this in a kiosk environment, in an industrial control installation where the computer's job is simply to run some specialized software, or in a *very* trusting home or work environment with just one user.

To bypass the Welcome Screen or logon dialog, open a Command Prompt window, type the command **control userpasswords2**, and press Enter. Uncheck Users Must Enter a User Name and Password to Use This Computer and click OK. You'll be prompted for a username and password. (If the account has no password, leave the password fields blank.) The next time Windows boots up, it will automatically log on using this account information. You can use shortcuts placed in the Startup folder to automatically run applications. And, you can use Local Security Policy to disable any features you don't want this unprotected computer to make available.

If you want to log on using another user account you can simply log off or switch users, and then log back on using the alternate account.

To change Windows back so that it presents the Welcome Screen or logon dialog, use the `control userpasswords2` command again, and check Users Must Enter a User Name.

Dealing with a Lost Password

It will eventually happen that you or one of your users will forget his password, or worse, the Administrator password.

In this case, there are only a few things you can do. You should try them in the following order.

1. If the user created a Password Reset disk as discussed earlier, use it as described earlier under "Local Accounts and Password Reset Disks" to log on. The first thing that the user should do after that is to set a new password.

2. On a domain network, the network administrator can reset the password for any domain account. For standalone computers, workgroup computers, or local accounts, continue....

3. On XP Home Edition, boot your computer in Safe mode. From the Welcome Screen, select the "Administrator" account, which by default has no password. Use the Users control panel applet to reset the password on the desired account.

4. There are other things that can be done, but on XP Professional, all of the remaining methods will cause the user to lose any encrypted files she has. If there *are* any encrypted files, now is the time to stop and try to remember that password one more time.

5. If you have access to any Computer Administrator account, any Computer Administrator account, log on using that account, and use the User Accounts control panel to change the other account's password, or remove the password entirely. Then, the user can log on and select a new password.

   If it's the Administrator account password you're trying to reset, and Administrator doesn't appear in the User Accounts control panel, use the Local Users and Groups Management Console, described earlier. Open the Users list, right-click Administrator, and select Set Password.

6. If you get here, it means you have no way to log on as a Computer Administrator. Oh dear. Things get very dicey from here on down.

   One way to reset the Administrator password is to use a special-purpose "cracking" tool developed just for this purpose. You can visit www.winternals.com and purchase ERD Commander or their entire Administrator's Pak package. Windows XP/2000/NT Key from LostPassword.com also works well. Both programs require you to boot up from a floppy disk or CD, which runs a program that clears out the Administrator password. I know of two other such programs, although I haven't personally tested them: NTAccess from www.sunbelt-software.com and NTAccess (same name, different program) from www.mirider.com.

7. If you have a second hard drive or disk partition on your hard drive with at least 2GB of free space, you can install a second copy of Windows XP into the alternate partition or drive, and boot it up. You can then copy files from the original installation, or reset the permissions on the original files so that any other user can read them. This doesn't fix the lost password problem but it does let you rescue your data.

8. Equivalently, you can remove your hard drive and install it in another computer running Windows XP or 2000, and copy or at least unsecure your files.

9. Finally, you can perform a clean install of Windows on your original disk partition. This will erase all of your existing user accounts and preferences, and you will have to reinstall your applications. But, your files will be intact. When you re-create user accounts, Windows will create new profile folders with different names. Files in the previous installation's My Documents folders will be the original profile folders. You'll have to use Windows Explorer to dig into \Documents and Settings to find them.

Prevention is the best medicine in this case, so you might want to take a minute now to create a password reset disk for your personal account and your computer's Administrator Account. If you manage many computers, it also can't hurt to get a copy of the Administrator Pak from winternals.com now, before you run into a crisis.

Note

This section's given you just the basics of user management. As you might guess, it's a large topic. If you want to get into more detail, I recommend you pick up a copy of *Special Edition Using Microsoft Windows XP Professional, 3rd Edition* (or the *Home Edition*), published by Que.

Managing Hardware

Over the past several years, Windows and hardware compatibility have improved immensely, mostly because Windows XP is now ubiquitous and device driver writers have essentially only one target to aim at. Also, modern plug-and-play PCI bus hardware has now entirely replaced the previous generation of manually configured ISA bus devices, so configuration errors are nearly impossible, resource conflicts are essentially a thing of the past, and contention for resources a non-issue, as modern busses provide for many more interrupt and IO port options.

The end result is that I've found that I can summarize just about all you need to know about hardware management in just four bullet points:

- Always check the manufacturer's instructions *before* you install or plug in a new device. Sometimes you need to install the driver software package before Windows sees the device for the first time.

- If Windows crashes after you've installed the device, shut Windows down, remove the device and replace any original hardware. That should get you back on the air. The device driver was almost certainly at fault, and the manufacturer will most likely have a new one on its website. Install the update.

- Driver problems are actually rare, but are most common in display adapters. If you've made several changes, suspect the display adapter first.

- Cheap hardware devices always work. It's the expensive ones you have to watch out for.

There's a bit more to it than that, so I'll explain how to use the Windows Device manager to update drivers and diagnose problems. But the first time you run into trouble, come back to this page and see whether the issue wasn't covered in those four bullet points.

Using Device Manager

To manage hardware devices, Windows XP uses a tool called—not surprisingly—Device Manager. This applet is very similar to that provided in Windows 98 or Windows Me. It can be accessed from the

Computer Management application in the Administrative Tools menu folder, or, more commonly, from the Control Panel System applet's Hardware properties page as shown in Figure 5.10.

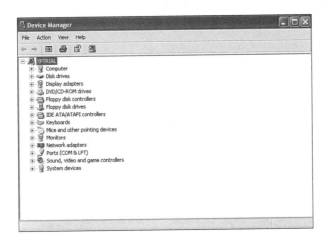

Figure 5.10   The Windows XP Device Manager.

You must be logged on as a Computer Administrator to use the tool; if you're not, but you know the Administrator password, you can use the Run As method to start it up. Click Start, Administrative Tools, right-click Computer Management, and select Run As. Then, check The Following User, select an administrator account and enter the password.

Note

If Administrative Tools doesn't show up under your Start menu, you can add the link. Right-click on Start, and then select Properties, Start Menus, Customize, Advanced, Display.

Viewing Devices

As you can see in Figure 5.10, devices are categorized into types. Each type has a + next to it that can be expanded to show the devices contained within the type. (Windows Explorer uses the same sort of display.) If Windows knows of any problems with any hardware devices, those categories will be opened by default, and Windows will display a yellow exclamation point icon next to each of the problem devices.

You can also view devices in the following formats:

- *Devices by connection*—This view lists devices based on their connection to each other. It may be useful to determine how multiple devices are connected to an external bus (USB or PCMCIA), for example.

- *Resources by type*—This view, which is the default, lists devices by the type of resource—Direct Memory Access (DMA) channel, Input/Output ports, Interrupt Request (IRQ), or Memory.

- *Resources by connection*—This view lists devices by the resource (Direct Memory Access [DMA] channel, Input/Output ports, Interrupt Request [IRQ], or Memory) and how they are connected.

Configuring Devices Manually

Sometimes, a device fails to function after the Windows XP PnP subsystem configures it. This is an extremely rare occurrence, but might occur if you are using a legacy ISA bus device. Windows XP allows you to manually configure a device, as long as it is not configured as an ACPI-compliant device, by following these steps:

1. Open the Device Manager.

2. Right-click the device and choose **Properties** from the pop-up menu.

3. Select the **Resources** property page shown in Figure 5.11.

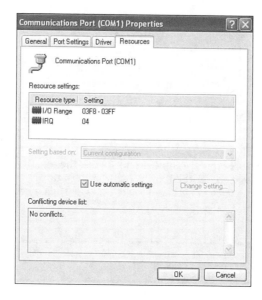

Figure 5.11 The Resources device properties page in the Windows XP Device Manager.

4. Clear the **Use Automatic Settings** check box (if the box is grayed out, the device is managed by ACPI and you can't configure it manually).

5. Choose an alternate configuration in the Setting Based On list box. If no alternate configuration will work, you can then manually select a resource and click the **Change Setting** button to manually assign a resource. It's best to select resource settings that are not already in use by other devices. If in doubt, switch the Device Manager view to Resources by Type to see what DMA channels, interrupts, I/O addresses, and I/O ports are already in use.

6. Repeat step 7 for each resource in question.

7. Click the **OK** button to save your changes.

Forcing Detection and Reinstallation

If you've installed a new device and afterward discover that you should have installed its device drivers before the hardware, or if Windows for some reason fails to locate the correct driver for the device, or if you inadvertently mislead it so it *can't* find the correct driver, you can force Windows to begin the detection and installation process again. Here are the steps:

1. In the Device Manager, locate the device, which will most likely have a yellow exclamation point icon next to it. Right-click it and select Uninstall.

2. If the manufacturer provided a device driver installer disk or if you have downloaded such an installer, run it now. This usually puts the drivers in your Windows folder along with files that help Windows locate the correct driver the next time it identifies the device.

3. If the device is an internal device and is not currently installed, shut down Windows and install it, and then restart Windows. For an external USB/Firewire device, just unplug and then plug the device back into a USB or Firewire port.

4. Go back to the Device Manager, right-click your computer's name at the top of the device list, and select Scan For Hardware Changes. This will start the detection process and pop up the New Hardware Wizard. You should be able to select all the "automatic" choices, to let Windows locate and install the drivers itself.

Dealing with the Blue Screen of Death

When a regular application program crashes, Windows displays the familiar message "Such-and-such application has encountered a problem and needs to close," and then terminates the application. However, when a device driver or a part of the Windows kernel itself fails, Windows can't just carry on. It halts and displays an error message in white text on a blue screen, at which point all you can do is write down the cryptic message and cycle the power on your computer. This display is known as the *Blue Screen of Death*, and was so common with earlier versions of Windows that it was reduced to the acronym BSOD.

BSODs have three main sources: failed disk drives, failed memory chips, and buggy device drivers. If you get a BSOD after installing a new device or updating a device driver, restart Windows in Safe mode by pressing F8 immediately after your BIOS screen disappears. Then, either perform a device driver rollback, use System Restore to restore the most recent saved configuration, or use the Device Manager to delete the device. Restart Windows, and it should now boot up correctly. Get an updated driver from the device's manufacturer before attempting to reinstall it.

For detailed instructions about starting in Safe mode, how to deal with a BSOD, and using Driver Rollback, see Chapter 12, "Windows Troubleshooting."

▶▶ For instructions on performing a system restore, see "Restoring a Point" p. 227.

Updating Device Drivers

If you suspect that a device driver is causing system problems, or if you find that a hardware vendor has released a newer version with additional features, you can use the Device Manager to perform a driver update.

Caution

Check the manufacturer's website for upgrade instructions, as they may use a different procedure than the one I'll describe here. If the manufacturer does describe its own procedure, ignore my instructions and follow their instructions carefully.

In the absence of specific manufacturer instructions, here are the steps:

1. You will usually obtain a driver update as on a CD, or through a download from the manufacturer's website. The CD can be used as is. In the case of a download you will usually obtain either an .EXE installer file or a .ZIP file.

If you download an .EXE file, run it while logged on as a Computer Administrator. It may update the drivers itself and exit. Or, it may indicate that it wants to store extracted files in a directory. I usually direct such programs to store files in a folder named c:\drivers\ *manufacturer* substituting the device manufacturer's name.

If you get a .ZIP file, open it using WinZip, Windows Explorer, or another ZIP utility, and again, extract the files into c:\drivers*manufacturer*.

If you have the updated drivers on a CD, insert it now.

2. Open the Device Manager, right-click the device you want to update, and select Update Driver.

3. If you want, check the box to let Windows check Windows Update. Then, click Next.

4. Select Install from a List or Specific Location (Advanced) and click Next.

5. If the driver is on a CD, check Search Removable Media. If the driver is in your hard disk, check Include This Location in the Search, click Browse, and locate the manufacturer-specific folder in which you expanded the driver files.

6. Click OK, and then follow the remaining prompts to complete the wizard. You may be asked to select the correct device from a list of devices supported by the same driver.

Windows will install the driver, and may or may not ask you to restart the computer.

Selecting an Older Device Driver

In some rare cases you may find that your hardware device's manufacturer has not provided a driver for Windows XP, even on its website; this should happen only in cases of older devices no longer being sold or supported. In this case, you *may* be able to install and use a Windows 2000 version of the driver, or a "Windows Driver Model" (WDM) driver. Windows Me drivers are WDM-compatible.

Before installing an older driver for your device, you should check for new versions. The very first place you should check is the Windows Update website. You can search the Windows Update website as part of the Device Manager Wizard. If you don't find a driver there, try the manufacturer website. If you don't know what the manufacturer website is, try one of the following websites:

http://www.driversplanet.com/

http://www.driverzone.com/

http://www.driverguide.com/

http://www.windrivers.com/

If you still can't find a newer certified Windows XP driver you can try to install either a Windows Driver Model (WDM) driver or a Windows 2000 driver. This usually requires a manual install using the following steps:

1. Select the device in Device Manager and click Properties.

2. Click the Update Driver button to start the Hardware Update Wizard.

3. Enable the Install from a List or Specified Location (Advanced) radio button and click Next.

4. Click Don't Search. It will choose the Driver to Install radio button. Click Next.

5. Click the Have Disk button, and then Browse.

6. Locate the disk and directory containing the driver's .INF file, and then click OK.

7. Select the appropriate device, click the Next button, and then click Finish.

Replacing Hardware

Sooner or later, everyone has to replace some hardware on his computer. It might be the replacement of a malfunctioning network card, a disk drive that is starting to fail, or just installing a faster video card. If your version of Windows XP is not part of an Open License or Enterprise purchase, you may find that when you have replaced a new piece of hardware, your installation will require that you reactivate Windows XP to continue to use it.

Microsoft created Windows Product Activation (WPA) to discourage casual copying of Microsoft products. For security reasons, Microsoft does not provide much information on exactly what type of hardware is used to create the hardware key contained in your Windows XP product ID, but we do know that somehow the specific set of hardware devices in your computer factors into WPA's identification scheme. Nor is Microsoft providing information on exactly how many changes are allowed before the product will be required to be reactivated. What is important to know is that if you change your hardware sufficiently, you may be required to reactivate Windows, as it will think that it may have been illegally copied to another computer. We believe that as long as major hardware changes occur no more often than every six months, WPA will not get agitated. In any case, while it may be irritating and offensive, the worst that should happen is that you may have to make a toll-free call to Microsoft to get a verbal authorization code.

Note

For the curious, and technical minded, take a look at the Fully Licensed home page at http://www.licenturion.com/xp/. You'll find an in-depth discussion of the Installation ID and hardware key as well as an application to examine the Installation ID.

Troubleshooting Problem Devices

The key to troubleshooting devices is interpreting the messages that Device Manager provides. Between the message the Device Manager provides, the event log, and the information displayed in the following sections, you should be able to narrow down the source of the problem. I can tell you that in almost all cases, it's the device driver's fault.

To use this section, open the problem device's properties page in Device Manager, and view the General tab. Look at the error message displayed under Device Status, locate it in the lists of error messages that follow in this section, and then follow the corresponding fix-it procedure.

Note

If the addition of a new hardware device has damaged Windows so badly that you can't get it to start up, go to the end of this chapter and follow the instructions under "Restoring a Point."

Bad Driver or Incorrect Driver

Device Status says:

> This device is not configured correctly. (Code 1)
>
> The *bustype* device loader(s) for this device could not load the device driver. (Code 2)
>
> The driver for this device might be corrupted, or your system may be running low on memory or other resources. (Code 3)
>
> The driver for this device might be bad, or your system may be running low on memory or other resources. (Code 3)

This device is not working properly because one of its drivers may be bad, or your Registry may be bad. (Code 4)

The driver for this device requested a resource that Windows does not know how to handle. (Code 5)

The drivers for this device need to be reinstalled. (Code 7)

This device is not working properly because Windows cannot load the file *name* that loads the drivers for the device. (Code 8)

This device is not working properly because Windows cannot find the file *name* that loads the drivers for the device. (Code 8)

This device is not working properly because the file *name* that loads the drivers for this device is bad. (Code 8)

Device failure: Try changing the driver for this device. If that doesn't work, see your hardware documentation. (Code 8)

This device is not working properly because the BIOS in your computer is reporting the resources for the device incorrectly. (Code 9)

Windows stopped responding while attempting to start this device, and therefore will never attempt to start this device again. (Code 11)

The driver information file *name* is telling this child device to use a resource that the parent device does not have or recognize. (Code 17), where *<name>* is the .INF file for the device.

Reinstall the drivers for this device. (Code 18)

The drivers for this device need to be reinstalled. (Code 18)

Windows cannot start this hardware device because its configuration information (in the Registry) is incomplete or damaged. To fix this problem you can first try running a troubleshooting wizard. If that does not work, you should uninstall and then reinstall the hardware device. (Code 19)

Your Registry may be bad. (Code 19)

Windows could not load one of the drivers for this device. (Code 20)

This display adapter is not functioning correctly. (Code 23)

The loaders for this device cannot load the required drivers. (Code 23)

Windows can't specify the resources for this device. (Code 27)

The drivers for this device are not installed. (Code 28)

Windows cannot install the drivers for this device because it cannot access the drive or network location that has the setup files on it. (Code 32)

Windows cannot initialize the device driver for this hardware. (Code 37)

Windows cannot load the device driver for this hardware. The driver may be corrupted or missing. (Code 39)

Windows cannot access this hardware because its service key information in the Registry is missing or recorded incorrectly. (Code 40)

The software for this device has been blocked from starting because it is known to have problems with Windows. Contact the hardware vendor for a new driver. (Code 48)

Fix: Click on the device's Driver tab. Click the Driver Details button. If no driver has been installed click the Update Driver button. This will invoke the Hardware Update Driver Wizard and walk you through installing a driver for the device.

If this fails, close the dialog, right-click the device, and click Uninstall. You may need to install a driver manually using your manufacturer-supplied software. Usually this means executing a program (often called setup.exe or install.exe) that will install a driver on the computer. See "Forcing Detection and Reinstallation," earlier in this section.

Code 39 may also indicate a problem with your hard disk itself; you might use CHKDSK to perform a disk check before continuing.

Bad Bus Detection

Device Status says:

> Windows could not load the driver for this device because the computer is reporting two *bustype* bus types. (Code 2)

> Your computer's system firmware does not include enough information to properly configure and use this device. To use this device, contact your computer manufacturer to obtain a firmware or BIOS update. (Code 35)

Fix: Check with your computer or motherboard manufacturer for a BIOS update.

Resource Conflict

Device Status says:

> Another device is using the resources this device needs. (Code 6)

> This device cannot find enough free resources that it can use. If you want to use this device, you will need to disable one of the other devices on this system. (Code 12)

> This device is causing a resource conflict. (Code 15)

> Windows cannot identify all the resources this device uses. (Code 16)

> Windows could not identify all the resources this device uses. (Code 16)

> Windows cannot determine which resources are required for this device. (Code 33)

> This device is requesting a PCI interrupt but is configured for an ISA interrupt (or vice versa). Please use the computer's system setup program to reconfigure the interrupt for this device. (Code 36)

Fix: A resource (I/O port, interrupt, or DMA channel) conflict has occurred. It can also occur if a required resource was not allocated to the device, or if an incorrect device driver was selected.

Verify that the resources requested by the device are available using the Device Manager or System Information tool (WinMSD.EXE). If another device is using the requested resources, you can resolve the problem by disabling the conflicting device, reconfiguring either the conflicting device or the failed device using the Device Manager, or reconfiguring the conflicting or failed device using your BIOS configuration program.

Verify that the BIOS is not disabling a required interrupt or DMA channel or not reserving a resource for a legacy device. Resource problems of this type usually fall into three categories:

- USB devices—Verify that interrupts have not been disabled for the USB controller in the BIOS.

- PCI bus devices—Verify that the requested interrupt or DMA channel has not been reserved for a specific legacy (ISA) device.

- ISA bus devices—Verify that the required interrupt or DMA channel has been reserved by the BIOS for the device.

If the steps under "Bad Driver or Incorrect Driver" do not resolve the problem, you may need to manually configure resources, disable the conflicting device, or remove it physically from the computer.

Failed Hardware, Missing Hardware, or Incorrect Driver

Device Status says:

> This device cannot start. (Code 10)
>
> This device is either not present, not working properly, or does not have all the drivers installed. (Code 10)
>
> This device is either not present, not working properly, or does not have all the drivers installed. (Code 13)
>
> This device is not present, is not working properly, or does not have all its drivers installed. (Code 24)
>
> This device is not working properly because Windows cannot load the drivers required for this device. (Code 31)
>
> This device is not working properly because <*device*> is not working properly. (Code 31)
>
> Windows successfully loaded the device driver for this hardware but cannot find the hardware device. (Code 41)
>
> Currently, this hardware device is not connected to the computer. (Code 45).

Fix: First, the peripheral may have failed or may not be installed correctly. To check for this possibility, remove the peripheral in question and physically reinstall it. If the peripheral is an internal peripheral on the PCI or ISA bus, clean the copper contacts using an eraser before reinstalling it. If the peripheral is connected via a cable, verify that all cable connections are clean, not damaged, and that the cables themselves are not routed by any device that may cause interference (power supply, monitor, speakers, and so on).

Second, the peripheral may have a resource conflict. Verify that the resources requested by the device are available. This can be accomplished using the Device Manager or System Information tool (WinMSD.EXE). If another device is using the requested resources you can resolve the problem by disabling the conflicting device, reconfiguring either the conflicting device or the failed device using the Device Manager, or reconfiguring the conflicting or failed device using your BIOS configuration program.

Finally, the device driver may not be installed correctly, or the wrong device driver (such as one designed for a prior version of Windows) may be installed. To resolve the former, first uninstall the device driver and then reinstall it as described previously for Error Code 1.

Restart Required

Device Status says:

> This device cannot work properly until you restart your computer. (Code 14)
>
> Windows is in the process of setting up this device. (Code 26)
>
> Windows cannot gain access to this hardware device because the operating system is in the process of shutting down. (Code 46)

Fix: Restart Windows. If the problem persists after a restart, right-click the device, select Uninstall, and have Device Manager scan for new devices to reinstall it.

Device Driver Shutdown Problem

Device Status says:

> Windows is removing this device. (Code 21)
>
> Windows cannot load the device driver for this hardware because a previous instance of the device driver is still in memory. (Code 38)
>
> Windows cannot load the device driver for this hardware because there is a duplicate device already running in the system. (Code 42)

Fix: Wait for 15 seconds or so. If the device entry still appears, reboot the computer. If the problem persists, uninstall and reinstall the device driver as discussed in previous entries.

Disabled Device

Device Status says:

> This device is disabled. (Code 22)
>
> This device is not started. (Code 22)

Fix: Right-click the device in question and choose Enable from the pop-up menu.

Incomplete Windows Setup

Device Status says:

> Windows is in the process of setting up this device. (Code 25)

Fix: This error message usually occurs during the initial setup of Windows XP during the first or second reboots. It usually indicates an incomplete file copy. Restart the computer. If that fails to resolve the situation, reinstall Windows XP.

Device Disabled by BIOS

Device Status says:

> This device is disabled because the firmware of the device did not give it the required resources. (Code 29)
>
> This device is disabled because the BIOS of the device did not give it the required resources. (Code 29)

Fix: Refer to the onscreen message provided by the peripheral's BIOS during startup (for example, Adaptec SCSI controllers may display a message instructing you to press Ctrl+A to access its BIOS setup), or refer to the peripheral documentation to enable the device.

Disabled Service

Device Status says:

A driver (service) for this device has been disabled. An alternate driver may be providing this functionality. (Code 32)

Fix: If the driver is actually a service, you can edit the startup value in the Registry by using the Service MMC snap-in to resolve the problem. For a device, you can either uninstall and then reinstall the driver as described for Error Code 18, or edit the Registry directly and change the start type.

Manual Device Configuration Required

Device Status says:

Windows cannot determine the settings for this device. Consult the documentation that came with this device and use the Resource tab to set the configuration. (Code 34)

Fix: Manually allocate the resources for this device.

Device Reported Problems

Device Status says:

Windows has stopped this device because it has reported problems. (Code 43)

An application or service has shut down this hardware device. (Code 44)

Fix: Restart the computer. Errors of this nature should be logged in the System or Application event log. If the error continues, review the event log to determine the cause of the error. If that doesn't help, request help from the manufacturer or try to get an updated driver.

Device Prepared for Removal

Device Status says:

Windows cannot use this hardware device because it has been prepared for "safe removal," but it has not been removed from the computer. (Code 47)

Fix: Remove and reinsert the peripheral, or restart the computer.

Registry Size Limit Exceeded

Device Status says:

Windows cannot start new hardware devices because the system hive is too large (exceeds the Registry Size Limit). (Code 49)

Fix: Your best bet is to add more memory (RAM) to your computer.

Using Driver Rollback

If after installing a device driver you find that the driver did not work, has caused a system instability, or caused another problem, you can easily replace it with the previous driver using driver rollback.

You can accomplish this task by following the directions found on p. 552 ("Device Driver Rollback") of Chapter 12, "Troubleshooting Windows."

Disk Management

Regardless of what file system or storage types you have in place on your hard drives, all routine disk maintenance and configuration is done from one place: the Disk Management console, shown in Figure 5.12.

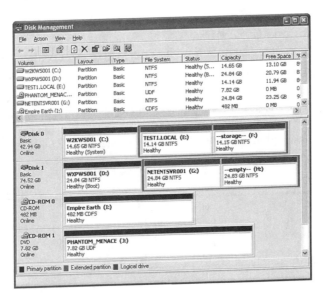

Figure 5.12   The Disk Management console.

You must be logged on as a Computer Administrator to use this tool. You can open the Disk Management console in several different ways, the two easiest being as follows:

- From within the Computer Management console, click Start, Programs, Administrative Tools, Computer Management (or right-click on My Computer and choose Manage). Then, from within the Computer Management console, expand the Storage node and then select Disk Management.

- From the command line, type `diskmgmt.msc`.

The following are just some of the tasks that can be performed using the Disk Management console:

- Create new partitions and logical drives.

- Create new volumes.

- Determine disk size, file system, disk health, and other pertinent information. This can easily be done by looking at each volume in the Disk Management console as shown in Figure 5.12.

- Format volumes and partitions.

- Assign drive letters or paths to hard drives and removable storage drives. This can be done by right-clicking on the volume of concern and selecting Change Drive Letter and Paths.

- Mount and unmount drives.
- Upgrade basic storage to dynamic storage.
- Extend the size of dynamic volumes.

Some of the more complex of these tasks are discussed in more detail in the following sections, but most can be explained in brief.

▶▶   For more information about the disk formats and their options and functions, see "Disks, Partitions, and Volumes," p. 446.

Creating New Partitions and Logical Drives

To create a new partition or logical drive from the Disk Management console, follow these steps:

1. Open the Disk Management console as discussed previously.
2. To create a new partition, right-click an unallocated region of a basic disk, and select New Partition. To create a logical drive, right-click in an extended partition, and select New Logical Drive.
3. Follow the onscreen prompts in the New Partition Wizard to enter the desired partition size and so on.

Note

The `diskpart` command-line utility can also manage disk partitions. For more information, search the Windows Help and Support Center for `diskpart`. There are two "Overview" articles named DiskPart; one is the diskpart program in the Recovery Console, and the other is for the full version. You want to read the article that starts "DiskPart.exe is a text-mode command interpreter..."

Creating New Simple Volumes

To create a new simple volume from the Disk Management console, follow these steps:

1. Open the Disk Management console as discussed previously.
2. Right-click the unallocated space on the dynamic disk on which you want to create the simple volume, and then click New Volume.
3. In the New Volume Wizard, click Next and then click Simple. Follow the onscreen prompts to complete the process.

You can create other types of volumes on dynamic disks in much the same fashion. Dynamic disk volumes, however, can't be read by Windows 9x or MS-DOS, so you may not want to use them if you dual-boot your computer.

Formatting Disks and Volumes

Formatting storage media is a fairly common task you can easily accomplish using the Disk Management console. Windows XP supports formatting numerous kinds of media, partly due to its excellent multimedia support. You can format hard drives, removable storage media (such as ZIP drives), and DVD-RAM disks to name a few of your options.

Note

Although you can format removable media from within the Disk Management console, you most likely won't. Instead it's more likely that you will use Windows Explorer, simply because it's easier to get to an Explorer window and because many of the advanced Disk Management console tools for fixed drives don't apply to removable storage.

Windows XP is fairly intelligent and self-protective, and will not allow you to format the system or boot partitions from within the Disk Management console. Those options will be grayed out. To begin the process of formatting a hard drive or removable media device, right-click the volume (or unallocated space) of interest from within the Disk Management console and select Format, which opens the window shown in Figure 5.13. Depending on how large the volume to be formatted is, you will have the choice to format it as FAT16, FAT32, or NTFS. For hard disks, you probably want to use NTFS formatting, unless you have to be able to read and write the disk volume from MS-DOS, Windows 9x, or Linux. To share the volume with MS-DOS, use FAT16; to share with Windows 9x or Linux, choose FAT32.

Note

We haven't mentioned standard floppy disks. Does anyone use them anymore? I have a huge pile of them sitting around gathering dust. The only way to format standard floppy disks is using Windows Explorer. Standard floppy disks are formatted using a special file system called FAT12, incidentally.

Formatting removable media such as DVD-RAM, Flash, or ZIP disks follows the same process, except that you will not have the choice of file systems; all removable media (other than floppies) are formatted with the FAT (which is really to say FAT16) file system.

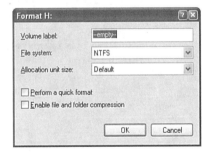

Figure 5.13 Formatting a new drive or partition.

Remember that in order to convert a basic disk to dynamic later on, be sure to select 512 bytes as the sector size. In most cases, this is the smallest size available (due to the physical construction of the hard drive itself) and will be selected by Windows XP automatically if the Allocation Unit Size setting is left as Default, as shown in Figure 25.6.

The other options available to you during a format operation are fairly simple, but still deserve some mention.

- The volume label can be a descriptive name that you use to readily identify the volume. You should keep the label as short as possible and avoid using the following reserved characters: < > : " / \ | * ? + and . because they will cause problems when accessing volumes over the network. Note that Windows XP will not stop you from using the characters for a volume name—you have to do that for yourself. If a disk is formatted with the FAT file system, the label can contain up to 11 characters. If the disk is formatted with the NTFS file system, the limit is 32 characters.

- The file system will be a choice of FAT16, FAT32, or NTFS as previously mentioned.

- Selecting to perform a quick format removes files from the disk but does not scan the disk for bad sectors. You should only use this option if the disk has been previously formatted and is known to not have any damage to it.

- Selecting the last option, Enable File and Folder Compression, will configure the newly format-ted volume for file and folder compression. Remember that this will prevent you from later using EFS encryption unless compression is removed.

Of course, should you need to format drives from the command prompt, you still can. The format command has the following syntax:

```
format volume [/fs:filesystem] [/v:label] [/q] [/a:unitsize] [/c]
```

The parameters for the format command are outlined in Table 5.6.

Table 5.6 Parameters for the *format* Command

Parameter	Description
Volume	Specifies the mount point, volume name, or drive letter of the drive you want to format.
/fs:filesystem	Specifies the file system to use: FAT, FAT32, or NTFS. Floppy disks can use only the FAT file system.
/v:label	Specifies the volume label. If you omit the /v command-line option or use it with-out specifying a volume label, format prompts you for the volume label after the formatting is completed.
/q	Performs a quick format. Deletes the file table and the root directory of a previously formatted volume but does not perform a sector-by-sector scan for bad areas.
/a:unitsize	Specifies the cluster size, also known as allocation unit size, to use on FAT, FAT32, or NTFS volumes. If *unitsize* is not specified, it will be chosen based on volume size.
/c	NTFS only. Files created on the new volume will be compressed by default.

Creating Mounted Drives

Windows 2000 and XP let you join two separate drives or volumes into one larger, virtual volume. It's called *mounting*, and it works by making the entire contents of one volume appear in the place of a specified folder on another volume. For example, if I created a new empty folder named c:\mounted, I could format a new hard disk, and mount it to c:\mounted. The root folder of the new volume will appear as the contents of c:\mounted, and subdirectories in the new volume will appear as subdirecto-ries of c:\mounted...it's all very UNIX-like. One reason you might want to do this is if you needed to add space to an existing file system but don't want to change the directory structure. As long as you don't mind that the added space is only available in a specific set of folders, mounting a new drive is a nifty way to do it.

To create a mounted drive from the Disk Management console, follow these steps:

1. Open the Disk Management console as discussed previously.

2. Right-click the partition or volume you want to mount, and then click Change Drive Letter and Paths.

3. To mount a volume, click Add. Click Mount in the following empty NTFS folder and enter or browse to the empty folder. To unmount a volume, click it and then click Remove.

Converting Basic Disks to Dynamic Disks

Dynamic disks have a slightly different partition structure than the basic disks that we inherited from MS-DOS. Dynamic disks have some advantages; they can have their partition sizes changed, for one thing. They can't be read by older operating systems, so if you dual-boot your computer you probably don't want to use them, but if you're running straight XP and use NTFS-formatted disks already, you might consider it. To convert a basic disk to dynamic from the Disk Management console, follow these steps:

1. Open the Disk Management console as discussed previously.

2. Right-click the basic disk you want to convert and select Convert to Dynamic disk. Follow the onscreen prompts to complete the process. Looking at Figure 5.10, the area to click in is that area on the left side of each disk in the bottom frame.

Extending Dynamic Volumes

To extend a dynamic volume from the Disk Management console, follow these steps:

1. Open the Disk Management console as discussed previously.

2. Right-click the simple or spanned volume you want to extend and click Extend Volume. Follow the onscreen prompts to complete the process.

A few things to keep in mind when attempting to extend volumes:

■ You cannot extend a system volume or a boot volume.

■ You cannot extend striped volumes.

■ You cannot extend a dynamic volume that was upgraded from a basic volume to a dynamic volume in Windows 2000 if you've subsequently upgraded to Windows XP.

■ You cannot extend a simple volume onto additional dynamic disks to create a spanned volume. Spanned volumes cannot be mirrored or striped.

■ If you extend a spanned volume, you cannot delete any portion of it without deleting the entire spanned volume.

Resizing Basic Disks

If you are using basic storage on your disk drive and you decide that you need to adjust your partition layout after it has been initially created, you have three possible means to this end: You can use the diskpart utility, you can delete and re-create partitions, or you can use a third-party utility such as Partition Magic.

Using the extend command within the diskpart utility, you can add more space to existing primary partitions and logical drives as long as you meet the following requirements:

- The basic volume must be formatted with NTFS.

- You can extend a basic volume using space from the same physical hard disk only (unlike dynamic volumes). The basic volume must be followed by contiguous unallocated space.

- You can extend a logical drive only within the contiguous free space that exists in the partition that contains the logical drive.

If you meet all the aforementioned requirements, you can extend a basic disk as follows:

1. Open a command window by clicking Start, Run and entering **cmd** into the Run box. Press Enter.

2. Type **diskpart**.

3. Type **list volume**. Write down what volume you want to extend.

4. Type **select volume** *n*, where *n* is the volume you identified in the previous step.

5. Type **extend [size=n]**, where *n* is the extended size of the volume in MB.

If working from the command line is not your thing, and you are not ready to perform mass deletions (as required by the third method), you may want to consider using a third-party disk utility, such as Partition Magic from Symantec. Partition Magic allows you to redesign your partition table graphically within the Windows XP GUI and then on the subsequent restart performs the required actions to carry out your wishes.

If you choose not to use either of the other methods presented, you can still resize your basic disks, with no out-of-pocket cost. It is more laborious, however. You'll need to back up all pertinent data on the partition(s) in question, delete the partitions, and then re-create them sized to your liking. After formatting the new partitions, you can then restore your data onto them. Yuck.

If you are running with dynamic storage volumes, resizing your volumes is an easy process. You simply right-click on the volume that you want to extend and select Extend Volume. This will open the Extend Volume Wizard, which will allow you to enter the size you want to extend the volume to. After the wizard has finished, which is a relatively quick process, you will have a volume that is now larger...all without a restart of the computer or the time-intensive process of copying and recopying all the files in that volume. It's quite a time saver.

Converting FAT16/FAT32 File Systems to NTFS

Should you make the decision to upgrade your hard disk's file system from FAT16 or FAT32 to NTFS, you will need to perform the upgrade from the command line by using the convert command. The convert command has the following syntax:

```
convert [volume] /fs:ntfs [/v] [/cvtarea:FileName] [/nosecurity] [/x]
```

The parameters for the convert command are outlined in Table 5.7.

Table 5.7   Parameters for the *convert* Command

Parameter	Description
Volume	Specifies the drive letter (followed by a colon), mount point, or volume name to convert to NTFS.
/fs:ntfs	Required. Converts the volume to NTFS.
/v	Specifies verbose mode; that is, all messages will be displayed during conversion.

Table 5.7 Continued

Parameter	Description
`/cvtarea:FileName`	Specifies that the Master File Table (MFT) and other NTFS metadata files be written to an existing, contiguous placeholder file. This file must be in the root directory of the file system to be converted. Use of the `/cvtarea` parameter can result in a less fragmented file system after conversion. For best results, the size of this file should be 1KB multiplied by the number of files and directories in the file system; however, the convert utility accepts files of any size. You must create the placeholder file using the `fsutil file createnew` command prior to running `convert`, which does not create this file for you. `convert` overwrites this file with NTFS metadata. After conversion, any unused space in this file is freed.
`/nosecurity`	Specifies that the converted files and directory security settings are accessible by everyone.
`/x`	Dismounts the volume, if necessary, before it is converted. Any open handles to the volume will no longer be valid.

To convert your C: drive and apply standard security restrictions, for example, the command is

```
convert c: /fs:ntfs
```

Only hard disks can be updated; NTFS isn't used on removable media like floppies, flash disks and CD-RWs. You *can* format a USB or Firewire-attached hard drive with NTFS, however.

Caution

Converting your existing FAT or FAT32 volume to the NTFS file system will preclude you from uninstalling Windows XP at a later date. This is no big loss of freedom if you are upgrading from Windows 2000 or NT because those upgrades are not reversible anyway. But if you hoped to return to Windows 98 or Me, for example, because they don't read NTFS, it's obvious why uninstallation would be problematic. This sort of limitation is one reason why people who deal with multiboot scenarios stick with FAT-based disks.

Note

Unknown to most people, the **convert** command has quietly received an upgrade from the Windows 2000 version. Using the **convert** command in Windows 2000 would produce a volume that did not have the default NTFS permissions settings that you would get after installing Windows itself. The version of **convert** that comes with Windows XP fixes this problem by automatically applying the correct default permissions to all folders. When used with the `/cvtarea` switch to create an unfragmented MFT, there is virtually no difference anymore between a volume converted to NTFS during setup of Windows or by using the **convert** command.

Converting the NTFS File System to FAT16/FAT32

Reversion from NTFS to FAT16 or FAT32 is not supported by Windows XP; however using a third-party disk utility such as Partition Magic will allow you to perform this task.

Hard Drive Cleaning

It may seem that after getting your hard drives set up and configured to your liking all of your work is done. Nothing could be further from the truth, unfortunately. Over time, as I'm sure you know,

Windows systems do accumulate hundreds and possibly thousands of unnecessary files and folders on your hard drives. Not only do these files and folders waste valuable space, they can slowly degrade system performance. In this section, I am going to blow the top off of some of Windows's secrets and show you how to keep your hard drives slim and trim.

Temporary Files—To Be Eliminated at Any Cost

Windows XP likes to store its temporary files in three places, more often than not. That is not to say that some rogue program will not deposit some temporary files in another location; just that in most cases you can look in three places to find the dead wood you've been collecting on your system. These three places are

- %USERPROFILE%\Local Settings\Temp—Here you will typically find temporary files that were not properly cleaned up by the application that created them.

- %USERPROFILE%\Local Settings\Temporary Internet Files—Here you find the cache used by applications such as Outlook and Internet Explorer. The files are usually hidden, but they are there in droves.

- %SYSTEMROOT%\Temp—Another dumping ground that some applications like to use for their temporary files.

There are two methods for cleaning up temporary files: the GUI-based Disk Cleanup utility and a command-line–based script you can use.

Using the Disk Cleanup Utility

The easiest way to help clean the dead wood from your hard drives is to use the Disk Cleanup utility on a regular basis. The Disk Cleanup utility is launched by clicking Start, All Programs, Accessories, System Tools, Disk Cleanup. You can also launch it by right-clicking on a drive icon in any Explorer window and choosing Properties, Disk Cleanup.

There are two useful tricks to getting more out of Disk Cleanup. The first thing is to make use of two undocumented switches for the Disk Cleanup utility that can be accessed from the command line. The second is to schedule the Disk Cleanup utility to run automatically, using advanced settings of your choice, thus purging your hard disk of specific types of unwanted types of files on a regular basis.

You can use the command line to gain additional categories of files to delete, as shown in Figure 5.14.

To use them, follow these steps:

1. Start the Disk Cleanup utility from the command line by opening a Command Prompt window and typing **cleanmgr /d x /sageset:n**, where x represents the drive letter you want to clean, and n is any number between 1 and 65535. The /sageset:n value provides a means for you to create multiple preconfigured Disk Cleanup instances, each with the specific drives and options selected that you desire. Which value you choose for the /sageset:n value doesn't matter; it is only used to store your settings in the Registry to allow you to run Disk Cleanup with those options again in the future.

2. After you press Enter, the hard disk will grind a bit. Then up will pop the Disk Cleanup Settings dialog. The actual categories offered may be different on your computer. Select the categories of files you want to delete and click OK to save these settings into the Registry. You can click on each option to read a description of it. Note that choosing to compress files that are not often used could take a while, during which time the compression occurs.

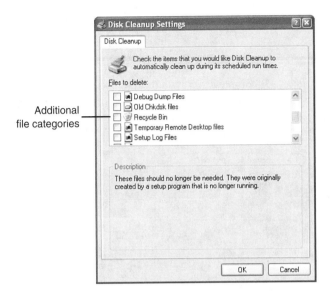

Additional file categories

Figure 5.14   Additional, more-or-less hidden configuration settings for Disk Cleanup.

3. Create a shortcut to `cleanmgr /sagerun:`*n*, where *n* is the number you chose previously in step 1.

4. Using the Scheduled Task Wizard (Start, Settings, Control Panel, Scheduled Tasks), create and configure a scheduled task to run daily or weekly using the shortcut you created in step 3.

You will probably want to create a Disk Cleanup setting and shortcut for each drive on your system.

Defragmenting for Greater Speed

Computers store information on their hard disks in a disorganized fashion, using whatever bits and pieces of free space they find, and as files are added and deleted, the unused space gets more and more spread out in tiny little bits. Imagine if you had to place 50 pieces of paper flat on your desk, without overlapping. You would line them up nicely, one next to the other, in order, although it might nearly cover your desk. Now take 20 pages away at random, and put a 20 page essay down in their place. They can't all get put down side by side now, so you'll have to put each page wherever you can, in any empty space you can find. Fine, but now try to pick them up, in order. Oops! They're all scattered all over the place, and to find page 1, then page 2, then page 3...you're going to be at this for a while.

That's fragmentation. And on your hard drive, there aren't just 50 places for pages to be scattered, but tens of millions. Over time, the slowdown from increasing fragmentation becomes significant. Cleaning it up by collecting the scattered pieces of each of your files and moving them into consecutive spaces on the disk is called *defragmentation*, and Windows comes with a tool to do a fair-to-middlin' job of it. To use the tool:

- From within the Computer Management console, choose Start, All Programs, Administrative Tools, Computer Management. From within the Computer Management console, expand the Storage node and then select the Disk Defragmenter tool.

   Or

- From the command line: type **dfrg.msc**.

No matter which way you launch the GUI version of the disk defragmenter; your options are the same.

To see whether defragmentation is severe (or more precisely, to see whether the Windows defragmenting tool is going to do anything about it) you can run an analysis on a volume by clicking the Analyze button. When the analysis is complete, you will receive a report similar to the one shown in Figure 5.15.

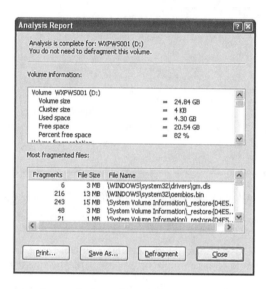

Figure 5.15 The defragmentation analysis results window.

Should you decide to perform the defragmentation, click the Defragment button and watch the progress as shown in Figure 5.16.

Defragmenting a volume is an extremely CPU- and hard drive-intensive operation, and it is severely hampered if you continue to work with the computer while it's going on. In particular, saving documents or otherwise writing files to the disk can make the defragmenter have to start over from scratch. As with the Disk Cleanup utility, the true power of the Disk Defragmenter comes if you use the Windows Task Scheduler to create a scheduled event for it and allow it run weekly during a low-usage time, such as early in the morning every Sunday.

Tip

The defragmentation tool provided with Windows is a "lite" version of a commercial product called Diskeeper. You can also buy disk defragmenters that do a more thorough job, and which, for example, can defragment the Windows page file. Check out PerfectDisk at www.raxco.com and Diskeeper at www.diskeeper.com (with one k) for two such products.

Although you can perform disk deframentation with the GUI, you can also do it from the command line, which is helpful if you want to create a cleanup batch file or script. You can defragment a volume with the defrag command, which has the following syntax:

```
defrag volume [/a] [/v] [/f]
```

The parameters for the defrag command are outlined in Table 5.8.

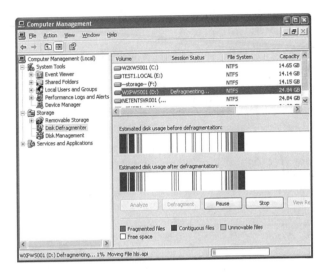

Figure 5.16 Defragmenting a volume.

Table 5.8 Parameters for the *defrag* Command

Parameter	Description
volume	The drive letter or a mount point of the volume to be defragmented.
/a	Analyzes the volume and displays a summary of the analysis report.
/v	Displays the complete analysis and defragmentation reports.
/f	Forces defragmentation of the volume regardless of whether it needs to be defragmented.

Without options /a or /f, defrag makes its own decision whether to defragment or not.

A few points should be kept in mind when attempting to perform disk defragmentation:

- A volume must have at least 15% free space to be defragmented. Defrag uses this space as a sorting area for file fragments. If a volume has less than 15% free space, defrag will only partially defragment it.

- You cannot defragment volumes that the file system has marked as "dirty." A volume that is marked as dirty may be in an inconsistent status, which will require the CHKDSK utility to be run to verify the consistency of the volume. A volume could be marked as dirty if it is online and has outstanding changes that must be made at the next successful startup or if the volume is corrupt. To solve this, restart Windows.

- You cannot run the defrag command and GUI Disk Defragmenter utility simultaneously. And, you cannot defragment more than one volume at a time.

Backing Up Your Disk

I'm sure I don't need to warn you of the importance of backing up your hard drive. Computers are *so* much more reliable today than they were even a decade ago, but they do still fail, and you can be sure that one day when you turn on your computer you'll see nothing on the screen but "Hard Drive

Failure." All those photographs, emails, songs, all that work...all gone. It's a sickening feeling. And it could happen tomorrow. So: You have to back up.

The good news is that it's not expensive, and it's not difficult. You can get a high-capacity tape drive, but these days, I find it's just as easy to use a 200 or 250GB Firewire or USB-2 portable hard drive. These currently cost less than $200—less if you find a sale or rebate promotion, and the security they give you is *well* worth the cost (if it makes you feel better, when the first hard drive came out in 1956, that much disk space would have cost $13.6 billion in today's dollars). My own backups are about 40GB in size, so I can do one a week and easily fit four on a single portable drive.

Windows XP (as well as Windows 2000) comes with a backup program that you can use to perform system backups. It's not very sophisticated; you can buy better, but this one is free, and it's provided with every copy of Windows. If you have a larger network, you should seriously think about acquiring an enterprise backup solution, such as Backup Exec or NetBackup.

Note

NTBackup is provided with Windows XP Home Edition, but it's not installed when you set up Windows. To install it, insert your Windows XP setup CD-ROM, and use Windows Explorer to browse to `\VALUEADD\MSFT\NTBACKUP`. Double-click `ntbackup.msi` to install the program. If you're not a Computer Administrator, right-click `ntbackup.msi`, select Run As, and use an Administrator account.

The backup utility in Windows XP has undergone some changes from its predecessor in Windows 2000. The two major changes are support for XP's Volume Shadow Copy feature, and the replacement of the Emergency System Recovery disk with the Automated System Recovery feature on XP Professional.

Volume Shadow Copy

When Windows 2000 performed a backup, files that were in use while the backup was performed were often omitted from the backup set, including important user Registry files. Files that were actively being updated that did get backed up could be saved in an inconsistent state, with different parts of the file saved before, during, and after changes were made.

Windows XP's Volume Shadow Copy feature solves both problems by letting Windows present the backup program with a view of the entire file system frozen at a moment in time. Internally, Windows keeps a copy of the original versions of any individual disk data blocks that are modified after the moment that the Shadow copy is created. The backup program can then be fed this original data, while every other application sees ongoing, changing data from moment to moment. When the backup has completed, Windows releases the frozen copies of the changed data, so overall there is no cost to the file system.

Automated System Recovery

Automated System Recovery (ASR) is an advanced restoration option of the Backup utility available only on Windows XP Professional, not on Home Edition. ASR can be used to restore your system if other disaster recovery methods fail or are not available for use. Using ASR, you can restore the operating system back to a previous state, which will allow you to start Window XP Professional in the event that other methods do not work. You should always consider ASR your last resort for recovery, after Safe mode, the Recovery Console, and Last Known Good Configuration, which are detailed in Chapter 12, "Windows Troubleshooting." You should make a point to keep your ASR media up to date as you make configuration changes to your computer in order to minimize the amount of recovery required should you ever need to use ASR. To use the ASR Wizard to create a set of ASR media, you only need to click on the Automated System Recovery Wizard button on the main page of the Backup tool, as shown in Figure 5.17.

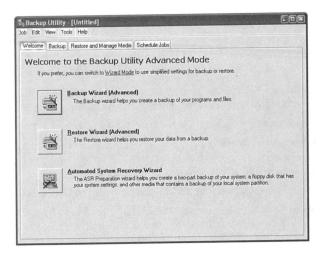

Figure 5.17 Start the Automated System Recovery Disk Wizard from the main page of the Backup utility.

Using Windows Backup

Using the Backup utility consists of three distinct processes: creating one or more backup configurations, scheduling backups to occur automatically, and performing restorations.

There are five types of backups you can perform:

- *Normal backup*—Copies all selected files and marks each file as having been backed up (the archive bit—the "changed since last backup" file attribute—is cleared). Only the most recent backup set is required to perform restoration.

- *Incremental backup*—Copies only those files created or changed since the last normal or incremental backup; the archive attribute is then cleared. Using normal and incremental backups, you will require the last normal backup and *all* intervening incremental backups in order to perform restoration.

- *Differential backup*—Copies files created or changed since the last normal backup; the archive bit is left alone. Differential backup set will get larger over time, as more and more files are changed since the last normal backup. Eventually a new normal backup has to be performed. The benefit is that only two backup sets are needed to restore all files: the last normal backup, and the most recent differential backup.

- *Copy backup*—Copies all selected files but does not mark each file as having been backed up (the archive attribute is not cleared). Copy backups have no effect on any other type of backup operation.

- *Daily backup*—Copies all selected files that have been modified the day the daily backup is performed; the archive attribute is not cleared in this case. This is a risky procedure as files modified right around midnight could be left behind, and missing a day leaves files unprotected.

In addition to your system's drives, you will see that NTBackup has a choice to back up something called System State. This is a collection of Registry data, device drivers, and system programs. When you back up your entire hard drive, this stuff is included, so you don't need to specify it in that case. It's mainly an option you can use to back up Windows itself before installing a new driver or application. The new System Restore feature does just as good a job of this, so System State is less necessary now than in the past. System Restore is discussed later in this chapter.

Creating the Backup Configurations

The Windows Backup utility makes it extremely simple to create a backup configuration. The basic steps to create the configuration are outlined here, although your options and decisions will vary depending on how your system and backup media devices are configured.

1. Log on as a Computer Administrator user. Start the Backup Wizard by clicking Start, All Programs, Accessories, System Tools, Backup; or, at the command prompt, type **ntbackup**.

2. Start the Backup Wizard by clicking the Backup Wizard (Advanced) button.

3. Click Next to dismiss the opening page of the Wizard. From the What to Back Up page, select the scope of the backup: everything, selected files, or System State, which includes the Registry and Windows' protected files. Click Next.

   If you chose to back up selected files and folders, proceed to step 4, otherwise skip to step 5.

4. From the Items to Back Up page, choose the files and folders to back up, as shown in Figure 5.18, and then click Next. If you have mapped network drives to drive letters, you can also back up these folders even though they are stored on other computers.

5. From the Backup type... page, choose the backup filename and location and click Next. In the case of a removable hard drive, enter the drive letter for the drive, followed by a filename that identifies your backup. You can also store the backup on another computer, using a network drive. For the filename, you might want to use names that incorporate the name of the computer and the date and type of the backup. For example, I might name a full backup of my computer named JAVA on July 4 as java_full_0704.bkf.

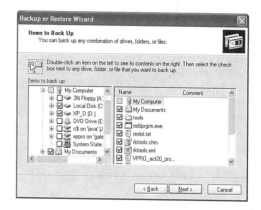

Figure 5.18 Selecting files to back up. In this example, both the C: and D: drives will be backed up.

6. To configure advanced options, including scheduling and disabling volume shadow copy, click Advanced and proceed to step 7. If you want to perform this backup immediately, click Finish.

7. From the Type of Backup page, select the type of backup you want (the default is Normal) and click Next. I personally perform Normal backups monthly, and Differential backups weekly or more often, but you can use a different schedule; certainly do it no less often than I do!

8. From the How to Back Up page, select your preferences as they relate to verification and volume shadow copy and select Next. It's generally not necessary to verify backups written to a disk. If you're backing up to tape, you may want to verify.

9. From the Backup Options page, select whether to append or overwrite existing data and select Next. For backups to a disk, select overwrite rather than append.

10. From the When to Back Up page, select when you want to perform this backup and click Next. If you selected Now, click Finish to start the backup.

11. If you selected Later, you will be able to configure scheduling options. When you have completed setting all scheduling options, click Next. Enter the username and password information of a Computer Administrator account when requested (to ensure that this user has permissions to perform backups). Click Finish to complete the procedure.

Additionally, you can choose to create a backup configuration manually, however you will still make all of the same decisions as when using the Backup Wizard.

Excluding Files from Backups

If you watch the backup procedure in action, you may see it copying large files that you know aren't valuable, and which you would just as soon not have backed up at all. Although you could manually locate and uncheck these files in the list of files to back up, you can also make settings in NTBackup to exclude them automatically.

NTBackup ignores all files listed under Registry key HKEY_LOCAL_MACHINE\system\ CurrentControlSet\Control\BackupRestore\FilesNotToBackUp (exclusions for all users), and under HKEY_CURRENT_USER\system\CurrentControlSet\Control\BackupRestore\FilesNotToBackUp (exclusions for the user running NTBackup).

The FilesNotToBackUp list is also excluded by the System Restore feature, discussed in Chapter 12. Many file types are excluded by default. The default list of files types designated for exclusion are listed in Table 5.9.

Table 5.9   Default *FilesNotToBackUp* Categories

File Categories
Automated System Recovery Error File
Automated System Recover Log File
Background Transfer (Automatic Updates) metadata
Catalog Database
Client Side Cache (offline files)
Digital Rights Management
Internet Explorer cache index
Memory Page File
Microsoft Writer (Bootable State)
MS Distributed Transaction Coordinator database
Netlogon
Files manually listed for exclusion in NTBackup
Hibernation file
Registry Writer data
SUS (Software Update) Client

(continues)

Table 5.9   Continued

File Categories
System Restore index data
Task Scheduler log
Temporary files (TEMP environment variable)
Winlogon debugging information

You can add exclude additional files by following these steps:

1. Start NTBackup, and select the link for Advanced mode.
2. Select Tools, Options, and view the Exclude Files tab.
3. Click one of the Add New buttons, under All Users or under your user account name.
4. Select a listed file extension (file type), such as .xyz to eliminate all .xyz files, or enter a file matching pattern such as DATA*.Z*, to match files based on name as well as extension, as shown in Figure 5.19.

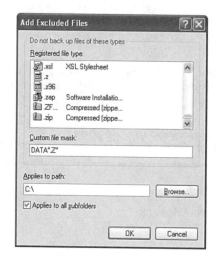

Figure 5.19   Listing files or file types for exclusion.

5. Select or type a path, and check or uncheck Applies to All Subfolders.
6. Click OK, and either add more entries, or click OK again to save the updated list.

Scheduling Your Backups

Managing a backup schedule is very easy in Windows XP. Simply switch to the Schedule Jobs tab from the Backup utility advanced view (see Figure 5.20). Each day on the calendar will show what type of backup is scheduled for that day. Holding the cursor over a backup will display the backup name. You can edit the backup properties, including rescheduling the backup, by clicking it. You can also create new backup configurations by clicking the Add Job button. Figure 5.20 shows the schedule of Normal backups I have in place on one of my Windows XP Professional computers.

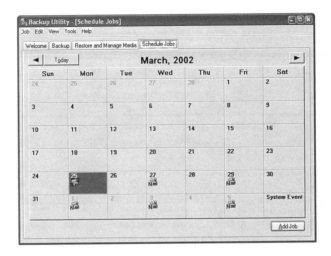

Figure 5.20   Scheduling backup jobs.

After a Disaster: Performing the Restoration

Should the day actually come that you need to put your backup system to the test, the actual process of performing the restoration is a relatively easy task in Windows XP Professional—as long as you are ready for the task. The basic steps to perform a restoration are outlined here, although your options and decisions will vary depending on how your system and backup media devices are configured.

1. You will need a working copy of Windows XP. If your original installation of Windows is work-ing, and you just need to recover a few files, this isn't a concern. But if you lost your entire hard drive, you'll need to install a fresh copy of Windows XP. You'll be replacing this installation with the version saved on your backup, so don't spend any time configuring it, just get it to the point of being able to run ntbackup and read the saved backup files.

2. Log on as a Computer Administrator user. Start the Backup Wizard by clicking Start, Programs, Accessories, System Tools, Backup, or click Start, Run and enter **ntbackup**.

3. Start the Backup Wizard by clicking the Restore Wizard (Advanced) button from the main page of the Backup utility.

4. Click Next to dismiss the opening page of the wizard.

5. From the What to Restore page, select the backup set and the files you want to restore (all, or just some). If your desired backup set is not listed, click the Browse button to locate it. You will need to browse to the disk files that you stored on the removable disk or on a network folder. After making your selections, click Next.

6. To configure advanced options, such as changing the restoration location, click Advanced and proceed to step 7. Otherwise, click Finish to start the restoration.

7. From the Where to Restore page, select the restoration location for the files and click Next. Generally you will want to restore files to their original location, unless you want to be able to compare the files you have on your disk now with the files in the backup set; in that case, you must restore them to a different folder.

8. From the How to Restore page, select your option in regards to overwriting existing files and click Next. In most cases, you will want to replace all files in all circumstances; this will get you

back to the original version you had in the backup set. If you are just recovering files you accidentally deleted, you do not want the restore operation to overwrite newer files.

9. From the Advanced Restore Options page, select the options you want, and click Next.

10. Click Finish to start the restoration.

Note

Before performing a restore that includes the Registry, NTBackup examines Registry value `HKEY_LOCAL_MACHINE\` `system\CurrentControlSet\Control\BackupRestore\KeysNotToRestore`. Keys listed here are not restored. If a key name ends with \, the key's subkeys are also not restored. If a key name ends with *, the subkeys are merged based on Start values. This helps when restoring Windows onto a computer with a different hardware setup. For more information see support.microsoft.com/default.aspx?kbid=249694.

The following list provides some additional help when deciding which advanced restore options to choose.

- *Restore Security*—Restores security settings for each file and folder. You usually want this enabled.

- *Restore Junction Points, and Restore File and Folder Data Under Junction Points to the Original Location*—Restores junction points on your hard disk as well as the data that the junction points point to. If you are restoring a mounted drive, and you want to restore the data that is on the mounted drive, you must select this check box. If you do not select this check box, you will only restore the folder containing the mounted drive. This applies to very few users, so if you don't know what a Junction Point is, you don't need to worry about it.

- *Preserve Existing Volume Mount Points*—Prevents the restore operation from writing over any volume mount points you have created on the partition or volume you are restoring data to. Again, if you haven't created mount points, leave the default setting alone.

- *Restore Removable Storage Database*—Restores the Removable Storage database and deletes the existing Removable Storage database. If you are not using the Removable Storage manager to manage storage media (tapes, for instance), you do not need to select this option.

Note

After restoring a full system, restart Windows. You may find that some of your hardware doesn't work when Windows comes back up. To fix this, open the Device Manager, right-click each of the non-functioning devices in turn, and select Uninstall. Restart Windows again. Log back on as a Computer Administrator, and the Found New Hardware wizard should pop up. Let it locate device drivers automatically. This *ought* to get everything working again.

If you really do need to restore the Registry and Windows itself, however, you might be better off using the System Restore feature that's built into Windows. It does require that your hard disk is intact, but it's a more sophisticated system that's better for recovering from serious configuration goof-ups.

System Restore

Sometimes, installing a device driver causes such severe instability that you need to restore your system to a previously known good state. In the old days, the only way to do this was to restore your system from a backup. Today, however, Windows XP has a System Restore application that can be used to restore a previous configuration of Windows XP. Windows keeps a list of *restore points*, backup files containing critical system information and driver files, that you can use to take a step back in time.

What Restore Points Actually Restore

A *Restore Point* is actually a `.CAB` file, a compressed file much like a `.ZIP` file, that contains driver files, configuration data, and the Registry. A restore point contains

- The Registry, including all of the per-user Registry sections from the user profiles under `\Documents and Setting`, but excluding the security (SAM) sections that contain user passwords
- The COM+ database
- File system configuration data
- The Windows File Protection `.DLL` cache
- The WMI database
- The IIS Metabase (if IIS is installed)
- Files with extensions in the Monitored File Extensions list, which is listed in Table 5.10.

It does *not* include

- Digital Rights Management settings
- SAM Registry hives (System Restores does not restore passwords)
- Windows Product Activation data
- Documents or other user files in user profile folders
- Files with extensions not listed in the Monitored File Extensions list
- Files listed under the Registry keys `FilesNotToBackUp`, and Registry keys listed in under the key `KeysNotToRestore`, both under `HKEY_LOCAL_MACHINE\system\CurrentControlSet\Control\BackupRestore`. The `FilesNotToBackUp` list is also excluded when you use the NTBackup utility to perform backups, as discussed earlier in the chapter.
- Contents of redirected (network) folders
- Settings stored in Roaming User Profiles

The list of file types monitored is amazingly long. The default entries are listed in Table 5.10. Any file on any protected drive with one of the listed extensions is saved in the System Restore database, unless it is also listed in the `FilesNotToBackUp` Registry key. The default categories of files under `FilesNotToBackup` were listed in Table 5.9; the actual filenames and paths will vary from system to system.

All system and user-specific Registry keys are backed up as well. During a restore operation, Registry keys that describe the current hardware environment are *not* restored, as they are re-created every time Windows boots, nor is the SAM security database. This prevents System Restore from restoring an old password that you've already forgotten. The default list of KeysNotToRestore is listed in Table 5.11.

Note

In KeysNotToRestore, if a key name ends with \, the key's subkeys are also excluded from the restore. If a key name ends with *, its subkeys are merged into existing keys. This assumes that the keys specify service and device drivers, and the merging is controlled by the entry's Start value. A subkey is restored only if it has a lower Start value.

Table 5.10 File Types Protected by System Restore

Protected File Types

~~C	~~D	12A	1PA	1st
386	8BA	8BY	8LI	A2A
AAS	AAX	ABM	ABR	ACF
ACG	ACO	ACS	ADK	ADW
ADX	AFM	AID	AIP	ALT
AM	AMB	APL	APM	APP
APV	AR	ARX	AS	AT
ATC	ATL	ATM	ATN	AW
AWE	AWX	AX	B0	BAT
BCF	BD	BDR	BE	BGB
BGR	BID	BIT	BK1	BLD
BM	BMA	BND	BNF	BOF
BPP	BPT	BPX	BT	BTN
BUC	CAG	CAO	CAT	CBS
CC	CF	CFG	CHA	CIK
CL	CLW	CLX	CLY	CMD
CNT	CNV	COL	COM	CPB
CPL	CQM	CR	CRL	CRS
CRV	CS	CSB	CSI	CSL
CSW	CTB	CTG	CTY	CUS
CW_	D01	D02	D03	D04
D05	D32	DATA	DB0	DB1
DB2	DC2	DCA	DCF	DCI
DCL	DDB	DDD	DEP	DES
DESKLINK	DET	DGM	DIALOG	DID
DIR	DISABLED	DIX	DLL	DOB
DOS	DRC	DRS	DRV	DS
DSC	DSK	DSN	DSR	DSX
DT	DTT	DUN	DVB	DWT
DXT	DYNCMD	ECF	EFF	EFM
EID	EL	ELM	END	ENU
ENV	EOT	EPF	ET	EX_
EXA	EXCLUDE	EXE	EXL	F32
FAE	FAM	FAS	FFP	FIN
FIO	FLL	FLW	FMC	FMP
FNT	FON	FSG	FSS	GCS
GDB	GI_	GMS	GNG	GPD
GS	GSF	GST	GUIATN	GUICMD

Table 5.10   Continued

Protected File Types

GVT	GWD	H16	HCT	HDC
HDI	HDP	HFX	HGD	HHC
HHK	HK0	HK1	HK2	HK3
HLP	HM	HTA	HTC	HTZ
HU	HWL	HYP	IAT	IBD
ICD	ICM	ICO	ICR	ICW
ID	IDS	IFA	ILF	ILG
ILM	IN_	INCL	INF	INI
INK	INL	INO	INS	INV
IP	IRS	ISA	ISS	ISU
ITF	J0	JA	JBR	JCM
JGD	K01	K02	K03	KBD
KNN	KO	L0	L2L	L2P
LAB	LAM	LAST	LCA	LCK
LDA	LEX	LGC	LGD	LGE
LGF	LIC	LID	LIM	LIVEREG
LLI	LMC	LMG	LMP	LNK
LO~	LRD	LRS	LSM	LSO
LSQ	LSS	LSX	LT	LTS
LV	M20	MANIFEST	MAPIMAIL	MC
MCD	MCM	MD2	MDM	MDP
ME	MFL	MHK	MIL	MLN
MMC	MMM	MMX	MNC	MNL
MNR	MNS	MOF	MOR	MP
MPD	MPT	MSB	MSC	MSE
MSI	MST	MSK	MSO	MXT
MYDOCS	N0	NAM	NAME	NDX
NEW	NFO	NIB	NMD	NOD
NPM	NQM	NQV	NSI	NSW
NTE	NU4	NUM	NUS	NV
OBE	OCM	OCX	ODE	ODL
OLB	OLD	OLE	OP	OPG
OR5	OSD	OUT	P2A	PAG
PBC	PBK	PBV	PC3	PCI
PDI	PDR	PEN	PER	PFB
PFM	PFR	PH	PHO	PHX
PID	PIF	PL3	PLY	PMT
PNF	POC	POF	POL	PPD

(continues)

Table 5.10 Continued

Protected File Types

PR4	PROPERTIES	PRX	PSC	PSF
PSP	PT	PTH	PTX	PV
Q0	Q32	Q3X	QDAT	QJF
QRS	QTC	QTD	QTW	QUE
QUF	QUT	R0	R98	RAD
RAT	RC2	RCP	RCT	RDB
RDC	REF	REG	RGS	RH
RI	RJS	RO	ROB	RPR
RPS	RSD	RSP	RSRC	RTA
RTR	RU	S98	SAM	SAX
SCK	SCR	SCS	SECURITY	SELFREG
SFP	SG	SG0	SG1	SHARED
SHR	SHX	SIF	SK	SLL
SMC	SMM	SNP	SOF	SPC
SPE	SPM	SPT	SPX	SR
SRC	SRG	SRT	SSM	SST
ST4	STB	STD	STF	STP
SWB	SYM	SYN	SYS	T32
TAG	TB	TDF	TH	THE
THK	THS	TID	TIE	TIP
TLB	TLD	TLF	TLT	TLU
TLX	TMC	TNL	TOL	TPA
TR	TRE	TRG	TRO	TSK
TSP	TTF	TTS	TUB	TUM
TUW	TV	TVC	TWD	TXR
TYM	TZD	UBM	UCM	UCP
UCT	UDC	UDI	UDL	UDT
UID	UIL	UK	ULG	ULK
UNT	US	USA	USERPROFILE	USP
USR	UTX	V10	VBS	VBX
VBZ	VCPREF	VDB	VER	VFM
VFX	VIL	VLX	VM	VOF
VPH	VPX	VQA	VQM	VSC
VSH	VWP	VXD	W32	W98
WA_	WBD	WBM	WCD	WDL
WDS	WINSYS	WIPEINFO	WIPESLACK	WMZ
WPC	WPX	WRF	WSL	WTB
WTR	XLL	XMX	XRS	XTU
ZFSENDTOTARGET	ZH	ZH_TW	ZRW	

Table 5.11   Default *KeysNotToRestore* Entries

File Categories
Active Directory Restore
Automated System Recover information
Disk fault tolerance (RAID) configuration
Installed Services
Disk Manager boot information
Mounted Devices
File rename operations pending until next reboot
Plug and Play discovery data
Removable Storage import database
Session Manager Allow Protected Renames entries
Certain Windows Setup file location data

By default, all hard drives are protected by System Restore. If you have extra disk drives that that don't contain Windows components or application programs, you can disable System Restore on those drives to save disk space. To do this, follow these steps:

1. Log on as a Computer Administrator.
2. Click Start and right-click My Computer. Select Properties.
3. Select the System Restore tab.
4. Select a drive from the Available Drives list and click Settings.
5. Check Turn Off System Restore on This Drive, or lower the amount of disk space that System Restore is allowed to use for its backups.

Restore point .CAB files are stored in folder \System Volume Information on each monitored drive, and are kept 7 to 90 days, depending on the amount of free disk space and the maximum disk space that System Restore is permitted to use. By default, on an NTFS-formatted disk, these folders are not accessible by any user, not even Administrator, although you can make them readable by typing these commands at the command prompt:

```
cd \
cacls "System Volume Information" /E /G Administrator:R
```

on Windows XP Professional; for Home Edition you must substitute another Computer Administrator user's name for Administrator. Enable the display of Hidden and System files in Windows Explorer using Tools, Folder Options, View, and then you can browse the folder.

Caution

Do not delete or modify any files in a System Volume Information folder under any circumstances. To save space, unmodified files are not saved in successive .CAB files, so Windows could conceivably need *all* of the files to perform a successful system restore.

When you are finished poking around, be sure to type the command

```
cacls "System Volume Information" /E /R Administrator
```

to restore the folder's security settings.

Creating Restore Points

Windows XP automatically creates a restore point when any of the following occurs:

- You start Windows XP for the first time after its initial installation and setup

- You install an application that uses the Microsoft Installer or a modern installation program like InstallShield as its setup program

- Windows is about to install updates received via Automatic Updates, or Windows Update

- You have restored files using Microsoft Backup (described earlier in this chapter)

- 24 hours have elapsed since the last restore point was created, whether your computer was turned on or not

If you're concerned that something you're about to do might cause damage, you can also manually create a restore point by following these steps:

Note

It's worth noting that XP's System Restore does *not* back up documents or user files, only system files. If you want a backup utility that makes it possible to roll back documents and files in the same way that System Restore does with system files, check out GoBack at www.symantec.com/goback.

1. Open the System Restore application from the System Tools folder located in the Accessories folder on the All Programs menu. The System Restore application, shown in Figure 5.21, will be displayed.

2. Select the Create a Restore Point radio button and click the Next button.

3. Specify a description for the restore point in the Restore point description field; for example, "Just before installing Dangerously Buggy Program."

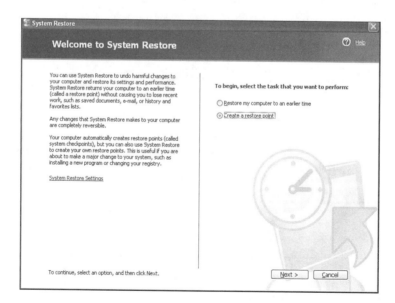

Figure 5.21   The System Restore application.

4. Click the Create button.

5. The Restore Point will be created. When finished, click the Close button to close the application.

Restoring a Point

Assuming your computer will boot into Normal mode or Safe mode, and you either manually created a system restore point, or Windows XP created one for you when you installed your now-deprecated device driver, you can restore a previous configuration.

Caution

System Restore protects all files with file types listed earlier in that staggeringly long list of extensions. This means that any file with a protected extension could get rolled back to an earlier version, or even deleted, if it was not present in the restore point. This includes *your* files, not just files in the Windows folder.

First, you need to get Windows up and running. Often you can use Safe mode; reboot your computer and start tapping the F8 key down as soon as the system BIOS startup message appears. When Windows Advanced Startup Options menu appears, select Safe Mode and press Enter.

Then, follow these steps to restore the system to its previous state.

1. Open the System Restore application from the System Tools folder located in the Accessories folder on the All Programs menu.

2. Select the Restore My Computer to an Earlier Time and click the Next button.

3. Select the desired restore point, as shown in Figure 5.22.

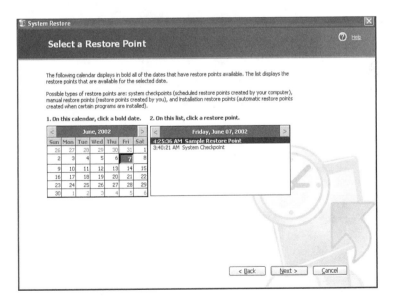

Figure 5.22 Choosing a system restore point to restore.

4. Click the Next button.

5. Confirm that you do want to continue with the restore.

6. Click the Next button to install the system restore point.

7. If you had added or removed hardware, shut Windows down, and restore your original hardware setup before turning the computer back on. Otherwise, just restart Windows. When Windows is up and running again, find out what went wrong before reinstalling the troublesome hardware. You may need to download and install updated device drivers.

If you are unable to boot your system to Windows or if Windows, once booted, is too unstable to activate System Restore, see "Using the System Restore Tool," in Chapter 12. This section explains how to use System Restore from Safe mode or from a command prompt.

Note

As I mentioned earlier, this chapter has a lot to cover, more than we can fit here. If you want more detail, we have books that dish it out in spades…check out *Special Edition Using Microsoft Windows XP Professional, 3rd Edition* (or the *Home Edition*), both published by Que.

CHAPTER 6

Tweaking and Tuning Windows

Configuration Settings

When you install Windows XP or turn on a new computer that has XP preinstalled, you'll find that it works pretty darn well right out of the box. There are several reasons for this. First, modern computer hardware is *really* fast, and many things that used to cause irritating delays have sped up to the point that they're barely noticeable.

Second, PC hardware standards have evolved and matured, and virtually all hardware you can buy now is compliant with various standards for Plug and Play operation, inter-vendor operation, and so on. The software standards for driver architecture have stabilized to the point that almost all drivers install themselves automatically, configure the hardware automatically, tune themselves for best performance automatically, and don't leave much for you to worry about. Drivers for the new generation of 64-bit processors may take a while to become ubiquitous, but other than that, I haven't seen a piece of basic hardware not work instantly upon installation in at least five years. If you've already followed the advice in *Upgrading and Repairing PCs* for selecting and connecting your computer's hardware, there's not a lot left for you do on the configuration front.

Finally, the minimum requirements for the hardware on which Windows can run have increased to the point that Windows no longer has to keep its default settings tuned for computers far below our current expectations. For example, Windows now assumes that your display can handle at least 800×600 resolution, rather than the minimum 640×480 standard that dates back to 1987. If it detects that your monitor can work at 1024×768 resolution (and with a modern Plug and Play monitor, it *can* detect that), it automatically switches up to the higher resolution.

So, if adequate raw performance was your only concern, you wouldn't need this chapter. That's why this chapter is focused on *usability*, which encompasses not only raw performance, but also ease of use, efficiency, "friendliness," and other subjective attributes. This chapter is about making the *experience* of using Windows more pleasant and efficient, removing impediments to effective use, and in general, making Windows better fit your way of working and thinking.

However, what helps one person work faster may not help you at all, and vice versa, so you'll have to test the ideas presented here to see which ones will work for you. Effective tuning depends on what *you* do frequently and personal taste. I've found that the biggest paybacks come from tiny improvements in activities that I perform over and over, rather than large improvements in things that I do rarely. If you use Microsoft Word frequently, shaving a half-second off the time it takes to be able to start using Word may help more than making a once-a-month tune-up run in 15 minutes instead of 30. If you frequently log on and off, minimizing the number of automatic-startup programs is something you will want to focus on. If you frequently use a few applications or certain network resources, you can really help by giving yourself instant access to those resources, even at the expense of others.

Finally, it's worth considering that there is a trade-off involved when you make customizations. The more you customize, the less your computer will look and act like other Windows computers. If you frequently work with other peoples' computers, or if other people often use your computer, major changes in the way the Windows interface works can actually slow you down. You'll have to stop and hunt around for the right way to do something that you're used to doing by habit, and it's irritating.

So, with the philosophy out of the way, let's go over some Windows configuration settings that you might be able to use to make your use of your computer more effective and pleasant. At the end of the chapter, under "Tuning for Maximum Performance," I'll summarize the most important recommended settings.

Note

Although it's helpful to adjust the GUI tools for better usability, remember that you can often perform a job with the command line much faster than you can with a GUI interface. And, you can set up command line "aliases" to abbreviate common functions. For example, on my system I just have to type the letter **n** and press Enter to start Notepad, which takes only a fraction of a second. For more about using and configuring the command line, see Chapter 9, "Windows Commands and Scripting."

Display Settings

As I mentioned earlier, Windows automatically takes good advantage of modern high-resolution displays. There are, however, some settings you can do to get better performance and make the display easier on your eyes.

Adjusting Resolution and Refresh Rate

It's likely that your monitor can handle several different screen resolutions. The higher the resolution, the finer the detail Windows can display, and the more information you can display on the screen at once. This is a more important issue with CRT monitors, and less so with LCD monitors. If you have an LCD monitor be sure to read the additional information on resolution settings after this section.

To adjust the screen resolution, right-click the desktop, select Properties, and select the Settings tab. The dialog's appearance may change depending on whether you have one monitor (see Figure 6.1) or multiple monitors (see Figure 6.2). The procedures for making adjustments are the same in either case, except that in the case of multiple monitors you must click on one of the monitor icons to indicate which monitor's settings you want to change.

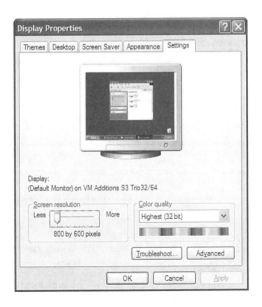

Figure 6.1 Display Properties Settings Page for a single monitor.

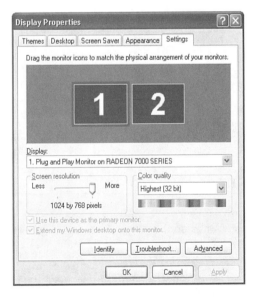

Figure 6.2 Display Properties Settings Page for dual monitors.

A display's resolution is the number of pixels or dots drawn on the screen, horizontally and vertically. The optimum resolution for different monitor sizes has proven to be that which gives you about 86 to 96 pixels per inch (also called dots to the inch, or dpi), or equivalently, a *dot pitch* of about 0.27 mm. The resolution can be decreased to make the display elements bigger and easier to read—those of us over 40 understand this well. For various monitor sizes, the typical maximum resolution is listed in Table 6.1.

Table 6.1   Typical Maximum Display Resolution for Various Monitor Sizes

Diagonal Size	Resolution
15"	1024×768
17"	1280×1024
19"	1280×1024*
21"	1600×1200

Some monitors can be set for higher resolutions than this, but the dot pitch will be significantly lower than .27mm and possibly difficult to read.

To adjust the monitor's resolution, drag the Resolution slider to the left or right. In most cases, Windows will only offer choices that it knows the graphic card can generate *and* that the monitor can accept. When you have made a selection, click Apply and wait for Windows to switch to the new display mode. If the screen does not become readable within 5 to 10 seconds, press the Esc key.

Tip

Do not press the Enter key if you cannot read the screen, or Windows will lock in the nonfunctional setting. If this happens, try this: Press the Esc key 10 times. Press Windows+D. Move the mouse in the direction that takes it away from the taskbar. Right-click the mouse and press the letter R. Press Shift+Tab once, and then press the right arrow key five times. Press Alt+S. Press the left arrow key five times, and then press Alt+A. This should set the resolution to its minimum setting. If this doesn't work, reset or cycle the power on your computer, and when the BIOS screen appears, press F8 until you see the Windows Advanced Options menu. Select Enable VGA mode; this starts Windows with your current display driver set to 640×480 resolution. You can then reset the resolution to something appropriate.

Note

Some display adapters will let you set the screen resolution higher than is physically displayable. In this case, part of the desktop will be hidden, and it will "pan" when you move the mouse to the edge of the screen. If you see this happen and don't like it, just reduce the resolution setting.

If you have a CRT monitor, it's best to adjust the refresh rate—the rate at which the display is repainted on the screen—to around 70Hz or higher if your monitor is capable of it. LCD monitors are fine at 60Hz, but CRTs at this speed have a faint flicker, more noticeable in your peripheral vision than at the center of your field of vision, that can give you a headache or cause eye strain.

To adjust the screen refresh rate, open the Display Properties Settings tab, click the Advanced button, select the Monitor tab, and select a higher refresh rate from the drop-down box. I typically use 70 or 72Hz for CRT monitors, as most can handle this without problems, and 60Hz for LCD monitors. Again, most modern monitors are Plug-and-Play capable and tell Windows what rates they can accommodate, but if you select too high a rate on a non–Plug-and-Play monitor, you can make the display inoperative, and can actually burn out your monitor. Click Apply after changing the rate, and be prepared to press Esc if the display doesn't come back within five to ten seconds.

Resolution Issues on LCD Monitors

If you have a flat-panel LCD monitor, it's best to always run it at its native hardware resolution. LCD monitors can be fed a lower resolution signal, but the pixels on an LCD screen are physical, and can't simply be drawn farther apart as they can be on a CRT display. The LCD monitor or its driver must internally expand a lower resolution display to the higher, physically determined resolution. The result is that at lower resolution settings, the screen will always be slightly blurry.

If your aim is to make desktop elements, icons, and text larger and more readable, you might consider leaving the resolution at its native 1024×768 or 1280×1024, and instead adjust Windows Display Properties to draw larger elements and text, as discussed in the next section.

If you have an LCD monitor, be sure to read the section "Font Smoothing and ClearType" later in this chapter.

Adjusting Text, Icon, and Window Element Sizes

If you find the items on the screen difficult to read or see, you can either lower the screen resolution, which makes everything larger but blurrier, or ask Windows to make the elements themselves larger while keeping a crisper, high screen resolution.

There are two ways you can do this. Here's the first procedure:

1. Right-click the Desktop and select Properties.
2. Save the current screen settings so if you're unhappy with the results, you can back the changes out. Select the Themes tab, click Save As, and enter the name **Original Display Settings**. Click OK.
3. Select the Appearance tab, change the Font Size drop-down to Large Fonts, and click Apply to view the new text size. The text in the dialog won't change but the desktop and Start menu will. You can also try the Extra Large Fonts setting.
4. You can also click Advanced, select individual elements of the Windows display, and change their sizes, although this is more difficult to do and the results are less rewarding.
5. If want to back out all of the changes you made, go back to the Themes tab, open the Theme drop-down, select the entry that says Original Display Settings Without "(Modified)", and clickOK.

With this change, application programs won't necessarily know to make their displays more readable, but many have settings that will enlarge the display. You can Zoom the display in Microsoft Word, alter your email program's default font size, and so on.

There is another method you can use to make *all* Windows display appear larger; this involves lying to Windows to tell it that the dot-pitch (physical pixel spacing) of your monitor is greater than it really is, which will make Windows draw sized elements such as fonts larger than it would otherwise. To do this, follow these steps:

1. Right-click the Desktop and select Properties.
2. Select the Settings tab and click the Advanced button.
3. Select the General tab and make a note of the DPI setting. It's usually set to 96 DPI, although some monitors may cause Windows to use a larger or smaller value. Change the setting to the

next higher value, or use Custom to enter a number about 1.2 times the original value. Click OK, and then restart Windows.

4. Experiment with the DPI setting at a higher value and the Font Size setting (discussed previously) at both the Normal and Large Fonts settings.

Configuring Multiple Monitors

Windows quite nicely supports the use of two or more monitors; Windows can stretch your desktop across up to 16 of them. Sixteen may be overkill, but even two 15" monitors, with about the same area as one 21" monitor, make it easier to stretch out several application windows. And you should see what three 21" monitors in a row look like!

To get a multiple monitor setup, you'll need to install multiple display adapters, use a display adapter that supports more than one monitor (a "dual head" or "quad head" adapter), or both.

Note

Be careful when buying additional adapters. The faster the adapter's connection to the computer, the better, but most motherboards support just one high-speed AGP-bus adapter, and additional adapters must be PCI. Many newer motherboards have one or more PCI-Express (PCI-E) adapters, but only one will be high speed. The latest Serial Link Interface (SLI) motherboards and display adapters let you gang two adapters together, but when SLI mode is enabled, they apply their processing power to *one* display, and all additional monitors will go dark. If you're into computer gaming, it's great because most games use just one display anyway, but it's no help for multiple monitor use. For more information about selecting display hardware, check out Scott Mueller's *Upgrading and Repairing PCs*.

Some laptops also support multiple monitors. The method varies between manufacturers; some require you to make a Control Panel setting (enable DualView), but on some you must use a function key to scroll between display modes. You want the one that enables both monitors with separate displays.

To enable the multiple monitor feature, connect your monitors to the display adapter connectors, turn them on, and then boot up Windows. The initial boot screen will appear on one monitor, or perhaps all the monitors connected to the primary adapter card.

When Windows starts, log on, right-click the desktop, and select Properties. View the Settings tab. The display will appear like that in Figure 6.2. To activate additional displays, click on the numbered monitor icons and check Extend My Windows Desktop Onto This Monitor; then click Apply. (If additional icons don't appear, you may need to select them in the Display drop down.)

It's important to arrange the monitor icons in the Settings dialog exactly as the monitors on your desk are arranged, so that your mouse will move between the monitors in the right order. Click the Identify button to display numerals on your monitors. If necessary, rearrange the icons in the Settings dialog to appear in the same physical order, and then click Apply. The mouse should now move smoothly from monitor to monitor, left to right (or top to bottom, if you've stacked your monitors vertically). To eliminate any vertical jumping as the mouse crosses between the monitors, move the icons slightly up or down to exactly match the exact physical arrangement of your monitors, and click Apply to test the smoothness of the mouse movement. To move an icon one pixel at a time, click it, and then use the up or down arrow key. You must click Apply before testing the adjustment.

Tip

If your computer has multiple monitors and you connect to the computer using Remote Desktop, you may find that an application seems to be running, but you can't make its window appear. What's happened is that it's positioned offscreen, where it would be if there was a second monitor. To move it into view, right-click the application's button in the taskbar. If Minimize is grayed out, click Restore, and then right-click again. If Maximize is grayed out, click Restore, and then right-click again. Select Move, and use the left or right arrow key to bring the window onto the primary monitor.

Also, if you have monitors set to different screen resolutions, you may find that application windows and dialogs can open up with the title bar and menu out of view. To move them fully into view, select the window (click it anywhere), press Alt+spacebar followed by the letter M, and then use the arrow keys to move the window into view. Press Enter to lock in the new position.

Getting the Highest Quality Drivers

Although CPU speeds increase only fractionally from year to year, the special-purpose Graphical Processing Units (GPUs) built into display adapters are being improved in leaps and bounds and their processing speeds now reach into the *teraflop* (trillion floating-point operations per second) range. In fact, some researchers are now exploiting graphics adapters' blazing mathematical computation speeds to perform scientific calculations at supercomputer rates, with the main CPU left to handle mundane tasks like shuffling data and performing I/O.

If you have a pricey high-speed graphics display adapter, perhaps because you're into computer games or graphical design, you should know that the drivers provided by Microsoft with Windows usually (a) are more reliable and (b) perform more slowly than drivers provided directly by the adapter's manufacturer. The reason is that Microsoft's drivers usually undergo more rigorous testing before being released as part of the Windows Setup CD or Windows Update, but they are also usually written to the lowest-common-denominator capabilities of the manufacturer's product line, and may not take best advantage of built-in acceleration capabilities.

The Microsoft drivers are the ones you'll get if you simply install your new graphics adapter and start up Windows. The manufacturer's drivers must usually be installed from a CD, or downloaded from the manufacturer's website. My experience is that new drivers for high-end graphics adapters are released fairly frequently, so you may want to make a note to check for updates every two or three months, at least until the updates for your model taper off.

When you test an upgrade to your drivers, you can usually use Driver Rollback if you encounter a problem, but problems with graphics drivers sometimes make Windows completely unbootable. Frequently, what you will observe is that Windows makes it partway through its startup process, something flashes briefly on the screen, it goes black, and the boot process starts over. This repeats indefinitely. Or, the boot process may halt with white text on a blue background—this is the infamous Blue Screen of Death. If you've just installed a new graphics adapter, power off your computer, unplug it, remove the new adapter and/or replace the original one, and then power back up. If Windows boots successfully, download and install an updated driver before attempting to reinstall the new adapter.

◀◀ For more on testing an upgrade to your drivers, see "Updating Device Drivers", p. 195.

If Windows continues to fail to boot even without new hardware, you'll need to boot Windows in a special VGA mode, where it expects nothing but the most primitive graphics capability. Immediately after your system BIOS message flashes on the screen during bootup, start pressing the F8 key repeatedly until the Advanced Boot Options menu appears. (For more information about the Advanced Boot Options menu see Chapter 4, "Windows Startup.") Select Enable VGA Mode and press Enter. This should let you get in, albeit at 640×480 resolution. Then, perform a driver rollback, or update your device driver.

Note

As you might guess, you're most likely to run into problems with the most up-to-date drivers for the latest, most expensive graphics adapters. Welcome to the leading edge of technology.

Font Smoothing and ClearType

You've probably noticed that with computer displays, as the size of displayed text get smaller and smaller, its appearance gets more and more jagged. The reason is that the curves and diagonal lines in the typeface are being drawn with a very limited number of square pixels on the screen, and the size of those pixels is fixed by the resolution of the monitor. At a certain point, your eye no longer glosses over the square edges, and you start to notice them. Figure 6.3(b) shows what happens to the letter *D* when it's drawn so small that it's just seven pixels high—the boxy pixels in the curved part are quite noticeable.

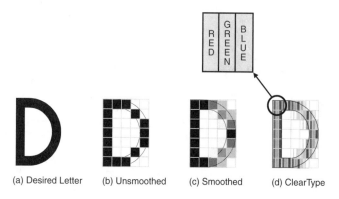

(a) Desired Letter   (b) Unsmoothed   (c) Smoothed   (d) ClearType

Figure 6.3   Font Smoothing and ClearType use shading to reduce jagginess.

Windows can help reduce this jagginess using a technique called *antialiasing*, or *font smoothing*, illustrated in Figure 6.3(c). Instead of being drawn only all-black or all-white, each pixel is shaded to the degree that it would have been filled in by the shape of the desired letter. If the shape would only have filled in half of the area of the pixel, it's displayed at half intensity. You can see that the jagginess is greatly diminished, but the shape also becomes blurred. It's a trade-off, and whether it's worthwhile or not is a judgment that you have to make for yourself. To change the setting, open a document or web page with a small typeface. Then, right-click the Desktop, select Properties, select the Appearance tab, click Effects, and check or uncheck Use the Following Method To Smooth The Edges of Screen Fonts, with the drop-down box set to Standard. Click OK, then Apply, and see what you think of the effect. Switch back and forth a few times to see which display you prefer.

If you have an LCD monitor, you can choose between two different methods of smoothing fonts. The full-pixel method shown in Figure 6.3(c) is available on both CRT and LCD monitors. A second smoothing method trademarked by Microsoft as *ClearType* is available for LCDs only and takes advantage of the fact that each pixel on an LCD monitor is laid out as a set of parallel stripes of red, green, and blue, as illustrated in Figure 6.3(d). When the antialiasing concept is applied to each of these subpixels independently, the horizontal resolution for text is effectively tripled, and the blurred areas around curves are much smaller.

You could switch the effect on and off using the drop-down list on the Effects dialog that you used to turn smoothing on and off, but there's a much better way. Microsoft has released a ClearType Tuning program that displays a series of text samples using different degrees of smoothing, and lets you decide which you like best. (It's a lot like a visit to the ophthalmologist: "Which looks better, A or B?") After several comparisons, this tuning utility is able to set some ClearType smoothing options that aren't reachable directly, and the result can be a much-improved display. To get the tool, follow these steps:

1. Visit www.microsoft.com, search for "powertoys for windows xp," and follow the link to download the ClearType Tuner PowerToy.

2. Save the file setup.exe on your desktop and double-click it to run it. You may have to enter a Computer Administrator account name and password to begin the installation.

3. When the installation is complete, open Control Panel, select the Appearance and Themes category, and select the ClearType Tuning icon.

4. Follow the Wizard's directions; at each step, click on the best-looking text sample, and then click Next.

When the Wizard is finished, if you don't like ClearType, you can disable it. Just run the Wizard again, uncheck Turn On ClearType, and click OK. Personally, I don't like it. Although the smoothing effect is quite remarkable, to my eyes ClearType text is too thin and blurry, and has an odd "unstable" quality—it seems to swim around a bit.

Note

For a comprehensive and interesting article on the concepts behind antialiasing and ClearType, with excellent illustrations, check out www.grc.com/ct/cleartype.htm. The nifty downloadable "Free and Clear" program lets you experiment with sub-pixel rendering and zoom in on the results. It's really fun.

Updating DirectX

Although most Windows applications place fairly low demands on the display system, putting up fairly static displays and updating them relatively infrequently, interactive games and video displays are very graphics intensive. Game players pay big bucks for *fps*, or *frames per second*, which is a measure of how fast the hardware and software can generate new images as the scene changes and objects move. Under about 30fps, the image flickers and motion is noticeably jerky. Beyond 30fps, faster updates aren't noticeable, and the extra processing power can be put to work by reconfiguring the game to generate more complex, detailed images.

The problem is that the software overhead that Windows places between applications and the graphics hardware in order to foster good cooperation, nicely rendered text, and cleanly overlapping windows can slow down a game program or DVD video player and hinder its ability to crank out images. Enter *DirectX*, a set of application software interfaces (drivers, really) that let applications have much more direct, faster access to underlying display hardware. DirectX also provides hardware-independent image rendering and sound-producing tools that applications and games can rely on; these can take advantage of the hardware adapters' built-in computing abilities, but are guaranteed to work—if slowly—even on inexpensive adapters without hardware acceleration.

Microsoft updates DirectX on a schedule independent of its updates to Windows, and although some software setup CDs come with a version of DirectX, if you play video-intensive games or watch movies on your computer you're better off getting the latest DirectX package directly from Microsoft. To find out what version of DirectX is installed on your computer, click Start, Run, and in the command box, type **dxdiag** and press Enter. On the System tab, near the bottom of the System Information list, you should see an entry labeled DirectX Version.

DirectX updates are usually not security-related fixes, so they will not be delivered through Automatic Updates, nor will they appear in the "High Priority" section in Windows Update. To check for a DirectX update, click Start, All Programs, Windows Update. Select Custom updates, and view any entries in the "Optional Software" category. Check and install DirectX if it appears.

You can also download and install the latest version of DirectX from www.microsoft.com/directx.

Menu Accelerator Keys

In all versions of Windows prior to Windows XP, Window menus used underscores (as in File) to indicate Alt key shortcuts. For touch typists, these so-called *menu accelerators* can save a lot of time and trouble; it's much easier to type Alt+F, Alt+A than to take your hands off the keyboard, reach for the mouse and click File, Save As, and then go back to the keyboard to enter a filename. And, you didn't even have to memorize these shortcuts; they were always displayed on the screen.

By default, however, Windows XP hides the telltale underscores until you press down the Alt key. Unless you think to press the Alt key, you won't even know that the shortcuts are available, or which menu functions even have them. To make Windows display accelerators by default, right-click the Desktop, select Properties, view the Appearance tab, click Effects, uncheck Hide Underlined Letters... and click OK. Some applications, such as Word, control the appearance of menu accelerators themselves and are not affected by this setting.

Start Menu Settings

Windows XP introduced a radically new Start menu, shown in Figure 6.4, and while some of the changes may please the casual user, not all of them contribute to efficiency and greater usability. The self-reorganizing Recent Application list on the Start menu is one example. While a "most recently used" list for applications sounds like a good idea, and may be for some users, it drives me crazy to have menu items appear and disappear and move around by themselves; usually I'm already moving my mouse to a favorite item before I can even read the menu titles, and I hate a moving target. Luckily, the Start menu and its submenus are eminently configurable. In this section I'll list some changes you may want to make.

To customize the Start menu, right-click the Start button and select Properties. From the Start Menu tab, you can elect to use the original Windows 2000-style Start menu by selecting Classic Start Menu—this is essentially what Windows displays from the XP Start menu when you select All Programs, with the Control Panel and Log Out options added.

The XP style Start menu can be much handier, so you may want simply to customize it instead. Click Customize, and investigate the following options:

- You can eliminate the ever-changing most-recently used program icons, shown in the bottom left part of Figure 6.4, by changing Number of Programs on Start Menu to 0. Or, you can adjust the number of recent applications listed to another number.

- You can control whether Internet (web browser) or email icons are displayed, and what applications are launched.

- You can add program shorts to the "fixed" upper-left part of the Start menu by locating items in the Start menu, holding down the right mouse button, and dragging them to the left into the desired position in the main Start Menu panel. To remove an item from the fixed area, right-click the icon and select Remove From This List.

On the Advanced tab, shown in Figure 6.5, there are several other useful options:

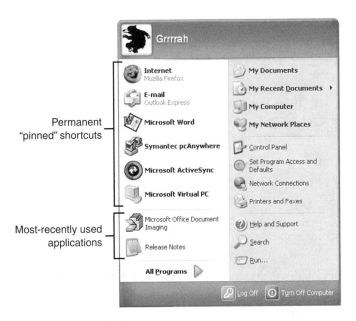

Permanent "pinned" shortcuts

Most-recently used applications

Figure 6.4 The Customizable Start menu.

Figure 6.5 The Advanced tab on the Start Menu customization dialog lets you enable or disable many Start menu items.

■ Under Start Menu Items, you can have the Control Panel, My Computers, My Music, My Pictures, and Network Connections entries act as links, which when clicked open the associated window, or as menus, which when opened display a submenu of Control Panel applets, My Computer drives and items, documents and so on. You can also elect not to display them on the Start menu at all.

- Favorites adds an item to the Start menu that, opened, lists all of your web browser bookmarks.

- You can elect to show or hide entries for Help and Support, My Network Places, Printers and Faxes, the Run command dialog, Search, and Set Program Access and Defaults.

- The System Administrative Tools entry is especially helpful to set. By default it's disabled entirely; select Display on the All Programs menu to enable the Administrative Tools submenu. (It's always available from the Control Panel in any case.)

- If you want, you can disable the list of most-recently opened documents. Clicking Clear List will remove existing entries, but won't keep the list from rebuilding itself.

Once you've removed any unwanted Start menu features, you can add desired startup items of your own.

Organizing Menus for Efficient Use

Although menus that reorganize themselves can hinder you by short-circuiting your natural tendency to (eventually) learn where menu items are, you *can* move menu items to more convenient places, and have them stay put.

Simply open the Start menu, hold down the right mouse button, and select and drag a menu item to a new position. A thin black line will appear where the menu will land if you release the mouse button. If the menu item above the mouse pointer has submenus, the submenus will open and if desired, you can move the menu item into the submenu.

Remember that the entire contents of the All Programs menu is actually a set of shortcuts stored in the folders `\Documents and Settings\All Users\Start Menu` and `\Documents and Settings\` *your_login_name*`\Start Menu`. Subfolders in these folders appear as submenus under All Programs, and any items in these folders are the menu items. As you might guess, entries in the All Users profile folder appear in everyone's Start menu, whereas the ones in your own profile folder appear only on your Start menu. The contents of the two folders are merged to create the list of submenus and shortcuts.

Creating QuickLaunch Icons

The taskbar has a place that can hold tiny icons for favorite applications or folders, called the QuickLaunch menu. The selected applications can be launched with a single click without even opening the Start menu, and the icons don't clutter up your desktop. I strongly suggest that you customize your QuickLaunch menu by following these steps:

1. Right-click the taskbar. If Lock the Taskbar is checked, uncheck it and right-click the taskbar again.

2. Select Toolbars, and check Quick Launch.

3. If necessary, enlarge the QuickLaunch menu and/or adjust the height of the taskbar to make room for the QuickLaunch buttons. Some people keep 20 icons in it, but I like to keep it down to under a dozen; any more and I have trouble finding them more quickly there than I could in the Start menu.

4. Right-click any icons you don't want to have there, and select Delete.

5. Populate the QuickLaunch menu with icons from your desktop or Start menu. To get items from the Start menu, locate the desired Start menu item, right-click and hold the button down, and drag the icon to the desired position on the QuickLaunch menu. When you release it, select Copy Here from the menu that pops up. (If you inadvertently select Move Here, it will disappear from its original location in the Start menu. Immediately right-click the desktop and select Undo Move to fix this.) You can also open Windows Explorer and Alt+drag a shortcut to a

favorite folder to the Quick Launch menu. Be sure to use the Alt key while dragging, otherwise you will copy the folder's contents.

6. When you've added icons for your most common applications, resize the QuickLaunch menu down to the minimum necessary size, and if you want, relock the taskbar.

Some surprisingly big-name software applications install icons in your Quick Launch bar whether you want them there or not, and occasionally reinstall them even after you've deleted them. It's arrogant and rude, but they do it anyway. You may have to weed your Quick Launch bar from time to time.

Internet and Email Options

You have control over which programs are launched when you use the Internet or email icons on the Start menu. If you've installed an alternate web browser or email program and want to use it as your primary program from the Start menu, right-click the Start menu, select Properties, and click Customize. At the bottom of the dialog you can select from among the web browsers and email programs installed on your computer. (Non-Microsoft applications must have registered themselves correctly in order to appear in this list.) Microsoft products may not be available if you or your computer manufacturer disabled them—click Start, All Programs, Set Program Access and Defaults to show or hide applications.

Changing the applications displayed as the Internet and Email programs in the Start menu changes the programs launched from the Quick Launch menu as well.

Tuning System Properties

There are some important system environment settings that you can control through the System Properties dialog. To open this dialog, right-click My Computer and select Properties, or open the Control Panel, select Performance and Maintenance, and open the System icon. You can make the following adjustments from this dialog, shown in Figure 6.6:

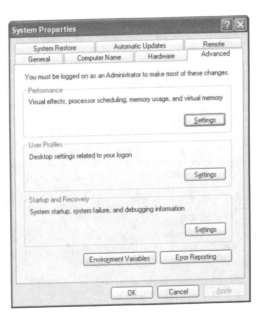

Figure 6.6 The System Properties dialog lets you make many startup, performance, and configuration adjustments.

- *Computer Name tab*—Computer description, computer name, workgroup or domain network type, workgroup or domain name. These items are covered in Chapter 7, "Networking Windows."

- *Hardware tab*—Launch Device Manager, enable/disable installation of unsigned drivers, use of Windows Update during driver installation, management of hardware profiles (sets of different hardware configurations). These items are covered in Chapter 5, "Managing Windows."

- *Advanced tab*—Performance (CPU scheduling) adjustments, User Profile management, System startup/crash recovery options, Environment Variables, configuration of crash reporting to Microsoft. User profiles and environment variables are covered in Chapter 5, and the remaining items are covered in the following sections.

- *System Restore tab*—Selection of protected drives. This feature is covered in Chapter 5 and in Chapter 12, "Windows Troubleshooting". Chapter 12 deals with using System Restore to fix a non-bootable system.

- *Automatic Updates tab*—Configuration of automatic update download and installation. These items are covered in the following sections.

- *Remote tab*—Configuration of access to this computer via Remote Assistance and Remote Desktop. This tab is covered in Chapter 7.

You must be logged on as a Computer Administrator to change most of these settings, though any user can change his personal Environment Variables list. Power users (on XP Professional), which I covered in Chapter 5, can change the default operating system in the Startup and Recovery options, Virtual Memory settings, Visual Effects, Error Reporting, and Driver Signing options.

Application Performance Settings

There are some settings you can use to adjust Windows performance. Virtual memory settings are the most important, and to a lesser extent, you can also instruct Windows to give slightly greater emphasis to either running programs or creating a smooth visual display.

To adjust these performance settings, right-click My Computer and select Properties to open the System Properties dialog. Select the Advanced tab, and click the top Settings button under Performance.

In the unlikely event that your computer will be running as a server of some sort, and is to expend as much of its processing power as possible running a constant CPU-intensive workload, you can disable Windows' slicker graphical features. On the Performance Options dialog, select the Visual Effects tab and check Adjust for Best Performance. If the processing is to be done by a Service rather than an application launched on the desktop, select Background Services.

If your computer will be performing a large amount of data reading and writing using relatively small programs, you can tune Windows for faster I/O by selecting System Cache. This can take away from application memory space, so you should compare performance with and without this setting; a reboot is required to put the change in effect.

Virtual Memory and Page File Settings

Windows Virtual Memory system works by writing data that won't fit into RAM into a *page file* that holds the overflow. For efficient operation the page file should be unfragmented and positioned either on its own separate physical disk drive (preferably a disk that's seldom used), or on the Windows disk, but not on a drive that's really just an alternate partition on the same physical drive as the Windows installation drive.

▶▶ To determine what your system's RAM and page file requirements should be, see "How Much Memory Is Enough," p. 284.

To configure Page File sizes and locations, you must be logged on as a Computer Administrator. Right-click My Computer and select Properties to open the System Properties dialog. Select the Advanced tab, and click the top Settings button under Performance. Select the Advanced tab and click the Change button under Virtual Memory. The page file configuration dialog appears as shown in Figure 6.7.

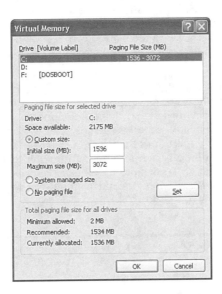

Figure 6.7 The Virtual Memory dialog lets you specify the location and size of page files.

After first installing Windows, there will probably be a page file located on drive C: (or the boot drive) with the System Managed Size option selected. You can create page files on more appropriate, faster drives and either leave the original file as is, or delete it.

To create a new page file, select a drive letter in the upper part of the dialog and select either Custom Size or System Managed Size. If you want to prevent the page file from fragmenting, create it on a freshly formatted or defragmented drive and set a custom initial size at 1.5 to 3 times the amount of physical RAM installed in your computer. To prevent the page file from growing or fragmenting, set its maximum size at the same amount. The new file will be created and used immediately.

If you are not sure what your system's memory demands will be, leave the page file set to System Managed Size and let Windows manage it.

To delete a page file, select a drive letter in the upper-hand part of the dialog and select No Paging File. The file will be freed and deleted when you restart Windows.

Note

Page files are created in the root folder of the selected drive(s) with the name `pagefile.sys`, with the System and Hidden attributes. The file will be locked and unreadable as long as Windows is running.

For some tips on selecting appropriate page file settings, see the discussion "Placing the Page File" later in this chapter.

Data Execution Prevention

Starting with Windows XP Service Pack 2, Windows XP supports a feature called Data Execution Prevention (DEP) that prevents programs from replacing the original, intended machine instructions in memory with new instructions that could perform malicious acts. This feature became necessary when virus writers and hackers began exploiting bugs in software that can result in malicious program instructions sent from the attacker being written in memory that was supposed to hold just program data. These are often referred to as *buffer overrun exploits* or *stack overflow exploits*. If the program's path through memory eventually takes it into the malicious code, the injected instructions can do anything *you* can do; that is, the program has your privileges, can access any file you can, can infect other programs, and so on.

Data Execution Prevention uses two different mechanisms to guard against this type of attack: First, it uses Windows software mechanisms to prevent programs from writing any new instructions into sections of memory that were originally designated as holding instructions. Second, it prevents programs from executing instructions from any section of memory that was originally designated as holding only data. The second form of protection is the stronger of the two, but it is only available with some CPU chips, including all 64-bit processors from AMD and Intel, Intel's Pentium D and Pentium 840 Extreme Edition processors, and AMD's Sempron processors. This second mechanism is called *Execute Disable* or *ED* by Intel, and *No Execute* or *NX* by AMD, and it's used when available whenever Data Execution Prevention is enabled in Windows.

Note

On a corporate network, Data Execution Prevention is probably enabled and managed by the network Group Policy. Individual applications that are known to be safe but which modify their own executable instructions on purpose can be marked to "opt out" of protection using the Application Compatibility Toolkit. For more information about this mechanism, see www.microsoft.com/windows/appcompatibility/default.mspx.

By default, when Windows XP Service Pack 2 is installed, DEP is enabled only for Windows components themselves. To protect all applications, right-click My Computer and select Properties to open the System Properties dialog. Select the Advanced tab, and click the top Settings button under Performance. Select the Data Execution Prevention tab, shown in Figure 6.8.

To enable DEP for all applications, select Turn On DEP for All Programs and Services Except Those I Select.

If you change Data Execution Prevention settings, you'll need to restart Windows. When enabled for all applications, you may find that an application that used to work suddenly fails with a dialog box that says "Data Execution Prevention—A Windows security feature has detected a problem and closed this program." In this case, you should contact the manufacturer's tech support to see whether this is a known issue, or if an update is available.

If you determine that the application is actually safe but just happens to require the ability to write modified instructions in order to work, you can instruct Windows to disable DEP for this application. Back in the DEP setup dialog (refer to Figure 6.8), click Add, and then browse to select the .EXE file that corresponds to the application in question. Click OK to save it in the list of exceptions.

Caution

If you enable Hardware Data Execution Prevention and have a flaky device driver, the driver may prevent Windows from booting. Use the following procedure to recover.

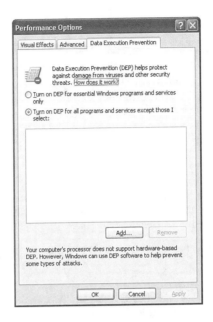

Figure 6.8   Enabling Data Execution Prevention.

If Windows halts with a blue screen, or reboots repeatedly when you restart it after enabling Hardware DEP (or after updating a device driver when Hardware DEP is enabled), one of your device drivers is executing code from "No Execute" memory and terminating. Use one of the following methods to disable DEP. First, try to boot Windows in Safe mode:

1. When your computer's BIOS startup screen appears, press F8 repeatedly until Windows' Advanced Startup Options menu appears. Select Safe Mode and press Enter.

2. When Windows has started, log on as a Computer Administrator, go back to the Data Execution Prevention setup tab, and disable hardware protection. Restart Windows to test.

If Windows won't even boot in Safe mode, you'll need to take the more drastic step of manually editing the boot.ini file on the hard drive that contains Windows. To do this, follow these steps:

1. Remove the hard drive from your computer and install it in another computer, which, if your Windows partition uses NTFS formatting, must be running Windows XP or Windows 2000. If you need to change the drive's master/slave jumpers, be sure to make a note of the original setting before changing them.

2. Start up the alternative computer, and view My Computer to identify the drive letter that was assigned to your relocated drive; let's say it's E. (If a different drive letter is assigned, use that letter instead of E in the next step.)

3. Open a command prompt window and type the following commands:

```
e:
attrib -r -h -s boot.ini
notepad boot.ini
```

4. In Notepad, locate the line under [operating systems] that has /NoExecute=OptIn, /NoExecute=OptOut or /NoExecute=AlwaysOn in it. Carefully change it to read /NoExecute=AlwaysOff.

5. Save boot.ini (Alt+F, Alt+S) and close Notepad (Alt+X).

6. Type the following command:

   `attrib +r +h +s boot.ini`

7. Shut down the computer, remove your hard drive, reset the master/slave jumpers if you changed them, put it back in your computer, and restart Windows.

When Windows boots successfully, log on as a Computer Administrator and check the Event Log for an indication of which driver failed during startup. Update it or roll it back before enabling hardware DEP again.

Setting Environment Variables

Environment variables are used by Windows to communicate the locations of certain folders to application programs. Environment variables are set through the System Properties dialog, but the process can be somewhat tricky, especially for the PATH variable.

▶▶ For instructions on managing environment variables, see "Setting Default Environment Variables," p. 394. (Chapter 9).

System Startup Options and Crash Recovery

The Startup and Recovery Options dialog lets you specify what operating system choices are available when your computer boots, and what action Windows should take when Windows itself crashes and cannot continue. To set these options, right-click My Computer and select Properties to open the System Properties dialog. Select the Advanced tab, and click the Settings button under Startup and Recovery.

If Windows crashes due to a bad device driver, hardware failure, or software error in an internal part of Windows itself, it will halt without performing a proper shutdown. It will usually display the now infamous Blue Screen of Death, which displays code numbers indicating the type of failure detected. What happens next depends on the options selected in the System Failure section of the Startup and Recovery dialog, which you can see in Figure 6.9.

By default all three options are checked:

- *Write an Event to the System Log*—Information about the crash is stored in memory, and when Windows restarts, if it is able to progress far enough that the system event logging service starts, the information will be recorded in the Event log. The entry will not be written if the PC is shut off before Windows restarts, or if Windows fails to find the crash information left in memory when it restarts.

- *Send an Administrative Alert*—Like the preceding option, when Windows restarts, if it is able to detect that it had previously crashed, it will send an inter-computer message to any logged-on Administrators. Unless you're on a network and actually use Alerts, you can disable this option.

- *Automatically Restart*—If this option is unchecked, Windows displays the blue screen after a crash, and the PC will have to be restarted using its reset button (or power switch) to reboot. If this option is checked, the blue screen will be displayed for only an instant, and Windows will automatically restart. This can be problematic if you never get to see what's wrong.

I recommend that for a server or other computer that must run unsupervised all of the time, you check Automatically Restart, but for all other uses, uncheck Automatically Restart. Otherwise, after a crash, you will likely never get to see the information displayed on the blue screen, and if Windows is crashing before you have a chance to log on, you'll only be able to watch it boot up, crash, reboot, crash, over and over.

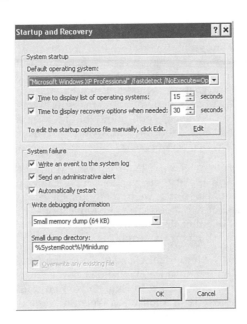

Figure 6.9 The Startup and Recovery Options dialog lets you specify boot crash restart behavior.

Note

If Windows does crash and restart in endless loop, try pressing F8 as soon as the reboot starts, and try to boot in Safe mode. If this works, go into the Startup and Recovery dialog and uncheck Automatically Restart. Then restart Windows, and you should be able to see what the blue screen says.

If Safe mode doesn't work, remove the disk drive from the computer, install it in another computer running Windows XP, and use the Registry Editor to mount the hive file `\windows\system32\config\system` on the crashed computer's hard drive (see "Editing a Hive File" later in this chapter for instructions). Find key `SYSTEM\Select` in the mounted hive. Locate value `Current` and note the number. Open key `System\ControlSet00n`, replacing *n* with the number you saw in value `Current`. Locate key `Control\CrashControl`. Edit value `AutoReboot` and change its value to 0. Shut down the computer, remove the drive, reinstall it in the original computer, and power it up. You should now be able to see what the blue screen says. If you don't have another computer you can use for this, you can add another hard drive to your original computer, install Windows on that drive, and then use this procedure to edit the Registry of the original drive.

The Write Debugging Information option can make Windows store a copy of the contents of memory in a disk file after a crash (assuming that the disk hardware and file system drivers are still operative). I recommend that you set this option to (none) unless requested to change it by a tech support person, or unless you are a device driver developer and need to use debugging tools to analyze the crash dumps. Saving crash dumps takes time and disk space and a Complete Memory Dump can take a *very* long time.

Tip

Chapter 12 has more information on working through Blue Screen of Death issues.

Error Reporting

Windows has an application error reporting feature that collects information about the circumstances of application failures and Windows crashes and sends them back to Microsoft headquarters over your Internet connection. The purpose is to gather statistics about the types of crashes that occur, and enough information to identify what part of the program had the problem. It's a voluntary program and won't benefit you directly (that is, nobody from Microsoft is going to call you to ask whether they can come right over to fix the buggy application), but the idea is that over time, statistical fingers will point toward the most error-prone programs, and with the necessary repairs, this will lead to improvements in future releases and service packs.

For the most part it makes sense to let Error Reporting send Microsoft reports about failures in Windows itself and in Microsoft applications. Vendors of big-name applications probably purchase crash report information from Microsoft as well, so it's probably worth reporting other commercial applications. It doesn't make sense to report errors in applications you develop yourself or those from your own company, so you can either elect not to send them when an error box pops up, or you can tell Windows not to even offer to report these applications.

To change the Error Reporting settings, right-click My Computer and select Properties to open the System Properties dialog. Select the Advanced tab, and click the Error Reporting button at the bottom. The configuration dialog is shown at the left in Figure 6.10. Here you can disable error reporting entirely, or enable it for Windows itself, Application Programs, or both. For more detailed control over which programs are reported, click Choose Programs to get the dialog at the right side of Figure 6.10.

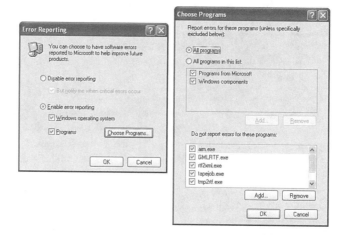

Figure 6.10   You can control which programs' crashes get reported to Microsoft.

In the Choose Programs dialog you can select All Programs to report everything, All Programs in this list to report only Microsoft products or selected programs of your own; click the Add button and locate the .EXE files of any applications you want to include by name. You can also exclude specific programs using the list at the bottom of the dialog. Click Add to locate specific programs.

Note

When programs are listed for inclusion or exclusion, only the filename itself is recorded, not the full path. For example, if program name **AIM95.EXE** is listed, any program file named **AIM95.EXE** will be included or excluded no matter what folder it resides in.

When an error report is sent, it includes the name of the application that crashed, and a minimal amount of data copied from the memory stack. This stack data could conceivably contain a tiny bit of confidential information. It's very unlikely, but if you're seriously concerned about this, you can tell Windows never to send reports.

Configuring Automatic Updates

Automatic Updates is a mechanism with an awkwardly plural-sounding name by which Microsoft or corporate network managers distribute critical security updates to Windows users. Fixes sent by this means are considered so important for adequate security in the hostile Internet environment that Microsoft prefers that you configure it to download and install the updates, and if necessary even restart your computer without your being aware of it.

There are four levels of Automatic Updates protection to which you can subscribe:

- *Automatic*—Windows will query Microsoft or your corporate network servers every day or on a specified day of the week, or whenever Internet access is available, will download the updates when they become available, and will install the updates at a designated time, if the computer is on at that time, or the next time you shut the computer down, or when you log on as a Computer Administrator and open the Update Notification icon in the taskbar, whichever occurs soonest. This is the option recommended by Microsoft.

- *Download updates*—Windows will download the updates automatically, but will not automatically install them until you ask for them to be installed. You will be prompted to do this when you log on as a Computer Administrator; a balloon tip will pop up from the taskbar informing you that updates are ready to install.

- *Notify me*—Windows will not download updates automatically. You will have to log on as a Computer Administrator to receive the pop-up notification that updates are available for download and activate the pop-up icon to begin the download process.

- *Turn off*—Windows will neither download nor notify you of the availability of updates. This option should be used only on a corporate network where the administrators will take responsibility for all updates, but no Automatic Updates server is installed locally.

In most cases the Automatic method is best, for as long as your computer is turned on and has frequent Internet access, you will get these critical security fixes within hours or days of their release. The Download Updates option is recommended only if your computer is running important services and cannot be allowed to shut itself down for a restart without your consent and supervision, and you will be sure to log on as a Computer Administrator frequently so that you see the update notification; or, your computer is not connected to the Internet so is not vulnerable to the attacks that these fixes are designed to ward off.

To modify the Automatic Updates settings, right-click My Computer and select Properties to open the System Properties dialog. Select the Automatic Updates tab, shown in Figure 6.11, and make the appropriate selection. Click OK to save the change.

It is quite important that the vast majority of Windows computers do use Automatic Updates so that in the future there will not be large numbers of unprotected, vulnerable computers for software viruses and worms to prey upon. Keeping the number of vulnerable systems under a certain "critical mass" will help minimize the number of virus storms that occur.

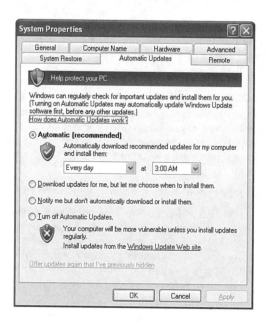

Figure 6.11   Critical security updates can be downloaded and installed automatically.

Managing Startup Programs

Besides ensuring that your computer has adequate memory, one of the next best ways to improve your subjective experience of Windows' speed is to make the logon process faster. The logon process can be greatly slowed by large numbers of programs that are launched automatically upon logon; the desktop and Start menu don't respond until all of the login programs have been activated.

Keeping the list of startup programs short is a constant struggle, however. To hide the fact that many common programs are poorly written and bloated in size, software vendors have taken to stealthily having Windows start them up when you log on, where they remain hidden. If you later launch the application, its window pops right up, because it was actually already running in the background. The software vendors fool you into thinking that its product is fast, and that it's the Windows logon process that is slow. What's even worse, because you have to wait for their clunky software to start up *every time you log on,* even if you rarely actually use the application, over time they waste hours of your time to make their program start up 10 or 20 seconds faster. And, like virus authors, they usually have their software rigged to keep adding itself back as a startup program even after you've told it not to, especially after software updates. It's shameful, and what's amazing is that the vendors that practice this include large companies like Apple (Quick Time Player and iTunes), Microsoft (Windows Messenger), and Real Audio (Real Player).

So, to avoid ongoing theft of your time, you need to know how startup programs are run, how to find them, and how to manage them.

There are several places to specify programs that are to be run upon logon:

- Shortcuts in the Startup folder in the All Users Start Menu folder, usually `C:\Documents and Settings\All Users\Start Menu\Startup`
- Shortcuts in the Startup folder in your personal Start Menu folder, usually `C:\Documents and Settings\`*your logon name*`\Start Menu\Startup`

- Values in Registry key `HKEY_LOCAL_MACHINE\Software\Microsoft\Windows\CurrentVersion\Run`

- Values in Registry key `HKEY_LOCAL_MACHINE\Software\Microsoft\Windows\CurrentVersion\RunOnce`

- Values in Registry key `HKEY_LOCAL_MACHINE\Software\Microsoft\Windows\CurrentVersion\RunOnceEx`

- Values in Registry key `HKEY_CURRENT_USER\Software\Microsoft\Windows\CurrentVersion\Run`

- Values in Registry key `HKEY_CURRENT_USER\Software\Microsoft\Windows\CurrentVersion\RunOnce`

- Values in Registry key `HKEY_CURRENT_USER\Software\Microsoft\Windows\CurrentVersion\RunOnceEx`

- Entries under the `[run]` section in `\windows\win.ini` (these are a holdover from Windows 3.1. Run entries in `win.ini` now would come only from truly ancient applications or viruses)

- Commands in logon scripts specified through Group Policy or Local Security Policy, on Windows XP Professional

▶▶ Two other potential sources of startup programs are the `Winlogon\Shell` Registry value and print monitors. For more information, see "Startup Programs," p. 130.

You can manually scan through all of these locations using Windows Explorer and the Registry Editor, or you can use the msconfig tool described in the next section. In some cases the program being run will be obvious but in other cases you will need to do some research to determine what the startup program is. I've found that a Google search on the name of the `.EXE` file (for example, something like `ssmmgr.exe`) will usually lead me to a clue, although there are now dozens of fairly useless websites that simply contain pages for all known programs, with advertising and links to very dubious "anti-spyware" products. Another good site to check out is www.sysinfo.org/startuplist.php. There you can search a database of known good and bad programs.

Some programs definitely should be run at startup. These include special purpose printer monitors, certain backup applications, antivirus and antispyware user interfaces, PDA synchronizers, and such programs. Even programs like Apple's Quicktime player startup program `qttask.exe` might be worth allowing to remain active as startup programs *if* you use these applications during nearly every logon session.

Some programs can be cajoled into at least temporarily removing themselves as startup programs. QuickTime Player, for example, has a Preferences setting under its Browser Plug-In category called "Quick Time System Tray Icon." Unchecking this removes the `qttask.exe` startup program for a while, usually until the next update to QuickTime Player.

You should still check the Run Registry entries after doing this, as some programs still leave a startup entry in place in order to check with the manufacturer for software updates; if no updates are found, the program quits without creating a System Tray icon. But this stealth tactic takes up a significant amount of your time *every time you log on*, so if you find that a program keeps its Run startup entry after you've disabled its "quick start" feature, delete the Run entry (and send a complaint to the software vendor).

If you decide to manually eliminate a startup program, it can't hurt to make a note of the corresponding entry before you delete it, in case you want to manually restore it later. Deleting startup programs requires deleting shortcuts from the Startup folder (or moving them out of the Startup folder), or deleting specific Registry values using the Registry editor. (Editing the Registry is discussed later in this chapter.)

msconfig

To quickly see what programs are run when you log on and to test what happens without them, use msconfig, a little-known system configuration utility provided with some versions of Windows; I'll describe the XP version here.

To start msconfig, log on as a Computer Administrator, click Start, Run, and then enter **msconfig** (see Figure 6.12). To run it from the command line, type **start msconfig**. If you are not currently logged on as a Computer Administrator, open Windows Explorer and browse to \Windows\PCHEALTH\ Binaries. Right-click msconfig.exe and enter Administrator credentials.

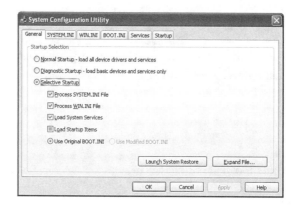

Figure 6.12   msconfig lets you test Windows with and without startup programs.

The program's main window is shown here. On the General tab, you can select what sets of programs Windows starts up at boot time and when you log on:

- boot.ini controls which version of Windows is run at boot time, and what diagnostic options are enabled. (Boot.ini is discussed in detail in Chapter 4.)
- System Services are started when Windows starts.
- Startup Items, discussed earlier in this section, are run when you log on, from Registry values and Startup folder shortcuts.
- win.ini and system.ini entries are also processed when you log on; usually these contain only entries inserted by 16-bit Windows applications.

The Diagnostic Startup mode loads an absolute minimum number of drivers and services. Selective Startup lets you individually control which programs and Services are run at startup and logon.

Individual Services and startup programs can be disabled using check boxes on the other five tabs. For a minimal startup that preserves the ability to perform maintenance, Microsoft recommends that you do *not* disable the following services:

- Cryptographic Services
- Event Log
- Logical Disk Manager
- Help and Support
- Plug and Play

- Remote Procedure Call (RPC)
- System Restore Service
- Windows Management Instrumentation

msconfig does not permanently disable services or delete entries that initiate startup programs. It simply inhibits them temporarily, and in fact when you log on while items are disabled, you will see a dialog box warning you of this. msconfig is meant to be used to identify which services or startup programs are causing specific problems by process of elimination, so that you can then disable or delete the service or program by the usual means, and use msconfig to restore "normal startup" operation.

Antispyware and Antivirus Programs

As I discuss in more detail in Chapter 8, "Protecting and Securing Windows," if your computer is infected with spyware or viruses, you will likely not be able to remove their associated startup programs nor their executable files for more than a few seconds at a time. They're devious. Use a good antispyware or antivirus program to clean and protect your computer.

Be very careful when researching antispyware and antivirus programs on the Internet, however. The Web is filled with bogus advertisements and "reviews" for products that actually *install* spyware and viruses on your computer. Remember that no reputable software vendor would *ever* advertise with a pop-up ad, an offer to scan your computer for free over the Internet, or an ad that looks like a Windows error dialog box saying "Your computer is unprotected!"

Tip

If you do want to have a go at removing spyware manually, boot Windows in Safe mode with Command Prompt; this prevents all Startup programs from running, even the desktop GUI, so you'll have a better chance of deleting the executables and the startup entries. Also, many spyware programs deliberately attack any setup programs they believe to be antispyware installers. If your antispyware program's installer hangs up or crashes, reboot in Safe mode and try again.

Most viruses and spyware programs use several different means to get themselves running when you log on, so, if you find an entry that's starting a dubious program, don't just delete that one entry and assume the problem is fixed.

Internet Explorer

Internet Explorer (IE) is a significant application and, assuming you don't use an alternative browser, you probably open it more than any other application on your computer. It has a little start-up system of its own that you can tune to minimize the time it takes for IE to open and become available.

First off, Microsoft and nearly every computer manufacturer seem to think that it is *their website* that you want to visit every time you open a copy of IE, but they're wrong. You can control where IE goes when it opens. If you really do visit the same site nearly every time you open IE, then set that page to be your start page: visit the page, and then click Tools, Internet Options and under Home Page, click Use Current. If you're like me, though, and head off to visit all sorts of random pages, set IE to display a blank screen when it opens: Click Tools, Internet Options, Use Blank. This will save you a few seconds every time you open IE.

Furthermore, if you type an invalid URL, you probably *don't* want to send the mistyped entry to Microsoft for their recommendation of what you ought to view. Although you're changing IE settings, select the Advanced tab, scroll down to Search from the Address bar, and select Do Not Search from the Address Bar. You may have to reset this option from time to time, as Microsoft occasionally changes it back to their preferred setting (little wonder, when you realize that they *sell* positioning on those helpful search results they offer you).

Also, software vendors and ISPs seem very interested in installing add-on toolbars and "Browser helper" agents into IE, which you pay for with your time every time IE starts and has to load them. Click View, Toolbars and disable any toolbars you don't want or use. Click Tools, Manage Add-Ons to disable any browser plug-ins that you don't recognize, don't want, or don't use.

TweakUI

TweakUI is a program that you can download for free from Microsoft, and it's a veritable Swiss Army knife for Windows configuration. TweakUI lets you configure many Windows features that aren't adjustable from standard Windows dialogs or control panels. I'll give you a tour in this section, but I recommend that you download and install a copy—you may find that something I've passed over as uninteresting is just what you've been looking for.

Obtaining and Installing TweakUI

TweakUI is available in two versions, one designed for Windows XP and Windows Server 2003, and another version that's designed for Windows 2000, Me, 98, and 95. They're installed and opened somewhat differently, so I'll cover both procedures here.

TweakUI PowerToy for Windows XP and Windows Server 2003

To obtain TweakUI for Windows XP Home Edition, Professional, Media Center Edition, and Tablet Edition, as well as Windows Server 2003, visit www.microsoft.com and search for "Powertoys for Windows XP". That should lead you to a page from which you can download the TweakUI PowerToy.

To obtain and install it, follow these steps:

1. From the Microsoft website, download the installer program (it's named `TweakUiPowertoySetup.exe` despite what the link on the web page says) and save it on your desktop or in a temporary folder.

2. You have to run the installer as a Computer Administrator. If you are currently logged on as an administrator, just double-click the installer file. If you're not, right-click the installer file icon, select Run As, select The Following User, and enter a Computer Administrator username and password.

3. After the installer finishes, you can drag `TweakUiPowertoySetup.exe` to the Recycle Bin, or to a shared network folder where you can use it to set up TweakUI on other computers.

The program will be installed in your Start menu under Start, All Programs, Powertoys for Windows XP, TweakUI for Windows XP. I'll delve into its use shortly, after discussing TweakUI for older versions of Windows.

TweakUI Control Panel for Windows 2000, Me, and 9x

The XP version of TweakUI can't be used on earlier versions of Windows. But, you can use the earlier version of TweakUI written for Windows 2000, Me, 98, and 95. To get it, visit www.microsoft.com and search for "tweakui windows 2000". Look for the entry for Tweak UI 1.33. (It's *possible* that a newer version will become available, but I doubt it; the last update was in 2002.)

To obtain and install it, follow these steps:

1. Download file `tweakui.exe` from the Microsoft website, save it to your desktop, and double-click it.

2. The WinZip Self-Extractor dialog appears. In the Unzip To Folder field, enter `c:\tooltemp` and click Unzip. You can now drag `tweakui.exe` to the Recycle Bin.

3. Open My Computer, open the C: drive (you may need to click Show Contents if Windows thinks you're too naïve to be allowed to view a root directory), and open folder `tooltemp`.

4. Right-click file `tweakui.inf` and select Install.

5. When the "About Tweak UI" help window appears, close it.

6. In the Explorer window, click to "Up" folder button to view the C:\ drive contents again. Drag folder `tooltemp` to the Recycle Bin.

Now, you should find the TweakUI icon in your control panel. The tool (shown in Figure 6.13) looks somewhat different than the Windows XP version, but the categories and settings are similar. I won't cover this version of TweakUI in this chapter, but you can quickly view its various tabs to see what it can do.

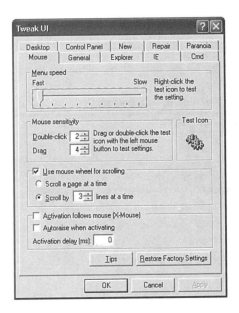

Figure 6.13   Tweak UI for Windows 2000, Me, and 98.

TweakUI Categories and Adjustments

To run TweakUI for Windows XP, click Start, All Programs, Powertoys for Windows XP, TweakUI for Windows XP. Figure 6.14 shows the TweakUI window with all the option subcategories in the left pane opened up for easier viewing. Table 6.2 lists the categories of adjustments TweakUI can make, with a brief description of the items available in each category.

To view the various categories, click on the category name in the tree-view list in the left-hand pane. Several adjustable items are shown in the right-hand pane.

For each item, you can see a fairly detailed description by clicking on the name of the item as opposed to its check box, although in a few cases this also toggles the check box. Where there are several categories of options, you can also click the ? button at the upper-right corner of the window, and then click the item's name. (If the Description text doesn't change, the same description applies to all the displayed items.)

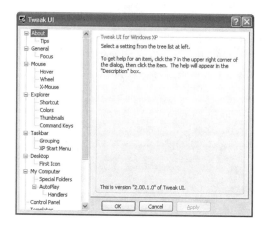

Figure 6.14 TweakUI PowerToy for Windows XP and Windows Server 2003.

Table 6.2 Adjustments Available via TweakUI

Category	Adjustments
About	None
Tips	None; here you can view the tips that Windows offered to show you the first time you logged on, which you didn't read but instead clicked "Don't show these ever again." These tips refer to Windows itself, not TweakUI.
General	Beep-on-error, menu animation and fading
Focus	Focus-stealing prevention, taskbar flashing
Mouse	Speed, double-click, and drag sensitivity
Hover	Balloon-tip hover sensitivity
Wheel	Mouse-wheel sensitivity
X-Mouse	"Activation follows mouse" option
Explorer	Double-click action, scrolling, search behaviors
Shortcut	Visual appearance of shortcut icons
Colors	Colors for compressed, tracked, encrypted files
Thumbnails	Image quality and size for Thumbnail view
Command Keys	Assignments for special keyboard function keys such as Email and speaker volume
Taskbar	Balloon tips
Grouping	Grouping of multiple copies of applications into a single toolbar button
XP Start Menu	Applications that can be added to Frequently Used Programs list
Desktop	Visibility of icons for IE, Recycle Bin, My Computer, Documents, Network Places
First Icon	Order of My Desktop/Computer icons
My Computer	Visibility of icons for Control Panel, Mobile Devices, other special displays
Special Folder	Location of files held for burning to CD

Table 6.2   Continued

Category	Adjustments
AutoPlay	None; reminds you how to enable/disable autoplay and select autoplay applications
Handlers	Autoplay players and actions, associated commands, and media types
Control Panel	Visibility of control panel icons
Templates	Document types for "New" context menu
Internet Explorer	Toolbar background
Search	Search shortcut keywords for Address field
View Source	Program used to display page source
Command Prompt	Filename and directory completion keys, word separators recognized by Ctrl+Left, Right
Logon	Parsing of `autoexec.bat` for SET commands
Unread Mail	Notification of new mail on Welcome screen
Repair	None; repairs missing or incorrect desktop icons

Using TweakUI to...

As you can see in Table 6.2, there are quite a few adjustments you can make with TweakUI. Here are a few that I find interesting, keeping in mind my earlier comments about the trade-off between making Windows easier to use versus the irritation of finding that everyone's computer behaves differently.

Speed Up XP's Menus

Although XP's fading menus are nice, and perhaps easier on the eyes than the older instant-pop-up kind, I don't like waiting for them, and on some computers, they're too slow and jerky. You can eliminate all fades and UI animation from TweakUI's General page by unchecking Enable Combo Box Animation, Enable List Box Animation, Enable Menu Animation, Enable Menu Fading, and Enable Tooltip Fade. Leave Window Animation (that swoopy thing windows do when you minimize and reopen them) checked; it's too helpful to disable.

Set Mouse Sensitivity

On the Mouse and Mouse, Hover pages, I personally like to set the double-click speed as fast as possible, and keep the hover time low (about 10ms). If you have mobility limitations, you can increase the double-click time to give you more time between clicks. If you have difficulty keeping the mouse still, increase the hover sensitivity and hover time.

Set Scroll Wheel Sensitivity

You can modify the sensitivity of your mouse's scroll wheel, should it have one, on the General, Mouse page. If you often have to scroll through *very* long documents, you can make the scroll wheel scroll by whole pages rather than by lines.

Hide or Show Desktop Icons

You can use the standard desktop Display Properties dialog to hide or show icons for My Computer, My Documents, and so on, but TweakUI can also make the Recycle Bin disappear. I prefer to have a completely clean desktop and hide Recycle Bin, because I always press the Del key to delete files anyway. This is a per-user setting.

Hide or Show Document Templates

Document templates come into play when you right-click the desktop or a folder and select New. You can make this context menu more friendly by unchecking the document types you know you'll never use. You can also add new types, if you want. Just create an empty document (or song or drawing or whatever) using the desired application, and click Create in TweakUI to locate the empty file.

Perform Instant Searches from Internet Explorer

You can add a special form of shortcut to Internet Explorer that lets you perform searches from the Address bar. For instance, I defined "gg" as a shortcut for Google searches, so I can type gg `Windows XP tweakui` in the Address field to perform a Google search for the words `Windows XP tweakui`.

To define a prefix, open TweakUI, select Internet Explorer, and Search in TweakUI, and click Create. Enter a desired prefix and the query URL with %s in place of the search words, and click OK to save. The next time you start Internet Explorer, the prefix will be available. Here are some ways you can use this feature:

Google Search: gg `words to find`

> Prefix: gg
> URL: www.google.com/search?q=%s

Yahoo! Search: yy `words to find`

> Prefix: yy
> URL: search.yahoo.com/search?p=%s

United Parcel Service Package Tracking: ups `1z2345678901234567`

> Prefix: ups
> URL: wwwapps.ups.com/WebTracking/processInputRequest?TypeOfInquiryNumber=
>   T&InquiryNumber1=%s

FedEx Package Tracking: fedex `1234567890`

> Prefix: fedex
> URL: www.fedex.com/Tracking?tracknumbers=%s

To design your own prefix URL, perform a search, take the URL from the results page, and replace the query words you had typed in with %s. This search method only works with websites that transmit the query string in the URL; not all of them do.

Enable Filename and Directory Completion

If you use the command prompt a lot, you can save a lot of typing if you take advantage of Filename and Directory completion. When you're entering a command line, by default, if you press the Tab key, Windows will take whatever you've typed so far and perform a directory search to see whether any file or folder names match. If one or more does, Windows finishes typing it for you; successive Tabs scroll through other matching files. You can designate a separate key to be used only to match folder names using TweakUI's Command Prompt page. I use Ctrl+D.

Most Windows settings (and in fact, all of the settings made by TweakUI) are controlled by entries in the Windows Registry, and you may run into articles on various websites that tell you how to adjust many of the same settings by editing the Registry. It's neither necessary nor advisable to do so when a nifty, comprehensive graphical tool like TweakUI can do the job. However, there may on rare occasion be times when you need to make Registry changes directly. The next section covers this process.

Other Useful PowerToys

Besides the TweakUI PowerToy, you may want to download and install some or all of the others. I've found several of them to be very helpful:

- *Open Command Window Here*—This PowerToy adds an "Open Command Window Here" context menu option on file system folders, giving you a quick way to open a command window (cmd.exe) preset to use the selected folder.

- *Alt-Tab Replacement*—With this PowerToy, when you press Alt+Tab to switch between applications, in addition to seeing the icon of the application window you are switching to, you will also see a preview of the window and its contents. This helps particularly when multiple sessions of an application are open.

Microsoft has an additional tweaking tool for Windows XP Media Center Edition 2005 and later called TweakMCE. You can get it by searching www.microsoft.com for "Tweak MCE." It lets you alter remote control settings, skip and replay times, user interface options, and more. It also lets you adjust MCE for plasma and LCD displays.

The Windows Registry

The Windows XP Registry is the central repository in which Windows and most Windows applications store configuration information, such as hardware settings, software configuration, licensing and registration data, associations between filename extensions and applications, and user preferences.

For most of your daily tasks with Windows XP, you will never need to touch the Registry. Almost everything you'll ever need to configure that shows up in the Registry can be handled through a Control Panel applet, application option dialogs, or, as discussed in the last section, TweakUI. But, there are some adjustments that can only be made through direct Registry settings, so you should know the basics of safe Registry editing.

There are hundreds of websites offering advice about performance improvements you can gain by altering Registry settings. My advice is to *ignore these entirely*. My experience is that much such advice is either out of date, specific to particular situations (but not yours), or flat-out wrong. (As a perfect example, while writing the previous section, I tried a Registry hack that purported to make the TweakUI XP Power Toy appear in the Control Panel, and it did do that, but it also made Explorer crash every time I clicked on a Control Panel icon.) There are, however, times when Registry editing is necessary; usually on the advice of a Microsoft Knowledge Base article, tech support person, or a helpful book like this one.

Structure of the Registry

The Registry is a specialized database of *values*, which can be compared to files, that are stored in a hierarchical structure of *keys*, which can be compared to folders. There are five *top-level keys*, under which all of the Registry's keys reside. Logically, then, each top-level key contains a plethora of hierarchically related keys, subkeys, values, and data. The top-level keys (in order of appearance) are as follows:

- **HKEY_CLASSES_ROOT** (HKCR)—This contains file association data. For example, when you click on a file ending in .TXT, the .TXT subkey contains the information that tells Windows to display the file using NOTEPAD.EXE. HKEY_CLASSES_ROOT builds itself by combining the values from HKEY_LOCAL_MACHINE\Software\Classes, which contains systemwide default application associations, and from HKEY_CURRENT_USER\Software\Classes, which contains user-specified preferences for application associations. If any keys appearing in both locations are in conflict, the settings specified under HKEY_CURRENT_USER will win. HKCR also contains the configuration information for COM and ActiveX objects and document type/MIME type associations.

- **HKEY_CURRENT_USER (HKCU)**—This is a "virtual" top-level key that actually references the subsection of HKEY_USERS pertaining to the currently logged-on user.

- **HKEY_LOCAL_MACHINE (HKLM)**—This stores all hardware and machine-specific setup information for your computer. For example, this key lists every device driver to load, all of your hardware's settings, all services and service configurations, and any software setup and configuration data that is common to all users.

- **HKEY_USERS (HKU)**—This contains a subkey for each user of the computer. Under each user's key, Windows stores user-specific information such as file locations, display preferences, software preferences, and recently accessed file lists. These keys are only loaded when the associated user is logged on.

- **HKEY_CURRENT_CONFIG (HKCC)**—This is another "virtual" top-level key whose contents are actually the contents of HKEY_LOCAL_MACHINE\System\CurrentControlSet\Hardware Profiles\ Current. This key is the selected hardware configuration specific to your current hardware profile.

Note

When referencing the Registry via a script or command-line utility—as well as in much of the documentation available for the Registry—the parent Registry hives are often referred to only by their three- or four-letter standard abbreviations. The accepted abbreviations are listed in parentheses behind their associated full names in the preceding list.

Physically, the Registry's data are stored in a small collection of files called *hives*. For each hive file there is corresponding file called a *change log*, which protects against corruption from system crashes. Most hive files can be found in folder %systemroot%\System32\Config.The Registry hive used to store per-user preference settings is named ntuser.dat (with corresponding change log file NTUSER.DAT.LOG), and is stored in each user's profile folder, which is by default %systemdrive%\ Documents and Settings*username*. This hive's data is loaded as a subkey under top-level key HKEY_USERS when a user logs on, and the same data appears under top-level key HKEY_CURRENT_USER when the user is the current primary user.

Another file, UsrClass.dat (and UsrClass.dat.LOG), can be found a bit deeper under each user profile in %systemdrive%\Documents and Settings*username*\Local Settings\Application Data\Microsoft\Windows. This second hive holds the list of keys that *add to* and *override* systemwide settings that are specified in the HKEY_CLASSES_ROOT key. This feature makes it possible for users to have individualized document type/application associations (which used to be applied throughout the system) and for individual users to have customized application and ActiveX/COM object installations.

Note

You can see a complete listing of the full paths to all currently loaded Registry hives under **HKEY_LOCAL_MACHINE** SYSTEM\CurrentControlSet\Control\hivelist.

Backing Up and Restoring the Registry

Before diving into Registry modifications, I'll talk about backing them up. Every computer book I've seen (including those I've written) stresses these facts:

1. There is no Undo key in the Registry Editor.

2. Improper changes to the Registry can keep Windows from booting, or can make subsystems fail to work.

3. You should always perform a system backup, or at least back up the entire Registry before you make *any* changes to the Registry.

In the spirit of full disclosure, I have to tell you that items 1 and 2 are completely true, and I've never followed the advice of item 3 myself. Maybe I'm an idiot, maybe the warnings are a bit too strident, or maybe it's something in between. But, especially with Windows XP's System Restore feature to do all of the work for you, there's really no harm in taking a few extra moments to protect yourself against a preventable bad outcome.

You can back up the Registry in Windows XP in five ways: You can back it up as part of a regular disk backup; you can selectively back up portions of the Registry by exporting the keys with the Registry Editor; you can create a System Restore Point; you can use the command-line application REG.EXE; or you can use a special-purpose Registry backup program.

Registry Backup and Recovery with Windows Backup

As discussed in Chapter 4, Windows XP includes a simple, straightforward backup and restore utility called NTBackup that you can use to back up your entire system, including data files, system files, and Registry files. (NTBackup is not installed by default on XP Home Edition; see Chapter 5 for instructions on installing it from your Setup CD.)

To back up only the Registry, follow these steps:

1. Click Start, Run, and type **ntbackup** in the open box. Click OK.

2. If the backup utility starts in the wizard interface, click the Advanced Mode option in the body of the main paragraph to take you out of the wizard and display the tabbed Backup Utility interface.

3. Select the Backup tab and select the System State option in the tree in the left pane. The System State is composed of the Registry, the boot files, the Active Directory files, and the certificates.

4. Enter a backup filename in the designated box. You should see something similar to what is displayed in Figure 6.15. It's best if you save this backup in another computer's shared network folder, or on a removable disk.

5. Click the Start Backup button. You are then prompted for a backup description. Select the option to Replace the Data on the Media with This Backup.

6. Click the Advanced button and uncheck the option to Automatically Backup System Protected Files with the System State. This ensures that you're grabbing only a backup of the Registry and cuts your backup file down from 1GB to somewhere between 10 and 50MB, depending on your Registry size. Click OK, and then click Start Backup.

7. The Backup Progress dialog displays. When the job completes, click Close.

To restore the Registry from a backup made with NTBackup, follow these steps:

Caution

Do not test this procedure out on a properly functioning system. This is a drastic procedure meant only for recovering from Registry-related disasters and should not be attempted unless absolutely necessary, or if you are working on a lab machine specifically set up to test this process.

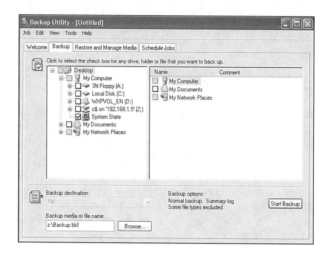

Figure 6.15 The tabbed interface of the Windows XP Backup Utility application.

1. Click Start, Run, and type **ntbackup** in the open box. Click OK.

2. If the backup utility starts in the wizard interface, click the Advanced Mode option in the body of the main paragraph to take you out of the wizard and to display the tabbed Backup Utility interface.

3. Select the Restore and Manage Media tab.

4. Select Tools, Options, Always Replace the File on My Computer because your Registry files already exist. Click OK.

5. In the right pane, expand the list of catalogued backups until you find the one you want to restore. If you do not see your backup job in the list, click Tools, Catalog a Backup File, and enter the location for the backup file in the resulting box. Select the applicable backup set and select System State in the left pane.

6. Click Start Restore. A dialog warns you that System State is always restored to the current location. Because that's what you want to happen, click OK.

7. Click OK on the Advanced Options dialog.

8. Confirm the proper name and location of the backup set, and then click OK.

9. When the restore completes, you must restart the system to successfully load the restored Registry files.

Exporting and Importing Registry Files with the Registry Editor

The Registry Editor that is included with Windows XP allows you to selectively export anything from a single subkey to an entire Registry key. If you're performing significant modifications, this is a good way to ensure that you can figure out what the original values were if you need to roll back your changes.

To back up a key including all subkeys and values, follow these steps:

1. Click Start, Run, type **regedit**, and click OK.

2. Select the key you want to back up from the list in the left pane.

3. Select File, Export.

4. In the Common File dialog, select a directory and enter the filename where you would like to save the exported Registry entries.

Caution

The default extension for an exported Registry file is `.REG`. Double-clicking on a `.REG` file automatically imports the file into the Registry after providing a single confirmation box. To prevent too-easy accidental Registry imports, I suggest you save exported Registry files as text files, with the `.TXT` extension.

5. Select Selected Branch in the Export Range option box, and click Save.

Because this is a plain-text file, you can open it in Notepad to see the contents. I often use this method to deploy changes to several computers: I make limited Registry changes on a single system, export the change as a `.REG` file, edit the file down to just the modified entries, move the file to a network folder, and import the file on other machines.

Importing a Registry file exported through the Registry Editor is just as straightforward as exporting:

1. Click Start, Run, type **regedit**, and click OK.

2. Select File, Import.

3. In the Common File dialog, enter the filename containing the data you want to import.

4. Select Open.

Importing a Registry setting through the Registry Editor overwrites existing keys or values and adds missing keys or values, but it does *not* delete extra keys or values that are not contained in the Registry file. However, you can use a Registry file to explicitly specify subkeys or values to delete. I'll show you how in the section "Deploying Registry Settings with `.REG` Files," later in this chapter.

Note

Remember when I suggested changing the extension of the previous Registry file from `.REG` to `.TXT` so you wouldn't accidentally import the settings? You can use the inverse to enable a two-step, REGEDIT-free Registry file import. Simply rename the Registry file you want to import with a `.REG` extension. Then double-click the Registry file to quickly import the contents of the file into your Registry. You can't back out of the import after you've confirmed it exists, so ensure you know what you're importing before you run the **REG** file.

Backing Up with System Restore

A System Restore Point allows you to restore your computer to a previous state, rolling back changes to device drivers, system files, and the Registry. By manually requesting that Windows create a Restore Point before you forage into the Registry, you can make changes and easily roll them back if something doesn't work.

▶▶ For instructions on creating and restoring a Restore Point, see "System Restore," p. 220.

Command-Line Backup and Restore Using reg.exe

A command-line Registry manipulation tool called `reg.exe` is included with Windows XP. This tool is useful for selectively backing up or restoring specific Registry subkeys. Numerous functions are available in `reg.exe`, including Registry exporting and importing.

Note

You can do quite a few things with **reg**. Use the command **reg /?** for a complete usage syntax of the command.

To back up a Registry key using reg.exe, use the following syntax:

```
reg export rootkey\subkey filename
```

For rootkey, you can use the abbreviations HKLM, HKCU, HKCR, HKU, or HKCC. Subkey must be the full name of a Registry key under the selected root. Filename is the name of the file to which you want to save the exported data.

To restore a Registry key using reg, use the following syntax:

```
reg import filename
```

When importing, filename can be any file created by reg export, from the regedit Registry Editor's Export command, or created manually with a text editor.

Editing the Registry

The primary interface to the Registry, the Registry Editor, displays a representation of the Registry using an interface that is similar to the familiar layout of folders and files as viewed through Windows Explorer. To run it, click Start, Run and enter **regedit**.

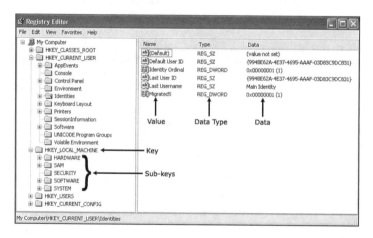

Figure 6.16 The Registry Editor: unfiltered access to your system's configuration database.

Figure 6.16 shows a Registry Editor window. The left pane contains the five top-level keys. The status bar along the bottom displays the full path of the currently selected key. I've expanded the HKEY_CURRENT_USER and HKEY_LOCAL_MACHINE keys to show the first round of subkeys beneath each. The right pane shows values assigned to the key selected in the left-hand pane.

Just as a disk's folders can contain subfolders, and in each there may be files as well, Registry keys can contain subkeys, and each key can contain *values* as well. Most Registry editing tasks consist of locating one or two existing values and changing them. Occasionally, you will need to add new values or subkeys; it is impossible for you to add a new top-level Registry key.

The five main value data types in the Registry are as follows:

- **REG_DWORD**—This is a single hexadecimal or decimal number. You can select decimal or hexadecimal display when you're editing a particular value.

- **REG_BINARY**—This is a block of binary data displayed in the REGEDIT interface in hexadecimal format.

- **REG_SZ**—This is a plain-text string of alphanumeric characters.

- **REG_MULTI_SZ**—This is similar to REG_SZ, but it can contain multiple lines of text.

- **REG_EXPAND_SZ**—This is similar to REG_SZ, but the string can contain environment variables such as %SYSTEMROOT% or %USERNAME%. When a program requests such a value from Windows, the environment values are automatically substituted in before the program sees the data.

There are other data types, but they are rarely encountered, and never need to be edited by hand.

To open the Registry Editor, click Start, Run, type **regedit** in the Open field, and click OK. You can dig through the top-level keys into subkeys in the left pane. Values associated with each key are displayed in the right pane.

To change the data associated with a value, double-click the value and change the value data in the resulting dialog. For numeric (DWORD) values, you can select a decimal or hexadecimal display; use whichever mode is more convenient for you.

Keep in mind that all changes are final. There is no Undo. If you delete a key or value, the only way to put it back is to manually re-add it or restore it from backup.

Caution

Here's that strident warning again: Editing the Registry can change the configuration of your system. Therefore, by nature, it is a potentially dangerous task. Do not directly manipulate the Registry when using a GUI setting can do the same job, and never blindly fiddle with the Registry unless you are aware of what the potential consequences are.

Some Registry-based settings take effect immediately; others require a restart of an associated application or a reboot of the system.

Editing the Registry Remotely

If you need to edit the Registry of a system other than your own, you can connect to a Registry over the network. To perform this function on a Workgroup network, three conditions must be met:

- The remote computer must have an account with the same logon name and password as the account you're currently using.

- The account on the remote computer must be a Computer Administrator account.

- Simple File Sharing must be disabled on the remote computer. This means that the remote computer cannot be running Windows XP Home Edition, but it can be running Windows XP Professional with Simple File Sharing disabled. Windows 2000 Professional or a Server version are editable as well.

If your network meets these conditions, in the Registry Editor, simply click File, Connect Network Registry, and enter the computer name for the remote system in the resulting dialog. The remote computer's HKEY_CURRENT_USER section will not be displayed.

Editing a Hive File

At some point you may find that you need to edit the Registry of a Windows system that cannot boot. To edit a dead system's Registry, you can install its boot drive in another computer and use that computer's Registry Editor to mount and edit the Registry files on the added disk. Once the hard drive from the dead computer is running in a new computer, follow these steps:

1. Log on as a Computer Administrator and start regedit.

2. Select HKEY_USERS in the left pane, and from the menu select File, Load Hive.

3. In the Load Hive (open file) dialog, click My Computer, open the drive that came from the dead computer, and browse to the file corresponding to the Registry section that you need to edit (see Table 6.3). Click Open.

4. For a key name, enter **xxx** or something clearly not normal.

5. Browse into key xxx and make the necessary changes, as shown in Figure 6.17.

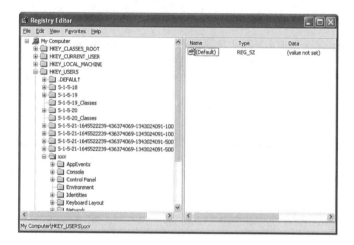

Figure 6.17 Editing a Registry hive mounted from another computer's disk.

6. Hightlight xxx under HKEY_USERS in the left pane and from the menu select File, Unload Hive. Confirm by checking Yes.

Now you can shut down Windows and return the hard disk to the original computer.

Table 6.3   Hive Files for Various Registry Sections

Registry Section	Hive File
HKEY_CLASSES_ROOT	\windows\system32\config\software (look at subkey Classes)
HKEY_CURRENT_USER	\Documents and Settings\username\ntuser.dat
HKEY_LOCAL_MACHINE\Hardware	(none, this is created dynamically when Windows boots)
HKEY_LOCAL_MACHINE\SAM	\windows\system32\config\sam
HKEY_LOCAL_MACHINE\Security	\windows\system32\config\security
HKEY_LOCAL_MACHINE\Software	\windows\system32\config\software
HKEY_LOCAL_MACHINE\System	\windows\system32\config\system

(Alternatively, if the disk in the dead system has more than one partition, you can leave the disk in the original computer, and install a fresh copy of Windows into an alternative partition. Boot that copy of Windows and locate and edit the hive files from the original partition.)

Deploying Registry Settings

When a Registry change has to be made in several computers, it can be impractical to visit each one and manually make the changes. On a corporate domain network, Registry settings can easily be deployed through Active Directory. If don't have a domain network, there are still some ways to quickly install Registry changes in multiple computers.

Deploying Registry Settings with .REG Files

The easiest method for distributing Registry settings is through the use of a `.REG` file. You saw how to export and import `.REG` files earlier in this chapter, in the section "Exporting and Importing Registry Files with the Registry Editor" (**page 262**), but in that section you were exporting an entire Registry key. Let's take a look at using `.REG` files to deploy a limited group of settings.

In the earlier example, you selected the top-level Registry key and exported the entire thing to a `.REG` file. If you viewed the resulting file in the Registry Editor, you probably noticed fairly significant and unruly content. That is because the `.REG` file contained all keys, subkeys, values, and data in the branch of the Registry that you exported. Let's manually create a `.REG` file that adds a key and some values to `HKEY_CURRENT_USER`. Create the following file in a plain-text editor, such as Notepad:

```
Windows Registry Editor Version 5.00

[HKEY_CURRENT_USER\My Settings]
@="this is the default value"
"ValueName1"="String Value"
"ValueName2"="String Value"
"ValueName3"=dword:0000002a
```

Save this file as `mysettings.reg`. To import the settings, follow these steps:

1. Double-click the `mysettings.reg` file.

2. You see a pop-up confirmation message that asks `Are you sure you want to add the information in c:\mysettings.reg to the registry?` Click Yes to import the file.

3. You then receive a confirmation box stating `Information in C:\mysettings.reg has been successfully entered into the registry`. Click OK.

After you import the `.REG` file, open the Registry Editor (Start, Run, regedit). Expand `HKEY_CURRENT_USER`, and you should see a subkey named `My Settings` that contains values as displayed in Figure 6.18.

Note

Importing a `.REG` file by double-clicking it is pretty straightforward, but what about those two confirmation boxes? What if you don't want your users to know that you are importing Registry settings? And what's more, you don't want them having an opportunity to reject the setting by clicking No on the confirmation dialog. Fortunately, you can silently install a Registry file from the command line using the following command:

```
regedit /s mysettings.reg
```

Add a line like the preceding to a logon or startup script, and you can quickly, easily, and silently deploy Registry settings to users and computers throughout your environment.

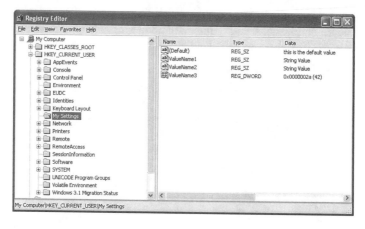

Figure 6.18   The Registry key and values created by `mysettings.reg`.

Deploying Registry settings using `.REG` files overwrites existing keys, values, or data and adds missing keys, values, or data. `.REG` files do *not* delete extra keys, values, or data that are in the Registry but not in the Registry file. To delete information in the Registry, you must use `regedit`, remove the key using a script (as demonstrated in the next section), or explicitly define the keys or values you want to delete within the `.REG` file. To demonstrate, I show you how to manually create two `.REG` files to manipulate values created under the `HKEY_CURRENT_USER\My Settings` key created earlier in this section.

First, create the following file in a plain-text editor, such as Notepad, and save the file as `WhackOneValue.reg`:

```
Windows Registry Editor Version 5.00

[HKEY_CURRENT_USER\My Settings]
"ValueName2"=-
```

Notice the minus (-) sign where the data normally goes for the value. This directs the Registry Editor to delete the associated name and data pair when you run or import the `.REG` file. After you run `WhackOneValue.reg`, open the Registry Editor. You no longer find ValueName2 under `HKEY_CURRENT_USER\My Settings`. Note that if you had the Registry Editor open when you ran the script, you might need to press F5 to refresh the display before seeing the effect of the script.

Next, create the following file in Notepad and save the file as `WhackMySettings.reg`:

```
Windows Registry Editor Version 5.00

[-HKEY_CURRENT_USER\My Settings]
```

Notice the minus (-) sign in front of `HKEY_CURRENT_USER`. This directs the Registry Editor to delete the following key when you run or import the `.REG` file. After you run `WhackMySettings.reg`, open the Registry Editor. You no longer find the `My Settings` key under `HKEY_CURRENT_USER`. Again, if you had Registry Editor open when you ran the script, you might need to press F5 to refresh the display before seeing the effect of the script.

Deploying Registry Settings with VBScript

Managing the Registry with VBScript is amazingly straightforward using the `RegRead`, `RegWrite`, and `RegDelete` methods against the `WScript.Shell` object.

Note

For full downloadable Windows Scripting Host documentation in the Windows Help File format, see the Microsoft Developers Network Scripting resources at http://msdn.microsoft.com/scripting.

The following code listing creates a Registry subkey named My Settings under the HKEY_CURRENT_USER key. The script uses the RegWrite method to populate the default value, plus three additional values under the new subkey. Each new value is populated with data. After populating the key, values, and data, the script displays the data values by reading the Registry with the RegRead method. Enter the following lines of code into a plain-text editor, such as Notepad, and save the file as mysettings.vbs.

```
Set myReg = CreateObject("WScript.Shell")
key = "HKEY_CURRENT_USER\My Settings"

'Write the keys
myReg.RegWrite key & "\",                "this is the default value"
myReg.RegWrite key & "\Boolean Value", "True"
myReg.RegWrite key & "\String Value",  "Upgrading and Repairing", "REG_SZ"
myReg.RegWrite key & "\DWORD Value",    42, "REG_DWORD"

'Read the keys
WScript.Echo "Default Value: " & myReg.RegRead(key & "\")
WScript.Echo "Boolean Value: " & myReg.RegRead(key & "\Boolean Value")
WScript.Echo "String Value:  " & myReg.RegRead(key & "\String Value")
WScript.Echo "DWORD Value:   " & myReg.RegRead(key & "\DWORD Value")
set myReg = Nothing
```

After you type the command cscript mysettings.vbs, open the Registry Editor (Start, Run, regedit). Expand HKEY_CURRENT_USER, and you should see a subkey named My Settings, containing values created by the script.

To demonstrate the use of the RegDelete method—and to clean up the useless Registry key created previously—create a script file named delkey.vbs containing the following five lines.

```
'Delete the keys
Set myReg = CreateObject("WScript.Shell")
key = "HKEY_CURRENT_USER\My Settings"
myReg.RegDelete key & "\"

Set myReg = Nothing
```

After you run the command cscript whackmysettings.vbs, open the Registry Editor. You should no longer see the My Settings key under HKEY_CURRENT_USER. If you had Registry Editor opened when you ran the script, you might need to press F5 to refresh the display before seeing the effect of the script.

Because startup, shutdown, logon, and logoff scripts can all be written using VBScript, the previous samples give you an easy way to deploy scripted changes to the Registry of any systems on which you control the related script policies.

Caution

Often, deploying settings through the startup, shutdown, logon, or logoff scripts is your only way to distribute Registry edits now that .REG and .VBS files effectively function as a sort of poor man's virus for virus authors who can't afford compilers. You definitely don't want to get your users in the habit of opening .VBS or .REG attachments from their

(continues)

email. In fact, many corporate email scanners automatically delete attachments of these types, and Outlook XP automatically blocks both types of attachments. Therefore, a user might not even be able to open or run `.VBS` or `.REG` files if you don't deploy them through the system scripts.

Managing Windows Services

Services are programs that are started independently of your logging on. For the most part, they are started up in a specific sequence when Windows boots up, and they perform their jobs without directly interacting with the keyboard, mouse, or display. Services are used to perform such tasks as indexing your hard disk for faster searching, managing various types of storage devices, providing networking functions and more. On other operating systems, they might be called *daemons* or *background processes*. Services are described in detail in Chapter 4. Here, I'll cover the tools used to manage them.

Managing Services with the GUI

Figure 6.19 shows the Services management tool, from which you can manage the services available on your computer. (The services themselves are described in Chapter 4.) You must be logged on as a Computer Administrator, or on Windows XP, as a Power User.

To open the Services management tool, right-click My Computer and select Manage; then in the left-hand pane, open Services and Applications and select Services. Alternatively, you can type `services.msc` at the command prompt or the run dialog.

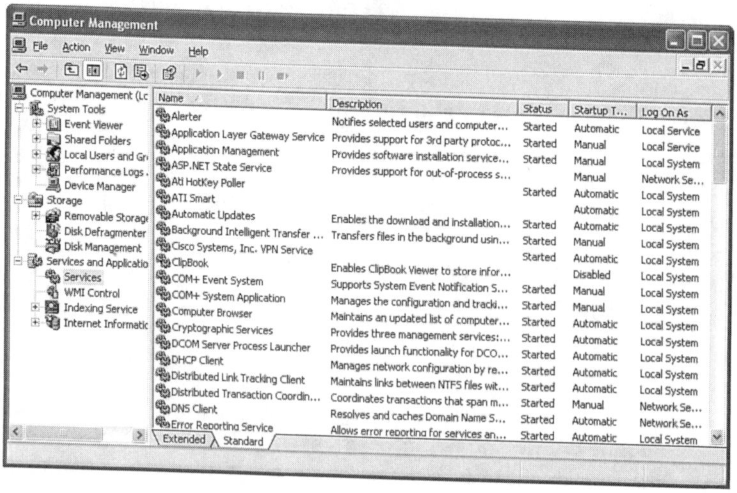

Figure 6.19   The Services management tool allows you to monitor and change the status of services.

The columns in the management display list the name of each service, a description of its purpose, its current status, its startup type, and its logon account. The Status column can display any of the following values:

(blank)	The service is not running (is stopped).
Starting	The service is starting up but is not yet operational.
Started	The service is operational.
Stopping	The service is in the process of shutting down.

Pausing   The service is in the process of suspending its activity.

Paused   The service is running, but has been instructed to suspend activity.

Continuing   The service is resuming normal activity after having been paused.

The startup type can have any of the following values:

Automatic   The service is started automatically as Windows boots up. Services with no dependencies are started first, followed by any services that depend on them.

Manual   The service is not started unless requested to by an application, another service, or by a Services management tool.

Disabled   The service has been designated as disabled and will not be started under any circumstances.

Services can run in the context of a user account in order to control the privileges they have; for best security, a service should run with only the privileges it absolutely needs and no more, in order to limit the damage it could do should it crash or get compromised by a hacker. Most of the standard services run under the Local System context, which means they have total privileges, but some are run using the special built-in Network Service or Local Service user accounts. These accounts do not appear in the account manager. Other special services could conceivably be configured to standard user accounts.

Note

Each installed service registers with Windows the names of any services that it requires to get its job done. These are called *dependencies*, and as it starts services during the boot process, Windows first starts services that have no dependencies, and only when depended-upon services are operational does it start up dependent services. This process is automatic.

Current Status and Startup Options

To manage or monitor a service, double-click it in the Services list, or right-click and select Properties (see Figure 6.20).

On the General tab, shown in Figure 6.20, you can perform the following maintenance tasks:

- Start, stop, pause, resume, or restart the service. Restarting a service stops it and then immediately starts it again. It's like "rebooting" the service. This can be especially useful in cases where you need to restart a service that either is not working, which has failed and is consuming 100% of the CPU doing nothing (I have seen the Printer Spooler service do this), or is working with corrupt data (for example, restarting the DNS Client clears stale entries from the local DNS cache).

- View the command line that is used to run the service. You will see that many services use the program svchost.exe; this is a "shell" program that interacts with the service management system. The real work is performed by a Dynamic Link Library (DLL) whose name is stored in the Registry. See Chapter 4 for more information on svchost.exe.

- Set the startup type to automatic, manual, or disabled. This can be useful in cases where you want to prevent a service from starting for one reason or another.

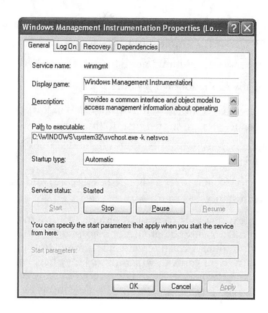

Figure 6.20   A Service's Properties page lets you specify startup, logon, and failure recovery settings.

Caution

Disabling a service also disables any dependent services, which you can view using the Dependencies tab.

Note

Some services don't accept the Stop or Restart functions; they'll be grayed out. If such a service is not functioning correctly, you will probably have to restart Windows itself to get it going again.

Log On Account

On the Log On tab, you can define the login account used for the service. This is most useful when you are configuring additional third-party services or services for a very specific task where you want to confine the service to an account that has only the specific privileges it requires to perform its function. Do not change the logon account for standard services.

Note

If you specify an account and password to be used by a service, and later change the account's password, you must come back to the Services snap-in and re-enter the logon password for the service.

From this tab you can also specify whether the service is to be run in each of the computer's hardware profiles.

Crash Recovery Options

The Recovery tab, shown in Figure 6.21, lets you specify actions to be taken if the service fails, that is, it crashes or stops unexpectedly. The options for the first, second, and subsequent crashes can be set separately, and the following choices are available:

Figure 6.21   The Recovery tab lets you determine what Windows should do if the service crashes.

Take No Action—A note will be written to the Event Log, but that's all. The service will be left unavailable.

Restart the Service—Windows will attempt to restart the service.

Run a Program—Windows will run the program specified in the properties dialog that can take any action you want.

Restart the Computer—Windows will shut down and restart.

In addition, you can specify the time frame over which successive failures are considered sequential.

This configuration scheme is meant primarily for servers or computers that run unattended and perform some critical function. It might be reasonable to attempt to restart a service once, but if it fails again shortly afterward, something is probably seriously wrong, and it may make more sense than to try something else, perhaps reboot Windows, or perhaps run a program that invokes a repair procedure or sends a text page to a network administrator.

View Dependencies

Finally, on the Dependencies tab, you can view the service's dependency tree. This is the list of other services that a given service requires to do its job, and the list of services that depend on this service to do their jobs. If you start a service that has dependencies, the other services will be started first. If you shut down a service that has dependents, the dependents will be shut down first.

Managing Services on Another Computer

Network managers frequently have to manage large numbers of computers, and it's often inefficient to have to physically visit them when there's trouble. Like most Windows management utilities, the Services management console can request to manage services for a remote computer over the network.

To manage another computer's services using the GUI, right-click the icon at the top of the list in the upper-left pane of the management window (it will be labeled Computer Management or Services, depending on how you opened the window), and select Connect to Another Computer. Enter the name of the other computer, or click Browse to select it from your workgroup or domain. You must have an account on the remote computer with the same login name and password as the account you're currently using, or you must have a domain logon valid on that computer.

You can also manage services on other computers using the sc command discussed in the next section.

Managing Services from the Command Line

You can manage services through the command-line interface as well as the GUI; in some cases, the command line can be faster and easier.

There are two ways to do this. The first is with the net command. The commands net start *servicename* and net stop *servicename* start and stop a service on the local computer. If the service name has spaces in it, you must enclose the name in quotation marks ("), and you can specify either the service's Display Name (the name listed in the Services management display), or the shorter Service Key name.

◄◄ For a list of Service Key names, see Table 4.5 on p. 143.

These commands can be used to quickly and easily restart a service. For example, if you had recently accessed a network host by its DNS name and the host's IP address is now changed, or if the host was offline but is now online, your computer's DNS cache will still hang on to the out-of-date address or the failure result for several minutes. Restarting the DNS service will make it discard the old, incorrect information and refresh itself. You can do this with

```
net stop dns
net start dns
```

A more powerful command-line service management utility is sc, which can manage services on other computers, change service settings, and list information about installed services.

However, to manage services with sc, you must know the service's "Service Key name", which is usually not the name displayed in the Services management window. You can use sc to get a list of all installed services and their Service Key names, or you can refer to Table 4.8 for the names of common Windows services; the key names are printed in boldface.

Here are some sample uses of the sc utility:

■ Print a list of all services installed on the local computer, including their Automatic/Manual/Disabled setting and their Service Key names (labeled SERVICE_NAME)

```
sc query
```

■ Print a list of services installed on another computer named otherhost:

```
sc \\otherhost query
```

- Restart the IIS web server service on computer otherhost

```
sc \\otherhost w3svc stop
sc \\otherhost w3svc start
```

To get a listing of sc's full command syntax, type these three lines in a command prompt window:

```
sc ? >x.txt
y
notepad x.txt
```

(You will not be prompted for the y line.) Open the Windows Help and Support Center and search for sc for details on each subcommand.

Running Your Own Program as a Service

Developing a Windows service program requires a fair bit of effort and programming skill. In addition to writing code to do whatever job the service has to do, you must add extra code that lets the service program communicate with the Windows Service Manager, so that the service can be started, stopped, and can communicate its status and dependencies to the manager.

Still, in some cases it's nice to be able to have a program run when Windows boots up and have it stay running 24×7, whether you're logged on or not, and no matter what else is going on. And, in fact you can do this, using a utility program from the Windows 2000 Resource Kit that runs a program of your choice as if it were a service; the utility takes care of communicating with the Service manager, and runs your program using a specified command-line when the service manager starts it up. Your program can be a Windows application, command-line program, batch file, Windows Script Host script, database application, or a program written in another scripting language such as Perl. I've used this method to create a web server database back-end written in the FoxPro database language, and an interface to the SpamAssassin spam-filtering program written in Perl.

A program that is to act as a service needs to function with no interaction from the keyboard, mouse, or screen. To communicate with the outside world, it can create and listen on network sockets, or it can scan a specified directory every so many seconds for the appearance of files. It should *not* run in an endless loop waiting for work to do, or it will slow performance of your computer. Instead, it should use Windows synchronization tools like Events, or at least it should "sleep" for periods of time in order not to consume any CPU power when it's idle. Test the program from the command line to be sure it works before trying to run it as a service.

Then, when you are ready to install it as a service, follow these steps.

Caution

Running a program as a service this way has some risks. In fact, the Windows AntiSpyware program reports the presence of Srvany as a risk every time it runs. If a hacker replaces the program that the service manager starts up, the bogus program will run with whatever privileges the service would have run with. You should follow the steps listed here to ensure that your service is safe from hacking.

1. Log on as a Computer Administrator.

2. Download the Windows 2000 Server or Windows Server 2003 Resource Kit Tools package from microsoft.com, as discussed in Appendix A. Install the package.

3. Click Start, All Programs, and find the new Resource Kit Tools entry. Open the Resource Kit Tools help file, and search for srvany. On the srvany page, there are several links to other pages that you'll need to read: Installing Srvany, Running an Application as a Service, Starting and Stopping a Service, and Srvany Notes. You may want to print these documents.

4. Create a special user account to be used just for your service, and set a password for it.

5. Create a special folder for the service's files on a drive that is formatted with the NTFS file system (do *not* use a FAT-formatted disk). For these instructions, I'll assume that the folder is `C:\myservice`.

6. In the Resource Kit tools folder under Program Files, locate files `instsrv.exe` and `srvany.exe`. Copy `instsrv.exe`, `srvany.exe`, the program file(s) for your service, and any data files it needs to the service's folder (`c:\myservice` in this example).

7. Set NTFS permissions for this folder so that only Administrator and the new user account have access to it. Use the Advanced button to reset permissions on all objects in the folder. (Simple File Sharing must be disabled in order to set permissions.)

8. Open a command prompt window and change to the service's folder, for example, with `cd /d c:\myservice`.

9. Choose a name for your service; it must be different than any other service, and should describe in a word or two what the service does.

10. Follow the instructions for installing `srvany` as a service, and for creating the `Application` and `AppParameters` values that specify your program and its command line parameters. Table 6.4 lists the correct Application values for various types of programs; replace the filename in italics with the appropriate filename for your program.

11. Create the `AppDirectory` value and set it to the full path of your service's folder.

12. When the service has been installed, open the Services management tool, locate your service, and use the Log On tab to specify that it's to run under the special user account.

Now, you should be able to start the service and press Ctrl+Alt+Del to see that the associated program appears in the Windows Task Manager's Processes display. If it doesn't, it may be exiting prematurely, or there may be a problem starting the service. In the latter case there should be a record in the Event log.

Table 6.4   Application and AppParameters Values for Various Types of Service Programs

Program Type	Registry Values
Standard `.EXE` AppParameters *any needed parameters*	Application *myprogram.exe*
Batch file AppParameters `/c` *mybatch.bat*	Application `c:\windows\system32\cmd.exe`
Script AppParameters *myscript.vbs*	Application `c:\windows\system32\cscript.exe`

Monitoring Your System to Identify Bottlenecks

Sometimes you get the feeling that your computer is not performing at full capacity. The indication might anything from a momentary lag between typing and having characters appear on the screen, to applications taking far too long to open when you start them. Sometimes these slowdowns can be caused by momentary network outages, the automatic installation of Windows Updates downloads, or the Windows Indexing Service deciding that the middle of your workday is a good time to scan through every document on your disk. Sometimes they fix themselves and don't occur again. But sometimes they don't, and you need to know how to find the source of the problem.

Using the Task Manager

The first place I go when my computer is acting sluggish is the Task Manager. Type Ctrl+Alt+Del to open it, view the Processes tab, and click the title of the CPU column twice to show the processes using the greatest percentages of available CPU cycles.

Note

If you are logged on via Remote Desktop, you might only be able to see processes running under your own username. To view all active processes, you must run the Task Manager as a Computer Administrator and check Show Processes From All Users. If you don't want to log off and back on as an Administrator to do this, open a command prompt window and type **runas /user:Administrator taskmgr**.

If a single task is consuming a large percentage of the CPU, it's either very busy, or it's stuck in an infinite loop doing nothing. It's difficult to tell which, sometimes. One helpful indicator is the amount of disk activity the program is doing. Click View, select Columns and check PID, I/O Read Bytes, and I/O Write Bytes, and click OK. The result is shown in Figure 6.22.

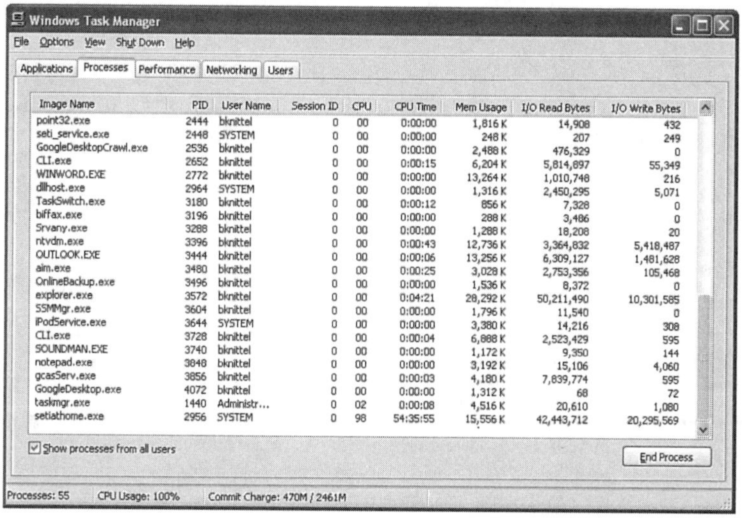

Figure 6.22 Task Manager display showing %CPU usage and total disk activity.

Watch the I/O Read Bytes and I/O Write Bytes numbers. If they are increasing, the program is actively reading and writing data. A program that is consuming nearly 100% of the CPU with no I/O activity is probably hung up; a program that is using a large CPU percentage and is also performing I/O is just working hard.

If you suspect that a program is hung up, you can try to terminate it from the Task Manager. Select the program in the list and click End Process. In most cases, this will have no effect, so the next step is to open a command prompt window. If you are using Windows XP Professional, type the command **taskkill /pid *nnn*** with the number from the process's PID column in place of *nnn*. If you are using

XP Home Edition, try the command `tskill`, although it may not work. Hopefully you had previously downloaded installed the Resource Kit Tools described in Appendix A, and can type `kill /f nnn` which is more likely to work.

Reading the Event Log

The Windows Event log is a sort of collective blog written by Windows, its services, and applications as they go about their business, and it records errors, warnings, and observations that aren't necessarily displayed on the desktop or in message boxes. To read these messages, open the Event Viewer by right-clicking My Computer, selecting Manage, and then selecting Event Viewer in the left pane. Alternatively, type `eventvwr.msc` at the command prompt.

The Event Viewer displays at least three different log sections:

- *Application log*—Contains events logged by applications or programs running on the computer. For example, a program might record a file error in the application log. Each program's developer decides which, if any, events to record.

- *Security log*—Records security events such as valid and invalid logon attempts as well as audit events related to resource use such as creating, opening, or deleting files. The administrator can specify which events will be recorded in the Security log by enabling specific logging actions.

- *System log*—Contains events logged by Windows system components. For example, the failure of a driver or other system component to load during startup is recorded in the System log. The event types logged by system components are predetermined by Windows and can't be changed by users or administrators.

The EventLog service starts automatically early in the bootup process. All users of a computer can view the Application and System logs, but only Administrators can view the Security log. Special services may also create other logs. My computer, for example, gained a log named ACEEventLog when I installed a new ATI display adapter driver recently; it appears to contain debugging information written by the driver. Windows Server installations may have several additional logs relating to server functions such as DHCP, File Replication, and Active Directory.

Log entries are categorized into one of five Event Types, which are listed in Table 6.5.

Table 6.5   Windows Event Types

Event Type	Description
Error	Indicates a serious problem that has occurred, such as a loss of data or degradation in usability or reliability. A service that fails to load or a domain controller that is unavailable for contact will cause an Error event. More often than not, you will receive an onscreen warning concerning the Error event.
Warning	Indicates that a less serious event has occurred that should not normally have an immediate adverse effect on the computer. Low disk space or failure to contact a time server to update the clock might cause a Warning event.
Information	Indicates the successful completion of a task or the successful operation of an application, device, or service. Many occurrences will create an Information event, such as the starting of a network service or the loading and configuring of a driver.
Success Audit	Indicates that an action that was configured for success auditing was attempted and was successful. Auditing can monitor access to files or folders, logging on to the network, use of privileges, and so on.

Table 6.5   Continued

Event Type	Description
Failure Audit	Indicates that an action that was configured for failure auditing was attempted and was unsuccessful. Failure audit events can be used to identify users who are attempting to gain access to files or privileges for which they are not authorized.

You can easily scan through the logs for events that might shed light on a problem you're investigating, or events that may predict an upcoming problem; double-click an entry to view detailed information.

Some of other possible activities include the following:

- To save a log file for archival purposes, select Save Log File As. You will need to select from three file types: .EVT, .TXT, or .CSV. If you plan on opening the log later in the Event Viewer, you should save it in .EVT format. If you save a log in .TXT (plain text) or .CSV (comma-delimited) format, you can import the data into a spreadsheet or database for further processing.

- To open a saved log file, select Open Log File. This comes in handy if you've saved and cleared out Event logs.

- Clicking New Log View simply creates a copy of the selected log, allowing you to create a custom view of it without changing the view of the original.

- After you've archived a log, you can Clear All Events in the log to start with a clean slate again.

- Export List is a nice feature that allows you export a log file to a text file for easy transport and viewing in any text editor.

You can configure maximum log size and specify event retention polices by right-clicking a log name in the left pane and selecting Properties. Figure 6.23 shows the General tab, from which you can configure most of the basic options for a log.

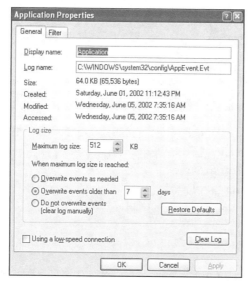

Figure 6.23   You can configure log sizes and event retention limits.

Caution

A common hacker trick is to do something improper, and then flood the log with innocuous entries to flush out any record of their misdeeds. On important servers, then, it's a common security practice to disable automatic overwriting of the security log. However, if you disable the overwriting of old events and your log grows to the maximum configured size, the logging of new events will not occur. Always pay careful attention to your logs when you have selected to manually clear log entries.

Security Logging and Auditing

By default, security logging is turned off and must be enabled through Local Security Policy, or on a domain network, Group Policy. Security logging can record attempts to log on with incorrect passwords.

The Administrator can also set auditing policies to enable logging of auditing events, which can help you determine whether an application or service is failing because it cannot gain access to needed files, or which can help you watch for attempts by people to access things they shouldn't. Files and folders to be so monitored must be stored on NTFS-formatted disks, and must be marked separately for auditing using their Advanced security properties dialogs. In addition, Simple File Sharing must be turned off. Auditing is not available on Windows XP Home Edition.

To enable Security logging, log on as a Computer Administrator, open the Administrative Tools menu from the Start menu or Control Panel, and select Local Security Policy. Alternatively, at the command prompt, type the command `gpedit.msc`. View Local Policies, Audit Policy, as shown in Figure 6.24.

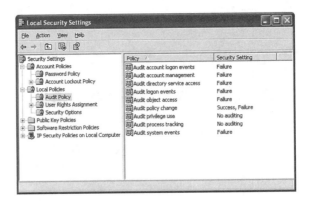

Figure 6.24   Enable Security and Audit logging from the Local Security Policy editor.

To have the Security log record failed logon attempts, set Audit Logon Events to Failure. To record all logons, set Audit Logon Events to Success, Failure.

To permit the recording of file and folder Audit activity, set Audit Object Access to Failure, or Success, Failure. Then, modify the Security permissions of the files and/or folders you want to monitor. To do this, follow these steps:

1. Use Windows Explorer to locate and right-click the file or folder you want to audit. Select Properties.

2. Select the Security tab. (If it does not appear, either the file is on a FAT-formatted disk or Simple File Sharing has not been disabled.)

3. Click the Advanced button and select the Auditing tab. (If Auditing does not appear, you are not logged on as a Computer Administrator.) Click Add.

4. You may select specific users and groups to be monitored. Enter a username, group name, or Everyone to monitor all access.

5. Select the type of activity you want to monitor (see Figure 6.25), and click the check box in the Successful and/or Failed column. Only the selected activities and results will be considered for logging in the Event log, and then, only the result types for Object Access set earlier in the policy editor will actually be recorded.

Figure 6.25 Select access types and results for auditing.

6. Save the changes by clicking OK.

When you have enabled auditing for debugging purposes, it's best to disable it immediately after solving the problem to avoid having the security log grow unnecessarily large.

Using the Performance Monitor

The System Monitor and Performance Logs and Alerts management tools are available in the Computer Management console. These tools let you plot and monitor all sorts of internal measurements inside Windows, view recorded performance data, and configure management alerts to be sent when system measurements stray from preset bounds.

If you type **perfmon.msc** at the command line, or choose Start, All Programs, Administrative Tools, Performance, you'll get a console with Performance Logs and Alerts, plus the more useful System Monitor tool, which plots system activity in real-time, as shown in Figure 6.26. (For some strange reason, System Monitor is not available as a selection when building custom consoles in MMC.)

Note

If Administrative Tools doesn't appear under All Programs in your Start menu, right-click the Start button, select Properties, click Customize and select the Advanced tab. Locate System Administrative Tools under Start Menu Items, and select Display On The All Programs Menu. Click OK twice to close the dialogs and Administrative Tools will now be available.

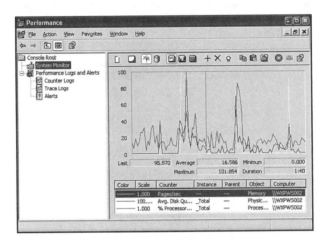

Figure 6.26   The Performance console is the powerhouse of performance monitoring.

Monitoring performance begins with the collection of data. The Performance console provides you with various methods of working with data, although all methods use the same means of collecting data. Data collected by the Performance Monitor is broken down into objects, counters, and instances.

- An *object* is the software or device being monitored, such as memory or processor.

- A *counter* is a specific statistic for an object. For instance, Memory has a counter called Available Bytes, and a processor has a counter called % Processor Time.

- An *instance* is the specific occurrence of an object you are watching; in a multiprocessor server with two processors, or a single CPU system with dual cores or hyperthreading, you will have three instances: 0, 1, and Total.

The primary difference between using the System Monitor and Counter Logs/Trace Logs is that you typically watch performance in real-time in System Monitor (or play back saved logs), where you use Counter Logs and Trace Logs to record data for later analysis. Alerts function in real-time by providing you with (you guessed it) an alert when a user-defined threshold is exceeded. Collecting data and displaying it will be discussed at length in the following section, "Using System Monitor." Counter Logs, Trace Logs, and Alerts will be discussed in great detail in the "Using Performance Logs and Alerts" section later in this chapter.

Using System Monitor

The System Monitor (shown previously in Figure 6.26) enables you to view statistical data either live or from a saved log. You can view the data in three formats: graph, histogram, or report. Graph data is displayed as a line graph; histograms are incorrectly named and are actually just bar graphs; and reports are text-based displays that show the current numerical information available from the statistics.

To add counters to the Performance Monitor, click the "+" icon, which is the eighth icon from the left in the System Monitor; this opens the Add Counters dialog box shown in Figure 6.27. At the top of the dialog box is a set of radio buttons with which you can obtain statistics from the local machine or a remote machine. This is useful when you want to monitor a computer in a location that is not within a reasonable physical distance from you. Under the radio buttons is a pull-down list naming the performance objects that can be monitored. Which performance objects are available depends on the features (and applications) you have installed on your server. Also, some counters come with specific applications. These performance counters enable you to monitor statistics relating to that application from the Performance Monitor.

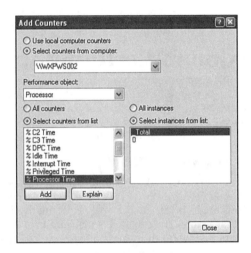

Figure 6.27   Use the Add Counters dialog box to add counters to the System Monitor.

Under the performance object is a list of counters. When applied to a specific instance of an object, counters are what you are really after, and the object just narrows down your search. The counters are the actual statistical information you want to monitor. Each object has its own set of counters from which you can choose. Counters enable you to move from the abstract concept of an object to the concrete events that reflect that object's activity. For example, if you choose to monitor the processor, you can watch for the average processor time and how much time the processor spent performing non-idle activity. In addition, you can watch for %user time (time spent executing user application processes) versus %privileged time (time spent executing system processes).

To the right of the counter list is the instances list. In most cases where instances are listed, selecting Total will give you the most useful results.

You can make several modifications to the System Monitor to improve how it functions in your environment. To access the properties page for the System Monitor, right-click the graph and select Properties from the menu that appears.

Using Performance Logs and Alerts

Using the Performance Logs and Alerts section of the Performance Monitor, you can log counter and event trace data. Additionally, you can create alerts triggered by performance that can notify the administrator of critical changes in monitored counters, to give advance warning of impending problems. The following three items are located in the Performance Logs and Alerts section of the Performance Monitor:

- *Counter Logs* enable you to record data about hardware usage and the activity of system services from local or remote computers. You can configure logging to occur manually or automatically based on a predefined schedule. If you desire, continuous logging is available, but it consumes large amounts of disk space quickly. You can view the logs in System Monitor or export the data to a spreadsheet or database program, such as Microsoft Excel and Microsoft Access, respectively.

- *Trace Logs* are used to record data as certain activity, such as disk I/O or a page fault, occurs. When the event occurs, the provider sends the data to the log service.

- *Alerts* can be set on a specific counter defining an action to be performed when the selected counter's value exceeds, equals, or falls below the specified setting. Actions that can be set include sending a message, running a program, and starting a log.

Tuning for Maximum Performance

In this section you'll learn some specific settings you can make to tune Windows for peak performance. Of course there are always trade-offs to be made, and you'll have to make personal judgments as to whether a feature is worth its cost in computer time, or whether it should be disabled to gain speed, or whether you should spend more money to speed your computer with better hardware, *or* gain speed through software settings and feature sacrifices.

Installing Sufficient Memory (RAM)

The most important thing you can do to make sure your computer runs at top speed it to make sure that you have enough main memory (RAM) installed. Here's why: Windows uses a system called *virtual memory* to let applications use as much memory as they want, even if they want to use more memory than the system has available. The shortfall is made up by using space in a hidden disk file called the *page file* to store data that won't fit into main memory. When a program wants more memory than is currently free, Windows freezes the application, finds a block of memory that hasn't been recently accessed, writes its contents to the page file (*pages it out*), and then lets the frozen application use this block of memory. When the application whose memory got shuffled off to the disk drive gets its turn to run again, and tries to read or write to the memory block that got taken away, Windows has to repeat the process, shuffling some other application's memory off to disk and paging the first application's data back in.

This decades-old technique lets multiple applications share limited memory, lets an application run even if it needs more memory than the computer has, and it's been made as efficient as possible, but it has a cost: Reading and writing to the hard disk is thousands of times slower than reading or writing data from RAM. Each time Windows has to stop to move memory in or out of the page file, it delays the frozen application by several tens of milliseconds at least, and if this happens several dozen times a second, the application slows to a crawl. There's even a technical term for this: *thrashing*, which means expending a lot of effort and getting little done. If you ever used Windows 95 or 98 on an old computer with 32MB of memory, you know well what this is like. And even a current computer with 512MB of memory can start thrashing if you load in a big video clip for editing.

The good news is that even while Windows and applications have bloated to the point that they require hundreds of megabytes just to boot up, memory has gotten so cheap that there's virtually (ha!) no reason to suffer with a computer that's having to page data to disk.

How Much Memory Is Enough?

So how much memory is enough? You can actually do some calculations to find out. After going through a demanding work session, type Ctrl+Alt+Del to open the Task Manager, and view the

Performance tab. Under the graphs are some numbers the list amounts of memory in K (thousands of bytes). This is what they mean:

- *Physical Memory, Total*—The amount of RAM you've installed in your computer, less any "borrowed" by a low-end "shared memory" motherboard-based graphics adapter.

- *Physical Memory, System Cache*—The amount of physical RAM being used just to speed up file operations.

- *Physical Memory, Available*—The amount of memory that is either totally unused or could be taken away from the System Cache if needed by applications.

- *Commit Charge, Total*—The amount of *virtual* memory actually in use by Windows, drivers, services, and applications; in other words, the amount of memory your system thinks it's using at this moment.

- *Commit Charge, Peak*—The largest Total Commit Charge since Windows was last booted.

- *Commit Charge, Limit*—The amount of physical memory plus the current size of the page file; this is the most virtual memory that could be in use at once. If necessary, Windows will increase this quantity automatically by enlarging the page file(s), if the page file(s) can be increased in size.

Now, here's how to use these numbers:

- If the Commit Charge Peak is equal to the Commit Charge Limit, your page file filled up at some point, and either had to be extended, which means it's now fragmented and slowing you down, or it has reached its maximum size, which means you've pushed your computer to the proverbial wall and held it there. Check the page file settings to see whether your total page space is limited in size to this amount. If so, you should increase the limit. You may also want to use a third-party disk defragmenter that is able to defragment your page file. Alternatively, move the page file to a different physical disk drive with more room and less fragmentation.

- Calculate the approximate amount of "working memory" in your system by calculating (0.9 × Physical Memory Total) – Kernel Memory Nonpaged.

- If this working memory amount is *greater* than Commit Charge Peak, you have sufficient memory installed in your computer. (Of course, having more wouldn't slow it down any.)

- If the working memory amount is *less* than the Commit Peak, calculate the shortfall as Commit Charge Peak – working memory. Divide this shortfall amount by 1,024 to get the number of MB that you need to add. You may have to replace your current memory modules or add additional modules, depending on what you have now; *Upgrading and Reparing PCs* goes into these details.

Here's an example. From my computer, I recorded the following numbers:

Physical Memory Total	1048096
Commit Charge Total	505712
Commit Charge Limit	2520816
Commit Charge Peak	649472
Kernel Memory Nonpaged	19288

The interpretation is:

- Commit Charge Peak is much less than Commit Charge Limit, so the Page File is currently large enough.

■ Working memory is $(0.9 \times 1048096) - 19288 = 923988$KB.

■ 923988 is greater than the Commit Charge Peak of 649472, so there is sufficient RAM.

Now, if my computer had only 512MB (524,288K) of memory installed, the results would have been different:

■ Working memory would be $(0.9 \times 524288) - 19288 = 452571$ KB.

■ The working memory would be less than the Commit Charge Peak, with a shortfall of $(649472 - 452571) = 196900$KB, or 192MB.

In this case, the indication would be that I would have to add at least 192MB of memory to prevent memory paging from slowing me down. You can live with some paging, of course, but it definitely drags performance down. This is why, despite Microsoft's recommendation of a 256MB minimum, 512MB is a functional *minimum* memory size for Windows XP.

Placing the Page File

If the preceding calculation shows that you need to increase the size of your page file, consider where you should put the page file for best performance. Paging needs to be as fast as possible. You can configure Windows to put page files on more than one drive, and you can set maximum and minimum page file sizes or let Windows manage the size automatically, as discussed earlier in this chapter. Here are the things you should consider to make the most efficient page file setup:

■ Your total page file size should be 1.5 to 3 times the amount of physical memory in your computer; tending toward the smaller factor if you are sure you have adequate physical RAM, and toward the larger if you know you don't. Don't allocate less than 512MB of page file space.

■ If Windows is reading or writing to the page file, it means that some application, or Windows itself, is frozen and waiting for the disk operation to complete. Reading and writing data to and from disk is slow enough, but having to mechanically reposition the little recording head that swings back and forth across the disk surface is even slower, thus costlier. Therefore, you don't want your page file to get fragmented, forcing Windows to move the recording head all over the disk to pick up the scattered data. As soon as you install Windows, set a very large minimum page file size, 2 or 3 times the amount of physical memory in your computer, so that this block is allocated all in one piece.

■ If your page file grows during normal operation, the Windows Defragmenter can't put the pieces back together. Only third-party applications like Diskkeeper can do this.

■ The best place to put a page file is on a fast disk drive that is *physically* separate from your primary Windows disk drive, preferably one used only occasionally for other purposes. This way, the disk's read head will be positioned once and left in the location of the page file. The disk drive should be an internal SATA drive, internal or external fast SCSI drive, or an IDE drive *not* on the same controller cable as a CD-ROM or DVD drive.

■ The second best place to put a page file is on the same drive as Windows.

■ The worst place to put a page file is in a separate partition on the same physical disk as your Windows drive. In this case, the disk's read head has to travel a large distance every time it needs to switch between the page file and an operating system file.

■ If you have several otherwise equally desirable choices, dig into the specifications for the disk drives involved, and place your page file on the disk with the lowest track-to-track positioning time and the highest data transfer rate.

Defragment the Disk

Another key factor in achieving top performance is the speed at which data can be moved between your computer's CPU and its hard disk. Having the latest high-speed disk interface hardware won't help you if your files and data are widely scattered across the disk. Disk data gets scattered, or fragmented, over time, and to maintain peak disk performance, you should periodically run a disk defragmenting utility.

Windows XP comes with a defragmenting tool that is discussed under "Defragmenting for Greater Speed" in Chapter 5. However, it's not the sharpest knife in the drawer, so to speak, and you can get much better disk performance improvements if you buy a better "defragger" and run it on a regular schedule. Check out Raxco's PerfectDisk (www.raxco.com) and Diskeeper Corporation's Diskeeper (www.diskeeper.com, with just one k).

◀◀ To learn more about defragmenting, see "Defragmenting for Greater Speed," p. 211.

Note

To help Windows XP meet its goal of keeping its boot time under 30 seconds, there is a special service that automatically runs every few weeks or so, which identifies the files Windows uses when it boots, and reorganizes them on the disk so that they're placed in the order in which they're used, in consecutive unfragmented disk blocks. This helps reduce boot time but doesn't speed up subsequent disk operations.

Disk Interface Tuning

Having data neatly organized on disk won't help if the pipeline between the disk and the CPU is restricted. Hard drives can achieve the highest transfer rates if they transfer data directly into the memory on your motherboard using Direct Memory Access (DMA), but they can be prevented from doing this if they share a controller cable with a slower Zip Disk, optical, or other ATA disk device. To verify that your disk drives are using DMA transfers, log on as a Computer Administrator, right-click My Computer and select Manage, and open the Device Manager. Select View, Devices by Connection and locate the entries for any IDE-type disk controllers. You will have to open the items in the tree view to find them (see Figure 6.28).

Find the channel entry that connects to your Windows hard drive, such as "Primary IDE Channel"; double-click it and select the Advanced Settings tab, shown in Figure 6.30, and examine the Current Transfer Mode for each device. Disk devices should be using a DMA mode, not Programmed I/O (PIO), which requires the CPU to intervene in transferring every byte to and from the device. Higher DMA transfer modes are faster. Transfer modes and rates for standard parallel ATA devices are listed in Table 6.6. If a disk is listed as using a mode that is slower than the disk drive's peak transfer rate, you may have incorrectly arranged or cabled disks, or an inadequate disk controller.

Table 6.6   IDE Disk Transfer Modes and Rates

Mode	Also called	Maximum Transfer Rate, MBps
Ultra DMA Mode 6	UDMA/133 or Ultra ATA/133	133
Ultra DMA Mode 5	UDMA/100 or Ultra ATA/100	100
Ultra DMA Mode 4	UDMA/66 or Ultra ATA/66	67
Ultra DMA Mode 3		44
Ultra DMA Mode 2	UDMA/33	33
Ultra DMA Mode 1		25

Table 6.6   Continued

Mode	Also called	Maximum Transfer Rate, MBps
Ultra DMA Mode 0		16.7
DMA Mode 2	Multiword DMA mode 2	16.7
DMA Mode 1	Multiword DMA mode 1	13.3
DMA Mode 0	Multiword DMA mode 0	4.2
PIO Mode 4		16.7
PIO Mode 3		11.1
PIO Mode 2		8.3
PIO Mode 1		5.2
PIO Mode 0		3.3

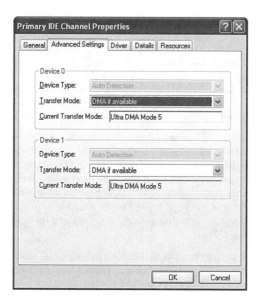

Figure 6.28   Verify that your disk controller channels are using DMA.

Repeat this check for any other channels that connect to hard drives. If DMA transfers are prevented by a slower device on the same channel as a disk, you may want to reconfigure the hardware so that slower devices are on a separate channel.

What to Enable and Disable

Earlier in the chapter you read about ways to eliminate unwanted startup programs run when you log on and when you start Internet Explorer.

In addition, you can disable some Windows services and graphical functionality to gain additional performance. There aren't many such items that make the trade-off worthwhile, but we'll cover a few of them here.

Graphical Niceties

You can make Windows' responses to menu operations somewhat snappier by disabling some of the shading, shadows, and smooth scrolling features that have crept into the Windows user interface. You can see a list of optional graphical effects in the Display Properties dialog, Settings tab, and Effects button, and the TweakUI PowerToy discussed earlier in this chapter also has check boxes that you can use to disable graphics effects.

On my computer, I've disabled the fade-in of pop-up submenus, which occasionally seems to take more time than I would like it to, and font smoothing, which I personally don't like.

Unnecessary Services

You can eke out some small gains in performance by disabling system services that aren't necessary. This will decrease the time it takes Windows to boot, will free some memory (usually not enough to have been worried about), and will prevent these services from running and taking CPU cycles away from your interactive work. The only truly egregious CPU and disk hog in the Services list is the Indexing service. If you don't use the search for keywords within files option in the standard Windows Search utility, or if you use a more advanced search tool like Google Desktop Search instead, you can disable the Indexing service using the Services management utility discussed earlier in the chapter.

If you do need to use the Indexing service because you use search functions in web pages hosted by Internet Information Services on your computer, you can restrict Indexing Service so that it searches only web content and not your entire disk. As a Computer Administrator, open the Computer Management window, open the Indexing service entry under Services and Applications, and dig down to System, Directories. Delete the entry for C:\ and for any other drive root folders. This will prevent the indexing of your disks for general searches. Leave the other entries, and all entries under the web branch, alone.

If you installed the Internet Information Services (IIS) web server suite out of curiosity but don't use it, this is another candidate to be disabled.

CHAPTER 7

Networking Windows

Setting Up a Network

In this chapter, we're assuming that you are creating or adding to a network for a home or small office network, which in Microsoft's jargon is called a Workgroup network.

We assume that you've purchased and installed the necessary hardware components:

- An Ethernet (wired) or wireless network adapter for each computer. (Most new desktop and laptop computers have an Ethernet adapter built onto the motherboard, so you may not have to purchase these.)

- For a wired network, an Ethernet switch or hub, or a cable/DSL sharing router with a built-in switch, and CAT-5 cables to run from each computer to the switch, as shown in Figure 7.1.

- For a wireless network, a wireless router or access point. The router or access point will usually have Ethernet connections so that wired connections can be made as well, if desired, as shown in Figure 7.2.

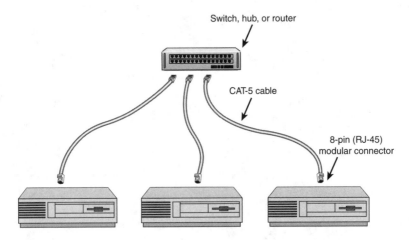

Figure 7.1   A basic wired Ethernet network, using CAT-5 cabling.

If you need information on selecting and installing network hardware, refer to *Upgrading and Repairing Networks* or *Upgrading and Repairing PCs*, both by Que.

Note

If you have cable or DSL Internet service, we strongly recommend that you use a router (wired or wireless) to share the Internet connection with your network, rather than using Windows Internet Connection Sharing. These inexpensive ($10 to $40) devices simplify setup and provide increased security against hackers. Be sure to purchase a router that supports Universal Plug and Play, and if you want to be able to access your Windows XP Professional computer from the Internet using Remote Desktop, be sure the router supports Dynamic DNS (DDNS).

When the hardware has been connected, you're ready to configure the network.

If you are creating a wired network, skip ahead to the section "Configuring a Workgroup Network."

If you are creating a wireless network, install your access point or wireless router according to the manufacturer's instructions. Then proceed to the next section to set up wireless networking on your Windows XP computers.

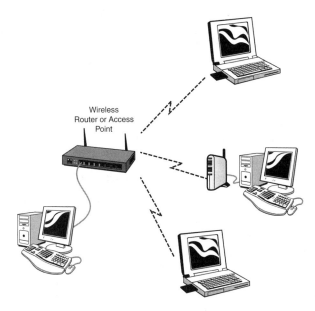

Figure 7.2   A wireless network with an "access point" or wireless Internet sharing router, and optional wired Ethernet connections.

Wireless Networking

Wireless networking has become much faster, more reliable, and *much* less expensive year by year. At the time this book was written, 802.11g adapters costs about $40 per computer, less when on sale or with a rebate, and a wireless router costs about the same. The next generation of 802.11n (WiMax) equipment, when the specifications are finalized, promises even faster speeds and greater range, and "pre-n" equipment is already being sold. (It's fast, and its range is good, but it may not be compatible with future equipment when the specification is finalized.) The Multiple-Input Multiple-Output (MIMO) technology promises to extend the range of wireless networking from the current effective limit of about 100 feet indoors to considerably more.

If you do want to install a wireless network, you need to know that there are security risks involved:

- If you don't enable Wireless security, any passerby can connect to your network.
- If you use the old 54-bit encryption option, a determined passerby can still easily connect.
- With Windows Simple File Sharing enabled, anyone who connects can read or modify your shared files. (Simple File Sharing is discussed later in this chapter.)
- Even without Simple File Sharing, anyone who connects could send spam or viruses from *your* Internet connection.

So, wireless security is important, but fortunately, it's not that difficult to manage.

Note .

This section tells how to configure wireless networking for Windows XP Service Pack 2 or later, in a home or small office. If you are using an earlier version of Windows, consult the manual provided with your hardware for setup instructions. On a corporate wireless network, your network administrator will most likely be the one to configure the wireless adapter and security settings.

Caution

If you want to set up an "open" wireless hotspot to share your Internet connection with friends, neighbors, customers, or the world, that's great, but you must not use file and printer sharing on the same network. If you use a wireless network for your own file sharing, configure your network with security enabled, and then plug into it a second wireless router, set with a different ssid and a different channel, and disable security on that second network.

To be able to distinguish your network's signal from others, and to secure your network, you must make four choices when you set up a wireless network:

- A SSID (Service Set Identifier), a short name that you give your network, up to 32 characters in length. This could be your last name, company name, a pet's name, whatever makes sense to you.

- An encryption type, a choice of protocol, and "strength" of the code used to secure the network against eavesdropping. The choices are, in order of increasing security, none, WEP 40 bit (also called 64 bit), WEP 128 bit, or WPA 128 bit. WEP stands for Wired Equivalent Privacy, but that turned out to be overoptimistic as WEP security can be broken in as little as a few hours by a determined interloper. WPA, or "Wi-Fi Protected Access," is the new improved encrypting scheme, and it's the preferred choice, *if* all of your network adapters and drivers support it. Select the highest security method supported by *all* of your network gear, including any access points or routers. (If your router doesn't support WPA, you may be able to install updated firmware to get it. Windows XP Service Pack 2 provides WPA support for Windows XP. You would need to download updated driver software to get WPA support for older versions of Windows.)

  A new, even stronger standard called WPA2 is now out, as well. If your router supports the WPA2 standard, you can download an update for Windows XP Service Pack 2 from Microsoft. Visit support.microsoft.com and search for KB893357.

- An encryption key, a string of hexadecimal digits—that is, the numbers 0 through 9 and the letters A through F. Some wireless networking software lets you generate a key from an ordinary text password, but this method doesn't work when you use equipment from different manufacturers. I recommend that you just deal with the cumbersome numeric key. 128-bit WEP security requires a 26-character key, which would look like this: 47A014C65F92305B6000C3D639. (If you're doing the math, you're right, that adds up to only 104 bits, but that's the way it works). If you're lazy, you might use a key like this: 112233445566778899AABBCCDD.

  This should be kept secret, as it's the key to your network and your shared files.

- A channel, which selects the frequency used to transmit your network's data. In the U.S., this is a number between 1 and 11; the numbers may be different in other countries. The most common channels used are 1, 6, and 11. Start off with channel 6.

- MAC-level security, which lets you specify which network adapters can connect to your router, is cumbersome and does nothing to repel a determined hacker.

If you have a router or access point, you are setting up what is called an *infrastructure network*. Windows XP has a wizard to help you choose the correct settings. To set up a new wireless network, follow this procedure:

1. Open My Network Places from the Start menu. In the Network Tasks list, select Set Up a Wireless Network for a Home or Small Office. When the wizard appears, select Set Up a New Wireless Network.

2. In the first screen (see Figure 7.3), enter a name for your wireless network, and indicate whether you want Windows to create a random key for you, or if you want to enter your own. Also, if *all* of your wireless equipment supports WPA encryption, check the Use WPA box at the bottom of the screen. Then, click Next.

Figure 7.3 The first page of the Wireless Network Setup wizard lets you select a network name and choose what type of encryption to use.

3. If you elected to enter the key manually, Windows will display a page asking for the network key. Unless you're concerned that someone is peeking over your shoulder, uncheck Hide Characters as I Type. Enter 26 hexadecimal digits (digits 0–9 and/or letters A–F; upper/lowercase doesn't matter), as shown in Figure 7.4, and enter it again to confirm. Click Next to proceed.

Figure 7.4 If you're entering a key manually, uncheck Hide Characters as I Type so you can see what you're typing.

4. Now for the clever part (see Figure 7.5). If you have one of those USB-based keychain Flash memory devices, or if you have a USB-connected digital camera memory card reader that presents the memory cards as disk drives on your computer, you can use this device to copy the settings from one computer to another, and even to your wireless router if it has a USB port. What Windows will do is to copy a file containing the settings, *and* an "autoplay" program that will load the settings when you plug the card into each computer. (You can also make this selection and use a floppy disk, if you want.) You can also choose to copy the settings manually. Make your selection and click Next.

Figure 7.5 Select the means you want to use to copy the wireless settings.

5. If you chose to use the USB device, Windows will ask you to insert the device, and then select the corresponding drive letter. You can also select your floppy drive here. Click Next and Windows will copy the necessary files.

After Windows copies the files, click Print Network Settings to get a copy of the settings. You'll need this as a backup and may need it to configure your router. Click Next and Windows will prompt you to configure your access point and other computers before proceeding. (When you've done that, come back to this computer, reinsert the USB drive, and click Next so Windows can erase the secret key information from the USB drive.)

If you chose to copy the settings manually, click the Print button and Windows will open up a Notepad window containing the wireless settings. Click File, Print to print a copy. The printout will look like this:

```
Wireless Network Settings

Print this document and store it in a safe place for future reference.
You may need these settings to add additional computers and devices to your
network.

Wireless Settings

Network Name (SSID): brians network
Network Key (WEP/WPA Key): bb5976c32f3f4e8d9fc6a0a969
Key Provided Automatically (802.1x): 0
```

```
Network Authentication Type: open
Data Encryption Type: WEP
Connection Type: ESS
Key Index: 1
```

6. At this point, the wizard has already set up the Windows XP computer you're using to automatically connect to your new network, once it's up and running.

7. Configure your router or access point next. If it has a USB port and you're using a USB device, plug the USB memory unit into the router. It should blink its lights and load the settings within 30 seconds. If you're using a manual setup, use the printed list of settings and enter this information into your router's setup screens.

8. Finally, configure the other computers on your network, using one of these methods:

- If you're using a USB device, plug the device into the computer. The Wireless Network Setup Wizard should run automatically, and will add the computer to the wireless network.

- If you're using a floppy disk, insert the disk in each computer, and use My Computer or Windows Explorer to locate and double-click file `SetupSNK.EXE`. This will add the computer to the wireless network.

- If you're adding computers manually, go to each computer. Use the printed sheet of setup information to add the computer to the network. I'll cover this procedure in the next section.

9. If you're using a USB device, when you're finished with the other computers, go back to the first computer, reinsert the disk, and click Next on the screen remaining from when you first ran the wizard. This will erase the sensitive key information from the USB drive.

If you later need to add more computers to the network, you can rerun the wizard on the computer you started with, and it will walk you through the process of reinstalling the setup software on your USB drive, or reprinting the instruction sheet. Or, you can follow the procedure in the next section to join them to the network manually.

After all your computers have joined the wireless network, skip the next section and continue with "Setting Up a Network."

Joining an Existing Wireless Network

If you are using a wireless connection on a corporate network, your wireless configuration can and should be managed by your network administrators. Most likely, your administrator will install a security "certificate" file that will identify your computer as one authorized to use the wireless network. And it's also likely that you won't have to make any manual settings to use the network.

However, if your home or small office wireless network has already been configured and you're just adding a new computer, or, if you are taking your computer into someone's work or home and want to use his or her wireless network, you will have to take some steps to be able to use the network. You can use the Wireless Network Setup Wizard discussed in the previous section, or you can connect to and use the network by following this manual procedure:

1. In the notification area at the bottom corner of your screen, locate the Wireless Connection icon (shown here to the left). Double-click it.

2. Windows will display a list of the names (SSIDs) of the wireless networks that it "hears," as shown in Figure 7.6. Click on the network you want to use and click Connect.

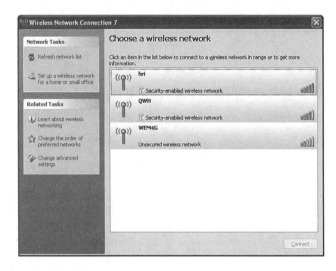

Figure 7.6   Windows displays the names of the networks whose signals it can receive.

Note

If the network you want to use doesn't appear, it could be because the signal is too weak. Also, some people prevent their router from broadcasting the SSID name over the airwaves. (This doesn't really provide much extra security, as hackers can find the network anyway.) If the network you want to use isn't broadcasting its SSID, you'll have to enter the information manually.

3. Windows will determine what type of security the network is using, and if the network is encrypted, will prompt you to enter the network key. Enter the 10- or 26-digit key that was used to set up the network to begin with.

After the wireless connections are made, you can continue setting up the rest of your network, as described in the following section.

Configuring a Workgroup Network

After your network hardware has been installed, whether it's wired or wireless, the next step in setting up a workgroup network is to run the Network Setup Wizard. This isn't optional. For security reasons, Windows won't enable file and printer sharing until this wizard has been run at least once. Beyond the settings made by the Network Setup Wizard, there are several features that you should consider and adjust manually. After discussing the wizard, this chapter covers the following topics:

- IP addressing options
- Networking with Windows 9x and Me
- Designating a master browser
- Providing a shared Internet connection

You may want to review these topics before starting to set up your network.

Using the Network Setup Wizard

Windows XP comes with a Networking Setup Wizard program that can automatically configure file sharing and Internet access for each of the computers on your network. The wizard lets you make a few basic choices, but otherwise takes care of all of the technical details for you. As I mentioned earlier, you *have* to run the Network Setup Wizard at least once in order to enable File and Printer sharing.

Note

If you're going to use Microsoft's Internet Connection Sharing to share an Internet connection over your LAN, configure the computer that will be sharing its Internet connection first. Establish and test its Internet connection, and then configure the other computers. Internet Connection Sharing is discussed later in this chapter.

To start the wizard, click Start, Control Panel, Network and Internet Connections, and Set Up or Change Your Home or Small Office Network. Read the "Checklist for Creating a Network" if you want, and then click Next. Follow the wizard through the following steps.

Select a Connection Method

The wizard asks you to select a statement that best describes your computer. The choices can be confusing, so consider them each carefully. They are

■ *This Computer Connects Directly to the Internet. The Other Computers…Connect…Through This Computer.* Choose this if you want this computer to share its Internet connection with the rest of your LAN using Windows Internet Connection Sharing, which is discussed later in the chapter. *This* computer will connect to the Internet through a dial-up modem or a cable/DSL modem. In the latter case, you'll need two network adapters in this computer: one for the LAN connection and one to connect to the DSL or cable modem. In any case, be sure that you've already configured and tested your Internet connection before setting up the LAN.

■ *This Computer Connects to the Internet Through Another Computer on My Network or Through a Residential Gateway.* Choose this if your network has a hardware Internet connection sharing router, or if you've set up some *other* computer to share its connection with Internet Connection Sharing.

Also, use this choice if your LAN has routed Internet service, such as that provided by a DSL, cable, ISDN, or Frame Relay router connected to your network hub, *and* the router for that service has been configured to filter out Windows networking traffic, which we'll discuss later in this chapter.

To get to the next three options, click Other. These alternatives are as follows:

■ *This Computer Connects to the Internet Directly or Through a Network Hub. Other Computers on My Network Also Connect [this way].* Select this if your computer uses its own dial-up or direct DSL/cable Internet connection, but you do *not* want to use Windows's Internet Connection Sharing to share the connection with the rest of your LAN.

Also, use this selection if you use "multiple-computer" cable Internet service with no router. Please read "Providing Shared Internet Access" later in this chapter for important warnings.

■ *This Computer Connects Directly to the Internet. I Do Not Have a Network Yet.* You would use this choice if you had a direct Internet connection (that is, a cable or DSL modem that uses a network adapter), but no LAN. Because you're setting up a LAN, this choice probably isn't appropriate.

You *do* want to use this choice if you are setting up a network *only* to use a shared Internet connection, and don't want to share files with other computers. This might be the case if you are sharing an Internet connection in an apartment building or other public space, for instance. In this case, this choice indicates that you consider your network to be as untrustworthy as the Internet itself.

- *This Computer Belongs to a Network that Does Not Have an Internet Connection.* Select this if your computer will connect to the Internet using Dial-Up networking or AOL, or if your computer will never connect to the Internet.

Make the appropriate selection and click Next.

Select Your Internet Connection

If you chose one of the "This computer is directly connected to the Internet" choices, Windows presents a list of options for making that connection, listing your network adapters and your configured dial-up connections. Choose the connection that is used to reach the Internet and click Next. If you use a dial-up or PPPoE connection (frequently used with DSL service), choose the appropriate dial-up connection. Otherwise choose the network adapter that connects to your broadband modem.

Give This Computer a Description and Name

Enter a brief description of the computer (such as its location or primary user) and a name for the computer. Choose a name using just letters and/or numbers with no spaces or punctuation. Each computer on your LAN must have a different name.

If you're hard pressed to come up with names, try the names of gemstones, composers, Impressionist painters, or even Star Wars characters, as long as Mr. Lucas' lawyers don't hear about it. I use the names of islands in the Indonesian archipelago—with more than 25,000 to choose from there's little chance of running out of unique names!

Some Internet service providers, especially cable providers, require you use a name that they provide. (If you have a hardware connection sharing device hooked up to your cable modem, enter that name into the hardware device and use any names you want on your LAN.)

Name Your Network

Choose a name for your network workgroup. This name is used to identify which computers should appear in your list of network choices later on. All computers on your LAN should have the same workgroup name. If you have an existing network, enter the same workgroup name that the other computers use. Otherwise, you could pick a creative name like "WORKGROUP," or accept the Wizard's default "MSHOME."

Caution

Beware! If you run the wizard a second time, it will try to change your workgroup name to MSHOME. Re-enter the name you used the first time.

Also: The workgroup name *must* be different than all of the computer names.

File and Printer Sharing

The Wizard will ask whether you want turn on file and printer sharing, or turn it off. Select Turn On File and Printer Sharing unless your network will contain computers that you don't trust; that is, computers in a public area, or computers whose users you don't know, and so on. (If you later change your mind, or move your computer from one network to another, you can turn file sharing on or off using the Exceptions tab on the Windows Firewall control panel.)

Ready To Apply Network Settings

The wizard will let you review your selections. Click Next to proceed.

You're Almost Done...

You'll need to run the wizard on all of the computers on your LAN at least once. If all the computers use Windows XP, select Just Finish the Wizard, and then run the wizard each of your other computers. If you have computers running versions of Windows 95, 98, Me, NT, or 2000, you can create a disk that will let you run the wizard on these older machines, or you can use your Windows XP CD-ROM in these computers.

To use a disk, choose Create a Network Setup Disk, and insert a blank, formatted floppy disk. If you ran the wizard earlier and just changed some of the settings, choose Use the Network Setup Disk I Already Have, and re-insert the setup disk you created earlier. Otherwise, choose Just Finish the Wizard; I Don't Need to Run the Wizard on Other Computers."

Note

If you need to adjust the computer or workgroup name later, log on as a Computer Administrator, right-click My Computer, select Properties, and view the Computer Name tab. You can use a name-assignment wizard by clicking Network ID, or you can enter the information manually by clicking Change.

Note

If your network includes computers running Windows 95, 98 or Me, and you are using a shared Internet connection, I recommend that you install only the TCP/IP protocol on all computers, and configure them for Automatic TCP/IP configuration.

If your network includes computers running Windows 95, 98, or Me, and you are *not* using a shared Internet connection, I recommend that you install the NetBIOS protocol on Windows XP, as discussed later in this chapter under "Networking with Windows 9x and Me."

Now, continue with the next section to review the IP addressing choices made on your network.

IP Addressing Options

Windows uses TCP/IP as its primary network protocol. Each computer on the network needs to have a unique IP address assigned to it. There are three ways that IP addresses can be assigned:

- Manually, in what is called *static* IP addressing. You would select an address for each computer and enter it manually.

- Dynamically, through the DHCP service provided by Internet Connection Sharing, a Windows NT/200x Server, or a hardware router.

- Automatically, though Windows' Automatic Private Internet Protocol Addressing (APIPA) mechanism. If Windows computers are configured for dynamic IP addressing but there is no DHCP server present, Windows automatically assigns IP addresses.

By default, a newly installed network adapter will be set up for dynamic addressing. I recommend that you do *not* rely on APIPA to configure your network. In my experience, it can cause horrendous slowdowns on your computers. If you don't have a device or computer to provide DHCP service, configure static TCP/IP addresses.

Configuring Dynamic (DHCP) IP Address Assignment

By default, Windows sets up new network adapters to use dynamic IP address assignment, so for new adapters, you don't need to take any additional configuration steps.

Note

If you used static addressing in the past, just view the properties page for your network adapter, select Internet Protocol (TCP/IP), click Properties, and set both the IP Address and DNS settings to Obtain an Address Automatically.

You will need a computer or hardware device to provide DHCP service to provide configuration information to the other computers. This is provided automatically by any Windows computer that runs Windows Internet Connection Sharing (there can be at most one such computer on a network), or by a connecting sharing router device. And, you can run the DHCP service on Windows NT or 200x Server; these operating systems can be used on Workgroup networks as well as domain networks.

If you are using Windows Internet Connection Sharing, it will assign IP address 192.168.0.1 with a network mask of 255.255.255.0 to the network adapter in the sharing computer. Other computers should be configured for dynamic addressing and will receive addresses from 192.168.0.2 on up.

If you are configuring a hardware Internet Connection Sharing router, you will need to enable and configure its DHCP server. Usually, the DHCP feature is enabled by default, so you will not need to configure it. If you do, you can use the following settings:

DHCP server:	Enabled
Server IP address:	192.168.0.1
DHCP starting address:	192.168.0.100
Number of addresses:	100
DNS server(s):	(as provided by your ISP)

Some routers prefer to use a different subnet (range of network addresses), for instance 192.168.1.*x*. Whichever range you use, be sure to use the same subnet range for any static IP addresses you assign. There is more information on setting up IP address ranges later in this chapter in the discussion of enabling Remote Desktop.

Configuring Static IP Addresses

There are three situations where you'll want to set up static (fixed) IP addresses for some or all of your computers:

■ If your network has no shared Internet connection and no router, you'll want to assign static IP address for all of your computers, so you won't be slowed down by the Automatic IP configuration mechanism.

■ If you have computers that you want to reach from the Internet—for example, one or more computers that you want to be able to use via Remote Desktop—you'll want to assign a static IP address at least to those computers; the others can have their IP addresses assigned automatically.

■ If you have network-attached printers or print servers, you'll need to assign static IP addresses to these devices. You'll need to enter these addresses when you're setting up Windows to use the printers.

The goal in assigning static IP addresses is to ensure that each computer on your network has a unique IP address, shared by no other, and that the other TCP/IP setup information for each computer is the same.

I suggest you make a worksheet that lists the setup information for your network. Determining what settings to use depends on the type of network you have, which will be one of the following three choices:

- If your network does not have a router, *and* you are not using Windows Internet Connection Sharing, use the following values for your computers:

IP Address:	192.168.0.x, where x is a number from 200 on up
Network Mask:	255.255.255.0
Gateway Address:	leave blank
DNS Server:	leave blank

- If your network has a router, connect it and turn on one of your computers. Be sure that the router is configured and working, according to the manufacturer's instructions, and be sure that you can view web pages from the attached computer. Then, Click Start, All Programs, Accessories, Command Prompt. In the command prompt window, type **ipconfig /all** and press Enter. Make a note of the IP address, network mask, gateway address, and DNS server listed in the window.

Then, use the following values for any computers and devices that need a static IP address:

IP Address:	a.b.c.x, where a.b.c are the first three numbers of the IP address you saw in the Command Prompt window, and x is a number from 200 on up. This might end up being something like 192.168.1.200.
Network Mask:	As noted in the command prompt window, usually 255.255.255.0.
Gateway Address:	As noted in the command prompt window, usually something like 192.168.0.1.
DNS Server:	As noted in the command prompt window, usually the DNS addresses supplied by your ISP, or in some cases the same as the gateway address.

- If you are using Windows Internet Connection Sharing, use the following values for those computers and devices that need a static IP address:

IP Address:	192.168.0.x, where x is a number from 200 on up
Network Mask:	255.255.255.0
Gateway Address:	192.168.0.1
DNS Server:	192.168.0.1

I suggest that you then list on your worksheet all of your computers and any printer devices. Next to each, write down "automatic" if you are letting the computer get its address automatically, or write down the IP address that you will be setting manually. This way you can keep track of which numbers have been used already. The finished worksheet might look something like this:

```
My Network:
Information from command prompt window:
IP Address:      192.168.0.2    (so: all IP addresses will start with 192.168.0)
Network Mask:    255.255.255.0
Gateway Address: 192.168.0.1
DNS Servers:     10.11.12.13
                 10.21.22.23
```

```
My IP Address assignments:
java            192.168.0.200    (want to access from Internet with Remote Desktop)
sumatra         automatic
bali            automatic
HPJetDirect     192.168.0.201    (print server)
```

With this worksheet in hand, configure each computer or device that requires a static IP address.

To assign an IP address to a computer running Windows XP, use the following steps:

1. Log on as a Computer Administrator.

2. Open the Network Connections window. Right-click the entry or icon for your LAN adapter (usually labeled Local Area Connection) and select Properties.

3. Select Internet Protocol (TCP/IP) and click Properties.

4. On the General tab, enter the selected IP address, subnet mask, default gateway, and one or two DNS server IP addresses, as shown in Figure 7.7.

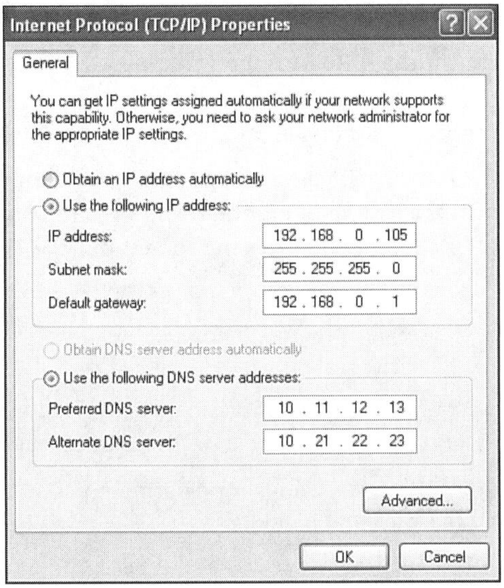

Figure 7.7   Enter static IP address information on the General tab.

5. You can configure your preferred Internet domain name (called the *preferred DNS suffix*) on the Network Identification page in the System Properties dialog. To get there, right-click My Computer and select Properties, or select Advanced, Network Identification in the Network Connections window. View the Computer Name tab, click Change, and then click More.

   You can also enter a preferred Internet domain name for each individual network or Internet connection. You might want to use your company's domain name on the Network connection, and your ISP's domain name on a dial-up connection. To do this, view the network connection's properties dialog, click the Advanced button, select the DNS tab, and enter the domain name under DNS Suffix for This Connection, as shown in Figure 7.8.

   Also, if your ISP has provided you with more than two DNS server addresses, click Add to enter additional addresses on this same tab.

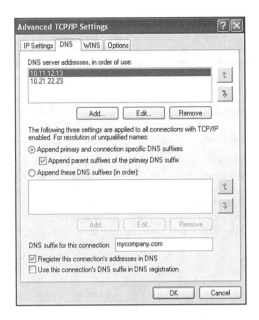

Figure 7.8   Enter per-connection DNS information on the connection's Advanced Properties DNS tab.

6. Unless your network's DNS server supports dynamic IP address registration, uncheck Register This Connection's Addresses in DNS.

7. Click OK to close the dialogs.

Configuring Additional Useful Network Services

Besides the TCP/IP protocol and network services that are installed by default with Windows XP, there are some additional services that you may want to install manually as part of your network setup.

Internet Gateway Device Discovery and Control Client

If you are using a hardware Internet sharing router or Windows Internet Connection Sharing, you should install the Internet Gateway Device Discovery and Control Client on all of your Windows XP computers. This service places an icon in each computer's Network Connections folder that lets users monitor and manage the Internet connection that is hosted on the sharing computer or the router.

To install the Discovery and Control Service, follow these steps on each computer:

1. Log on as a Computer Administrator.

2. Open the Network Connections window.

3. From the menu, select Advanced, Optional Networking Components.

4. Select Networking Services and click Details.

5. Check both Internet Gateway Device Discovery and Control Client and UPnP User Interface, and click OK.

6. Click Next.

A comparable service is available on Windows 98 and Me computers as well.

When this service has been installed, an icon will appear in your Network Connections window for your router or other network devices. You can double-click this icon to open the device's setup and control page. What appears will vary from device to device, but it's usually the device's built-in setup web page.

Universal Plug and Play

If you use a hardware connection sharing router or Internet Connection Sharing, you may also want to consider enabling a feature called Universal Plug and Play (UPnP). UPnP provides a way for software running on your computer to communicate with the router. Here's what UPnP can do:

- It provides a means for the router to tell software on your computer that it is separated from the Internet by Network Address Translation. Some software—Remote Assistance and the video and audio parts of Windows Messenger in particular—ask the computer on the other end of the connection to establish a connection back to your IP address. On a network with a shared connection, however, the IP address that the computer sees is not the public IP address that the shared Internet connection uses. UPnP lets software like Remote Assistance find out what its public IP address is. It also provides a way for the router to suggest alternate port numbers if several computers on the network want to provide the same service (for example, if several users send Remote Assistance requests).

- It provides a means for software running on the network to tell the router to forward expected incoming connections to the correct computer. Remote Assistance and Windows Messenger again are two good examples. When the computer on the other end of the connection starts sending data, the router would not know to send it to your computer. UPnP lets UPnP-aware application programs automatically set up forwarding in the router.

- UPnP provides a means for printers and perhaps other types of as-yet-undeveloped hardware devices to announce their presence on the network, so that Windows can automatically take advantage of the services they provide.

UPnP has a downside, however—it has no built-in security mechanism, so any program on any computer on your network could potentially take control of the router and open "holes" for incoming connections. (I am confident that we will soon see computer viruses and Trojan Horses that take advantage of this.) However, Windows Firewall or your third-party firewall package will still provide some protection. Windows Firewall will warn you if an undesired program prepares to receive incoming network connections, and this cannot be disabled as long as you are not using a Computer Administrator user account. In addition, most third-party firewalls inform you if an unrecognized program requests either incoming or outgoing network connections. UPnP abuse is not yet a serious problem. If you use Remote Assistance or Windows Messenger, the benefits that UPnP provides outweigh the risks.

To use UPnP, you must enable the feature in your router. It's usually disabled by default. If your router doesn't currently support UPnP, you may have to download and install a firmware upgrade from the manufacturer. Most routers now do support UPnP.

By default, Windows XP provides support for detecting UPnP enabled routers. If you have a UPnP router or Windows Internet Connection Sharing running on your network, the Network Connections screen should display an icon for the router as shown in Figure 7.9.

Note

If the icon doesn't appear, click Advanced, Optional Networking Components, select Networking Services, and click Details. Be sure that Internet Gateway Device Discovery and Control Client is checked. While you're here, check UPnP User Interface as well—this enables support for future UPnP devices.

Then, on the task list, click Change Windows Firewall Settings. View the Exceptions tab and be sure that UPnP Framework is checked.

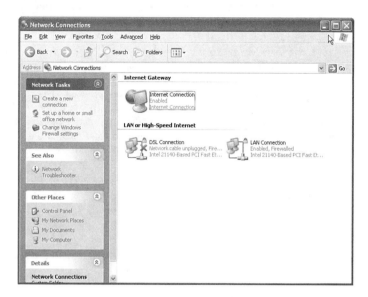

Figure 7.9 If your router supports UPnP, an Internet Gateway icon should appear in Network Connections.

If you right-click the Internet Connection icon and select Status, you'll see a dialog similar to the one shown in Figure 7.10, displaying the status of the router's connection. If your Internet service uses a connection-based system like PPPoE or standard dial-up service via a modem, this dialog may display a button that lets you connect to and disconnect from your ISP.

Figure 7.10 Router Status displayed via UPnP.

Click Properties and then Settings to display a list of network services for which the router is forwarding incoming connections to computers on your network. This list shows only forwarding settings made via UPnP. Services you've forwarded using the setup screens on your router, for example, Remote Desktop, as discussed later in this chapter, do not appear here and new settings should not be made here—they usually disappear when the router is reset.

Networking with Windows 9x and Me

If you have computers running older versions of Windows as well as XP, you'll very likely want to network them—if not permanently, at least long enough to transfer files from an old computer to a newer one. What most people quickly find out is that it's not as simple as they would hope. Although all versions of Windows use the same basic networking protocols to share files and printers, compatibility problems crop up more often than not. And although some of the problems are easily explained and fixed, others remain mysterious and intermittent. (We Windows users are used to that, aren't we?) The most significant issue is that Microsoft has changed the default networking protocol from NetBEUI to TCP/IP. Windows XP doesn't even overtly offer NetBEUI as an option, while older versions of Windows installed NetBEUI by default, and often didn't install TCP/IP at all. Unless you take steps to give all of your computers one common protocol, they won't be able to talk to one another.

There are three ways to get around this problem:

- You can install TCP/IP on your older computers.

- You can install NetBEUI on Windows XP (it's there, for the time being, but it's hard to find).

- You can use the IPX/SPX-Compatible Protocol as the common protocol.

The best route to follow won't be clear until you consider these other points:

- NetBEUI is not compatible with large, routed networks. In the future, NetBEUI may not be available at all. So, although it's an acceptable approach on small networks for the present, it's not a good long-term solution. It probably won't be usable at all with XP's successor, Windows Vista.

- NetBEUI and IPX/SPX require no configuration, so they work "out of the box." TCP/IP has to be properly configured to work. If you're not using a shared Internet connection, using one of these two protocols will simplify your life.

- If your network includes Macs, UNIX, and/or Linux and you want to share files with them as well, you'll definitely want to use TCP/IP for file sharing. TCP/IP is also the standard on all enterprise networks.

- Windows networks definitely don't like to have different mixes of protocols installed on different machines. It's best to install the same protocol or set of protocols on every computer. It doesn't matter which, as long as every computer has the same mix.

With this in mind, I recommend that you follow one of these three plans:

- On a home or small-office network, if you plan on retiring the older Windows computers within the next couple of years, go ahead and install NetBEUI on Windows XP (as well as all of your older computers). In the next section, I'll tell you how to install NetBEUI on Windows XP.

  Install TCP/IP on your older computers, as well.

  For a one-time network copy from an old computer to a new one, this is probably the best option. After the old computer is gone, you can uninstall NetBEUI from Windows XP.

■ If you have a larger number of computers and don't want to rely on NetBEUI's remaining available in the future, install the IPX/SPX-Compatible Protocol on all computers. Remove or disable NetBEUI from all computers on which it is installed.

■ If you're using a shared Internet connection, disable or remove NetBEUI and IPX/SPX from all computers. You'll have to expect some flakiness and sensitivity to the order in which your computers are booted up. You may find that some computers see others but not vice versa. If possible, boot a Windows XP machine first and keep it running all the time.

Installing NetBEUI on Windows XP

If you want to install the NetBEUI protocol on Windows XP in order to network with older version of Windows, follow these steps. You'll need your Windows XP Installation CD:

1. Log on as a Computer Administrator user.

2. Insert the Windows Installation CD into your computer's CD or CD/DVD drive.

3. Open Windows Explorer and locate folder `\Valueadd\MSFT\Net\NetBEUI` on the installation CD.

4. Drag file `nbf.sys` to `C:\Windows\System32\Drivers` (or wherever Windows XP is installed on your computer).

5. Drag file `netnbf.sys` to `C:\Windows\inf`. Now, you can install the NetBEUI protocol using the usual procedure, which I'll recap here.

6. Click Start, Network Connections (or click Start, and then right-click My Network Places).

7. Open the connection corresponding to your network adapter (usually Local Area Connection). Click Properties.

8. Click Install. Select Protocol, and click Add.

9. Select NetBEUI and click OK.

10. Close all the dialogs by clicking OK.

You won't need to restart Windows XP, but it may take a few minutes for your Windows XP computer to appear in the Network Neighborhood lists of other computers on your network. If it doesn't appear within 20 minutes, restart all of your computers, starting with the XP machine.

Installing SPX/IPX

If you want to install SPX/IPX as a network protocol, follow these steps:

1. View the Network Connections window, right-click the Local Area Connection icon and select Properties.

2. Click Install, select Protocol, and click Add.

3. Hightlight NWLink IPX/SPX/NetBIOS Compatible Transport Protocol and click OK.

Designating a Master Browser

Windows uses a database of known online computers to build the display known variously as "Network Neighborhood, "Computers Near Me," or "View Workgroup Computers." The service runs on one primary computer called the "master browser," which is determined by an automatic "election" held by the computers on the network. In addition, on a larger network some computers may be elected as backup browser servers.

When you are running a network with different versions of Windows, this service will not function correctly; the election goes haywire or the database is filled incorrectly or other problems occur, and the Network Neighborhood display won't function correctly even though the computers clearly can communicate with each other (for example, one can map network drives to folders shared by the invisible computers).

If you find that this occurs on your network, you may want to force the master browser service to run on a designated Windows XP computer that is always left on. This can help stabilize the list of local computers.

To make this work you have to (a) configure one computer to always be the master browser, and (b) configure all of the other computers never to offer to be the master.

To force the setting in Windows XP, 2000, and NT computers, you have to edit the Registry key `HKEY_LOCAL_MACHINE\System\CurrentControlSet\Services\Browser\Parameters`. There are two values that can be altered (refer to Chapter 6, "Tweaking and Tuning Windows," for more details on editing the Registry):

Value	Possible Settings
IsDomainMasterBrowser	True—This computer is master browser
	False—Master is determined by election
MaintainServerList	No—Never serve as master
	Yes—Ask to be the preferred master
	Auto—Offer to be master if needed

For Windows 98, the setting is made in the Control Panel. Open the Network applet, select File and Print Sharing for Microsoft Networks, and click Properties. Under Browse Master, change the setting from Default to Disabled.

Simple File Sharing

Although most home users are typically happy letting anyone at any computer read or modify any file, business users need to restrict access to files with payroll, personnel, and proprietary information. Windows XP and its predecessors, Windows NT and Windows 2000, were primarily designed for business use, so they require usernames and passwords for identification, and have a security system that lets computer owners restrict access to sensitive files on a user-by-user and file-by-file basis on each computer.

Unfortunately, on a Windows workgroup network, there is no centralized list of authorized usernames. This makes maintaining control of who is and isn't permitted to access network files on each computer difficult. Here's why: When you attempt to use a file or printer shared by another computer, Windows sends your username and password to the other computer. In versions of Windows *prior* to XP

- If the username and password matched a user account already set up on the other computer, Windows used that account's permission settings to determine whether to grant you access to the file.

- If the user information didn't match, Windows prompted you to enter a username and password that the other computer will recognize.

- If you failed to provide a valid password, the remote Windows computer gave you the permissions assigned to the "Guest" account, which was usually disabled or didn't have permission to access the resource you wanted.

The advantage of this system was that it let you determine precisely which users could access specific files and printers. The disadvantage was that it required you to set up identical user accounts for each network user on every computer, and then grant these users permissions to view and modify shared files and folders.

Smaller business and home users found this security setup cumbersome to use and difficult to set up properly. This pushed people into sharing accounts and passwords, and otherwise avoiding good security practices, just to get the network to work. That's a risky approach, so Microsoft gave Windows XP a new feature called *Simple File Sharing*.

When Simple File Sharing is enabled

- Network users are always given access to shared folders and printers, without being prompted for a username or password. They are automatically granted access to files and folders using the permissions granted to the Guest account, even if Guest is disabled for direct logins.

- The Security properties tab that is normally used to assign per-user permissions to files and printers is not displayed, even for files that are stored on a drive formatted with the NTFS file system. Files stored in directories in a user's profile folder (My Documents, for example) are automatically set up to permit access only by the owner, and files stored elsewhere are set up to permit access by anyone.

- Windows automatically assigns appropriate security permissions to folders and printers when you share them. If you check Allow Network Users to Change My Files, all network users can read, write, rename, or delete the contents of the shared folder. If you don't check this option, network users can view but not modify the contents.

The result is that, with Simple File Sharing in effect, anyone who connects to your network will have access to all files, folders, and printers shared from a Windows XP computer, with no security enforcement of any kind. This has the advantage of eliminating all worries about having to manage accounts and passwords on multiple computers, but it does mean that you have to keep in mind these points:

- The "Shared Documents" folder that appears under My Computer is automatically set up as a shared folder, the idea being that any files you place in it will be available not only to other users on your computer, but to other users anywhere on your network.

- You don't get to pick and choose who gets access and who doesn't. Everyone gets access to every shared resource.

- If you have an unsecured wireless network with no WEP or WPA security key, anyone driving by your home or office will not only be able to connect to your network, they'll be able to see and/or modify your shared files.

In the end, it's a reasonable trade-off, as long as keep in mind the fact that all shared files and folders are available to anyone who can connect to your network. You should also keep in mind that

- Simple File Sharing is always used on XP Home Edition, and cannot be disabled. This means that anyone can use any resource shared by a computer running XP Home Edition.

- Simple File Sharing is optional on XP Professional, when the computer is part of a workgroup network. It's enabled by default when Windows is installed, but you can disable it if you want to use the user-level security on files and/or shared resources.

- Simple File Sharing is always disabled on an XP Professional computer when it's joined to a domain network. User-level security is always used in this case.

- Simple File Sharing applies only to the resources shared by the computer running Windows XP. If you use XP to used folders shared by a computer running some other operating system, Windows Me or Mac OS X, for example, that operating system's security system will be used.

On an XP Professional computer that is not a member of a domain network, the Simple File Sharing feature can be disabled from the Tools, Folder Options, View tab in any Windows Explorer window, as shown in Figure 7.11. You must be logged on as a Computer Administrator to change the setting.

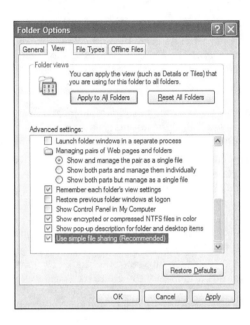

Figure 7.11 Simple File Sharing is enabled by default; disable it to use the old Windows NT/2000 access control system on a peer-to-peer network.

Tip

If you disable Simple File Sharing, a remote user will have to supply a username and password valid on your computer in order to use a shared resource on your computer. In this case, it vastly simplifies things if you set up an identical account for each user on each of your computers. For each user, pick a username and password, and use that same name and password on every computer.

Also, if Simple File Sharing is disabled, your computer will display different dialog boxes when you go to share a folder, and you'll have access to the Security properties page on folders and printers. We'll show both versions in the next section.

Sharing Resources

After your network is working, each computer can share selected resources—that is to say, folders and printers. The purpose of sharing is to make these folders and printers available to other computers, where they look and act *exactly* like folders on your own hard drive and printers connected to your own computer. This section briefly describes how to make resources available to other computers on the network.

Sharing Folders and Drives

By default, on a workgroup network Windows XP automatically shares the "My Documents" folder in the All Users profile folder; this is the folder that is listed as "Shared Documents" in My Computer. In some cases this may be sufficient. To make a file available to other users, simply drag it to the Shared Documents folder on your computer, and other users will be able to locate it on the network and read or copy it.

You can share other folders as well. To do so, locate the folder in Windows Explorer, right-click it and select Sharing. If you have Simple File Sharing enabled, the dialog in Figure 7.12 will appear.

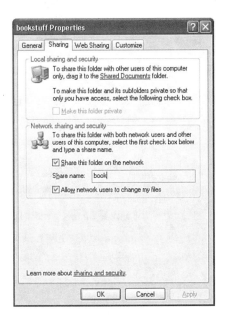

Figure 7.12   To share a folder, check Share This Folder and enter a share name.

Check Share This Folder On The Network and enter a share name, a name of up to 14 characters with no punctuation characters other than the underscore (_) or hyphen.

On an XP Professional computer on a workgroup network with Simple File Sharing enabled, or on a Windows XP Home Edition computer, you will see a check box labeled Allow Network Users to Change My Files. If you do not check it, network users can view and copy the files, but they cannot modify or delete them.

On an XP Professional computer with Simple File Sharing disabled, or on a domain network, the Sharing tab appears as shown in Figure 7.13.

In this case, permissions to read and write files can be controlled on a per-user or per-group basis by clicking the Permissions button. These permissions work as *additional restrictions* to any imposed by NTFS file security, if the folder is on a drive formatted with NTFS.

For example, if the sharing permissions grant read/write access to Everyone, the file will still be protected by whatever per-user permissions are assigned to the file; a network user will simply have the same rights to the file that he or she would have if seated right at the computer. If the sharing permissions give Everyone just Read access, users will be able to read files *if* the NTFS permissions let them, but in any case no network user will be able to modify or delete files.

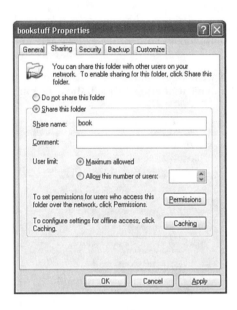

Figure 7.13   When Simple File Sharing is not active, there are more specific permission controls.

From the command line, you can share a folder or drive with the command

`net share sharename=drive:\fullpath`

For example,

`net share music=c:\musicfiles`

or

`net share cddrive=d:\`

and can cancel a share with the command

`net share sharename /delete`

Note

You can prevent a share from being displayed when other users browse the network by adding a dollar sign ($) to the share name. For example, the share name **secret$** will not appear in the My Network Places display. This won't deter a motivated hacker, but it does discourage casual browsing. To use a resource that's been hidden this way, you have to explicitly use its name. For example you can open **\\computername\sharename$** in Windows Explorer or you can map a network drive to this network path.

Note

Administrators may be used to using the built-in whole-drive shares that are automatically created for each disk drive on a Windows NT/2000/XP computer, for example, C$. However, these shares are only available to Computer Administrator users. You cannot reach these "admin" shares on a Windows XP computer that has Simple File Sharing enabled because all network access takes place using the Guest user account.

You can also share entire drives by viewing and right-clicking the drive icon in My Computer. This is a great way to make a DVD-ROM, CD-ROM, floppy disk, or other disk available to all users on a network. In the case of DVD and CD drives, you will be able to read but not write to these disks.

Sharing Printers

You can share any printer that is controlled by your computer. This includes printers directly cabled to your computer, and printers driven using LPR or other direct network protocols.

To enable printer sharing, do the following:

1. Choose Start and view the Printers and Faxes folder.
2. Right-click the printer icon and choose Sharing, or select Properties and then select the Sharing tab.
3. Select Share This Printer, and enter a network name for the printer, as shown in Figure 7.14. Enter up to 14 characters, avoiding punctuation characters.

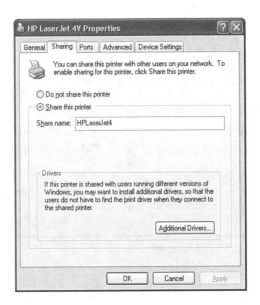

Figure 7.14   Enabling sharing for a printer.

4. If your network has only Windows XP/2000 computers, click OK, and you're finished. Other network users can now use the shared printer.

Otherwise, continue to the next section to add extra printer drivers for other operating systems.

Installing Extra Printer Drivers

If you have computers running other versions of Windows or other CPU types, you can load the appropriate printer drivers for those operating systems now, and network users will receive them automatically when they connect to your printer. This step is optional, but it's the friendly thing to do.

View the Sharing tab in your printer's Properties dialog box, and select the Additional Drivers button. Windows displays a list of supported operating systems and CPU types, as shown in Figure 7.15. (By the way, "Intel" refers to any Intel or compatible chips like those made by AMD or VIA/Cyrix.)

Figure 7.15   You can install drivers for additional operating systems or CPUs to make it easy for network users to attach to your printer.

Check the boxes for operating systems you want to support, and click OK. Windows then goes through these one by one and asks for the appropriate driver disks. You can find these drivers on the original installation disks for the alternative operating system, or often on disks provided with the printer, which might contain support for many operating systems on the same disk.

When installed, the alternative drivers are sequestered in your Windows folder and delivered to users of the other operating systems when they elect to use the networked printer.

Setting Printer Permissions

If you're on a domain network or have chosen to disable Simple File Sharing, you can control access to your shared printers with three security attributes that can be assigned to users or groups:

Permission	Lets User or Group
Print	Send output to the printer
Manage Printers	Change printer configuration settings, and share or unshare a printer
Manage Documents	Cancel or suspend other users' print jobs

You can use the Security tab in the printer's Properties dialog box to alter the groups and users assigned each of these permissions. The CREATOR OWNER name applies to the user who submitted a given print job.

You probably don't have to change the default permission settings unless you want to limit use of the printer by outside users in a domain environment only. In this case, delete Everyone, and add specific groups with Print permission.

Notifying Users When Printing Is Complete

You can have Windows send a pop-up message to remote users when print jobs they send to your printer have completed. By default, this feature is turned off when you install Windows XP.

To enable remote user notification, do the following:

1. Open the Printers and Faxes window.

2. Choose File, Server Properties.

3. Select the Advanced tab.

4. Check Notify When Remote Documents Are Printed.

5. If users on your network tend to use more than one computer at a time, check Notify Computer, Not User, When Remote Documents Are Printed. This option sends the notification to the computer where the print job originated rather than to the user who submitted the print job.

6. Click OK.

With remote notification enabled, when a print job has completed, a notification pops up on the sender's desktop. No message is sent if the print job is canceled, however.

Sharing Fax Modems and Other Devices

The software provided with Windows does not permit you to share a data modem, fax modem, scanner, or other input/output device over your network. You may find it as annoying as I do that the Windows Fax service is built to provide shared fax sending and receiving for a network, but the sharing capability is disabled in Windows XP.

If you want to be able to send faxes through a single phone line from several networked computers, the Windows Fax service on Windows 2000 Server or Windows Server 2003 *can* be shared. You can also purchase a third-party fax sharing program such as Symantec WinFax.

Shared scanners are a more complex matter. Some high-end printer/scanners have network capability built in. But this may not really be necessary. Because a scanner will have to be connected to one of your computers anyway, and you will need to stand there to put pages into the scanner, you can simply save the scans to a network shared folder, and later pick up the files from another computer.

Avoiding Firewall Issues

If you find that you cannot access shared folders or printers on another network computer, or if other users cannot access resources that are shared by your computer, it's possible that Windows Firewall or a third-party firewall is interfering. You may need to make a configuration change in order to let file and printer sharing work. However, in doing so, you must be *very careful* not to make your computer more accessible than absolutely necessary.

Use this checklist to enable file and printer sharing on both the computer that is sharing resources and the computer that is attempting to use them.

■ Be sure that you have run the Network Setup Wizard at least once. File and Printer sharing are silently disabled until you do so.

■ If the computer is running Windows XP Service Pack 2 or later, be sure that the Windows Firewall service is not blocking you. Open the Control Panel, and open Windows Firewall. On the General tab, the Firewall should be On, and Don't Allow Exceptions should *not* be checked. On the Exceptions tab, be sure that File and Printer Sharing are checked.

■ If you are using a third-party firewall service such as Norton Internet Security, be sure that this firewall is also configured to permit Windows File and Printer Sharing between computers on your subnet. The exact method for doing this varies from one product to another, but most have a fairly easy and explicit way to enable Windows File and Printer sharing.

In general you will *not* be able to safely share files and printers between computers that are not on the same network subnet; that is, directly connected on a network that is controlled by a single router.

Caution

If your computer is directly connected to the Internet, it is exceedingly dangerous to disable Windows Firewall or your third-party firewall package. Your computer may quickly become infected by viruses and Trojan Horse programs that are constantly scouring the Internet looking for unprotected Windows computers.

Providing Shared Internet Access

Although you could give each computer its own dial-up modem or broadband modem, one of the principal advantages of installing a network is gaining Internet access for all of your computers through a single connection. There are two simple ways to provide shared Internet access for a home or small office network:

- If you have cable or DSL broadband Internet service, get a hardware Internet connection sharing router. It's easy to set up, costs little or nothing, provides a certain amount of added security to your network, lets you add on additional computers with no setup effort, and can let you use both wired and wireless connections at the same time.

- If you use standard dial-up Internet service (not AOL dial-up service), use the Windows Internet Connection Sharing service to share the connection with others through your network. This is an acceptable solution although the "sharing" computer must be turned on in order to use the Internet from your other computers.

Note

You cannot share an AOL dial-up connection, nor can you share connections to discount ISPs that require the use of proprietary dial-up software.

Caution

For homes with more than one computer, cable Internet providers used to require you to connect your computers and cable modem to a hub, rather than to a router. However, this is dangerous—it exposes all of your computers directly to the Internet. If you still have this sort of setup, I strongly recommend that you purchase a hardware cable/DSL connection sharing router to place in between your cable modem and your computers. Otherwise, you *must not* enable File and Printer Sharing on your network.

Shared network connections provided by hardware routers and Windows Internet Connection Sharing (ICS) use a mechanism called *Network Address Translation* (NAT) to mediate between the computers on your network and the Internet via a single connection and single public IP address. The router or ICS computer has two connections, one to the Internet via a dial-up, cable, or DSL modem, and one to your LAN, as illustrated in the top part of Figure 7.16.

When one of your computers attempts to contact a website, it sends a data packet to the router or computer running ICS to be forwarded to the Internet, as illustrated in the bottom part of Figure 7.16. As it passes the outgoing network data packet to the Internet, the router replaces the packet's "from" address—the private IP address assigned to your computer—with the router's public address, so that the reply from the remote server will be returned through the Internet to the router. The router remembers from whom the request came, replaces the response's "to" network address with your computer's private address, and transmits it on its LAN connection.

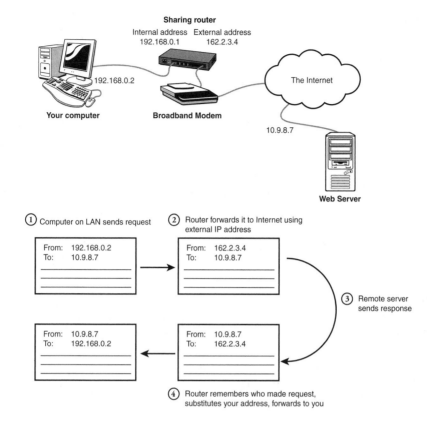

Figure 7.16   A Connection Sharing Router acts as an intermediary between your LAN and the Internet.

This mechanism works quite well for communication initiated by computers on your network. When outside computers attempt to contact you, however, it's another story. If you have a web or email server on your network, for instance, the connection sharing router or computer must be configured to send packets for particular network services to the correct computer; this is called "port forwarding." Otherwise incoming connection attempts are simply discarded. In this way NAT protects you against random probing by hackers, and it's very helpful to have this as a second level of protection in addition to Windows Firewall.

Adding a Connection Sharing Router

Connection sharing routers almost always have one 10Mbps Ethernet port that is used to connect to a cable or DSL modem, and have a second connection for your LAN. This LAN connection can take several forms:

- There may be a single 10/100Mbps Ethernet port.
- There may be four or more 10/100Mbps Ethernet ports, giving you a built-in switching hub.
- There may be a built-in Wireless networking access point.
- There may be a combination of the above.

Because wireless devices and laptops are becoming so common, and because it's very nice to be able to offer wireless connectivity to friends and visitors even if you don't use it yourself, I recommend purchasing an 802.11g wireless router with a built-in four port switch. If you shop carefully and look for a sale or rebate offer, wireless routers with four-port switches can frequently be purchased for $10 to $40.

Note

If you are planning to use Voice over IP (VoIP) telephone service, contact your VoIP provider to see what sort of routers they support.

You will need to ensure that your ISP provides you with a cable or DSL modem with an Ethernet port; USB or internal PCI adapters will not work with a router. Use a standard Ethernet patch cable to connect the modem to the Internet or WAN port on the router.

Then, connect one of your computer's LAN adapters to one of the ports on the router using another standard Ethernet patch cable.

Note

Even if you're going to use wireless connections, it's usually required, or at least easier, to use a wired connection to set up the router.

When you connect your computer's Ethernet port to the router, Windows will automatically request an IP address and configure the port's TCP/IP settings from default values provided by the router. You should then be able to open your web browser and view the router's setup web page using the URL //192.168.0.1 or //192.168.1.1, as instructed by your router's installation manual.

Your router will be establishing the connection to your ISP on your behalf, so you'll need the same information that you'd need to establish the connection directly through Windows. For a DSL connection, this often involves a username and password. For a cable connection, this often requires that you set the router's hostname to a specific name, or, you may have to provide the router's MAC address (its Ethernet hardware address code) to your ISP; this number is usually printed in tiny letters on a label on the bottom of the router. Alternatively, if you've already used your cable internet service by directly connecting your computer, you might be able to have the router *clone* your computer's MAC address, that is, copy your computer's address and use it on its Internet port so that your ISP doesn't have to make any changes.

Tip

If you previously had your computer connected directly to your cable or DSL modem, power the modem off and back on after you've connected it to the sharing router. This removes your computer's physical (MAC) address from the modem and from your ISP's end of the connection.

After installing the router, run the Network Setup wizard on all of your Windows XP computers. The Wizard is described earlier in this chapter under "Configuring a Workgroup Network." When asked to select a connection method, select This Computer Connects to the Internet Through Another Computer on My Network or Through a Residential Gateway.

Using Windows Internet Connection Sharing

Windows versions 98 Second Edition, Me, 2000, and XP have a software version of NAT called Internet Connection Sharing (ICS). It does in software what a connection sharing router does in hardware. If you have cable or DSL Internet service, I strongly recommend that you use a hardware router.

But, if you have standard dial-up Internet service, Internet Connection sharing can let you use the Internet from two or more computers at once, without tying up additional phone lines—a neat trick. It does, however, require you to leave the computer that is set up to share its connection turned on all of the time, at least, it must be on anytime anyone wants to use the Internet.

To set up ICS, select a computer to use to share the connection. Set up and test its Internet connection first, before creating a LAN. Then, if necessary, add a network adapter, and hook up your computers.

While logged on as Computer Administrator, run the Network Setup Wizard. We covered this wizard earlier in the chapter, under "Configuring a Workgroup Network." The important steps are as follows:

- When you're asked to selection a connection method, select the first choice, "This Computer Connects Directly to the Internet. The Other Computers…Connect…Through This Computer."

- When asked to choose a connection, select the entry for the dial-up connection to your ISP.

Complete the rest of the Network Setup Wizard as described earlier in the chapter. If you had set up your LAN previously, be sure to enter the same Workgroup name you used originally, as the wizard wants to change the setting to MSHOME every time you run it.

When the wizard completes, go to the Network Connections window and locate the icon that represents your Internet connection. It should now say "Firewalled, Shared" and possibly "Disconnected." Right-click it and select Properties. View the Networking tab. In the list of Components used by the connection, be sure that *only* Internet Protocol (TCP/IP) and QoS Packet Scheduler are checked. This will prevent file sharing from being exposed to the Internet. The Firewall will do that, too, but it doesn't hurt to be extra safe.

Then, restart your computer. Log on again, and try to view a web page (such as www.google.com). Your computer should automatically connect to your ISP, dialing or signing on if necessary. If the web page doesn't appear you'll have to resolve the problem before continuing.

When the sharing computer can connect properly, run the Network wizard on your other Windows XP computers, except for one detail: When you run the wizard, select This Computer Connects to the Internet Through Another Computer on My Network or Through a Residential Gateway.

Remote Desktop and Remote Assistance

Windows XP has two remote access features that are worth getting to know. The first is Remote Assistance. Its purpose, as its name suggests, is to let someone connect to your computer via the Internet or a LAN to work with you on a problem or project. Both of you can see the screen, and you can trade off using the mouse and keyboard to control the computer. Likewise, you can use Remote Assistance to assist someone else. However, connections can't be made arbitrarily—the "assistee" must invite the assistant via an encrypted message sent via email or Microsoft Messenger, and must indicate acceptance of the connection when the assistant response to the invitation. A Remote Assistance scenario is illustrated in Figure 7.17.

In contrast to Remote Assistance, the purpose of Remote Desktop is to let you remotely connect to your own computer; for example, to use your office computer from home, or your home computer from out of town. While you're connected, it's almost as if you were "there," because the controlled computer's display and sound are brought to you, and the remote computer's keyboard, mouse, and even COM ports and hard disk can function as if they were connected to the "home" computer, as illustrated in Figure 7.18.

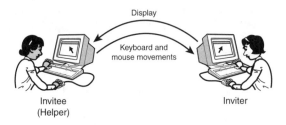

Figure 7.17 With Remote Assistance, you can work collaboratively with someone else.

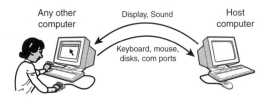

Figure 7.18 With Remote Desktop, you can use your own computer from any computer running Windows or Mac OS X.

Remote Desktop works in much the same way as other remote control products such as VNC, PCAnywhere, and CarbonCopy. Personally, it seems to me to be somewhat faster than these other programs, although it has some limitations:

- Remote Desktop is only available on Windows XP Professional, not Home Edition. However, this applies only to the host (controlled) computer. The Remote Desktop Client program, which you use to connect to the controlled computer, can run on Windows 9x, ME, 2000, or XP, and there is an Apple Mac OS X version as well.

- Only one person can use the host computer at a time. If you connect remotely, the controlled computer's own monitor switches to the Welcome Screen. And if someone then logs on locally, the remote user is disconnected.

- Remote Desktop works only over a TCP/IP network such as the Internet; it doesn't directly support modem access as PCAnywhere and CarbonCopy do. However, Windows XP does provide a way for you to establish a network connection to your computer via modem, so with a few extra steps you *can* actually a use modem to connect to your computer for Remote Desktop access.

Remote Desktop Connection is one of the spiffiest features of Windows XP Professional, and for me, reason enough to use XP Pro instead of Home Edition. It lets me use my office computer (and thus my email, documents, notes, and everything) from anywhere in the world, from nearly any Windows or Macintosh computer. Because it's quite difficult to set up, we thought it would be useful to go into the details in this chapter.

Making Your PC Available for Remote Desktop Connection

To use Remote Desktop to reach your computer from the Internet, both the computer and your Internet connection must always be up and running. In addition, you must be able to make connections from the outside world to your computer, so there are additional requirements:

- If you use dial-up Internet service, you'll need someone at home to establish the connection before you can connect to your computer.

- If you use cable or DSL Internet service, you must either have a static IP address assigned by your ISP, or, you must use a dynamic DNS client on your computer or router to notify a dynamic DNS name service provider every time your connection's IP address changes.

- If you use a connection sharing router or use an Internet connection provided through Windows Internet Connection Sharing on a different computer, you must configure the sharing device or computer to forward incoming TCP connections on port 3389 to your computer.

If you can forgo access from the outside world, you also use Remote Desktop just within your own private network at home or work with far less setup trouble, as I'll note later on. The initial steps are the same.

Note

If your computer is part of a corporate network, be sure that your organization's security policies permit you to enable Remote Desktop connection. On a Windows Domain network, Remote Desktop might even be disabled by the Group Policy feature.

Also, if your Internet Service Provider is AOL, or if you use a free advertisement-subsidized Internet service, you will not be able to establish Remote Desktop access to your computer.

The following sections describe the setup procedure. Perform all of these steps while logged in as a Computer Administrator.

Step 1—Enable Remote Desktop

The first step in configuring Remote Desktop Connection is to enable the connections at your computer, using this procedure:

1. Right-click My Computer and select Properties. Or, open the System control panel applet.

2. Select the Remote tab and check Allow Users to Connect Remotely to This Computer.

3. Computer Administrator users can connect without explicit permission. If you want to grant Remote Desktop access to Limited Access or Power User user accounts, click Select Remote Users and check the boxes next to the usernames.

   In any case, however, *only* accounts with passwords can be used. Windows will not grant access to any user account that does not have a password set.

4. Click OK to close the dialogs.

Enabling Remote Desktop *should* automatically create an exception in Windows Firewall so that connections will be allowed in. However, you should confirm this.

Step 2—Open Your Firewall

To check the Firewall settings, open the Control Panel and Windows Firewall. Select the Exceptions tab and locate the entry for Remote Desktop Connection. Select the entry and check its check box if it is not checked already. Then, click Edit, and be sure that under Scope the word *Any* appears. If it doesn't, click Change Scope and select Any Computer. Click OK to close all of the dialogs.

If you use a third-party firewall program, you must instruct it to open access to TCP Port 3389 for all IP addresses, following the instructions for your particular firewall product.

At this point you should be able to connect to your computer from any other computer on your network using Remote Desktop Connection. If you do have another networked computer, you should test this now to be sure that the first two steps have worked. Note the name of the computer you just set up (if you don't know it, right-click My Computer, select Properties, view the Computer Name tab, and make a note of the name after Full Computer Name). However, if the name ends with a period, drop the period. Now, go to another computer on your network, skip ahead to "Connecting to Your Computer with Remote Desktop," on page 333 and try connecting to your computer using this name.

Note

If you only want local remote desktop access, you can stop at this point. This is actually useful enough—my friend Bob totes a small, slow, wireless-enabled laptop around his house, and uses it to access his primary desktop Media Center computer, mainly for email, but also to control his sound system, TV recorder, and so on.

When you know that Remote Desktop is working correctly in-house, you'll have to provide a way to access to your computer from the outside world.

Step 3—Set a Static IP Address

If your computer makes its Internet connection directly, has a fixed IP address assigned by your network manager, or gets its Internet connection through Windows Internet Connection Sharing, you can skip this step.

However, if you use a hardware connection sharing router device, you'll have to configure your router and your computer so that your computer has a *static* or fixed IP address. We discussed this earlier in the chapter.

There are two steps involved: You must select a fixed address in the correct range for your network, and, you must configure your router so that it does not give this address to any other computer.

Most routers automatically assign IP addresses to the computers on your network, and they typically look like 192.168.0.3 or 192.168.1.101. The first two numbers are almost always 192 and 168. The third number varies from manufacturer to manufacturer. It's usually 0 or 1, but it doesn't really matter, so in this section I'll use x in its place; just be sure to make note of the actual number your router happens to use. The fourth number is the only number that is different for each device and computer. It's usually 1 for the router itself, and a number between 2 and 254 for computers.

My recommendation is that you use addresses 192.168.x.200 through 192.168.x.254 for any computers or devices such as print servers that need a fixed address, and let your router pass out dynamic addresses from 192.168.x.2 up or 192.168.x.100 up. Most routers have a configuration screen that lets you set this; it may be on the main LAN setup page or it may be on a menu labeled DHCP. A typical setup screen is shown in Figure 7.19.

While you are doing this, also make a note of the IP address assigned to the router itself (it's 192.168.0.1 in the figure), and the Network Mask or Subnet Mask value.

For the static addresses in the range 192.168.x.200 to 192.168.x.254, you'll have to manually keep track of which addresses are available and which are free.

Tip

I recommend keeping a list of used and unused IP addresses on paper, in a file folder along with printed screen shots of all of your computer and network configuration screens and dialogs, to have on hand in case of an emergency—your network setup is too valuable to lose in a disk crash!

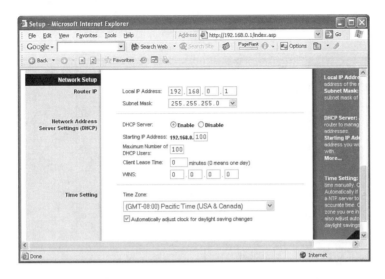

Figure 7.19   Configure DHCP to pass out addresses 100 and up.

You will also need to know IP address or addresses of the Domain Name Service (DNS) Servers pro-vided by your ISP. To find them, check your ISP's tech support web pages, view the setup screen on your router to see if you entered this information there, or, go to a computer that has a functioning Internet connection, open a command Prompt Window, type the command **ipconfig /all** and press Enter, and note the address or addresses listed after DNS Servers. Jot this information down for use later on.

To configure your computer, select an unused number from the list of static addresses, and follow these steps:

1. Open Network Connections, right-click the network adapter's icon (usually labeled Local Area Connection) and select Properties.

2. Select Internet Protocol (TCP/IP) and click the Properties button.

3. On the General tab (see Figure 7.20), select Use the Following IP Address.

4. For the IP address, enter one of the available IP addresses from your list, for example, 192.168.*x*.2, but with the correct digit instead of *x*.

5. For the Subnet mask, enter the mask value you recorded from the router's setup screen. It's usu-ally 255.255.255.0.

6. For the Default Gateway, enter the IP address of the router itself. It usually ends in .1.

7. For the Preferred DNS Server, enter the first DNS server address you noted earlier. If there was just one, leave the Alternate DNS server blank; otherwise enter the second address.

8. Click OK, wait 10 seconds or so, and then test the Internet connection by trying to view a web page.

Remember to write down the IP address you used, and the name of the computer to which you assigned it.

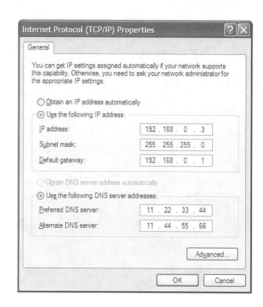

Figure 7.20   Configuring a static IP address.

Step 4—Enable Port Forwarding

If you use Windows Internet Connection Sharing or a connection sharing router, you'll have to instruct your sharing computer or router to forward incoming Remote Desktop connections from the router's public connection to your private network and thence to your computer. Specifically, you'll have to set up your sharing computer or router to forward incoming requests on TCP port 3389 to the computer that you want to reach through Remote Desktop.

If you use a connection-sharing router, it will have a setup menu option titled Port Forwarding or Applications. You sometimes have to select the Advanced menu to find it. Make an entry to forward TCP port 3389 to the IP address of the host computer. A typical configuration screen is shown in Figure 7.21.

If you use Windows Internet Connection Sharing, go to the computer that is sharing its Internet connection, log on as a Computer Administrator, and follow these steps:

1. Open Network Connections and locate the icon for the shared connection (it will be labeled as Shared).

2. Right-click the icon and select Properties. View the Advanced tab. Under Internet Connection Sharing, click the Settings button.

3. In the Services list, locate Remote Desktop Connection and check it. The Services Settings dialog will appear, as shown in Figure 7.22. Enter the name of the computer that you will be connecting to with Remote Desktop, or, if it has a static (fixed) IP address, enter the IP address.

4. Click OK to close the dialogs.

The next step is to ensure that your computer will be reachable when it's needed.

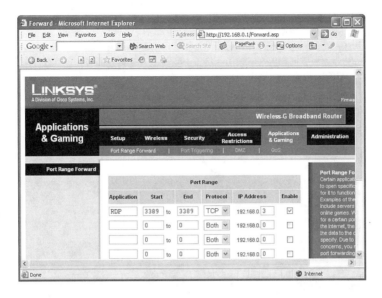

Figure 7.21   Make your router forward TCP Port 3389 to your computer.

Figure 7.22   Enter the name or static IP address of the computer to be reached via Remote Desktop.

Step 5—Establish a Permanent Connection

Many consumer-grade broadband Internet services provide temporary connections, requiring a user-name and password to establish a connection that lasts until a certain amount of time has passed with no data traffic, or until you force a disconnection. Dial-up Internet service is always connection-based, and DSL service often is as well, using a scheme called Point-to-Point Protocol over Ethernet, or

PPPoE. Cable Internet service is usually "always on" but some cable providers also use PPPoE. This helps conserve the limited number of IP addresses allotted to your Internet Service Provider, but it's no good if you have to be sitting in front of your computer to establish a connection in order to connect to it remotely! So, if you have a connection-based Internet service, you'll need to configure your computer or sharing router to keep the connection open all of the time.

If you are using a broadband connection sharing router device, its setup screen should have an option to keep the connection on permanently. The means varies from one manufacturer to another, but it's usually there. Enable any settings that mention establishing a connection automatically, sending Keep Alive packets, and if there is a setting for disconnecting after a certain amount of time idle, set it to zero or Never. A typical setup screen is shown in Figure 7.23.

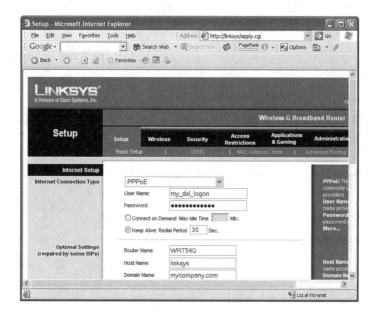

Figure 7.23 Use your router's setup screen to establish an always-on connection.

If you establish your Internet connection directly from Windows XP using an icon on the Network Connections window, either at a solo computer, or on a computer that shares its connection with Internet Connection Sharing, follow these steps:

1. Open Network Connections, and locate the icon for your Internet connection; this is the one that you set up with the username and password required by your ISP.

2. Right-click the icon and select Properties.

3. View the Options tab, and make the following changes: Set Redial Attempts to 20, Time Between Redial Attempts to 10 seconds, Idle Time Before Hanging Up to Never, and check Redial If Line Is Dropped.

4. Click OK, and establish the connection.

If your computer is sharing this connection with Internet Connection Sharing, the connection should stay up as long as your computer is powered on. If the connection is not shared, it will stay up as long as your computer is turned on and your account stays logged on. It's not ideal, but it'll work for a while. (You might consider getting a connection-sharing router device just so that you can let *it* do the job of keeping your connection up; it shouldn't cost more than $20, and will do a much better job.)

Caution

This type of always-on connection can be even be set up with a standard dial-up or ISDN connection, but before you try it be *sure* that you aren't going to be charged on a per-minute basis, or you could be in for a very nasty surprise when the next phone bill arrives.

Additionally, if you want your computer to be remotely accessible at all times, you should anticipate that a power failure might occur while you're away. You may want to configure your PC's BIOS to automatically turn the computer on after a power outage. Dell computers label this setting "AC Power Recovery." Other manufacturers use different terms.

Step 6—Obtain a Domain Name Service (DNS) Name

Lastly, to reach your computer from the Internet, you'll need to know the IP address of the Internet connection used by the computer you're contacting. If you have business-class Internet service, your computer may have a public, static (fixed) IP address and you may have domain name service set up so that you can use a name like "maggie.mycompany.com" to reach your own computer. If so, you're finished, and can go ahead and try to connect to your computer using Remote Desktop. Some ISPs will also provide static IP addresses for single-computer customers, for a moderate fee.

However, the majority of us use consumer-grade dial-up or broadband Internet service, where your IP address can change every time a connection is made, or at least every few days or weeks. In this case, you present a moving target to the Internet, and in order to connect to your computer from "outside" you need a way to find out what its IP address is.

What you need is called Dynamic Domain Name Service (DDNS). There are several free DDNS services, but to keep this short I'll describe how to use only one, dyndns.org. Dyndns.org maintains DNS servers whose job it is to turn hostnames like joebob.homedns.org into IP addresses. You simply register and set up an account, choose a hostname, and configure your computer or router to automatically notify dyndns.org when your network's external IP address changes. That's the dynamic part—the address gets updated without any manual intervention. When this has been set up, the selected hostname will be recognized anywhere on the Internet and will return your router's current external IP address.

There are two steps to setting up DDNS service: creating an account at dyndns.org, and configuring your network to send updates when its IP address changes. I'll describe the basic, free service here.

To set up service at dyndns.org, follow these steps:

1. Visit www.dyndns.org and click Sign Up Now. Read and check acceptance of the Acceptable Use Policy, select and enter a username, enter your email address, select a password, enter any optional information you feel like entering, and click Create Account. Be sure to write down your logon name and password to keep in your network setup file.

2. Check your email for a message from dyndns.org, and double-click the URL it contains to confirm your account.

3. Click login, and enter your username and password. Click Login.

4. Click My Services, Add Host Services, Add Dynamic DNS Host.

5. Make up a hostname, and select a domain name from the drop-down list, as illustrated in Figure 7.24. The combination of the two will be the name you'll use when you connect to your computer with Remote Desktop, so choose something easy to remember; it might be something like joebob.homedns.org. Write the combined hostname and domain name down to keep in your network setup file.

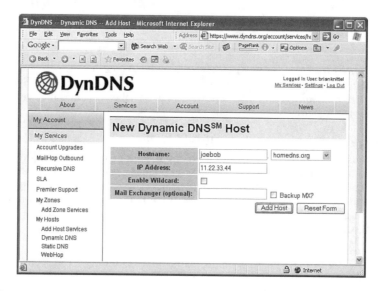

Figure 7.24   Select the hostname and domain name you'd like to use to access your computer.

6. Leave the IP address as is, leave Enable Wildcard unchecked, and leave the Mail Exchanger field blank. Click Add Host to create the entry. If no one else has used the same combined hostname and domain name, it should work; otherwise you might be asked to make a different selection.

You can return to the My Hosts list later and edit this information. To change the host or domain name, however, you must delete the host and add a new one.

Now, the host and domain name combination you selected is online and available anywhere on the Internet. It will resolve to your current IP address, though, and you must now take steps to ensure that it's updated when your IP address changes.

If you use a hardware connection sharing router, see whether it has built-in support for DDNS. Some do, including some models by DLink, Linksys, and others. If it does have DDNS support, enable it and enter the dyndns.org account name, password, and full host name (including the domain name) that you set up in the previous steps; a typical router setup screen is shown in Figure 7.25. When you save the settings, see if your router displays a status message indicating that it successfully contacted and updated dyndns.org's records. If so, it should now keep your selected hostname updated with your current IP address at all times.

Note

Although dyndns.org updates its database instantly when your router or DDNS client program notifies it of a change, ISPs can elect to hang on to (cache) address information for an arbitrary amount of time—minutes to hours. If your home network's connection goes down and comes back up with a new IP address, you might have trouble re-establishing a

Remote Desktop connection to it until the ISP you're using allows the cached address to expire and finally queries dyn-dns.org for the current one.

Also, dyndns.org will drop any hostnames that are not updated at least once a month, unless you upgrade to a higher service level for a fee. Some routers fail to send DDNS updates if their IP address never changes, which often is the case with cable Internet service. So if you get an email saying your hostname was deleted, you'll have to re-create it, and do one of these four things to prevent it from being dropped again: (1) see whether your router manufacturer has a firmware upgrade that fixes this problem, (2) get a new router with better ddns firmware, (3) upgrade your dyndns.org service to eliminate the six-month limit, or (4) use a software DDNS update client.

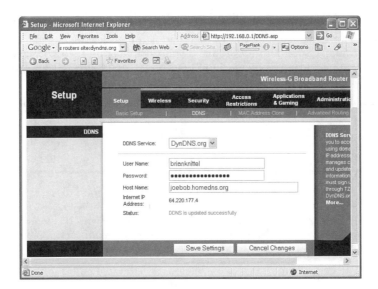

Figure 7.25   Enable DDNS on your router.

If your router can't send DDNS updates or you do not use a hardware connection sharing router, you can still maintain your DDNS records using a software DDNS update client. This is a program that runs on one of your computers and periodically updates dyndns.org whenever your IP address changes, but at least once every few weeks so that your hostname is not dropped. Dyndns.org has a recommended DDNS update client it calls the "Official Windows Update Client," but unfortunately this program runs only when you are logged on, which is of no use if you're away for an extended period. You should use a DDNS update client that runs as a Windows service on one of your computers—the Remote Desktop host computer would be the best candidate—so that it is always active whether anyone is logged in or not.

Some DDNS update clients that run as Windows services you might want to investigate are inadyn from inadyn.ina-tech.net (free, but with the current version, installation is not for the faint of heart), myDynamicIP from www.roconsoftware.com (shareware, $15 Canadian), and DirectUpdate from www.directupdate.net (shareware, $19 US). By the time you read this, a new version of inadyn should be available that is easy to install and use, so I'd check it out first.

When your dynamic DNS hardware or software configuration is set up and working, you should be able to test the connection to your computer by connecting to it with the Remote Desktop client from another computer, via the Internet. The instructions for doing so appear after the next section.

Providing Access to More than One Computer

Once you have one computer configured, tested, and reachable by Remote Desktop from the Internet, you can consider making other computers on your network available as well. If your computers all have their own public IP addresses, you can just repeat the previous steps. But, if you have a shared Internet Connection, there are some additional considerations.

By default, Remote Desktop uses TCP Port 3389 for its connection. This works fine *within* a given network, because each computer has its own IP address and network name. However, when you use a shared Internet connection, there is only one IP address visible to the outside world, so another means must be used to designate which of your computers you want to connect to. What you'll need to do is designate different ports to be used to reach each the additional computers. I use port numbers 3390, 3391, and so on for my additional computers.

The setup screens for some hardware connection sharing routers let you designate different external and internal port numbers for port forwarding. If yours permits this, then setting up additional computers is a snap. Simply direct incoming connections on different ports to your various computers, as in this sample router forwarding configuration:

External Port	Internal Port	Protocol	Internal IP Address
3389	3389	TCP	192.168.0.3
3390	3389	TCP	192.168.0.5
3391	3389	TCP	192.168.0.6

With this setup, from the outside world a Remote Desktop Connection to, say, `remote.mycompany.com`, which uses the default port, would go to the computer with IP address 192.168.0.3. A connection to `remote.mycompany.com:3391` would be forwarded to the computer with IP address 192.168.0.6. The router will take care of translating not only the IP address of the connection, but also the port, so that the target computer receives the connection on the standard port #3389.

Within your private network you can still use Remote Desktop to connect to these computers using their assigned computer names and no specified port number.

If your router does not permit you to specify different external and internal port numbers, your additional computers must be configured so that Remote Desktop listens on alternate ports. The router's Port Forwarding setup might look something like this:

Port	Protocol	IP Address
3389	TCP	192.168.0.3
3390	TCP	192.168.0.5
3391	TCP	192.168.0.6

In this example, we would have the computer at IP address 192.168.0.3 use the default Remote Desktop port, and would configure the computers with addresses 192.168.0.5 and 6 to use alternate ports 3390 and 3391.

Make a list of computers that are to be reachable by Remote Desktop. Select a port number for each computer that you want to reach, starting with 3389 and going up or down from there. Unless you're using Microsoft Internet Connection Sharing, each of these computers must also be configured to use a fixed IP address, which you should also write down along with the chosen port number.

Now, perform the following steps on each of the computers that will use a non-standard port:

1. Log on as a Computer Administrator, enable Remote Desktop, and designate authorized users as described earlier.

2. Open the Registry Editor by clicking Start, Run, regedit and pressing Enter.

3. In the left hand pane, view the key `HKEY_LOCAL_MACHINE\System\CurrentControlSet\Control\ TerminalServer\WinStations\RDP-Tcp`.

4. In the right hand pane, double-click the value PortNumber. Select Decimal, and change the port number from 3389 to the chosen value for this particular computer. Then, click OK and close the Registry editor.

5. Open Control Panel, Security Center, Windows Firewall and select the Exceptions tab. Click Add Port. For the name, enter **Remote Desktop (Alternate Port)**. For the port, enter the number you used in step 4. Select TCP. Click Change Scope and verify that All Computers is checked. Click OK three times to close everything.

6. Restart the computer.

Now, if you're using Windows Internet Connection Sharing, configure the sharing computer to forward incoming connections on the additional ports to the selected computers. You can specify the computers by name.

Otherwise, configure your router to forward the additional ports to the selected computers. Specify the computers by their IP addresses, which must be configured as fixed addresses.

If you want to use Remote Desktop Connection to control any of the additional computers from *within* your private network, you will have to specify the correct port number as well as the computer name.

Connecting to Your Computer with Remote Desktop

To establish a connection to a computer that's been set up to receive Remote Desktop connections, you'll need a copy of the Remote Desktop Client, also called the Terminal Services Client. There are several ways you can get this program:

- It's preinstalled on Windows XP computers. Select Start, All Programs, Accessories, Communications, Remote Desktop Connection.

- It's on your Windows XP CD-ROM. Insert it in another Windows computer, and from the setup program select Perform Additional Tasks, and then Set Up Remote Desktop Connection. This will run the installation program.

- You can download it from www.microsoft.com. Search for Remote Desktop Client.

- On Apple Macintosh computers running OS X, download the Mac version from www.microsoft.com/mac; click on View All Downloads and scroll down to Other Products to find it.

- For UNIX and Linux, there is an open-source version under development that runs under X11. Check www.rdesktop.org or sourceforge.net/projects/rdesktop.

- If you are using a Windows computer on which you don't have sufficient privileges to install new software, you can use an ActiveX version of the client that runs within Internet Explorer. Search microsoft.com for Remote Desktop Connection Web Connection Software Download. Download and run the software and install it in a temporary folder. Open Internet Explorer and click File, Open, Browse, and then locate the file `default.htm` in the folder into which you installed the software. If Internet Explorer warns you about running Active content, permit it to do so. You should then be able enter the DNS name of the remote computer and click Connect.

When you run the Remote Desktop Client, you'll see the Remote Desktop Connection dialog, as shown in Figure 7.26.

Figure 7.26   The Remote Desktop Connection dialog lets you configure the connection and select the remote computer to use.

Enter the IP address or registered DNS name of the computer you'd like to use. If you want to connect to a computer using an alternative TCP port number, enter a colon and the port number after the IP address or name, as in `remote.mycompany.com:3391`.

Entering a username and password at this point is optional. If you don't enter them now, you'll be asked for them when the connection is established. Click Connect to establish the connection immediately, or click Options to adjust the connection properties first. The properties tabs are described in Table 7.1.

Table 7.1   Remote Desktop Connection Properties

Tab	Properties
General	*Connection Settings* saves the configuration for a particular remote computer as a shortcut for quick access later.
Display	Sets the size and color depth of the window used for your remote connection's desktop. Display size can be set to a fixed window size, or Full Screen.
Local Resources	Connects devices on the local computer so that you can use them as if they were part of the remote computer. (This feature does not work when connecting to Windows NT and Windows 2000 Terminal Services.) The Keyboard setting determines whether special Windows key commands like Alt+Tab apply to your local computer or the remote computer.
Programs	Lets you automatically run a program on the remote computer upon logging on.
Experience	Lets you indicate your connection speed, so that Windows can appropriately limit display-intense features like menu animation.

When you establish the connection, you'll see a standard Windows logon dialog. Enter your username and password to sign on. It may take awhile for the logon process to complete, if Windows has to switch out a logged-on user.

When you're logged on, you'll see the remote computer's desktop, and you can use it as if you were actually sitting in front of it. Keyboard, mouse, display, and sound should be fully functional. If you maximize the window, the remote desktop will fill your screen. It all works quite well—it can even be difficult to remember which computer you're actually using!

In addition, any printers attached to your local computer will appear as choices if you print from applications on the remote computer, and you enabled them before you established the connection, the local computer's drives will appear in the list in My Computer, as shown in Figure 7.27. You can take advantage of this to copy files between the local and remote computers, although it's rather slow.

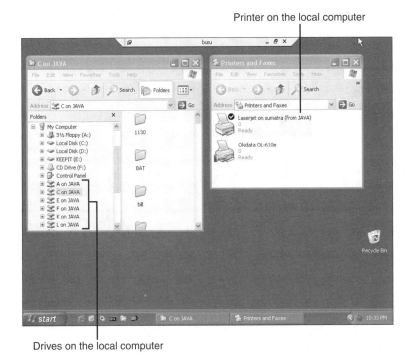

Printer on the local computer

Drives on the local computer

Figure 7.27   When connected to Windows XP via Remote Desktop, your local computer's drives and printers can be made available.

Finally, your local computer's serial (COM) ports will also be available to the remote computer. (My friend Norm syncs his Palm Pilot to his Windows XP Professional computer at home using this feature.)

Tip

If the computer to which you connect has multiple monitors, you may find that an application seems to be running, but you can't make its window appear. What's happened is that it's positioned offscreen, where it would be on the second monitor that doesn't exist in the Remote Desktop world. To move it into view, right-click the application's button in the task bar. If Minimize is grayed out, click Restore, and then right-click again. If Maximize is grayed out, click Restore, and then right-click again. Select Move, and use the left or right arrow key to bring the window into view.

While you're connected, you might want to use keyboard shortcuts like Alt+Tab to switch between applications on the remote computer. By default, this won't work, because they will be interpreted by the local computer and Alt+Tab will simply switch you away from the Remote Desktop application. However, you can specify which computer should be the one to interpret special key combinations on the Local Resources properties page, as I described earlier, or you can use alternate key combinations to ensure that the desired actions take place on the remote computer. The alternate keyboard shortcuts are shown in Table 7.2.

Table 7.2   Some of the Remote Desktop Keyboard Shortcuts

Use These Keys:	To Transmit This to the Remote Computer:
Alt+PgUp, Alt+PgDn	Alt+Tab (switch programs)
Alt+End	Ctrl+Alt+Del (task monitor)
Alt+Home	(Displays the Start menu)
Ctrl+Alt+Break	Alt+Enter (toggle full screen)
Ctrl+Alt+Plus	Alt+PrntScrn (screen to clipboard)

When you've finished using the remote computer, choose Start, Log Off to sign off and end the connection. If you want the remote computer to continue running an application, though, you can simply close the Remote Desktop window or select Disconnect. Your account will stay active on the remote computer until you reconnect and log off, or until a user at that computer logs on. I use this feature extensively: My spam filter is very slow, so I find it better to leave my account logged in all the time, and leave the email program open all the time. When I leave work I use Windows+L to switch off but stay logged on. Then, from home I can reconnect with remote Desktop to check email.

Note

Windows XP Professional only permits one person to use each computer. If you attempt to connect to a computer while another user is logged on, you'll have the choice of disconnecting or forcing them off. If Fast User Switch is enabled, they'll simply be switched out. Otherwise they're summarily logged off. This is somewhat brutal as the other user might lose work in progress.

If you log on using the same username as the local user, though, you simply take over the existing desktop without forcing a logoff, with any applications that were running still active.

If someone logs on to the remote computer while you're connected from afar, *you'll* be disconnected. Again, if Fast User Switch is enabled, you can reconnect later and pick up where you left off. Otherwise, the same deal applies: If they used a different username, your applications will be shut down.

Finally, you may notice that the TEMP environment variable is not what you expect when you log on using Remote Desktop. When a second or subsequent session is created with the Welcome Screen, or if you create a new logon session through Remote Desktop—as opposed to connecting to one initially started at the computer itself—the Terminal Services system will create a subfolder under your usual temporary folder named 1 or 2 or another digit, and TEMP will point to this subfolder. If you disconnect without logging out and later reconnect to the session at the computer console itself, TEMP will still refer to this subfolder.

CHAPTER 8

Protecting and Securing Windows

Protecting and securing your computer is a major concern with the growing number of malicious software applications circulating on the Internet. The days of just applying the latest Windows security patches to your computer are over. New vulnerabilities or security holes are found almost daily and it usually takes Microsoft several days, if not weeks, to write and test a security patch to fix the hole. The slow response by many of the software companies combined with the fact that most vulnerabilities are not widely known about until they are used to attack thousands of computers are why it is now necessary to take an active approach to protecting your Windows computer.

Using various security tools and techniques, it is possible to greatly reduce how vulnerable your computer is, even when new security vulnerabilities are discovered.

By taking an active approach to securing your computer, you can easily protect your computer from the three core security threats to all PCs:

- Viruses that may infect all of the documents on your computer and may even erase or corrupt critical operating system files.

- Spyware that monitors activity on your computer and is often used to display annoying advertisements.

- Trojans that have the possibility of giving an attacker full access to your computer files over the Internet.

While these threats are an obvious concern to system administrators in enterprise level networks, they are no less a problem for the at-home user of Windows XP. Taking the steps outlined in this chapter to protect your Windows PC is an essential part of protecting both its data and its operating stability. The first of these essential steps is to make sure all user accounts on your PC are password protected.

Windows Passwords

Passwords are your first line of defense for both local and remote attacks on your computer. However, the vast majority of home users simply do not use passwords for their Windows user accounts. For some it is too much of an inconvenience, while others just do not see why they need to use one because they trust everyone (family and friends) who has physical access to their computer. If your computer is never connected to any type of a network, including the Internet, then you are in the clear. But if you are like the majority of computer users and connect to the Internet through some type of medium, even if just for a few minutes at a time via a dial-up connection, you are leaving the door wide open.

The fact that your computer is in a secure location (a home, office, and so on) will protect physical access to your computer. But the moment that you log on to the Internet, or turn your PC on (if you are a broadband user), you could potentially be sharing all of your data files with the world. Basically, anyone who knows your user name can access your computer. And for those who don't, it only takes a little effort from a clever attacker to figure out your user name.

There is a reason why more and more people are getting their identity stolen every year. Many are not taking the steps necessary to protect their sensitive data. A password on all of the user accounts on your computer will not solve all of your security problems, but it's a necessary first step that goes a long way in protecting access to your computer by shutting the door to attackers looking for easy access.

If you do not already have a password assigned to all of the accounts on your computer, it is very easy to set it up. Just open the Control Panel and click on User Accounts. Then click on the name of the account and click the Create Password button. To set a password for a user, right-click on the name of the account and select Set Password. (General management of user accounts is covered in Chapter 5, "Managing Windows.")

Tip

In Windows 2000/XP, you can just run `lusrmgr.msc` from either the command prompt or the Run box in the Start menu (click Start, Run). This starts up the Local User and Group manager.

Keep in mind that a password is only as good as an attacker's ability to guess or crack it using any number of simple brute-force utilities. Here are my recommendations for a good password:

- The password contains numbers and special characters such as ")(*&^%$#".
- The password contains both upper- and lowercase letters.
- Common words are not used.
- Personal information such as variation of name, address, and phone number is not used.
- Your password is at least 8 characters long.
- You change your password at least twice a year.

Aside from these guidelines, I also recommend you use different passwords for each of your online accounts. Using the same one is like using the same exact key for your car, your home, your office, and your safety deposit box. If someone discovers your password, a lot of your personal information as well as any financial data could be at risk.

Tip

Following the good password security guidelines and using different passwords for all of your online accounts can result in a big variety of passwords that you have to remember. I have dozens of online accounts and trying to remember them all is next to impossible. If you have a lot of passwords as well, or just have a hard time remembering them all, I recommend using a password utility such as the free application called Password Safe, located at http://passwordsafe.sourceforge.net. This handy tool makes it possible to securely store all of your passwords for all of your accounts in a single location using an encrypted file.

How Windows Implements Passwords

The early versions of Windows had a very different method of implementing passwords than the NT-based operating systems NT, 2000, and XP. In Windows 98/Me, passwords were encrypted in a very weak encryption and then stored in a password file on the file system, available to anyone who wanted to play with it. This was extremely insecure, as anyone could just delete the password file and then have full access to your computer.

Starting with Windows NT, passwords were handled much more securely. Today, with Windows 2000 and Windows XP Home and Pro, user passwords are stored in what is called the Security Account Manager, commonly known as the SAM, similar to how Unix password protection works. The SAM is placed in a restricted part of the system registry that can only be accessed by the system account. This prevents a user, either locally or remotely, from loading up the registry editor and retrieving password information. To add another level of security, the passwords are stored in a 128-bit one-way hash with an industry standard encryption method known as MD4 Message Digest. This makes the password very difficult to crack even if access is somehow gained to the SAM database.

You can find more information on user passwords and account management in the "Managing Users" section of Chapter 5, "Managing Windows."

Recovering a Lost Password

Forgetting a password to an account on your computer can be very frustrating. In Windows 2000/XP, a new security mechanism based on Windows NT was used to replace the extremely vulnerable mechanism used in Windows 98/Me. Back in the Windows 98/Me days, you could very easily get into any account on the computer. With the help of a DOS boot disk, all you had to do was delete the Windows password file. Because Windows 2000 and XP are based on the NT kernel, a much more robust and secure system is in place.

This system makes it next to impossible to figure out what a user's password is because all of the password data is encrypted. In theory, it would be possible to use an application that would try to "crack" the encryption on the password data and recover the actual password. However, with the large number of bits that are used in encryption these days, it would take you several years on the fastest hardware available to "crack" the password. Unless you have your own super computer, this is not a valid solution for most of us.

If you know the Administrator user account password on your computer then you can log in with that account and then run `lusrmgr.msc` from the command prompt to get to the Local User and Group Manager (or activate it from the Control Panel). From there, you can right-click on any account and use its password.

Tip

In Windows XP the Administrator account will not be shown on the Welcome screen. In order to log on with the Administrator account on Windows XP, you will need to press **CTRL+ALT+DEL** twice to get the Windows 2000–style logon screen to show up. Then just manually type in the username and enter your password.

If you do not remember the Administrator password, the only feasible way to get into an account that you forgot the password for is to use a third-party utility to essentially overwrite the specific account's password data. This will not allow you to recover the password, but it will allow you to get into any account on your machine because the account will be assigned a new password.

Using a third-party utility to assign any account a new password is straightforward but there are a lot of steps are involved. They all work in a similar method but can be stored on either a floppy boot disk or a bootable CD-ROM. In general, you would turn on your computer with the utility disk in the drive so that the computer loads the utility's operating system instead of Windows. Then, a utility is run that will do the work of replacing the password.

There are hundreds of password utilities available for use. Some are free and others cost hundreds of dollars. The majority of these utilities work similarly so it really does not seem worthwhile to pay for something that is so widely available for free on the Web. From all of the available utilities, I selected two of the leading utilities that are used to replace Windows account passwords. One utility is booted from a floppy disk, and the other is burned to a CD-ROM and booted from the CD drive.

Caution

Before you get started, you should be aware of the consequences of replacing user account passwords. Because of the more robust security system in Windows 2000/XP, when a password for a user is replaced, any encrypted files, folders, and saved passwords will be lost. The files will still exist, but they will be encrypted with a key that your account with the replaced password will not have, leaving them inaccessible and essentially lost forever.

Using a Floppy Boot Disk to Change Passwords

To replace a user's password with a floppy boot disk, I recommend using the Offline NT Password & Registry Editor located at http://home.eunet.no/~pnordahl/ntpasswd/. While it's not exactly the most user-friendly tool, it is by far one of the most popular and reliable utilities in its class.

1. To get started, visit the site and download the disk image using the download links located near the bottom of the page. If your computer has SCSI hard drives, make sure that you download the version that has driver support for those drives.

2. Once you have the correct version downloaded, extract the zip file into any folder. Place an empty and formatted floppy disk into your disk drive and run `install.bat` from the folder to which you extracted the zip file. When prompted for the Target Disk Drive, enter the drive letter of the drive the floppy is in (this is usually drive "a"). After you confirm the drive, the utility copies the boot image to the floppy.

3. Now that your password recovery floppy disk has been created, you are ready to get started using it. Take the floppy disk and place it in the floppy drive of the computer containing the password(s) you want replaced. Next, just turn on the computer and it should start to boot from the floppy drive. If it does not, check the computer's BIOS to make sure that the floppy drive is first in the boot order.

◀◀ For more information on creating password reset disks, see "Local Accounts and Password Reset Disks" on p. 180.

4. Once the disk finishes loading, you're asked to select the disk where Windows is installed. Enter the corresponding number for the list of drives on the screen. The default of **1** should work for the vast majority of Windows installations, especially if your system has just one hard drive and one partition. If you do not see any drives listed, press **d** and **Enter** to load more drivers. After you have selected the drive and pressed Enter, you are ready for the next step.

5. Next, the screen asks where the Registry is stored as shown in Figure 8.1. For Windows XP, this directory is **Windows/System32/Config**. For Windows 2000 users, this directory is **Winnt/System32/Config**. The onscreen default is the directory for Windows XP, so you can just press **Enter** for this step if you are running XP.

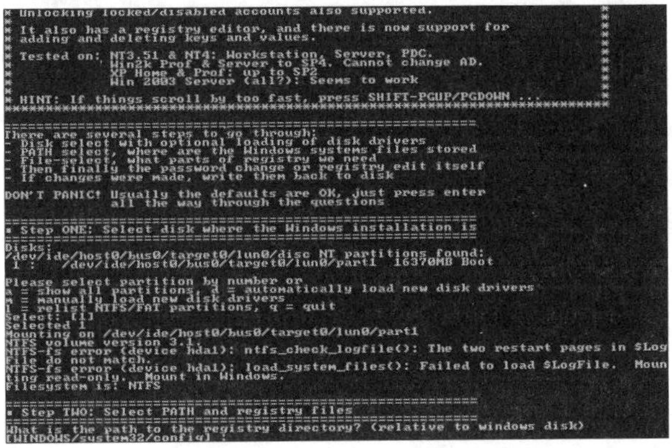

Figure 8.1   Selecting the location of the system registry with the Offline NT Password & Registry Editor.

6. The software then asks you what part of the registry you would like to load. Because we want to work with the passwords, press **1** and **Enter** to continue.

7. Password data from the registry will now be loaded. Next, press **1** (to edit user password information) and **Enter** to edit user password information.

8. All of the users configured for use with that PC are listed. Type in the name of the user for which you want to replace the password and press **Enter**. If you want to replace the Administrator's password, just press **Enter** because it is the onscreen default.

9. Next, enter the new password, or the software recommends that you enter in a * for a blank password as shown in Figure 8.2 (you can always change this later once you log in to Windows). Press **Enter** to go to the next step.

10. You will be asked to confirm your change; press **y** to continue.

11. Now you are almost done; you just need to quit and save your password changes back to the registry. Press **!** and **Enter** on this screen to quit back to the main menu. And press **q** and **Enter** to quit the password change program.

12. You will be asked if you want to write your changes to the registry. Press **y** and press **Enter**. This may take a few minutes. Once it says "***** Edit Complete *****" you can take the disk out and reboot your computer.

If all went well, when your computer reboots, you should be able to log in to the account you edited with either a blank password or with the password you supplied.

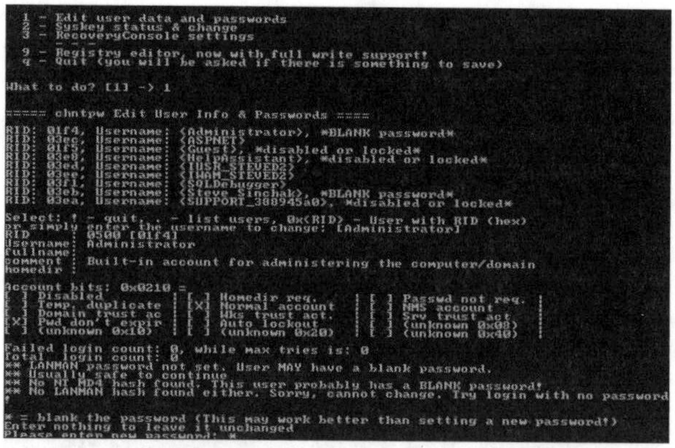

Figure 8.2   Enter a * for a blank password.

Tip

If while using the Offline NT Password & Registry Editor you experience any onscreen errors or if the application just does not work for you, check out the software developer's FAQ located at http://home.eunet.no/~pnordahl/ntpasswd/faq.html.

Using a Bootable CD-ROM to Change Passwords

If the floppy boot method does not work for you or if you just don't have a floppy disk drive on your computer, there are other tools you can use to reset a user's password. I personally like to use a suite of utilities called the Emergency Boot CD. The EBCD is a collection of useful utilities that you can use to fix your computer from a wide variety of disasters. It also has the ability to reset passwords, which makes it a great tool for any IT professional or power user.

Note

Emergency Boot CD requires the use of a separate CD burning software utility, such as Nero Burning ROM from Ahead Software or Easy CD Creator, published by Roxio.

Follow the procedure below to make your own bootable CD and replace passwords with it:

1. Visit http://ebcd.pcministry.com and download a copy of either the lite or pro version of the CD. The only difference between the two is that pro contains additional utilities that we do not need for this task. (You may, however, find them useful.)

2. Once you have downloaded a version of the CD, run the file and extract the files to your hard drive. Because the CD allows you to customize its contents, the CD image is not yet created. Just open up the folder to which you extracted the files and run `makeebcd.exe` to automatically create the image file.

3. This creates an ISO image file of the CD on your hard disk. From here, you need to use any one of several popular CD burning software applications to burn the ISO file to a CD-R or CD-RW disk.

4. Once you have burned the ISO image file, place the newly created Emergency Boot CD into the computer that contains the passwords you want to change. Restart the computer, and if the BIOS is configured to boot from the CD drive, the computer should load the boot program on the CD instead of Windows. If the computer does not boot from the CD, make sure that your BIOS is configured properly and that it supports booting from the CD-ROM drive.

Note

For more information on the BIOS and the Windows boot process, see Chapter 4, "Windows Startup."

5. Once the computer boots to the CD, launch the NT Password Utility by pressing **5** as shown in Figure 8.3 and then **Enter**.

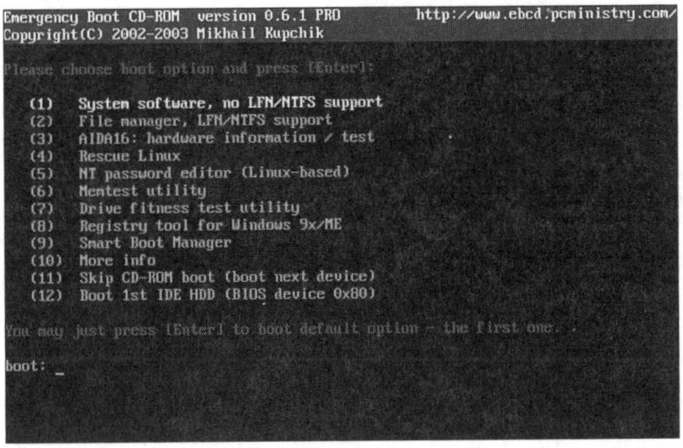

Figure 8.3 Select option 5 from the Emergency Boot CD-ROM to launch the NT password editor.

6. Once the utility loads, press **Enter** to continue after the initial welcome message. You will be asked to probe for SCSI drives; press **n** and then **Enter** if you do not have any SCSI hard drives.

7. A list of drive partitions will be shown. Enter the full name of the partition where Windows is installed as shown on the screen and press **Enter**. Most users can just press **Enter** to select the onscreen default of **/dev/hda1**.

8. Next, enter the location to the Windows registry data (refer to step 5 in the previous section). Most users can press **Enter** again to select the onscreen default of **Windows/System32/Config** for Windows XP.

9. The next prompt asks you which hives, another name for a location in the registry, to edit. The default values for this are the same for everyone so you can just press **Enter** to continue.

10. Select Option **1** to edit passwords and press **Enter**.

11. Type the name of the user whose password you need to change and press **Enter** (see Figure 8.4).

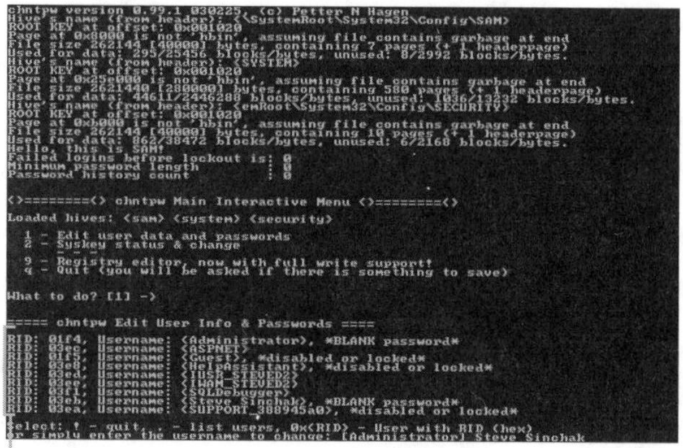

List of user accounts

Figure 8.4 Using the Emergency Boot CD to change the password of a Windows user account.

12. Enter * for the password so that it is blank and press **Enter**. Alternatively, you can enter in a new password, but the software recommends that you just set it to a blank password.

13. On the confirmation screen, press **Y** and then press **Enter**. Then quit out of user edit mode by pressing ! and then **Enter**, and quit out of the NT Password application with **q** and **Enter** to save your changes.

14. You will need to press **Y** twice more to confirm the writes back to the registry. Once that's done, your task is complete.

Now that you have reset the password for the account, it is a good idea to log in and change the password to one that follows the guidelines mentioned earlier to make your data secure.

Windows Update

As I mentioned at the start of this chapter, new vulnerabilities are discovered in Windows all the time. Keeping your computer up to date and secure from newly discovered vulnerabilities is a big part of the game. Using free services such as Microsoft Windows Update allows you to easily make sure that your computer is always up to date. Additionally, with the release of Windows XP, the operating system can be configured to automatically check for updates and update itself without having you do anything.

A Brief History of Windows Security

Throughout the history of Windows, Microsoft has had to come up with numerous methods of correcting the various security problems found in its operating systems. When security vulnerabilities are discovered, work begins on developing a patch to correct the problem. Once the patch has passed internal testing, Microsoft would release it through both Windows Update and Microsoft TechNet. Over the years, this method of releasing security patches has changed from releasing patches randomly during the month to batching a bunch of patches to be released at once. Currently Microsoft releases patches only once a month unless there is an immediate need for a quick fix.

About every two years, Microsoft takes all of the security patches and additional features that it has been working on and bundles them all together into one big package called a service pack. One reason this is done is to make updating a PC that has never been updated much easier, because you only have to apply one update, instead of dozens of individual patches and additional features. More recently, Microsoft has been using service packs, such as Windows XP Service Pack 2, to deliver significant changes to the operating system. In the case of Windows XP Service Pack 2, many components of Windows XP were rewritten to operate more securely, and additional features such as a more intelligent firewall were included to help users better protect their computers.

The Windows Update service is a valuable tool that helps you keep on top of the monthly security patches that Microsoft releases (and the occasional critical update). Using Windows Update ensures that your computer will get that update when it is released, minimizing the amount of time your computer is potentially vulnerable to security threats.

Using Windows Update

Windows Update is very easy to use. It can be accessed a number of ways within Windows. You can launch it using the Windows Update shortcut found at the top of the All Programs menu in the Start menu or by opening up a copy of Internet Explorer and selecting Tools, Windows Update, or by navigating IE directly to www.WindowsUpdate.com.

If it's been a while since your last visit, or if you are visiting the website for the first time, you may be required to install a special control that detects which of the available updates your PC needs. This control is itself updated frequently, so over time you may have to permit its installation more than once.

Once the site has loaded and the control has initialized, you will have two options, Express and Custom, that allow you to manually update your computer with the latest security patches as well as bonus applications, as shown in Figure 8.5.

If you are in a rush and don't care about which updates are getting installed and why, select Express Install. Choosing Custom Install allows you to see exactly which updates are available for your system and gives you the option of which ones to install. I personally like the Custom Install because I like to see what updates are available.

After you select the method of updating your computer, Windows Update launches the update utility and checks your computer for available updates. If any updates are available, they will be displayed. If you selected the Express Install, just click the Install button to begin installing the updates if any are available. If you selected Custom Install, browse through the provided list of updates and click the Add button for any that you want downloaded and installed to your PC. When you're done, click the Install button.

At this time the download utility will be launched, which will automatically download the updates and install them one by one. If a restart is required, you will be prompted with the option to restart immediately or restart later.

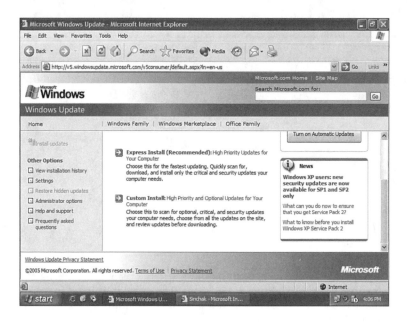

Figure 8.5   Windows Update options.

Occasionally an update available on the Windows Update service must be installed by itself, without any other of the available updates. If that is the case for an update you select, you will notice that any other updates that you had selected will become unselected and you won't be able to select any other updates. In this case, you should download and install the lone update and perform the required system reboot. After rebooting, restart the Windows Update service and select the remaining updates you want to install.

Note

For more information on Windows Update and Windows Service Packs, see Chapter 2, "Installing Windows."

Configuring Automatic Updates

Automatic Updates are a great feature of Windows XP that has been enhanced with the various service pack releases since the initial release of Windows XP. Configuring your computer to automatically update itself is the best way to keep on top of the latest security patches, and doing so is very easy with Windows XP once Service Pack 2 has been installed.

Tip

If you do not already have Windows XP Service Pack 2 installed, just run Windows Update manually as mentioned previously and make sure to select the service pack as an update. This update implements many new security measures and refines a lot of features of Windows XP.

If you have not already installed Windows XP Service Pack 2, you will have the option of enabling Automatic Updates during the final phases of the setup. If you missed those screens or did not turn on the feature at the time, you can always easily turn the feature on using the following procedure:

1. Open up Control Panel by clicking Start, Control Panel.

2. If Classic View is not already on, click Switch to Classic View on the left pane. Then, launch System Properties by clicking on the System icon.

3. Next, click on the **Automatic Updates** tab as shown in Figure 8.6 to reveal the update settings. On this screen you have four different update options. You can have Windows

   - Fully automate downloading and installing the updates at a specific time
   - Automate the downloading but have you confirm the installation
   - Just notify you of new updates
   - Disable automatic updates

   I suggest that at the bare minimum you have Windows automatically download the latest updates and notify you when they are ready to be installed. Ideally, the best option is to have Windows handle both the downloading and the installation.

Figure 8.6 The Automatic Updates tab of the System Properties dialog sheet gives you control over how Windows XP deals with updates to the operating system.

4. Once you have selected the update method, click the **OK** button and you are finished.

Most users already know that Automatic Updates are a great feature of Windows XP, but many don't know or forget to utilize the fact that Microsoft currently has similar services that update other software, such as the popular Office series of products. I highly recommend that you visit Microsoft Update, the new centralized site for updating all of Microsoft products, to make sure that any known vulnerabilities in those products are fixed as well. Microsoft Update can be accessed through http://www.microsoft.com.

Updating all of the software on your computer on top of the operating system is very important to securing your computer. Even if the operating system is secure, vulnerabilities in any software application that you run on top of your operating system could give an attacker another door into your computer.

Firewalls

The moment that your computer connects to the Internet by any means, it becomes vulnerable to just about anyone else on the Internet. Anyone who knows the IP address of your computer, or is scanning blocks of IP addresses, could be looking for known and unknown vulnerabilities that they can use to compromise your Windows installation. Quite often your computer is scanned by viruses and Trojans that have infected other computers on the Internet and are trying to spread themselves to more systems.

Tip

An IP address, which is short for Internet Protocol address, is a value assigned to your computer by your Internet service provider or network administrator to identify your computer on a local or wide area network (like the Internet). For more information on IP addresses, refer to Chapter 7, "Networking Windows."

There is a lot of junk traffic on the Internet that is caused by these viruses, Trojans, and attackers. Applications that filter out a lot of this junk and block it from ever getting to the core of your operating system are called firewalls. This very intelligent software works closely with the various layers of network communications. When information is sent across a network using the most popular protocols, a connection is established between the two computers at specific port numbers. For example, when I visit a website, my computer connects to port 80 on the machine the domain name points to. Firewall software works by blocking anyone from trying to connect to the ports on your computer, except the ones you tell it people are allowed to connect to.

By using firewalls, you are greatly limiting the ways your computer can be attacked on the Internet. Even if new vulnerabilities are discovered, the use of a firewall alone may protect your computer because attackers or viruses and Trojans cannot connect to your computer on the port the vulnerability exists on because the firewall is blocking them. As you can see, a firewall is one of the greatest defenses against getting attacked on the Internet.

There are two different variations of firewalls on the market: hardware firewalls and software firewalls. Software and hardware firewalls behave and work similarly; the difference is that hardware firewalls are separate physical machines that are located on a network and filter all network traffic going through them. Software firewalls are just special software applications that run on your computer on top of the operating system. The advantage of a hardware firewall is that it can protect a number of computers while a software firewall can only protect the computer on which it is installed. This book focuses exclusively on software firewalls.

How Software Firewalls Protect Your PC from Attacks

Software firewalls all operate using a similar methodology. All data routed into and out of your PC is done using *ports*. The firewall software is configured to monitor these ports and only allow traffic on those that are specifically enabled to do so, while blocking all other traffic. When a remote computer attempts to connect to your computer on a port that the firewall has blocked, the connection is prevented. Most software firewalls have no ports open by default, blocking all of them. This protects your computer from attacks because even if your computer may be vulnerable to a specific security hole, a remote computer trying to infect you cannot connect to it in the first place.

Obviously, blocking every port on your system at all times is impractical. Completely closing off all traffic into your system would cause problems for any applications on your system that make use of the of a LAN or the Internet, including web browsers, instant messenger applications, or online computer games. Consequently, it is possible to open up ports to allow required network traffic into your computer. Most firewalls allow you to specifically set permissions for allowing specific programs to use specific ports while denying all others. However, whenever you open up a port, both good and bad traffic can get through.

To fight that problem, most modern firewalls have a feature called *packet inspection*. Packet inspection looks at the packets that it lets through for known vulnerabilities. This is a good feature to have, because it helps protect you even when you open up some holes in your firewall by opening up ports. Currently the firewall that comes with Windows XP does not support this feature.

Most third-party software firewalls not only inspect incoming network traffic, but also outgoing data. This is an important feature, because there are any number of ways for a virus or Trojan to infect your system and then send data out to the Internet from your PC. Firewalls that monitor outgoing traffic stop any unknown transmissions from leaving your PC until you specifically allow them to go through.

When you are configuring your software firewall's settings, keep in mind that the best policy is to block everything. Only open up the ports you absolutely need!

Windows Firewall

Any user who is connected to the Internet should have some form of firewall protecting their computer from the outside world. The Windows Firewall is the perfect solution for most computer users.

Windows XP has been shipped with a firewall ever since it was released and it's the first Windows OS to do so. However, because it was not enabled by default, many users never even knew that it was there to protect them. Initially, it was also far weaker than many of the third-party software firewalls available. Windows XP Service Pack 2 has made many changes to the Windows Firewall. It has made it more powerful and more effective. Additionally, it has made it much easier to turn it on, as users have the opportunity to do so during the installation of Service Pack 2.

Windows Firewall is a very basic firewall when compared to all of the options out there. More advanced firewalls not only monitor incoming traffic but also monitor outgoing traffic, and can tell you if you have some program on your computer trying to send information out without your knowledge, such as a program that is stealing your personal information.

If you do not already have the Windows Firewall enabled on your computer and you want to do so, it is easy to enable. First, make sure that you are using Windows XP and have Service Pack 2 installed. Then open Control Panel in Classic view and click on the Windows Firewall icon. Select **On** and click **OK**.

Configuring the Windows Firewall is also very simple, because it is a very basic firewall. To configure its options, just open up the firewall settings again using the icon in Control Panel and select the **Advanced** tab. This is where you can specify which connections the firewall will protect, the individual port settings for each connection, the ICMP settings, and logging information, as well as the ability to restore the firewall to the default settings as shown in Figure 8.7.

Individual Connection Settings

Each of the network connections that you have the firewall enabled for can be configured separately to have different ports opened and closed. This allows you to run various services on your computer, such as an FTP or web server, and allow access to the data behind your software firewall by the outside world.

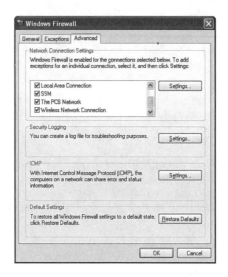

Figure 8.7 Windows Firewall advanced settings.

If you have more than one connection on your computer, such as a wired network connection and a wireless, you can configure each separately so that you only need to open the ports on the connection that you use an application on for greater security. For example, you may play games on your computer that require a specific port to be opened while you are at home using your wired network connection. Opening the port on your wireless connection as well is not needed in this situation and just poses a security risk.

To allow the outside world to access services, you will need to open "holes" in the firewall so that it does not filter out traffic on that port. Opening holes in the Windows firewall is very simple. While on the Advanced tab of the Firewall Settings window, highlight the connection you want to edit from the list and click the Settings button. This displays the Advanced Settings window, as shown in Figure 8.8, listing some predefined services that you can check to open up access to through the firewall.

To open a service for access from the outside world, just check the box next to the service if it is already on the list. Otherwise, you will need to click on the Add button to create a custom service.

If you need to create a custom service and have clicked the Add button, just enter in the name of the application you are opening a port for in the Description box. Then enter the port number that you need to open in the External and Internal port boxes and click **OK** (this port should be specific by the developer or publisher of the software).

ICMP Settings

ICMP is short for Internet Control Message Protocol, which is normally used by network administrators as a suite of commands that can be used to monitor and diagnose network issues. Unfortunately these commands can also be used to create excessive traffic on a user's connection and slow down networks. One of the most popular ICMP commands that you have probably heard of is the ping command.

These commands, as shown in Figure 8.9, can be very useful if you are trying to test and configure a local area network or work on your Internet connection, but they have no other practical uses in the general business of using the Internet.

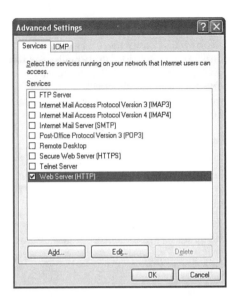

Figure 8.8 Windows Firewall service settings.

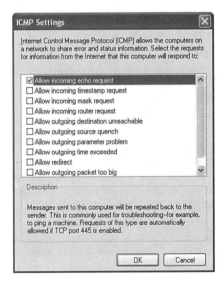

Figure 8.9 Windows Firewall ICMP settings.

Because of their nature, it is best to have the firewall disable them unless you temporarily have a use for them. To do this, on the Advanced tab of Firewall Properties, click on the Settings button under the ICMP section. Then, just check or uncheck the various types of messages allowed.

Limitations of the Windows Firewall

The Windows firewall is a basic firewall. It only monitors incoming traffic and does not monitor outgoing traffic as many other software firewalls do. Additionally, the firewall does not do any sophisticated packet inspection to see what is really inside the traffic that it does allow through the firewall, which more complex third-party firewalls usually check. That said, even though the Windows Firewall has its limitations, it still provides a big help in securing your computer and offers far more protection for your system than not using a firewall at all.

Third-Party Firewalls

There are a wide variety of software firewalls on the market. Most of them are not free but offer a level of protection much higher than the Windows Firewall that comes with Windows XP. Some of the common features that add another level of protection provided by commercial third-party firewalls includes

- Intrusion Detection Systems. These are advanced systems that do packet inspection looking for known signatures of "bad" data trying to get into your computer.

- Process Communication Monitoring. PCM looks at the traffic that is sent between services running on your computer.

- Outgoing Data Monitoring. Firewalls with this feature look at all of the outgoing data that is sent from your computer. Many firewalls just block incoming data, but firewalls with this feature also can block data from going out. This would be especially useful if your computer got infected with spyware. In this scenario, the spyware would not be able to phone home your personal information.

Norton Personal Firewall 2005

Norton Personal Firewall, available as part of Norton's Internet Security suite of applications, is one of the most popular firewalls used to protect Windows. It has all of the features that the built-in Windows Firewall has, plus additional features such as intelligent packet filtering, intrusion detection systems, and monitoring of all outgoing traffic to make sure that none of your files or other sensitive data are sent over the Internet without your knowing about it.

With Norton Personal Firewall 2005, new features were added to help users with the growing number of phishing scams on the Web. With Norton Personal Firewall 2005, when you submit your personal information to a website, the firewall makes sure that your data is going to a site that you configured as a site you trust. Now, when you get those one of those emails and accidentally take it for real, the firewall will catch your error for you.

Note

Phishing scams are fake websites that are made to trick visitors into giving their personal information, such as social security number and bank account numbers, to websites that they feel are of legitimate origin. One common Phishing scam is an email sent from a person pretending to be your bank asking you to log in to their website to verify your account information. When you click the link you do not go to the real website, but the fake one they set up.

Using Norton Personal Firewall is fairly simple. Once the application is installed, the main interface is shared with any other Symantec software you have installed on your computer. Figure 8.10 shows the home screen of Norton Personal Firewall integrated with Norton Anti-Virus.

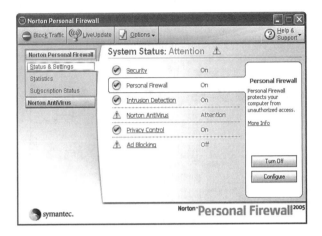

Figure 8.10 Norton Personal Firewall.

Configuring Norton Personal Firewall is very easy compared to some other third-party firewalls. Just select the area of the program that you want to configure on the main screen and click the **Configure** button.

Configuring the firewall can be done on a per-location basis, which is very useful if you have a laptop that you carry around to many different networks. Most likely, you will want to have your laptop more secure on a public Wi-Fi network at a coffee shop than at work on the corporate network. Additionally, your needs will be different at each location, so it is a big advantage that you can customize the "holes" in the firewall depending on the location.

To make managing the firewall easier, pre-configured security levels are set up within the firewall configuration settings. However, specifically opening up a port for a service such as a web or FTP server is a little more difficult and buried in the application. To open up a specific port, after you click on the Configure button when Personal Firewall is selected on the main screen, you must then select the Advanced tab and then click the General button. On this screen, you can click the Add button as shown in Figure 8.11 to add additional rules to the selected network connection firewall settings. An easy-to-use wizard will guide you through the steps of setting up the new rule that will open up your firewall on a specific port.

Norton Personal Firewall is not free but is priced on the lower range of the commercial firewalls. Although it has some of the best features in commercial software firewalls, it lacks some of the control and flexibility over firewall rules some other firewalls provide.

A trial version as well as more information on Norton Personal Firewall can be found at http://www.symantec.com.

Using Tiny Personal Firewall Professional 2005

Tiny Personal Firewall is an advanced firewall that is aimed at users who want total control in customizing traffic rules for both incoming and outgoing traffic. Published by Tiny Software, Inc., it can be downloaded at http://www.TinySoftware.com. Tiny Personal Firewall is also one of the more expensive software firewall options, retailing close to $100.

Tiny Personal Firewall provides all of the features the basic Windows Firewall provides in addition to the ability to automatically filter outgoing traffic. One nice feature of Tiny Personal Firewall is it already knows which processes running on the computer are operating system processes and adds them to the trusted list automatically. This spares you from getting bombarded by dozens of notifications regarding whether to allow or block certain types of traffic as you do with other third-party firewalls. However, if you want to block all outgoing traffic whether it is legitimate or not, this feature could be more of a hassle for you.

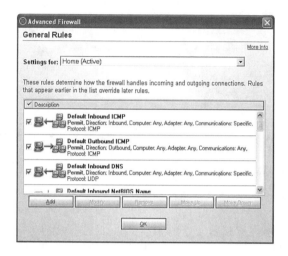

Figure 8.11   Opening a port with Norton Personal Firewall.

The core of the firewall is the Activity Monitor, which shows you all of the current network connection attempts, both incoming and outgoing. I personally like the Connections tab, which shows you all of the current connections established to and from your computer, how much data has been received and transmitted through them, and the current speed of transfer, as shown in Figure 8.12.

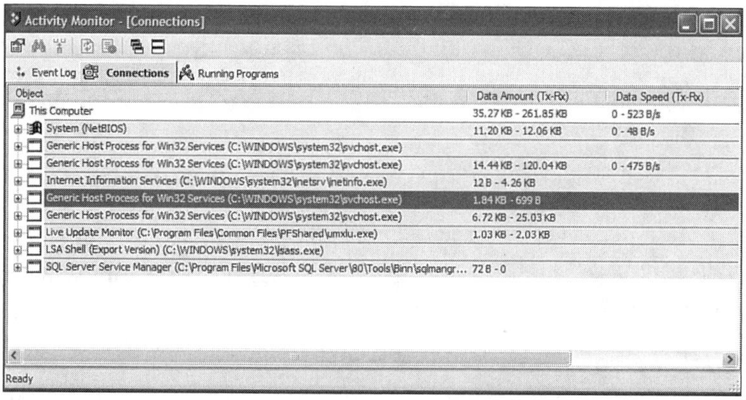

Figure 8.12   Tiny Personal Firewall network connection information.

The Administration Center is where all of the network access policies are managed. The management of network policies is similar to Microsoft's enterprise firewall software called ISA Server. Anyone familiar with that system will be right at home with Tiny Personal Firewall. However, using the extensive options of Tiny Personal Firewall may be frustrating and annoying for some users.

Because the administration is much more complex and extensive than other software firewalls I recommend that you use a more simple to administer firewall such as the Norton Personal Firewall or the free Sygate Personal Firewall if you just want basic functionality plus the ability to monitor and control outgoing traffic. If you want the maximum amount of flexibility over what is going on with your network connection, Tiny Personal Firewall is the firewall for you.

Using Sygate Personal Firewall

The Sygate Personal Firewall (non-professional version) is a free third-party firewall that replicates all of the functionality of the built-in Windows Firewall but also adds the ability to block outgoing traffic for all applications or just specific applications.

After installing the firewall, you will be surprised how many processes running on your computer request to have access to the Internet. Every time a process attempts to access the Internet, a screen will pop up as shown in Figure 8.13.

Figure 8.13   Sygate Personal Firewall—application access notification.

As shown in Figure 8.13, the user has a few options to handle the requests. After the first couple of times you boot your computer, the mass amount of notifications will subside as the program learns what to do with your normal traffic.

Another feature of Sygate Personal Firewall is the graphical charts, shown in Figure 8.14, and the extensive logs that show all incoming traffic attempts and outgoing traffic attempts that were blocked.

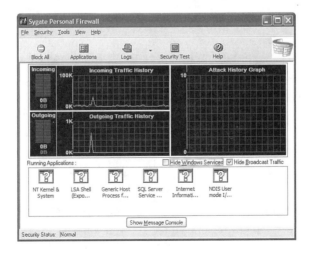

Figure 8.14   Sygate Personal Firewall in action.

Sygate also offers a professional version of its personal firewall software, which has additional protection similar to Norton Personal Firewall and Tiny Personal Firewall. It is also priced similar to other "professional version" firewalls. More information on Sygate Personal Firewall, both the free and professional versions, can be downloaded at http://smb.sygate.com.

Viruses

Viruses have been around for a very long time, and while the Internet is still rampant with these dangerous programs, they are finally starting to become a little less common in favor of other forms of destructive malware and spyware. Fortunately, out of all of the different computer menaces in existence, computer viruses are one of the easiest to defend yourself from. Because of advances in anti-virus software, a good, frequently updated anti-virus utility is really all that is needed.

Initially anti-virus software took a more passive role in protecting your computer. It would scan, on demand, any file you specified. Then anti-virus software vendors realized that a proactive solution was needed. Now anti-virus utilities can be configured to scan all files that the computer attempts to read or execute as well as automatically block the methods most viruses use to spread themselves around. This is very useful, because most anti-virus utilities detect viruses based on virus definitions that constantly must be updated to know about the latest viruses. By blocking certain extensions of files attached to e-mail messages and blocking the running of various types of scripts, anti-virus software can protect you from potential viruses that it does not yet have definitions for.

Tip

If you are working on a computer that does not have any anti-virus software installed and want to do a quick check for viruses, check out Trend Micro's Housecall website located at http://housecall.trendmicro.com for a free online virus scan. Then, get yourself a dedicated AV program that pro-actively protects your PC.

AVG Anti-Virus Free Edition

There are many vendors that provide anti-virus utilities but very few provide the software for free. AVG Anti-Virus Free Edition by Grisoft is a standard anti-virus utility. It has all of the basic features of anti-virus applications currently on the market and is also available free of charge for personal use. Grisoft has a professional version of AVG Anti-Virus that is designed for commercial use; however, it is not free.

Nonetheless, if you are looking for a good anti-virus utility for your personal computer and don't want to pay for Norton Anti-Virus or Mcafee Anti-Virus then AVG will get the job done for you.

To get started using AVG Anti-Virus Free Edition, you will need to visit http://free.grisoft.com to download a copy of the latest version.

Follow the procedure below to install, configure, and update AVG Anti-Virus:

1. Download and install AVG Anti-Virus. Once setup finishes, the application will automatically launch and you will see the First Run wizard. You may also see a pop-up notification saying that your internal virus database is out-of-date. Disregard this message for now; you will update the database shortly. On the First Run wizard, click **Next**.

2. Now it is time to update the database; just click on the **Check for Updates** button. Then, click on the **Internet** button to download updates automatically from Grisoft's web servers.

3. If new updates are found, they will be listed and you will have to option to select the update (if it is not already selected) and click **Update** to initiate the downloading and installation of the new update.

4. After the installations of any updates are finished, you are returned to the First Run wizard. Click on the **Next** button once again.

5. At this point, you have the option to create rescue disks that can be used to repair your computer if a virus infects certain system files. This step is not required but I recommend you do it. Just click on the **Create Rescue Disks** button and follow the wizard. Make sure you have some floppy disks available. Once you are finished, or if you want to skip this step, just click **Next**.

Note

You cannot create a rescue CD using this process.

6. If this is the first time you are installing an anti-virus utility on this computer, it is a good idea to do an initial scan that will analyze all of the files on your computer to make sure they are virus free. Click the **Scan Computer!** Button to start a scan. The initial virus scan can take anywhere from a few minutes to more than an hour depending on the number of files on your hard drive. Once the scan is finished, you will be presented with the results as well as options to remove any viruses found. When everything is finished, click on the **Next** button of the First Run wizard to continue.

7. The final step of configuration is the registration step. This step is up to you, as registering the free version really does not give you any other benefits other than providing your personal information to Grisoft. Click **Next** when you are finished and **Continue** on the final screen to close the wizard.

AVG Anti-Virus is now installed and running on your computer. By default, all of its monitoring agents, such as the active file scanner that automatically scans any opened documents in word processors and the email attachment scanner, are operational. If you want to manually configure any of the settings of these agents, just click on Control Center from the main Test Center window of AVG. Once the Control Center is loaded, you will see all of the different protection agents, as shown in Figure 8.15.

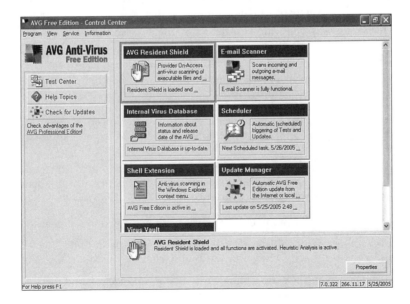

Figure 8.15   AVG Anti-Virus Control Center.

Click on any of the agents you want to configure, and then click on the **Properties** button or any other option in the lower-right portion of the window.

Keeping your virus database up to date is critical to the utility. AVG Anti-Virus Free Edition comes with a scheduler that is configured by default to automatically check for updates and scan for new viruses on a daily basis.

Norton AntiVirus 2005

Norton AntiVirus is the leading anti-virus utility for Windows. It has all of the features of AVG Anti-Virus Free Edition plus a more sophisticated database that also checks for Trojans, worms, and other types of malware. Developed by Symantec, Norton AntiVirus retails for under $50. Using Norton AntiVirus is similar to using any other anti-virus utility, as it monitors files the same way, just with a different engine.

Like all other anti-virus applications, keeping the virus definition database up to date is critical. Norton AntiVirus uses Symantec's LiveUpdate service to update the definitions weekly. Installing and configuring Norton AntiVirus is also fairly simple. Just follow the procedure below to set up Norton AntiVirus on your computer:

1. After you have purchased and begun installing Norton AntiVirus, it will conduct a pre-setup scan for viruses. Symantec has placed this feature in the setup program so that before Norton Antivirus is installed, the computer is cleared of any existing viruses that may try to sabotage the installation. This step is not required, so you may just click **Next** to continue. However, it is recommended that you click **Start Scan** to make sure your computer is clean to ensure a good install.

2. After the scan is completed, you can continue with the installation by clicking **Next**. After installation is completed, you will be asked to restart your computer.

3. When your computer restarts and after you log in, the configuration Wizard will launch. On the initial screen, click Next to begin configuring Norton AntiVirus.

4. The next screen is where you will need to activate the software and enter in your product key Symantec provided when you purchased the software.

5. On the security screen, you will have the option to allow Norton AntiVirus the ability to share the status of the software with other software products. It is best to just leave the option checked and continue.

6. The wizard is now completed but LiveUpdate will be launched to update the software and download the latest virus definitions. Once LiveUpdate checks your software for updates and presents you with a list of available updates, click the Next button to have them downloaded and automatically installed. Depending on your Internet connection speed, this may take a while. And, depending on the updates installed, you may be required to restart your computer afterward.

7. Usually after your computer restarts, Norton AntiVirus will automatically launch a scan of all files on your computer again, this time using the latest virus/trojan/worm definitions. Once this scan is complete, the configuration is finished.

After a full system scan has been completed, you will be shown a window similar to Figure 8.16.

In most cases, Norton Antivirus will automatically delete any viruses it finds. If you want to see the details of the scan and see exactly what virus was found, click on the More Details button.

If you want to disable any of the extra features such as worm protection and instant messaging protection because they are interfering with your applications by blocking network access, you can permanently disable them by clicking on the Options button at the top of the main screen.

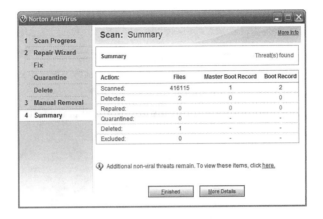

Figure 8.16 Norton AntiVirus—Virus Found.

Spyware

Spyware has become the fastest growing concern among computer users today. It is uncommon to find a computer that has never been infected with some sort of a spyware application. Because of vulnerabilities discovered mostly in Internet Explorer and other software and the bundling of spyware with some common applications, spyware is often secretly installed on a user's machine. The first time most users notice an indication of the presence of spyware on their system is when, out of nowhere, an advertisement pops up relevant to something they are or had been doing on their computer. In other instances, the spyware may just record what is happening on your computer, such as the websites you visit, and never give any clues to you that it is there.

Because spyware is often very difficult to detect for the average user, using utilities to detect and remove spyware may be necessary. Currently there are dozens of spyware removing utilities. Ironically, some of them are spyware themselves. It seems that everyone wants to make some money from the use of spyware. Thankfully, there are a few utilities that are both free and also happen to be the best utilities to remove spyware from your computer and protect it from getting infected in the future.

Similar to anti-virus software, spyware utilities detect spyware based on their database of known spyware. Each utility has a database that is updated at different times. This makes it necessary to use a combination of utilities to make sure your computer is clean of all spyware. The utilities are getting much better, but quite often, when I do a scan with Ad-Aware and then do a scan with Spybot Search & Destroy after my computer is supposedly cleaned of all Spyware, spybot sometimes finds more. The reverse is also true. It is not that either of the utilities is better than the other; it is a matter of different spyware information in their databases.

LavaSoft Ad-Aware

LavaSoft Ad-Aware SE Personal Edition is the free version of the popular Ad-Aware spyware removal utility that can be downloaded from http://www.lavasoftusa.com. Ad-Aware SE Personal Edition is a great utility to search for spyware and clean your computer of it. To get started using Ad-Aware, make sure that you have a copy of Ad-Aware SE Personal Edition downloaded and installed, and then follow this procedure:

1. Launch Ad-Aware and start downloading the latest version of the definitions database. Once the definitions are downloaded and automatically installed, the main application screen will be displayed. Because the definitions are now up to date, it is time to do a full system scan. Click on the **Scan Now** button.

2. Now you will see the different types of scans that can be done with Ad-Aware. If this is your first time, it is best to do a full system scan as shown in Figure 8.17. In the future, you can get away with doing a smart system scan, which only checks for spyware in the most common places instead of the entire hard drive. As you can imagine, that scanning method is much faster. But for now, select **Perform full system scan** and click **Next** to begin.

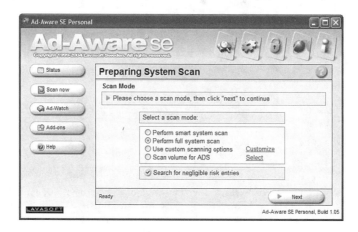

Figure 8.17 Ad-Aware SE Personal Edition full system scan.

3. Once the scan is complete, click the Next button to view the results. The Critical Objects tab displays any spyware found. To remove it, click on each of the entries or right-click on the list and click **Select All Objects**. Then, click **Next** to remove the spyware.

4. A confirmation screen will pop up asking whether you are sure if you want to delete the spyware. Click **OK** and you are finished.

It is recommended that you manually check for spyware at least once a week to make sure that your personal information is safe and your computer is clear. Also, before each scan, make sure to get the latest spyware definitions.

Tip

The Ad-Aware SE Personal Edition spyware definitions can be updated by clicking on the globe icon on the main screen. Once the Web Update window pops-up, just click on the Connect button for Check For and Download New Updates.

Spybot Search & Destroy

Spybot Search & Destroy, developed by Patrick Kolla, is another free and very popular spyware utility. Spybot operates in the same fashion of Ad-Aware but it also has the ability to configure Internet Explorer to automatically block some of the most well known spyware applications from ever getting a chance to tricking you into installing them.

Using Spybot is different than Ad-Aware but it just as easy. You can visit http://www.safer-networking.org to download and install a copy and then use the following procedure to scan and repair your computer with Spybot:

1. Launch Spybot S&D Wizard from the Windows Start menu (or desktop icon). If this is the first use of Spybot Search & Destroy, the Spybot S&D Wizard will be loaded. The first screen gives you the option of creating a backup of your registry. This is very useful if, after you remove a spyware application, your computer stops working properly. In that situation, you can use the backup you made to restore any changes made to the registry. If you would like to create a backup, click **Create registry backup**. Otherwise, click **Next** to continue.

2. On the next screen of the wizard, you have the option to check for updates before scanning your computer. Click **Search for Updates** to get the list of the latest program and definition updates available. If any updates are available, click the **Download all available updates** button.

3. After the updates are installed, Spybot will restart itself and you will be shown the main screen (see Figure 8.18). Click **Check for problems** to begin scanning your computer.

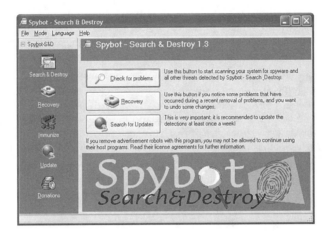

Figure 8.18 Spybot Search & Destroy.

4. When the search for spyware is completed, if anything is found, you will be shown a list of identified spyware. To remove all of the spyware on the list, click **Fix Selected Problems**. Spybot will first create a system restore point for backup and then will remove all instances of the spyware found. In certain situations, Spybot may not be able to remove all of the spyware files. Usually this occurs if the files are in use and Spybot cannot terminate the process that is making use of them. In these situations, Spybot will inform you that your computer needs to be restarted to remove the spyware. Once your computer restarts, right after you log on, Spybot S&D will launch again, automatically scan, and give you the option to fix all of the problems. However, this time, because it is the first application to run after the reboot and is holding up all startup items, no other processes, including spyware, will be able to start up, making it possible to remove any file needed.

Tip

Spybot Search & Destroy should always be updated before every scan to make sure that you will find the latest spyware infecting the computer. Launch the application and click the Search for Updates button to automatically get the latest spyware definitions.

Now that you have finished using Spybot Search & Destroy to remove all of the spyware from your computer, you can use its advanced features to secure Internet Explorer by preventing the installation of known spyware in the first place.

To enable these advanced features of Spybot, launch Spybot and then click on the Immunize button on the left menu of the application. There are more than 2,000 different spyware applications that can be automatically blocked in Internet Explorer. Just click on the Immunize button with the big plus sign on it to enable the protections.

If you ever experience any problems in the future, such as web pages that you normally visit not working properly in Internet Explorer, I suggest you try undoing the Immunization Spybot applied to Internet Explorer. This can be done by clicking on the Undo button within the Immunize section of Spybot Search & Destroy.

Microsoft Windows AntiSpyware

Microsoft Windows AntiSpyware is Microsoft's answer to battling the growing amount of spyware affecting Windows. Originally developed by Giant Software before Microsoft acquired the company in 2004, AntiSpyware is a comprehensive package, offered for free, that not only removes spyware, but actively protects against it similar to the way Norton AntiVirus uses its Auto Protect feature to actively protect users from viruses.

When you are running Microsoft Windows AntiSpyware and visit a web page that attempts to secretly install anything, you are notified by a pop-up message and given the option to allow or disable the action as shown in Figure 8.19. Similar notifications are also given when any application on your computer attempts to modify the startup programs and modify other Internet related settings. This has proven to be a very effective measure of instantly letting you know that your computer may be infected with spyware as well as preventing spyware from changing any settings on your computer.

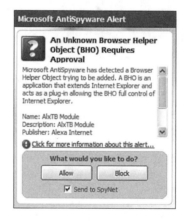

Figure 8.19   Microsoft Windows AntiSpyware notification.

Installing Microsoft Windows AntiSpyware is very simple; just visit http://www.microsoft.com to download a copy. Once you have AntiSpyware installed, click on the desktop icon to start the utility and follow these steps to set up AntiSpyware:

1. When you start Microsoft Windows AntiSpyware, the Setup Assistant will be loaded to guide you through the steps of configuring your spyware protection. Click **Next** to continue.

2. Step 1 of 3 will ask you whether you want to enable AutoUpdate. AutoUpdate automatically downloads the latest spyware definitions for you on a regular basis, unlike the other utilities mentioned earlier. It is highly recommended that you enable this option and click **Next**.

3. The next step gives you an opportunity to enable or disable the real-time protection agents I mentioned earlier that require a response from you before any Internet settings can be changed. This is one of the best features of Microsoft Windows AntiSpyware and should definitely be left enabled. Click **Next** to continue to the final step.

4. The final step gives you the opportunity to participate in what they call SpyNet. SpyNet is basically a method that allows you to report the results of your personal spyware scan back to Microsoft so they can use the information to update their definitions database. In general, it is best when everyone uses this feature because then the definitions will be better; however, some people concerned about their privacy may want to disable this feature. Either way, click **Finish** to close the Setup Assistant.

5. The next screen gives you the opportunity to run a full system scan. I suggest you click **Run Scan Later** and update the definitions first.

6. Once the main interface loads, click on the **File** menu bar item and select **Check for Updates**. If any updates are available, they will be automatically installed. Click on **Close** to continue.

7. Now you are ready to do a scan for Spyware. Click the **Run Quick Scan Now** button to start the scan.

8. After the scan is over, if anything is found, a summary of the results will be shown. Click **View Report** to view the details and to remove any spyware found.

9. On the Scan Results screen, you will see a list of every item found with a drop-down box for the recommended action to be taken (Ignore, Quarantine, Remove, or Always Ignore). By default, Microsoft AntiSpyware selects what it believes is the appropriate action for the severity of the spyware. However, you can always override that selection by selecting a new option in the drop-down menu for the item on the left. Once you have all of the items actions selected, click **Continue** and then **Yes** on the confirmation screen to execute the actions.

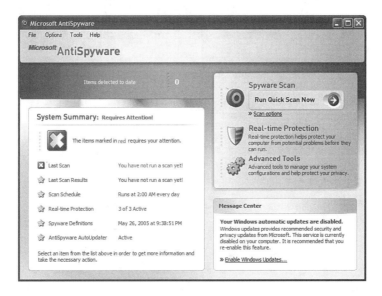

Figure 8.20 Microsoft Windows AntiSpyware.

Tip

Microsoft AntiSpyware has a lot of features that you would not expect to find in a spyware utility. Click on the Advanced Tools icon on the main program screen and explore the System and Privacy tools for some useful utilities.

Recovering from Browser Hijacks

For your convenience, spyware often automatically changes your home page in Internet Explorer as well as your default search page. This way, as soon as you open Internet Explorer or attempt to do a search, you are bombarded with even more opportunities to get spyware. While sometimes these incursions are innocuous, far too often they cross the line, motivating users to take control of their browsers again.

Recovering from a browser hijack caused by spyware is often a very annoying event. Quite often you run a spyware utility to clean the spyware off of your computer only to find it returns when you open up your web browser because the utility isn't necessarily capable of detecting hacks to your browser. Spyware designers are usually clever in their work, and they design software that doesn't always go away without a fight. Thankfully, with the help of Microsoft Windows AntiSpyware, it is very easy to reset all of Internet Explorer's settings back to the default settings, so you can reset everything that spyware may have modified. Of course, you may lose some of your own browser tweaks in the process.

The feature that can help you with this is buried within the application. Launch Microsoft Windows AntiSpyware and then click on the Advanced Tools icon in the upper-right corner of the screen and follow this procedure:

1. Locate and click on the **Browser Restore** icon located under System Tools.

2. Click on the **Check all** text button as shown in Figure 8.21.

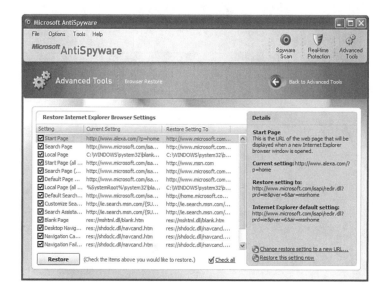

Figure 8.21   Microsoft Windows AntiSpyware browser restore.

3. Next, just click the **Restore** button and everything will be reset back to the factory default.

Now recovering from a browser hijack has never been easier.

What to Do When the Automated Utilities Fail

Spyware is constantly evolving to try to get ahead of the spyware removal utilities. One of the biggest problems with the spyware removal industry is that it relies very heavily on known definitions. While this passive approach can be effective and is far better than nothing, it means that new malware must cause damage for it to become known in the first place. To get rid of spyware that just wont go away, it may take someone who is very well experienced with removing spyware to help you out.

To help the countless spyware victims, various websites have dedicated support for fighting spyware. Most of these sites use the popular diagnosis software called HijackThis. HijackThis is a great little utility that examines various parts of the system configuration and Internet Explorer settings and displays their current values. The software allows a user to save a copy of the results, which can then be posted on one of the various websites dedicated to this utility. Dedicated individuals who volunteer their time are available at a variety of these sites to take a look at your log and help you figure out what entry is causing the problem. Then, using HijackThis again, you can easily check that entry and have it removed to solve your problem.

To get started, visit http://www.merijn.org to download the latest copy of HijackThis. Then, follow this procedure to generate your log:

1. Once you have HijackThis downloaded, launch the application (it doesn't require an installation).

2. Click on the **Scan** button to reveal your log (see Figure 8.22).

3. Next, click the **Save Log** button to save a text file with the contents of the scan on your computer.

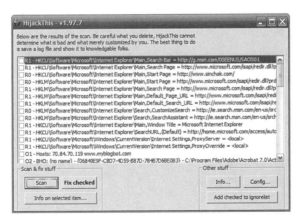

Figure 8.22 Generating the HijackThis log.

Now that you have your log generated, post it on one of these popular websites that are known for their dedicated HijackThis support:

- http://forum.tweakxp.com
- http://forums.spywareinfo.com
- http://forums.tomcoyote.org

Once you have posted your HijackThis log on one or a few of the websites, you will most likely get a response within a day. When the culprit is identified, just open up HijackThis again and check the box next to the line you want to be removed and click **Fix Checked**. You will be asked to confirm the delete and then the operation will be completed. After a reboot, the problem should now be solved.

CHAPTER 9

Windows Commands and Scripting

The Windows Command Prompt

The Windows GUI is fine for the casual user, but for tasks that you have to perform over and over every day, the Command Prompt window is your best friend. Visualize the difference between a hunt-and-peck typist and a Mavis Beacon Teaches Typing *summa cum laude* graduate. That's the difference between someone who uses only the GUI, and someone who knows how and when to take advantage of Windows' command line interface. Once you've committed the necessary commands to memory, you can type them *much* more quickly than you can take your hands off the keyboard, grab the mouse, and navigate through endless menus.

If you don't believe me, do an experiment: See how long it takes to get to the Windows Firewall control panel using the GUI, versus typing **control firewall.cpl** followed by the Enter key. The command line is also less distracting: You can just type the command you want without having to read and scroll through all of the commands you *don't* want to use.

Speed-typing aside, there are several other important reasons to know how to use the command line, batch files, and Windows Script Host:

- There are some commands and management tools available through the command line that aren't available through the GUI.

- You can put often-used sequences of commands into a batch file or script, and repeat complex tasks (or even simple tasks) with just a few keystrokes.

- Batch files and scripts serve as a form of documentation. Not only do they perform a job, they are themselves a description of a procedure, step by step, with nothing left out.

- Batch files and scripts encapsulate skill and knowledge. If you write one to perform a complex task, it will be much easier to teach someone else how to use the batch file than it would be to show him how to perform all of the individual steps inside.

The Windows Command Prompt window looks and behaves a lot like the screen you may remember from the pre-Windows days of MS-DOS. But, the Command Prompt window is a gateway to a full 32-bit environment closer to UNIX than MS-DOS. Command prompt programs (technically, they're called *console applications*) are actually full-fledged Windows programs; the only difference is that their window displays text output with no graphics, and it accepts typed text input; it's like using a very powerful electric typewriter.

Note

The next few sections describe how the Command Prompt environment works in some detail. If you want to skip ahead to the "how to" information, jump over to "Editing Command Lines" on page 382.

What the Command Prompt Really Does

When you use the Start menu to open a Command Prompt window, what's actually happening is that you're running a program named `cmd.exe`, the Windows command shell. Cmd is defined as a console application, as opposed to a GUI application, so as the program is started up, Windows opens a blank, black window. Cmd prints a prompt, a bit of text to indicate that it's waiting for you to type something; it might look like this:

```
C:\Documents and Settings\brian>
```

When you respond by typing a command and pressing Enter, cmd looks at the first word in the line of text you typed. It interprets this as the name of the program you want to run. It searches for an executable program file with this name, and if it finds one, starts up the program. Any other text on the line you typed is provided to the program for it to interpret, according to its own conventions, telling it what you want it to do.

For example, if I type the command

```
ping www.mycompany.com
```

cmd will search several standard folders for a program named "ping". It will find `ping.exe`, which is a network testing utility, in `\windows\system32`. Cmd will instruct Windows to run `ping.exe` and provide it with the additional text I typed, `www.mycompany.com`. Ping interprets this additional text as the name of another computer whose network connection I'd like to test. It will perform the network test and print a few lines into the Command Prompt window. When the ping program exits (finishes), `cmd.exe` prints another prompt, and the cycle starts over.

Environment Variables

Where exactly does cmd look for these program files? The list of locations is defined by a setting called the *PATH environment variable*. The Environment is a set of text values that Windows makes available to all programs. Each one consists of a name like PATH or USERNAME, followed by an equals sign and additional text. You can see them by opening a command prompt window and typing **set** followed by the Enter key. The output will look something like this:

```
ALLUSERSPROFILE=C:\Documents and Settings\All Users.WINDOWS
APPDATA=C:\Documents and Settings\brian\Application Data
CLIENTNAME=Console
CommonProgramFiles=C:\Program Files\Common Files
COMPUTERNAME=JAVA
ComSpec=C:\WINDOWS\system32\cmd.exe
HOMEDRIVE=C:
HOMEPATH=\Documents and Settings\brian
⋮
```

Each of these lines shows the name of an environment variable and its value. Windows defines most of these variables and values for you, though you can define environment variables for your own use in batch file programming. Of the predefined variables, Windows uses PATH and PATHEXT to locate programs that you want to run.

Note

Actually, Windows uses the **PATH** to locate *any* program it's told to run, whether it's from the command line, a line in a batch file, the Start menu's Run dialog, a shortcut, or from inside another program. It also uses the **PATH** to locate the Dynamic Link Libraries (DLLs) used by most Windows programs. When a program needs to use a DLL, Windows first looks in the folder that contains the calling program's **.EXE** file, and then it searches through the folders in the **PATH**.

Of course, if a command or DLL file is specified using a full pathname, the **PATH** list isn't used.

When you type a command on the command line, cmd first checks to see whether the command is one of the *built-in* commands that it handles directly, by itself, without any program file at all. Built-in commands include `dir` and several others, which are discussed later in this chapter.

If the command isn't recognized as a built-in command, cmd looks at the PATH environment variable and interprets it as a list of folders to search for a program file. The folder names are separated by semicolons, so for the PATH in the environment variable list you saw earlier, cmd will look at the following folders, in this order:

```
C:\WINDOWS\system32
C:\WINDOWS
C:\WINDOWS\system32\WBEM
c:\bin
c:\bat
```

The first three folders were put into the PATH list by Windows so that cmd can find the standard programs provided with Windows: notepad, ping, and so on. I added the second two folders myself, so that cmd can find some additional programs and batch files that I wrote; I'll tell you how to do this later in this chapter.

As it scans through these folders, Windows looks for a file whose name matches the name you typed on the command line, and whose extension (file type) is any one of those listed in the PATHEXT environment variable. Table 9.1 lists the most common file extensions used on executable files, batch files and scripts.

Table 9.1   Common Program File Extensions

Extension	Type of Program
.COM	MS-DOS executable file, absolute binary format
.EXE	Standard MS-DOS, Windows, OS/2, or other application
.BAT	Batch file, written for cmd.exe or MS-DOS command.com
.CMD	Batch file, written for cmd.exe
.VBS	Windows Script Host script, written in VBScript
.VBE	Encrypted VBScript script
.JS	Windows Script Host script, written in JScript
.JSE	Encrypted JScript script
.WSF	Windows Script Host script, in XML format
.WSH	Windows Script Host settings file

To continue with our sample command,

```
ping www.mycompany.com
```

Because ping isn't one of the built-in commands, cmd looks in the first folder listed in the PATH environment variable for a file named ping.com. If a file with this name is present, cmd instructs Windows to run the program. If ping.com isn't found, cmd checks for ping.exe, then ping.bat, and so on, through the PATHEXT list. If no file is found in the first PATH folder, cmd goes to the second folder and repeats the process. If a file can't be found in any of the folders, cmd prints an error message and gives up.

Of course, if you type a specific file extension as part of your command line, for example, if you type

```
ping.exe www.mycompany.com
```

Windows will look through the PATH folders only for a file with the specified extension, and will not use the PATHEXT list. Likewise, if you specify the command using a specific path, as in

```
c:\windows\system32\ping www.mycompany.com
```

Windows will not search through the PATH list.

Tip

If the same program or batch file is in more than one folder in your search path, and the first one that cmd finds is not the one you want, type the full pathname before the command to eliminate any ambiguity about which copy of the program you want to use. For example

```
c:\windows\system32\ping
```

tells cmd exactly where to find the ping program.

In any case, when Windows has located a program file that matches the command name you typed, it uses the file's extension to see what type of program it is to run. The extension .COM indicates a very old-style MS-DOS application. .BAT and .CMD files contain commands that cmd.exe is to interpret one line at a time just as if you were typing them at the command prompt. .EXE files are executable program files that could be MS-DOS programs, 16-bit or 32-bit Windows applications, console applications, or they could be programs that are associated with other add-on program environments including Interix (POSIX UNIX) or OS/2—Windows has to examine the contents of the file to see exactly what it is.

Executable Program Types

When Windows is instructed to run an .EXE file, Windows has to examine the file to determine what type of program it represents.

All executable files start with a block of data in the standard format used by all versions of Windows and MS-DOS versions 2.0 and later (see Table 9.2 for the gory details). The file starts with the ASCII characters "MZ", followed by values that describe the location within the file of the executable instructions.

Table 9.2   Microsoft Executable File Header Format

Offset (Hex)	Bytes	Description
0000	2	ASCII characters 'MZ'
0002	2	Number of bytes in last 512-byte page of executable code
0004	2	Total number of 512-byte pages of executable code (including last page)
0006	2	Number of relocation entries
0008	2	Header size in 16-byte paragraphs
000a	2	Minimum paragraphs of memory to allocate in addition to the executable code
000c	2	Maximum paragraphs of memory to allocate in addition to the executable code
000e	2	Initial Stack Segment register (SS) value relative to start of executable
0010	2	Initial Stack Pointer (SP) value
0012	2	Checksum value for executable data
0014	4	Initial Code Segment and Instruction Pointer (CS:IP) relative to start of executable (that is, program start address)
0018	2	Offset of relocation table. For a Windows GUI or console application (that is, for anything beyond an MS-DOS application), this value is always 40 hex and points to the relocation table of the MS-DOS stub program.
0020-0019		(data varies depending on linker used)

(continues)

Table 9.2   Continued

Offset (Hex)	Bytes	Description
001a	2	Overlay number (0 for main program)
003c	4	Offset of Windows "NE" or "PE" header from start of file; 0 if plain MS-DOS .EXE file

In the case of a true MS-DOS application, this "header" data describes the actual MS-DOS program. For Windows and console applications, the header fields point to a tiny MS-DOS program contained within the file that simply prints "This program cannot be run in DOS mode" and exits. This is called the "MS-DOS stub," and it ensures that if you attempt to run the application under MS-DOS, it will not crash the older operating system. Windows knows to look past the "stub" for a second descriptive data block called a "New Executable" (NE) or "Portable Executable" (PE) header, farther in the file.

The second header describes where within the file to find the program's executable code, its resources (dialog and text data), debugging information, and other file sections, and also indicates the CPU type and Windows subsystem to which the program belongs. The CPU type indicates the instruction set for which the program is designed, and can specify the x86 (32-bit), x86-64 (64-bit), Itanium 2, Alpha, or MIPS instruction sets. (Alpha and MIPS processors, alas, are no longer supported.) The subsystems include the following:

- 16-bit Windows GUI application
- 32-bit Windows GUI application
- 64-bit Windows GUI application
- 32-bit Windows console application
- 64-bit Windows console application
- OS/2 1.x console application
- POSIX (Interix or UNIX) console application
- Other types including device driver, DLL, and so on

Thus, between the file extension and, for .EXE files, the two header structures, Windows can determine whether it's being asked to run a script or batch file, an MS-DOS program, a Windows program, or a program designed for another supported operating system; and whether the application uses a GUI or the console window's character-oriented interface.

Program Subsystems

In addition to standard Windows GUI applications, Windows supports several sorts of console-mode applications. Windows console programs are actually full-fledged Windows programs that can use the standard Windows application programming interface (API); they just don't have graphical windows of their own. Instead, they interact through the text window of the Command Prompt window that started them.

Windows can also run programs based on other operating system standards. It does this using additional software, installed with Windows, that provide the system functions these other programs expect. This is called *emulation*, where Windows makes itself look and act like another operating system. Several emulation environments are available, listed in Table 9.3.

Table 9.3   Windows Emulation Subsystems

Subsystem	Description
MS-DOS	MS-DOS applications (.COM and .EXE files) are run inside of an emulation program named NTVDM.EXE ("NT Virtual DOS Machine"), which emulates standard PC hardware, and provides the DOS and BIOS system call support expected by MS-DOS applications. The Virtual DOS Machine is described later in this chapter.
Interix (POSIX)	A POSIX-compliant (UNIX-like) environment is provided as part of the Services for UNIX package, a free download available from microsoft.com for Windows 2000 Professional, XP Professional, and the various Windows Server versions. Services for UNIX are described in Appendix A, "Windows Tool Reference."
16-bit Windows	16-bit Windows applications are supported by the "WinOldAp" system, which translates 16-bit Windows function requests into the appropriate 32-bit requests. Emulation is provided by ntvdm.exe (NT Virtual DOS Machine) and wowexec.exe (Windows on Windows); 16-bit Windows programs run inside a virtual Windows 3.1 environment provided by these programs.
OS/2 1.x	Windows NT 3.51, NT 4.0, 2000 Professional, and 2000 Server include a subsystem that runs IBM OS/2 version 1.x (character mode) applications. The OS/2 subsystem is not included in Windows XP.

Note

The 64-bit versions of Windows do not support 16-bit Windows (Windows 3.1) applications nor MS-DOS applications; the necessary emulation environments are not and will not be provided as an integral part of 64-bit Windows. If you need to use these older applications under 64-bit Windows, you must install a full-scale emulator program like VMWare or Microsoft Virtual PC, install a 16-bit or 32-bit operating system in an emulated PC, and run the old applications there.

The goal of the subsystem mechanism is that any supported program should run exactly as it would under its native operating system, yet to you, the user, it should appear and act like any other Windows console-mode application.

MS-DOS Emulation

MS-DOS applications performed disk, printer, keyboard, and mouse input/output operations through support routines provided by MS-DOS. The application would store a code number corresponding to a desired system service in a CPU hardware register, and then execute a CPU interrupt instruction, which would transfer control to DOS or the Basic Input/Output System (BIOS) routines in the lower range of system memory. These services provided a way for an application program to display text output on the screen, read characters from the keyboard and coordinates from the mouse, and to create, read, and write disk files, without the program's having to contain the code to handle the details of these operations.

However, instead of using interrupt instructions, Windows applications read and write files by calling functions in Dynamic Link Libraries provided into Windows. An interrupt instruction would simply make Windows display the message "Your program has performed an illegal operation" and terminate the program. Therefore, MS-DOS applications are run inside a "container" program called ntvdm.exe that provides code to simulate the DOS functions. Ntvdm.exe intercepts CPU interrupt instructions, and calls the appropriate Windows library functions on the program's behalf. It also contains code to mimic the MS-DOS segmented memory structure. When you attempt to run an MS-DOS application, Windows actually runs ntvdm.exe; it reads the desired MS-DOS program into its own address space and lets it run. At this point, the MS-DOS application cannot tell it is not running on an old-fashioned PC over MS-DOS*.

To achieve better performance, MS-DOS programs frequently bypassed MS-DOS's limited input/output support and took direct control of some hardware devices, including graphics adapters, parallel ports (LPT ports), and serial ports (COM ports). This was necessary because there was no standardized way of addressing graphics adapters, and on the slower computers of that era, it was not possible to process thousands of characters per second for a high-speed modem or printer when there were several layers of software involved. Windows NT, 2000, and XP do not allow any user program to have direct access to hardware devices. So, ntvdm.exe emulates the graphics adapter and COM1, COM2, LPT1, LPT2, and LPT3 hardware as well; that is, it intercepts attempts by an MS-DOS application to manipulate these hardware devices directly, and uses the appropriate Windows system functions to get the intended results.

Ultimately, the MS-DOS environment provides support for the following MS-DOS services and emulates standard hardware devices, through code built into ntvdm.exe:

- All standard BIOS and DOS function interrupts.
- Mouse support (MOUSE.COM) interrupts.
- Display and keyboard hardware.
- PC-standard timers, Programmable Interrupt Controllers, and the speaker interface.
- Soundblaster-compatible sound adapter hardware. (No matter what sort of sound hardware your computer has, MS-DOS applications "see" a standard, low-end SoundBlaster adapter.)
- Intel 386 memory management hardware.
- Up to 16MB of memory, which the MS-DOS application thinks is the entirety of system memory, but which is simply a standard block of memory in ntvdm's address space.

Ntvdm's emulation works pretty well for graphics and LPT printer devices, but the serial (COM) port simulation is iffy, and network printing support is sometimes troublesome. I've run into these sorts of problems:

- DOS programs that use network printers, such as the old DOS FoxPro database program, don't always eject a page after printing, or sometimes eject too many pages.
- Modem software like Norton-Lambert's Close-Up remote-control software doesn't work perfectly. Data is lost between the software and the modem, resulting in slow communications and even modem hang-ups.
- Games that attempt to use ntvdm's Sound Blaster emulation may generate hideous screeching sounds or may crash entirely.

Unfortunately, when problems like these do occur, there is little or nothing you can do about it. I keep an old laptop with Windows 95 on hand for the rare occasion that I really have to run an MS-DOS communications program that fails under Windows XP.

Special versions of some standard MS-DOS device drivers are provided with Windows XP. These are true MS-DOS style drivers, although they are specially coded to work in this emulation environment. They are loaded into the MS-DOS environment when ntvdm.exe starts up through configuration files

---

* Ntvdm.exe *is a descendant of SoftPC, an early 1990's PC emulator that let people run DOS and Windows 95 on Apple Macintosh computers. The original Insignia Solutions, Ltd copyright is still tucked away inside* ntvdm.exe, *as is the cryptic comment "NtVdm : Using Yoda on an x86 may be hazardous to your systems' health"*

config.nt and autoexec.nt, which are discussed later in this chapter. The additional standard services are

- High memory access service, provided by himem.sys.
- CD-ROM extensions, provided by mscdexnt.exe (a special version of mscdex.exe that doesn't expect to connect to a DOS-mode CD-ROM device driver).
- Networking support (access to shared files and printers), provided by redir.exe. If you have installed a Novell NetWare client, a partial implementation of the NetWare interface is provided to DOS programs by nw16.exe and vwipxspx.exe.
- DOS Protected Mode Interface (memory support) provided by dosx.exe, which replaces DOS's emm386.exe.

Additional support for ANSI screen output and national language support can be loaded as well; see "Configuring the MS-DOS command environment" (this chapter) for more information.

Interpreting Command-Line Syntax

Commands entered at the command prompt start with the name of the command to run, but there may be more. Any additional text items on the command line after the program name are called *arguments*, and they are given to the program to interpret. For example, the command

```
ping mycompany.com
```

runs the program ping.exe, and the extra text mycompany.com is given to ping.exe to interpret. Each program interprets its command-line arguments in its own way, according to the design of the programmer who created it.

Most programs expect to see some fundamental information like the name of a file to process or the name of a website to test. Some programs require more than one argument like this, for example, an input filename and an output filename. (The order in which they're entered usually matters! For example, the first name might always be interpreted as the name of the input file, and the second name as the name of the output file.)

Then, many programs can be made to adjust their behavior by specifying additional arguments variously called *options, switches*, or *flags*. For example

```
ping www.mycompany.com
```

tests the network connection to a given Internet host by sending four test data packets. You can tell ping to send eight test data packets by adding the -n option:

```
ping -n 8 www.mycompany.com
```

Things get decidedly hairier at this point, for there is little consistency in how these options are specified. Some programs don't want a space between an option and value; for example, the author of ping might just as well have required you to type

```
ping -n8 www.mycompany.com
```

Other programs, mostly those that were originally written by Microsoft or borrowed from the earlier CP/M operating system, use options that start with a slash rather than the UNIX tradition of using a dash; for example,

```
dir /b
```

There's simply no way to know what options are available, or how to format them, other than to look at the documentation. What you want to know is the program's *command-line syntax*, which is a formal way of saying "what it expects to see."

There are several possible ways to get a description of a program's command-line syntax. For a given program, which for the sake of example let's call xxx, you can try these things:

- Type **xxx /?** Some programs recognize /? as a plea for help, and print out a description of the command-line syntax.

- Type **help xxx**, which invokes the Windows command-line help system.

- Click Start, Help and Support and search for xxx.

- Search Help and Support for the string command line reference, and click the link to Command Line Reference A-Z.

- Perform an Internet search for xxx.

There's no way to tell beforehand which of these will work; you may want to try all five.

Command-line syntax is usually described in a way that indicates what parts you *have* to type, what parts are optional, and what parts have to contain names or other information particular to your situation. The documentation will usually define its particular conventions somewhere, but this is a very common format:

- **boldface** indicates text that you have to type literally.

- *italics* indicate something that's just representative; you don't type this literally, but replace it with your own information. In some Microsoft documentation, angle brackets < > are used for this purpose also.

- Square brackets [ ] enclose optional parts; you can type them or leave them out.

- Ellipses (…) indicate that you can type more, or repeat the previous items as many times as desired.

- The vertical bar | separates a series of choices; you are to enter just one of the listed options. Sometimes, alternate choices of long sequences of options are printed on separate lines.

For example, the command to create directories (folders) can be typed as mkdir or md, and this is how Microsoft describes its syntax:

   mkdir [*drive:*]*path*

   md [*drive:*]*path*

The two lines indicate two alternate choices. The boldface mkdir or md is something that is to be typed literally. You don't type the word *path* literally; *path* just shows where you are to type the name of the folder you want to create. *Drive* and its following colon are optional; they can be typed, or omitted. You do have to read the description of the command to know that *drive* is supposed to be a single letter representing a disk drive; the syntax description can't provide that information symbolically.

This stuff may be confusing at first, but you'll soon get the hang of it, and you'll find that a glance at syntax description will convey a lot of information about what a program can and can't do.

Environment Variable Substitution

As it examines command lines that you've typed or that it has read from a batch file, cmd replaces strings of the form %*name*% with the value of the named environment variable. (*Environment variables* are named text strings used by Windows to communicate information to programs, batch files, and scripts, and also by batch files to hold and modify data.) For example, the command

   echo %path%

is interpreted as the command

```
echo c:\windows\system32;C:\WINDOWS;C:\WINDOWS\System32\Wbem
```

and echo prints out whatever is on its command line. Thus the command echo %path% displays the value of the path variable. Environment variable substitution can be used anyplace on any command line, as long as the resulting text is a valid command.

Note

Environment variable names are not case sensitive. To cmd, **%path%**, **%Path%**, and **%PATH%** are all the same.

Input and Output Redirection

Console programs read interactive input from the keyboard and display it on the screen. They do this through a mechanism called *standard I/O streams*. Each console program has available to it a stream or source of input called the *standard input*, and two output streams, *standard output* and *standard error*. By default, keyboard input to the console window goes to the applications standard input, and anything the application prints on the standard output or standard error streams appears in the console window, as illustrated in Figure 9.1. As you might guess, the standard output stream is used for the program's principal output, while the standard error stream is used for error messages and warnings.

Note

The concept of redirectable standard I/O has a long history. It started in the Multics operating system developed at MIT in the late 1960s. In the 1970s, the developers of the UNIX operating system adopted the idea and added the < and > syntax. The 8-bit CP/M operating system "borrowed" it from UNIX, MS-DOS took it from CP/M, and Windows XP inherited it from MS-DOS. This reminds me of the Tom Lehrer song "I Got It From Agnes," but maybe we shouldn't go there.

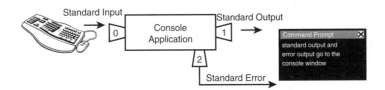

Figure 9.1   Console applications have three standard input/output streams.

You can think of console applications as having a sort of "plumbing." The standard I/O streams can easily be *redirected*, or connected, to files or other console applications. For example, the standard output stream, which usually appears in the console window, can be directed to a file using the > character on the command line. Placing >output.txt on the command line redirects what would have appeared in the console window into the file named output.txt. Similarly, the < character redirects the standard input. Placing <input.txt on the command line connects file input.txt to the standard input, so the application will read from that file instead of the keyboard. For example, the command

```
sort <input.txt >output.txt
```

runs the sort console application; when it reads from the standard input, it reads file input.txt, and whatever it writes to the standard output stream goes into file output.txt, as illustrated in Figure 9.2. Of course, you can specify any filenames that you want to use; it doesn't have to be input.txt or output.txt. Also, the files input.txt and output.txt will be read from and written to in the current directory, but you can control this by specifying a path as part of the redirection command; for example:

```
sort <c:\myproject\rawdata\input.txt >c:\myproject\results\output.txt
```

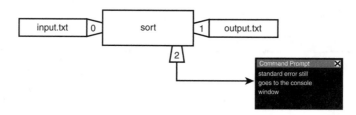

Figure 9.2 The standard I/O streams can be redirected to files.

Notice that in this command the standard error stream is not redirected. If the `sort` command runs into any sort of problem and prints an error message on the standard error stream, the message will appear in the console window where you can see it.

However, if you want to, you *can* redirect the standard error to a file. You might want to do this in a batch file that will be run when nobody is logged on, to collect any error messages in a log file so they can be printed or viewed later. To redirect the standard error stream, put `2>filename` on the command line. For example, if you typed the command

```
sort <input.txt >output.txt 2>error.txt
```

and `sort` printed any error messages, they would appear in file `error.txt` rather than in the console window.

What's this business with the number 2? If you look back at Figures 9.1 and 9.2, you'll see that the little pipe fittings for the standard I/O streams have numbers attached to them. The standard output is designated as stream #1, and the standard error as stream #2. A number before > redirects a specific stream. So, `2>error.txt` indicates that the program's standard error output stream is to be redirected into file `error.txt`.

You can also instruct Windows to write both the standard output and standard error streams to the same file. This will produce one file with the output of both streams mixed together. The syntax for this is `2>&1`, as in the command

```
sort <input.txt >output.txt 2>&1
```

It means "Stream 2 goes to the same place as stream 1." It's peculiar, but it's a very handy thing when you need it.

Finally, you should know that if the filename you specify when redirecting data output exists before you run the command, the > redirection feature erases that file. That is, after you type these three commands:

```
dir >file.txt
ping mycompany.com >file.txt
echo This is the third command >file.txt
```

`file.txt` will contain only one line of text, reading "This is the third command." The first command puts the output of the `dir` command into `file.txt`, and then `ping` overwrites that with its output, and then `echo` replaces that.

To get around this problem you can use the append operator >>. When you add >>filename to a command line, the standard output is *added to* the file if it already exists; if the file didn't exist, it is created. The commands

```
dir >file.txt
ping mycompany.com >>file.txt
echo This is the third command >>file.txt
```

will create a file named file.txt that contains the output of all three commands: first the dir listing, followed by the output of the ping command, followed by the line This is the third command from the echo command.

Table 9.4 has a complete listing of all of the redirection variations. You can use any name in the place of filename, and you can enter a plain filename or a path and filename.

Table 9.4   Input/Output Redirection Functions

Syntax	Result
<filename	Standard input is read from filename
>filename	Standard output is written to filename
1>filename	(equivalent to >filename)
2>filename	Standard error is written to filename
>>filename	Standard output is appended to filename
1>>filename	(equivalent to >>filename)
2>>filename	Standard error is appended to filename
>filename 2>&1	Standard output and standard error are both written to filename
>>filename 2>&1	Standard output and standard error are both appended to filename

Tip

You can add a space between the > or >> and the filename; it works with or without the space. You might want to get into the habit of adding a space, as it will help you if you want to use the name completion feature that is discussed later in the chapter.

Tip

If the file that you want to create has a space in its name, put quotes around the name. You can put the > or >> inside or outside of the quotes; ">filename with space" and > "filename with space" work equally well. But again, it's probably better to get in the habit of putting the > outside the quotes, so that you can use name completion.

By the way, the older command.com shell used by MS-DOS, Windows 9x, and Me does not support any of the numeric variations of output redirection, such as 2>&1 and 2>. These are part of the enhancements made to cmd.exe.

Finally, if you are familiar with the UNIX operating system and shell script programming, you should know that the << input redirection mechanism is *not* available in the Windows command shell.

Command Pipelines

You can direct the output of one command to the input of another using the pipeline operator (|). The concept is illustrated in Figure 9.3. The command

```
tasklist | findstr "winword"
```

runs the Windows XP Professional `tasklist` program, which writes a listing of all running programs to the standard output. The pipeline operator (|) redirects this output to the input of the `findstr` command, which writes to *its* standard output only lines containing the text string `winword`. This combined command thus prints a listing of just information about running instances of Microsoft Word.

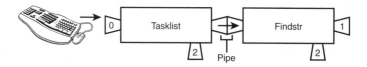

Figure 9.3   The Pipeline operator (|) connects the output of one program to the input of another.

You could accomplish the same thing by redirecting the output of the first command to a file, and then running the second command with input from the same file, like this:

```
tasklist >filex
findstr "winword" <filex
delete filex
```

but the pipeline mechanism actually runs the two programs simultaneously, and doesn't store the intermediate output in a disk file; the pipeline is more efficient because it all takes place in the computer's main RAM.

Pipelines aren't limited to two commands; if you need to, you can hook up several commands in sequence. For example,

```
dir /b /s c:\ | findstr "net" | more
```

uses `dir` to list the entire contents of the C drive; its output is passed to `findstr`, which filters out only those lines containing the string `net`, and *that* output is passed to `more`, which displays one screen of text at a time and waits for you to press the spacebar before displaying the next screen.

Command Separators

You can type several commands on one input line using the special *command separator* delimiters that `cmd.exe` recognizes. The delimiters are described in Table 9.5.

Table 9.5   Command Separators

Syntax	Description
command1 & command2	Runs command1, then command2. Example: `dir >listing.txt & notepad listing.txt`
command1 && command2	Runs command1, and only if it is successful (that is, if command1 sets its error status value to 0), runs command2. If the command1 indicates an error, the remainder of the command line is discarded. Example: `copy file.dat a: && copy second.dat a:`

Table 9.5   Continued

Syntax	Description
command1 || command2	Runs command1, and only if it fails (that is, if command1 sets its error status value to something other than 0), runs command2.
	Example:
	`copy file.dat a: || goto copyfailed`

In addition, parentheses can be used to group multiple commands. We'll talk about that later in the chapter when we cover batch file programming.

Command-Line Quoting

When a command-line program requires you to specify information such as the name of a file to process or an option to use, you usually type this information after the command name, with the items separated by spaces. For example, the `delete` command erases the file or files named on its command line:

```
delete somefile.txt anotherfile.txt
```

Unfortunately, because Windows filenames can contain spaces in the middle of the name, the command

```
delete C:\Documents and Settings\brian\My Documents\a.txt
```

will attempt to delete four files: `C:\Documents`, `and`, `Settings\brian\My`, and `Documents\a.txt`. To solve this problem, cmd interprets quotation marks (`" "`) to mean that the text enclosed is to be treated as part of one single argument. For example, the command

```
delete "C:\Documents and Settings\brian\My Documents\a.txt"
```

deletes the one indicated file. The quotation marks are not seen as part of the filename; they just keep it all together.

Note

You can also separate command-line arguments with the semicolon (;) or comma (,), but not all programs accept them. I recommend that you don't use these characters to separate arguments—use spaces. But, some programs do see them as separators, so, as with spaces, if you have a filename with a comma or semicolon in the name you'll have to put quotes around the name.

Escaping Special Characters

As you've already seen, the following characters have special meaning to cmd:

```
< > ( ) & | , ; "
```

If you need to use any of these characters as part of a command-line argument to be given to a program (for example, to have the `find` command search for the character >), you need to *escape* the character by placing a caret (^) symbol before it. This indicates that the character is to be treated like any other character and removes its special meaning. To pass a ^ character as an argument, type ^^.

For example, the `echo` command types its arguments in the Command Prompt window. The command

```
echo <hello>
```

would cause a problem because cmd would think that you want to redirect input from a file named hello and that you want to redirect output to...well, there is no filename after >, so cmd would print an error message. However, the command

```
echo ^<hello^>
```

prints <hello>.

Because the characters ( ) < > & | and ; have special meaning to cmd.exe (they are the command separators and redirection operators), if you want to specify one of these characters as part of an argument to a command-line program, you have to tell cmd to ignore its special meaning. To do this, you have to precede the character with a caret (^) character. This is called *escaping* it. For example, if you wanted to use the findstr command to search a file named listing.txt for lines containing &, you would have to type the command this way:

```
findstr ^& listing.txt
```

Without the ^, cmd would treat the & as a command separator and would see the line as two separate commands.

To pass the ^ character itself as part of a command-line argument, you have to escape it in the same way, as in the command

```
findstr ^^ listing.txt
```

The first ^ means, "take the following character literally and ignore its special meaning." The second ^ is passed to findstr. This command searches file listing.txt for lines containing the caret symbol.

Editing Command Lines

One big area of improvement in cmd.exe over the old MS-DOS command.com shell is its command-line editing feature. I don't know about you, but while I'm a fast typist, my error rate is about 20%. A few letters forward, a backspace, a few more forward, another backspace. Luckily, it's very easy to edit the input to console windows. If you used the DOSKEY utility under MS-DOS, you'll find some of this familiar, but cmd.exe's editing features are even further improved. The backspace, Delete, and left and right arrow keys work as you would expect. Table 9.6 lists additional keys you can use to edit command lines.

Table 9.6   Command-Line Editing Keys

Key	Effect
Esc	Erases the current input line and returns the cursor to the left margin.
Ctrl+left arrow	Moves the cursor one word to the left.
Ctrl+right arrow	Moves the cursor one word to the right.
Home	Moves the cursor to the beginning of the current input line.
End	Moves the cursor to the end of the current input line.
Ins	Toggles between overwrite and insert mode. In overwrite mode, keystrokes replace previously entered characters. In insert mode, keystrokes insert new characters at the cursor position sliding previous text to the right. The initial setting—Insert or Overwrite—can be set in the console window's Properties page.
F1	Copies one character from the previous command into the current command line.
F2 *x*	F2 followed by any character (for example, *x*) retypes text from the previous command line up to and but not including the character *x*.

Table 9.6   Continued

Key	Effect
F3	Retypes the remainder of the previously entered command line, from the cursor point forward to its end.
F4 x	F4 followed by any character (for example, x) deletes characters in the current line from the cursor point up to but not including the character x.
F5	Retypes the entire text of the previous input line into the current input line.
F6	Types Ctrl+Z; not really useful in Windows 2000 or XP.
F7	Displays a pop-up box containing the previously entered input lines. You can scroll through them with the arrow keys and press Enter to retype the selected line, or Esc to cancel.
Alt+F7	Deletes the command history.
xxx F8	F8 typed after any text will recall the most recent command from the history list whose first characters match the characters typed. Repeated F8's will search back for the next most recent matching command.
F9	Prompts you for a number n, then retypes the nth command back in the history list.
Up arrow	Recalls the previously entered line; repeated use scrolls through the last 20 or so input lines.
Down arrow	Used after the up arrow key, scrolls back down through the last few input lines.
PgUp	Recalls the oldest command in the history list.
PgDn	Recalls the most recently typed command.
Alt+Space, E	Displays the Edit menu, from which you can choose Mark, Paste, Find, or Scroll.
	Paste takes whatever text is in the clipboard and "types" it into the console window.
	Mark lets you select a rectangular block of text with the mouse or cursor keys; press Enter to copy the marked text to the clipboard.
	We'll go into this in more detail in the next section.

The ability to use the up and down arrow keys to recall previously entered lines is especially useful, as you can quickly fix incorrectly entered commands, or simply save yourself typing when entering a series of similar commands.

Command-line editing works not only when typing commands at the command prompt itself, but also when typing text input to most console programs. However, the history list (the list of input lines that you can scroll through with the up and down arrow keys) is maintained separately for the input to the command prompt and for each program you run.

Name Completion

When you are typing command lines to cmd, you'll often need to type file and folder names. Name completion makes this easier—you can type just the first few letters of a file or folder name, press a control key, and cmd will finish typing the name for you. This is called *pathname completion* or *filename completion*, a nifty but not widely known feature that, like most of the other fun new features in cmd, Microsoft has borrowed from the UNIX operating system.

By default, the Tab key is used for both filename and pathname completion. That is, if you type a partial filename or pathname and press the Tab key, cmd will automatically add on the remainder of the first filename or folder name that matches what you've typed up to that point. If this is the correct name, you can just continue typing on the command line. This is a great timesaver!

If the name that cmd types is not the one you were looking for, you can press the Tab key again to see the next matching name. Pressing Tab repeatedly cycles through all matching names. What's more, you can hold the Shift key down while pressing Tab to cycle backward.

If cmd finds no matching file or folder name, it beeps and does nothing.

Tip

If you have to type a long pathname such as `\Documents and Settings\brian\My Documents`, you can use name completion for each part of the name. For this example, you could type the following:

`dir \d` (Tab) `\b` (Tab) `\m` (Tab)

Try this on your own computer (and use your own username instead of **brian**). It's pretty slick—cmd adds the required quotation marks and moves them into the correct positions automatically.

Cmd is smart enough to know that certain commands expect only a folder name. For example, if you've typed cd or rd on the command line, name completion will match only directory names and will ignore filenames. It's clever (if a bit spooky) but this mechanism only kicks in for the few commands that are "obviously" directory-only commands.

If you want to take explicit control of whether cmd should match file or folder names, you can use the TweakUI Power Toy (discussed in Chapter 6, "Tweaking and Tuning Windows") to specify different control keys for filename and pathname completion. For example, you can set the filename completion character to Ctrl+F and the pathname character to Ctrl+D. When you type Ctrl+F cmd will match only to filenames, and will ignore any potential matching subdirectory names. Likewise, Ctrl+D will match only folder names.

There are other ways to make these settings, but TweakUI is the easiest. For more information, see Microsoft Knowledge Base article number 310530.

Copy and Paste in Command Prompt Windows

Although console programs don't have the display windows and menus of ordinary Windows programs, you can still use the mouse to copy and paste text to and from Command Prompt windows.

The usual Ctrl+C shortcut doesn't work to copy text from a Command Prompt window. To copy text to the Clipboard, you have to extract a rectangular block of text—you can't select text line by line as you're used to. Position the mouse at the upper-left corner of the block of text you want, drag it down to the bottom-right corner, and then press Enter. While you're selecting text, the word *Select* appears in the window's title. Figure 9.4 shows how a Command Prompt window looks when selecting text.

You can also select text using the window's System menu. Click the upper-left corner of the window or press Alt+space and then select Edit, Mark. Use the arrow keys to move the cursor to the upper-left corner of the desired area; then hold the Shift key down while moving the cursor to the lower-right corner. Press Enter to copy the selected text.

Also, in a Command Prompt window, the usual Ctrl+V shortcut doesn't perform a paste operation. You *can* paste text into a Command Prompt window using the System menu: press Alt+space and then select Edit, Paste. The program running in the window has to be expecting input; otherwise it's just ignored.

Tip

The keyboard shortcut for Paste is worth memorizing: Alt+space, E, P.

Figure 9.4   To copy text to the Clipboard, select a block of text with the mouse and press Enter.

By the way, "cut" isn't available—once something is typed in a Command Prompt window, it can't be removed.

If you need to run a mouse-aware MS-DOS program in a Command Prompt window, you'll want to disable the Select feature so that mouse movements will be sent to the program rather than being interpreted by the console program window. To disable the use of the mouse for copying text, select the window's Properties dialog box and uncheck Quick Edit mode, as shown in Figure 9.5.

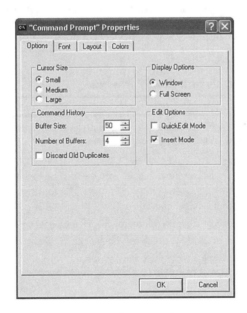

Figure 9.5   A Command Prompt window's Properties dialog box lets you select the Quick Edit mode, Screen mode, scroll length, editing properties, and screen colors.

DOSKEY Macros

DOSKEY is a command-line helper program that originated in MS-DOS, where it provided the up-and-down arrow key command recall feature that's now a standard part of the 32-bit Windows command window. DOSKEY is also provided with Windows XP and 2000. You don't need to run DOSKEY to get the command-line editing features, but you can use it to print out the command history, and more importantly, to define *macros*, which are keyboard shortcuts. For example, I use the command

```
doskey n=notepad
```

to define n as a command macro, and henceforth I can edit a text file by typing a command line like

```
n myfile.bat
```

instead of having to type

```
notepad myfile.bat
```

Once the macro is defined, n is seen as the word notepad whenever it's typed as the first word on a command prompt line. In the long run, this really does save time and frustration—you can't imagine how many times I've typed ntoepad instead of notepad!

By default, DOSKEY macros affect only text read by cmd.exe, that is, commands typed at the command prompt itself. You can define macros that will affect the input of specific command-line programs using the /EXENAME option. For example, the command

```
doskey /exename=ftp.exe anon=anonymous
```

defines anon as a macro that turns into the word anonymous when it's typed as the input to ftp.exe, the command-line File Transfer Protocol client.

Table 9.7 lists symbols that have special meaning inside a DOSKEY macro. You can use these symbols to construct macros complex enough to handle jobs that you would otherwise have to write small batch files to accomplish. With these symbols, upper/lowercase does not matter; $g and $G are treated the same.

Table 9.7   Special Symbols in DOSKEY Macros

Symbol	Function
$G	Works like > on the command line; lets you perform output redirection when the macro is run. Use GG to put >> in the macro, to append output.
$L	Works like < on the command line; lets you perform input redirection when the macro is run.
$B	Works like | on the command line; lets you create a pipeline when the macro is run.
$T	Works like & on the command line; lets you specify several commands that are to be run in sequence when the macro is encountered.
$n	Where n is a single digit, is replaced by the nth argument on the macro's command line.
$*	$* is replaced by all of the arguments on the macro's command line.
$$	Appears as a single $ when the command is run.

For example, after the macro definition

```
doskey fs=findstr /i /c:"$1" $2.log $B more
```

the command

```
fs index ww3svc
```

will be treated like the command

```
findstr /i /c:"index" ww3svc.log | more
```

which will search for a specified string in a specified log file and page the results through more.

It's important to know that unless you use $*, $1, $2 or the other $*n* symbols to explicitly tell DOSKEY to copy command-line arguments from your typed command line to the replacement line, they will be discarded. For example, with the definition

```
doskey n=notepad
```

the command

```
n myfile.txt
```

will open Notepad but the filename will not be seen. You have to define the macro this way:

```
doskey n=notepad $*
```

to ensure that any arguments on the command line after n are passed along to notepad.

The command doskey /macros:all will list all defined macros.

To load your favorite DOSKEY macros every time you open a Command Prompt window, it won't help to put the DOSKEY command in autoexec.bat (which is ignored) or \windows\system32\ autoexec.nt (which is used only by the MS-DOS emulation system). Instead, you have to put the desired macro definitions into a text file (one macro per line with the format name=replacement) and make an entry in the Registry to tell cmd.exe to load these settings every time it starts up.

You can define DOSKEY macros for all users by setting a Registry value named AutoRun under key HKEY_LOCAL_MACHINE\Software\Microsoft\Command Processor, or just for yourself by setting value AutoRun under HKEY_CURRENT_USER\Software\Microsoft\Command Processor. The entry should be a String (REG_SZ) or Expandable String (REG_EXPAND_SZ) with the name AutoRun and the value

```
doskey /macrofile="full path to macro definition file"
```

A helpful shortcut here is to define the value as an Expandable String (REG_EXPAND_SZ) under HKEY_CURRENT_USER... with the text

```
doskey /macrofile="%userprofile%\doskey.macros"
```

You can then create file doskey.macros in your own profile folder (for example, in C:\Documents and Settings\Brian). My own doskey.macros file contains the following entries:

```
n=notepad $*
e=explorer .
home=cd /d %userprofile%
desktop=cd /d %userprofile%\Desktop
macdef=start /wait "" notepad "%userprofile%\doskey.macros" $T doskey /reinstall $T
    ➥ doskey /macrofile="%userprofile%\doskey.macros"
u=cd /d d:\project
```

Here's what they do:

- Macro n lets me run Notepad with one character.
- Macro e pops open a Windows Explorer window in the current directory.
- Home sets the current directory to my Windows profile folder and desktop sets the current directory to my Desktop folder.
- Macdef (whose definition is displayed on two lines here but is actually typed all on one line in doskey.macros) lets me modify my macro definitions and have the changes take effect without having to close the Command Prompt window and open a new one. It opens the macro definition file for editing, clears the defined macros, and then reloads the definitions. Start /wait is used here so that DOSKEY doesn't run until after Notepad exits.

■ The last macro u is a quick shortcut to a commonly used folder. I add and delete macros like this all the time, as my work projects come and go. They save a lot of typing.

Note

The version of DOSKEY provided with Windows 2000 and XP works only in the 32-bit command prompt environment, not the 16-bit emulated MS-DOS environment. Running DOSKEY inside `autoexec.nt` or after running `command.com` has no effect. This means that the up and down arrow keys will not recall commands in the 16-bit command shell.

The version of DOSKEY provided with Windows 98 and Me is the original 16-bit version that does work inside the `command.com` shell. It's most effectively loaded in `autoexec.bat`, before Windows is loaded.

For a full description of all of DOSKEY's features, type

```
help doskey | more
```

at the command prompt.

Command Extensions

Under Windows 2000 and XP, lines into a Command Prompt window or listed in a batch file are processed by `cmd.exe`, which is known as the command shell or command-line processor. It performs the same function that `command.com` did under DOS and earlier versions of Windows, but it has been expanded and includes many additional features. If you haven't used the command-line environment since the days of MS-DOS, and especially if you write batch files, you need to know about cmd's important and useful enhancements. Table 9.8 lists some of the ways that cmd handles commands differently than `command.com`. For more information, search Windows Help for "cmd."

Table 9.8 Command Extensions provided by *cmd.exe*

Command	Enhancement
Cd	The cd (Change Directory) command can change the current drive letter as well as the current directory. For example, `cd /d w:\serverfolder` changes the drive letter to W: as well as changing the current directory to \serverfolder. This is especially useful in batch files where you may have an environment variable that contains a drive letter and path, as in cd /d %userprofile%.
pushd *path* popd	Pushd is a new command that also changes the current directory (or drive and directory), but also "remembers" the previous drive and directory. Popd returns to the previous drive and directory. Pushd and popd commands can be nested—three pushds followed by three popds get you back to where you started. Pushd can take a network path name as its argument, for example, pushd \\server\do files. This will automatically map a drive letter to the network path, starting with drive z: and working backwards.
for	The for command has been extensively enhanced and now has the ability to scan directories, scan directories recursively, iterate through number ranges, scan the lines of a file or the output of a command-line program, and more. Special substitution operators let you extract specific parts of the any matched filenames or tokens. For more information type the command help for | more.
set	The set command, which lets you define environment variables, has been enhanced to let you perform mathematical calculations on environment variables, extract substrings, and prompt for user input. For more details, type help set | more.

Table 9.8 Continued

Command	Enhancement
`call`	The batch file command `call` can now call subroutines defined within the same batch file, using the syntax `call :label [arguments...]`.
`goto`	The batch file command `goto` can now jump directly to the end of the file, to terminate the batch procedure or return from the batch subroutine, with the syntax `goto :EOF`.
`setlocal` `endlocal`	In a batch file, `setlocal` saves a copy of the environment variables, and subsequent changes to or additions to the environment will not persist after the batch file exits. An `endlocal` command inside the batch file will restore all environment variables to their value at the time of `setlocal`. `Setlocal` can also be used to enable and disable all of these command extensions, and to enable or disable delayed expansion, a complex but important feature that comes into play when you write complex batch files. Delayed expansion is disabled by default, and must be enabled in a batch file with the command `setlocal enabledelayedexpansion`. Delayed expansion is described in more detail shortly.

In addition, input and output redirection operators have been enhanced, as described earlier in this chapter under "Input and Output Redirection." Multiple commands can be typed on one command line, using the separators discussed earlier under "Command Separators."

Printing in the Command-Line Environment

Windows applications generate printed output through calls to the Windows programming interface. Output is page oriented; that is, applications generate output by describing to Windows what to draw on successive whole pages of paper. Output is graphical in nature; lines, images, and text are all drawn pixel by pixel. The application doesn't know how to tell the printer how to draw these things; it simply tells Windows what it wants drawn, and Windows communicates this to a printer driver that sends the appropriate manufacturer-specific commands to the printer.

Console applications are distinctly different. Windows console applications have no concept of formatting; they simply spit text out character by character, line after line. The output from these programs is plain text, with no font, pagination or formatting information whatsoever. If you used MS-DOS you may be familiar with the technique of directing output to the lpt1 device, as in the command

```
dir >lpt1
```

On Windows, this does direct the directory listing to device LPT1, your computer's parallel port device, but there are several reasons this might not produce the listing you intended:

- If you are using a laser or inkjet printer, this inherently page-oriented device will not "kick out" the printout until it receives a form-feed instruction. Most likely, nothing will come out until you try to print the next document. And then, the page margins and default font will likely be unsatisfactory.

- If your printer is connected to a USB port, this won't work at all unless you share the printer on your network, and then use the net command to redirect LPT1 output to the printer via the network share.

- Many cheap inkjet and laser printers cannot interpret ASCII text directly and will generate no output at all. Postscript printers will likely simply generate an error page. Only dot-matrix printers and page printers with a built-in page-description language (for example, printers with Hewlett-Packard PCL support) will generate valid text.

The best way to get printed output from Windows console applications is to redirect their output to a file on your hard disk, and then open and print the file with Notepad or your favorite word processor.

For example, to get a printed listing of the files in your My Documents folder, you might open a command prompt window and issue these commands:

```
cd My Documents
dir >listing.txt
notepad listing.txt
```

You can then print this listing from within Notepad. To get printed output from a batch file, you can use this command line:

```
notepad /p listing.txt
```

which makes Notepad open the file, print it, and then immediately exit, without any manual interaction. The printout will use Notepad's default font and margins, which you should set beforehand.

MS-DOS applications like WordPerfect take full responsibility for communicating with the printer, and want to send specific formatting codes to the printer. The MS-DOS emulation subsystem simply passes these codes directly to the printer, so you must configure the MS-DOS program to tell it what make and model printer you are using. The issues I discussed previously still apply: USB printers and inexpensive page printers will likely not work at all.

Some MS-DOS applications can use printers shared on your network, as long as the share names of the devices are 8 characters in length or less, and the names of the computers are 15 characters in length or less. For example, WordPerfect 5.1 can be told to use network printers given the printer's network share name, which will look something like \\mycomputer\laserjet.

If your MS-DOS application doesn't know explicitly how to use networked printers, you may also be able to let it use a network printer by redirecting an MS-DOS LPT printer port to a network printer. You must use an LPT port number for which there is no physical LPT port on your computer. Because most computers do have an LPT1 parallel printer port, you must use LPT2, LPT3, up to LPT9. (Some MS-DOS programs can only use printers up to LPT3.) The command

```
net use lpt2: \\mycomputer\laserjet
```

makes the MS-DOS LPT2 device point to the shared printer named laserjet on the computer named mycomputer. Once this is done, you can configure your MS-DOS application to print to LPT2.

You can even use this technique to let MS-DOS applications print to USB printers attached to your own computer. Set up sharing on your USB printer, and then issue the net use command using the name of your own computer on the command line. Again, remember that this will work only if the USB printer can accept raw text, or if it uses a page description language (formatting code set) that your MS-DOS application knows how to use.

To stop redirecting an LPT port to a network printer, issue the command

```
net use lpt2: /d
```

substituting lpt3 for lpt2 if that's what you were using.

Print Screen

On Windows XP, the MS-DOS Print Screen function does not work as it did in the real MS-DOS. When an MS-DOS program is running in window mode, the PrtScr key works just as it normally does in Windows: It copies a bitmap picture of the screen or current window to the Clipboard. You have to paste the bitmap into a document (in, say, Word or WordPad), and then print that document.

When an MS-DOS program is running in full-screen mode, the PrtScr key still doesn't send the screen to the printer. Instead, it copies the screen's *text* to the Clipboard. To print it, again, you'll need to paste the text into a document and print it as a separate step.

Stopping Runaway Programs

Occasionally you'll type a command that starts spewing page after page of text to the screen, or one that displays some sort of ominous warning about making a change to Windows that can't be undone, and you'll want to stop it—pronto.

Most command-line programs will quit if you press Ctrl+C. If that doesn't work, Ctrl+Break often works. As a last resort, you can simply close the Command Prompt window by clicking its close box in the upper-right corner. This will kill the program in at most a few seconds.

On Windows XP Professional, you may also find the tasklist and taskkill command-line programs useful. Type **tasklist** to get a list of active programs. This will display something like this:

```
Image Name                    PID Session Name      Session#   Mem Usage
========================== ====== ================ ======== ============
System Idle Process             0 Console                 0         16 K
System                          4 Console                 0        216 K
smss.exe                      876 Console                 0        372 K
csrss.exe                     924 Console                 0      3,320 K
winlogon.exe                  948 Console                 0      5,584 K
setiathome.exe               1072 Console                 0     20,252 K
...
winword.exe                  2756 Console                 0     22,784 K
cmd.exe                      1904 Console                 0      4,320 K
tasklist.exe                  488 Console                 0      4,148 K
```

The PID column contains the Process Identification number (PID) of each running program. You can kill a program with the command

```
taskkill /force /pid nnn
```

with the PID of the program you want to stop in place of *nnn*.

Configuring the Command-Line Environment

In this section, I'll tell you a bit about how cmd may be adjusted to better meet your own needs. Some of these settings change how the Command Prompt window appears, whereas others change the software environment itself. If you were used to the MS-DOS environment, some of the software settings will be familiar, although the method of changing them is quite different.

Console Window Properties

You can make several changes to the appearance of console program windows. For better visibility, or to make a program look more like it's running under MS-DOS, you can press Alt+Enter to run the program in *full-screen* mode. If you run a DOS graphics program, this will happen automatically. In this mode, the program takes over the whole screen and all other Windows features disappear. You can always press Alt+Enter to bring back the Windows desktop.

You can set the screen mode and the number of lines that the window can scroll using the window's Properties dialog box, as shown earlier in Figure 9.5. You can also set the window's colors and font. Usually, you won't need to adjust the font. It's best to simply resize the window in the normal way and Windows will size the characters accordingly.

Changing the Search Path

By default, Windows sets the PATH environment variable to a standard list of Windows folders. If you plan on writing your own programs, batch files, Windows Script Host scripts, or other application programs, it's a good idea to place them in a folder of their own and then add that folder to the path.

You can change the search path in any of three ways.

First, you can set a new value for the PATH environment variable using the set command, as in this example:

```
set path=c:\bat;%path%
```

This makes the folder c:\bat the first folder in the path. The ;%path% ensures that the prior PATH folders are retained in the path list, otherwise you wouldn't be able to run programs not in c:\bat.

Second, you can use the path command, which is a "shortcut" version of set path:

```
path c:\bat;%path%
```

These commands have the same effect: They set the environment variable PATH to c:\bat, followed by the previous PATH definition.

Note

If the folder you're adding to the path has spaces in its name, put quotes around the name.

You could also add a new folder to the *end* of the search path with a statement like this:

```
set path=%path%;"c:\bat"
```

The ordering only matters if there are versions of the same command in more than one folder in the path; the version in the first folder to be searched will be the one that Windows runs.

Tip

If you mess up the path and cmd stops working, just close the Command Prompt window and open another. You'll be back in action.

Putting your own folders ahead of the Windows folders in the list can be a blessing or a curse. If you create a program or batch file with the same name as a standard Windows program, yours will run instead of the standard program. If this is what you want, great, but if not...the result can be very confusing.

The path and set commands only change environment variables for the current instance of the cmd program. If you close the Command Prompt window and open a new one, you'll be back to the initial default PATH.

The third way of changing the PATH makes the change appear in all future cmd prompt windows. To do this, you'll need to make the change on the System Properties dialog box, as I'll discuss shortly under "Setting Default Environment Variables."

Predefined and Virtual Environment Variables

Environment variables can be set in any of six places. If a given variable name is set in more than one place, the last definition encountered is used. The sources are processed in the following order:

1. Predefined, built-in system variables (for example, APPDATA).

2. Systemwide variables defined in the System Properties dialog box.

3. User-specific variables defined in the System Properties dialog box. However, a user-specific PATH definition does *not* replace the systemwide definition. Instead, it's *added* to the beginning of the system-wide definition.

4. Variables defined in logon scripts (batch or WSH-type).

   These first four sources are processed when a user logs on, and they form the user's default environment; the remaining sources are processed each time a new CMD process is started, and any changes are lost when cmd is closed.

5. Variables defined in AUTOEXEC.NT, when *and* only when a DOS program is run.

6. Variables defined on the command line, in batch files, or in Windows Script Host scripts through WshShell.Environment("Process").

The following variables are defined by default for all users (systemwide):

Variable Name	Usual Value
ALLUSERSPROFILE	C:\Documents and Settings\All Users
APPDATA	C:\Documents and Settings*username*\Application Data
CommonProgramFiles	C:\Program Files\Common Files
COMPUTERNAME	*computername*
ComSpec	C:\WINDOWS\system32\cmd.exe
HOMEDRIVE	C:
HOMEPATH	\Documents and Settings*username*
LOGONSERVER	(Varies)
NUMBER_OF_PROCESSORS	(Varies)
OS	Windows_NT
Path	C:\WINDOWS\system32;C:\WINDOWS;C:\WINDOWS\System32\Wbem (this entry varies depending on the location of Windows)
PATHEXT	.COM;.EXE;.BAT;.CMD;.VBS;.VBE;.JS
PROCESSOR_ARCHITECTURE	(Varies)
PROCESSOR_IDENTIFIER	(Varies)
PROCESSOR_LEVEL	(Varies)
PROCESSOR_REVISION	(Varies)
ProgramFiles	C:\Program Files
PROMPT	PG
SESSIONNAME	(Varies)
SystemDrive	C:
SystemRoot	C:\WINDOWS
TEMP	C:\DOCUME~1*username*\LOCALS~1\Temp
TMP	C:\DOCUME~1*username*\LOCALS~1\Temp

Variable Name	Usual Value
USERDOMAIN	*computername* or *domainname*
USERNAME	*username*
USERPROFILE	C:\Documents and Settings*username*
windir	C:\WINDOWS

In addition, when command extensions are enabled, several "virtual" environment variables are available. The following environment variable names are computed dynamically if used on a command line or in a batch file:

Name	Value
CD	The current directory drive and path
DATE	The current date, formatted as by the DATE command
TIME	The current time, formatted as by the TIME command
RANDOM	A random number between 0 and 32,767
ERRORLEVEL	The exit status of the previous program
CMDEXTVERSION	The version number of command extensions
CMDCMDLINE	The command line used to start cmd itself

These entries don't really exist in the environment; cmd just fakes it by substituting the appropriate value when it runs into, for example, %date%. If you define an environment variable with one of these names, your fixed defined value will always supercede the dynamic value.

The maximum size for an individual environment variable (name, equals sign, and value) is 8,192 bytes. The total size of all environment variables must be less than 65,536KB.

Setting Default Environment Variables

To define environment variables permanently so that they are defined whenever you log on, click Start, right-click My Computer, and select Properties. Next, view the Advanced tab and click Environment Variables. Windows will display the dialog box shown in Figure 9.6.

The top part of the dialog box lets you define the default variables for your account. You can click New to add a new variable, or you can click Edit or Delete to modify an existing entry.

The lower part of the dialog box edits the default variables provided to *all* user accounts. These settings can only be edited by an Administrator account, and the settings may be overridden by user-specific entries.

An interesting feature of this dialog is that in *most* cases, if a variable is defined in the User Variables list, the user version overrides the System version. However, in the case of the PATH variable, the User version is *prepended* to the System version. This helps prevent users from accidentally ending up with a PATH that is missing all of the standard Windows program folders. Here's an example. If the System PATH is defined as

```
C:\WINDOWS\system32;C:\WINDOWS;C:\WINDOWS\system32\WBEM
```

and the User PATH is defined as

```
c:\bat;"c:\program files\my special stuff"
```

then the user's actual PATH environment variable will be set to

```
C:\WINDOWS\system32;C:\WINDOWS;C:\WINDOWS\system32\WBEM;c:\bat;
➥ "c:\program files\my special stuff"
```

at logon.

Figure 9.6   The Environment Variables dialog box lets you edit default environment variables for your account or for all users.

Note

If you're familiar with Windows Script Host, you can also modify the default environment variables with WSH scripts by modifying the WshShell.Environment("system") and WshShell.Environment("user") collections.

I recommend that you create a folder to contain your own personal batch files and scripts, perhaps named c:\bat, and add it to your user PATH as discussed here. This way, your scripts and batch files can be run from any command prompt you own, without worrying about where they're stored.

The Adjustable Prompt

I mentioned earlier that the command prompt shows you the shell's current directory. For example, the prompt

```
C:\Documents and Settings\brian>
```

shows that my current drive is C: and the current directory is C:\Documents and Settings\ brian. If you manage computers or use networking software to work with several computers at once, you may find yourself confused at times, wondering to which computer a Command Prompt window belongs! You can modify the command prompt to display more (or less) information using the hieroglyphics listed in Table 9.9. cmd examines the PROMPT environment variable for any of the character codes listed in the table and replaces them with the appropriate information.

Table 9.9   Prompt Codes

Code	Prints	Example
$$	Dollar sign	$
$	(Dollar sign followed by a space)	A new line
$a	Ampersand	&
$b	Pipe character	|
$c	Left parenthesis	(
$d	The current date	Wed 04/24/2002
$e	ANSI escape (code 27)*	
$f	Right parenthesis	)
$g	Greater-than sign	>
$h	A backspace	
$l	Less-than sign	<
$n	The current drive	C:
$p	The current drive and path	C:\windows
$q	Equal sign	=
$s	Space	
$t	The current time	19:13:37.21
$v	The Windows version number	Microsoft Windows XP [Version 5.1.2600]
$+	Zero or more + signs to show depth of pushd commands.	+++
$m	The UNC name of the network drive plus a space, if the current drive is not local; otherwise, nothing.	\\sumatra\cdrive
Any other	Any other character is printed literally.	

This was used in earlier Windows versions to construct ANSI screen control escape codes such as color changes, which would be interpreted by the ANSI.SYS screen driver. This is not helpful in the cmd.exe shell because ANSI.SYS is an MS-DOS driver and does not work in 32-bit console mode.

To set the prompt, construct the desired series of codes and issue the command

```
set prompt=codes
```

or use the shortcut

```
prompt codes
```

For example,

```
prompt $t$h$h$h$h$h$h $m$p$g
```

prints the time, backspaces over the number of seconds, adds a space, and then prints the network path and current drive and directory. The resulting command prompt looks like this:

```
19:19 \\sumatra\cdrive K:\>
```

If you mess things up, prompt pg restores the prompt to its default value.

Tip

To make a permanent change to your prompt, right-click My Computer, choose Properties, Advanced, Environment Variables and then add a **PROMPT** definition under User Variables for….

AutoRun

Normally, when it first starts, cmd examines the Registry for a value named AutoRun under the keys

```
HKLM\Software\Microsoft\Command Processor
```

and

```
HKCU\Software\Microsoft\Command Processor
```

(HKLM and HKCU are short for HKEY_LOCAL_MACHINE and HKEY_CURRENT_USER, respectively.) AutoRun values with type REG_SZ (string) or REG_EXPAND_SZ (string with environment variables to be expanded) are taken as commands to be run when an instance of cmd first starts up; first the HKEY_LOCAL_MACHINE value is examined, and if defined, run, and then the HKEY_CURRENT_USER value is checked.

AutoRun settings can be used to perform some of the functions that used to be provided by the AUTOEXEC.BAT file in DOS. In particular, you can use it to run DOSKEY to set macros via an AutoRun command (we'll discuss this later in the chapter).

If you want to run more than one command with the AutoRun feature, create a batch file, and have the AutoRun value specify this batch file's name.

If necessary, you can disable AutoRun commands by starting cmd with /D on its command line, as I'll discuss later in this appendix.

Note

This "autorun" setting is not related to the Autorun feature that launches applications or plays media when you insert a CD or DVD.

Configuring the MS-DOS Command Environment

As mentioned earlier, Windows XP uses a command prompt shell program named cmd.exe. As it turns out, to maintain maximum compatibility with old MS-DOS programs and old batch files, the original MS-DOS command.com shell is actually still available. The clunky old batch file language we all knew—and loved?—is still there.

Here's how it works: If you run an MS-DOS program in a Command Prompt window, cmd assumes that you're going to work in the 16-bit world for a while. So, when the DOS program finishes, the window switches to the command.com shell. You'll notice several differences:

- The current directory name is changed to its old-style 8.3 equivalent. For example, if your current directory had been C:\Documents and Settings\naleks, when the DOS program exits, the directory will be displayed as C:\DOCUME~1\NALEKS.
- Environment variable names change to all uppercase letters.
- The extended versions of the built-in commands will be unavailable.
- If you've run command.com explicitly, you cannot close the window by clicking its Close button—command.com doesn't get the message to quit. You'll have to type **exit** to close the window.

These changes make it more likely that old programs and batch files will be able to run. However, if you want, you can keep cmd.exe as your command shell even when using MS-DOS programs, by configuring the MS-DOS environment.

To maintain compatibility with as many old DOS programs as possible, ntvdm can be configured to mimic an older environment. You can configure ntvdm's memory and window options through a properties dialog box, and you can configure the virtual DOS environment itself through configuration files that mimic the old CONFIG.SYS and AUTOEXEC.BAT files. Here is how the default configuration works:

- By default, ntvdm gives an MS-DOS program as much regular and DOS Protected Mode Interface (DPMI) memory as it asks for. No Extended (XMS) or Expanded (EMS) memory is available.

- Ntvdm reads configuration options from \windows\system32\config.nt and executes the batch file \windows\system32\autoexec.nt before running the program. These files are installed along with Windows and contain important default settings that permit the use of high memory, networking, and emulated Sound Blaster sound hardware.

These settings should work for most MS-DOS programs. You can modify these files to make changes that will apply to all MS-DOS programs, or you can create customized versions for specific applications; we'll discuss this in the next section.

If you need specially tuned DOS environments for special applications, you may want to configure Windows shortcuts for these applications, or at least create shortcuts that open custom-configured Command Prompt windows. To create a customized MS-DOS environment, right-click the name of the MS-DOS program you want to run and select Properties. If you change any of the default properties and save the settings, Windows will create a file with the same name as the program file, but with extension .PIF. This .PIF file holds the customized settings. It is listed in Explorer as a "Shortcut to MS-DOS Program." Use this shortcut to run the program. If you need to run a batch file before running the program, follow this same procedure, but create a shortcut to the batch files instead of the program itself.

Note

You must use the shortcut to start the MS-DOS program in order to take advantage of any configuration changes you've made. If you run the .EXE file directly, Windows will not know to look at the .PIF (shortcut) file.

Window and Memory Options

The Properties dialog box for an MS-DOS application shortcut (.PIF file) lets you set the virtual MS-DOS environment's memory display and mouse properties. To customize these properties, right-click the MS-DOS application file itself, or if you've already created customized properties, you can right-click the MS-DOS Application Shortcut icon, and then select Properties.

Here are the most common settings to change:

- The working folder on the Program page
- The Extended Memory and Initial Environment options on the Memory page
- The Always Suspend option on the Misc page

In the next sections, I'll describe all the property pages in more detail so you can see what configuration options are available. The General, Security, Summary, and Backup pages (if they appear on your system) are the same as for any other Windows file, so I won't describe them here.

Program Settings

The Program tab displays a typical Shortcut property page and has the following settings (see Figure 9.7):

- *Cmd Line*—The path to the MS-DOS program file or batch file, and any additional command-line arguments you need. If you enter **?** on the command line, Windows will prompt you for command-line arguments when you run the shortcut. Whatever you type will be used in place of **?**.

- *Working*—The drive and folder to use as the initial working directory for the program. If you leave this field blank, the initial directory will be the one containing the MS-DOS program. If the shortcut will be used by several people, you may want to use environment variables in this path. For example, `"%userprofile%\My Documents"` will specify the user's own My Documents folder.

- *Batch File*—Ostensibly, the name of a batch file to run before starting the program. As far as I can tell, however, this feature does not work.

- *Shortcut Key*—Optional. Specifies a hotkey that is supposed to start the program. However, this feature does not appear to work either.

- *Run*—Selects the initial window size: Normal, Maximized, or Minimized (icon). Full Screen is different; see the screen settings.

Figure 9.7   The MS-DOS Shortcut Program tab. The Advanced button lets you specify a custom `config.nt` or `autoexec.nt` file.

- *Close on Exit*—If this option is checked, the window will close when the program exits. If this option is unchecked, the window will remain open but inactive, and the title will include the word "Inactive." You will want to leave this checked in most cases.

Tip

If a DOS program fails to run, uncheck this box and try to run the program again. You'll then have time to read any error messages that appear.

The Program tab also lets you specify alternate configuration and startup batch files to use instead of CONFIG.NT and AUTOEXEC.NT. To change the configuration files associated with a shortcut, click the Advanced button and enter the paths and names of the desired files. The default values are %SystemRoot%\SYSTEM32\CONFIG.NT and %SystemRoot%\SYSTEM32\AUTOEXEC.NT. I will describe the settings in these files shortly.

Tip

If your MS-DOS program has timing or speed problems, it may be that it expects to be able to change the settings of the PC's timer chips. If you click the Advanced button and check the Compatible Timer Hardware Emulation option, the problem may go away.

Font Settings

The Font tab lets you select the font used when the program is running in a window. The default setting, Auto, lets Windows resize the font as you resize the window, but you can specify a fixed size. If you do, the window will not be resizable.

Tip

If you want to switch to a fixed font size, you can do it while the program is running. Right-click the upper-left corner of the program's window, select Properties, and view the Font tab. Make any desired changes and then choose Save Properties for Future Windows with the Same Title when Windows offers you this option.

Memory Settings

The Memory tab, shown in Figure 9.8, lets you specify the type and amount of memory to make available to the MS-DOS program. The plethora of memory types came about as different ways of coping with the original PC's limited memory hardware options. Some programs can use any type of memory, but others specifically require access to XMS or EMS memory—your program's installation instructions will tell you what type of memory it requires or can take advantage of. Here's a list of the settings:

- *Conventional Memory, Total*—The amount of memory between 0 and 640KB. The Auto setting provides up to 640KB. You will probably never need to alter this setting.

- *Initial Environment*—The number of bytes to set aside for environment variables. Auto directs ntvdm to use the amount specified in the SHELL setting in CONFIG.NT. If you use complex batch files, you may want to increase this setting to 2000 bytes or more.

- *Protected*—If checked, this option prevents the program from altering memory in the range occupied by the simulated MS-DOS system components. Check this box only if you experience unexplained crashes.

- *Expanded (EMS) Memory*—If your program requires EMS (paged) memory, set this to Auto or a fixed number. (Your program's installation instructions will tell you if it needs EMS memory.)

- *Extended (XMS) Memory*—If your program can use XMS expanded memory, set this to Auto or a fixed number.

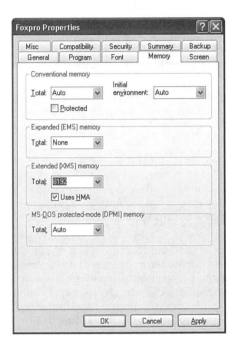

Figure 9.8   The Memory tab lets you make various memory formats available to the DOS program.

- *Uses HMA*—This option normally has no effect because the High Memory Area is used by the simulated MS-DOS program.

- *MS-DOS Protected-Mode (DPMI) Memory*—By default, this option is set to Auto. You can disable or permit a fixed amount of DPMI memory, if necessary.

Screen Settings

The screen settings let you determine whether the program has "direct" access to the whole screen at startup. These settings include the following:

- *Usage*—Lets you select between full-screen and window as the initial display mode. In full-screen mode, the MS-DOS program takes over the primary display and can display graphics.

- *Restore Settings at Startup*—If this option is checked, the last-used window size and font will be reused the next time you start the program. If you want to provide a consistent environment for multiple users, uncheck this box, make the appropriate initial settings, and then make the PIF file nonwritable by other users using file security settings.

- *Fast ROM Emulation*—When this option is checked, the Virtual DOS Machine emulates the graphics functions normally provided by the display adapter's built-in (read-only memory) BIOS program.

- *Dynamic Memory Allocation*—When this option is checked, Windows releases memory assigned to the virtual graphics display when the program switches from graphics to text display. If you get a blank screen when the program switches back, try unchecking this box.

When the MS-DOS program is running and attempts to change the display from text-based to graphical, Windows will automatically switch to full-screen mode. You can manually switch back and forth between full-screen and window mode by pressing Alt+Enter. If the program is using a text display, you can continue using it in window mode. If it is displaying graphics, however, the program will be suspended (frozen) and minimized unless it's in full-screen mode. Windows, unfortunately, can't display a little windowed version of the DOS graphical display.

Miscellaneous Settings

The Miscellaneous Settings tab determines how the program behaves when it's running in a window. Most of the settings are self-explanatory. The tab is shown in Figure 9.9. Here are the less obvious settings:

- *Always Suspend*—If this option is checked, the MS-DOS program will be frozen when it's not the active window. Because MS-DOS programs didn't anticipate multitasking, they tend to burn lots of CPU time even when idle. Suspending the program when you're not using it makes your system more responsive. However, if you are running a communications or database program that needs to run while you do other things, uncheck this box.

- *Idle Sensitivity*—This is also related to the idle CPU issue. Windows tries to guess when the DOS program is just spinning its gears doing nothing and gives it a lower priority when it thinks this is the case. A high Idle Sensitivity setting means that Windows will lean toward thinking the program is idle, resulting in snappier performance for other applications. A lower Idle Sensitivity setting will make Windows give the DOS application more time. The DOS application will be better able to perform background (noninteractive) processing, while making your Windows applications more sluggish. Raise this setting if your DOS program makes everything else too slow, or lower it if your DOS program can't get its job done. In the latter case, also uncheck Always Suspend.

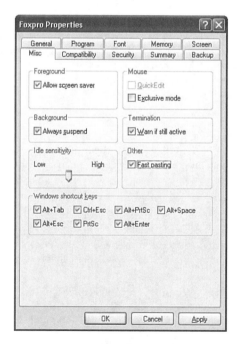

Figure 9.9 The Miscellaneous Settings tab lets you control the program's use of the mouse and keyboard.

■ *Exclusive Mode*—Dedicates the mouse to the DOS program.

■ *Fast Pasting*—Determines how quickly Windows will stuff simulated keystrokes into the MS-DOS programs when you paste in text from the Windows clipboard using Alt+space, Edit, Paste. If characters are lost when pasting, uncheck this option.

■ *Windows Short Keys*—These check boxes let you determine which special keystrokes should be passed to Windows rather than to the MS-DOS programs. If your MS-DOS program needs key combinations such as Alt+Tab and Alt+Enter, you will need to uncheck the relevant boxes on this page. The DOS program will get these keystrokes in full-screen mode or when its window is active, so be prepared to lose the corresponding Windows shortcut.

It's especially tricky if you uncheck Alt+Enter and the program switches to full-screen mode. You will have to type Ctrl+Alt+Del to open the Task Manager if you want to switch back to the Windows desktop before the program exits.

Compatibility Settings

Windows XP compatibility settings let you limit the abilities of the virtual display adapter seen by the MS-DOS program. The relevant settings are Run in 256 Colors and Run in 640×480 Screen Resolution. If your MS-DOS program has problems displaying graphics screens, try checking these boxes.

CONFIG.NT

Just as MS-DOS used CONFIG.SYS to make initial memory allocations and to load device drivers, ntvdm uses CONFIG.NT to configure the virtual DOS environment.

The default CONFIG.NT file as installed by Windows is located in \windows\system32 and contains several pages of comment text, which you may want to read. Here are the default settings in this file:

```
dos=high,umbdevice=%systemroot%\system32\himem.sys
files=40
```

You can edit CONFIG.NT to modify the defaults for all MS-DOS applications, or you can create alternate files using a different name for use with specific applications. In the latter case, use the Advanced button on the Program Settings properties page for the program's shortcut to enter the alternate filename. I'll use the name CONFIG.NT in the discussion that follows to refer to any config file.

Note

For starters, if you use MS-DOS database applications, you will probably want to increase the **FILES=** setting in CONFIG.NT to **100** or more. You may also want to add the ANSI cursor control module with the line

```
device=%systemroot%\system32\ansi.sys
```

Other than these two adjustments, it's unlikely that you'll need to make any other changes.

The full set of options for CONFIG.NT is listed in the rest of this section.

COUNTRY=*xxx*[,[*yyy*][,[[*path*]]*filename*]]

tells MS-DOS to use an alternate character set and date/time format. *xxx* is a country/region code, *yyy* is an optional code page designator, and *filename* designates an optional driver containing country code information. If you use the virtual MS-DOS environment outside the U.S., view the Help and Support Center and search for "country."

DEVICE=[*path*\]*filename* [*parameters*]

loads a device driver. Hardware device drivers will almost certainly *not* work in Windows XP, but certain software services implemented as drivers will. Examples include `himem.sys`, which is required to let MS-DOS programs access memory above 640KB, and `ansi.sys`, which interprets character sequences that some DOS programs use to control the cursor. These drivers are located in folder `%systemroot%\system32`.

DEVICEHIGH=[*path*]*filename* [*parameters*]

or

DEVICEHIGH [**SIZE**=*xx*] [*path*]*filename* [*parameters*]

similar to *device* but attempts to load the device driver into upper memory blocks, leaving more conventional memory for MS-DOS applications. If there is insufficient room in upper memory or if the device `himem.sys` has not been loaded, the driver will be loaded into conventional memory. The alternate `size=`*xx* format lets you specify the number of bytes of high memory that must be free; *xx* must be specified in hexadecimal.

DOS=[**HIGH**|**LOW**][, **UMB**|**NOUMB**]

`DOS=HIGH` specifies that MS-DOS should move parts of itself into the high memory area (the first 64KB past 1MB). The default is `LOW`, where DOS resides entirely in conventional memory. The optional keyword `UMB` indicates that DOS should make upper memory area blocks (the memory beyond 1MB+64KB) available for DOS, devices, and programs.

DOSONLY

If this keyword is present in `CONFIG.NT`, `COMMAND.COM` will only be permitted to run MS-DOS programs. Normally, if you typed the name of a Windows program at its command prompt or in a batch file, it would run the Windows program in a separate environment. This may disrupt some DOS terminate-and-stay-resident (TSR) programs, so the `DOSONLY` option lets you prevent this from happening.

ECHOCONFIG

If the command `ECHOCONFIG` appears, `CONFIG.NT` commands are echoed to the Command Prompt window while ntvdm is initializing. The default is for the commands not to be displayed.

FCBS=*n*

File Control Blocks (FCB) is an archaic structure used by DOS version 1.0 programs to manage files. Few, if any, surviving MS-DOS programs require FCB, but if you have one, you can use the `FCBS` statement to instruct ntvdm to allocate space for *n* of them. (At this late date, if you do need them, you'll already know it, as you'll have had to deal with this on every prior version of DOS and Windows.)

FILES=*n*

sets the maximum number of concurrently open files available to MS-DOS applications. The default value is `20`. You may want to increase this number to `100` or more if you use database applications such as MS-DOS FoxPro.

INSTALL=[path\]*filename* [*parameters*]

loads a TSR into memory prior to running `AUTOEXEC.NT`.

One program that you may need to install in `AUTOEXEC.NT` is `setver.exe`. Setver intercepts programs' requests to find out what version of DOS is running, and it lies to them. Its purpose is to let you run programs that would otherwise be unhappy to find that they're running on DOS version 5.0, which is what ntvdm would tell them. If your MS-DOS application complains about the DOS version number, open the Help and Support Center and search for "setver."

NTCMDPROMPT

By default, when an MS-DOS program is run from the command line or a batch file and exits, cmd runs command.com to handle all further commands. This makes it possible to run old MS-DOS batch files. If you specify NTCMDPROMPT in CONFIG.NT, cmd will not run command.com, but will remain in control between MS-DOS programs. This lets you write modern batch files to use with MS-DOS programs.

SHELL=[path\]filename [parameters]

specifies an alternate shell program to use if you do not want to use command.com as the MS-DOS shell. You can also use this command to specify command.com with startup options. For example, the entry

```
shell=%systemroot%\system32\command.com /E:2048/P
```

requests 2048 bytes for environment variables. The /P option is required to prevent command.com from exiting after processing one command.

STACKS=n,s

When a hardware interrupt occurs, ntvdm needs "memory stack" space to temporarily store information for the interrupt handler. The stacks option lets you instruct ntvdm to allocate separate stack space for interrupt handlers. The numbers n and s instruct ntvdm to allocate n blocks of s bytes each. n can be 0 or 8 through 64. s can be 0 or 32 to 512. The default values are 9 and 128, respectively. If necessary, you can save memory for program use by specifying stacks=0,0; this may or may not cause a program crash. You can specify stacks=8,512 to allocate plenty of stack space if you suspect that interrupt handlers are causing DOS crashes.

SWITCHES=/K

makes MS-DOS programs treat the keyboard as a "conventional" 96-key keyboard even if it uses the extended 102+ key layout. If you use this switch and also load ansi.sys, specify /k after ansi.sys as well.

The following items are permitted in CONFIG.NT for compatibility with historical CONFIG.SYS settings but have no effect in Windows XP:

- buffers
- driveparm
- lastdrive (lastdrive is always Z)

AUTOEXEC.NT

AUTOEXEC.NT serves the same purpose AUTOEXEC.BAT did on MS-DOS systems: It is a batch file that lets you run programs that set up the command environment before you begin working. The default version of AUTOEXEC.NT installed with Windows is located in \windows\system32 and contains the following commands:

```
lh %SystemRoot%\system32\mscdexnt.exe
lh %SystemRoot%\system32\redir
lh %SystemRoot%\system32\dosx
SET BLASTER=A220 I5 D1 P330 T3
```

MSCDEXNT provides support for CD-ROM drives, REDIR is the network interface, DOSX provides upper-memory support (it serves the same purpose EMM386.EXE did on MS-DOS), and the SET command provides DOS programs with information about the simulated Sound Blaster sound hardware. No matter what kind of sound system your computer has, MS-DOS programs "see" a Sound Blaster–compatible card (although the emulation is less than perfect).

In addition, if you've installed the Client for Novell Networks, AUTOEXEC.NT will also run nw16.exe and vwipxspx.exe, which give DOS applications access to the Novell application programming interface (API).

You can load other programs and set environment variables in AUTOEXEC.NT, but remember that they will be loaded every time you run an MS-DOS program. If you need particular terminate-and-stay-resident programs only for some MS-DOS applications, set up a customized AUTOEXEC file just for those applications.

Tip

One program that's handy to add to **AUTOEXEC.NT** is **doskey**, which gives **command.com** the same editing commands as those provided by **cmd.exe**, and in addition, it lets you define abbreviated commands called *aliases*. To read about this program, start the Help and Support Center and search for "doskey."

MS-DOS Environment Variables

In MS-DOS, memory is a limited resource, and MS-DOS is particularly stingy with environment variable space. If you need to define more than a dozen or so environment variables in any MS-DOS–style batch files, you'll probably need to extend the amount of space allocated to environment variables either on the Properties dialog box of an associated shortcut or in a shell= command in a CONFIG.NT file. These techniques were described earlier in this appendix.

When you first start an MS-DOS program or command.com, ntvdm inherits the default Windows environment, but with the following changes:

- All variable names are changed to uppercase. MS-DOS programs do not expect to find lowercase letters in environment variable names.
- The COMSPEC variable is added, which contains the path and filename of the command shell, usually command.com.
- The TEMP and TMP variables are reset to the system default, rather than the user-specific setting.
- Path names in all environment variables are changed to use DOS-compatible 8.3-character names.

Important Commands

There are several commands that you should become very familiar with...these are some of the command-line tools that you'll use nearly every day once you've become a master of command line-fu.

Note

There are, of course, hundreds of others. Appendix B, "Windows Command Reference," contains a listing of all standard Windows programs, and the ones marked **CMD** are command-line programs. You might want to scan through that listing to see the range of programs that is available. For some tips about getting usage instructions for programs that interest you, see "Interpreting Command Line Syntax" earlier in this chapter. And Appendix A lists hundreds more add-on tools that you can obtain.

cd

Each Command Prompt window has the concept of a *current drive* and *current directory* (also called the *default directory*), which is its starting place when looking for files. Although Windows Explorer displays its current directory in its status and address bars, it's most common for the Command Prompt window to show the current directory name in its prompt; the indicator it prints to tell you it's ready to accept another command. For example, the prompt

```
C:\Documents and Settings\brian>
```

indicates that the current drive is C: and the current directory is \Documents and Settings\brian.

You can change the current drive by typing a command line that consists only of a drive letter and colon, for example

```
d:
```

You can change the current directory by typing the cd or equivalently the chdir command, followed by a path name:

```
cd \documents and settings\brian
```

Note

For the **cd** command (only), quotes around a pathname that contains spaces are optional.

Each drive letter has its own default directory, so the commands

```
cd c:\program files
cd d:\setup
cd e:\temp
```

set the default directory on c:, d:, and e: drives without changing the default drive letter.

You can specify full or relative paths. If the path doesn't start with a \ character, it's interpreted relative to the current directory. For example, if the current directory is \Documents and Settings, the commands cd \Documents and Settings\brian and cd brian are equivalent. The command

```
cd \
```

returns to you the current drive's root (top level) directory.

The special directory name .. is interpreted as "the directory above," or the *parent* directory, so if the current directory is C:\Documents and Settings\brian, the command cd .. changes to C:\Documents and Settings, and cd ..\scott changes to C:\Documents and Settings\scott.

You can make the cd command change the drive and directory by adding /D to the command line, as in

```
cd /D d:\setup\english
```

This is especially useful in batch files, where you might want to change to a specific drive and directory whose name is specified in an environment variable, as in

```
cd /d %userprofile%\My Documents
```

which changes to your My Documents folder no matter the drive on which it's located.

pushd *and* popd

The command **pushd** *path* changes the current directory to the specified *path*. The previous current drive and directory are remembered, and the command popd restores the previous path. Pushd saves as many directory changes as you care to make, and each popd returns to the directory in use before the corresponding pushd.

If the path specified to pushd contains a drive letter, the current drive is changed as well.

When command extensions are enabled (which they are, by default), you can specify a network path, for example, \\server\sharename\path, and pushd will automatically map a drive letter to the network path, starting with the letter *Z* and working backwards. Popd automatically deletes the temporary drive mappings.

Note

If you search your hard drive for **cd.exe**, **pushd.exe**, or **popd.exe**, you'll find that they don't exist. There are no executable files corresponding to these commands. They are built-in commands handled directly by **cmd.exe**.

dir

The dir command lists the contents of directories (folders). It's handy enough to know that the command dir by itself lists the contents of the current directory; with this and cd, you can explore the entire hard disk.

Dir has dozens of options. I won't list them all here; you can see the entire list by typing dir /? at the command prompt. Here are a few of the most useful variations:

Command	Description
dir /p	Prints a listing, pausing when the screen fills with text. Press Enter to continue the listing. You can use /p with any of the command variations.
dir *filename*	Lists just files matching *filename*. You can use wildcard characters in the *filename*: * matches anything; ? matches exactly one character. For example, dir *.exe lists all files ending with .exe, and dir print*.* lists all files whose names start with print. Put the *filename* in quotes if the name contains spaces. You can also specify a drive letter and/or path to search a particular drive or directory.
dir ... /od	Sorts the files from youngest to oldest.
dir ... /oen	Lists files sorted by extension (.*xxx*), then by name.
dir ... /ah	Lists hidden files.
dir ... /s	Lists the current or specified directory and its subdirectories as well; for example, dir /s "c:\program files*.exe " lists all .EXE files in c:\program files and all of its subdirectories.
dir ... /b	Removes the file date, size and other information. Prints just the names of matched or located files.

The last variation I've found especially useful when I'm creating a batch file that is to perform some operation on a list of files. I use a command line

```
dir /b *.txt >mybatch.bat
```

which puts all of the names into file mybatch.bat. Then I can edit mybatch.bat and put commands before each of the filenames.

more

Many command-line programs print out more text than fits in the console window. In most cases, you can resize the window or scroll the window contents up to read it all, but there's another way. The utility more displays text a screen at a time, letting you press a key when you're ready to move on to the next screen.

There are two easy ways to use more: You can view a file with the command

```
more filename
```

but most often, you'll use more to page through the output of another program. With no filename argument, more reads the standard input, so you can pipe text to it like this:

```
dir /s | more
```

Because the command dir /s lists the contents of the current directory and all subdirectories, its output is often quite long. Piping the output through more pauses it after each screen. When more has halted, it will display -- More -- at the bottom of the screen. Press the space or Enter key to move on to the next screen.

There are some command-line options and other functions available as well. To read about the type more /? or rather,

```
more /? | more
```

runas

runas lets you run a program using the credentials of another user. The program will appear in your command prompt window (or, if it's a GUI program, on your desktop), but it will have the rights and privileges of another user. It's especially handy when you want to quickly run an administrative program as Administrator without logging on using that privileged account.

The full syntax of the runas command is

```
runas [/noprofile] [/env] [/netonly] [/smartcard]
      [/user:username] command line
```

The command line options are:

Command	Description
/noprofile	Specifies that the user's profile (Registry settings) should not be loaded. This causes the application to load more quickly, but can make some applications malfunction.
/env	Uses the current environment variables instead of the user's default variables.
/netonly	The credentials specified are for remote access only, not local file access.
/smartcard	Uses the credentials on a smart card. If this option is used, the /user option may be omitted.
/user	Specifies the user account to use to run the program. Can be a local account (for example, Administrator), or a domain account in the format user@domain or domain\user.
command line	The command to run, and any additional arguments.

I've found that I use runas frequently, but in only three ways:

- runas /user:Administrator mmc opens the Microsoft Management Console. From there, you can click File, Add/Remove Snap In to open management tools.

- runas /user:Administrator control *panelname*.cpl, where *panelname* is the name of a Control Panel applet file. I'll talk about this more in the next section.

- runas /user:Administrator cmd opens a Command Prompt window with Administrator privileges. The new window will run under the Administrator logon name, and any programs you run from this command prompt will also have Administrator privileges. The only exception to this is that you can't run Explorer from this new window, or any window derived from Explorer, for example, Printers and Faxes. Explorer is an odd program, and you can't have two copies running under two different accounts at the same time.

control

You can run Control Panel applets from the command line using the control command. There are three reasons you might want do to this:

- To more quickly open a control panel. If you already have a command prompt window open, it's faster to type control firewall.cpl than to poke your way through the Start menu, open the Control Panel, and then open the Windows Firewall window.

- To run a control panel applet as a Computer Administrator. Again, it's much faster to type runas /user:Administrator "control firewall.cpl" than to log off and back on, or to switch users.

- To run a control panel applet that is not listed in the Control Panel window. For example, to configure Windows to log on automatically at startup, you have to type control userpasswords2, or if you're not logged on as a Computer Administrator, runas /user:Administrator "control userpasswords2"

The syntax for the control command has three variations:

control *filename*.**cpl**	Opens the primary control panel applet contained in the file *filename*.cpl stored in \windows\system32 or elsewhere in the PATH.
control *filename*.**cpl** *appletname*	Opens an alternate applet contained in a .CPL file; some .CPL files contain code for more than one control panel applet.
control *specialname*	Opens a control panel applet or system configuration window corresponding to a special name recognized by control.exe, or listed in the Registry under HKEY_LOCAL_MACHINE\SOFTWARE\Microsoft\Windows\CurrentVersion\Control Panel\Cpls or HKEY_CURRENT_USER\SOFTWARE\Microsoft\Windows\CurrentVersion\Control Panel\Cpls.

Table 9.10 lists the various control panel applets and system windows you can open from the command line. Not all versions or installations of Windows will have all these control panels.

To run a control panel as the Computer Administrator, the control command must be enclosed in quotes, and preceded by the runas command, as in

```
runas /user:Administrator "control appwiz.cpl"
```

Table 9.10   Control Panels Applets from the Command Line

Argument(s) after `control`	Applet Title
`access.cpl`	Accessibility Options
`admintools`	Administrative Tools*
`appwiz.cpl`	Add/Remove Programs
`bthprops.cpl`	Bluetooth Properties
`color`	Display Properties, Appearance tab
`cttune.cpl`	ClearType Tuning (source: PowerToys for Windows XP download)
`date/time`	Date and Time Properties
`desk.cpl`	Display Properties, Themes tab
`desktop`	Display Properties, Themes tab
`fax.cpl`	Fax Properties (Windows 2000)
`firewall.cpl`	Windows Firewall
`folders`	Folder Options
`fonts`	Fonts*
`hdwwiz.cpl`	Add Hardware
`inetcpl.cpl`	Internet Options
`infrared`	Wireless Connection (IRDA infrared)
`international`	Regional and Language Options
`intl.cpl`	Regional and Language Options
`irprops.cpl`	Wireless Link (IRDA infrared)
`joy.cpl`	Game Controllers
`main.cpl mouse`	Mouse Properties
`main.cpl keyboard`	Keyboard Properties
`main.cpl pc card (PCMCIA)`	PCMCIA or Removable Hardware
`main.cpl power`	Power Management (Windows 95 only)
`mlcfg32.cpl`	Windows Messaging profile manager (Windows 98/Me only)
`mmsys.cpl`	Sounds and Audio Devices
`modem.cpl`	Modem properties (Windows 98/Me only)
`mouse`	Mouse Properties
`msmq.cpl`	Microsoft Message Queuing Service
`ncpa.cpl`	Network Connections, but much slower to open than `control netconnections`*
`netconnections`	Network Connections*
`netcpl.cpl`	Network Configuration (Windows 98/Me only)
`netsetup.cpl`	Network Setup Wizard
`NetWare`	Client Services for NetWare
`nusrmgr.cpl`	User Accounts
`nwc.cpl`	Client Services for NetWare

(continues)

Table 9.10   Continued

Argument(s) after `control`	Applet Title
`odbccp32.cpl`	ODBC Data Source Administrator
`password.cpl`	Change Passwords/Remote Administration/User Profiles (Windows 98/Me only)
`ports`	System Properties, Computer Name tab
`powercfg.cpl`	Power Options
`printers`	Printers and Faxes*
`sapi.cpl`	Speech Properties
`scannercamera`	Scanners and Cameras*
`schedtasks`	Scheduled Tasks*
`speech`	Speech Properties
`sticpl.cpl`	Scanners and Cameras
`sysdm.cpl`	System Properties
`sysdm.cpl add new hardware`	Add New Hardware wizard
`telephon.cpl`	Phone and Modem options
`telephony`	Phone and Modem options
`themes.cpl`	Desktop themes (Windows 98/Me only)
`timedate.cpl`	Date and Time Properties
`tweakui.cpl`	Tweak UI (Windows 98, ME, and 2000 version only; Windows XP version is a Start menu item)
`ups.cpl`	UPS properties or Power Management
`userpasswords`	User Accounts
`userpasswords2`	On Windows XP, displays Windows 2000 version of User Accounts. Allows setting of automatic logon account. Prompts for Administrator password if necessary, no need to use `runas`.
`wgpocpl.cpl`	Workgroup Postoffice Admin (Windows 98/Me only)
`wscui.cpl`	Security Center
`wuaucpl.cpl`	Automatic Updates

*This control panel does not work when started by `runas`

net

The `net` command is a universe of its own; it performs 22 different functions involving networking and (strangely enough) Windows service management. The `net` command by itself lists these functions. These are very handy commands to know if you spend a lot of time working with networked computers. The functions available under Windows 2000 and XP are listed in Table 9.11.

Table 9.11 *net* **Subcommands**

net Subcommand	Function
net accounts	Adjusts the password requirements settings for local accounts on this computer
net computer	Adds or deletes computers from a domain network
net config	Displays or sets parameters for the server (file sharing server) or workstation (file sharing client) Microsoft networking components
net continue	Reactivates a paused service
net file	Lists your files that are being used by others, and optionally can disconnect the file and clear its "locked" status
net group	Lists, adds, or modifies global user groups on the local computer or domain
net help	Displays help information for these subcommands
net helpmsg	Prints a text description of a network error code number
net localgroup	Lists, adds, or modifies local user groups on the local computer or domain server
net name	Lists the names or aliases for the Windows Message service (this is not the same as Windows Messenger; it's a rarely used notification service)
net pause	Pauses a Windows service on the local computer
net print	Lists and manages print jobs queued on the local computer or another networked computer
net send	Sends a message to another user or computer (again, this service is rarely used and is likely disabled on Windows XP)
net session	Lists network files in use by the local computer or another networked computer; can also disconnect open files
net share	Lists, adds, or removes shared folders
net start	Starts a Windows service
net statistics	Prints network data transfer statistics
net stop	Stops a Windows service
net time	Synchronizes the computer's clock with another computer or time server
net use	Maps a drive letter to a shared folder, or a printer LPT port to a shared printer
net user	Lists, adds, or manages local user accounts
net view	Lists computers in a network workgroup or domain, and can also list folders and printers shared by a specific computer

You can get help for any of these commands by typing

```
net help subcommand
```

on the command line. The most important uses are listed in the following sections. These are especially useful in batch files that have to access shared folders; the batch file can create drive mappings on demand.

net view

The net view subcommand has several useful variations:

Command	Description
net view	Lists all of the computers in the current domain or workgroup
net view /domain	Lists all of the domains on the network
net view /domain:*xxx*	Lists all of the computers in the specified domain *xxx*
net view /network:nw	Lists all available Novell NetWare Servers
net view *computername*	Lists all of the printers and folders shared by the specific computer

net use

The net use subcommand lets you map networked files and folders to drive letters or printer devices on your computer. There are several variations:

Command	Description
net use x: *computer**sharename*	Maps drive letter *x*: to shared folder *sharename* on computer named *computer*.
net use x: *computer**sharename*\\ *subfolder*\\...	Maps drive letter *x*: to a subfolder of the shared folder *sharename* on computer *computer*. The apparent "root" directory of the mapped drive will be the subfolder.
net use x: *computer**sharename* /user:*username*	Maps drive letter *x*: to shared folder *sharename* on computer *computer* using an alternate user's credentials. net use will prompt for a password if necessary.
net use x: *computer**sharename* /user:*username password*	As in the preceding command, but the password is specified on the command line. This is a security risk but may be your only option when mapping drives using an alternate username from a batch file.

Command	Description
net use lpt*n*: *computer**printername*	Maps a specified LPT printer port (for example, LPT2) to a network shared printer, for use by MS-DOS applications. Note: You cannot map an LPT port that corresponds to a physical printer port in your computer.
net use ... /persistent:yes|no	On a net use command line, /persistent:yes stores the current and subsequent drive mapping in your profile so that the mapping is restored the next time you log on. /persistent:no makes the current and subsequent mapping appear in the current logon session only.
net use x: /d	Unmaps drive letter *x*:, that is, disconnects it from a shared folder.
net use lpt*n*: /d	Disconnects the specified LPT port from a network shared printer.

net share

The `net share` command shares an existing folder on your computer to the network, or cancels file sharing. The most important variations are:

Command	Description
`net share` *sharename drive:path*	Shares the specified folder under the specified share name
`net share` *sharename* `/delete`	Cancels the specified share

Additional options can specify how files are cached if a remote user requests offline access to the shared folder; type **net help share** for details.

net start and net stop

`net start` and `net stop` have nothing to do with networking. Instead, they can start and stop Windows services on your computer. The argument after `start` or `stop` is the "short" name of the service.

Note

Each Windows service has a "short name" (also called the "service name") and a "long name" (also called the "display name"). The Services management window lists only the display names. To see the short names of the services on your computer, type the command **sc query**. The **sc** command is a more comprehensive command-line service manager, which is also worth learning about; see "Managing Services from the Command Line" in Chapter 6 for more information.

I've found this command to be most helpful on Windows Server computers, where it's easier to type

```
net stop dns
net start dns
```

at a command prompt than to use Computer Management to restart the service when it's gone haywire.

findstr

`findstr` searches text files and folders for strings, optionally using a powerful pattern matching scheme called *regular expressions*. (If you're familiar with UNIX or Linux, `findstr` is a lot like grep.) Findstr has a slew of options. You can see the whole list by opening a command prompt window and typing `help findstr`, which prints the following:

```
FINDSTR [/B] [/E] [/L] [/R] [/S] [/I] [/X] [/V] [/N] [/M] [/O] [/P] [/F:file]
        [/C:string] [/G:file] [/D:dir list] [/A:color attributes] [/OFF[LINE]]
        strings [[drive:][path]filename[ ...]]

  /B          Matches pattern if at the beginning of a line.
  /E          Matches pattern if at the end of a line.
  /L          Uses search strings literally.
  /R          Uses search strings as regular expressions.
  /S          Searches for matching files in the current directory and all
              subdirectories.
  /I          Specifies that the search is not to be case sensitive.
  /X          Prints lines that match exactly.
  /V          Prints only lines that do not contain a match.
  /N          Prints the line number before each line that matches.
```

```
/M          Prints only the filename if a file contains a match.
/O          Prints character offset before each matching line.
/P          Skip files with non-printable characters.
/OFF[LINE]  Do not skip files with offline attribute set.
/A:attr     Specifies color attribute with two hex digits. See "color /?"
/F:file     Reads file list from the specified file(/ stands for console).
/C:string   Uses specified string as a literal search string.
/G:file     Gets search strings from the specified file(/ stands for console).
/D:dir      Search a semicolon delimited list of directories
strings     Text to be searched for.
[drive:][path]filename
            Specifies a file or files to search.
```

Use spaces to separate multiple search strings unless the argument is prefixed
with /C. For example, 'FINDSTR "hello there" x.y' searches for "hello" or
"there" in file x.y. 'FINDSTR /C:"hello there" x.y' searches for
"hello there" in file x.y.

In the form

```
findstr /c:"whatever string you want to find" filename…
```

findstr scans through every file named on the command line (you can use wildcards), and prints out each line that contains the exact string. Some of the more useful options that you can put on the command line between findstr and /c are

/B   Matches the string only if occurs at the beginning of the text line. findstr /b
     /c:"mouse" will match the line "mouse ate my cheese" but not "my house has a
     mouse."

/E   Like /B, but makes findstr print lines only if the search text is found at the end of the
     input line.

/I   Ignores case; lines with mouse, MOUSE, or Mouse will match /c:"mouse".

/S   Searches for files in the current directory and all subdirectories. This is especially useful
     if you specify the filenames with wildcards, for example:
     findstr /s /c:"mouse" *.txt

findstr can also search for complex patterns using a pattern matching formula called a *regular expression*. Regular expressions are complex and beyond our scope here, but if you need to pull information out of or rearrange text files, they're an *extremely* powerful tool. You can find lots of information about them on the Net. The regular expressions used by findstr can use any of the following elements:

Pattern item	Matches...
.	Any one character
*	Zero, one, or more occurrences of the item immediately before *
^	Beginning of the line; ^abc matches abc only if it occurs at the beginning of a line
$	End of the line; abc$ matches abc only if it occurs at the end of a line
[xyz]	Any one character listed in the set of characters between the brackets
[^xyz]	Any one character not in the set of characters listed between the brackets
[x-y]	Any one character in the range from x to y
\<	The beginning of a word (that is, printing text preceded by whitespace or a line break)

Pattern item	Matches...
\>	The end of a word (that is, whitespace following printing characters or a line break)
x	The character x
\x	The character x, where x would otherwise have special meaning, that is, . * ^ $ [ ] or \

For full information on `findstr` regular expressions refer to the online Command Reference.

Batch Files

Batch files are, in essence, command-line commands typed into a text file rather than typed directly at the command prompt. You can tell the command shell to read this text file and interpret its commands as if you were typing them. This serves several purposes:

- It can save you a lot of typing, as you only need to type the batch file commands once, but you can have Windows run the commands as many times as you want. This is really important with long sequences of commands, but I even more frequently write what I call "tiny handy batch files," with single letter names, and perhaps only one command inside, to do things like change the current directory to a commonly used folder. These batch files can save you quite a bit of time and trouble.

- You can write the batch file in such a way that it records *steps* of a particular job without storing the *particulars*; you can then provide the particulars when you use the batch file. For example, if you repeatedly have to extract and print information from different data files, you might write a batch file that performs these steps but doesn't contain the name of the actual data file to be processed. You can supply that name when you use the batch file. This, again, can save you time and mental energy: After the batch file is written, you don't have to think about what's inside the batch file. It's just a new Windows command that you can use whenever you need.

- The contents of the batch file serve as a form of documentation, which lists the steps necessary to perform a particular job. A year after you've completed some project, you might have forgotten the steps involved in processing your data files, but you can always read the batch file yourself to refresh your memory.

Batch files can also use primitive programming commands to handle varying situations: "if a particular situation arises, do this, otherwise, do that" or "repeat this step for every file in a certain folder."

Creating and Editing Batch Files

You can place batch files in any folder you want. You can place them on your own hard drive, or you may want to place your batch files on a shared network folder so they can be used from any computer. I place my personal batch files in a folder named c:\bat and put this folder in the PATH so that I can run them by name from any command prompt.

Regardless of their folder location, batch files should be given the extension .CMD or .BAT. Either is fine. The .BAT extension is more traditional, whereas .CMD makes it clear that the batch file is written for Windows NT/2000/XP, because DOS and Windows 9x will not recognize such files as batch files.

To create a sample batch file, open a Command Prompt window or use the one opened earlier in this section. Type the command

```
notepad test.bat
```

and then click Yes when Notepad asks, Do you want to create a new file? In the empty Notepad window, type the following lines:

```
@echo off
cls
echo The command line argument is %1
pause
```

Save the file and at the command line type:

```
test xxx
```

The Command Prompt window should clear, and you should see the following:

```
The command line argument is xxx
Press any key to continue . . .
```

Press Enter, and the command prompt should return. You can use this same procedure to create any number of batch files.

Later, if you want to edit the files, you can use the name notepad command to open and modify the files and make changes.

One batch file you may want to create right now is named bat.bat, with this one line inside:

```
pushd c:\bat
```

With this file in place, if you type bat at any command prompt, your current directory will be instantly changed to c:\bat so that you can edit or create new batch files. Type popd to go back to whatever directory you were using beforehand.

Of course, you could just type pushd c:\bat directly. It may seem silly to create a batch file just to save nine keystrokes, but when you're actively developing batch files, you'll quickly find that this really does make life easier.

I have about a dozen batch files like this that I use on a daily basis to move into directories for specific projects. For projects that use special command-line programs, the batch file has a second line that adds the program directory to the beginning of the search path, using a command such as this:

```
path c:\some\new\folder;%path%
```

If you find yourself frequently working with command-line programs, you will want to make "tiny handy batch files" for your projects as well.

Batch File Programming

The following sections discuss programming techniques that take advantage of the extended commands provided by the cmd shell. The commands that are most useful in batch files are listed in Table 9.12.

Table 9.12   Batch File Commands

Command	Use
call	Calls a batch file subroutine
echo	Displays text to the user
setlocal/endlocal	Saves/restores environment variables
exit	Terminates batch file
for	Iterates over files, folders, or numbers
goto	Used for flow control

Table 9.12 Continued

Command	Use
if/else	Executes commands conditionally
pause	Lets the user read a message
pushd/popd	Saves/restores the current directory
rem	Used for comments and documentation. Windows ignores any lines that start with the word rem or remark.
set	Sets environment variables, performs calculations, and prompts for user input
shift	Scans through command-line arguments
start	Launches a program in a different window

If you've written batch files for DOS, Windows 9x, and Windows NT, you'll find that most of these commands have been significantly enhanced, so even if you are familiar with these commands, you should read the discussions in this chapter, and check out the online Command Line Reference in Windows Help and Support.

Argument Substitution

Many times you'll find that the repetitive tasks you encounter use the same programs and steps, but operate on different files each time. In this case, you can use command-line arguments to give information to the batch file when you run it. When you start a batch file from the command line with a command such as

```
batchname xxx yyy zzz
```

any strings after the name of the batch file are made available to the batch program as arguments. The symbols %1, %2, %3, and so on are replaced with the corresponding arguments. In this example, anywhere that %1 appears in the batch file, cmd replaces it with xxx. Then, %2 is replaced with yyy, and so on.

Argument substitution lets you write batch files like this:

```
@echo off
notepad %1.vbs
cscript %1.vbs
```

This batch file lets you edit and then run a Windows Script Host program. If you name the batch file ws.bat, you can edit and test a script program named, say, test.vbs just by typing this:

```
ws test
```

In this case, cmd treats the batch file as if it contained the following:

```
@echo off
notepad test.vbs
cscript test.vbs
```

This kind of batch file can save you many keystrokes during the process of developing and debugging a script.

Note

The command @echo off at the top of a batch file keeps cmd from printing out each of the program steps as it encounters them. This reduces "clutter" in the Command Prompt window. If your batch file is behaving in some way you don't understand, you can temporarily change this to @echo on, to see the steps as they are run.

Besides the standard command-line arguments %1, %2, and so on, you should know about two special argument replacements: %0 and %*. %0 is replaced with the name of the batch file, as it was typed on the command line. %* is replaced with *all* the command-line arguments as they were typed, with quotes and everything left intact.

If I have a batch file named test.bat with the contents

```
@echo off
echo The command name is %0
echo The arguments are: %*
```

then the command test a b c will print the following:

```
The command name is test
The arguments are: a b c
```

%0 is handy when a batch file has detected some problem with the command-line arguments the user has typed and you want it to display a "usage" message. Here's an example:

```
if "%1" == "" (
    rem - no arguments were specified. Print the usage information
    echo Usage: %0 [-v] [-a] filename ...
    exit /b
)
```

If the batch file is named test.bat, typing test would print out the following message:

```
Usage: test [-v] [-a] filename ...
```

The advantage of using %0 is that it will always be correct, even if you rename the batch file at a later date and forget to change the "usage" remarks inside.

Argument Editing

cmd lets you modify arguments as they're replaced on the command line. Most of the modifications assume that the argument is a filename and let you extract or fill in various parts of the name. You might want to use this feature when, say, a batch file argument specifies a Microsoft Word file with the .DOC extension, and you want the batch file to construct a new filename with the same root name but a different extension.

When command extensions are enabled, cmd can insert edited versions of the arguments by placing a tilde (~) and some additional characters after the % sign. The editing functions let you manipulate filenames passed as arguments. Table 9.13 lists the edit options, using argument number 1 as an example.

Table 9.13 Argument Editing Expressions

Expression	Result
%~1	Removes surrounding quotes (").
%~f1	Fully qualified pathname.
%~d1	Drive letter only.
%~p1	Path only.
%~n1	Filename only.
%~x1	File extension only.

Table 9.13   Continued

Expression	Result
%~s1	Short DOS 8.3 file and path.
%~a1	File attributes.
%~t1	Modification date/time of file.
%~z1	Length of file in bytes.
%~$PATH:1	Fully qualified name of the first matching file when searching PATH. If no file is found, the result is a zero-length string. The filename must include the proper extension; PATHEXT is not used.

For example, if I ran a batch file with the argument `"under the hood.doc"`, the results might be as follows:

Expression	Result
%~1	under the hood.doc
%~f1	C:\book\ch11\under the hood.doc
%~d1	C:
%~p1	\book\ch11
%~n1	under the hood
%~x1	.doc
%~s1	C:\book\ch11\UNDERT~1.DOC
%~a1	--a------
%~t1	04/20/2002 12:42 PM
%~z1	45323
%~$PATH:1	

Here's how these features might be used: Suppose I have a series of files that I need to sort. The input files could come from any folder, but I want to store the sorted files in C:\sorted and give them the extension .TAB regardless of what the original extension was. I can write a batch file named sortput.bat to do this:

```
@echo off
sort <%1 >c:\sorted\%~n1.tab
```

The sort command will read the file as I've specified it on the command line, but the output file will use only the base part of the input file's name. If I run the command

```
sortput "c:\work files\input.txt"
```

the substituted command will be

```
sort <"c:\work files\input.txt" >c:\sorted\input.tab
```

Conditional Processing with *if*

One of the most important capabilities of any programming language is the ability to choose from among different instructions based on conditions the program finds as it runs. For this purpose, the batch file language has the if command.

The Basic `if` Command

In its most basic form, `if` compares two strings and executes a command if the strings are equivalent:

```
if string1 == string2 command
```

This is used in combination with command-line variable or environment variable substitution, as in this example:

```
if "%1" == "ERASE" delete somefile.dat
```

If and only if the batch file's first argument is the word `ERASE`, this command will delete the file `somefile.dat`.

The quotation marks in this command aren't absolutely required. If they are omitted and the command is written as

```
if %1 == ERASE delete somefile.dat
```

the command will still work as long as some command-line argument is given when the batch file is run. However, if the batch file is started with no arguments, `%1` would be replaced with nothing, and the command would turn into this:

```
if == ERASE delete somefile.dat
```

This is an invalid command. cmd expects to see something before the `==` part of the command and will bark if it doesn't. Therefore, it's a common practice to surround the items to be tested with some character—any character. Even `$` will work, as shown here:

```
if $%0$ == $ERASE$ delete somefile.dat
```

If the items being tested are identical, they will still be identical when surrounded by the extra characters. If they are different or blank, you'll still have a valid command.

The `if` command also lets you reverse the sense of the test with the `not` option:

```
if not "%1" == "ERASE" then goto no_erase
```

Checking for Files and Folders

The `exist` option lets you determine whether a particular file exists in the current directory:

```
if exist input.dat goto process_it
    echo The file input.dat does not exist
    pause
    exit /b
:process_it
```

Of course, you can specify a full path for the filename if that's appropriate, and you can use environment variables and `%` arguments to construct the name. If the filename has spaces in it, you'll need to surround it with quotes.

The not modifier can be used with `exist` as well.

Tip

The **exist** test only checks for files, not folders. However, the special file **nul** appears to exist in every folder. You can perform the test

```
if exist c:\foldername\nul command
```

to see whether the folder *c:\foldername* exists.

Checking the Success of a Program

When a command line or even a Windows program exits, it leaves behind a number called its *exit status* or *error status* value. This is a number that the program uses to indicate whether it thinks it did its job successfully. An exit status of zero means no problems; larger numbers indicate trouble. There is no predetermined meaning for any specific values. The documentation for some programs may list specific error values and give their interpretations, which means that your batch files can use these values to take appropriate action. How? Through the `errorlevel` variation of the `if` command.

After running a command in a batch file, an `if` statement of the form

```
if errorlevel number command
```

will execute the command if the previous program's exit status value is the listed number or *higher*. For example, the `net use` command returns 0 if it is able to map a drive letter to a shared folder, and it will return a nonzero number if it can't. A batch file can take advantage of this as follows:

```
@echo off

net use f: \\bali\corpfiles
if errorlevel 1 goto failed
    echo Copying network data...
    if not exist c:\corpfiles\nul mkdir c:\corpfiles
    copy f:\*.xls c:\corpfiles
    exit /b
:failed
    echo Unable to access network share \\bali\corpfiles
    pause
```

You can also use not with this version of the `if` command. In this case, the command is executed if the error status is *less* than the listed number. The error testing in the previous example can be rewritten this way:

```
if not errorlevel 1 goto success
    echo Unable to access network share \\bali\corpfiles
    pause
    exit /b
:success
    echo Copying network data...
    if not exist c:\corpfiles\nul mkdir c:\corpfiles
    copy f:\*.xls c:\corpfiles
```

In this version, the flow of the batch file is a bit easier to follow. However, even this can be improved upon, as you'll see next.

Grouping Commands with Parentheses

Often, you'll want to execute several commands if some condition is true. In the old days, before the extended cmd shell came along, you would have to use a `goto` command to transfer control to another part of the batch file, as in the `if exist` example given in the previous section. With the extended version of `if`, this is no longer necessary.

The extended `if` command lets you put more than one statement after an `if` command, by grouping them with parentheses. For example, you can place multiple commands on one line, as shown here:

```
if not errorlevel 1 (echo The network share was not available & exit /b)
```

Or you can put them on multiple lines:

```
if not errorlevel 1 (
    echo The network share was not available
    pause
    exit /b
)
```

I recommend the second version, because it's easier to read. Look how much clearer the network file copying example becomes when parentheses are used instead of goto:

```
@echo off

net use f: \\bali\corpfiles
if errorlevel 1 (
    echo Unable to access network share \\bali\corpfiles
    pause
    exit /b
)
echo Copying network data...
if not exist c:\corpfiles\nul mkdir c:\corpfiles
copy f:\*.xls c:\corpfiles
```

You can also execute one set of commands if the if test is true and another if the test is false by using the else option, as in this example:

```
if exist input.dat echo input.dat exists else echo input.dat does not exist
```

You can use else with parentheses, but you must take care to place the else command on the same line as if, or on the same line as the closing parenthesis after if. You should write a multiple-line if...else command using the same format as this example:

```
if exist input.dat (
    echo Sorting input.txt...
    sort <input.txt >source.data
) else (
    echo Input.txt does not exist. Creating an empty data file...
    echo. >source.data
)
```

Extended Testing

The extended if command lets you perform a larger variety of tests when comparing strings, and it can also compare arguments and variables as numbers. The extended comparisons are listed in Table 9.14.

Table 9.14   Comparison Operators Allowed by the *if* Command

Variation	Comparison
if *string1* **EQU** *string2*	Exactly equal
if *string1* **NEQ** *string2*	Not equal
if *string1* **LSS** *string2*	Less than
if *string1* **LEQ** *string2*	Less than or equal to
if *string1* **GTR** *string2*	Greater than
if string1 **GEQ** string2	Greater than or equal to

Table 9.14   Continued

Variation	Comparison
`if /i` (comparison)	Not case sensitive
`if defined` *name*	True if there is an environment variable *name*
`if cmdextversion` *number*	True if the cmd extensions are version *number* or higher

As a bonus, if the strings being compared contain only digits, cmd compares them numerically. For example, you could test for a specific exit status from a program with a statement like this:

```
some program
if %errorlevel% equ 3 (
    echo The program returned an exit status of 3 which
    echo means that the network printer is offline.
)
```

Processing Multiple Arguments

When you have many files to process, you may get tired of typing the same batch file commands over and over, like this:

```
somebatch file1.dat
somebatch file2.dat
somebatch file3.dat
...
```

It's possible to write batch files to handle any number of arguments on the command line. The tool to use is the `shift` command, which deletes a given command-line argument and slides the remaining ones down. Here's what I mean: Suppose I started a batch file with the command line

```
batchname xxx yyy zzz
```

Inside the batch file, the following argument replacements would be in effect before and after a `shift` command:

Before Shift	After Shift
%0 = batchname	%0 = xxx
%1 = xxx	%1 = yyy
%2 = yyy	%2 = zzz
%3 = zzz	%3 = (blank)
%4 = (blank)	%4 = (blank)

This lets a batch file repeatedly process the item named by %1 and shift until %1 is blank. To process a variable number of command-line arguments, use the `shift` command to delete arguments until they're all gone, as in this example:

```
@echo off
if "%1" == "" (
    rem if %1 is blank there were no arguments. Show how to use this batch
    echo Usage: %0 filename ...
    exit /b
)

:again
```

```
rem if %1 is blank, we are finished
if not "%1" == "" (
    echo Processing file %1...

    rem ... do something with file %1 here

    rem - shift the arguments and examine %1 again
    shift
    goto again
)
```

If you want to have the program process a default file if none is specified on the command line, you can use this variation of the pattern:

```
@echo off

if "%1" == "" (
    rem - no file was specified - process the default file "test.for"
    call :process test.for
) else (
    rem - process each of the named files
:again
    rem if %1 is blank, we are finished
    if not "%1" == "" (
        call :process %1
        rem - shift the arguments and examine %1 again
        shift
        goto again
    )
)
exit /b

:process
echo Processing file %1...
 .
 .
 .
```

In this version, if no arguments are specified on the command line, the script will process a default file—in this case test.for. Otherwise, it will process all files named on the command line. This version of the pattern uses batch file subroutines, which are discussed later in this chapter under "Using Batch Files Subroutines."

The extended version of the shift command, shift /n, lets you start shifting at argument number n, leaving the lower-numbered arguments alone. The following illustrates what shift /2 does in a batch file run with the command "batchname xxx yyy zzz":

Before Shift	**After Shift**
%0 = batchname	%0 = batchname
%1 = xxx	%1 = xxx
%2 = yyy	%2 = zzz
%3 = zzz	%3 = (blank)
%4 = (blank)	%4 = (blank)

In actual use, you might want to use this feature if you need to have the batch file's name (%0) available throughout the batch file. In this case, you can use shift /1 to shift all the remaining arguments, but keep %0 intact. You may also want to write batch files that take a command line of the form

```
batchname outputfile inputfile inputfile ...
```

with an output filename followed by one or more input files. In this case, you could keep the output filename %1 intact but loop through the input files with shift /2, using commands like this:

```
@echo off

rem be sure they gave at least two arguments
if "%2" == "" (
    echo Usage: %0 outfile infile ...
    exit /b
)

rem collect all input files into SORT.TMP

if exist sort.tmp del sort.tmp

:again
if not "%2" == "" (
    echo ...Collecting data from %2
    type %2 >>sort.tmp
    shift /2
    goto again
)

rem sort SORT.TMP into first file named on command line

echo ...Sorting to create %1
sort sort.tmp /O %1
del sort.tmp
```

Working with Environment Variables

Although environment variables were initially designed to hold system-configuration information such as the search path, they are also the "working" variables for batch files. You can use them to store filenames, option settings, user input from prompts, or any other information you need to store in a batch program. The set command is used to set and modify environment variables.

However, you should know that, by default, changes to environment variables made in a batch file persist when the batch file finishes because the variables "belong" to the copy of cmd that manages the Command Prompt window and any batch files in it. This is great when you want to use a batch file to modify the search path so that you can run programs from some nonstandard directory. However, it's a real problem if your batch file assumes that any variables it uses are undefined (empty) before the batch file starts. Here's a disaster waiting to happen:

```
@echo off
set /p answer=Do you want to erase the input files at the end (Y/N)?
if /i "%answer:~,1%" EQU "Y" set cleanup=YES
... more commands here
... then, at the end,
if "%cleanup%" == "YES" (
    rem they wanted the input files to be erased
    del c:\input\*.dat
)
```

If you respond to the prompt with Y, the environment variable cleanup will be set to YES, and the files will be erased. However, the next time you run the batch file, cleanup will *still* be set to YES, and the files will be erased no matter how you answer the question. Of course, the problem can be solved by adding the statement

```
set cleanup=
```

at the beginning of the batch file. In fact, good programming practice requires you to do so in any case (you should always initialize variables before using them), but the point is still important: Environment variables are "sticky."

In the old DOS days, a batch file program would usually add set statements to the end of batch files to delete any environment variables used by the program. However, cmd provides an easier method of cleaning up.

If you plan on using environment variables as working variables for a batch file, you can use the setlocal command to make any changes to the variables "local" to the batch file. At the end of the batch file, or if you use an endlocal command, the environment will be restored to its original state at the time of the setlocal command. It would be prudent to put setlocal at the beginning of any batch file that does not require its environment changes to persist outside the batch file itself.

Environment Variable Editing

As with the old command.com, in any command, strings of the form %var% are replaced with the value of the environment variable named var. One of cmd's extensions is to let you modify the environment variable content as it is being extracted. Whereas the edits for command-line arguments are focused around filename manipulation, the edits for environment variables are designed to let you extract substrings.

The following types of expressions can be used:

Expression	Result
%name:~n%	Skips the first n letters and returns the rest
%name:~n,m%	Skips n letters and returns the next m
%name:~,m%	First (leftmost) m letters
%name:~-m%	Last (rightmost) m letters

Using the environment variable var=ABCDEFG, here are some examples:

Command	Prints
echo %var%	ABCDEFG
echo %var:~2%	CDEFG
echo %var:~2,3%	CDE
echo %var:~,3%	ABC
echo %var:~-3%	EFG

Expressions of the form %name:*str1*=*str2*% replace every occurrence of the string *str1* with *str2*. *str2* can be blank to delete all occurrences of *str1*. You can start *str1* with an asterisk (*), which makes cmd replace all characters up to and including *str1*.

Using the environment variable var=ABC;DEF;GHI, here are some examples:

Command	Prints
echo %var:;= %	ABC DEF GHI
echo %var:;=%	ABCDEFGHI
echo %var:*DEF=123%	123;GHI

The first example listed is particularly useful if you want to use the PATH list in a for loop; for wants to see file or folder names separated by spaces, whereas PATH separates them with semicolons. I'll discuss this in more detail later on.

Processing Multiple Items with the *for* Command

You'll often want to write batch files that process "all" of a certain type of file. Command-line programs can deal with filename wildcards: For example, you can type delete *.dat to delete all files whose names end with .dat. In batch files, you can accomplish this sort of thing with the for loop.

Note

If you have a UNIX background, the need for special statements to deal with wildcards may seem confusing at first. On UNIX and Linux systems, the command shell expands all command-line arguments with wildcards into a list of names before it starts up the command, so to the command it appears that the user typed out all of the names. This is called *globbing*. On DOS and Windows, the shell doesn't do this. When command-line arguments contain wildcard characters, it's up to the command or batch file to expand the name into a list of filenames.

The basic version of the for command scans through a set or list of names and runs a command once for each. The format for batch files is

```
for %%x in (set of names) do command
```

where *set of names* is a list of words separated by spaces. The for command executes *command* once for each item it finds in the set. At each iteration, variable x contains the current name, and any occurrences of %%x in the command are replaced by the current value of x. You can choose any alphabetic letter for the variable name. Also, upper- and lowercase matters, meaning *a* and *A* are different to the for command.

Note

When you type a **for** command directly at the command prompt, you only use single percent signs. In a batch file, you must double them up. Otherwise, they confuse cmd because they look sort of like command-line arguments. cmd could have been written to know the difference, but it wasn't, so we're stuck with this.

For example, the command

```
for %%x in (a b c d) do echo %%x
```

prints four lines: a, b, c, and d. What makes for especially useful is that if any item in the set contains the wildcard characters ? or *, for will assume that the item is a filename and will replace the item with any matching filenames. The command

```
for %%x in (*.tmp *.out *.dbg) do delete %%x
```

will delete any occurrences of files ending with .tmp, .out, or .dbg in the current directory. If no such files exist, the command will turn into

```
for %%x in () do delete %%x
```

which is fine...it does nothing. To get the same "silent" result when specifying the wildcards directly in the delete command, you would have to enter

```
if exist *.tmp delete *tmp
if exist *.out delete *.out
if exist *.dbg delete *.dbg
```

because delete complains if it can't find any files to erase.

As another example, the command

```
for %%F in ("%ALLUSERSPROFILE%\Documents\➥
    My Faxes\Received Faxes\*.tif") do echo %%~nF: received %%~tF
```

prints a list of all faxes received from the Windows Fax service and the time they were received.

Note

If you use variable substitution edits, choose as your **for** variable a letter that you don't need to use as one of the editing letters. **for** stops looking at the editing expression when it hits the **for** variable letter. For instance, in the example, if I had needed to use the ~f editing function, I would have had to choose another variable letter for the **for** loop.

The extended for command lets you scan for directories, recurse into subdirectories, and several other useful things that you can't do any other way.

Using Multiple Commands in a for Loop

cmd lets you use multiple command lines after a for loop. This makes the Windows XP for command much more powerful than the old DOS version. In cases where you would have had to call a batch file subroutine in the past, you can now use parentheses to perform complex operations.

For example, this batch file examines a directory full of Windows bitmap (BMP) files and makes sure that there is a corresponding GIF file in another directory; if the GIF file doesn't exist, it uses an image-conversion utility to create one:

```
@echo off
setlocal
echo Searching for new .BMP files...

for %%F in (c:\incoming\*.bmp) do (
    rem output file is input file name with extension .GIF
    set outfile=c:\outgoing\%%~nF.gif
    if not exist %outfile% (
        echo ...Creating %outfile%
        imgcnv -gif %%F %outfile%
    )
)
```

Therefore, every time you run this batch file, it makes sure there is a converted GIF file in the \outgoing folder for every BMP file in the \incoming folder. This sample script uses several of the techniques we've discussed in this chapter:

- A setlocal statement keeps environment variable changes in the batch file from persisting after the batch is finished.

- The for loop and if command use parentheses to group several statements.

- The environment variable `outfile` is used as a "working" variable.
- The batch file uses `echo` statements to let you know what it's doing as it works.

A batch file like this can make short work of maintaining large sets of files. You might accidentally overlook a new file if you were trying to manage something like this manually, but the batch file won't.

As a final example, the following handy batch file tells you what file is actually used when you type a command by name. I call this program `which.bat`, and when I want to know what program is run by, say, the `ping` command, I type the following:

```
which ping
```

The batch file searches the current folder, and then every folder in the PATH list. In each folder, it looks for a specific file, if you typed a specific extension with the command name, or it tries all the extensions in the PATHEXT list, which contains `.EXE`, `.COM`, `.BAT`, and the other usual suspects:

```
@echo off

if "%1" == "" (
    echo Usage: which command
    echo Locates the file run when you type 'command'.
    exit /b
)

for %%d in (. %path%) do (
    if "%~x1" == "" (
        rem the user didn't type an extension so use the PATHEXT list
        for %%e in (%pathext%) do (
            if exist %%d\%1%%e (
                echo %%d\%1%%e
                exit /b
            )
        )
    ) else (
        rem the user typed a specific extension, so look only for that
        if exist %%d\%1 (
            echo %%d\%1
            exit /b
        )
    )
)
echo No file for %1 was found
```

As you can see, the `for` command lets you write powerful, useful programs that can save you time and prevent errors, and the syntax is cryptic enough to please even a Perl programmer.

Delayed Expansion

Environment variables and command-line arguments marked with % are replaced with their corresponding values when cmd reads each command line. However, when you're writing `for` loops and compound `if` statements, this can cause some unexpected results.

For example, you might want to run a secondary batch file repeatedly with several files, with the first file handled differently, like this:

```
call anotherbatch firstfile.txt FIRST
call anotherbatch secondfile.txt MORE
call anotherbatch xfiles.txt MORE
```

You might want to do this so that the first call will create a new output file, while each subsequent call will add on to the existing file.

You might be tempted to automate this process with the for command, using commands like this:

```
set isfirst=FIRST
for %%f in (*.txt) do (
    call anotherbatch %%f %isfirst%
    set isfirst=MORE
)
```

The idea here is that the second argument to anotherbatch will be FIRST for the first file and MORE for all subsequent files. However, this will not work. cmd will replace %isfirst% with its definition MORE when it first encounters the for statement. When cmd has finished processing % signs, the command will look like this:

```
set isfirst=FIRST
for %%f in (*.txt) do (
    call anotherbatch %%f FIRST
    set isfirst=MORE
)
```

Because FIRST is substituted before the for loop starts running, anotherbatch will not see the value of isfirst change, and the result will be

```
call anotherbatch firstfile.txt FIRST
call anotherbatch secondfile.txt FIRST
call anotherbatch xfiles.txt FIRST
```

which is not at all what you wanted.

There is a way to fix this: Delayed expansion lets you specify environment variables with exclamation points rather than percent signs, as an indication that they are to be expanded only when cmd actually intends to really execute the command. Because ! has not traditionally been a special character, this feature is disabled by default. To enable delayed expansion, specify /V:ON on the cmd command line or use SETLOCAL to enable this feature inside the batch file. The statements

```
setlocal enabledelayedexpansion
set isfirst=FIRST
for %%f in (*.txt) do (
    call anotherbatch %%f !isfirst!
    set isfirst=MORE
)
```

will work correctly.

Although delayed expansion is disabled by default in Windows XP, you can change the default setting through the Registry key HKLM\Software\Microsoft\Command Processor\EnableExtensions. If this DWORD value is present and set to 0, command extensions are disabled by default. Any nonzero value for EnableExtensions enables them.

Another place delayed expansion is useful is to collect information into an environment variable in a for list. The following batch file adds c:\mystuff and every folder under it to an environment variable named dirs:

```
setlocal ENABLEDELAYEDEXPANSION
set dirs=
for /R c:\mystuff %%d in (.) do set dirs=!dirs!;%%d
```

The `for` statement recursively visits every folder, starting in `c:\mystuff`, and `%%d` takes on the name of each folder in turn. The `set` statement adds each directory name to the end of the `dirs` variable.

Using Batch Files Subroutines

The cmd shell lets you write batch file subroutines using the `call` command. Although the new capability to group statements with parentheses makes batch file subroutines somewhat less necessary than they were in the past, the subroutine is still an important tool in batch file programming.

For example, in a task that involves processing a whole list of files, you might write a batch file subroutine to perform all the steps necessary to process one file. Then, you can call this subroutine once for each file you need to process.

In the old days of `command.com`, batch file subroutines had to be placed in separate `.BAT` files. You can still do this, but with cmd, you can also place subroutines in the same file as the main batch file program. The structure looks like this:

```
@echo off

rem MAIN BATCH FILE PROGRAM -----------------------

rem call subroutine "onefile" for each file to be processed:
cd \input
for %%f in (*.dat) do call :onefile %%f    ← subroutine called here

rem main program must end with exit /b or goto :EOF
exit /b

rem SUBROUTINE "ONEFILE" --------------------------
:onefile
echo Processing file %1...
echo ... commands go here ...
exit /b
```

The `call` command followed by a colon and a label name tells cmd to continue processing at the label. Any items placed on the `call` command after the label are arguments passed to the subroutine, which can access them with `%1`, `%2`, and so on. The original command-line arguments to the batch file are hidden while the call is in effect.

Processing returns to the command after the call when the subroutine encounters any of these conditions:

- The end of the file is reached.
- The subroutine deliberately jumps to the end of the file with the command `goto :EOF`.
- The subroutine executes the command `exit /b`.

Normally, any of these conditions would indicate the end of the batch file, and cmd would return to the command prompt. After `call`, however, these conditions Ï end the subroutine, and the batch file continues.

Caution

You must be sure to make the main part of the batch file stop before it runs into the first subroutine. In other scripting languages such as VBScript, the end of the "main program" is unmistakable, but in the batch file language it is not. You must use `goto :EOF` or `exit /B` before the first subroutine's label; otherwise, cmd will plow through and run the subroutine's commands again.

Tip

When I have a bunch of files that I have to process in some way, I often don't like to use the **for** command. Instead I use the command `dir /b >filename.bat` to create the beginnings of the batch file. I edit the batch file with Notepad and put `call :process` before each filename. I put `@echo off` at the top. At the bottom, I put the lines

```
    goto :EOF
:process
    echo Processing file %s...
    ...
    (commands go here)
```

The reason I go to this trouble is that I can manually delete from the list any files that I want to skip—you can't do that with **for**! And if I have to interrupt the procedure before it finishes, I can delete the **call** lines for any files that had already been processed, or use a **goto** to skip over them, before running the batch file again.

Prompting for Input

If your batch file has to print a message you definitely don't want the users to miss, use the pause statement to make the batch file sit and wait until they've read the message and acknowledged it. Here's an example:

```
echo The blatfizz command failed. This means that the world as
echo we know it is about to end, or, that your input file needs to
echo be corrected.
pause
exit /b
```

If you want to ask a user whether to proceed after a mishap, or if you want the batch file to prompt for input filenames or other data, you can use the new extended set /p command. set /p reads a user's response into an environment variable, where it can be tested or used as a command argument. Here's an example:

```
:again
    echo The input file INPUT.DAT does not exist
    set /p answer=Do you want to create it now (Y/N)?
    if /i "%answer:~,1%" EQU "Y" goto editit
    if /i "%answer:~,1%" EQU "N" exit /b
    echo Please type Y for Yes or N for No
    goto again
```

These commands ask the user to type a response, examine the leftmost letter with %answer:,1%, and take the appropriate action only if the user types a valid response. To prompt a user for a yes/no answer, use a series of commands following this pattern:

```
:again
    echo If the question is long or requires an explanation,
    echo use echo commands to display text before the question.
```

```
set /p answer=Ask the question here (Y/N)?
if /i "%answer:~,1%" EQU "Y" command to execute for Yes
if /i "%answer:~,1%" EQU "N" command to execute for No
echo Please type Y for Yes or N for No
goto again
```

Put a single space after the question mark on the set /p command. If you use this pattern more than once in the same batch file, be sure to use a different label for each one. I used again in this version, but you can use any word as the label.

If the work that has to be done given either the Yes or No answer is more than a few commands (placed in parentheses), you can use be a goto :label command to continue execution in another part of the batch file.

You can modify this pattern to create a menu. You can write a prompt like this:

```
echo Options: [A]dd, [D]elete, [P]rint, [Q]uit, [H]elp"
set /p answer=Enter selection:
```

In this example, instead of comparing the response to the letters Y and N, you would compare it to A, D, P, Q, and H.

Scripting

As you saw in the previous sections, batch files give you a means to automatically run programs. There is some limited programming capability; that is, you have the means to take different actions depending on the conditions encountered, but for the most part, as helpful as they are, batch files just let you push data into and pull data out of existing programs.

Scripts, on the other hand, give you access to full-scale programming languages that can more easily manipulate data, and from which you can not only run existing command-line programs, but can also

- Use the features of many Windows programs such as Word and Excel to create documents or perform calculations.

- Gain access to Windows files, folders, network settings, the Registry, disk configuration and just about every other part of Windows.

- Write your own programs from scratch, to manage data, manage Windows, send email, or... well, just about anything else.

The range of what you can do with scripting is pretty much limited only to your imagination and your skill as a programmer. And that's the rub, as it does take some training and practice to build up that skill. Scripting is a complex subject that could easily fill several books of this size, so here we'll just be able to scratch its surface. I'll give you an overview. And, I hope that you'll be intrigued enough to learn more through other books and resources. I'll give you some suggestions for follow-up reading at the end of this chapter.

Script Languages

Windows scripting is managed through a program called *Windows Script Host* or WSH. The word "host" here is significant. It refers to the fact that Windows Script Host is a "framework" program that provides support for scripting without being tied to a specific script programming language. Out of the box, Windows comes with the VBScript and JScript languages, so you can use whichever of these two programming languages you prefer. Or, if you're already more familiar with one of the other programming languages available from third-party vendors, you can download and install one of these other languages, usually for free. Table 9.15 lists several widely used languages for which WSH versions are available.

Note

Windows Script Host is installed by default with Windows XP and 2000. For Windows 98 and Me you must download it from microsoft.com; search for "download windows script 98." At the time this was written, version 5.6 was the current version.

Table 9.15   Windows Script Host Languages*

Language	Description
VBScript	VBScript is a version of Microsoft Visual Basic used in Windows Script Host, Internet Explorer, and Internet Information Services. It's *very* similar to Visual Basic for Applications (VBA), which is used as the scripting or macro language for Microsoft desktop products such as Word and Excel. If you know how to write macros for Word and Excel, you know VBScript. VBScript is installed by default with Windows Script Host.
JScript	JScript is a programming language modeled after Netscape's JavaScript language. Microsoft made its own version just to keep things interesting and incompatible. If you've written client-side web page scripts, you're probably already familiar with JScript; now you can use it to manage and manipulate Windows. JScript is installed by default with Windows Script Host.
Perl	Perl was developed in 1987 by developers in the Unix community. From the very start, Perl was an "open" language—its writing, debugging, and subsequent development were carried out by the public, for free. It's a very popular, powerful language that's especially well suited for manipulating text. It has powerful string-handling and pattern-matching capabilities, and huge repositories of free Perl scripts are available on the Internet. As a programming language, though, it's on the strange side, and may not be a good choice if you're new to programming. A free version for Windows called ActivePerl can be downloaded from www.activestate.com.
Python	Python is another very popular scripting/programming language from the UNIX world. It originated at the National Research Institute for Mathematics and Computer Science (CWI) in Amsterdam. It's a portable object-oriented language and is much less cryptic than Perl. A free Windows Script Host plug-in called ActivePython is available at www.activestate.com.
Object REXX	REXX is a language that originated in 1979 as a scripting language for IBM mainframes. Since then, IBM has made it available for IBM Linux, AIX, OS/2, and Windows as well as its mainframe operating systems. Object REXX began as an IBM product but is now a free, open-source project. For information, visit www.rexxla.org.
Ruby	Ruby is a fairly new language that originated in Japan. It's currently more popular in Europe and Japan than in the U.S., but it's picking up steam. A port of Ruby to the Windows Script Host environment is available at http://isweb27.infoseek.co.jp/computer/arton/index.html. You might also search the Web for "ActiveScriptRuby."

*A few other language plug-ins have been made by independent developers, but they appear to be partial implementations and so are not listed here. For a survey, see www.mvps.org/scripting/languages.

Unix and Linux enthusiasts loudly sing the praises of Perl and Python, and in fact each of the languages has its disciples, but for a first-time programmer, VBScript is probably the easiest of these languages to learn. If you use Microsoft desktop applications, VBScript is definitely an important language to know because it's used inside Word, Excel, Access—in fact *most* Microsoft products—as the built-in macro language. You'll get a double payoff for learning VBScript because experience you gain writing scripts will help you write macros, and vice versa.

With this in mind, for this chapter, I'll provide the examples in VBScript.

Creating and Editing Scripts

Scripts are plain text files with a special file extension that tells Windows Script Host what language the script is written in; the most common extensions are listed in Table 9.1. The two most common are .VBS for a VBScript script, or .JS for a JScript script.

As stated previously, I suggest that you create a special folder to hold your scripts and batch files, for example c:\bat, so that you can put this folder into the search path and thus have access to them from any command prompt. For instructions, see "Creating and Editing Batch Files" earlier in this chapter. When you've done this, open a command prompt window and type the command bat to change to your batch file directory.

It's easy to create and edit scripts using the Notepad accessory. Let's create a simple script to display your logon (user) name. In the command prompt window you just opened, type **notepad myname.vbs** and press Enter. When Notepad asks whether you want to create a new file, click Yes. Then, type the following lines into the Notepad window:

```
set wnet = CreateObject("WScript.Network")
uname = wnet.UserName
wscript.echo "Your user name is " & uname
```

Save the file by clicking File, Save, or equivalently, by typing Alt+F, and then Alt+S.

Now, type the following line in the command prompt window:

```
cscript myname.vbs
```

This will run your script as a console (command line) application, and the result will print out in the console window. In my case, it prints:

```
Your user name is brian
```

Now, type the command

```
wscript myname.vbs
```

This runs your script as a Windowed (GUI) application. Instead of printing text at the command prompt, a dialog box pops up, as shown in Figure 9.10.

Figure 9.10   The WScript command runs scripts as GUI applications, and text output is displayed in dialog boxes.

In most cases, it's easier to run script applications using the command-line interface. You can set cscript to be the default, so that it is used to automatically run a script when you enter only its name. To do this, enter this command at the command prompt:

```
cscript //nologo //h:cscript //s
```

being sure to double-up the slashes as shown. You only need to do this once; this setting will "stick" permanently.

Now, you can run a script simply by typing its name. Type the command `myname` and press Enter. Recall that `.VBS` is in the `PATHEXT` list of executable file types, so when Windows looks for a program named `myname` it finds `myname.vbs`, and uses `cscript` to run it.

Note

If you have Microsoft AntiSpyware or another antispyware package installed, running a script by name may trigger a security warning. Click the appropriate button to allow the script to run. You may need to retype the command to get the script run. You should only have to go through this once for each new script you write.

Security Issues

When you run a script (or batch file, or any other program, for that matter), the script can do anything that your user account's permissions let it do. If you are using a Computer Administrator account, this means the script can do *anything*, including deleting Windows entirely.

You should take a moment to consider what might happen if some other user was able to modify your script file to so something other than what you intended. The next time you run the script, it will run with your account's permissions. Another user could use this technique to have you inadvertently give him or her Administrator privileges, cause damage, or, well…the mind boggles.

Here's what you can do to prevent this from happening:

■ Be sure that your scripts are stored on a disk formatted with the NTFS file system. The FAT file system offers no user-level security whatsoever.

■ On Windows XP Home Edition or Windows XP Professional with Simple File Sharing enabled, open a command prompt window and, assuming the batch file folder is `c:\bat`, type this command:

```
cacls c:\bat /T /G "%username%":F Users:R
```

This replaces the permissions on this folder and its contents to give you (and only you) read/write privileges, and gives all other users read-only access.

■ On Windows XP Professional with Simple File Sharing turned off, or on Windows 2000 Professional, you can use the preceding method, or if you want to do it the hard way, you can use the GUI: Open Windows Explorer and locate the folder that contains your scripts. Right-click the folder and select the Security tab. Add your user account to the list of names, and click Full Control. For the Users or Power Users entries, uncheck everything but Read & Execute. If you can't change these entries, log on as a (or contact your) system administrator, or click the Advanced button, uncheck the Inherit from Parent setting. Click OK, and then make the changes. Then, click Advanced again, and check "Replace Permission Entries…" and click OK to close the dialogs. (I told you it could be easier to use the command line to manage Windows!)

Running Scripts

As I mentioned in the previous section, if the folder that contains your scripts is listed in the `PATH` environment variable, and if you've set `cscript` (the command line version of Windows Script Host) to be the default script processor, you can run your scripts just as you would any other Windows command, by typing its name.

If your script contains a programming error, Windows Script Host may either refuse to run it, or may stop in the middle of running it. Let's demonstrate this. Open a Command Prompt window and switch to your scripts directory (type **bat**, if you're using the method I suggested). Edit the sample script by typing **notepad myname.vbs**, and add on to the third line so that it reads

```
wscript.echo "Your user name is " & uname & " no closing quote here
```

Save the file, and run it again by typing **myname** at the command prompt. This time you will see this message:

```
C:\Documents and Settings\brian\myname.vbs(3, 68) Microsoft VBScript
compilation error: Unterminated string constant
```

This message tells us three things:

- VBScript found an error in the script program
- The error occurred on the third line in the file; the (3, 68) part tells you this. The 3 is the number of the line in the file with the error, and the 68 is a number that tells what sort of problem VBScript found. You don't need to know what 68 means because its meaning is written in plain English:
- The message `Compilation error: Unterminated string constant` means that a text message was missing the second quotation mark (") that should have been there to indicate its end.

When errors like this occur, you'll need to determine what's wrong with the script before you can continue. The description of the message will often help you figure out what's wrong; you may have this sort of "syntax error," that is, there may be a missing keyword, quotation mark, or other typographical error, or the program might be attempting to work with invalid data.

Tip

To view and edit the script line that caused the error, open the script with Notepad. Turn line wrapping off by clicking Format and unchecking Word Wrap. (You just need to do this once; it will still be unchecked the next time you run Notepad.) Now, press Ctrl+G. Windows will pop up the Goto Line dialog. Type the line number reported by Windows Script Host (3, in the example you just saw), and press Enter. This will move the cursor right to the offending line.

Scripting and COM Objects

Although the programming languages that you can use with Windows Script Host are powerful programming tools by themselves, most of their usefulness comes from their ability to work with external software components called *Component Object Model (COM) objects*.

In the most general sense, objects are little program packages that manipulate and communicate information. They're a software representation of something tangible, such as a file, a folder, a network connection, an email message, or an Excel document. You interact with objects through their properties and methods. *Properties* are data values that describe the attributes of the thing the object represents. For example, a file or folder object might have a name property that represents the associated file or folder's name. *Methods* are actions—program subroutines—you can use to alter or manipulate whatever the object represents. For example, a file object might have a delete method that, if activated, would delete the associated file.

Most importantly, objects extend the abilities of the language from which they're used. Although VBScript doesn't know how to manage network printers, it does know how to let you use a COM object that *can* manage network printers.

Hundreds of different COM objects are available in Windows, representing things like network connections, files and folders, printers, user accounts, email messages, and Active Directory information. In addition, many application programs such as Word and Excel are totally accessible as COM objects themselves, so if you have Microsoft Office or another desktop suite installed, your scripts can create documents, spreadsheets, and charts.

In VBScript, the statement used to create an instance of a particular object is

```
set variable = CreateObject("objectname")
```

where *variable* is the name of the variable you want to use to refer to the object reference, and *objectname* is the type of object you want to create.

Once an object has been created, you refer to its properties and methods as `variable.name`, where `variable` is an object variable, and `name` is the name of a method or property. Let's look again at the sample script you created at the beginning of this section on scripting:

```
set wnet = CreateObject("WScript.Network")
uname = wnet.UserName
wscript.echo "Your user name is " & uname
```

The first line creates a `WScript.Network` object, and stores it in variable `wnet`. WScript.Network objects provide properties and methods for working with—you guessed it—Windows networking.

The second line sets a normal VBScript variable with the value of the object's `UserName` property, which is the name of the currently logged-on user.

The third line uses the built-in `WScript` object, an object that is automatically provided by Windows Script Host. Its `echo` method prints whatever text is provided on the program line into the console window or a dialog box (depending on whether the script is being run as a console program with `cscript` or a GUI program with `wscript`).

The point I want to make here is that VBScript itself doesn't know how to determine your username, but Windows comes with a component called the `WScript.Network` object that does. And, there are thousands of object types provided with Windows.

Some of the most important objects used for management scripting in Windows Script Host are listed in Table 9.16.

Table 9.16   Some Windows Management COM Objects

Object Name	Representations
`Scripting.FileSystemObject`	Drives, files, folders, text file contents
`WScript`	Command-line arguments, script input and output streams
`DOMDocument`	XML and HTML files
`WScript.Shell`	Windows desktop, special folders, the Registry, command-line programs
`WSHShortcut`	Desktop shortcuts
`WSHEnvironment`	Environment settings (current and default)
`WHSNetwork`	Network printer icons, network drive mappings, current computer name, and username
`CDO.Message`	Email message (outgoing) with optional attachments

Table 9.16   Continued

Object Name	Representations
SWbemServices	Windows Management Instrumentation (WMI); provides access to Services, device drivers, running tasks, network configuration, user accounts, and more than 100 other aspects of Windows configuration
IADs	Active Directory users, groups, containers, domains, computers, and all other AD objects

In addition, applications such as Microsoft Word and Excel provide objects such as Word.Document and Excel.Sheet. You can create and manipulate these objects as well; for instance, a script could easily create a telephone directory Word document by pulling information out of Active Directory.

Sample Scripts

Here are a few practical scripts that demonstrate the kinds of things you can accomplish with scripting in Windows. They range from information gathering to workflow management.

Listing Network Printer Connections

The following script, listprinters.vbs, lists the computer's printer mappings:

```
set wshNetwork = CreateObject("WScript.Network")

set maps = wshNetwork.EnumPrinterConnections
for i = 0 to maps.Length-2 step 2
    WScript.echo "Port:", maps.item(i), "  Name:", maps.item(i+1)
next
```

The output on my computer looks like this:

```
Port: USB002    Name: Samsung ML-1710 Series
Port: Microsoft Document Imaging Writer Port:   Name: Microsoft Office Document
    ➡ Image Writer
Port: HPLaserJet4V    Name: HP LaserJet 4V JetDirect
Port: SHRFAX:    Name: Fax
Port: C:\Documents and Settings\All Users.WINDOWS\Desktop\*.pdf    Name: Acrobat
    ➡ Distiller
```

Reading and Writing Registry Values

The following script, countme.vbs, shows how a script may read and write Registry values. This demonstration script just prints a running count of how many times it has been run.

```
set shell = CreateObject("WScript.Shell")

nruns = shell.RegRead("HKCU\Software\MyScripts\countme\number of runs")
nruns = nruns+1
wscript.echo "Number of runs:", nruns

Shell.RegWrite "HKCU\Software\MyScripts\countme\number of runs", nruns, "REG_DWORD"
```

If you create this script and type

```
countme
countme
countme
```

at the command prompt, you'll see the count increase by one each time. In addition, if you use regedit to view key HKEY_CURRENT_USER\Software\MyScripts\countme, you'll see that the program indeed saves a value in the Registry (click View, Refresh after running countme to see that the value changes).

Sending Email from a Shortcut

Finally, there is a long-ish but practical script meant for someone who regularly has to email files to a colleague as part of their day-to-day job. With this script, you can simply drag files on the Desktop and drop them onto a shortcut icon, and they'll be mailed without your having to do anything else.

The script takes any files named on its command line and sends them to a specific person as email attachments. To use this script, you would first edit it to use the correct email addresses, and you'll need to add the name of your organization's SMTP mail server (the server for outgoing mail). Then, create a shortcut to the script on your desktop.

When you drop files on a shortcut, Windows runs the associated program with the names of the dropped files as command-line arguments. In our case, the program is the following script. It uses the Collaboration Data Objects (CDO) tool provided with Windows 2000 and XP.

```
if WScript.arguments.count <= 0 then      ' no files were specified
    MsgBox "Usage: mailfiles filename..., or drag files onto shortcut"
    WScript.quit 0
end if

const cdoSendUsingPort = 2                ' standard CDO constants
const cdoAnonymous     = 0

sender    = "brian@mycompanyxyz.com"      ' sender of message
recipient = "sheila@mycompanyxyz.com"     ' recipient of this message
subject   = "Attached: sales lead form"

set msg  = CreateObject("CDO.Message")    ' create objects
set conf = CreateObject("CDO.Configuration")
set msg.configuration = conf

With msg                                  ' build the message
    .to      = recipient
    .from    = sender
    .subject = subject
    .textBody = "Attached to this message are files for you."

    nfiles = 0                            ' count of files attached
    for each arg in WScript.arguments     ' treat each argument as a
        .AddAttachment arg                ' file to be attached
        nfiles = nfiles+1
    next
End With

prefix = "http://schemas.microsoft.com/cdo/configuration/"
With conf.fields                          ' set delivery options
    .item(prefix & "sendusing")           = cdoSendUsingPort
    .item(prefix & "smtpserver")          = "mail.mycompanyxyz.com"
    .item(prefix & "smtpauthenticate")    = cdoAnonymous
.update                                   ' commit changes
End With
```

```
on error resume next        ' do not stop on errors
msg.send                    ' deliver the message
on error goto 0             ' restore normal error handling

if err then                 ' if something went wrong...
    MsgBox "Error sending message"
else
    if nfiles = 1 then plural = "" else plural = "s"
    MsgBox "Sent " & nfiles & " file" & plural & " to " & recipient
end if
```

Learning More About Scripting

Useful scripting is at first a complex undertaking, as you have to learn about programming *and* about Windows management scripting tools at the same time. It's far too much to cover in a single chapter of single book; I've just tried to give you a taste.

For more in-depth coverage of the command line, batch files, and scripting, check out Brian's book *Windows XP Under the Hood: Hardcore Scripting and Command Line Power*, published by Que, which is a tutorial as well as a handy desk reference.

For a detailed reference to all VBScript statements, functions, objects, and constants, see the online or downloaded version of the VBScript Language Reference, which you can get at msdn.microsoft.com/scripting.

Finally, I've found that some of the Microsoft public newsgroups can be a great source of information for everyone from beginners to old hands. The newgroups `microsoft.public.scripting.vbscript` and `microsoft.public.scripting.wsh` are particularly valuable. You can learn a lot by watching the discussions, and unlike most newsgroups I've tried, in these you have a reasonably good chance of getting a useful answer if you post a concise, realistic question. Although some of the conversation on these newsgroups concerns the use of VBScript in web server and web browser applications, most of the discussion is applicable to scripting as well.

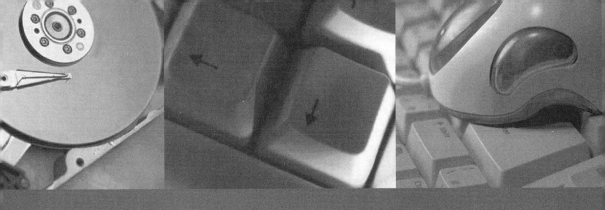

CHAPTER 10

Windows File Systems

The file system is the structure used by the OS to name, store, and organize files on the various storage devices that can be connected to a computer. The primary goal of a file system is to allow the efficient storage and retrieval of data in the form of files, to control access to those files, as well as to keep them safe and secure. Good file systems store not only the file itself, but also *metadata* for the file. Metadata literally translates as "data about data," and is used by the file system to help categorize, organize, control, manipulate, secure, and protect the files. Simple examples of file metadata include the date and timestamp that a file was created, file attributes, pointers to the location of the file on the media, and more. More sophisticated file systems such as NTFS store additional metadata, giving greater control and integrity to the files. This chapter covers the various file systems and related structures that are used by Windows to manage drives, volumes, directories (folders), and files.

Disks, Partitions and Volumes

In order to understand the structures and concepts in this chapter, some basic terminology must be defined and understood.

The file system is part of a hierarchical storage system, which means that the system has successive nested levels or layers. Physically it begins with a disk drive, such as a hard disk. A physical hard disk drive is divided into one or more *partitions*, which are physical areas of the disk. Windows normally uses two types of partitions, called *primary* and *extended*. Primary partitions are assigned drive letters directly by the operating system and are also called *volumes*, and volumes are also called *logical drives*. Think of the partition as the raw physical space on the disk used by the volume, and think of a volume as the space after it is formatted with a file system, after which it appears to the OS as a drive letter. Extended partitions can contain one or more logical drives or volumes. Each volume must be *formatted* before it can be used, a process which writes the file system to the volume. The file system then manages the directories (also called folders) and files stored on the volume.

Basic Disks and Volumes

A disk set up with the standard system of using primary and extended partitions is referred to as a *basic disk*, and the volumes on a basic disk are also called *basic volumes*. Basic disks and volumes are accessible by virtually all operating systems, and represent the default setup used on most drives.

Basic disks can have up to four primary partitions, or up to three primary and one extended partitions. Each primary partition is a basic volume, and the extended partition can contain an unlimited number of logical drives, which are also basic volumes. Each basic volume must use contiguous physical space on the disk, and can only be extended in size if there is unallocated (non-partitioned) space immediately following the end of the volume. Aftermarket utilities can be used to extend a volume if there is available space before the volume as well.

Dynamic Disks and Volumes

Windows 2000 and later versions can create and use a special partitioning scheme called a *dynamic disk*, which contains *dynamic volumes*. Dynamic disks use a special hidden database in the last megabyte of the disk to manage information about the dynamic volumes on the disk, as well as any other dynamic volumes on other dynamic disks in the system. Once a new dynamic disk is created or imported into a system, the hidden database for the new disk is added to the database on all dynamic disks in the system. Because each dynamic disk contains the same database, if the database on one is corrupted Windows can rebuild it from the database on any of the other dynamic disks.

Dynamic volumes support several features not possible with basic volumes, such as:

- A dynamic volume can be extended to include non-contiguous unallocated space on a single drive.

- A dynamic volume can be extended to span multiple (up to 32) drives.
- A dynamic volume can be striped (written distributively across multiple drives) for greater performance.

Windows 2000 and later Server editions also support these additional features:

- A dynamic volume can be mirrored (identical data written to two drives) for fault tolerance.
- A dynamic volume can be RAID-5, which divides the volume among three or more physical drives and stripes data and error correcting (parity) information for performance and fault tolerance.

There are unfortunately many limitations to the use of dynamic disks and volumes:

- Dynamic disks and volumes are only supported by Windows 2000 and later versions.
- All volumes on a physical disk must be either basic or dynamic.
- Spanned dynamic volumes cannot be striped.
- Striped dynamic volumes cannot be extended or spanned.
- Removable media disks (Floppy, Optical, SuperDisk, Jazz, Zip) cannot be dynamic.
- USB or FireWire disks cannot be dynamic.
- Portable (that is, laptop) systems do not support dynamic disks, even on internal drives.
- Mirrored or RAID-5 dynamic volumes are supported only by Windows 2000 or later Server Editions.

Because of the features, differences, and limitations of working with dynamic disks and volumes, they are mostly suited for server systems and not standard desktop or laptop PCs. As such, all further discussion of disks and volumes in this chapter will be about standard basic disks and volumes.

Creating Partitions

Partitioning a hard disk is the act of defining areas of the physical disk for an operating system to use as a logical volume. A volume is a formatted area of storage that has a drive letter assigned to it.

When you partition a disk for the first time, the partitioning software writes a master partition boot sector at Cylinder 0, Head 0, Sector 1—the first sector on the hard disk. This sector contains data that describes the partitions by their starting and ending cylinder, head, and sector locations. When a system starts up, the motherboard ROM BIOS reads the partition table to determine which of the primary partitions is *active* (bootable) and, therefore, where to look for an operating system to load.

The standard disk partitioning tools provided in Windows vary according to the Windows version. Windows 9x/Me and earlier include the FDISK program, while Windows NT/2000/XP and later include both the DISKPART program and the much easier to use Disk Management tool (called Disk Administrator in Windows NT). The FDISK program is a text-based menu-driven utility that is run from a command prompt, while DISKPART is a text-based command-line utility (not menu-driven), and Disk Management is a tool that runs under the Windows graphical user interface (GUI) environment. In most cases you would use FDISK if partitioning under Windows 9x/Me or earlier, or the Disk Management tool if partitioning under Windows NT/2000/XP or later. The command-driven DISKPART utility is somewhat difficult to use interactively, because it is entirely command driven; however, it is very useful if you want to write scripts that automate its operation.

No matter which tool you use, the primary and extended partitions are created at the same, and as such are compatible across OS boundaries. For example, I can use the Disk Management tool in

Windows XP to partition a drive that will later be installed in a system running Windows 98. Likewise, I can use the FDISK tool from Windows 98 to partition a drive that will later be installed on a system running XP.

The partitioning rules for a single drive are as follows:

- There can be up to four total partitions on a drive.
- There are two main types of partitions, primary and extended.
- There can be only one extended partition on a drive.
- A primary partition is a single volume (drive letter).
- An extended partition is not a volume, but instead may contain one or more logical drives, each of which is a volume (drive letter).
- Only primary partitions can be marked *active* (bootable).
- Only one primary partition on a drive can be *active* at any given time.

If you combine these rules, you see that a single drive can have up to four primary partitions (with no extended partition), or up to three primary partitions along with a single extended partition. It is also possible to create only an extended partition containing one or more logical drives, but since only primary partitions can be bootable, that would not be suitable for a hard disk on which you want to load a bootable OS.

The limit of four partitions per drive dates all the way back to March 1983, when IBM and Microsoft released DOS 2.0 along with a ROM BIOS designed to boot from a hard disk. Together the updated BIOS and DOS defined the structure of the Master Boot Record (MBR), which contained a partition table with entries for up to four partitions. Originally this limited a single drive to supporting up to only four volumes (drive letters), but in 1987, IBM and Microsoft released DOS 3.3 which first included the extended partition with logical drives. Think of the logical drives as sub-partitions inside a single extended partition, thus allowing a single drive to be divided into more than four volumes. Using an extended partition, the number of total volumes on a drive is technically limited only by the size of the drive, but the OS can only handle up to a total of 24 drive letters (C: through Z:) at a time. In addition to the standard partitioning tools, the Windows SETUP program in Windows 95 and later can also partition (and format) drives during the start of the Windows installation process. In other words, you don't have to partition and format volumes in advance; if the drive is blank, you will be prompted at the start of the Windows installation process to partition and format the drive.

Note

Because FDISK, DISKPART, SETUP, and the Disk Management tool all depend on the BIOS Setup information about the hard disk to determine the size and drive geometry of the hard disk, having correct drive settings saved in the BIOS Setup is vital to the correct operation of these programs. If a 100GB hard drive is defined in the BIOS as a 100MB hard drive, for example, all these programs will see is 100MB. Fortunately most BIOS Setup programs feature auto-detect capabilities that automatically identify drives properly. However, problems can arise if somebody uses manual settings and enters them incorrectly.

Don't get hung up on the fact that FDISK calls partitions primary or extended "DOS" partitions or logical "DOS" drives. This is true even though the operating system you are running or installing is a version of Windows. Primary partitions, extended partitions, and logical drives are essentially the same no matter what tool you use or OS you are running.

However, it is also true that older versions of Windows may be limited in the size of partitions that are supported as well as the different types of file systems supported on those partitions. For example, the original release of Windows 95 and all MS-DOS versions 6.x and earlier support only the FAT16 file system, which allows a single volume size of no more than 2GiB. Thus, a 20GiB hard disk prepared with the original Windows 95 (called 95a) or MS-DOS 6.x and earlier must have a minimum of 10 volumes (drive letters) to allocate all of the space on the drive. Fortunately Windows 95B and later versions support single volumes of up to 2TiB or more, which is larger than any currently available drive, meaning that separating a single drive into multiple partitions is more of an option or personal preference instead of a necessity.

Even though you can partition and format even the largest drives as a single volume today, many people prefer to divide their drives into multiple volumes for organizational or data security reasons. For example, many people suggest a two-volume partitioning scheme that looks like this:

C: for the operating system and applications

D: for user data only

In this example, you could create two primary partitions or a primary partition along with an extended partition containing a single logical drive.

This two-volume arrangement makes backing up the data easier; just set the backup program to back up all of D:.

If a catastrophic failure in the file system wipes out or corrupts the C: volume, drive D:—which contains the data—may still be intact. Note however that multiple volumes like this will not protect against hardware failures. Because both volumes are on the same physical drive, if the drive fails, files on both volumes will be lost.

Note

Although external USB and FireWire (IEEE 1394) drives normally come pre-partitioned and formatted as a single FAT32 volume to allow immediate use on the widest variety of systems, you can use FDISK, DISKPART, or the Disk Management tool to delete and re-create the partitioning and file systems used on external drives to suit your specific needs.

Assigning Drive Letters to Volumes

When assigning drive letters to volumes, Windows normally assigns drive letters to primary partitions before assigning drive letters to logical drives in extended partitions. Because of this, using extended partitions with logical drives can often result in confusion over drive letter assignments.

As an example, let's say we have a system with a single 75GiB primary master ATA drive (physical disk 0) that we want to partition into three equal-sized (25GiB) volumes, with the first one bootable. This can be done several different ways. One method would be to simply create three 25GiB primary partitions, with the first one set active (bootable). Another would be to create a single 25GiB primary partition (set active) along with a 50GiB extended partition, and then further divide the extended partition into two 25GiB logical drives. Using three primary partitions, Windows would assign default drive letters as in Table 10.1:

Table 10.1   Drive Letter Allocations by Drive, Partition Order, and Type

Physical Disk	Partition Order	Partition Type	Drive Letter
0	1st	Primary (active)	C:
0	2nd	Primary	D:
0	3rd	Primary	E:

Using one primary partition plus an extended partition with two logical drives, Windows would assign default drive letters as in Table 10.2:

Table 10.2   Drive Letter Allocations by Drive, Partition Order, and Type

Physical Disk	Partition Order	Partition Type	Drive Letter
0	1st	Primary (active)	C:
0	2nd	Extended/1st Logical Drive	D:
0	2nd	Extended/2nd Logical Drive	E:

So far these different partitioning methods produce pretty much the same results as far as drive letters being assigned to physical parts of the disk. However if we add another drive to the system, the default drive letter assignments for volumes on the new drive will vary. As an example. let's add a second physical drive to the system (ATA Primary Slave, physical disk 1) and create a single primary partition on it. What drive letter will the new partition on the new drive assume? That depends on how your first drive was partitioned. If disk 0 was partitioned using three primary partitions, the default drive letter assignments would be as in Table 10.3:

Table 10.3   Drive Letter Allocations by Drive, Partition Order, and Type

Physical Disk	Partition Order	Partition Type	Drive Letter
0	1st	Primary (active)	C:
0	2nd	Primary	D:
0	3rd	Primary	E:
1	1st	Primary	F:

That seems perfectly normal; the partition on the new drive is assigned the next available letter F:. However if disk 0 had been partitioned using a primary partition plus an extended partition with logical drives, the default drive letter assignments would be as in Table 10.4:

Table 10.4   Drive Letter Allocations by Drive, Partition Order, and Type

Physical Disk	Partition Order	Partition Type	Drive Letter
0	1st	Primary (active)	C:
0	2nd	Extended/1st Logical Drive	E:
0	2nd	Extended/2nd Logical Drive	F:
1	1st	Primary	D:

This can be really confusing, as the primary partition on the new drive would be assigned as D:, and the existing logical drives in the extended partition on the first drive would change from D: to E: and from E: to F:. This will not only confuse the user, but it can also confuse any previously installed applications as well. Fortunately Windows NT/2000/XP and later can easily change drive letter assignments for all except the boot volume using the Disk Management tool, but unfortunately such drive letter changes are not possible for Windows 9x/Me or earlier. If the second drive also has an extended partition with logical drives, it can get even more confusing, as shown in Table 10.5:

Table 10.5   Drive Letter Allocations by Drive, Partition Order, and Type

Physical Disk	Partition Order	Partition Type	Drive Letter
0	1st	Primary (active)	C:
0	2nd	Extended/1st Logical Drive	E:
0	2nd	Extended/2nd Logical Drive	F:
1	1st	Primary	D:
1	2nd	Extended/1st Logical Drive	G:
1	2nd	Extended/2nd Logical Drive	H:

The basic rule is that all primary partitions on any internal (ATA, SATA, or SCSI) drives are assigned letters before any logical drives in extended partitions on those same drives. To keep things simple as far as future drive assignments no matter what version of Windows you are using, I recommend creating only primary partitions on all drives, which will limit you to a maximum of four volumes per drive.

If you set up both drives using only primary partitions, the default drive assignments would be as shown in Table 10.6:

Table 10.6   Drive Letter Allocations by Drive, Partition Order, and Type

Physical Disk	Partition Order	Partition Type	Drive Letter
0	1st	Primary (active)	C:
0	2nd	Primary	D:
0	3rd	Primary	E:
1	1st	Primary	F:
1	2nd	Primary	G:
1	3rd	Primary	H:

This is obviously much simpler and more straightforward, and would be the recommended setup if you were using Windows NT/2000/XP or later. Unfortunately due to an artificially imposed limitation, such a setup is not possible with the FDISK program included with Windows 9x/Me or earlier.

Another alternative that is possible using the standard FDISK program is to create a single extended partition only on all drives except the first drive, and then divide the partition into one or more logical drives. For example, let's take the second physical drive (physical disk 1) in the previous example and set it up as a single extended partition with three logical drives. In that case, the drive letters for the new volumes would always be F:, G:, and H:, as shown in Table 10.7.

Table 10.7   Drive Letter Allocations by Drive, Partition Order, and Type

Physical Disk	Partition Order	Partition Type	Drive Letter
0	1st	Primary (active)	C:
0	2nd	Extended/1st Logical Drive	D:
0	2nd	Extended/2nd Logical Drive	E:
1	1st	Extended/1st Logical Drive	F:
1	1st	Extended/2nd Logical Drive	G:
1	1st	Extended/3rd Logical Drive	H:

This would be true no matter whether the first drive was partitioned as three primary partitions or as a single primary and an extended with two logical drives. Also, in either case, the drive letter assignments would remain the same both before and after the second drive was added.

My personal preference is to keep things as simple as possible by avoiding extended partitions entirely, and instead create only primary partitions on all drives. This does limit the total number of volumes on a single drive to four or less, but I would rarely need to divide a single drive into five or more volumes anyway. The only problem with this recommendation is that if you are using Windows 9x/Me or earlier, the standard FDISK program included with those operating systems is artificially limited to create only a single primary partition on a drive. This means that if you want to divide a drive into two or more volumes, you are forced to use an extended partition with one or more logical drives. Fortunately this limitation is only in the FDISK program, and not in the actual operating systems. Windows 9x/Me and even DOS will support up to four primary partitions on a single drive, if you use a utility program other than the standard FDISK to create them.

Because the DISKPART utility or Disk Management tool included with Windows NT/2000/XP or later is not limited to creating only one primary partition per drive, you could temporarily boot those OSs from a CD or a set of startup floppies in order to use DISKPART to partition a drive, or you could temporarily connect a drive to a system currently running Windows NT/2000/XP or later in order to partition it. But probably the easiest solution would be to simply use a third-party partitioning program to partition the drive as you like. One program I recommend as a replacement for FDISK is the "Free FDISK" program (the official FDISK of FreeDOS), which is available from www.23cc.com/free-fdisk. Free FDISK can be copied to a Windows 9x/Me startup floppy in place of the standard FDISK program and will allow you to create up to four primary partitions on a single drive with no artificial limitations.

Running FDISK

If you run the Windows 95B (Win95 OSR 2.x) or later (Windows 9x/Me) version of FDISK with a hard drive greater than 512MB, FDISK offers to enable large disk support by prompting you with the following question:

```
Your computer has a disk larger than 512MB. This version of Windows
includes improved support for large disks, resulting in more efficient
use of disk space on large drives, and allowing disks over 2GB to be
formatted as a single drive.

IMPORTANT: If you enable large disk support and create any new drives on this
disk, you will not be able to access the new drive(s) using other operating
systems, including some versions of Windows 95 and Windows NT, as well as
earlier versions of Windows and MS-DOS. In addition, disk utilities that
were not designed explicitly for the FAT32 file system will not be able
```

to work with this disk. If you need to access this disk with other operating
systems or older disk utilities, do not enable large drive support.

Do you wish to enable large disk support (Y/N)..........? [Y]

If you answer *Yes* to this question, FDISK creates FAT32 volumes for all volumes larger than 512MB.
Answering *No* to this question forces FDISK to create only FAT16 volumes. Choosing to enable large
disk (meaning FAT32) support provides several benefits:

- *You can use a large hard disk (greater than 2GiB) as a single drive letter.* In fact, your drive can be as
  large as 2TiB and still be identified by a single drive letter. This is because of the FAT32 file system, which allows for many more files per drive than FAT16.

- *Because of the more efficient storage methods of FAT32, your files will use less hard disk space overall.*

However, keep in mind that FAT32 volumes will only be recognized by operating systems with FAT32
support (Windows 95B or later, but not including Windows NT). If booting old MS-DOS games or
applications via an MS-DOS 6.x or earlier startup floppy or CD, you won't be able to access a FAT32
hard disk volume unless you replace the MS-DOS 6.x or earlier version on the disk with the MS-DOS 7
or later versions included with Windows 95B or 98. This normally can be done by using the SYS A:
command from the \Windows\Command folder. Another option is to use the Windows Startup menu in
Win95B or Win98 (press F8 as Windows starts to load) and select Command Prompt to get to a
FAT32-capable DOS. On the other hand, you can select Start, Shutdown, Restart the Computer in MS-
DOS Mode from the Windows desktop.

After answering the large disk support question, FDISK shows a menu similar to the following:

```
Current fixed disk drive: 1

    Choose one of the following:

    1. Create DOS partition or Logical DOS Drive
    2. Set active partition
    3. Delete partition or Logical DOS Drive
    4. Display partition information
    5. Change current fixed disk drive

    Enter choice: [1]
```

Option 5 is shown only if FDISK detects more than one drive on your system (if more than one is
entered via your BIOS Setup). In that case, FDISK defaults to the first drive, and via option 5 you can
cause FDISK to work with any of the other hard disks on the system.

To create partitions or logical drives in extended partitions, select option 1. You can use option 4 to
display the current partition layout of the drive.

After selecting option 1, the menu changes to enable you to create primary or extended partitions on
a drive as follows:

```
Create DOS Partition or Logical DOS Drive

    Current fixed disk drive: 1

    Choose one of the following:

    1. Create Primary DOS Partition
    2. Create Extended DOS Partition
    3. Create Logical DOS Drive(s) in the Extended DOS Partition

    Enter choice: [1]
```

FDISK forces you to create a primary partition first on the boot drive, but on a secondary or nonboot drive, you can create only an extended partition if you choose. So, if you are partitioning the first drive in a system and it will be bootable, you would choose option 1.

At this point, you are prompted to decide whether you want to use the maximum available size for a primary DOS partition. If you say yes and you've enabled large disk support (FAT32) then the primary partition will use the entire drive. Conversely, if you say yes and you did not enable large drive support (meaning you are using FAT16), the partition uses the entire drive or up to 2GiB of the drive, whichever is smaller.

Normally, I recommend making the primary partition the full size of the drive, keeping all of the drive as one letter. But there are various reasons you might want to split the drive into multiple partitions, such as for different operating systems, different file systems, applications, and so on.

However, if you decide to create a primary partition that is not the full drive, once that is done, you should then go back through the menus and create an extended partition using the rest of the drive, and then further divide it into logical drives. Or better yet, if you are using the *Free FDISK* program I mentioned earlier, you do not have to create an extended partition with logical drives, and instead you can simply create additional primary partitions to use the remaining space, up to a total of four per drive.

After all the partitions are created, the final operation is to make one of them active (bootable), which is option 2 from the main FDISK menu. Only primary partitions can be active. After that is done, all FDISK operations are complete, and you can exit the program.

When exiting FDISK after making partition changes, the system must be rebooted before these changes will be recognized. After rebooting, you must then format each of the volumes with the operating system FORMAT command, which creates the file system that allows the operating system to mange files on the volumes.

The C: volume usually must be formatted with the system files, although when you install Windows via the Windows Setup command, it detects whether the system files are present or not, and if not will install them for you.

Drive Partitioning and Formatting with Disk Management

Even though Windows 2000/XP and later have a very powerful command-line tool called DISKPART that can be used to partition and provides some FDISK-like capabilities, along with additional options useful for working with advanced disk structures such as RAID arrays and dynamic disks, most people should utilize the GUI-based Disk Management tool to perform hard disk partitioning and formatting when installing a new hard disk on an existing system.

Unfortunately DISKPART is a command-line program that is not really designed to be used interactively. It is definitely not a user-oriented tool, and has very little in the way of safety precautions to prevent one from setting up a disk improperly, or from destroying existing data on a disk. As such, it is highly recommended under Windows NT/2000/XP or later to use the Disk Management (also called Disk Administrator) tool instead.

Note

Note that DISKPART.exe is automatically installed in Windows XP and later as part of the base OS installation. It is not automatically installed with Windows 2000; however, DISKPART is included in the Windows 2000 Windows Recovery Console, which is on the Windows 2000 install CD. The Windows 2000 Recovery Console can also be installed to the hard drive if desired using the information in the following article:

"Description of the Windows 2000 Recovery Console"

http://support.microsoft.com/kb/229716

But perhaps the easiest way to get DISKPART for Windows 2000 is to simply download it for free from Microsoft at

http://www.microsoft.com/windows2000/techinfo/reskit/tools/new/diskpart-o.asp

---

The following list shows the major differences between FDISK and the Disk Management tool:

- *Disk Management is a true GUI-based utility.* Color-coded indicators for partition type and drive condition let you easily see which tasks you've performed with a drive. Wizards enable you to both partition and format a drive under the guidance of the tool.

- *Disk Management supports more file systems than FDISK.* Whereas FDISK is limited to FAT16 or FAT32, Disk Management also supports NTFS.

- *Disk Management partitions and formats hard disks with a simple process.* Unlike FDISK, which requires you to restart the system before a new volume can be formatted and uses a separate FORMAT program to finish the job, Disk Management can perform both tasks without the need to restart the computer.

- *Disk Management uses drive letters not already in use for hard disk or optical drives, regardless of the partition type.* Unlike FDISK, which can scramble existing drive letter assignments if you prepare a new hard disk with a primary partition, Disk Management assigns a drive letter(s) to the new hard drive that follows those already in use. And, if installing a new drive causes conflicts with removable-media drives such as USB keychain or flash memory card readers you use occasionally, you can use Disk Management to select a different drive letter for the new hard disk or for existing hard disks or optical drives.

To use Disk Management to partition a new hard disk

1. Open the Start menu, right-click My Computer, and select Manage from the context menu.

2. From the Computer Management screen, click Disk Management in the left window. The current hard disk drive letter is displayed in the upper-right window, and physical hard disks are displayed in the bottom-right window (see Figure 10.1). A newly installed drive is shown as unallocated space.

3. Select the new hard disk, right-click it, and select New Partition from the right-click menu to start the partitioning process.

4. Click Next at the opening screen of the New Partition Wizard.

5. Select Primary or Extended partition. Generally, you should choose an extended partition unless you want to create a primary partition that you can use to start the computer. Click Next to continue.

6. If you want to leave part of the hard disk unallocated, change the partition size. Otherwise, click Next to continue.

7. The New Partition Wizard displays the changes it's about to make to the new drive (see Figure 10.2). Click Finish to complete the partitioning process.

8. After the wizard finishes, the Computer Management view displays the newly partitioned hard disk as free space. Right-click the partition, and select New Logical Drive to continue.

9. Click Next to continue with the wizard. Click Next again to select a logical drive.

10. To create more than one logical drive, change the maximum size of the partition size. To create a single logical drive, click Next.

Primary partition
on Disk 0 (system)

Logical drive inside
an extended
partition on Disk 0

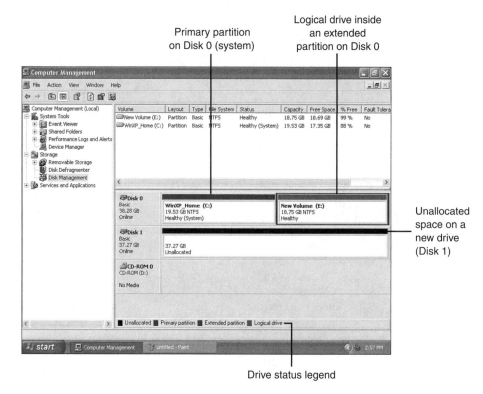

Unallocated
space on a
new drive
(Disk 1)

Drive status legend

Figure 10.1 The Computer Management view of a system with a newly installed hard disk (Disk 1). Because New Volume (E:) was prepared after the CD-ROM drive (D:) was installed, it has a higher drive letter.

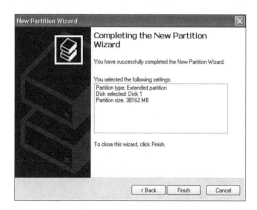

Figure 10.2 The New Partition Wizard prepares to create an extended partition from Disk 1.

11. Select the drive letter to assign. By default, the next available drive letter is displayed, but you can choose any unused drive letter. If you prefer, you can mount the new logical drive into an empty NTFS folder, or even not assign a drive letter or path. Click Next to continue.

12. Select the format options. By default, the new logical drive is formatted with NTFS, but you can choose FAT32 if the logical drive is 34.36GB (32GiB) or less. If the logical drive is larger than 32GiB, Windows can only format the drive using NTFS. You can also specify the volume label, select a particular allocation unit (cluster) size, enable file/folder compression, and perform a quick format. If you want to format the drive later, select Do Not Format This Partition. Click Next to continue.

13. Again, the New Partition Wizard displays a list of changes to be made. Click Back to return to a particular menu if you need to make any changes, or click Finish to format the logical drive with the options selected (see Figure 10.3).

14. Repeat steps 10–14 if you didn't use all the free space as a logical drive and want to prepare additional logical drives.

No rebooting is necessary, and the color-coded legend at the bottom of the Disk Management display helps you track the status of the disk preparation process.

Figure 10.3 The New Partition Wizard prepares to format a logical drive on Disk 1 with the options shown.

Drive Partitioning with Aftermarket Utilities

Often there are excellent free programs that are available to get around the limitations in the existing standard utilities. For example, previously in this chapter I recommended the *Free FDISK* program available from www.23cc.com/free-fdisk, because it can create multiple primary partitions on a single drive. This is useful because the standard FDISK is limited to creating only a single primary partition, forcing the use of an extended partition with logical drives in order to create multiple volumes on a single physical drive.

One might think that the Disk Management tool included with Windows NT/2000/XP and later would be free from artificial limitations, but unfortunately that is not the case. One major limitation with Disk Management is the artificially imposed inability to format a FAT32 volume larger than 32GiB. For example, if you have a 100GiB external USB drive that you would like to share between systems running Windows 9x/Me and/or Apple Macintosh systems as well as systems running Windows 2000/XP or later, using FAT32 would allow the drive to be both read and written by *all* of those systems. Unfortunately the Disk Management tool (as well as DISKPART and FORMAT) will only allow you to format a volume larger than 32GiB as NTFS, which will render it unreadable by most systems except those running Windows NT/2000/XP or later. One solution would be to connect the drive to a Windows 9x/Me system where you could use the standard FDISK and FORMAT programs there to format the entire drive (up to 2TiB) as FAT32. However if you don't have access to such a system, or don't want to try to create a bootable floppy or CD with USB support, then I recommend using the free *SwissKnife* utility, which can be downloaded from CompuApps at www.compuapps.com. The SwissKnife utility is a graphical program that runs under all versions of Windows 95B and higher, and for example will allow you to partition and format a FAT32 volume more than 32GiB on Windows NT/2000/XP or later as well.

These free tools are useful for creating new partitions and volumes that the standard utilities cannot; however, there are even more powerful tools available commercially that can modify existing partitions. Alternative partitioning programs such as PartitionMagic by Symantec and Partition Commander by V-Com enable you to take an existing hard drive and perform the following changes to it without loss of data:

- Create, resize, split, move, and merge partitions on the fly without losing data.
- Convert between file systems without losing data—conversions include FAT16 to FAT32 and NTFS; FAT32 to FAT16; NTFS to FAT16 and FAT32; primary to logical and vice versa; and FAT32 to NTFS under Windows 2000 and XP. It also includes support for Ext2 and Linux SWAP file systems.
- Move applications between partitions and automatically update the drive-letter references after partitioning with the DriveMapper utility.
- Undelete FAT16, FAT32, Linux Ext2, and NTFS partitions that have been deleted. You can restore partitions that have been deleted on disk as long as the space has not been reallocated or written over.
- Copy or move a partition to another partition or drive.

Note

I still recommend standard utilities such as FDISK, DISKPART, Disk Management, or Windows SETUP be used for initial partitioning and setup of most drives (these utilities destroy existing data), but these aftermarket utilities can be very useful for reconfiguring a system that is already partitioned.

Although the program recommends a full backup before starting, I've used these utilities many times to turn a single "big drive" into two or more drive letters in less than 10 minutes. Performing the same task with backup software and FDISK/FORMAT can take several hours because you must back up your existing drive, remove existing partitions with FDISK, create new partitions with FDISK, restart your computer, format the new drives, and reload your operating system and your backup.

High-level (Operating System) Formatting

As you learned in the previous section, Windows 2000 and Windows XP can automatically perform high-level formatting with the New Partition Wizard as part of the Disk Management tool. When using FDISK or DISKPART, a separate FORMAT utility must be used to format the volume once it is partitioned. The operating system format is called a *high-level format* to distinguish it from physical or *low-level format* that is sometimes used to initialize drives before they are partitioned. The primary function of the high-level format is to create the NTFS or FAT file system structures on the disk so the operating system can manage files. You must first partition a drive using FDISK, DISKPART, or Disk Management (or some third-party utility) before formatting a drive. Each volume (primary partition or logical drive in an extended partition) must be formatted before it can be used for data storage.

Usually, you perform the high-level format with the FORMAT.COM program or the formatting utility in Windows Explorer. FORMAT.COM uses the following syntax and optional parameters under Windows 2000/XP:

```
FORMAT volume [/FS:file-system] [/V:label] [/Q] [/A:size] [/C] [/X]
FORMAT volume [/V:label] [/Q] [/F:size]
FORMAT volume [/V:label] [/Q] [/T:tracks /N:sectors]
FORMAT volume [/V:label] [/Q]
FORMAT volume [/Q]
```

volume	Specifies the drive letter (followed by a colon), mount point, or volume name.
/FS:filesystem	Specifies the type of the file system (FAT, FAT32, or NTFS).
/V:label	Specifies the volume label.
/Q	Performs a quick format.
/C	NTFS only: Files created on the new volume will be compressed by default.
/X	Forces the volume to dismount first if necessary. All opened handles to the volume would no longer be valid.
/A:size	Overrides the default allocation unit size. Default settings are strongly recommended for general use. NTFS supports 512, 1024, 2048, 4096, 8192, 16K, 32K, 64K. FAT supports 512, 1024, 2048, 4096, 8192, 16K, 32K, 64K, (128K, 256K for sector size > 512 bytes). FAT32 supports 512, 1024, 2048, 4096, 8192, 16K, 32K, 64K, (128K, 256K for sector size > 512 bytes). Note that the FAT and FAT32 files systems impose the following restrictions on the number of clusters on a volume: FAT: Number of clusters <= 65526 FAT32: 65526 < Number of clusters < 4177918 Format will immediately stop processing if it decides that the above requirements cannot be met using the specified cluster size. NTFS compression is not supported for allocation unit sizes above 4096.
/F:size	Specifies the size of the floppy disk to format (1.44)
/T:tracks	Specifies the number of tracks per disk side.
/N:sectors	Specifies the number of sectors per track.

FORMAT.COM uses the following syntax with somewhat different optional parameters under Windows 9x/Me:

```
FORMAT drive: [/V[:label]] [/Q] [/F:size] [/B | /S] [/C]
FORMAT drive: [/V[:label]] [/Q] [/T:tracks /N:sectors] [/B | /S] [/C]
FORMAT drive: [/V[:label]] [/Q] [/1] [/4] [/B | /S] [/C]
FORMAT drive: [/Q] [/1] [/4] [/8] [/B | /S] [/C]
```

/V[:label]	Specifies the volume label.
/Q	Performs a quick format.
/F:size	Specifies the size of the floppy disk to format (such as 160, 180, 320, 360, 720, 1.2, 1.44, 2.88).

```
/B              Allocates space on the formatted disk for system files.
/S              Copies system files to the formatted disk.
/T:tracks       Specifies the number of tracks per disk side.
/N:sectors      Specifies the number of sectors per track.
/1              Formats a single side of a floppy disk.
/4              Formats a 5.25-inch 360K floppy disk in a high-density drive.
/8              Formats eight sectors per track.
/C              Tests clusters that are currently marked "bad."
```

Normally, the Windows FORMAT utility determines the cluster size used when you format the volume, based on the volume's size and the file system used. However, you can override the default using the /A:size parameter in the Windows NT/2000/XP FORMAT command, or a similar but undocumented switch /Z:size for the Windows 9x/Me FORMAT utility. Using the /A:size or /Z:size parameters, you can format the volume with cluster sizes that are larger or smaller than the defaults for the file system.

Caution

In general it is not recommended to override the default cluster sizes using the /A:size or /Z:size switches. Modifying the cluster size can increase or decrease the amount of slack on the partition, but it also can have a pronounced effect on the performance of the drive, and some disk utilities might not work with nonstandard cluster sizes.

Once a volume is formatted, the operating system can use the volume for storing and retrieving files.

During the high-level format, the program performs a defect scan. Defects marked by the drive manufacturer or low-level format (LLF) program as well as any newly unreadable sectors will show up during this scan as being unreadable tracks or sectors. When the high-level format encounters one of these areas, it automatically performs up to five retries to read these tracks or sectors. If the unreadable area was actually marked as such by the LLF, the read fails on all attempts.

After five retries, the FORMAT program gives up on this track or sector and moves to the next one. If an area remains unreadable after the initial read and five retries, it is marked in the FAT or MFT as a bad cluster.

Note

Because the high-level format doesn't overwrite data areas not actually used by the file system, in some cases it is possible to use programs such as Norton Utilities to unformat a hard disk that was accidentally formatted. Unformatting can be performed in some cases because the data from the drive's previous use might still be present.

File System Tool Limitations

The biggest problem with removing or creating a partition using the standard tools such as FDISK, DISKPART, or Disk Management is that the procedure is destructive. If you create a set of partitions but then change your mind about the disk structure, in almost all cases you must back up any data on those partitions, delete the partitions, and start over again. The standard tools have virtually no ability to move or change an existing partition while preserving data. That alone is cause for using these tools with care, but here are other limitations you should keep in mind:

- FDISK and DISKPART require FORMAT before the volume is ready for use.
- FORMAT must normally check an entire volume for defects before writing the file system. Its defect management is rudimentary and can waste a lot of disk space with older drives that have disk errors.

- FDISK, DISKPART, and Disk Management offer no standard procedure for migrating data to a new drive.

- FDISK forces the use of extended partitions with logical drives when multiple volumes are desired, often causing confusion with drive letter assignments.

Although Disk Management in Windows NT/2000/XP and later does a better job than FDISK, it's still a destructive process if you need to change your disk partitions, and there is no provision for migrating data.

For these reasons, many drive vendors offer some type of automatic disk installation software with their hard drives. These routines can make the task of disk installation and migration a fast, easy, and reliable operation.

Typical features of automatic disk installation programs include the following:

- *Replacement for FDISK/DISKPART and FORMAT.* A single program performs both functions more quickly than FDISK/DISKPART and FORMAT separately.

- *Database of drive jumpers for major brands and models.*

- *Drive copy function.* Copies contents of an old drive to the new drive, retaining full OS and file system functionality.

- *CD-ROM drive letter relocation utility.* Moves existing CD/DVD drives to new drive letters (in order to make room for new hard drive letters) and resets the Windows Registry and INI file references to the new drive letters so software works without reinstallation.

- *Menu-driven or wizard-driven process for installing a new hard drive.*

- *Optional override of existing BIOS limitations for installation of large hard drives (>528MB, 8.4GB, 137GB, and so on).*

Table 10.8 provides a basic overview of the most popular disk-installation programs. Most of these are only available in OEM versions that are included for free with drives sold retail. In some cases, the OEM versions can be downloaded from the drive manufacturer's website as well.

Table 10.8 Overview of Automatic Disk-Installation Programs

Vendor	Software	OEM	Retail
Ontrack	Disk Manager	Yes	Yes
Phoenix	DriveGuide	Yes	No
Western Digital	Data Lifeguard	Yes	No
Seagate	DiscWizard	Yes	No
Maxtor	MaxBlast	Yes	No

Note that while many of these utilities can override BIOS limitations on older systems, normally I recommend upgrading the motherboard BIOS instead to overcome such limitations.

Drive Capacity Limitations

There have been two main barriers in Windows maximum drive capacities, 8.4GB and 137GB. Using a drive larger than 8.4GB requires support for LBA (logical block addressing) in both the BIOS and Windows, where drives of 8.4GB or less use CHS (cylinder head sector) addressing instead. Motherboard BIOSes added LBA support during 1998, so most systems dated from 1998 or newer should have it. Windows added LBA support in Windows 95B and later versions as well. An interesting quirk to allow backward compatibility when you boot an older version of Windows that doesn't support LBA mode addressing (Windows 95A or earlier), drives larger than 8.4GB report as if they have 16,383 cylinders, 16 heads, and 63 sectors per track, which is 8.4GB. For example, this enables a 120GB drive to be seen as an 8.4GB drive by Windows 95A or earlier. That sounds strange, but I guess having a 120GB drive being recognized as an 8.4GB is better than not having it work at all. If you did want to install a drive larger than 8.4GB into a system with a BIOS dated before 1998, the recommended solution is either a motherboard BIOS upgrade or an add-on BIOS card with LBA support, and to install Windows 95B or later as well.

The 137GB drive capacity barrier has proven a bit more complicated than previous barriers because, in addition to BIOS and operating system issues, drive interface issues were also a problem. By 2001, the 137GB barrier had become a problem because 3 1/2" hard drives were poised to breach that capacity level. Supporting drives larger than this would require changes at the drive interface, the BIOS, and OS level. The drive interface solution came in the form of ATA-6, which was being developed during that year. To enable the addressing of drives of greater capacity, ATA-6 upgraded the LBA functions from using 28-bit numbers to using larger 48-bit numbers.

The ATA interface was originally designed using only 28-bit sector addressing (allowing up to 2^{28} sectors) at the interface level. This limited an ATA drive to 268,435,456 sectors, which was a capacity of 137,438,953,472 bytes, or 137.44GB. Thus, a barrier remained at 137GB because of the 28-bit LBA addressing used in the ATA interface. The numbers work out as follows:

```
                    Max. Values
-------------------------------------
Total Sectors       268,435,456
-------------------------------------
Total Bytes     137,438,953,472
Megabytes (MB)          137,439
Mebibytes (MiB)         131,072
Gigabytes (GB)           137.44
Gibibytes (GiB)          128.00
```

The ATA-6 and later specifications extended the LBA (logical block address) sector numbering to allow 48-bit addressing. This meant that the maximum capacity was increased to 2^{48} (281,474,976,710,656) total sectors. Because each sector stores 512 bytes, this results in a maximum drive capacity of

```
                        Max. Values
-------------------------------------------
Total Sectors       281,474,976,710,656
-------------------------------------------
Total Bytes     144,115,188,075,855,872
Megabytes (MB)          144,115,188,076
Mebibytes (MiB)         137,438,953,472
Gigabytes (GB)              144,115,188
Gibibytes (GiB)             134,217,728
Terabytes (TB)                  144,115
Tebibytes (TiB)                 131,072
Petabytes (PB)                   144.12
Pebibytes (PiB)                  128.00
```

As you can see, the 48-bit LBA in ATA-6 and later allows a maximum capacity of just over 144PB (petabytes = quadrillion bytes)! This applies to both ATA and SATA internal drives. Note that external USB or FireWire interfaces did not have any interface problems with respect to large drives; however, inside every external USB or FireWire drive enclosure is a standard ATA or SATA drive.

To take advantage of this, internal ATA and SATA drives larger than 137GB require 48-bit LBA (logical block address) support not only in the drive interface, but also in the OS as well as the motherboard BIOS.

To have 48-bit LBA support in the OS requires either

■ Windows XP with Service Pack 1 (SP1) or later.

■ Windows 2000 with Service Pack 4 (SP4) or later.

■ Windows 98/98SE/Me or NT 4.0 with the Intel Application Accelerator (IAA) loaded. This solution only works if your motherboard has an IAA-supported chipset. See www.intel.com/support/chipsets/IAA/instruct.htm for more information.

To have 48-bit LBA support in the BIOS requires either

■ A motherboard BIOS with 48-bit LBA support (usually dated Sept. 2002 or later).

■ An ATA or SATA host adapter card with onboard BIOS that includes 48-bit LBA support.

If your motherboard BIOS does not have 48-bit LBA support, and an update is not available from your motherboard manufacturer, then you can use a card with an on-board BIOS. ATA cards that offer 48-bit LBA support include the LBA Pro ISA card from eSupport at www.esupport.com/products/extenders/lbapro.htm or the Maxtor Ultra ATA/133 PCI card from www.maxtor.com/en/products/accessories/ultra_ata/ultra_ata_133_pci_adapter_card/index.htm. The Maxtor card has two additional ATA-133 ports that you can use to connect up to four additional drives, while the eSupport card has only a BIOS with no ports. In both cases you could continue to use your existing motherboard ports; the BIOS on the cards would allow 48-bit LBA support for both motherboard-based as well as card-based ports.

If you have both BIOS and OS support as well then you can simply install and use a drive over 137GB just like any other. If you have BIOS support, but you do have OS support, then portions of the drive past 137GB will not be recognized or accessible.

This can cause problems when installing Windows. For example, if you are installing Windows XP to a blank hard drive larger than 137GB, and you are booting from an original Windows XP CD (without Service Pack 1 or later integrated), then Windows will only see the first 137GB of the drive. During the installation you will only be able to create partitions using the first 137GB of the drive. Once Windows XP was installed, you could apply Service Pack 1 or later, which would enable Windows to "see" the rest of the drive up to its full capacity. In other words, after installing the service pack update, the rest of the drive will be available. However it won't automatically be used; it will simply be available as new unpartitioned space.

At that point you can either add one or more additional partitions to use the unpartitioned space with the standard partitioning software such as the Disk Management tool, or use a third-party partitioning program such as Partition Magic from Symantec or Partition Commander from V-Com to resize or extend the first partition to use the remainder of the drive. If you are booting from a Windows XP CD with Service Pack 1 or later fully integrated (or slip-streamed) then Windows will allow you to partition the full capacity of the drive (even over 137GB) during the Windows installation.

Operating system limitations with respect to large drives are shown in Table 10.9.

Table 10.9   Operating System Limitations

Operating System	Limitations for Hard Drive Size
DOS/Windows 3x	DOS 6.22 or lower can't support drives greater than 8.4GB. DOS 7.0 or higher (included with Windows 95 or later) is required to recognize a drive over 8.4GB.
Windows 9X/Me	Windows 95A (original version) does support the INT13h extensions, which means it does support drives over 8.4GB; however, due to limitations of the FAT16 file system, the maximum individual partition size is limited to 2GB. Windows 95B/OSR2 or later (including Windows 98/Me) supports the INT13h extensions, which allows drives over 8.4GB, and also supports FAT32, which allows partition sizes up to the maximum capacity of the drive. However, Windows 95 doesn't support hard drives larger than 32GB because of limitations in its design. Windows 98 requires an update to FDISK to partition drives larger than 64GB.
Windows NT	Windows NT 3.5x does not support drives greater than 8.4GB. Windows NT 4.0 does support drives greater than 8.4GB; however, when a drive larger than 8.4GB is being used as the primary bootable device, Windows NT will not recognize more than 8.4GB. Microsoft has released Service Pack 4, which corrects this problem.
Windows 2000/XP	Windows 2000/XP supports drives greater than 8.4GB; however to support drives greater than 137GB requires Windows XP with Service Pack 1 (SP1) or later, or Windows 2000 with Service Pack 4 (SP4) or later.
OS/2 Warp	Some versions of OS/2 are limited to a boot partition size of 3.1GB or 4.3GB. IBM has a Device Driver Pack upgrade that enables the boot partition to be as large as 8.4GB. The HPFS file system in OS/2 will support drives up to 64GB.
Novell	NetWare 5.0 or later supports drives greater than 8.4GB.

In some cases, the file system you select for a partition or volume may limit the capacity of an individual volume or even files on the volume. Table 10.10 shows the minimum and maximum volume size and file size limitations of the various Windows operating systems.

Table 10.10   Operating System Volume/File Size Limitations by File System

OS Limitations by File System	FAT16	FAT32	NTFS
Min. Volume Size (9x/Me)	2.092MB	33.554MB	—
Max. Volume Size (95)	2.147GB	33.554MB	—
Max. Volume Size (98)	2.147GB	136.902GB	—
Max. Volume Size (Me)	2.147GB	8.796TB	—
Min. Volume Size (NT/2000/XP)	2.092MB	33.554MB	1.000MB
Max. Volume Size (NT/2000/XP)	4.294GB	8.796GB	281.475TB
Max. File Size (all)	4.294GB	4.294GB	16.384TB

— = not applicable

MB = megabyte = 1,000,000 bytes

GB = gigabyte = 1,000,000,000 bytes

TB = terabyte = 1,000,000,000,000 bytes

As noted previously in this section, the original versions of Windows XP, Windows 2000/NT, and Windows 95/98/Me do not provide native support for ATA hard drives larger than 137GB. However, as indicated earlier, that can easily be solved by loading the appropriate Service Packs or Intel

Application Accelerator. Finally, note that the 137GB barrier affects internal ATA and SATA drives, and does not affect drives connected via USB, FireWire, SCSI, or other external interfaces.

Boot Sectors

To manage a disk and enable all applications to see a consistent interface to the file system no matter what type of storage hardware is being used, the operating system creates several structures on the disk. The most important of these are the boot sectors (also called boot records), of which there are two main types, called *Master Boot Records*, or *MBRs*, and *Volume Boot Records*, or *VBRs*.

There is only one MBR on a physical disk, and it is always found at the beginning of the disk. A single disk can contain multiple partitions (also called volumes), and there is a VBR at the start of each volume. The structure of the MBR is consistent among different operating systems and file systems, however the VBR depends mainly on the type of file system used on the volume. The following section looks into the structure and design of both MBRs and VBRs.

Figure 10.4 is a simple diagram showing the relative locations of the MBR and VBR on an 8.4GB disk with a single FAT partition.

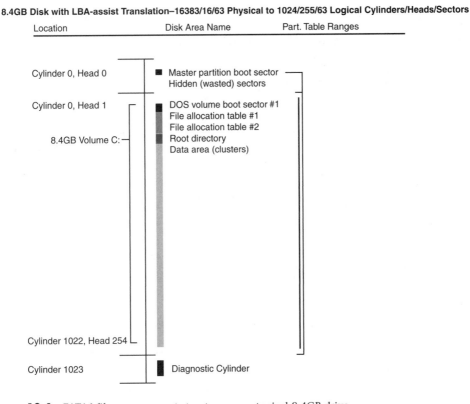

8.4GB Disk with LBA-assist Translation–16383/16/63 Physical to 1024/255/63 Logical Cylinders/Heads/Sectors

Location	Disk Area Name	Part. Table Ranges
Cylinder 0, Head 0	■ Master partition boot sector Hidden (wasted) sectors	
Cylinder 0, Head 1	DOS volume boot sector #1 File allocation table #1 File allocation table #2	
8.4GB Volume C:	Root directory Data area (clusters)	
Cylinder 1022, Head 254		
Cylinder 1023	■ Diagnostic Cylinder	

Figure 10.4 FAT16 file-management structures on a typical 8.4GB drive.

Note

Some removable cartridge drives, such as the SuperDisk (LS-120 and LS-240) and Iomega Zip drives, function like high-capacity floppy drives. They lack a master boot record (MBR) and can't be partitioned like hard disk drives. Other higher-capacity removable drives, such as the legacy Iomega Jaz or Castlewood Orb, function like hard drives and must be partitioned.

All PC hard drives using the FAT16 file system are similar.

Each disk area has a purpose and function. If one of these special areas is damaged, serious consequences can result. Damage to one of these sensitive structures usually causes a domino effect, limiting access to other areas of the disk or causing further problems in using the disk. For example, the OS normally can't access a drive at all if the MBR is corrupted. Therefore, you should understand these data structures well enough to be able to repair them when necessary. Rebuilding these special tables and areas of the disk is essential to the art of data recovery, which is covered in more detail in Chapter 11.

Master Boot Record

The first PC OS to support hard disks, DOS 2.0 (released on March 8, 1983), was also the first to introduce the capability to partition a drive. Partitioning assigns the available space on the drive to one or more volumes (drive letters). A common misunderstanding among newer users is to think that partitioning is necessary only if multiple volumes are desired, but the truth is that all drives that *can* be partitioned *must* be partitioned; in other words you have to partition a drive even if you are going to assign all of the space to a single volume.

Although the primary use for partitioning today is to divide a single drive into one or more volumes for use by a single OS, originally it was intended to allow multiple different operating systems, each with different file systems, to coexist on a single drive. This multi-OS capability still exists today; however, after-market utilities are often used to manage and boot multiple operating systems on a single machine.

Tip

If you want to dual-boot or multi-boot different Windows versions without purchasing after-market boot manager software, merely install the older versions such as Windows 95, 98, or Me first and then install newer versions such as Windows NT/2000/XP or later in succession, with the newest OS last. Each OS must be installed in a separate volume (drive letter) to prevent conflicts with shared folders and files. One rule is that you can only install one instance of either Windows 95, 98/98SE, or Me, because those operating systems share the same system files.

Another solution (which I prefer) is to use a virtual machine program such as Microsoft Virtual PC (www.microsoft.com/virtualpc) or VMware (www.vmware.com) to create multiple virtual machines, each capable of managing and loading a separate OS. This software allows you to run multiple instances of the same or different operating systems on a single machine without repartitioning or reformatting any drives.

To use a hard disk with different operating systems, you can create partitions to logically divide the disk. You can, for example, create one or more FAT or NTFS partitions for use with Windows and leave the rest of the disk storage area for use by another non-Windows OS, such as Linux. Each of the FAT or NTFS partitions appears to an OS that supports it as a separate drive letter. For example, Windows 9x/Me ignores any non-FAT partitions, whereas Windows 2000/XP and later sees both FAT and NTFS partitions but ignores others such as Linux and OS/2 HPFS partitions.

Even though Windows NT/2000/XP and later have an optional command-line disk partitioning program called DISKPART, disk partitions are usually prepared with the GUI-based Disk Management tool (also called Disk Administrator in some versions).

Information about each of the partitions on the disk is stored in a partition (or volume) boot record at the beginning of each partition. Additionally, a main table lists the partitions embedded in the master boot record.

The MBR, which is also sometimes called the master boot sector, is always located in the first physical sector of a disk (cylinder 0, head 0, sector 1) and consists of the following structures:

- *Bootstrap code*. The instructions used to locate and load the VBR from the active (bootable) partition.
- *Master partition table*. A table consisting of four 16-byte entries for up to four primary partitions, or three primary partitions and one extended partition. Each primary partition defines a logical drive, and an extended partition can be further partitioned into multiple logical drives. A given partition entry indicates which type of partition it is, whether it is bootable, where it is located physically on the disk, and how many sectors it occupies.
- *Signature bytes*. A 2-byte signature (55 AAh) used by the motherboard ROM and other code to validate the sector.

Primary and Extended Partitions

Most operating systems are designed to support up to 24 volumes on a single hard disk drive (represented by the drive letters C:–Z:), but the partition table in the master boot record (MBR) can have a maximum of only four entries. These entries can be for various types of partitions; however, Windows will normally recognize only primary and extended partitions.

An *extended* partition is listed in the master partition table the same as a primary partition, but it differs in that you can use its disk space to create multiple logical partitions, or *volumes*. You can create only one extended partition on a single drive, meaning that in many cases there will never be more than two entries in the master partition table, one primary and one extended.

The logical volumes you create in the extended partition appear as separate drive letters to the operating system, but they are not listed in the master partition table. Volumes in the extended partition are not normally bootable. You can create up to 23 volumes out of a single extended partition (assuming that you have already created a primary partition, which brings the total number of volumes to 24).

Each of the subpartitions in an extended partition includes an extended partition table located in the first sector of the subpartition. The first sector of the extended partition contains an extended partition table that points to the first subpartition and, optionally, another extended partition. The first sector of that extended partition has another extended partition table that can reference another volume as well as an additional extended partition. This chain of references continues, linking all the volumes in the extended partition to the master partition table. It is important to note that, if the entry for the extended partition in the MBR is lost or damaged, the chain will be broken at the start and all volumes contained within will be inaccessible—essentially meaning that they will disappear.

Few people have any reason to create 24 partitions on a single disk drive, but the extended partition can create a chain of linked partitions on the disk that makes it possible to exceed the four-entry limitation of the master partition table.

Because the master boot record contains the first program loaded from disk that the system executes when you boot a PC, it has been a frequent target for creators of computer viruses or other malicious software. A program that infects or destroys the MBR can make it impossible for the BIOS to find the active partition, thus preventing the operating system from loading. Because the MBR contains the first program executed by the system, a virus stored there loads before any antivirus code can be loaded to detect it. To remove an MBR virus, you must first boot the system from a clean, uninfected disk, such as a floppy, bootable CD/DVD, or USB drive, and then run an antivirus program to test and possibly repair or restore the MBR.

Each volume on a disk contains a volume boot record starting in the first sector. With FDISK, DISKPART, or Disk Management tools, you can designate a primary partition as active (or bootable). The master boot record bootstrap code causes the VBR from the active primary partition to receive control whenever the system is started.

Although FAT12, FAT16, FAT32, or NTFS partitions are mainly used when running Windows, you can also create additional disk partitions for Linux, Novell NetWare, OS/2's HPFS, AIX (Unix), XENIX, or other file systems or operating systems, using disk utilities provided with the alternative OS or in some cases a third-party disk partitioning tool such as PartitionMagic from Symantec. A partition that is not recognized by a particular operating system is simply ignored. If you install multiple operating systems on a single drive, a boot manager program (which might be included with the operating systems or installed separately) can be used to allow you to select which partition to make active each time you boot the system. As another alternative, you could install different operating systems in multiple different primary partitions and then use FDISK, DISKPART, Disk Management, or some other partitioning program to change the one you want to boot as active.

Table 10.11 shows the format of the master boot record and the included partition tables. The table lists the fields in each of the master partition table's four entries, the location on the disk where each field begins (the offset), and its length.

Table 10.11   Master Boot Record Format

		Master Boot Program Code		
Offset (hex)	**Offset (dec)**	**Name**	**Length**	**Description**
000h	0	Boot Code	446 bytes	Bootstrap code; loads the VBR from the active partition.
		Partition Table Entry #1		
Offset (hex)	**Offset (dec)**	**Name**	**Length**	**Description**
1BEh	446	Boot Indicator	1 byte	Boot status; 80h = active (bootable). Otherwise, it's 00h.
1BFh	447	Starting Head	1 byte	Starting head (or side) of partition in CHS mode.
1C0h	448	Starting Cylinder/ Sector	16 bits	Starting cylinder (10 bits) and sector (6 bits) in CHS mode.
1C2h	450	System Indicator	1 byte	Partition type/file system.
1C3h	451	Ending Head	1 byte	Ending head (or side) of partition in CHS mode.
1C4h	452	Ending Cylinder/ Sector	16 bits	Ending cylinder (10 bits) and sector (6 bits) in CHS mode.
1C6h	454	Relative Sector	4 bytes	Count of sectors before partition, which is the starting sector of partition in LBA mode.

Table 10.11   Continued

Partition Table Entry #1

Offset (hex)	Offset (dec)	Name	Length	Description
1CAh	458	Total Sectors	4 bytes	Total number of partition sectors in LBA mode.

Partition Table Entry #2

Offset (hex)	Offset (dec)	Description	Length	Description
1CEh	462	Boot Indicator	1 byte	Boot status; 80h = active (bootable). Otherwise, it's 00h.
1CFh	463	Starting Head	1 byte	Starting head (or side) of partition in CHS mode.
1D0h	464	Starting Cylinder/Sector	16 bits	Starting cylinder (10 bits) and sector (6 bits) in CHS mode.
1D2h	466	System Indicator	1 byte	Partition type/file system.
1D3h	467	Ending Head	1 byte	Ending head (or side) of partition in CHS mode.
1D4h	468	Ending Cylinder/Sector	16 bits	Ending cylinder (10 bits) and sector (6 bits) in CHS mode.
1D6h	470	Relative Sector	4 bytes	Count of sectors before partition, which is the starting sector of the partition in LBA mode.
1DAh	474	Total Sectors	4 bytes	Total number of partition sectors in LBA mode.

Partition Table Entry #3

Offset (hex)	Offset (dec)	Description	Length	Description
1DEh	478	Boot Indicator	1 byte	Boot status; 80h = active (bootable). Otherwise, it's 00h.
1DFh	479	Starting Head	1 byte	Starting head (or side) of partition in CHS mode.
1E0h	480	Starting Cylinder/Sector	16 bits	Starting cylinder (10 bits) and sector (6 bits) in CHS mode.
1E2h	482	System Indicator	1 byte	Partition type/file system.
1E3h	483	Ending Head	1 byte	Ending head (or side) of partition in CHS mode.
1E4h	484	Ending Cylinder/Sector	16 bits	Ending cylinder (10 bits) and sector (6 bits) in CHS mode.
1E6h	486	Relative Sector	4 bytes	Count of sectors before partition, which is the starting sector of partition in LBA mode.
1EAh	490	Total Sectors	4 bytes	Total number of partition sectors in LBA mode.

(continues)

Table 10.11   Continued

| | | Partition Table Entry #4 | | |
Offset (hex)	Offset (dec)	Description	Length	Description
1EEh	494	Boot Indicator	1 byte	Boot status; 80h = active (bootable). Otherwise, it's 00h.
1EFh	495	Starting Head	1 byte	Starting head (or side) of partition in CHS mode.
1F0h	496	Starting Cylinder/ Sector	16 bits	Starting cylinder (10 bits) and sector (6 bits) in CHS mode.
1F2h	498	System Indicator	1 byte	Partition type/file system.
1F3h	499	Ending Head	1 byte	Ending head (or side) of partition in CHS mode.
1F4h	500	Ending Cylinder/ Sector	16 bits	Ending cylinder (10 bits) and sector (6 bits) in CHS mode.
1F6h	502	Relative Sector	4 bytes	Count of sectors before partition, which is the starting sector of partition in LBA mode.
1FAh	506	Total Sectors	4 bytes	Total number of partition sectors in LBA mode.

| | | Signature Bytes | | |
Offset (hex)	Offset (dec)	Description	Length	Description
1FEh	510	Signature	2 bytes	Boot sector signature; must be 55 AAh.

CHS = Cylinder head sector
LBA = Logical block address

The data in the partition table entries tells the system where each partition starts and ends on the drive, how big it is, whether it is bootable, and which type of file system is contained in the partition. The starting cylinder, head, and sector values are used only by systems running in CHS mode, which is standard for all drives of 8.4GB or less. CHS values do not work past 8.4GB and therefore cannot represent partitions on drives larger than that. Drives larger than 8.4GB can be fully addressed only in LBA mode. In that case, the starting cylinder, head, and sector values in the table are ignored, and only the Relative Sector and Total Sectors fields are used. The Relative Sector field indicates the precise LBA where the partition begins, and the Total Sectors field indicates the length, which is always contiguous. Thus, from those two values the system can know exactly where a partition is physically located on a disk.

Note

The processors on which the PC is based have an interesting design characteristic that is important to know for anybody editing or interpreting boot sectors. Numbers larger than 1 byte are actually read backward! This is called *little endian format* (as in reading the number from the little end first) or *reverse-byte ordering*. People typically read numbers in *big endian format*, which means from left to right, from the big end first. However, because PC processors read in little endian format, most numeric values larger than 1 byte are stored so that the least significant byte appears first and the most significant byte appears last. For example, the value for the Relative Sector field in the MBR for the first partition is usually 63, which is 3Fh in hex, or 0000003Fh (4 bytes long) in standard big endian hexadecimal format. However, the same number stored in little endian format would appear as 3F000000h. As another example, if a partition had 23,567,292 total sectors (about 12GB), which is 01679BBCh in hexadecimal, the number would be stored in the MBR partition table Total Sectors field in reverse-byte/little endian format as BC9B6701h.

As an aside, the use of reverse-byte order numbers stems from the way processors evolved from 8-bit (1 byte) designs to 16-bit (2 byte), 32-bit (4 byte), 64-bit (8-byte) designs, and beyond. The way the internal registers are organized and implemented dictates how a processor deals with numbers. Many processors, such as the Motorola PowerPC chips used in older Macintosh systems, read numbers in big endian format. Intel and AMD processors, on the other hand, are based on Intel x86 processor designs dating back to the original Intel 8088 processor used in the first IBM PC. Of course, how a particular processor reads numbers doesn't make any difference to those using a system. In the PC, the only people who have to deal with reverse-byte order or little endian numbers directly are machine or assembly language program-mers—and of course those who also want to edit, modify, repair, or simply interpret raw boot sectors!

Each partition table entry contains a system indicator byte that identifies the type of partition and file system used in the partition referenced by that entry. Table 10.12 shows the standard values and meanings of the system indicator bytes for Microsoft operating systems, and Table 10.13 lists the values used by other systems.

Table 10.12   Standard System Indicator Byte Values

Value	Partition Type	Address Mode	Partition Size
00h	None	—	—
01h	Primary FAT12	CHS	0–16MiB
04h	Primary FAT16	CHS	16MiB–32MiB
05h	Extended	CHS	0–2GiB
06h	Primary FAT16	CHS	32MiB–2GiB
07h	NTFS/HPFS	Any	Any
0Bh	Primary FAT32	CHS	512MiB–2TiB
0Ch	Primary FAT32	LBA	512MiB–2TiB
0Eh	Primary FAT16	LBA	32MiB–2GiB
0Fh	Extended	LBA	2GiB–2TiB
42h	Dynamic	Any	Any

CHS = Cylinder head sector
LBA = Logical block address

Table 10.13   Nonstandard System Indicator Byte Values

Value	Partition Type	Value	Partition Type
02h	MS-XENIX Root	80h	Minix v.1.1–v1.4a
03h	MS-XENIX usr	81h	Minix v1.4b-up or Linux
08h	AIX File System Boot	82h	Linux swap file
09h	AIX Data	83h	Linux Ext native file system
0Ah	OS/2 Bootmanager	83h	Suspend to Disk (S2D)
12h	HP/Compaq EISA Configuration	93h	Amoeba file system

(continues)

Table 10.13   **Continued**

Value	Partition Type	Value	Partition Type
40h	ENIX 80286	94h	Amoeba bad block table
50h	Ontrack Disk Manager read-only DOS	B7h	BSDI file system (secondary swap)
51h	Ontrack Disk Manager read/write DOS	B8h	BSDI file system (secondary file system)
52h	CP/M or Microport System V/386	DBh	DR Concurrent DOS/CPM-86/CTOS
54h	Ontrack Disk Manager non-DOS	DEh	Dell OEM (hidden—system recovery/ diagnostic)
55h	Micro House EZ-Drive non-DOS	E1h	SpeedStor 12-bit FAT extended
56h	Golden Bow Vfeature Deluxe	E4h	SpeedStor 16-bit FAT extended
61h	Storage Dimensions SpeedStor	F2h	DOS 3.3+secondary
63h	IBM 386/ix or Unix System V/386	F4h	SpeedStor primary
64h	Novell NetWare 286	FEh	IBM OEM (hidden—system recovery/ diagnostic)
65h	Novell NetWare 386	FFh	Unix/Xenix Bad Block Table Partition
75h	IBM PC/IX		

These values can be useful for somebody trying to manually repair a partition table using a disk editor such as the DiskProbe utility (DSKPROBE.EXE) included with the free Windows Support Tools on the Windows NT/2000/XP or later install disc, the Disk Edit program included with Norton Utilities (now part of Norton SystemWorks), or WinHex from X-Ways Software (www.winhex.com).

Windows DiskProbe

DiskProbe (DSKPROBE.EXE) is a sector editor utility, and is one of the more powerful and interesting programs included in the Windows Support Tools package, which can be downloaded for free from Microsoft (the support tools can also be found on some of the Windows NT and later installation discs). DiskProbe allows you to read and write individual physical or logical sectors on a drive. This is similar in nature to the DiskEdit utility included with the Norton SystemWorks by Symantec as well as the WinHex utility from X-Ways Software (www.winhex.com). For the most part, DiskProbe does not have all of the features of DiskEdit, but it does have a slight advantage in decoding NTFS boot sectors.

DiskProbe can read any physical or logical sector on a drive, and has special features for decoding and editing the Master Boot Record (MBR), partition tables, and volume boot sectors (VBRs). Because some of these structures are literally outside of the file system on a drive, they are not accessible through most other applications. With this tool, a knowledgeable user can restore these important data structures if they are damaged, for example, by a boot sector virus. Using DiskProbe, data structures such as the MBR, partition tables, and VBRs can be edited directly.

In addition to editing, you can also use DiskProbe for preventive maintenance by making backups of these critical sectors as files, which can be stored on another removable disk or media (such as a floppy, CD, flash drive, and so on). Once saved, they can be later restored in the event that these sectors are corrupted on your hard drive.

To run DiskProbe, first download the Windows Support Tools from Microsoft (to find them, visit www.microsoft.com and search for "Windows Support Tools Download") or locate the tools on the Windows installation CD (they are normally in the \SUPPORT\TOOLS folder on the CD) and install them. Once the tools are installed, select Start, Windows Support Tools, and Command Prompt. At the prompt, enter Dskprobe. The program will then launch in a window. Optionally you can run the program by opening Windows Explorer and navigating to the \Program Files\Support Tools folder, and then click on Dskprobe. The documentation for the program is available via the Help command on the menu bar.

The following figure shows DiskProbe editing the MBR (Master Boot Record) on one of my systems:

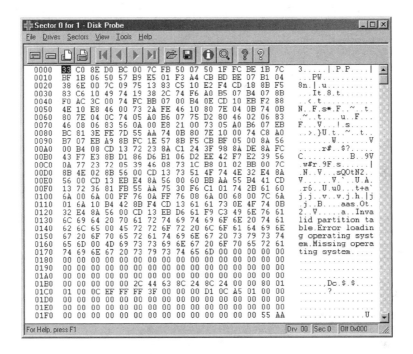

Figure 10.5 Editing an MBR with DiskProbe.

Note that editing critical sectors such as the MBR is like performing open-heart surgery on your system. DiskProbe and other sector editors such as Norton DiskEdit function at a level below the Windows file system, which means that the standard safety protocols are not in effect. DiskProbe gives you access to every byte on the physical disk without regard to normal security or access privileges, which makes it possible to damage or overwrite critical areas of the disk. If you change so much as a single byte inappropriately, you could render your system non-bootable, and possibly render the drive unrecognizable even if the system is booted from a floppy or CD. Fortunately the DiskProbe program defaults to read-only mode, which means you can run the program to view sectors without worrying about accidentally making changes. Before you do make any changes with a low-level tool such as DiskProbe, make sure you have a backup of any important data.

I have specialized in data recovery for many years, and in that line of work I regularly use sector editors such as DiskProbe to repair or restore critical boot sectors on hard drives that had otherwise been inaccessible by Windows. In a recent example, a client of mine was editing some rather large video files on an external FireWire drive. While working with the video editing program, the program crashed, and the system suddenly stopped recognizing the drive. Upon disconnecting and reconnecting the drive, Windows saw the drive as a new unformatted drive and offered to format it! Hundreds of hours of shooting and editing video seemed lost forever.

To solve the problem, I took the drive out of the FireWire enclosure and connected it internally as a standard ATA slave drive to one of my test systems running Windows XP. I then started up the test system, loaded DiskProbe, and did a manual inspection of the MBR and VBRs. As is the case with most external USB or FireWire drives, the drive had been formatted with the FAT32 file system, and I very quickly discovered that somehow the first sector of the 3-sector long FAT32 volume boot record, which was at Logical Block Address (LBA) 63, had been overwritten with zeros! I knew from experience that FAT32 keeps a backup copy of the 3-sector long VBR at LBAs 66 through 68. So I used DiskProbe to copy sector 66 and paste it over sector 63, thereby restoring sector 63 and instantly solving the problem. I then powered the system off, removed the drive from my test system, reinstalled it into the FireWire enclosure, and reconnected it to the client's system, whereupon the drive was instantly recognized and all data was fully accessible.

Total elapsed time from "zero" to "hero" was less than 10 minutes after I received the drive; needless to say the client was ecstatic. Even a relatively simple job like this would cost hundreds to possibly thousands of dollars if sent to a professional data recovery service. Now you see why most people who *know* data recovery don't like to *teach* it (except me, of course).

FIXMBR

The Windows NT/2000/XP Recovery Console has a special utility program called FIXMBR, which is designed to rebuild a corrupt MBR. FIXMBR overwrites only the master boot program code, leaving the existing partition table entries intact. This means that if the problem was in the boot code, FIXMBR will solve it by replacing the code; however, if the problem is instead with the actual partition tables, FIXMBR will not resolve the problem.

Caution

If your system uses non-standard MBR code, beware that FIXMBR will replace it with standard MBR code, meaning that whatever functionality was being provided by the non-standard code (such as a multi-boot loader) may be lost. Even more importantly, if you are using BIOS overlay software to override BIOS drive-size limitations (something I do not recommend in general), replacing the MBR code in this manner may result in your system becoming unbootable as well as losing access to any or all of the drives! Also, certain MBR virus programs (such as the infamous *Monkey* virus) relocate and encrypt the original MBR code before replacing it with virus code. If the MBR is rewritten by a program such as FIXMBR, you will lose access to the original MBR containing the partition tables. This means that unless you are able to re-create the partition table data manually using a sector editor you will lose access to all of the partitions on the drive. In that case a data recovery specialist should be able to rebuild the partition tables and recover the data if no further writing is done to the drive.

Use the following steps to start the Recovery Console and use FIXMBR to rewrite the MBR program code:

1. Ensure that your system is capable of booting from a CD, and that the CD/DVD drive precedes the hard disk in the boot sequence. Hint: You may need to change your BIOS setup to inspect or change the startup boot sequence.

2. Insert the Windows Setup CD into the CD/DVD drive, and restart the system.

3. If prompted to press a key to start the computer from the CD-ROM, press any key (such as the spacebar) to continue and start from the CD.

4. When the text-based part of Windows Setup begins, follow the prompts until the Welcome to Setup screen appears, then press the "R" key to Repair Windows, which also means to start the Recovery Console.

5. If you are repairing a system that has more than one operating system installed, from the Recovery Console, choose the Windows installation that you need to access or repair.

6. When you are prompted, type the Administrator password. If the Administrator password is blank, just press Enter. If a password has been set but you do not have the correct password, or if the security database for the installation of Windows you are attempting to access is corrupted, Recovery Console will not allow access to the disks.

7. To replace the MBR program code, at the Recovery Console command prompt, type

```
FIXMBR
```

8. Press the "Y" key to proceed, or press the "N" key to cancel. If you press "Y," the MBR program code will be replaced.

9. Finally, remove the CD and restart the system.

If you are using Windows 9x/Me or an older version of Windows or DOS, you can perform the same task as FIXMBR by using an undocumented feature in FDISK found in all versions of FDISK from MS-DOS 5.x to Windows Me. The undocumented FDISK feature can also be used on a Windows NT/2000/XP or later system by simply booting from a Windows 9x/Me startup floppy or installation CD, and running the command from the floppy or CD.

Undocumented FDISK

In DOS 5 and later versions, including Windows 9x/Me, FDISK gained some additional capabilities that were not originally documented by Microsoft. There are several undocumented FDISK parameters, but the one I am speaking about here is the /MBR (master boot record) parameter, which causes FDISK to rewrite the master boot record code, leaving the partition table area intact. This performs exactly the same function as the FIXMBR command included in Windows NT/2000/XP and later versions.

As with FIXMBR, the FDISK /MBR command is tailor-made for eliminating boot sector virus programs that infect the master boot record (located at cylinder 0, head 0, sector 1) of a hard disk. To use this feature, enter the following at a command prompt:

```
FDISK /MBR
```

FDISK then rewrites the boot record code, leaving the partition tables intact. This should not cause any problems on a normally functioning system, but just in case, I recommend backing up the partition table information to floppy disk before trying it. You can do this by using a third-party product such as Norton Utilities.

Be aware that using FDISK with the /MBR switch overwrites the partition tables if the two signature bytes at the end of the sector (55 AAh) are damaged. This situation is highly unlikely, however. In fact, if these signature bytes were damaged, you would know—the system would not boot and would act as though there were no partitions at all. If you are unable to access your hard disk after booting from a clean floppy or removable-media drive, your system might be infected with a boot sector virus. You should scan for viruses with an up-to-date antivirus program and use it to guide repair.

Caution

Also note that FDISK /MBR should be used only on systems using the normal master boot record structure. As with FIXMBR, if a BIOS overlay program such as Disk Manager, Disc Wizard, EZ-Drive, MaxBlast, Data Lifeguard Tools, or similar is being used to allow your system to access the drive's full capacity, do not use FDISK /MBR because these programs use a modified MBR for disk access. Using FDISK /MBR will wipe out the changes they made to your drive and could make your data inaccessible.

Volume Boot Records

The volume boot record (VBR) starts in the first sector on any area of a drive addressed as a volume, including primary partitions or logical volumes inside an extended partition. On a floppy disk or removable cartridge (such as a Zip disk), for example, the volume boot record starts at the physical beginning of the disk because the disk is recognized as a volume without the need for partitioning. On a hard disk, the volume boot record is located as the first sectors within any disk area allocated as a primary partition, or as a logical drive (volume) inside an extended partition. Refer to Figure 10.4 for an idea of the physical relationship between this volume boot record and the other data structures on a disk. The specific length and content of the VBR varies according to the specific file system, but all of them have certain similar features. The volume boot record loosely resembles the master boot record in that it contains several similar elements such as program code, disk-specific data, and signature bytes. The specific elements in the volume boot record include

- *Jump Instruction to Boot Code.* A 3-byte Intel x86 unconditional branch (or jump) instruction that jumps to the start of the operating system bootstrap code within the sector.

- *BIOS Parameter Block.* Contains specific information about the volume, such as its size, the number of disk sectors it uses, the size of its clusters, and the volume label name. Used by the file system driver to determine the type and status of the media. Varies according to the type of file system on the media.

- *Boot Code.* The instructions used to locate and load the initial operating system kernel or startup file, usually either IO.SYS or NTLDR (depending on the Windows version).

- *Signature Bytes.* A two-byte signature (55 AAh) used by the motherboard ROM and other code to validate the boot sector.

Either the motherboard ROM or the master boot record on a hard disk loads the volume boot record of the active partition on a disk. The program code in the volume boot record is given control of the system; it performs some tests and then attempts to load the first operating system file (in DOS/Windows 9x/Me the file is IO.SYS and in Windows NT/2000/XP the file is NTLDR). The volume boot record, similar to the master boot record, is transparent to the running system; it is outside the data area of the disk on which files are stored.

Note

Many of today's systems are capable of booting from drives other than standard floppy disk and hard disk drives. In these cases, the system BIOS must specifically support the boot drive. For example, some BIOS products enable you to select an ATAPI CD-ROM (or DVD) as a boot device, in addition to the floppy and hard disk drives. Many can also boot from drives connected to USB ports, adding even more flexibility to the system.

Other types of removable media, such as Zip cartridges and LS-120 disks, can also be made bootable. When the BIOS properly supports it, an LS-120 drive can replace the existing floppy disk drive as drive A:. Check the setup screens in your system BIOS to determine which types of drives can be used to start your system.

The VBR is typically created on a volume when the volume is high-level formatted. This can be done with the FORMAT command included with DOS and Windows, or you can also use Windows NT's Disk Administrator and Windows 2000/XP's Disk Management programs to perform this task after partitioning the disk. All volumes have a VBR starting in the first sector of the volume.

The VBR contains both program code and data. The single data table in this sector is called the media parameter block or disk parameter block. The operating system needs the information this table contains to verify the capacity of the disk volume as well as the location of important structures, such as the FATs on FAT volumes or the Master File Table on NTFS volumes. The format of this data is very specific.

Although all VBRs contain boot code in addition to the BIOS parameter block (BPB) and other structures, only the boot code from the VBR in the bootable volume is executed. The others are read by the operating system during startup to determine the volume parameters.

The VBR on FAT12 and FAT16 volumes is 1 sector long and contains the jump instruction, the main BPB, bootstrap code, and signature bytes. Table 10.14 shows the format and layout of the FAT12/16 VBR.

Table 10.14   FAT12/16 Volume Boot Record Format

Offset (hex)	Offset (dec)	Name	Length (bytes)	Description
000h	0	BS_jmpBoot	3	Jump instruction to boot code, usually EB3C90h.
003h	3	BS_OEMName	8	OEM ID. Indicates which system formatted the volume. Typically, it's MSWIN4.1. Not used by the OS after formatting.
00Bh	11	BPB_BytsPerSec	2	Bytes per sector; normally 512.
00Dh	13	BPB_SecPerClus	1	Sectors per cluster. It must be a power of 2 greater than 0; typically 1, 2, 4, 8, 16, 32, or 64.
00Eh	14	BPB_RsvdSecCnt	2	Number of sectors reserved for the boot record(s); it should be 1 on FAT12/16 volumes.
010h	16	BPB_NumFATs	1	Count of FAT structures on the volume; usually 2.
011h	17	BPB_RootEntCnt	2	Count of 32-byte folder entries in the root folder of FAT12 and FAT16 volumes; it should be 512 on FAT12/16 volumes.
013h	19	BPB_TotSec16	2	16-bit total count of sectors on volumes with less than 65,536 sectors. If 0, then BPB_TotSec32 contains the count.
015h	21	BPB_Media	1	Media descriptor byte; normally F8h on all nonremovable media, and F0h on most removable media.
016h	22	BPB_FATSz16	2	FAT12/16 16-bit count of sectors occupied by one FAT.
018h	24	BPB_SecPerTrk	2	Sectors per track geometry value for interrupt 13h; it's usually 63 on hard disks.
01Ah	26	BPB_NumHeads	2	Number of heads for interrupt 13h; it's usually 255 on hard disks.
01Ch	28	BPB_HiddSec	4	Count of hidden sectors preceding the partition that contains this volume; it's usually 63 for the first volume.
020h	32	BPB_TotSec32	4	32-bit total count of sectors on volumes with 65,536 or more sectors. If 0, then BPB_TotSec16 contains the count.

(continues)

Table 10.14   Continued

Offset (hex)	Offset (dec)	Name	Length (bytes)	Description
024h	36	BS_DrvNum	1	Int 13h drive number; it's usually 00h for floppy disks or 80h for hard disks.
025h	37	BS_Reserved1	1	Reserved (used by Windows NT); it should be 0.
026h	38	BS_BootSig	1	Extended boot signature; it should be 29h if the following three fields are present. Otherwise, it's 00h.
027h	39	BS_VolID	4	Volume serial number; used with BS_VolLab to support volume tracking on removable media. Normally generated using the date and time as a seed when the volume is formatted.
02Bh	43	BS_VolLab	11	Volume label. Matches the 11-byte volume label recorded in the root folder; it should be set to NO NAME if there is no volume label.
036h	54	BS_FilSysType	8	Should be FAT12, FAT16, or FAT. Not used by the OS after formatting.
03Eh	62	BS_BootCode	448	Bootstrap program code.
1FEh	510	BS_Signature	2	Signature bytes; should be 55 AAh.

The VBR on a FAT32 volume is 3 sectors long, although 32 sectors are reserved at the beginning of the volume for the default and backup VBRs. The default VBR is in sectors 0, 1, and 2, and the backup VBR is in sectors 6, 7, and 8. These are all created at the time the volume is formatted and do not change during normal use. The first sector contains a jump instruction, the BPB, initial bootstrap code, and signature bytes. The second sector is called the FSInfo (file system information) sector and contains signature bytes and information used to assist the file system software; the third sector contains only additional bootstrap code and signature bytes. Table 10.15 shows the format and layout of the first sector of the 3-sector long FAT32 VBR.

Table 10.15   FAT32 VBR Format, BPB Sector 0

Offset (hex)	Offset (dec)	Name	Length (bytes)	Description
000h	0	BS_jmpBoot	3	Jump instruction to boot code; it's usually EB5890h.
003h	3	BS_OEMName	8	OEM ID; indicates which system formatted the volume. It's typically MSWIN4.1. Not used by the OS after formatting.
00Bh	11	BPB_BytsPerSec	2	Bytes per sector; normally 512.
00Dh	13	BPB_SecPerClus	1	Sectors per cluster; it must be a power of 2 greater than 0. It's normally 1, 2, 4, 8, 16, 32, or 64.
00Eh	14	BPB_RsvdSecCnt	2	Number of sectors reserved for the boot record(s); it should be 32 on FAT32 volumes.
010h	16	BPB_NumFATs	1	Count of FAT structures on the volume; usually 2.

Table 10.15   Continued

Offset (hex)	Offset (dec)	Name	Length (bytes)	Description
011h	17	BPB_RootEntCnt	2	Count of 32-byte folder entries in the root folder of FAT12 and FAT16 volumes; should be 0 on FAT32 volumes.
013h	19	BPB_TotSec16	2	16-bit total count of sectors on volumes with less than 65,536 sectors. If 0, then BPB_TotSec32 contains the count. Must be 0 for FAT32 volumes.
015h	21	BPB_Media	1	Media descriptor byte, normally F8h on all non-removable media, F0h on most removable media.
016h	22	BPB_FATSz16	2	FAT12/16 16-bit count of sectors occupied by one FAT; it should be 0 on FAT32 volumes, and BPB_FATSz32 contains the FAT size count.
018h	24	BPB_SecPerTrk	2	Sectors per track geometry value for interrupt 13h; usually 63 on hard disks.
01Ah	26	BPB_NumHeads	2	Number of heads for interrupt 13h; usually 255 on hard disks.
01Ch	28	BPB_HiddSec	4	Count of hidden sectors preceding the partition that contains this volume; usually 63 for the first volume.
020h	32	BPB_TotSec32	4	32-bit total count of sectors on volumes with 65,536 or more sectors. If 0, then BPB_TotSec16 contains the count. Must be non-zero on FAT32 volumes.
024h	36	BPB_FATSz32	4	FAT32 32-bit count of sectors occupied by one FAT. BPB_FATSz16 must be 0.
028h	40	BPB_ExtFlags	2	FAT32 only: Bits 0–3. Zero-based number of active FAT. Valid only if mirroring is disabled (bit 7 = 1). Bits 4–6. Reserved. Bit 7. 0 indicates FAT is mirrored; 1 indicates only the FAT referenced in bits 0–3 is active. Bits 8–15. Reserved.
02Ah	42	BPB_FSVer	2	Version number of the FAT32 volume. A high byte is a major revision number; a low byte is a minor revision number. It should be 00h:00h.
02Ch	44	BPB_RootClus	4	Cluster number of the first cluster of the root folder; usually 2.
030h	48	BPB_FSInfo	2	Sector number of extended FSInfo boot sector structure in the reserved area of the FAT32 volume; usually 1.
032h	50	BPB_BkBootSec	2	Sector number of the backup copy of the boot record; it's usually 6.

(continues)

Table 10.15 Continued

Offset (hex)	Offset (dec)	Name	Length (bytes)	Description
034h	52	BPB_Reserved	12	Reserved; should be 0.
040h	64	BS_DrvNum	1	Int 13h drive number; it's usually 00h for floppy disks or 80h for hard disks.
041h	65	BS_Reserved1	1	Reserved (used by Windows NT); it should be 0.
042h	66	BS_BootSig	1	Extended boot signature; it should be 29h if the following three fields are present. Otherwise, it's 00h.
043h	67	BS_VolID	4	Volume serial number; used with BS_VolLab to support volume tracking on removable media. Normally generated using the date and time as a seed when the volume is formatted.
047h	71	BS_VolLab	11	Volume label. Matches the 11-byte volume label recorded in the root folder, should be NO NAME if there is no volume label.
052h	82	BS_FilSysType	8	Should be FAT32. Not used by the OS after formatting.
05Ah	90	BS_BootCode	420	Bootstrap program code.
1FEh	510	BS_Signature	2	Signature bytes; it should be 55 AAh.

Table 10.16 shows the format and layout of the FAT32 FSInfo sector, which is the second sector of the 3-sector-long FAT32 volume boot record.

Table 10.16 FAT32 VBR Format, FSInfo Sector 1

Offset (hex)	Offset (dec)	Name	Length (bytes)	Description
000h	0	FSI_LeadSig	4	Lead signature, validates sector; it should be 52526141h.
004h	4	FSI_Reserved1	480	Reserved; it should be 0.
1E4h	484	FSI_StrucSig	4	Structure signature; it validates sector and should be 72724161h.
1E8h	488	FSI_Free_Count	4	Last known free cluster count on the volume. If FFFFFFFFh, the free count is unknown and must be recalculated by the OS.
1ECh	492	FSI_Nxt_Free	4	Next free cluster; it indicates where the system should start looking for free clusters. Usually set to the last cluster number allocated. If the value is FFFFFFFFh, the system should start looking at cluster 2.
1F0h	496	FSI_Reserved2	12	Reserved; it should be 0.
1FCh	508	FSI_TrailSig	4	Trailing signature; it should be 00 00 55 AAh.

Table 10.17 shows the format and layout of the FAT32 Boot Code sector, which is the third and final sector of the 3-sector-long FAT32 volume boot record.

Table 10.17   FAT32 VBR Format, Boot Code Sector 2

Offset (hex)	Offset (dec)	Name	Length (bytes)	Description
000h	0	BS_BootCode	510	Boot program code
1FEh	510	BS_Signature	2	Signature bytes; should be 55 AAh

It is interesting to note that this third sector has no system-specific information in it, which means the contents are the same from system to system. Thus, if this sector (and its backup at LBA 8) were damaged on one system, you could obtain a copy of this sector from any other FAT32 volume and use it to restore the damaged sector.

The VBR on NTFS volumes is 7 sectors long, although 16 sectors are reserved at the beginning of the disk for the VBR. A backup of the 16 sector VBR area is reserved at the end of the volume, which contains a backup VBR. The first sector of the 7 is the BPB sector, and it contains a jump instruction, the BPB, and signature bytes. Sectors 2–7 contain only additional boot code, with no signature bytes or any other structures. Because the boot code is not system specific, all but the first VBR sector should be the same on any NTFS volume. Table 10.18 shows the format and layout of the first sector of the 7-sector-long NTFS VBR.

Table 10.18   NTFS VBR Format, BPB Sector 0

Offset (hex)	Offset (dec)	Name	Length (bytes)	Description
000h	0	BS_jmpBoot	3	Jump instruction to boot code; it's usually EB5290h.
003h	3	BS_OEMName	8	OEM ID; indicates which system formatted the volume. Typically, it's NTFS. Not used by the OS after formatting.
00Bh	11	BPB_BytsPerSec	2	Bytes per sector; it's usually 512.
00Dh	13	BPB_SecPerClus	1	Sectors per cluster; must be a power of 2 greater than 0. It's normally 1, 2, 4, or 8.
00Eh	14	BPB_RsvdSecCnt	2	Reserved sectors before the VBR; the value must be 0 or NTFS fails to mount the volume.
010h	16	BPB_Reserved	3	Value must be 0 or NTFS fails to mount the volume.
013h	19	BPB_Reserved	2	Value must be 0 or NTFS fails to mount the volume.
015h	21	BPB_Media	1	Media descriptor byte; it's normally F8h on all nonremovable media and F0h on most removable media.
016h	22	BPB_Reserved	2	Value must be 0 or NTFS fails to mount the volume.
018h	24	BPB_SecPerTrk	2	Sectors per track geometry value for interrupt 13h; usually 63 on hard disks.

(continues)

Table 10.18   **Continued**

Offset (hex)	Offset (dec)	Name	Length (bytes)	Description
01Ah	26	BPB_NumHeads	2	Number of heads for interrupt 13h; usually 255 on hard disks.
01Ch	28	BPB_HiddSec	4	Count of hidden sectors preceding the partition that contains this volume; normally 63 for the first volume.
020h	32	BPB_Reserved	4	Value must be 0 or NTFS fails to mount the volume.
024h	36	Reserved	4	Not used or checked by NTFS; it's normally 80008000h.
028h	40	BPB_TotSec64	8	Total count of sectors on the volume.
030h	48	BPB_MftClus	8	Logical cluster number for the start of the $MFT file.
038h	56	BPB_MirClus	8	Logical cluster number for the start of the $MFTMirr file.
040h	64	BPB_ClusPerMft	1	Clusters per MFT file/folder record. If this number is positive (00h–7Fh), it represents clusters per MFT record. If the number is negative (80h–FFh), the size of the record is 2 raised to the absolute value of this number.
041h	65	Reserved	3	Not used by NTFS.
044h	68	BPB_ClusPerIndx	1	Clusters per index buffer; it's used to allocate space for folders. If this number is positive (00h–7Fh), it represents clusters per MFT record. If the number is negative (80h–FFh), the size of the record is 2 raised to the absolute value of this number.
045h	69	Reserved	3	Not used by NTFS.
048h	72	BS_VolID	8	Volume serial number; used to support volume tracking on removable media. Normally generated using the date and time as a seed when the volume is formatted.
050h	80	Reserved	4	Not used by NTFS.
054h	84	BS_BootCode	426	Bootstrap program code.
1FEh	510	BS_Signature	2	Signature bytes; should be 55 AAh.

The Data Area

The data area of a partition is the place after the VBR where the actual files are stored. It is the area of the disk that is divided into clusters and managed by the file system. The specific content here varies based on what file system is used, the order in which the files are stored, the level of fragmentation of the files, and so forth. As such, it is not possible to show a specific structure here, because the structures are dynamic—that is, changing with the changing files and data on the drive.

Diagnostic Read-and-Write Cylinder

On older systems without LBA (logical block address) support, partitioning programs such as FDISK normally reserve the last cylinder of a hard disk for use as a special diagnostic test cylinder. Because this cylinder is reserved, FDISK might report fewer total cylinders than the drive manufacturer states are available. If present, operating systems do not use this cylinder for any normal purpose because it lies outside the partitioned area of the disk.

On systems using a Host Protected Area (HPA), the system can reserve space on the end of a drive for system recovery or restoration software, diagnostics, and other utilities. This situation can account for additional discrepancies between the total capacity reported by FDISK and the drive manufacturer's reported capacity.

The diagnostics area enables software such as a manufacturer-supplied diagnostics disk to perform read-and-write tests on a hard disk without corrupting any user data. Many of these programs also swap spare cylinders for damaged cylinders if damaged cylinders are detected during testing.

File Systems

Physically, the hard disks and other media provide the basic technology for storing data. Logically, however, the file system provides the structure of volumes and folders in which you store individual files and the organizational model that enables the system to locate data anywhere on a given disk or drive. File systems typically are an integrated part of an operating system (OS), and in general the newer versions of Windows provide support for several file systems from which you can choose.

Normally a file system is chosen for a volume when that volume is created or formatted. In some cases there are utility programs that can change a file system from one type to another on an existing partition. Depending on the version(s) of Windows you are running, several file systems are available from which to choose. Each file system has specific limitations, advantages, and disadvantages, and which ones you use can also be limited by the operating system you choose.

The primary file systems to choose from today include

- File allocation table (FAT), which includes FAT12, FAT16, and FAT32
- New Technology File System (NTFS)

Note that only Windows 2000/XP and later support all of these file systems; older or less capable versions of Windows generally support only some of these file systems. Table 10.19 lists the file systems supported by various Microsoft operating systems including various versions of DOS and Windows.

Table 10.19   Microsoft OS File Systems Support

Operating System	FAT12	FAT16	FAT32	NTFS
MS-DOS 1.x–2.x	X			
MS-DOS 3.x–6.x	X	X		
MS-DOS 7.x–8.x	X	X	X	
Windows 3.1	X	X		
Windows 95	X	X		
Windows 95B	X	X	X	
Windows 98/98SE	X	X	X	
Windows Me	X	X	X	

(continues)

Table 10.19   Continued

Operating System	FAT12	FAT16	FAT32	NTFS
Windows NT	X	X		X
Windows 2000	X	X	X	X
Windows XP	X	X	X	X

Although other operating systems may support other file systems, such as the Ext2FS supported by Linux or the HPFS (High Performance File System) supported by OS/2, this chapter focuses on the FAT and NTFS systems as supported by Windows.

Clusters (Allocation Units)

File systems store data in *clusters,* which are often called *allocation units.* The term *allocation unit* is appropriate because a single cluster is the smallest unit of the disk that the operating system can handle when it writes or reads a file. A cluster is equal to one or more 512-byte sectors, in powers of 2. Although a cluster can be a single disk sector, it is usually more than one. Having more than one sector per cluster reduces the size and processing overhead and enables the operating system to run faster because it has fewer individual units to manage. The trade-off is in wasted disk space. Because operating systems manage space only in full-cluster units, every file consumes space on the disk in increments of one cluster.

Because the operating system can allocate only whole clusters, inevitably a certain amount of wasted storage space results. File sizes rarely fall on cluster boundaries, so the last cluster allocated to a particular file is rarely filled completely. The extra space left over between the actual end of the file and the end of the cluster is called *slack.* A partition with large clusters has more slack space, whereas smaller clusters generate less slack.

The effect of larger cluster sizes on disk utilization can be substantial. A 2GiB partition containing about 5,000 files, with average slack of one-half of the last 32KiB cluster used for each file, wastes more than 78MiB (5000×(.5×32)KiB) of file space. When files under 32KiB in size are stored on a drive with a 32KiB allocation unit, waste (slack) factors can approach 40% of the drive's capacity. Newer file systems such as FAT32 and NTFS allow the use of smaller clusters, which use space on the disk more efficiently. For example, the same 2GiB partition with 5,000 files on it mentioned earlier would use 4KiB clusters with either NTFS or FAT32 instead of the 32KiB clusters used with FAT16. Assuming the same amount of slack for each file, the smaller cluster size reduces the average amount of wasted space on that partition from more than 78MiB to less than 10MiB.

Note

How much space does your current cluster size waste? To find out, you can download a free Windows utility called Karen's Disk Slack Checker from Karen Kenworthy's website. Go to http://www.karenware.com/powertools/ptslack.asp.

File Allocation Table (FAT)

Until the release of Windows XP, the most commonly used file systems were based on a file allocation table (FAT), which keeps track of the data stored in each cluster on a disk. FAT is still the most universally understood file system, meaning it is recognized by virtually every operating system that runs on PCs, and even non-PCs. For example, FAT is even recognizable on Apple Mac systems. For this reason, although NTFS (covered later in this chapter in the section "NTFS") is usually recommended with

Windows XP, for greater compatibility across systems and platforms, most external hard disks and removable-media drives still use FAT as their native file systems. Also, if you want to dual-boot Windows XP and Windows 9x/Me, you need to use FAT-based file systems even on your main drives.

Three main varieties of the FAT system exist, called FAT12, FAT16, and FAT32—all of which are differentiated by the number of digits used in the allocation table numbers. In other words, FAT16 uses 16-bit numbers to keep track of data clusters, FAT32 uses 32-bit numbers, and so on. The various FAT systems are used as follows:

- *FAT12.* Used on all volumes smaller than 16MiB (for example, floppy disks).
- *FAT16.* Used on volumes from 16MiB through 2GiB by MS-DOS 3.0 and most versions of Windows. Windows NT, Windows 2000, and Windows XP support FAT16 volumes as large as 4GiB. However, FAT16 volumes larger than 2GiB cannot be used by MS-DOS or Windows 9x/Me.
- *FAT32.* Optionally used on volumes from 512MiB through 2GiB, and required on all FAT volumes over 2GiB, starting with Windows 95B (OSR 2.x) and subsequent versions.

FAT12 and FAT16 are the file systems originally used by DOS and Windows and are supported by every other PC operating system from past to present. An add-on to the FAT file systems called VFAT is found in Windows 95 and newer. VFAT is a driver in Windows that adds the capability to use long filenames on existing FAT systems. When running Windows 95 or newer, VFAT is automatically enabled for all FAT volumes.

Although all PC operating systems support FAT12 and FAT16, Windows 2000 and XP also have support for FAT32 as well as non-FAT file systems such as NTFS.

FAT12

FAT12 was the first file system used in the PC when it was released on August 12, 1981, and because it is so efficient on small volumes, it is still used today on all floppy disks as well as hard disk and other removable storage media FAT volumes less than 16MiB. FAT12 uses a table of 12-bit numbers to manage the clusters (also called *allocation units*) on a disk. A *cluster* is the storage unit in the data area of the disk where files are stored. Each file uses a minimum of one cluster, and files that are larger than one cluster use additional space in cluster increments. FAT12 cluster sizes are shown in Table 10.20.

Table 10.20   FAT12 Cluster Sizes

Media Type	Volume Size	Sectors per Cluster	Cluster Size
5 1/4" DD floppy disk	360K	2	1KiB
3 1/2" DD floppy disk	720K	2	1KiB
5 1/4" HD floppy disk	1.2MB	1	0.5KiB
3 1/2" HD floppy disk	1.44MB	1	0.5KiB
3 1/2" ED floppy disk	2.88MB	2	1KiB
Other media	0–15.9MiB	8	4KiB

DD = Double density
HD = High density
ED = Extra-high density
KiB = Kibibyte = 1,024 bytes
MiB = Mebibyte = 1,048,576 bytes

Each cluster on a FAT12 volume is typically 8 sectors in size, except on floppy disks, where the size varies according to the particular floppy type. 12-bit cluster numbers range from 000h to FFFh (hexadecimal), which is 0–4,095 in decimal. This theoretically allows 4,096 total clusters; however, 11 of the cluster numbers are reserved and cannot be assigned to actual clusters on a disk. Cluster numbers start at 2 (0 and 1 are reserved), number FF7h is reserved to indicate a bad cluster, and numbers FF8h–FFFh indicate an end-of-chain in the FAT, leaving 4,085 clusters (4,096 − 11 = 4,085). Microsoft subtracts 1 from this to eliminate boundary problems, allowing up to exactly 4,084 clusters maximum in a FAT12 volume.

FAT12 volumes include 1 sector for the boot record and BPB (BIOS parameter block), two copies of the FAT (up to 12 sectors long each), up to 32 sectors for the root folder (less only on floppy disk media), and a data area with up to 4,084 clusters. Because each FAT12 cluster is 8 sectors (except on floppy disks), FAT12 volumes are limited to a maximum size of 32,729 sectors (1 sector for the boot record + 12 sectors per FAT × 2 FATs + 32 sectors for the root folder + 4084 clusters × 8 sectors per cluster). This equals 16.76MB or 15.98MiB. FAT12 volume limits are detailed in Table 10.21.

Table 10.21   FAT12 Volume Limits

Volume Limit	Clusters	Sectors per Cluster	Total Volume Sectors	Volume Size (Decimal)	Volume Size (Binary)
Maximum size	4,084	8	32,729	16.76MB	15.98MiB

MB = Megabyte = 1,000,000 bytes
MiB = Mebibyte = 1,048,576 bytes

PC/MS-DOS 1.x and 2.x use FAT12 exclusively, and all later versions of DOS and all Windows versions automatically create a FAT12 file system on any disks or partitions that are 32,729 sectors or less (16.76MB) in size. Anything larger than that is automatically formatted as FAT16, FAT32, or NTFS. Characteristics of FAT12 include the following:

- Is used on all floppy disks
- Has a default format on FAT volumes of 16.76MB (15.98MiB) or less
- Is supported by all versions of DOS and Windows
- Is supported by all operating systems capable of reading PC disks

FAT12 is still used in PCs today on very small media because the 12-bit tables are smaller than those for FAT16 and FAT32, which preserves the most space for data.

FAT16

FAT16 is similar to FAT12 except it uses 16-bit numbers to manage the clusters on a disk. FAT16 was introduced on August 14, 1984, along with PC/MS-DOS 3.0, with the intention of supporting larger hard drives. FAT16 picked up where FAT12 left off and was used on media or partitions larger than 32,729 sectors (15.98MiB or 16.76MB). FAT16 could theoretically support drives of up to 2GiB or 4GiB. However, even with FAT16, DOS 3.3 and earlier were still limited to a maximum partition size of 32MiB (33.55MB) because DOS 3.3 and earlier used only 16-bit sector addressing internally and in the BPB (BIOS parameter block, stored in the volume boot sector, which is the first logical sector in a FAT partition). The use of 16-bit sector values limited DOS 3.3 and earlier to supporting drives of up to 65,535 sectors of 512 bytes, which is 32MiB (33.55MB).

As a temporary way to address drives larger than 32MiB, PC/MS-DOS 3.3 (released on April 2, 1987) introduced the extended partition, which could internally support up to 23 subpartitions (logical drives) of up to 32MiB each. Combined with the primary partition on a disk, this allowed for a total of 24 partitions of up to 32MiB each, which would be seen by the operating system as logical drives C–Z.

To take full advantage of FAT16 and allow for larger drives and partition sizes, Microsoft collaborated with Compaq, who introduced Compaq DOS 3.31 in November 1987. It was the first OS to use 32-bit sector addressing internally and in the BPB. Then the rest of the PC world followed suit on July 19, 1988, when Microsoft and IBM released PC/MS-DOS 4.0. This enabled FAT16 to handle partition sizes up to 2GiB using 64 sectors per cluster.

Each cluster in a FAT16 volume is up to 64 sectors in size. 16-bit cluster numbers range from 0000h to FFFFh, which is 0–65,535 in decimal. This theoretically allows 65,536 total clusters. However, 11 of the cluster numbers are reserved and cannot be assigned to actual clusters on a disk. Cluster numbers start at 2 (0 and 1 are reserved), number FFF7h is reserved to indicate a bad cluster, and numbers FFF8h–FFFFh indicate an end of chain in the FAT, leaving 65,525 clusters (65,536 – 11 = 65,525). Microsoft subtracts 1 from this to eliminate boundary problems, allowing up to 65,524 clusters maximum in a FAT16 volume. FAT16 cluster sizes are shown in Table 10.22.

Table 10.22   FAT16 Cluster Sizes

Volume Size	Sectors per Cluster	Cluster Size
4.1MiB–15.96MiB[1]	2	1KiB
>15.96MiB–128MiB	4	2KiB
>128MiB–256MiB	8	4KiB
>256MiB–512MiB	16	8KiB
>512MiB–1GiB	32	16KiB
>1GiB–2GiB	64	32KiB
>2GiB–4GiB[2]	128	64KiB

1. Volumes smaller than 16MiB default to FAT12; however, FAT32 can be forced by altering the format parameters.

2. Volumes larger than 2GiB are supported only by Windows NT/2000/XP and are not recommended.

MB = Megabyte = 1,000,000 bytes

KiB = Kibibyte = 1,024 bytes

MiB = Mebibyte = 1,024KiB = 1,048,576 bytes

GiB = Gibibyte = 1,024MiB = 1,073,741,824 bytes

FAT16 volumes include 1 sector for the boot record and BPB, two copies of the FAT (default and backup) up to 256 sectors long each, 32 sectors for the root folder, and a data area with up to 65,524 clusters. Each FAT16 cluster can be up to 64 sectors (32KiB) in size, meaning FAT16 volumes are limited to a maximum size of 4,194,081 sectors (1 sector for the boot record + 256 sectors per FAT × 2 FATs + 32 sectors for the root folder + 65,524 clusters × 64 sectors per cluster). This equals a maximum capacity of 2.15GB or 2GiB. FAT16 volume limits are shown in Table 10.23.

Note

Windows NT/2000/XP can optionally create FAT16 volumes that use 128 sectors per cluster (64KiB) in size, bringing the maximum volume size to 4.29GB or 4GiB. However any volumes formatted in that manner are not readable in virtually any other OS. Additionally, 64KiB clusters cause many disk utilities to fail. For maximum compatibility, FAT16 volumes should be limited to 32KiB clusters and 2.15GB/2GiB in size.

Table 10.23   FAT16 Volume Limits

Volume Limit	Clusters	Sectors per Cluster	Total Volume Sectors	Volume Size (Decimal)	Volume Size (Binary)
Minimum size	4,167	2	8,401	4.3MB	4.1MiB
DOS 3.0–3.3 max.	16,343	4	65,533	33.55MB	32MiB
Win9x/Me max.	65,524	64	4,194,081	2.15GB	2GiB
NT/2000/XP max.	65,524	128	8,387,617	4.29GB	4GiB

MB = Megabyte = 1,000,000 bytes
GB = Gigabyte = 1,000
MB = 1,000,000,000 bytes
MiB = Mebibyte = 1,048,576 bytes
GiB = Gibibyte = 1,024MiB = 1,073,741,824 bytes

Some notable characteristics and features of FAT16 include

- FAT16 is fully supported by MS-DOS 3.31 and higher, all versions of Windows, and some UNIX operating systems.

- FAT16 is fast and efficient on volumes smaller than 256MiB but relatively inefficient on larger volumes because the cluster size becomes much larger than with FAT32 and NTFS.

- The boot sector information is not automatically backed up, and if damaged or destroyed, access to the volume is lost.

- In case of a problem, you can boot the system using any MS-DOS bootable floppy to troubleshoot the problem and if necessary, repair the volume. Many third-party software tools can repair or recover data from FAT16 volumes.

- The root directory (folder) can handle up to a maximum of 512 entries, which is further reduced if any root entries use long filenames.

- FAT16 has no built-in security, encryption, or compression capability.

- File sizes on a FAT16 volume are limited only by the size of the volume. Because each file takes a minimum of one cluster, FAT16 volumes cannot have more than 65,524 total files.

VFAT and Long Filenames

The original Windows 95 release introduced what is essentially the same FAT16 file system as was used in MS-DOS 6.x and earlier, except for a few important enhancements. Like much of the rest of Windows 95, the operating system support for the FAT file system was rewritten using 32-bit code and called *VFAT (virtual file allocation table)*. VFAT works in combination with the 32-bit protected mode VCACHE (which replaces the 16-bit real mode SMARTDrive cache used in DOS and Windows 3.1) to provide better file system performance. However, the most obvious improvement in VFAT is its support for long filenames. DOS and Windows 3.1 had been encumbered by the standard 8.3 file-naming convention for many years, and adding long filename support was a high priority in Windows 95—particularly in light of the fact that Macintosh and OS/2 users had long enjoyed this capability.

The problem for the Windows 95 designers, as is often the case in the PC industry, was backward compatibility. It is no great feat to make long filenames possible when you are designing a new file system from scratch, as Microsoft did years before with Windows NT's NTFS. However, the Windows 95 developers wanted to add long filenames to the existing FAT file system and still make it possible to store those names on existing DOS volumes and for previous versions of DOS and Windows to access the files.

VFAT provides the capability to assign file and folder names that are up to 255 characters in length (including the length of the path). The three-character extension is maintained because, like previous Windows versions, Windows 9x relies on the extensions to associate file types with specific applications. VFAT's long filenames can also include spaces, as well as the following characters, which standard DOS 8.3 names can't: +,;=[ ].

The first problem when implementing the long filenames was how to make them usable to previous versions of DOS as well as older 16-bit Windows applications that supported only 8.3 names. The resolution to this problem was to give each file two names: a long filename and an alias that uses the traditional 8.3 naming convention. When you create a file with a long filename in Windows 9x/Me, VFAT uses the following process to create an equivalent 8.3 alias name:

1. The first three characters after the last dot in the long filename become the extension of the alias.

2. The first six characters of the long filename (excluding spaces, which are ignored) are converted into uppercase and become the first six characters of the alias filename. If any of these six characters are illegal under the standard 8.3 naming rules (that is, +,;=[ ]), VFAT converts those characters into underscores.

3. VFAT adds the two characters ~1 as the seventh and eighth characters of the alias filename, unless this will result in a name conflict, in which case it uses ~2, ~3, and so on, as necessary.

Aliasing in Windows NT/2000/XP

Note that Windows NT/2000/XP creates aliases differently than Windows 9x/Me (as shown later).

NT/2000/XP begins by taking the first six legal characters in the LFN and following them with a tilde and number. If the first six characters are unique, a number 1 follows the tilde.

If the first six characters aren't unique, a number 2 is added. NT/2000/XP uses the first three legal characters following the last period in the LFN for a file extension.

At the fifth iteration of this process, NT/2000/XP takes only the first two legal characters, performs a hash on the filename to produce four hexadecimal characters, places the four hex characters after the first two legal characters, and appends a ~5. The ~5 remains for all subsequent aliases; only the hex numbers change.

For example, I created six files using long names under Windows XP, and the automatically generated alias (short names) were as follows:

Long File Name (LFN)	Alias (created by Windows)
New Text Document.txt	NEWTEX~1.TXT
New Text Document (2).txt	NEWTEX~2.TXT
New Text Document (3).txt	NEWTEX~3.TXT
New Text Document (4).txt	NEWTEX~4.TXT
New Text Document (5).txt	NE5A0A~1.TXT
New Text Document (6).txt	NE5A04~1.TXT

Note how the algorithm changes after the fifth file.

Tip

You can modify the behavior of the VFAT filename truncation mechanism to make it use the first eight characters of the long filename instead of the first six characters plus ~1. To do this, you must add a new binary value to the **HKEY_ LOCAL_MACHINE\System\CurrentControlSet\control\FileSystem** Registry key called **NameNumericTail**, with a value of **0**. Changing the value to **1** returns the truncation process to its original state.

Although this Registry change creates more "friendly" looking alias names, it causes many programs working with alias names to fail and is not recommended.

VFAT stores this alias filename in the standard name field of the file's folder entry. Any version of DOS or 16-bit Windows can therefore access the file using the alias name. The big problem that still remains, however, is where to store the long filenames. Clearly, storing a 255-character filename in a 32-byte folder entry is impossible (because each character requires 1 byte). However, modifying the structure of the folder entry would make the files unusable by previous DOS versions.

The developers of VFAT resolved this problem by using additional folder entries to store the long file-names. Each of the folder entries is still 32 bytes long, so up to 8 might be required for each long name, depending on its length. To ensure that these additional folder entries are not misinterpreted by earlier DOS versions, VFAT flags them with a combination of attributes that is not possible for a normal file: read-only, hidden, system, and volume label. These attributes cause DOS to ignore the long filename entries, while preventing them from being mistakenly overwritten.

Caution

When using long filenames on a standard FAT12 or FAT16 partition, you should avoid storing them in the root folder. Files with long names that take up multiple folder entries can more easily use up the limited number of entries allotted to the root folder than files with 8.3 names. On FAT32 drives, this is not a problem because the root folder has an unlimited number of entries.

In an experiment, I created a small (1KiB) text file on a floppy disk and gave it a 135-character long filename using Windows 98. I copied the file and pasted it repeatedly into the root folder of a floppy disk using Windows Explorer. Before I could make 20 copies of the file, the system displayed a **File copying** error. The disk could not accept any more files because the multiple copies of the extremely long filename had used up all the root folder entries.

This solution for implementing backward-compatible long filenames in Windows 9x is ingenious, but it is not without its problems. Most of these problems stem from the use of applications that can access only the 8.3 alias names assigned to files. In some cases, if you open a file with a long name using one of these programs and save it again, the connection to the additional folder entries containing the long name is severed and the long name is lost.

This is especially true for older versions of disk utilities, such as Norton Disk Doctor for MS-DOS, that are not designed to support VFAT. Most older applications ignore the additional folder entries because of the combination of attributes assigned to them, but disk repair utilities usually are designed to detect and "correct" discrepancies of this type. The result is that running an old version of Norton Disk Doctor on a partition with long filenames results in the loss of all the long names. In the same way, backup utilities not designed for use with VFAT can strip off the long filenames from a partition.

Note

When using VFAT's long filename capabilities, you definitely should use disk and backup utilities that are intended to support VFAT. Windows 9x includes VFAT-compatible disk repair, defragmentation, and backup programs. If, however, you are for some reason inclined to use an older program that does not support VFAT, Windows 9x includes a clumsy, but effective, solution.

A program is included on the Windows 9x CD-ROM called LFNBK.EXE. It doesn't install with the operating system, but you can use it to strip the long filenames from a VFAT volume and store them in a text file called **LFNBK.DAT**. You can then work with the files on the volume as though they were standard 8.3 FAT files. Afterward, you can use LFNBK.EXE to restore the long filenames to their original places (assuming the file and folder structure has not changed). This is not a convenient solution, nor is it recommended for use in anything but extraordinary circumstances, but the capability is there if needed. Some backup programs designed for disaster recovery (which enable you to reconstruct the contents of the hard drive without reloading Windows first) have used this feature to enable restoration of a Windows drive with long filenames from a DOS prompt (where only 8.3 alias names usually are supported).

Another problem with VFAT's long filenames involves the process by which the file system creates the 8.3 alias names. VFAT creates a new alias every time you create or copy a file into a new folder; therefore, the alias can change. For example, you might have a file called Expenses-January-Travel.doc stored in a folder with the alias EXPENS~1.DOC. If you use Windows 9x Explorer to copy this file to a folder that already contains a file called Expenses-December-Travel.doc, you are likely to find that this existing file is already using the alias EXPENS~1.DOC. In this case, VFAT assigns EXPENS~2.DOC as the alias of the newly copied file, with no warning to the user. This is not a problem for applications that support VFAT because the long filenames are unchanged, but a user running an older application might open the EXPENS~1.DOC file expecting to find the list of January travel expenses and see the December travel expenses list instead.

FAT32

FAT32 is an enhanced version of the FAT file system first supported by Windows 95B (also known as OEM Service Release 2, released in August 1996). FAT32 is also supported in Windows 98/Me and Windows 2000/XP. FAT32 is not supported in MS-DOS 6.xx or earlier, the original release of Windows 95 or in any release of Windows NT.

FAT32 works just like FAT16; the only difference is that it uses numbers with more digits, so it can manage more clusters on a disk. Unlike VFAT, which is a Windows innovation that used existing FAT12/16 file system structures to handle long filenames, FAT32 is an enhancement of the entire FAT file system. FAT32 was first included in the Windows 95 OEM Service Release 2 (OSR2, also known as Windows 95B) and is also part of Windows 98/Me, Windows 2000/XP and later.

One of the main reasons for creating FAT32 was to use disk space more efficiently. FAT32 uses smaller clusters (4KiB clusters for drives up to 8GiB in size), resulting in a 10%–15% more efficient use of disk space relative to large FAT16 drives. FAT32 also supports partitions of up to 2TiB in size, much larger than the 2GiB limit of FAT16. FAT32 cluster sizes are shown in Table 10.24.

Table 10.24 FAT32 Cluster Sizes

Volume Size	Sectors per Cluster	Cluster Size
32.52MiB–260MiB[1]	1	0.5KiB
>260MiB–8GiB	8	4KiB
>8GiB–16GiB	16	8KiB
>16GiB–32GiB	32	16KiB
>32GiB–2TiB[2]	64	32KiB

1. Volumes smaller than 512MiB will default to FAT16, although FAT32 can be forced by altering the format parameters.

2. Windows 2000 and XP format FAT32 volumes only up to 32GiB; however, they support existing FAT32 volumes up to 2TiB.

MB = Megabyte = 1,000,000 bytes

GB = Gigabyte = 1,000MB = 1,000,000,000 bytes

TB = Terabyte = 1,000GB = 1,000,000,000,000 bytes

KiB = Kibibytes = 1,024 bytes

MiB = Mebibyte = 1,024KiB = 1,048,576 bytes

GiB = Gibibyte = 1,024MiB = 1,073,741,824 bytes

TiB = Tebibytes = 1,024GiB = 1,099,511,627,776 bytes

Although the name implies that FAT32 uses 32-bit numbers to manage clusters (allocation units) on a disk, FAT32 actually uses only the first 28 bits of each 32-bit entry, leaving the high 4 bits reserved. The only time the high 4 bits are changed is when the volume is formatted, at which time the whole 32-bit entry is zeroed (including the high 4 bits). The high 4 bits are subsequently ignored when reading or writing FAT32 cluster entries; therefore, if those bits are non-zero, they are preserved. Microsoft has never indicated any purpose for them other than simply being reserved.

So, although the FAT32 entries are technically 32-bit numbers, FAT32 really uses 28-bit numbers to manage the clusters on a disk. Each cluster on a FAT32 volume is from 1 sector (512 bytes) to 64 sectors (32KiB) in size. 28-bit cluster numbers range from 0000000h to FFFFFFFh, which is 0–268,435,455 in decimal. This theoretically allows for 268,435,456 total clusters. However 11 of the numbers are reserved and cannot be assigned to actual clusters on a disk. Cluster numbers start at 2 (0 and 1 are reserved), the number FFFFFF7h is reserved to indicate a bad cluster, and numbers FFFFFF8h–FFFFFFFh indicate an end of chain in the FAT, leaving exactly 268,435,445 clusters maximum (268,435,456 – 11 = 268,435,445).

FAT32 volumes reserve the first 32 sectors for the boot record, which includes both the default boot record (3 sectors long, starting at logical sector 0) and a backup boot record (also 3 sectors long, but starting at logical sector 6). The remaining sectors in that area are reserved and filled with 0s. Following the 32 reserved sectors are 2 FATs (default and backup) that can be anywhere from 512 sectors to 2,097,152 sectors in length, with a data area 65,525–268,435,445 clusters.

Each FAT32 cluster is up to 64 sectors (32KiB) in size, so FAT32 disks or partitions could theoretically be up to 17,184,062,816 sectors (32 sectors for the boot record + 2,097,152 sectors per FAT × 2 FATs + 268,435,445 clusters × 64 sectors per cluster), which equals a capacity of 8.8TB or 8TiB. This capacity is theoretical because the 32-bit sector numbering scheme used in the partition tables located in the master boot record (MBR) limits a disk to no more than 4,294,967,295 (2^{32}–1) sectors, which is 2.2TB or 2TiB. Therefore, although FAT32 can in theory handle a volume of up to 8.8TB (terabytes or trillions of bytes), the reality is that we are currently limited by the 32-bit sector numbering in the partition table format of the MBR to only 2.2TB. At the current rate of hard disk capacity growth, single drives of that size will debut between the years 2009 and 2011. Of course, by that time the MBR limitation should be addressed.

Individual files can be up to 1 byte less than 4GiB in size and are limited by the size field in the folder entry, which is 4 bytes long. Because the clusters are numbered using 32-bit values instead of 16-bit ones, the format of the folder entries on a FAT32 partition must be changed slightly. The 2-byte Link to Start Cluster field is increased to 4 bytes, using 2 of the 10 bytes (bytes 12–21) in the folder entry that were reserved for future use.

Note

If you attempt to format a FAT32 volume larger than 32GiB on a system running Windows 2000 or Windows XP, the format fails near the end of the process with the following error:

```
Logical Disk Manager: Volume size too big.
```

This is by design. The format tools included with Windows 2000/XP and later will not format a volume larger than 32GiB using the FAT32 file system. Only the format tools are restricted as such; any preexisting volumes up to 2TiB are otherwise fully supported. The limitation is entirely voluntary; Microsoft is basically trying to force you to use NTFS on any newly created volumes larger than 32GiB. Unfortunately this means that if you are formatting an external USB or FireWire drive that will be moved between various systems, some of which include Windows 9x/Me or even Apple Mac systems, you must either format the drive on a Windows 98 or Me system, or use a third-party utility such as the SwissKnife program (available for free from www.compuapps.com) to partition and format the drive.

Windows 95 OSR2 and Windows 98 have additional limitations with FAT32. The ScanDisk tool included with those operating systems is a 16-bit program that has a maximum allocation size for a single memory block of 16MB minus 64KB. This means that ScanDisk cannot process volumes using the FAT32 file system that have a FAT larger than 16MB minus 64KB in size. Each FAT32 entry uses 4 bytes, so ScanDisk cannot process the FAT on a volume using the FAT32 file system that defines more than 4,177,920 clusters, which after subtracting the two reserved clusters leaves 4,177,918 actual clusters. At 32KiB per cluster—including the boot sector reserved area and the FATs themselves—this results in a maximum volume size of 136.94GB or 127.53GiB. The ScanDisk versions included with Windows Me and later do not have this limitation.

Table 10.25 lists the volume limits for a FAT32 file system.

Table 10.25   FAT32 Volume Limits

Volume Limit	Clusters	Sectors per Cluster	Total Volume Sectors	Volume Size (Decimal)	Volume Size (Binary)
Minimum size	65,535	1	66,601	34.1MB	32.52MiB
MBR max.	67,092,481	64	4,294,967,266	2.2TB	2TiB
Theoretical max.	268,435,445	64	17,184,062,816	8.8TB	8TiB

MB = Megabyte = 1,000,000 bytes

GB = Gigabyte = 1,000MB = 1,000,000,000 bytes

TB = Terabyte = 1,000GB = 1,000,000,000,000 bytes

KiB = Kibibytes = 1,024 bytes

MiB = Mebibyte = 1,024KiB = 1,048,576 bytes

GiB = Gibibyte = 1,024MiB = 1,073,741,824 bytes

TiB = Tebibytes = 1,024GiB = 1,099,511,627,776 bytes

FAT32 is more robust than FAT12 or FAT16. FAT12/16 uses the first sector of a volume for the volume boot record, which is a critical structure. If the boot sector is damaged or destroyed, access to the entire volume is lost. FAT32 improves on this by creating both a default and a backup volume boot record in the first 32 sectors of the volume, which are reserved for this purpose. Each FAT32 volume boot record is 3 sectors long. The default boot record is in logical sectors 0–2 (the first three sectors) in the partition, and the backup is in sectors 6–8. This feature has saved me on several occasions when the default boot record was damaged and access to the entire volume was lost. In these situations, I was still able to recover the entire volume by manually restoring the volume boot record from the backup by using a sector editor such as Norton Diskedit (included with Norton SystemWorks by Symantec). Because FAT12 and FAT16 do not create a backup boot sector, if the boot sector is destroyed on those volumes, it must be re-created manually from scratch—a much more difficult proposition.

Another important difference in FAT32 partitions is the nature of the root folder. In a FAT32 partition, the root folder does not occupy a fixed position on the disk as in a FAT16 partition. Instead, it can be located anywhere in the partition and expand to any size. This eliminates the preset limit on root folder entries and provides the infrastructure necessary to make FAT32 partitions dynamically resizable. Unfortunately, Microsoft never implemented that feature in Windows, but third-party products such as PartitionMagic from Symantec can take advantage of this capability.

As with FAT12/16, FAT32 also maintains two copies of the FAT and automatically switches to the backup FAT if a sector in the default FAT becomes unreadable. The root directory (folder) in a FAT16 system is exactly 32 sectors long and immediately follows the two FAT copies; however, in FAT32, the root folder is actually created as a subdirectory (folder) that is stored as a file, relocatable to anywhere in the partition, and extendable in length. Therefore, a 512-file limit no longer exists in the root folder for FAT32 as there was with FAT12/16.

The main drawback of FAT32 is that it is not compatible with previous versions of DOS and Windows 95. You can't boot to a previous version of DOS or (pre-OSR2) Windows 95 from a FAT32 drive, nor can a system started with an old DOS or Windows 95 boot disk see FAT32 partitions. Most recent distributions of Linux now support FAT32, and even the Mac OS 8.1 and later can read and write FAT32 volumes. For all but the oldest of equipment, FAT32 is the most universally understandable format that supports larger volumes.

Some notable characteristics and features of FAT32 include the following:

- FAT32 is fully supported by Windows 95B (OSR2), 98, Me, 2000, XP, and later versions.
- MS-DOS 6.22 and earlier, Windows 95a, and Windows NT do not support FAT32 and cannot read or write FAT32 volumes.
- Mac OS 8.1 and later support FAT32 drives.
- FAT32 is the ideal format for large, external USB or FireWire drives that will be moved between various PC and Mac systems.
- The root directory (folder) is stored as a subfolder file that can be located anywhere on the volume. Subdirectories (folders) including the root can handle up to 65,534 entries, which is further reduced if any entries use long filenames.
- FAT32 uses smaller clusters (4KiB for volumes up to 8GiB), so space is allocated much more efficiently than FAT16.
- The critical boot sector is backed up at logical sector 6 on the volume.
- Windows 2000 and XP format FAT32 volumes only up to 32GiB. To format FAT32 volumes larger than 32GiB, you must format the volume on a Windows 98/Me system.

- In case of a boot problem, you must start the system using a bootable disk created using Windows 95B (OSR2), 98, Me, 2000, or XP. A limited number of third-party software tools can repair or recover data from FAT32 volumes.

- FAT32 has no built-in security, encryption, or compression capability.

- File sizes on FAT32 volumes are limited to 4,294,967,295 bytes ($2^{32} - 1$), which is 1 byte less than 4GiB in size.

FAT Mirroring

FAT32 also takes greater advantage of the two copies of the FAT stored on a disk partition. On a FAT16 partition, the first copy of the FAT is always the primary copy and replicates its data to the secondary FAT, sometimes corrupting it in the process. On a FAT32 partition, when the system detects a problem with the primary copy of the FAT, it can switch to the other copy, which then becomes the primary. The system can also disable the FAT mirroring process to prevent the viable FAT from being corrupted by the other copy. This provides a greater degree of fault tolerance to FAT32 partitions, often enabling you to repair a damaged FAT without an immediate system interruption or a loss of table data.

Converting FAT16 to FAT32

If you want to convert an existing FAT16 partition to FAT32, Windows 98 and Me later include a FAT32 Conversion Wizard that enables you to migrate existing partitions in place.

The wizard gathers the information needed to perform the conversion, informs you of the consequences of implementing FAT32, and attempts to prevent data loss and other problems. After you have selected the drive you want to convert, the wizard performs a scan for applications (such as disk utilities) that might not function properly on the converted partition. The wizard gives you the opportunity to remove these and warns you to back up the data on the partition before proceeding with the conversion. Even if you don't use the Microsoft Backup utility the wizard offers, backing up your data is a strongly recommended precaution.

Because the conversion must deal with the existing partition data in addition to creating new volume boot record information, FATs, and clusters, the process can take far longer than partitioning and formatting an empty drive. Depending on the amount of data involved and the new cluster size, the conversion can take several hours to complete.

After you convert a FAT16 partition to FAT32, you can't convert it back with Windows tools, except by destroying the partition and using FDISK to create a new one. After-market partitioning utilities are available that can convert FAT32 back to FAT16 if you want. You should take precautions before beginning the conversion process, such as connecting the system to a UPS. A power failure during the conversion could result in a loss of data.

Third-Party Partitioning Utilities

Windows includes only basic tools for creating FAT32 partitions, but programs such as Partition Commander from VCOM (www.v-com.com) and PartitionMagic from Symantec (www.symantec.com) provide many other partition manipulation features. These programs can easily convert partitions back and forth between FAT16, FAT32, NTFS, and other file systems, as well as resize, move, and copy partitions without destroying the data they contain. They also allow changes in cluster sizes beyond what the standard Windows tools create.

File Allocation Table Tutorial

You can think of the FAT as a type of spreadsheet that tracks the allocation of the disk's clusters. Each cell in the spreadsheet corresponds to a single cluster on the disk. The number stored in that cell is a code indicating whether a file uses the cluster and, if so, where the next cluster of the file is located. Thus, to determine which clusters a particular file is using, you would start by looking at the first FAT reference in the file's folder entry. When you look up the referenced cluster in the FAT, the table contains a reference to the file's next cluster. Each FAT reference, therefore, points to the next cluster in what is called a FAT *chain* until you reach the cluster containing the end of the file. Numbers stored in the FAT are hexadecimal numbers that are either 12 or 16 bits long. The 16-bit FAT numbers are easy to follow in a disk sector editor because they take an even 2 bytes of space. The 12-bit numbers are 1 1/2 bytes long, which presents a problem because most disk sector editors show data in byte units. To edit a 12-bit FAT, you must do some hex/binary math to convert the displayed byte units to FAT numbers. Fortunately (unless you are using the DOS DEBUG program), most of the available tools and utility programs have a FAT-editing mode that automatically converts the numbers for you. Most of them also show the FAT numbers in decimal form, which most people find easier to handle.

With FAT16, the cluster numbers are stored as 16-bit entries, from 0000h to FFFFh. The largest value possible is FFFFh, which corresponds to 65,535 in decimal, but several numbers at the beginning and end are reserved for special use. The actual cluster numbers allowed in a FAT16 system range from 0002h to FFF6h, which is 2–65,526 in decimal. All files must be stored in cluster numbers within that range. That leaves only 65,524 valid clusters to use for storing files (cluster numbers below 2 and above 65,526 are reserved), meaning a partition must be broken up into that many clusters or less. A typical file entry under FAT16 might look like Table 10.26.

Table 10.26   FAT16 File Entries

	Folder	
Name	**Starting Cluster**	**Size**
USCONST.TXT	1000	4

	FAT16 File Allocation Table	
FAT Cluster #	**Value**	**Meaning**
00002	0	First cluster available
...	...	...
00999	0	Cluster available
01000	1001	In use, points to next cluster
01001	1002	In use, points to next cluster
01002	1003	In use, points to next cluster
01003	FFFFh	End of file
01004	0	Cluster available
...	...	...
65526	0	Last cluster available

In this example, the folder entry states that the file starts in cluster number 1000. In the FAT, that cluster has a nonzero value, which indicates it is in use; the specific value indicates where the file using it would continue. In this case, the entry for cluster 1000 is 1001, which means the file continues in cluster 1001. The entry in 1001 points to 1002, and from 1002 the entry points to 1003. The entry for 1003 is FFFFh, which is an indication that the cluster is in use but that the file ends here and uses no additional clusters.

The use of the FAT becomes clearer when you see that files can be fragmented. Let's say that before the USCONST.TXT file was written, another file already occupied clusters 1002 and 1003. If USCONST.TXT was written starting at 1000, it would not have been capable of being completely written before running into the other file. As such, the operating system would skip over the used clusters and continue the file in the next available cluster. The end result is shown in Table 10.27.

Table 10.27   Folder and FAT Relationship (Fragmented File)

Folder		
Name	**Starting Cluster**	**Size**
PLEDGE.TXT	1002	2
USCONST.TXT	1000	4
FAT16 File Allocation Table		
FAT Cluster #	**Value**	**Meaning**
00002	0	First cluster available
...	...	...
00999	0	Cluster available
01000	1001	In use, points to next cluster
01001	1004	In use, points to next cluster
01002	1003	In use, points to next cluster
01003	FFFFh	End of file
01004	1005	In use, points to next cluster
01005	FFFFh	End of file
...	...	...
65526	0	Last cluster available

In this example, the PLEDGE.TXT file that was previously written interrupted USCONST.TXT, so those clusters are skipped over, and the pointers in the FAT reflect that. Note that the defrag programs included with DOS and Windows take an example like this and move the files so they are contiguous, one after the other, and update the FAT to indicate the change in cluster use.

The first two entries in the FAT are reserved and contain information about the table itself. All remaining entries correspond to specific clusters on the disk. Most FAT entries consist of a reference to another cluster containing the next part of a particular file. However, some FAT entries contain hexadecimal values with special meanings, as follows:

- *0000h.* Indicates that the cluster is not in use by a file

- *FFF7h.* Indicates that at least one sector in the cluster is damaged and that it should not be used to store data

- *FFF8h–FFFFh.* Indicates that the cluster contains the end of a file and that no reference to another cluster is necessary

To compare FAT16 and FAT32, you can look at how a file would be stored on each. With FAT32, the cluster numbers range from 00000000h to 0FFFFFFFh, which is 0–268,435,455 in decimal. Again, some values at the low and high ends are reserved, and only values between 00000002h and 0FFFFFF6h are valid, which means values 2–268,435,446 are valid. This leaves 268,435,445 valid entries, so the drive must be split into that many clusters or less. Because a drive can be split into so many more clusters, the clusters can be smaller, which conserves disk space. The same file as shown earlier could be stored on a FAT32 system as illustrated in Table 10.28.

Table 10.28   FAT32 File Entries

Folder		
Name	**Starting Cluster**	**Size**
USCONST.TXT	1000	8
FAT32 File Allocation Table		
FAT Cluster #	**Value**	**Meaning**
0000000002	0	First cluster available
…	…	…
0000000999	0	Cluster available
0000001000	1001	In use, points to next cluster
0000001001	1002	In use, points to next cluster
0000001002	1003	In use, points to next cluster
0000001003	1004	In use, points to next cluster
0000001004	1005	In use, points to next cluster
0000001005	1006	In use, points to next cluster
0000001006	1007	In use, points to next cluster
0000001007	0FFFFFFFh	End of file
0000001008	0	Cluster available
…	…	…
268,435,446	0	Last cluster available

Because the FAT32 system enables many more clusters to be allocated, the cluster size is usually smaller. So, although files overall use more individual clusters, less wasted space results because the last cluster is, on average, only half filled.

Some additional limitations exist on FAT32 volumes. Volumes less than 512MiB default to FAT16, but FAT32 partitions as small as 32.52MiB can be forced using the proper utilities or commands. Anything smaller than that, however, must be either FAT16 or FAT12.

Using smaller clusters results in many more clusters and more entries in the FAT. A 2GiB partition using FAT32 requires up to 524,288 FAT entries, whereas the same drive needs only 65,536 entries using FAT16. Thus, the size of one copy of the FAT16 table is 128KiB (65,536 entries×16 bits = 1,048,576 bits/8 = 131,072 bytes/1,024 = 128KiB), whereas the FAT32 table is 2MiB in size.

The size of the FAT has a definite impact on the performance of the file system. Windows 9x/Me uses VCACHE to keep the FAT in memory at all times to improve file system performance. The use of 4KiB clusters for drives up to 8GiB in size is, therefore, a reasonable compromise for the average PC's memory capacity. If the file system were to use clusters equal to one disk sector (1 sector = 512KiB) in an attempt to minimize slack as much as possible, the FAT table for a 2GiB drive would contain 4,194,304 entries and be 16MB in size.

This would monopolize a substantial portion of the memory in the average system, probably resulting in noticeably degraded performance. Although at first it might seem as though even a 2MB FAT is quite large when compared to 128KiB, keep in mind that hard disk drives are a great deal faster now than they were when the FAT file system was originally designed. In practice, FAT32 typically results in a minor (less than 5%) improvement in file system performance. However, systems that perform a great many sequential disk writes might see an equally minor degradation in performance.

The partitioning program generally determines whether a 12-bit, 16-bit, or 32-bit FAT is placed on a disk, even though the FAT isn't written until you perform a high-level format (using the FORMAT utility). On today's systems, usually only floppy disks use 12-bit FATs, but FDISK also creates a 12-bit FAT if you create a hard disk volume that is smaller than 16MiB. On hard disk volumes of more than 16MiB, FDISK creates a 16-bit FAT. On drives larger than 512MiB, the FDISK program included in Windows 95 OSR2, and Windows 98/Me enables you to create 32-bit FATs when you answer yes to the question Enable Large Disk Support? when you start FDISK. You can also select FAT32 when you prepare a drive with the Windows 2000 or Windows XP Disk Management program (Windows NT doesn't support FAT32).

FAT volumes normally have two copies of the FAT. Each one occupies contiguous sectors on the disk, and the second FAT copy immediately follows the first. Unfortunately, the operating system uses the second FAT copy only if sectors in the first FAT copy become unreadable. If the first FAT copy is corrupted, which is a much more common problem, the operating system does not use the second FAT copy. Even the CHKDSK command does not check or verify the second FAT copy. Moreover, whenever the OS updates the first FAT, it automatically copies large portions of the first FAT to the second FAT. If the first copy was corrupted and subsequently updated by the OS, a large portion of the first FAT is copied over to the second FAT copy, damaging it in the process. After the update, the second copy is usually a mirror image of the first one, complete with any corruption. Two FATs rarely stay out of sync for very long. When they are out of sync and the OS writes to the disk, it updates the first FAT and overwrites the second FAT with the first. This is why disk repair and recovery utilities warn you to stop working as soon as you detect a FAT problem. Programs such as Norton Disk Doctor (included with the Norton Utilities which are a part of Norton SystemWorks) use the second copy of the FAT as a reference to repair the first one, but if the OS has already updated the second FAT, repair might be impossible.

Directories (Folders)

A *directory* is a simple database containing information about the files stored on a FAT partition. Directories are also called *folders* in Windows.

Each record in a folder is 32 bytes long, with no delimiters or separating characters between the fields or records. A folder stores almost all the information that the operating system knows about a file, including the following:

- *Filename and extension.* The eight-character name and three-character extension of the file. The dot between the name and the extension is implied but not included in the entry.

Note

To see how Windows extends filenames to allow 255 characters within the 8.3 folder structure, see the section "VFAT and Long Filenames," in this chapter.

- *File attribute byte.* The byte containing the flags representing the standard DOS file attributes, using the format shown in Table 10.32.
- *Date/Time of last change.* The date and time that the file was created or last modified.
- *File size.* The size of the file, in bytes.
- *Link to start cluster.* The number of the cluster in the partition where the beginning of the file is stored. To learn more about clusters, see the section "Clusters (Allocation Units)," in this chapter.

Other information exists that a folder does not contain about a file. This includes where the rest of its clusters in the partition are located and whether the file is contiguous or fragmented. This information is contained in the FAT.

Two basic types of directories exist: the root directory (also called the root folder) and subdirectories (also called folders). Any given volume can have only one root folder. The root folder is always stored on a disk in a fixed location immediately following the two copies of the FAT. Root folders vary in size because of the different types and capacities of disks, but the root folder of a given disk is fixed. Using the FORMAT command creates a root folder that has a fixed length and can't be extended to hold more entries. The root folder entry limits are shown in Table 10.29. Subfolders are stored as files in the data area of the disk and can grow in size dynamically; therefore, they have no fixed length limits.

Table 10.29   Root Folder Entry Limits

Drive Type	Maximum Root Folder Entries
Hard disk	512
1.44MB floppy disk	224
2.88MB floppy disk	448
Jaz and Zip	512
LS-120 and LS-240	512

Every folder, whether it is the root folder or a subfolder, is organized in the same way. Entries in the folder database store important information about individual files and how files are named on the disk. The folder information is linked to the FAT by the starting cluster entry. In fact, if no file on a disk were longer than one single cluster, the FAT would be unnecessary. The folder stores all the information needed by DOS to manage the file, with the exception of the list of clusters the file occupies other than the first one. The FAT stores the remaining information about the other clusters the file occupies.

To trace a file on a disk, use a disk editor, such as the Disk Edit program that comes with the Norton Utilities. Start by looking up the folder entry to get the information about the starting cluster of the file and its size. Then, using the appropriate editor commands, go to the FAT where you can follow the chain of clusters the file occupies until you reach the end of the file. By using the folder and FAT in this manner, you can visit all the clusters on the disk that are occupied by the file. This type of technique can be useful when these entries are corrupted and when you are trying to find missing parts of a file.

FAT folder entries are 32 bytes long and are in the format shown in Table 10.30, which shows the location (or offset) of each field within the entry (in both hexadecimal and decimal form) and the length of each field.

Table 10.30   FAT Folder Format

Offset (Hex)	Offset (Dec)	Field Length	Description
00h	0	8 bytes	Filename
08h	8	3 bytes	File extension
0Bh	11	1 byte	File attributes
0Ch	12	10 bytes	Reserved (00h)
16h	22	1 word	Time of creation
18h	24	1 word	Date of creation
1Ah	26	1 word	Starting cluster
1Ch	28	1 dword	Size in bytes

Filenames and extensions are left-justified and padded with spaces (which are represented as ASCII 32h bytes). In other words, if your filename is "AL", it is really stored as "AL---------", where the hyphens are spaces. The first byte of the filename indicates the file status for that folder entry, shown in Table 10.31.

Table 10.31   Folder Entry Status Byte (First Byte)

Hex	File Status
00h	Entry never used; entries past this point not searched.
05h	Indicates that the first character of the filename is actually E5h.
E5h	s (lowercase sigma). Indicates that the file has been erased.
2Eh	. (period). Indicates that this entry is a folder. If the second byte is also 2Eh, the cluster field contains the cluster number of the parent folder (0000h, if the parent is the root).

A word is 2 bytes read in reverse order, and a dword is two words read in reverse order.

Table 10.32 describes the FAT folder file attribute byte. Attributes are 1-bit flags that control specific properties of a file, such as whether it is hidden or designated as read-only. Each flag is individually activated (1) or deactivated (0) by changing the bit value. The combination of the eight bit values can be expressed as a single hexadecimal byte value; for example, 07h translates to 00000111, and the 1 bits in positions 2, 1, and 0 indicate the file is system, hidden, and read-only.

Table 10.32   FAT Folder File Attribute Byte

Bit Positions 7 6 5 4 3 2 1 0	Hex Value	Description
0 0 0 0 0 0 0 1	01h	Read-only file
0 0 0 0 0 0 1 0	02h	Hidden file
0 0 0 0 0 1 0 0	04h	System file
0 0 0 0 1 0 0 0	08h	Volume label
0 0 0 1 0 0 0 0	10h	Subfolder
0 0 1 0 0 0 0 0	20h	Archive (updated since backup)
0 1 0 0 0 0 0 0	40h	Reserved
1 0 0 0 0 0 0 0	80h	Reserved

(continues)

Table 10.32   Continued

Bit Positions 7 6 5 4 3 2 1 0	Hex Value	Description
	Examples	
0 0 0 0 0 1 1 1	07h	System, hidden, read-only
0 0 1 0 0 0 0 1	21h	Read-only, archive
0 0 1 1 0 0 1 0	32h	Hidden, subfolder, archive
0 0 1 0 0 1 1 1	27h	Read-only, hidden, system, archive

Note

The **ATTRIB** command can be used to change file attributes. In the Windows GUI, you can also use the properties sheet for a file or folder to change the attributes. The archive bit changes automatically when a file is backed up or changed.

FAT File System Errors

File system errors can, of course, occur because of hardware problems, but you are more likely to see them result from software crashes and improper system handling. Turning off a system without shutting down Windows properly, for example, can result in errors that cause clusters to be incorrectly listed as in use when they are not. Some of the most common file system errors that occur on FAT partitions are described in the following sections.

Lost Clusters

Probably the most common file system error, *lost* clusters are clusters the FAT designates as being in use when they actually are not. Most often caused by an interruption of a file system process due to an application crash or a system shutdown, for example, the FAT entry of a lost cluster might contain a reference to a subsequent cluster. However, the FAT chain stemming from the folder entry has been broken somewhere along the line.

Lost clusters appear in the file structure as shown in Table 10.33.

Table 10.33   Lost Clusters in a File Structure

	Folder	
Name	**Starting Cluster**	**Size**
(no entry)	0	0
	FAT16 File Allocation Table	
FAT Cluster #	**Value**	**Meaning**
00002	0	First cluster available
...	...	...
00999	0	Cluster available
01000	1001	In use, points to next cluster
01001	1002	In use, points to next cluster
01002	1003	In use, points to next cluster
01003	FFFFh	End of file

Table 10.33   Continued

FAT16 File Allocation Table

FAT Cluster #	Value	Meaning
01004	0	Cluster available
...	...	...
65526	0	Last cluster available

The operating system sees a valid chain of clusters in the FAT but no corresponding folder entry to back it up. Programs that are terminated before they can close their open files typically cause this. The operating system usually modifies the FAT chain as the file is written, and the final step when closing is to create a matching folder entry. If the system is interrupted before the file is closed (such as by shutting down the system improperly), lost clusters are the result. Disk repair programs check for lost clusters by tracing the FAT chain for each file and subfolder in the partition and building a facsimile of the FAT in memory. After compiling a list of all the FAT entries that indicate properly allocated clusters, the program compares this facsimile with the actual FAT. Any entries denoting allocated clusters in the real FAT that do not appear in the facsimile are lost clusters because they are not part of a valid FAT chain.

The utility typically gives you the opportunity to save the data in the lost clusters as a file before it changes the FAT entries to show them as unallocated clusters. If your system crashed or lost power while you were working with a word processor data file, for example, you might be able to retrieve text from the lost clusters in this way. When left unrepaired, lost clusters are unavailable for use by the system, reducing the storage capacity of your drive.

The typical choices you have for correcting lost clusters are to assign them a made-up name or zero out the FAT entries. If you assign them a name, you can at least look at the entries as a valid file and then delete the file if you find it useless. The CHKDSK and SCANDISK programs are designed to fix lost clusters by assigning them names starting with FILE0001.CHK. If more than one lost chain exists, sequential numbers following the first one are used. The lost clusters shown earlier could be corrected by CHKDSK or SCANDISK as shown in Table 10.34.

Table 10.34   Finding Lost Clusters

Folder

Name	Starting Cluster	Size
FILE0001.CHK	1000	4

FAT16 File Allocation Table

FAT Cluster #	Value	Meaning
00002	0	First cluster available
...	...	...
00999	0	Cluster available
01000	1001	In use, points to next cluster
01001	1002	In use, points to next cluster
01002	1003	In use, points to next cluster
01003	FFFFh	End of file

(continues)

Table 10.34   Continued

FAT16 File Allocation Table		
FAT Cluster #	**Value**	**Meaning**
01004	0	Cluster available
...	...	...
65526	0	Last cluster available

As you can see, a new entry was created to match the FAT entries. The name is made up because there is no way for the repair utility to know what the original name of the file might have been.

Cross-Linked Files

Cross-linked files occur when two folder entries improperly reference the same cluster in their Link to Start Cluster fields. The result is that each file uses the same FAT chain. Because the clusters can store data from only one file, working with one of the two files can inadvertently overwrite the other file's data.

Cross-linked files would appear in the file structure as shown in Table 10.35.

Table 10.35   Cross-Linked Files

Folder		
Name	**Starting Cluster**	**Size**
USCONST.TXT	1000	4
PLEDGE.TXT	1002	2
FAT16 File Allocation Table		
FAT Cluster #	**Value**	**Meaning**
00002	0	First cluster available
...	...	...
00999	0	Cluster available
01000	1001	In use, points to next cluster
01001	1002	In use, points to next cluster
01002	1003	In use, points to next cluster
01003	FFFFh	End of file
01004	0	Cluster available
...	...	...
65526	0	Last cluster available

In this case, two files claim ownership of clusters 1002 and 1003, so these files are said to be cross-linked on 1002. When a situation such as this arises, one of the files typically is valid and the other is corrupt, being that only one actual given set of data can occupy a given cluster. The normal repair is to copy both files involved to new names, which duplicates their data separately in another area of the disk, and then delete *all* the cross-linked files. Deleting them all is important because by deleting only one of them, the FAT chain is zeroed, which further damages the other entries. Then, you can examine the files you copied to determine which one is good and which is corrupt.

Detecting cross-linked files is a relatively easy task for a disk repair utility because it must examine only the partition's folder entries and not the file clusters themselves. However, by the time the utility detects the error, the data from one of the two files is probably already lost—although you might be able to recover parts of it from lost clusters.

Invalid Files or Folders

Sometimes the information in a folder entry for a file or subfolder can be corrupted to the point at which the entry is not just erroneous (as in cross-linked files) but invalid. The entry might have a cluster or date reference that is invalid, or it might violate the rules for the entry format in some other way. In most cases, disk repair software can correct these problems, permitting access to the file.

FAT Errors

As discussed earlier, accessing its duplicate copy can sometimes repair a corrupted FAT. Disk repair utilities typically rely on this technique to restore a damaged FAT to its original state, as long as the mirroring process has not corrupted the copy. FAT32 tables are more likely to be repairable because their more advanced mirroring capabilities make the copy less likely to be corrupted.

An example of a damaged FAT might appear to the operating system as shown in Table 10.36.

Table 10.36　Damaged FAT

	Folder	
Name	**Starting Cluster**	**Size**
USCONST.TXT	1000	4
	FAT16 File Allocation Table	
FAT Cluster #	**Value**	**Meaning**
00002	0	First cluster available
...	...	...
00999	0	Cluster available
01000	1001	In use, points to next cluster
01001	0	Cluster available
01002	1003	In use, points to next cluster
01003	FFFFh	End of file
01004	0	Cluster available
...	...	...
65526	0	Last cluster available

This single error would cause multiple problems to appear. The file USCONST.TXT would now come up as having an allocation error—in which the size in the folder no longer matches the number of clusters in the FAT chain. The file would end after cluster 1001 in this example, and the rest of the data would be missing if you loaded this file for viewing. Also, two lost clusters would exist; that is, 1002 and 1003 appear to have no folder entry that owns them. When multiple problems such as these appear, a single incident of damage is often the cause. The repair in this case could involve copying the data from the backup FAT back to the primary FAT, but in most cases, the backup is similarly damaged. Normal utilities would truncate the file and create an entry for a second file out of the lost clusters. You would have to figure out yourself that they really belong together. This is where having knowledge in data recovery can help over using automated utilities that can't think for themselves.

NTFS

Windows NT 3.1 (the first version of NT despite the 3.1 designation) was released in August 1993 and introduced the New Technology File System (NTFS), which is unique to NT-based operating systems (including Windows 2000 and Windows XP) and is not supported by Windows 9x/Me. NTFS includes many advanced features not found in the FAT file systems.

NTFS is the native file system of Windows NT/2000/XP and Vista. Windows 2000 and later use an enhanced version of NTFS called NTFS 5 or NTFS 2000; Windows NT 4.0 must have Service Pack 4 or above installed to be capable of accessing an NTFS 5/NTFS 2000 disk. Although NT/2000/XP support FAT partitions (and Windows 2000/XP even support FAT32), NTFS provides many advantages over FAT, including long filenames, support for larger files and partitions, extended attributes, and increased security. NTFS, like all of Windows NT, was newly designed from the ground up. Backward-compatibility with previous Microsoft operating systems was not a concern because the developers were intent on creating an entirely new 32-bit platform. As a result, few operating systems other than Windows NT and Windows 2000/XP, which are based on Windows NT, can natively read NTFS partitions. More recently that has been changing; for example Apple included the ability to read (but not write) NTFS volumes in the Mac OS X 10.3 (Panther) and later versions. Also NTFS drivers have become available for Linux, MS-DOS, and other OSs as well. Unfortunately most of these solutions have had to be reverse engineered because Microsoft has kept the internal technical details of NTFS mostly private.

NTFS supports filenames of up to 255 characters, using spaces, multiple periods, and any other standard characters except the following: *?/\;:<>|. Since Windows NT 3.51, NTFS has also supported compression on a file-by-file (or folder-by-folder) basis through each file or folder's properties sheet. No third-party program, such as WinZip or PKZip, is needed to compress or decompress files stored on an NTFS drive. NTFS 5 also supports encryption on a file-by-file or folder-by-folder properties sheet.

Tip

To access advanced file attributes under NTFS such as compression, encryption, and indexing, right-click the file or folder, select Properties, and click the Advanced button to bring up the Advanced properties dialog box.

NTFS supports larger volumes (up to 16TiB), larger files, and more files per volume than FAT. NTFS also uses smaller cluster sizes than even FAT32, resulting in more efficient use of a volume. For example, a 30GiB NTFS volume uses 4KiB clusters, whereas the same size volume formatted with FAT32 uses 16KiB clusters. Smaller clusters reduce wasted space on the volume. NTFS cluster sizes are shown in Table 10.37.

Table 10.37   NTFS Cluster Sizes

Volume Size	Sectors per Cluster	Cluster Size
16MiB–512MiB	1	0.5KiB
>512MiB–1GiB	2	1KiB
>1GiB–2GiB	4	2KiB
>2GiB–2TiB[1]	8	4KiB

1. Larger cluster sizes can be forced by altering the format parameters; however, file compression is disabled if clusters larger than 8 sectors (4KiB) are selected.

MB = Megabyte = 1,000,000 bytes

GB = Gigabyte = 1,000MB = 1,000,000,000 bytes

TB = Terabyte = 1,000GB = 1,000,000,000,000 bytes
KiB = Kibibytes = 1,024 bytes
MiB = Mebibyte = 1,024KiB = 1,048,576 bytes
GiB = Gibibyte = 1,024MiB = 1,073,741,824 bytes
TiB = Tebibytes = 1,024GiB = 1,099,511,627,776 bytes

NTFS uses a special file structure called a master file table (MFT) and metadata files. The MFT is basically a relational database that consists of rows of file records and columns of file attributes. It contains at least one entry for every file on an NTFS volume. NTFS creates file and folder records for each file and folder created on an NTFS volume. These are stored in the MFT and consume 1KiB each. Each file record contains information about the position of the file record in the MFT, as well as file attributes and any other information about the file.

NTFS was designed to manage clusters using up to 64-bit numbers, which is an astronomical amount, but the current implementations use 32-bit numbers instead. Using 32-bit numbers allows for addressing up to 4,294,967,295 clusters, each of which is typically up to 4KiB.

NTFS reserves a total of 32 sectors for a 16-sector-long default volume boot sector and a backup boot sector. The default boot sector is located at the beginning (logical sector 0) of the volume, whereas the backup boot sector is written at the logical center of the volume (if it was formatted using NT 3.51 and earlier) or at the end of the volume (if it was formatted with NT 4.0 or later, including 2000 and XP).

An NTFS volume can therefore contain up to 34,359,738,392 total sectors (32 sectors reserved for the default and backup boot sectors, plus 4,294,967,295 clusters × 8 sectors), which is 17.59TB or 16.00TiB. The 32-bit sector numbering scheme used in the partition tables located in the MBR limits a single disk to no more than 4,294,967,295 (2^{32}–1) sectors, which is 2.2TB or 2TiB.

Windows 2000 and later versions (including XP Pro) can get around this on nonbootable drives by using a *dynamic disk*. Windows 2000 and XP Professional (but not XP Home) offer two types of storage: basic disks and dynamic disks. *Basic disks* use the same structures as before, with an MBR on the disk containing a partition table limited to four primary partitions per disk, or three primary partitions and one extended partition with unlimited logical drives. Primary partitions and logical drives on basic disks are known as *basic volumes*.

Dynamic disks were first introduced in Windows 2000 and provide the capability to create dynamic volumes that can be simple (using only one drive), spanned (using multiple drives), or striped (using multiple drives simultaneously for increased performance). Dynamic disks use a hidden database (contained in the last megabyte of the disk) to track information about dynamic volumes on the disk and about other dynamic disks in the computer. Because each dynamic disk in a computer stores a replica of the dynamic disk database, a corrupted database on one dynamic disk can be repaired using the database on another. By spanning or striping multiple drives using dynamic disk formats, you can exceed the 2TiB limit of a single MBR-based partition. Note, however, that dynamic disks and volumes are intended for use on servers and not standard desktop PCs. As such this book won't be going into much more detail on dynamic disks and volumes, and in general one should not create them on standard desktop or mobile systems.

Although the 32-bit sector numbering in the partition tables on MBR disks limits NTFS basic disks to 2TiB volumes, you can use dynamic volumes to create NTFS volumes larger than 2TiB by spanning or striping multiple basic disks to create a larger dynamic disk. Because the dynamic volumes are managed in the hidden database, they are not affected by the 2TiB limit imposed by the partition tables in the MBR. In essence, dynamic disks enable Windows 2000 and XP Pro to create NTFS volumes as large as 16TiB. The volume limits for NTFS are listed in Table 10.38.

Table 10.38 NTFS Volume Limits

Volume Limit	Clusters	Sectors per Cluster	Total Volume Sectors	Volume Size (Decimal)	Volume Size (Binary)
Minimum size	32,698	1	32,730	16.76MB	15.98MiB
Basic disk max.	536,870,908	8	4,294,967,295	2.2TB	2TiB
Dynamic disk max.	4,294,967,295	8	34,359,738,392	17.59TB	16TiB

MB = Megabyte = 1,000,000 bytes

GB = Gigabyte = 1,000MB = 1,000,000,000 bytes

TB = Terabyte = 1,000GB = 1,000,000,000,000 bytes

KiB = Kibibytes = 1,024 bytes

MiB = Mebibyte = 1,024KiB = 1,048,576 bytes

GiB = Gibibyte = 1,024MiB = 1,073,741,824 bytes

TiB = Tebibytes = 1,024GiB = 1,099,511,627,776 bytes

Some notable characteristics and features of NTFS include

- *Files are limited in size to 16TiB less 64KiB or by the size of the volume, whichever is lower.* NTFS supports up to 4,294,967,295 (2^{32}–1) files on a volume.

- *NTFS is not normally used on removable media because NTFS does not flush data to the disk immediately.* In addition, removing NTFS-formatted media without using the Safe Removal application can result in data loss. For removable media that can be ejected unexpectedly, you should use FAT12, FAT16, or FAT32 instead.

- *NTFS incorporates transaction logging and recovery techniques.* In the event of a failure, upon reboot NTFS uses its log file and checkpoint information to restore the consistency of the file system.

- *NTFS dynamically remaps clusters found to contain bad sectors and then marks the defective cluster as bad so it will no longer be used.*

- *NTFS has built-in security features.* These enable you to set permissions on a file or folder.

- *NTFS has a built-in Encrypting File System (EFS).* This performs dynamic encryption and decryption as you work with encrypted files or folders, while preventing others from doing so.

- *It enables the setting of disk quotas.* You can track and control space usage for NTFS volumes among various users.

- *NTFS has built-in dynamic compression, which compresses and decompresses files as you use them.*

NTFS Architecture—The MFT

Although NTFS partitions are very different from FAT partitions internally, they do comply with the extra-partitional disk structures described earlier in this chapter. NTFS partitions are listed in the master partition table of a disk drive's master boot record, just like FAT partitions, and they have a volume boot record as well, although it is formatted somewhat differently.

When a volume is formatted with NTFS, system files are created in the root folder of the NTFS volume. These system files can be stored at any physical location on the NTFS volume. This means that damage to any specific location on the disk will probably not render the entire partition inaccessible.

Typically, 12 NTFS system files (often referred to as *metadata* files) are created when you format an NTFS volume. Table 10.39 shows the names and descriptions for these files.

Table 10.39   NTFS System Files

Filename	Meaning	Description
$mft	Master file table (MFT)	Contains a record for every file on the NTFS volume in its Data attribute
$mftmirr	Master file table2 (MFT2)	Mirror of the MFT used for recoverability purposes; contains the first four records in $mft or the first cluster of $mft, whichever is larger
$badclus	Bad cluster file	Contains all the bad clusters on the volume
$bitmap	Cluster allocation bitmap	Contains the bitmap for the entire volume, showing which clusters are used
$boot	Boot file	Contains the volume's bootstrap if the volume is bootable
$attrdef	Attribute definitions table	Contains the definition of all system- and user- defined attributes on the volume
$logfile	Log file	Logs file transactions; used for recoverability purposes
$quota	Quota table	Table used to indicate disk quota usage for each user on a volume; used in NTFS 5
$upcase	Upcase table	Table used for converting uppercase and lowercase characters to the matching uppercase Unicode characters
$volume	Volume	Contains volume information, such as volume name and version
$extend	NTFS extension file	Stores optional extensions, such as quotas, object identifiers, and reparse point data
(no name)	Root filename index	The root folder (directory)

An NTFS partition is based on a structure called the master file table (MFT). The MFT concept expands on that of the FAT. Instead of using a table of cluster references, the MFT contains much more detailed information about the files and folders in the partition. In some cases, it even contains the files and folders themselves.

The first record in the MFT is called the *descriptor*, which contains information about the MFT itself. The volume boot record for an NTFS partition contains a reference that points to the location of this descriptor record. The second record in the MFT is a mirror copy of the descriptor, which provides fault tolerance, should the first copy be damaged.

The third record is the log file record. All NTFS transactions are logged to a file that can be used to restore data in the event of a disk problem. The bulk of the MFT consists of records for the files and folders stored on the partition. NTFS files take the form of objects that have both user- and system-defined attributes. Attributes on NTFS partitions are more comprehensive than the few simple flags used on FAT partitions. All the information on an NTFS file is stored as attributes of that file. In fact, even the file data itself is an attribute. Unlike FAT files, the attributes of NTFS files are part of the file itself; they are not listed separately in a folder entry. Folders exist as MFT records as well, but they consist mainly of indexes listing the files in the folder—they do not contain the size, date, time, and other information about the individual files.

Thus, an NTFS drive's MFT is much more than a cluster list, like a FAT; it is actually the primary data storage structure on the partition. If a file or folder is relatively small (less than approximately 1,500 bytes), the entire file or folder might even be stored in the MFT. For larger amounts of storage, the MFT record for a file or folder contains pointers to external clusters in the partition. These external clusters are called *extents*. All the records in the MFT, including the descriptors and the log file, are capable of using extents for storage of additional attributes. The attributes of a file that are part of the MFT record are called *resident* attributes, whereas those stored in extents are called *nonresident* attributes.

NTFS 5 (NTFS 2000)

Along with Windows 2000 came a new variation of NTFS called NTFS 5 (also called NTFS 2000); NTFS 5 is also used by Windows XP. This update of the NT file system includes several new features that are exploited and even required by Windows 2000 and Windows XP. Because of this, when you install Windows 2000 or Windows XP, any existing NTFS volumes automatically are upgraded to NTFS 5 (there is no way to override this option). If you also run Windows NT versions earlier than Windows NT 4 Service Pack 4 (SP4), NT 4 is no longer capable of accessing the NTFS 5 volumes. If you want to run both NT 4 and Windows 2000 or Windows XP on the same system (as in a dual-boot configuration), you must upgrade NT 4 by installing Service Pack 4 or later. An updated NTFS.SYS driver in Service Pack 4 enables NT 4 to read from and write to NTFS 5 volumes.

New features of the NTFS 5 file system include

- *Disk quotas*. System administrators can limit the amount of disk space users can consume on a per-volume basis. The three quota levels are Off, Tracking, and Enforced.

- *Encryption*. NTFS 5 can automatically encrypt and decrypt files as they are read from and written to the disk (not available in Windows XP Home Edition).

- *Reparse points*. Programs can trap open operations against objects in the file system and run their own code before returning file data. This can be used to extend file system features such as mount points, which you can use to redirect data read and written from a folder to another volume or physical disk.

- *Sparse files*. This feature enables programs to create very large files as placeholders but to consume disk space by adding to the files only as necessary.

- *USN (Update Sequence Number) Journal*. Provides a log of all changes made to files on the volume.

- *Mounted drives*. You can attach volumes including drives and folders to an empty folder stored on an NTFS drive. For example, you can create a folder on one drive that allows you to access content stored on another drive.

Because these features—especially the USN Journal—are required for Windows 2000 to run, a Windows 2000/Server 2003 domain controller must use an NTFS 5 partition as the system volume.

NTFS Changes in Windows XP

The location of the MFT has changed in Windows XP versus Windows 2000 and Windows NT. In Windows 2000 and Windows NT, the MFT is typically located at the start of the disk space used by the NTFS file system. In Windows XP, the $logfile and $bitmap metadata files are located 3GB from the start of the disk space used by NTFS. As a result, system performance has been increased by 5%–8% in Windows XP over Windows 2000 or Windows NT.

Another improvement in Windows XP's implementation of NTFS is the amount of MFT information read into memory. During bootup, Windows XP reads only a few hundred kilobytes of MFT information if all drives are formatted with NTFS. However, if some or all of the drives are formatted with FAT32, many megabytes of information (the amount varies by the number of drives and the size of the drives) must be read during bootup. Thus, using NTFS utilizes system memory more efficiently.

NTFS Compatibility

Although NTFS partitions are not directly accessible by DOS and other operating systems, Windows NT/2000 is designed for network use, so other operating systems are expected to be capable of accessing NTFS files via the network. For this reason, NTFS continues to support the standard DOS file attributes and the 8.3 FAT naming convention.

One of the main reasons for using NTFS is the security it provides for files and folders. NTFS security attributes are called *permissions* and are designed to enable system administrators to control access to files and folders by granting specific rights to users and groups. This is a much more granular approach than the FAT file system attributes, which apply to all users.

However, you can still set the FAT-style attributes on NTFS files using the standard Windows NT/2000 file management tools, including Windows NT/2000 Explorer and even the command-prompt ATTRIB command. When you copy FAT files to an NTFS drive over the network, the FAT-style attributes remain in place until you explicitly remove them. This can be an important consideration because the FAT-style attributes take precedence over the NTFS permissions. A file on an NTFS drive that is flagged with the FAT read-only attribute, for example, can't be deleted by a Windows NT/2000 user, even if that user has NTFS permissions that grant her full access.

To enable DOS and 16-bit Windows systems to access files on NTFS partitions over a network, the file system maintains an 8.3 alias name for every file and folder on the partition. The algorithm for deriving the alias from the long filename is the same as that used by Windows 95's VFAT. Windows NT/2000 also provides its FAT partitions with the same type of long filename support used by VFAT, allocating additional folder entries to store the long filenames as necessary.

Creating NTFS Drives

NTFS is designed for use primarily on hard disk drives, and not removable storage. You can't create an NTFS floppy disk, although you can format some removable media (any that use an MBR and partitions), such as Iomega Zip and Jaz cartridges, to use NTFS. Three basic ways to create an NTFS disk partition are as follows:

- Create a new NTFS volume out of unpartitioned disk space during the Windows NT/2000 installation process or after the installation with the Disk Administrator utility.

- Format an existing partition to NTFS (destroying its data in the process), using the Windows NT Format dialog box (accessible from Windows NT Explorer or Disk Administrator) or the FORMAT command (with the /fs:ntfs switch) from the command prompt.

- Convert an existing FAT partition to NTFS (preserving its data) during the Windows NT/2000 installation process or after the installation with the command-line CONVERT utility.

NTFS Tools

Because it uses a fundamentally different architecture, virtually none of the troubleshooting techniques outlined for FAT are applicable when dealing with NTFS partitions, nor can the disk utilities intended for use on FAT partitions address them. Windows NT has a rudimentary capability to check a disk for file system errors and bad sectors with its own version of CHKDSK, but apart from that, the operating system contains no other disk repair or defragmentation utilities. Windows 2000 and Windows XP include a command-line and GUI version of CHKDSK and also include a defragmenting tool that is run from the Windows Explorer GUI. Windows XP Professional also includes DiskProbe (DSKPROBE.exe), a direct disk sector editor, in its Windows Support Tools (the Windows 2000 Resource Kit also contains DiskProbe).

One difference between Windows 2000/XP's CHKDSK and Windows 9x/Me's SCANDISK is that CHKDSK cannot fix file system errors if it is run within the Windows GUI. If you run CHKDSK and select the Automatically Fix File System Errors option, you must schedule CHKDSK to run at the next system startup. You can run CHKDSK without this option to find file system problems; you can also run CHKDSK within the Windows GUI to look for and attempt to fix bad sectors.

Tip

You can use the **FSUTIL** command-line program in Windows XP and later to learn more about a particular drive's file system, including whether you need to run **CHKDSK** or a third-party disk repair tool. For example, to determine whether drive D: is *dirty* (has file system errors requiring repair), you would open a command prompt and enter this command:

FSUTIL DIRTY QUERY D:

For more examples of **FSUTIL** commands and syntax, enter **FSUTIL** with no options at a command prompt. Note that **FSUTIL** is not included with Windows 2000 or earlier versions.

The NTFS file system, however, does have its own automatic disk repair capabilities. In addition to Windows NT/2000/XP's fault-tolerance features, such as disk mirroring (maintaining the same data on two separate drives) and disk striping with parity (splitting data across several drives with parity information for data reconstruction), the OS has two features to help improve reliability:

- Transaction management
- Cluster remapping

NTFS can roll back any *transaction* (its term for a change to a file stored on an NTFS volume) if it isn't completed properly due to disk errors, running out of memory, or errors such as removing media or disconnecting a device before the transaction process is complete. Each transaction has five steps:

1. NTFS creates a log file of the metadata operations of the transaction (file updates, erasure, and so on) and caches the file in system memory.
2. NTFS stores the actual metadata operations in memory.
3. NTFS marks the transaction record in the log file as committed.
4. NTFS saves the log file to disk after the transaction is complete.
5. NTFS saves the actual metadata operations to disk after the transaction is complete.

This process is designed to prevent random data (lost clusters) on NTFS drives.

With cluster remapping, when Windows (NT/2000/XP) detects a bad sector on an NTFS partition, it automatically remaps the data in that cluster to another cluster. If the drive is part of a fault-tolerant drive array, any lost data is reconstructed from the duplicate data on the other drives.

Despite these features, however, there is still a real need for third-party disk repair and defragmentation utilities for Windows NT/2000/XP. These were scarce when Windows NT was first released, but third-party utilities that can repair and defragment NTFS drives are now widely available. One I recommend is Norton Utilities 2004 (also included in Norton SystemWorks 2005) by Symantec, which works with Windows 98, Windows Me, Windows 2000, and Windows XP. Earlier versions work with Windows NT 4.0 and Windows 95. If you are looking for even faster defragmentation, Golden Bow's (www.vopt.com) VoptXP (which also supports Windows 9x, Me, and 2000) is a longtime favorite because of its incredible speed and efficiency.

File System Utilities

The CHKDSK, RECOVER, and SCANDISK commands are the core of the Windows damaged-disk recovery team. These commands are somewhat crude, and their actions sometimes are drastic, but at times they are all that is available or necessary. RECOVER is best known for its function as a data recovery program, and CHKDSK typically is used for inspection of the file structure. Many users are unaware that CHKDSK can implement repairs to a damaged file structure. DEBUG, a crude, manually controlled program, can also help in the case of a disk disaster—but only if you know exactly what you are doing.

SCANDISK is a safer, more automated, more powerful replacement for CHKDSK and RECOVER in Windows 9x/Me. Windows 2000 and XP do not include SCANDISK and instead have beefed up CHKDSK designed to handle NTFS.

CHKDSK Operation

CHKDSK reports problems found in a disk volume's file system with one of several descriptive messages that vary to fit the specific error. Sometimes the messages are cryptic or misleading. CHKDSK does not specify how an error should be handled. It does not tell you whether CHKDSK can repair the problem, whether you must use some other utility, or what the consequences of the error and the repair will be. Neither does CHKDSK tell you what caused the problem nor how to avoid repeating the problem.

The primary function of CHKDSK is to compare the folder and FAT or NTFS MFT (Master File Table) to determine whether they agree with each other—that is, whether all the data in the folder entries for the files (such as the starting cluster and size information) corresponds to what is in the FAT (such as chains of clusters with end-of-chain indicators). CHKDSK also checks subfolder file entries, as well as the special "dot" (.) and "double dot" (..) entries that tie the subfolder system together.

The second function of CHKDSK is to implement repairs to the disk structure. CHKDSK patches the disk so that the folder and FAT or MFT are in alignment and agreement. From a repair standpoint, understanding CHKDSK is relatively easy. On FAT volumes, CHKDSK almost always modifies the folders on a disk to correspond to what it finds in the FAT. There are only a few special cases in which CHKDSK modifies the FAT. When it does, the FAT modifications are always the same type of simple change.

Think of CHKDSK's repair capability as a folder patcher. Because CHKDSK cannot repair most types of FAT damage effectively, it simply modifies the disk folders to match whatever problems it finds in the FAT. On NTFS volumes, CHKDSK is very effective at correcting problems with the MFT.

Caution

You should never run **CHKDSK** with the **/F** parameter without first running it in read-only mode (without the **/F** parameter) to determine whether and to what extent damage exists.

Only after carefully examining the disk damage and determining how CHKDSK would fix the problems should you run CHKDSK with the /F parameter. If you do not specify the /F parameter when you run CHKDSK, the program does not make corrections to the disk. Rather, it performs repairs in a mock fashion. This limitation is a safety feature because you do not want CHKDSK to take action until you have examined the problem. After deciding whether CHKDSK will make the correct assumptions about the damage, you might want to run it with the /F parameter.

Problems reported by CHKDSK are usually problems with the software and not the hardware. You rarely see a case in which lost clusters, allocation errors, or cross-linked files reported by CHKDSK were caused directly by a hardware fault, although it is certainly possible. The cause is usually a defective program or a program that was stopped before it could close files or purge buffers. A hardware fault certainly can stop a program before it can close files, but many people think that these error messages signify fault with the disk hardware, which is almost never the case.

The *RECOVER* Command

The RECOVER command is designed to mark clusters as bad when the clusters contain unreadable sectors, and rewrite the entries for the file in the FAT or MFT in order to be able to read the remainder of the file past the unreadable sector. When the system can't read a file because of a problem with a sector on the disk going bad, the RECOVER command can essentially jump the pointers to the file data in the FAT or MFT so that the rest of the file can be read, as well as to mark the file system so another file does not use those clusters. When used improperly, this program can be dangerous. The RECOVER utility that was included in DOS 5.x and earlier was not supplied in Windows 9x/Me because its functionality has been replaced by SCANDISK. It was, however, re-introduced in Windows NT/2000/XP and later because SCANDISK had been replaced by an improved version of CHKDSK.

Caution

Be very careful when you use older versions of **RECOVER**. Used improperly, it can do severe damage to your files. If you enter the old DOS version of **RECOVER** command without a filename for it to work on, the program assumes you want every file on the disk recovered and operates on every file and subfolder on the disk. It converts all subfolders to files, places all filenames in the root folder, and gives them new names (**FILE0000.REC**, **FILE0001.REC**, and so on). This process essentially wipes out the file system on the entire disk.

Fortunately the newer version of **RECOVER** included with Windows NT/2000/XP and later will not accept wildcards, and will only work on the single specific filename you enter with the command.

An improved version of RECOVER that recovers data from a specified file is only one of the command-line programs provided with Windows NT, 2000, and XP. To use this version of RECOVER, which works with both FAT and NTFS file systems, open a command prompt and enter the command as shown here:

```
RECOVER (drive\folder\filename)
```

For example, to recover all readable sectors from a file called Mynovel.txt stored in C:\My Documents\Writings, you would enter the following command:

```
RECOVER C:\My Documents\Writings\Mynovel.txt
```

Because the NT/2000/XP version of RECOVER requires you to specify a filename and path, it cannot destroy a file system the way the old DOS RECOVER command could.

SCANDISK

You should check your FAT partitions under Windows 9x/Me regularly for the problems discussed in this chapter and any other difficulties that might arise. By far the easiest and most effective solution for disk diagnosis and repair under Windows 9x/Me is the SCANDISK utility, included with DOS 6 and higher versions, as well as with Windows 9x/Me. This program is more thorough and comprehensive than CHKDSK or RECOVER under those operating systems and can perform the functions of both of them—and a great deal more.

SCANDISK is similar to a scaled-down version of third-party disk repair programs such as Norton Disk Doctor, and it can verify both file structure and disk sector integrity. If SCANDISK finds problems, it can repair folders and FATs. If the program finds bad sectors in the middle of a file, it marks the clusters (allocation units) containing the bad sectors as bad in the FAT and attempts to read the file data by rerouting around the defect.

Windows 9x includes both DOS and Windows versions of SCANDISK, which are named SCANDISK.EXE and SCANDSKW.EXE, respectively. Windows scans your drives at the beginning of the operating system installation process and automatically loads the DOS version of SCANDISK whenever you restart your system after turning it off without completing the proper shutdown procedure. You can also launch SCANDISK.EXE from a DOS prompt or from a batch file using the following syntax:

```
Scandisk x: [/a] [/n] [/p] [dblspace.nnn/drvspace.nnn]
x: - designator of the drive that you want to scan
/a - scans all local fixed hard disks
/n - noninteractive mode; requires no user input
/p - scans only, without correcting errors
/custom - runs Scandisk with the options configured in the
➡[CUSTOM] section of the Scandisk.ini file
dblspace.nnn or drvspace.nnn - scans a compressed volume file,
➡where nnn is replaced by the file extension (such as 001)
```

The SCANDISK.INI file, located in the C:\WINDOWS\COMMAND folder on a Windows system by default, contains extensive and well-documented parameters you can use to control the behavior of SCAN-DISK.EXE. Note that the options in the SCANDISK.INI file are applied only to the DOS version of the utility and have no effect on the Windows GUI version.

You also can run the GUI version of the utility by opening the Start menu and selecting Programs, Accessories, System Tools. Both versions scan and repair the FAT and the folder and file structures, repair problems with long filenames, and scan volumes that have been compressed with DriveSpace or DoubleSpace.

SCANDISK provides two basic testing options: Standard and Thorough. The difference between the two is that the Thorough option causes the program to scan the entire surface of the disk for errors in addition to the items just mentioned. You also can select whether to run the program interactively or let it automatically repair any errors it finds.

The DOS and Windows versions of SCANDISK also test the FAT in different ways. The DOS version scans and, if necessary, repairs the primary copy of the file allocation table. After this, it copies the repaired version of the primary to the backup copy. The Windows version, however, scans both copies of the FAT. If the program finds discrepancies between the two copies, it uses the data from the copy that it judges to be correct and reassembles the primary FAT using the best data from both copies. If the FAT information is not reconstructed correctly, some or all of your data might become inaccessible.

SCANDISK also has an Advanced Options dialog box that enables you to set the following parameters:

- Whether the program should display a summary of its findings
- Whether the program should log its findings
- How the program should repair cross-linked files (two folder entries pointing to the same cluster)
- How the program should repair lost file fragments
- Whether to check files for invalid names, dates, and times

Although SCANDISK is good, and is certainly a vast improvement over CHKDSK (but not the CHKDSK included in Windows NT/2000/XP and later, which was greatly improved), I recommend using one of the commercial packages, such as the Norton Utilities (included with Norton SystemWorks), for any major disk problems. These utilities go far beyond what is included in DOS or Windows.

Disk Defragmentation

The entire premise of a file system is based on the storage of data in clusters that can be located anywhere on the disk. This enables the computer to store a file of nearly any size at any time. The process of following a chain to locate all the clusters holding the data for a particular file can force the hard disk drive to access many locations on the disk. Because of the physical work involved in moving the disk drive heads, reading a file that is heavily fragmented in this way is slower than reading one that is stored on consecutive clusters.

As you regularly add, move, and delete files on a disk over a period of time, the files become increasingly fragmented, which can slow down disk performance. You can relieve this problem by periodically running a disk defragmentation utility on your drives, such as the one included with Windows. When you run the Disk Defragmenter, the program reads the pointers to all of the clusters to all of the files on the drive, in order to determine which files are fragmented.

The program then writes any fragmented files to contiguous clusters and deletes the originals. By progressively reading, writing, and erasing files, the defragmenting program eventually leaves the disk in a state where all files exist on contiguous clusters. As a result, the drive is capable of reading any file on the disk with a minimum of head movement, thus providing what is often a noticeable performance increase.

The Windows Defragmentation utility provides this basic defragmenting function. It also enables you to select whether you want to arrange the files on the disk to consolidate the empty clusters into one contiguous free space (which takes longer). The Windows 98/Me version adds a feature that examines the files on the disk and arranges them with the most frequently used program files grouped together at the front of the disk, which can make programs load more quickly. Such a function is not necessary under Windows NT/2000/XP because those newer versions of Windows use a prefetch function to more quickly locate frequently accessed files.

To show how defragmenting works, see the example of a fragmented file shown in Table 10.40.

Table 10.40   Fragmented File

	Folder	
Name	**Starting Cluster**	**Size**
PLEDGE.TXT	1002	2
USCONST.TXT	1000	4

	FAT16 File Allocation Table	
FAT Cluster #	**Value**	**Meaning**
00002	0	First cluster available
...	...	...
00999	0	Cluster available
01000	1001	In use, points to next cluster
01001	1004	In use, points to next cluster
01002	1003	In use, points to next cluster
01003	FFFFh	End of file
01004	1005	In use, points to next cluster
01005	FFFFh	End of file
...	...	...
65526	0	Last cluster available

In the preceding example, the file USCONST.TXT is fragmented in two pieces. If you ran a defragmenting program, the files would be read off the disk and rewritten in a contiguous fashion. One possible outcome is shown in Table 10.41.

Table 10.41   Defragmented File

Folder		
Name	**Starting Cluster**	**Size**
PLEDGE.TXT	1004	2
USCONST.TXT	1000	4

FAT16 File Allocation Table		
FAT Cluster #	**Value**	**Meaning**
00002	0	First cluster available
...	...	...
00999	0	Cluster available
01000	1001	In use, points to next cluster
01001	1002	In use, points to next cluster
01002	1003	In use, points to next cluster
01003	FFFFh	End of file
01004	1005	In use, points to next cluster
01005	FFFFh	End of file
...	...	...
65526	0	Last cluster available

Although it doesn't look like much was changed, you can see that now both files are in one piece, stored one right after the other. Because defragmenting involves reading and rewriting a possibly large number of files on your drive, it can take a long time, especially if you have a large drive with a lot of fragmented files and not very much free working space on the drive.

Third-party defragmentation utilities, such as the Speed Disk program included in the Norton Utilities, provide additional features, such as the capability to select specific files that should be moved to the front of the disk. Speed Disk also can defragment the Windows swap file and files that are flagged with the system and hidden attributes, which Disk Defragmenter will not touch.

Caution

Although the disk-defragmentation utilities included with Windows and third-party products are usually quite safe, you should always be aware that defragmenting a disk is an inherently dangerous procedure. The program reads, erases, and rewrites every file on the disk and has the potential to cause damage to your data when interrupted improperly. Although I have never seen a problem result from the process, an unforeseen event—such as a power failure—during a defragmentation procedure can conceivably be disastrous. I strongly recommend that you always run a disk-repair utility, such as **CHKDSK** (Windows NT/2000/XP or later) or **SCANDISK** (Windows 9x/Me), on your drives before defragmenting them and have a current backup ready.

Windows NT 4.0 does not include a defragmentation utility, but Windows 2000 and Windows XP do include such a utility. Note that third-party defragmentation utilities available for recent and current versions of Windows, such as Golden Bow Systems' VoptXP (www.vopt.com), are often faster and offer more features than Windows's own defragmentation programs.

Third-Party Programs

When you have a problem reading a file or portions of a drive, the best course of action might be to use one of the more powerful third-party disk-repair utilities on the market. The Norton Utilities by Symantec (also included in Norton SystemWorks) stands as one of the more popular data recovery programs on the market today. This program is comprehensive and automatically repairs most types of disk problems.

Norton Utilities and Norton SystemWorks

Programs such as Norton Disk Doctor can perform much more detailed repairs with a greater amount of safety. Disk Doctor preserves as much of the data in the file as possible and can mark the FAT so the bad sectors or clusters of the disk are not used again. These programs also save Undo information, enabling you to reverse any data recovery operation.

Disk Doctor is part of Symantec's Norton Utilities package, which includes a great many other useful tools. For example, Norton Utilities has an excellent sector editor (Norton Disk Editor) that enables you to view and edit any part of a disk, including the master and volume boot records, FATs, and other areas that fall outside the disk's normal data area. Currently, no other program is as comprehensive or as capable of editing disks at the sector level. The disk editor included with Norton Utilities can give the professional PC troubleshooter or repairperson the ability to work directly with any sector on the disk, but this does require extensive knowledge of sector formats and disk structures. The documentation with the package is excellent and can be very helpful if you are learning data recovery on your own.

Note

Data recovery is a lucrative service that the more advanced technician can provide. People are willing to pay much more to get their data back than to replace a hard drive.

You also can create a rescue disk for restarting your system and testing the drive in case of emergencies, unerase accidentally deleted files (even if the Recycle Bin was bypassed), and unformat accidentally formatted drives.

Norton Utilities is now available in version 2005 as part of Norton SystemWorks 2005 (for Windows 98/Me/NT/2000/XP). SystemWorks 2005 also includes Norton Anti-Virus and CheckIt diagnostics; the SystemWorks 2005 Premier version also includes Norton Ghost disk imaging software. Some of the programs provided with Norton Utilities are designed to be run from the command line or from a DOS prompt, such as the following:

- Norton Disk Doctor (NDD.EXE)
- Disk Editor (DISKEDIT.EXE)
- UnErase (UNERASE.EXE)
- UnFormat (UNFORMAT.EXE)
- Rescue Restore (RESCUE.EXE)

Most Norton Utilities programs are designed to be run from within the Windows graphical user interface (GUI), and several of the utilities include both Windows and command-prompt versions. You should be careful not to use older versions of Norton Utilities, such as version 8.0 (designed for Windows 3.1 and MS-DOS), with 32-bit versions of Windows because of the possibility of data loss due to a lack of support for long filenames and large drives.

File Systems and Third-Party Disk Utilities

The most important consideration when you purchase third-party disk utilities is to choose products that support your file system. For example, Norton Utilities supports both FAT (including FAT32) and NTFS files systems, as does SpinRite 6. Beware of older utilities that don't support NTFS, for example. Never use a disk utility not designed for your file system, and never use an out-of-date disk utility (designed for an earlier operating system) on your disk. In both cases, you could cause irreparable damage to the data on your drive.

CHAPTER 11

Windows Data Recovery

Recovering lost data can be as simple as opening the Windows Recycle Bin, or it might require spending hundreds of dollars on specialized data recovery software or services. In the worst-case scenario, you might even need to send your drive to a data recovery center. Several factors affect the degree of difficulty you might encounter in recovering your data, including

- How the data was deleted
- Which file system was used by the drive on which the data was stored
- Whether the drive uses magnetic, optical, magneto-optical, or flash memory to store data
- Which version of Windows or other OS you use
- Whether you already have data-protection software installed on your system
- Whether the drive has suffered physical damage to heads, platters, or circuit board

The Windows Recycle Bin and File Deletion

The simplest data recovery of all takes place when you send files to the Windows Recycle Bin (a standard part of Windows since Windows 95). Pressing the Delete key or clicking the Delete button when you have a file or group of files highlighted in Windows Explorer or My Computer sends files to the Recycle Bin. Although a file sent to the Recycle Bin is no longer listed in its normal location by Windows Explorer, the file is actually protected from being overwritten. By default, Windows 95 and above reserve 10% of the disk space on each hard disk for the Recycle Bin (removable-media drives don't have a Recycle Bin). Thus, a 100GB drive reserves about 10GB for its Recycle Bin. In this example, as long as less than 10GB of files has been sent to the Recycle Bin, a so-called deleted file is protected by Windows. However, after more than 10GB of files has been sent to the Recycle Bin, Windows allows the oldest files to be overwritten. Thus, the quicker you realize that a file has mistakenly been sent to the Recycle Bin, the more likely it is you can retrieve it.

To retrieve a file from the Recycle Bin, open the Recycle Bin, select the file, right-click it, and select Restore. Windows lists the file in its original location and removes it from the Recycle Bin.

If you hold down the Shift key when you select Delete or press the Delete key, the Recycle Bin is bypassed. Retrieving lost data at this point requires third-party data recovery software.

Recovering Files That Are Not in the Recycle Bin

The Recycle Bin is a useful first line of defense against data loss, but it is quite limited. As you learned in the previous section, it can be bypassed when you select files for deletion, and files stored in the Recycle Bin are eventually kicked out by newer deleted files. Also, the Recycle Bin isn't used for files deleted from a command prompt or when an older version of a file is replaced by a newer version.

Products such as Norton UnErase (part of the Norton Utilities and Norton SystemWorks) are necessary if you want to retrieve files not in the Recycle Bin. However, the effectiveness of Norton UnErase and how you should use it depends on the version of Windows you use and the file system used by your drives.

Norton UnErase and Norton Protected Recycle Bin—Win9x/Me

With Windows 9x/Me, which use the FAT file system, retrieving data from a drive that doesn't have Norton Utilities installed isn't difficult. However, installing Norton Utilities before you start to delete files that you might want to retrieve makes it even easier. You can run Norton UnErase from the bootable CD included in current versions, and run it as a command-prompt program if you don't have it already installed and need to retrieve erased data. You will need to provide the first letter of each file you want to unerase.

Caution

Do *not* install data-recovery software to a drive you are attempting to retrieve data from because you might overwrite the data you are attempting to retrieve. If you are trying to recover data from your Windows startup drive, install another hard disk into your system, configure it as a boot drive in the system BIOS, install a working copy of Windows on it, boot from that drive, and install your data recovery software to that drive. If possible, install a drive large enough (at least 10GB or larger) so that you have several GB of free space on it for storing recovered data.

However, if you have already installed Norton Utilities, you probably have the Norton Protected Recycle Bin on your desktop in place of the regular Recycle Bin. Compared to the Windows standard-model Recycle Bin, the Norton Protected Recycle Bin protects files that have been replaced with newer versions and files that were deleted from a command prompt. To retrieve a file stored in the Norton Protected Recycle Bin, open the Recycle Bin, select the file you want to retrieve, right-click it, and select Retrieve to put it back in its original location.

Alternatively, you can start the Norton Unerase Wizard from the Norton Utilities menu. You can search for recently deleted files (these files are stored in the Recycle Bin), all protected files on local drives (also stored in the Recycle Bin), and any recoverable files on local drives. When you select the last option, you can narrow down the search with wildcards or file types and specify which drives to search. You must supply the first letter of the filename for files that were not stored in the Recycle Bin; you can also see which files were deleted by a particular program. To undelete a file with the Unerase Wizard, select the file, provide the first letter of the filename if necessary, click Quick View to view the file (if your file viewer supports the file format), and click Recover to restore the file to its original location.

With Windows 9x/Me, you can search both hard and removable-media (floppy, flash memory) drives for lost files, although the Recycle Bin works only for hard drives.

Norton UnErase and Norton Protected Recycle Bin—Win 2000/XP

Norton UnErase and Norton Protected Recycle Bin work in a similar fashion with Windows 2000/XP as with Windows 9x/Me, but with a significant exception: The Unerase Wizard can search only hard drives. Removable-media drives are not supported.

Alternatives to Norton UnErase

VCOM's System Suite 4.0 (previously sold by Ontrack) is an integrated utility suite that offers an undelete feature similar in many ways to Norton UnErase. However, System Suite's FileUndeleter works with removable-media drives as well as hard drives under all supported versions of Windows, including Windows XP.

Although it's not an automatic tool, you can use Norton's Disk Editor (DISKEDIT.COM) to retrieve lost data from hard, floppy, and most types of removable-media drives under any file system and most operating systems, including Linux. See the section "Using the Norton Disk Editor," later in this chapter.

Undeleting Files in NTFS

Because the file structure of NTFS is much more complex than any FAT file system version and some files might be compressed using NTFS's built-in compression, you should use an NTFS-specific file undeletion program to attempt to recover deleted files from an NTFS drive. For example, you should use a version of Norton Utilities or Norton SystemWorks compatible with NTFS, such as the 2002 or later versions. Also, you should enable the Norton Protection feature, which stores deleted files for a specified period of time before purging them from the system. Using Norton Protection will greatly enhance Norton UnErase's capability to recover deleted files.

If you need to recover deleted files and have not already installed an undelete program such as Norton Utilities or Norton SystemWorks' Norton UnErase, you should consider a standalone file recovery program, such as

- *Active Undelete.* This series of products also works with flash memory cards; more information and a free demo are available from http://www.active-undelete.com.
- *Restorer 2000.* Available in FAT, NTFS, and Professional versions; more information and a free demo are available from http://www.bitmart.net/r2k.shtml.
- *Ontrack EasyRecovery.* More information and a free demo are available from http://www.ontrack.com.

Tip

Some file-undelete products for NTFS can undelete only files created by the currently logged-in user, whereas others require the administrator to be logged in. Check the documentation for details, particularly if you are trying to undelete files from a system with more than one user.

Retrieving Data from Partitioned and Formatted Drives

When a hard disk, floppy disk, or removable-media drive has been formatted, its file allocation table, which is used by programs such as Norton UnErase or VCOM System Suite's FileUndeleter to determine the location of files, is lost. If a hard drive has been repartitioned with FDISK or another partitioning program (such as Windows 2000/XP's Disk Management), the original file system and partition information is lost (as is the FAT).

In such cases, more powerful data-recovery tools must be used to retrieve data. To retrieve data from an accidentally formatted drive, you have two options:

- Use a program that can unformat the drive.
- Use a program that can bypass the newly created FAT and read disk sectors directly to discover and retrieve data.

To retrieve data from a drive that has been partitioned, you must use a program that can read disk sectors directly.

Norton Unformat and Its Limitations

Norton Utilities and Norton SystemWorks offer Norton Unformat, which can be launched from the bootable CD to unformat an accidentally formatted FAT drive. However, Norton Unformat has significant limitations with today's file systems and drive types, including the following:

- *Norton Unformat doesn't support NTFS drives.* This means many Windows 2000 and XP-based systems can't use it for data recovery.
- *Norton Unformat cannot be used with drives that require device drivers to function, such as removable-media drives.*

- *Norton Unformat works best if the Norton Image program has been used to create a copy of the FATs and root directory.* If the image file is out-of-date, Unformat might fail; if the image file is not present, Unformat cannot restore the root directory and the actual names of folders in the root directory will be replaced by sequentially numbered folder names.

- *Norton Unformat cannot copy restored files to another drive or folder.* It restores data back to the same drive and partition. If Unformat uses an out-of-date file created by Norton Image to determine where data is located, it could overwrite valid data on the drive being unformatted.

For these reasons, Norton Unformat is not the most desirable method for unformatting a drive. You can use the powerful, but completely manual, Norton Disk Editor (DISKEDIT) to unformat a drive or retrieve data from a formatted drive, but other alternatives are simpler.

Retrieving Lost Data to Another Drive

Many products on the market can retrieve lost data to another drive, even if the data loss was due to accidental formatting or disk partitioning. One of the best and most comprehensive products is the EasyRecovery product line from Ontrack DataRecovery Services, a division of Kroll Ontrack, Inc. The EasyRecovery product line includes the following products:

- *EasyRecovery DataRecovery.* Recovers data from accidentally formatted or deleted hard, floppy, and removable-media drives and repairs damaged or corrupted Zip and Microsoft Word files. Local and network folders can be used for recovered files.

- *EasyRecovery FileRepair.* Repairs and recovers data from damaged or corrupted Zip and Microsoft Office (Word, Excel, Access, PowerPoint, and Outlook) files. Local and network folders can be used for recovered files.

- *EasyRecovery Professional.* Combines the features of DataRecovery and FileRecovery and adds features such as file type search, RawRecovery, and user-defined partition parameters to help recover data from more severe forms of file system corruption and accidental partitioning. A free trial version displays files that can be recovered (and repairs and recovers Zip files at no charge); it can be downloaded from the Ontrack website (http://www.ontrack.com).

An earlier version of EasyRecovery Data Recovery Lite can recover up to 50 files and is included as part of VCOM's System Suite (previously sold by Ontrack).

When you start EasyRecovery Professional, you can choose from several recovery methods, including these:

- *DeletedRecovery.* Recovers deleted files
- *FormatRecovery.* Recovers files from accidentally formatted drives
- *RawRecovery.* Recovers files with direct sector reads using file-signature matching technology
- *AdvancedRecovery.* Recovers data from deleted or corrupted partitions

In each case, you need to specify another drive to receive the retrieved data. This read-only method preserves the contents of the original drive and enables you to use a different data-recovery method if the first method doesn't recover the desired files.

Which options are best for data recovery? Table 11.1 shows the results of various data-loss scenarios and recovery options when EasyRecovery Professional was used to recover data from a 19GB logical drive formatted with the NTFS file system under Windows XP.

Table 11.1 Data Recovery Options and Results with EasyRecovery Professional

Type of Data Loss	Data Recovery Method	Data Recoverable?	Details	Notes
Deleted folder	DeletedRecovery	Yes	All files recovered.	All long file and folder names preserved.
Formatted drive (full format)	FormatRecovery	Yes	All files recovered.	New folders created to store recovered files; long filenames preserved for files and folders beneath root folder level.
Logical drive deleted with Disk Management	AdvancedRecovery	Yes	All files and folders recovered.	All long file and folder names preserved.
Formatted drive with new data copied to it	FormatRecovery	Partial	Files and folders that were not overwritten were recovered.	Long filenames and folders preserved.
Formatted, repartitioned drive reformatted as FAT32 (117MB Disk 1)	AdvancedRecovery	No	Could not locate any files to recover.	
	RawRecovery	Partial	Nonfragmented files recovered.	Original directory structure and filenames lost; each file type stored in a separate folder and files numbered sequentially.
Formatted, repartitioned drive formatted as NTFS (18.8GB Disk 2)	AdvancedRecovery	No	Could not locate any files to recover.	
	RawRecovery	Partial	Nonfragmented files recovered.	Original directory structure and filenames lost; each file type stored in a separate folder and files numbered sequentially.

As Table 11.1 makes clear, as long as the data areas of a drive are not overwritten, complete data recovery is usually possible—even if the drive has been formatted or repartitioned. Thus, it's critical that you react quickly if you suspect you have partitioned or formatted a drive containing valuable data. The longer you wait to recover data, the less data will be available for recovery. In addition, if you must use a sector-by-sector search for data (a process called RawRecovery by Ontrack), your original folder structure and long filenames will not be saved. You will therefore need to re-create the desired directory structure and rename files after you recover them—a very tedious process.

Tip

If you use EasyRecovery Professional or EasyRecovery DataRecovery to repair damaged Zip or Microsoft Office files, use the Properties menu to select a location for repaired files (the original location or another drive or folder). By default, repaired Outlook files are copied to a different folder, whereas other file types are repaired in place unless you specify a different location.

As you can see from this example, dedicated data-recovery programs such as Ontrack EasyRecovery Professional are very powerful. However, they are also very expensive. If you have Norton Utilities or Norton SystemWorks and don't mind taking some time to learn about disk structures, you can perform data recovery with the Norton Disk Editor.

Using the Norton Disk Editor

In my PC Hardware (Upgrading and Repairing) and Data Recovery/Computer Forensics seminars, I frequently use the Norton Disk Editor—an often-neglected program that's part of the Norton Utilities and Norton SystemWorks—to explore drives. I also use Disk Editor to retrieve lost data. Because Disk Editor is a manual tool, it can sometimes be useful even when friendlier automatic programs don't work correctly or are unavailable. For example, in physical sector mode, Disk Editor can be used with any drive regardless of what file system was used, since at that level it is working underneath the OS. Additionally, because Disk Editor displays the structure of your drive in a way other programs don't, it's a perfect tool for learning more about disk drive structures as well as recovering lost data. This section discusses two of the simpler procedures you can perform with Disk Editor:

- Undeleting a file on a floppy disk
- Copying a deleted file on a hard disk to a different drive

If you have Norton SystemWorks, SystemWorks Professional, or Norton Utilities for Windows, you have Norton Disk Editor. To determine whether it's installed on your system, look in the Norton Utilities folder under the Program Files folder for the following files: `DISKEDIT.EXE` and `DISKEDIT.HLP`.

If you don't find these files on your hard disk, you can run them directly from the Norton installation CD. If you have SystemWorks or SystemWorks Professional, look for the CD folder called `\NU` to locate these files.

Disk Edit is a command prompt program designed primarily to access FAT-based file systems such as FAT12 (floppy disks), FAT16 (MS-DOS and early Windows 95 hard disks), and FAT32 (Windows 95B/Windows 98/Me hard disks). You can use Disk Edit with Windows NT, Windows 2000, and Windows XP if you prepared the hard disks with the FAT16 or FAT32 file systems. Disk Edit will also work on NTFS volumes; however, in that case it can only be used in physical sector mode.

I strongly recommend that you first use Disk Editor with floppy disks you have prepared with noncritical files before you use it with a hard disk or vital files. Because Disk Editor is a completely manual program, the opportunities for error are high.

The Disk Edit files can easily fit on a floppy disk, but if you are new to the program, you might want to put them on a different drive from one you will be examining or repairing. *Never* copy Disk Edit files (or any other data recovery program) to a drive that contains data you are trying to recover because the files might overwrite the data area and destroy the files you want to retrieve. For example, if you are planning to examine or repair floppy disks, create a folder on your hard disk called `Disk Edit` and copy the files to that folder.

You can use Disk Editor without a mouse by using keyboard commands, but if you want to use it with a mouse, you can do so if your mouse attaches to the serial or PS/2 mouse ports (USB mice generally don't work from the command prompt, but if your USB mouse has a PS/2 mouse port adapter, you can use it by plugging the mouse and adapter into the PS/2 port). You must load an MS-DOS mouse driver (usually MOUSE.COM) for your mouse before you start Disk Editor. If you have a Logitech mouse, you can download an MS-DOS mouse driver from the Logitech website. If you have a Microsoft mouse, Microsoft doesn't provide MS-DOS drivers you can download, but you can get them from the following website:

http://www.bootdisk.com/readme.htm#mouse

For other mice, try the Microsoft or Logitech drivers, or contact the vendor for drivers. Keep in mind that scroll wheels and other buttons won't work with an MS-DOS driver. I recommend you copy your mouse driver to the same folder in which Disk Editor is located.

Using Disk Editor to Examine a Drive

To start Disk Editor:

1. Boot the computer to a command prompt (not Windows); Disk Editor needs exclusive access to the drives you plan to examine. If you use Windows 9x, press F8 or Ctrl to bring up the startup menu and select Safe Mode Command Prompt, or use the Windows 9x/Me Emergency Startup disk (make one with Add/Remove Programs). If you use Windows 2000 or XP, insert a blank floppy disk into drive A:, right-click drive A: in My Computer, and select Format. Select the Create an MS-DOS Startup Disk option and use this disk to start your computer.

2. Change to the folder containing your mouse driver and Disk Editor.

3. Type **MOUSE** (if your mouse driver is called MOUSE.COM or MOUSE.EXE; otherwise, substitute the correct name if it's called something else). Then press Enter to load the mouse driver.

4. Type **DISKEDIT** and press Enter to start the program. If you don't specify a drive, Disk Editor scans the drive on which it's installed. If you are using it to work with a floppy disk, enter the command **DISKEDIT A:** to direct it to scan your floppy disk. Disk Editor scans your drive to determine the location of files and folders on the disk.

5. The first time you run Disk Editor, a prompt appears to remind you that Disk Editor runs in read-only mode until you change its configuration through the Tools menu. Click OK to continue.

After Disk Editor has started, you can switch to the drive you want to examine or recover data from. To change to a different drive, follow these steps:

1. Press Alt+O to open the Object menu.

2. Select Drive.

3. Select the drive you want to examine from the Logical Disks menu.

4. The disk structure is scanned and displayed in the Disk Editor window.

Disk Editor normally starts in Directory mode, but you can change it to other modes with the View menu. When you view a drive containing data in Directory mode, you will see a listing similar to the one shown in Figure 11.1.

The Name column lists the names of the directory entries, and the .EXT column lists the file/folder extensions (if any). The ID column lists the type of directory entry, including

- *Dir.* A directory (folder).
- *File.* A data file.
- *LFN.* A portion of a Windows long filename. Windows stores the start of the LFN before the actual filename. If the LFN is longer than 13 characters, one or more additional directory entries is used to store the rest of the LFN. The next three columns list the file size, date, and time.

The Cluster column indicates the cluster in which the first portion of the file is located. Drives are divided into clusters or allocation units when they are formatted, and a *cluster* (allocation unit) is the smallest unit that can be used to store a file. Cluster sizes vary with the size of the drive and the file system used to format the drive.

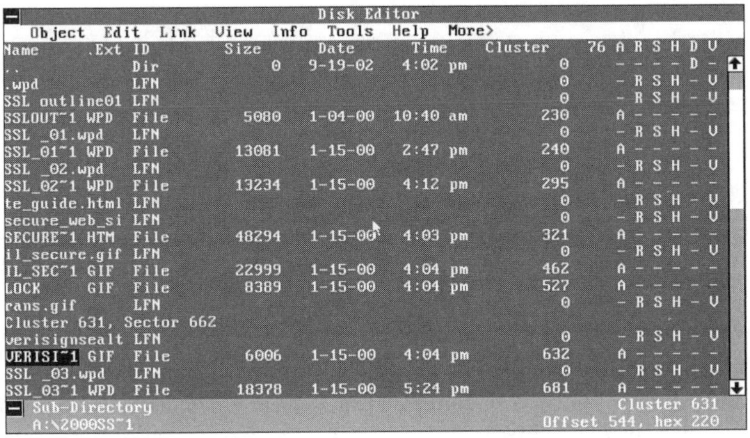

```
                         Disk Editor
   Object  Edit  Link  View  Info  Tools  Help  More>
Name      .Ext  ID       Size       Date     Time     Cluster    76 A R S H D V
..              Dir          0    9-19-02   4:02 pm          0       - - - - D -  ↑
.wpd            LFN                                              0       - R S H - V
SSL_outline01  LFN                                              0       - R S H - V
SSLOUT~1 WPD   File      5080    1-04-00  10:40 am        230       A - - - - -
SSL _01.wpd    LFN                                              0       - R S H - V
SSL_01~1 WPD   File     13081    1-15-00   2:47 pm        240       A - - - - -
SSL _02.wpd    LFN                                              0       - R S H - V
SSL_02~1 WPD   File     13234    1-15-00   4:12 pm        295       A - - - - -
te_guide.html  LFN                                              0       - R S H - V
secure_web_si  LFN                                              0       - R S H - V
SECURE~1 HTM   File     48294    1-15-00   4:03 pm        321       A - - - - -
il_secure.gif  LFN                                              0       - R S H - V
IL_SEC~1 GIF   File     22999    1-15-00   4:04 pm        462       A - - - - -
LOCK     GIF   File      8389    1-15-00   4:04 pm        527       A - - - - -
rans.gif       LFN                                              0       - R S H - V
Cluster 631, Sector 662
verisignsealt  LFN                                              0       - R S H - V
VERISI~1 GIF   File      6006    1-15-00   4:04 pm        632       A - - - - -
SSL _03.wpd    LFN                                              0       - R S H - V
SSL_03~1 WPD   File     18378    1-15-00   5:24 pm        681       A - - - - -  ↓
 Sub-Directory                                            Cluster 631
 A:\2000SS~1                                              Offset 544, hex 220
```

Figure 11.1 The Norton Disk Editor directory view of a typical floppy disk.

The letters *A*, *R*, *S*, *H*, *D*, and *V* refer to attributes for each directory entry. *A* (archive) means the file hasn't been backed up since it was last modified. *R* is used to indicate that the directory entry is read-only, and *S* indicates that the directory entry has the System attribute. *H* indicates that the directory entry has the Hidden attribute, whereas *D* indicates that the entry is a directory. Finally, *V* is the attribute for an LFN entry.

The file VERISI~1.GIF (highlighted in black near the bottom of Figure 11.1) is interesting for several reasons. The tilde (~) and number at the end of the filename indicate that the file was created with a 32-bit version of Windows. 32-bit versions of Windows (Windows 9x/Me, 2000, and XP) allow the user to save a file with a long (more than eight characters) filename (plus the three-character file extension such as .EXE, .BMP, or .GIF). In addition, long filenames can have spaces and other characters not allowed by earlier versions of Windows and MS-DOS. The process used by various versions of Windows to create LFN entries is discussed in Chapter 10, in the section called "VFAT and Long Filenames."

When you view the file in Windows Explorer or My Computer, you see the long filename. To see the DOS alias name within the Windows GUI, right-click the file and select Properties from My Computer or Windows Explorer. Or, you can use the DIR command in a command-prompt window. The LFN is stored as one or more separate directory entries just before the DOS alias name. Because the actual long name for VERISI~1.GIF (Verisignsealtrans.gif) is 21 characters, two additional directory entries are required to store the long filename (each directory entry can store up to 13 characters of an LFN), as shown in Figure 11.1.

Determining the Number of Clusters Used by a File

As discussed earlier in this chapter, an area of the disk called the file allocation table stores the starting location of the file and each additional cluster used to store the file. VERISI~1.GIF starts at cluster 632. Clusters are the smallest disk structures used to store files, and they vary in size depending on the file system used to create the disk on which the files are stored and on the size of the drive. In this case, the file is stored on a 1.44MB floppy disk, which has a cluster size of 512 bytes (one sector). The cluster size of the drive is very important to know if you want to retrieve data using Disk Editor.

To determine the cluster size of a drive, you can open a command-prompt window and run CHKDSK C: to display the allocation unit size (cluster size) and other statistics about the specified drive.

To determine how many clusters are used to store a file, look at the size of the file and compare it to the cluster size of the drive on which it's stored. The file VERISI~1.GIF contains 6,006 bytes. Because this file is stored on a floppy disk that has a cluster size of 512 bytes, the file must occupy several clusters. How many clusters does it occupy? To determine this, divide the file size by the number of clusters and round the result up to the next whole number. The math is shown in Table 11.2.

Table 11.2   Determining the Number of Clusters Used by a File

File Size (FS) of VERISI~1.GIF	Cluster Size (CS)	Result of (FS) Divided by (CS) Equals (CR)	(CR) Rounded Up to Next Whole Number
6,006	512	11.73046875	12

From these calculations, you can see that VERISI~1.GIF uses 12 clusters on the floppy disk; it would use fewer clusters on a FAT16 or FAT32 hard disk (the exact number depends on the file system and size of the hard disk). The more clusters a file contains, the greater the risk is that some of its data area could be overwritten by newer data if the file is deleted. Consequently, if you need to undelete a file that was not sent to the Windows Recycle Bin or was deleted from a removable-media drive or floppy drive (these types of drives don't support the Recycle Bin), the sooner you attempt to undelete the file, the more likely it is that you can retrieve the data.

The normal directory display in Norton Disk Editor shows the starting cluster (632) for VERISI~1.GIF. If a file is stored on a drive with a lot of empty space, the remainder of the clusters will probably immediately follow the first two—a badly fragmented drive might use noncontiguous clusters to store the rest of the file. Because performing data recovery when the clusters are contiguous is much easier, I strongly recommend that you defragment your drives frequently.

To see the remainder of the clusters used by a file, move the cursor to the file, press Alt+L or click the Link menu, and select Cluster Chain (FAT); you can also press Ctrl+T to go directly to this view. The screen changes to show the clusters as listed in the FAT for this file, as shown in Figure 11.2. The clusters used by the file are highlighted in red, and the filename is shown at the bottom of the screen. The symbol <EOF> stands for *end of file*, indicating the last cluster in the file.

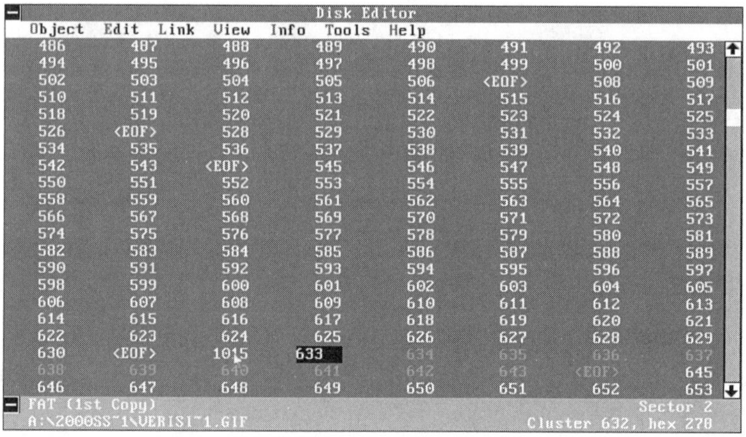

Figure 11.2   The FAT view of VERISI~1.GIF. All its clusters are contiguous.

How the Operating System Marks a File When It Is Deleted

If a file (VERISI~1.GIF, in this example) is deleted, the following changes happen to the disk where the file is stored, as shown in Figure 11.3:

■ The default directory view shows that the first character of the filename (V) has been replaced with a σ (lowercase sigma) character.

■ There are now two new types of entries in the ID column for this file and its associated LFN:

• *Erased.* An erased file

• *Del LFN.* An LFN belonging to an erased file

Note also that the beginning cluster (632) is still shown in the Cluster column.

```
                             Disk Editor
       Object  Edit  Link  View  Info  Tools  Help  More>
Name        .Ext ID       Size       Date       Time      Cluster    76 A R S H D V
Cluster 144, Sector 175
.                Dir         0    9-19-02   4:02 pm        144        - - - - D -
..               Dir         0    9-19-02   4:02 pm          0        - - - - D -
.wpd             LFN                                         0        - R S H - V
SSL outline01 LFN                                            0        - R S H - V
SSLOUT~1 WPD    File      5080    1-04-00  10:40 am        230        A - - - - -
SSL _01.wpd      LFN                                         0        - R S H - V
SSL_01~1 WPD    File     13081    1-15-00   2:47 pm        240        A - - - - -
SSL _02.wpd      LFN                                         0        - R S H - V
SSL_02~1 WPD    File     13234    1-15-00   4:12 pm        295        A - - - - -
te_guide.html    LFN                                         0        - R S H - V
secure_web_si    LFN                                         0        - R S H - V
SECURE~1 HTM    File     48294    1-15-00   4:03 pm        321        A - - - - -
il_secure.gif    LFN                                         0        - R S H - V
IL_SEC~1 GIF    File     22999    1-15-00   4:04 pm        462        A - - - - -
LOCK     GIF    File      8389    1-15-00   4:04 pm        527        A - - - - -
rans.gif     Del LFN                                         0        - R S H - V
Cluster 631, Sector 662
verisignsealt Del LFN                                        0        - R S H - V
σERISI~1 GIF   Erased     6006    1-15-00   4:04 pm        632        A - - - - -
  Sub-Directory                                                  Cluster 631
  A:\2000SS~1                                               Offset 544, hex 220
```

Figure 11.3   The Directory view after VERISI~1.GIF has been deleted.

Zeroes have also replaced the entries for the cluster locations after the beginning cluster in the FAT. This indicates to the operating system that these clusters are now available for reuse. Thus, if an undelete process is not started immediately, some or all of the clusters could be overwritten by new data. Because the file in question is a GIF graphics file, the loss of even one cluster will destroy the file.

As you can see from analyzing the file-deletion process, the undelete process involves four steps:

■ Restoring the original filename

■ Locating the clusters used by the file

■ Re-creating the FAT entries for the file

■ Relinking the LFN entries for the file to the file

Of these four, the most critical are locating the clusters used by the file and re-creating the FAT entries for the file. However, if the file is a program file, restoring the original name is a must for proper program operation (assuming the program can't be reloaded), and restoring the LFN entries enables a Windows user accustomed to long filenames to more easily use the file.

If you want to make these changes to the original disk, Disk Editor must be configured to work in Read-Write mode.

To change to Read-Write mode, follow these steps:

1. Press Alt+T to open the Tools menu.
2. Press N to open the Configuration dialog box.
3. Press the spacebar to clear the check mark in the Read Only option box.
4. Press the Tab key until the Save box is highlighted.
5. Press Enter to save the changes and return to the main display.

Caution

As a precaution, I recommend that you use DISKCOPY to make an exact sector-by-sector copy of a floppy disk before you perform data recovery on it, and you should work with the copy of the disk, not the original. By working with a copy, you keep the original safe from any problems you might have; plus, you can make another copy if you need to.

After you change to Read-Write mode, Disk Editor stays in this mode and uses Read-Write mode every time you use it. To change back to Read-Only mode, repeat the previously listed steps but check the Read-Only box. If you are using Disk Editor in Read-Write mode, you will see the message Drive *x* is Locked when you scan a drive.

Undeleting an Erased File

After you have configured Disk Editor to work in Read-Write mode, you can use it to undelete a file.

To recover an erased file, follow this procedure:

1. To change to the folder containing the erased file, highlight the folder containing the erased file and press Enter. In this example, you will recover the erased file VERISI~1.GIF.
2. Place the cursor under the lowercase sigma symbol and enter a letter to rename the file.
3. If the keyboard is in Insert mode, the lowercase sigma will move to the right; press the Delete key to delete this symbol.
4. This restores the filename, but even though the ID changes from Erased to File, this does *not* complete the file-retrieval process. You must now find the rest of the clusters used by the file. To the right of the filename, the first cluster used by the file is listed.
5. To go to the next cluster used by the file, press Ctrl+T to open the Cluster Chain command. Because you changed the name of the file, you are prompted to write the changes to the disk before you can continue. Press W or click Write to save the changes and continue.
6. Disk Editor moves to the first cluster used by the deleted file. Instead of cluster numbers, as shown earlier in Figure 11.2, each cluster contains a zero (0). Because this file uses 12 clusters, there should be 12 contiguous clusters that have been zeroed out if the file is unfragmented.
7. To determine whether these are the correct clusters for the file, press Alt+O or click Object to open the Object menu. Press **C** to open the Cluster dialog box (or press Alt+C to go to the Cluster dialog box). Enter the starting cluster number (**632** in this example) and the ending cluster number (**644** in this example). Click OK to display these clusters.

    Disk Editor automatically switches to the best view for the specified object, and in this case, the best view is the Hex view (see Figure 11.4). Note that the first entry in cluster 632 is GIF89a (as shown in the right column). Because the deleted file is a GIF file, this is what we expected. Also, a GIF file is a binary graphics file, so the rest of the information in the specified sectors should not be human-readable. Note that the end of the file is indicated by a series of 0s in several disk sectors before another file starts.

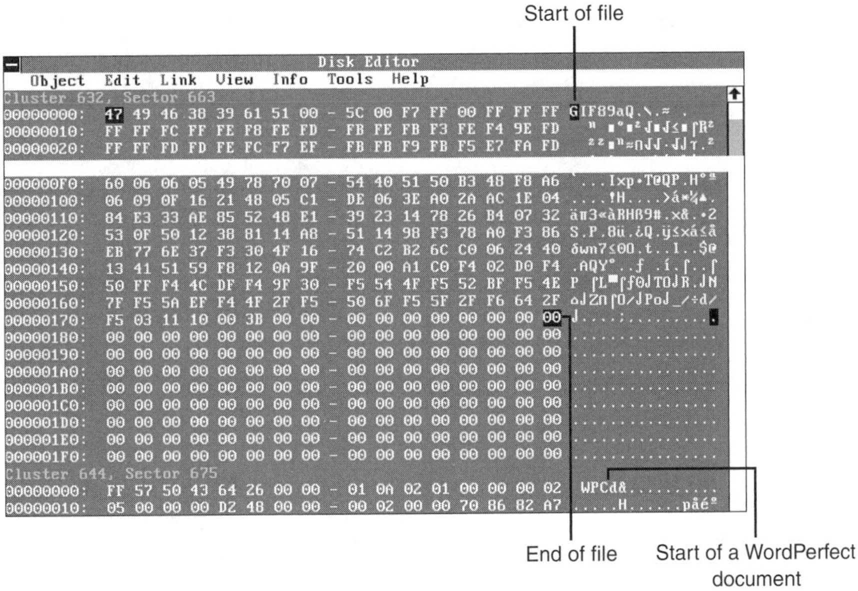

Start of file

```
                              Disk Editor
   Object  Edit  Link  View  Info  Tools  Help
Cluster 632, Sector 663
00000000:  47 49 46 38 39 61 51 00 - 5C 00 F7 FF 00 FF FF FF  GIF89aQ.\.÷
00000010:  FF FF FC FF FE F8 FE FD - FB FE FB F3 FE F4 9E FD   ÿ ■•²Jⁿ√≤■ ⌐R²
00000020:  FF FF FD FD FE FC F7 EF - FB FB F9 FB F5 E7 FA FD   ²²■ⁿ=∩√J.√J⌐.²

000000F0:  60 06 06 05 49 78 70 07 - 54 40 51 50 B3 48 F8 A6  `...Ixp•T@QP.H°ª
00000100:  06 09 0F 16 21 48 05 C1 - DE 06 3E A0 2A AC 1E 04  ....!H...>á■¼▲.
00000110:  84 E3 33 AE 85 52 48 E1 - 39 23 14 78 26 B4 07 32  äπ3«àRH89■.x&.•2
00000120:  53 0F 50 12 38 81 14 A8 - 51 14 98 F3 78 A0 F3 86  S.P.8ü.¿Q.ÿ≤xá≤ä
00000130:  EB 77 6E 37 F3 30 4F 16 - 74 C2 B2 6C C0 06 24 40  δwn7≤00.t..1..$ê
00000140:  13 41 51 59 F8 12 0A 9F - 20 00 A1 C0 F4 02 D0 F4  .AQY°..ƒ.í.Γ..Γ
00000150:  50 FF F4 4C DF F4 9F 30 - F5 54 4F F5 52 BF F5 4E  P ⌐L■ΓfθJTO↓R.JN
00000160:  7F F5 5A EF F4 4F 2F F5 - 50 6F F5 5F 2F F6 64 2F  ∆JZⁿ⌐O⌂JPoⱮ_⌂÷d⌂
00000170:  F5 03 11 10 00 3B 00 00 - 00 00 00 00 00 00 00 00  ∞J...;........ █
00000180:  00 00 00 00 00 00 00 00 - 00 00 00 00 00 00 00 00  ................
00000190:  00 00 00 00 00 00 00 00 - 00 00 00 00 00 00 00 00  ................
000001A0:  00 00 00 00 00 00 00 00 - 00 00 00 00 00 00 00 00  ................
000001B0:  00 00 00 00 00 00 00 00 - 00 00 00 00 00 00 00 00  ................
000001C0:  00 00 00 00 00 00 00 00 - 00 00 00 00 00 00 00 00  ................
000001D0:  00 00 00 00 00 00 00 00 - 00 00 00 00 00 00 00 00  ................
000001E0:  00 00 00 00 00 00 00 00 - 00 00 00 00 00 00 00 00  ................
000001F0:  00 00 00 00 00 00 00 00 - 00 00 00 00 00 00 00 00  ................
Cluster 644, Sector 675
00000000:  FF 57 50 43 64 26 00 00 - 01 0A 02 01 00 00 00 02  WPCd&........
00000010:  05 00 00 00 D2 48 00 00 - 00 02 00 00 70 86 82 A7  ....H......påé*
```

End of file   Start of a WordPerfect document

Figure 11.4   The start and end of the file VERISI~1.GIF.

Because the area occupied by the empty clusters (632–644) contains binary data starting with GIF89a, you can feel confident that these clusters contain the data you need.

8. To return to the FAT to fill in the cluster numbers for the file, open the Object menu and select Directory. The current directory is selected, so click OK.

9. Move the cursor down to the entry for VERISI~1.GIF, open the Link menu, and click Cluster Chain (FAT). The Cluster Chain refers to the clusters after the initial cluster (632); enter **633** in the first empty field, and continue until you enter **643** and place the cursor in the last empty field. This field needs to have the <EOF> marker placed in it to indicate the end of the file. Press Alt+E to open the Edit menu and select Mark (or press Ctrl+B). Open the Edit menu again and select Fill. Then, select End of File from the menu and click OK. Refer to Figure 11.2 to see how the FAT looks after these changes have been made.

10. To save the changes to the FAT, open the Edit menu again and select Write. When prompted to save the changes, click Write; then click Rescan the Disk.

11. To return to Directory view, open the Object menu and select Directory. Click OK.

12. The LFN entries directly above the VERISI~1.GIF file are still listed as Del LFN. To reconnect them to VERISI~1.GIF, select the first one (verisignsealt), open the Tools menu (press Alt+T), and select Attach LFN. Click Yes when prompted. Repeat the process for rans.gif.

13. To verify that the file has been undeleted successfully, exit Disk Editor and open the file in a compatible program. If you have correctly located the clusters and linked them, the file will open.

As you can see, this is a long process, but it is essentially the same process that a program such as Norton UnErase performs automatically. However, Disk Editor can perform these tasks on all types of disks that use FAT file systems, including those that use non-DOS operating systems; it's a favorite of advanced Linux users.

Retrieving a File from a Hard Disk or Flash Memory Card

What should you do if you need to retrieve an erased file from the hard disk or a flash memory card? It's safer to write the retrieved file to another disk (preferably a floppy disk if the file is small enough) or to a different drive letter on the hard disk. You can also perform this task with Disk Editor.

Tip

If you want to recover data from a hard disk and copy the data to another location, set Disk Editor back to its default Read-Only mode to avoid making any accidental changes to the hard disk. If you use Disk Editor in a multitasking environment such as Windows, it defaults to Read-Only mode.

The process of locating the file is the same as that described earlier:

1. Determine the cluster (allocation unit) size of the drive on which the file is located.

2. Run Disk Editor to view the name of the erased file and determine which clusters contain the file data.

However, you don't need to restore the filename because you will be copying the file to another drive.

The clusters will be copied to another file, so it's helpful to use the Object menu to look at the clusters and ensure that they contain the necessary data. To view the data stored in the cluster range, open the Object menu, select Cluster, and enter the range of clusters that the cluster chain command indicates should contain the data. In some cases, the first cluster of a particular file indicates the file type. For example, a GIF file has GIF89a at the start of the file, whereas a WordPerfect document has WPC at the start of the file.

Tip

Use Norton Disk Editor to view the starting and ending clusters of various types of files you create before you try to recover those types of files. This is particularly important if you want to recover files from formatted media. You might consider creating a database of the hex characters found at the beginning and ending of the major file types you want to recover.

If you are trying to recover a file that contains text, such as a Microsoft Word or WordPerfect file, you can switch Disk Edit into different view modes. To see text, press F3 to switch to Text view. However, to determine where a file starts or ends, use Hex mode (press F2 to switch to this mode). Figure 11.5 shows the start of a Microsoft Word file in Text format and the end of the file in Hex format.

To copy the contents of these clusters to a file safely, you should specify the sectors that contain the file. The top of the Disk Editor display shows the sector number as well as the cluster number. For example, the file shown in Figure 11.5 starts at cluster 75207, which is also sector 608470. The end of the file is located in sector 608503.

To write these sectors to a new file, do the following:

1. Open the Object menu.
2. Select Sector.
3. Specify the starting and ending sectors.
4. Click OK.
5. Scroll through the sectors to verify that they contain the correct data.

Start of file (text mode) End of file (hex mode)

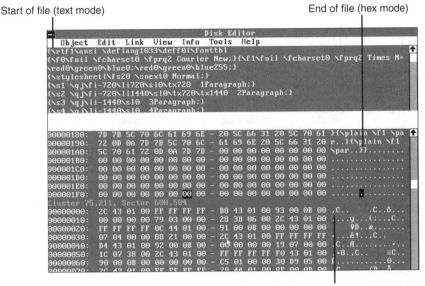

Junk data in cluster after end of file (hex mode)

Figure 11.5 Scrolling through an erased file with Disk Editor.

6. Open the Tools menu.

7. Click Write Object To.

8. Click To a File.

9. Click the drive on which you want to write the data.

10. Specify a DOS-type filename (8 characters plus a 3-character extension); you can rename the file to a long filename after you exit Disk Edit.

11. Click OK, and then click Yes to write the file. A status bar appears as the sectors are copied to the file.

12. Exit Disk Edit and open the file in a compatible program. If the file contains the correct data, you're finished. If not, you might have specified incorrect sectors or the file might be fragmented.

Norton Disk Editor is a powerful tool you can use to explore drives and retrieve lost data. However, your best data recovery technique is to avoid the need for data recovery. Think before you delete files or format a drive, and make backups of important files. That way, you won't need to recover lost data very often.

Data Recovery from Flash Memory Devices

Flash memory devices such as USB keychain drives and cards used in digital cameras and digital music players present a unique challenge to data recovery programs. Although, from a user standpoint, these devices emulate conventional disk drives, have file allocation tables similar to those found on floppy disks, and can usually be formatted through the Windows Explorer, many data recovery programs that work well with conventional drives cannot be used to recover data from flash memory devices—especially when the device has been formatted.

Under several conditions, data loss can occur with a flash memory device. Some of them, such as formatting of the media or deletion of one or more photos or files, can occur when the device is connected to the computer through a card reader or when the flash memory device is inserted into a digital camera. When photos are deleted, the file locations and name listings in the file allocation tables are changed in the same way as when files are deleted from magnetic media: The first character of the filename is changed to a lowercase sigma, indicating the file has been erased. Just as with magnetic media, undelete programs that support removable-media drives and the Norton Disk Editor can be used to retrieve deleted files on flash memory devices in the same way that they retrieve deleted files from magnetic media. Note that Disk Editor must be run in Read-Only mode and works best on systems running Windows 9x/Me. Data files can also be damaged if the flash memory card is removed from a device before the data-writing process is complete.

However, retrieving data from a formatted flash memory device, whether it has been formatted by a digital camera or through Windows, is much more difficult. Traditional unformat programs such as the command-line Norton Unformat program provided with Norton Utilities and Norton SystemWorks can't be used because flash memory devices are accessible only from within the Windows GUI, and command-line programs are designed to work with BIOS-compatible devices such as hard and floppy drives.

Programs that rely on the file system, such as Ontrack EasyRecovery Personal Edition Lite (incorporated into VCOM System's Suite) and Ontrack EasyRecovery Personal Edition, do not work either because the previous file system is destroyed when the flash memory devices are formatted.

Note

When a digital camera formats a flash memory card, it usually creates a folder in which photos are stored. Some cameras might also create another folder for storing drivers or other information.

If you need to recover data from a formatted flash memory device, the following programs work extremely well:

- *Ontrack EasyRecovery Professional Edition*; free evaluation and more information are available from http://www.ontrack.com
- *PhotoRescue*; free evaluation and more information are available from http://www.datarescue.com/photorescue/

Norton Disk Editor (incorporated into Norton SystemWorks and Norton SystemWorks Pro) can also be used to recover data if you can determine the starting and ending clusters used by the data stored on the device.

To recover data from a formatted flash memory card with EasyRecovery Professional Edition, the RawRecovery option (which recovers data on a sector-by-sector basis) must be used. This option bypasses the file system and can be used on all supported media types. A built-in file viewer enables you to determine whether the recovered data is readable.

PhotoRescue, which works only with standard photo image types such as JPG, BMP, and TIF, can access the media in either logical drive mode (which worked quite well in our tests) or physical drive mode. Physical mode uses a sector-by-sector recovery method somewhat similar to that used by EasyRecovery Professional Edition. PhotoRescue also displays recovered photos in a built-in viewer.

With both products, you might recover data from not just the most recent use before format, but also leftover data from previous uses. As long as the data area used by a particular file hasn't been overwritten, the data can be recovered—even if the device has been formatted more than once.

Table 11.3 provides an overview of our results when trying to recover data from two common types of flash memory devices: a Compact Flash card used in digital cameras and a USB keychain storage device.

Table 11.3   Retrieving Lost Data from Flash Memory Devices—Results by Data-Recovery Program

Device	Cause of Data Loss	Norton Utilities	Ontrack/Vcom System Suite	DataRescue Photo Rescue	Ontrack EasyRecovery Professional
Compact Flash 64MB	Deleted selected files in camera	Recovered data back to device when used with Windows 9x/Me only.[1, 2]	Recovered data to user-specified folder.[1, 3]	Recovered data from most recent format and from previous card uses to specified folder.[3, 4]	RawRecovery recovered deleted files from current and previous uses; refer to Table 11.1 for limitations.[3, 4]
Compact Flash 64MB	Deleted selected files with Windows Explorer	Recovered data back to device when used with Windows 9x/Me only.[1, 2]	Recovered data to specified folder when used with any supported version of Windows.[3]	Recovered data from most recent format and from previous card uses to specified folder (files and folders renamed).	DeletedRecovery recovered deleted data from current use (first character of file/folder name lost).
Compact Flash 64MB	Format in camera	Drive could not be unformatted; Disk Edit could retrieve data from current and previous uses to user-specified folder.[3, 5, 6]	Could not locate data. No data was recovered.	Recovered data from most recent format and from previous card uses to user-specified folder.[3, 4]	RawRecovery recovered all readable data, including data from previous card uses to user-specified folder.[3, 4]
Compact Flash 64MB	Format in card reader	Drive could not be unformatted; Disk Edit could retrieve data from current and previous uses.[5, 6]	Could not locate data. No data was recovered.	Recovered data from most recent format and from previous card uses to user-specified folder.[4]	RawRecovery recovered all readable data, including data from previous card uses to user-specified folder.[4]
USB keychain drive (128MB)	Deleted folder with My Computer	Disk Edit can retrieve data from current use.[3, 6]	Partial success: Recovered some files.[3]	Recovered photo files only.[3, 4]	RawRecovery retrieved most files.[3, 4]
USB keychain drive (128MB)	Formatted by Windows Explorer	Disk Edit can retrieve data from current use.[3, 6]	Partial success: Recovered some files (folder names and structure lost).[3]	Recovered photo files only.[3, 4]	RawRecovery retrieved most files.[3, 4]

1. *User supplied first letter of filename during undelete process.*
2. *Norton UnErase doesn't support removable-media drives in Windows NT/2000/XP.*

(continues)

3. *Program operates in read-only mode on the drive containing the lost data.*

4. *Original file and folder names were not retained; files are numbered sequentially and might need to be renamed after recovery.*

5. *Windows must be used to access flash memory devices, and Norton Unformat can't be used in a multitasking environment such as Windows.*

6. *Disk Edit requires the user to manually locate the starting and ending sectors of each file and write the sectors to another drive with a user-defined filename.*

FAT File System Troubleshooting

Here are some general procedures to follow for troubleshooting drive access, file system, or boot problems:

1. Start the system using a Windows startup disk, or any bootable MS-DOS disk that contains FDISK.EXE, FORMAT.COM, SYS.COM, and SCANDISK.EXE (Windows 95B or later versions preferred).

2. If your system can't boot from the floppy, you might have more serious problems with your hardware. Check the floppy drive and the motherboard for proper installation and configuration. On some systems, the BIOS configuration doesn't list the floppy as a boot device or puts it after the hard disk. Reset the BIOS configuration to make the floppy disk the first boot device if necessary and restart your computer.

3. Run FDISK from the Windows startup disk. Select option 4 (Display partition information).

4. If the partitions are listed, make sure that the bootable partition (usually the primary partition) is defined as active (look for an uppercase *A* in the Status column).

5. If no partitions are listed and you do not want to recover any of the data existing on the drive now, use FDISK to create new partitions, and then use FORMAT to format the partitions. This overwrites any previously existing data on the drive.

6. If you want to recover the data on the drive and no partitions are being shown, you must use a data recovery program, such as the Norton Utilities or Lost and Found, to recover the data.

7. If all the partitions appear in FDISK.EXE and one is defined as active, run the SYS command as follows to restore the system files to the hard disk:

   SYS C:

8. For this to work properly, it is important that the disk you boot from be a startup disk from the same operating system (or version of Windows) you have on your hard disk.

9. You should receive the message System Transferred if the command works properly. Remove the disk from drive A: and restart the system. If you still have the same error before after you restart your computer, your drive might be improperly configured or damaged.

10. Run SCANDISK from the Windows startup disk or an aftermarket data-recovery utility, such as the Norton Utilities, to check for problems with the hard disk.

11. Using SCANDISK, perform a surface scan. If SCANDISK reports any physically damaged sectors on the hard disk, the drive might need to be replaced.

NTFS File System Troubleshooting

The process for file system troubleshooting with Windows 2000/XP is similar to that used for Windows 9x. The major difference is the use of the Windows 2000/XP Recovery Console, which is clarified here:

- If the Recovery Console was added to the boot menu, start the system normally, log in as Administrator if prompted, and select the Recovery Console.

- If the Recovery Console was not previously added to the boot menu, start the system using the Windows CD-ROM or the Windows Setup disks. Select Repair from the Welcome to Setup menu, and then press C to start the Recovery Console when prompted.

If your system can't boot from CD-ROM or the floppy, you might have more serious problems with your hardware. Check your drives, BIOS configuration, and motherboard for proper installation and configuration. Set the floppy disk as the first boot device and the CD-ROM as the second boot device and restart the system.

After you start the Recovery Console do the following:

1. Type **HELP** for a list of Recovery Console commands and assistance.

2. Run DISKPART to examine your disk partitions.

3. If the partitions are listed, make sure that the bootable partition (usually the primary partition) is defined as active.

4. If no partitions are listed and you do not want to recover any of the data existing on the drive now, use FDISK to create new partitions, and then use FORMAT to format the partitions. This overwrites any previously existing data on the drive.

5. If you want to recover the data on the drive and no partitions are being shown, you must use a data recovery program, such as the Norton Utilities or Lost and Found, to recover the data.

6. If all the partitions appear in DISKPART and one is defined as active, run the FIXBOOT command as follows to restore the system files to the hard disk:

   FIXBOOT

7. Type **EXIT** to restart your system. Remove the disk from drive A: or the Windows 2000 or XP CD-ROM from the CD-ROM drive.

8. If you still have the same error after you restart your computer, your drive might be improperly configured or damaged.

9. Restart the Recovery Console and run CHKDSK to check for problems with the hard disk.

CHAPTER 12

Windows Troubleshooting

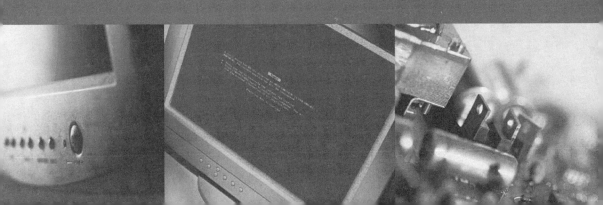

Troubleshooting Basics

Most experienced computer technicians will tell you that troubleshooting is a combination of skill and art. Troubleshooting is a skill, in that it can be learned as a process. It is an art, in that it also requires intuition, imagination, and even plain old dumb luck. Regardless of those factors, however, the more experience you gain, the better your troubleshooting ability becomes.

Troubleshooting can be a frustrating, anxiety-filled process, particularly if you are working on a mission-critical system, or if it is your personal machine that is malfunctioning. However, it is important to remain patient and objective when trying to resolve an issue and don't forget that the cause may not be related to Windows at all, but rather your hardware. Although I offer some basic guidelines here, I cover hardware problems in much more detail in *Upgrading and Repairing PCs* and *Upgrading and Repairing Laptops*.

Regardless of the source of your problems, it is crucial that you follow an organized method of troubleshooting rather than fiddling with things at random, hoping to get lucky. To troubleshoot a problem with Windows, you need to follow a deductive process. You are like Sherlock Holmes, eliminating the impossible until all that is left, however improbable, must be the cause of the problem. As you gain more experience troubleshooting Windows, you will begin to recognize problems that you have encountered before, which enables you to go straight to the root cause and apply a solution.

In this chapter, you will look at some of the more common errors encountered with Windows, and examine the tools that the Windows operating system provides to help solve these problems. Before we dive into these topics, here are some general tips for improving and refining your basic troubleshooting skills.

- *Always check the physical first.* Before you start drilling into the core of the operating system, always check the physical components of a malfunctioning machine first. For example, if you are troubleshooting a machine that is freezing during Windows startup, check to see whether all internal hard drive cable connections are secure.

  It is astonishing how many errors occur due to a simple physical fault, and how many times these faults are overlooked by troubleshooters. Don't assume that just because a machine worked the last time you used it that nothing has changed. Hard drive cables can vibrate loose from their connectors; RAM modules can thermal creep out of their sockets if the socket clasps are faulty or have come undone due to vibration; likewise power surges and overmatched power supplies can cause any number of obscure errors.

- *Never assume anything.* Faulty assumptions will absolutely kill a troubleshooting session. Don't take anything for granted when working on a problem. Verify your assumptions about the hardware and software status of a system before moving forward.

- *Document everything.* Before you begin to make changes to a malfunctioning system, you should record as much information about the problem as possible. Write down word for word any error messages that are being displayed. Sometimes, you only see an error message once, and chances are you won't remember exactly what it said if you don't write it down.

  Write notes detailing all of the symptoms of the problem. If troubleshooting an error that occurs repeatedly over a certain time interval, take note of the times when it occurs. If you are able to access Windows Event Viewer, copy down any pertinent error messages that appear in the logs.

  And, perhaps most important, create an ongoing record of any changes you make to the hardware and software while you are trying to solve the problem. It may seem absurd to think that you would forget a step you took during your troubleshooting process, but it happens more often than most technicians would care to admit.

- *If a change made to the system doesn't solve the problem, reverse it.* If you change a Windows setting in order to try to solve a problem, and making the change doesn't work, remember to change the setting back. If you don't do this while working on a system, you introduce an increasing amount of changing variables that will make it extremely difficult to isolate the source of a problem.

- *Create a summary once the problem is solved.* Once you have solved a problem, write down the details of the problem, the steps you took to solve the problem, and the appropriate dates and times. Don't leave these details solely dependent on your memory; a permanent record is much more reliable.

- *Know when to walk away.* When any of us experiences a problem with a computer, especially if it is our personal system, we always want to get the problem resolved as quickly as possible. However, there comes a time when it's best to walk away from a malfunctioning system for a little while, and come back to it fresh after a break.

  Very few people can maintain peak concentration for hours at a time. Taking a break isn't "giving up"; it's a necessary part of the troubleshooting process that keeps you from becoming part of the problem. If it's the end of the day, pack it up and get a good night's sleep. That's likely to do far more for your ability to identify and fix a problem than bouncing off the walls all night long.

- *You don't have to know everything in order to be a good troubleshooter.* Part of being a top-class troubleshooter is being able to effectively use external information resources. Remember that it is not only acceptable, but also often required to draw upon the experience of others to help you to solve a problem. This experience can be found in books, web resources, knowledgeable friends and family members, and especially with representatives of the technical support departments of hardware and software manufacturers.

Finally, if you ever get so frustrated that you want to take a sledgehammer to your PC, here's one last piece of troubleshooting advice from Confucius: "Do not use a cannon to kill a mosquito."

What You'll Find in This Chapter

In this chapter, you will look at a variety of different Windows problems and solutions. Specifically, you will split these problems into three categories:

- Problems encountered during Windows installation.
- Problems encountered during Windows startup.
- Problems encountered while Windows is running.

You'll also look at additional tools and resources that can be used to find solutions to problems, such as the Microsoft Knowledge Base (MSKB) and the Windows Support Tools located on the Windows XP installation CD.

Note

This chapter deals specifically with troubleshooting problems with the Windows XP operating system. If you are looking for more detailed information on PC hardware, check out *Upgrading and Repairing PCs* (ISBN 0-7897-3173-8) or *Upgrading and Repairing Laptops* (0-7897-2800-1) from Que Publishing. These are the definitive guides to everything that can be plugged into a tower case or crammed into a portable PC. For a no-holds barred troubleshooting book, check out Leo LaPorte's *PC Help Desk*, (0-7897-3394-3), also from Que.

A Word About Viruses and Spyware

If the top cardinal rule of troubleshooting is *check the physical first*, the next cardinal rule is *check for viruses or spyware second*.

There are two key reasons for this. The first is that both viruses and spyware can introduce several different behavioral variables into a Windows-based PC. Plainly speaking, viruses and spyware can cause more than one kind of problem behavior to appear. This can be incredibly misleading when you are trying to isolate the cause of the problem. More often than not, if you try to troubleshoot a malfunctioning Windows PC without first checking whether there is a virus or spyware present, you will end up chasing your tail.

The second reason is that if you make repairs to a malfunctioning Windows installation where the problem is attributable to a virus or spyware, you are only treating the symptom, not the disease. In fact, there is a good chance that the virus or spyware will undo the repairs you have made as soon as you restart the system, which will send you running down another false trail.

After you have verified that there are no physical problems with a sick computer, your second step should always be to scan the system for viruses and spyware. There are a number of free and commercially available programs you can use to find and eliminate viruses and spyware. Ideally, you should have two variations of such programs: one version that is used on a system while Windows is up-and-running, and another version that is "bootable"; that is, that you can use from system startup to scan the machine before Windows is loaded. You'll find more information an antivirus and antispyware programs in Chapter 8, "Protecting and Securing Windows."

Windows "Sickbed" Symptoms

Generally speaking, Windows XP will exhibit one of five major symptoms when it encounters a problem that causes a core component of the operating system to malfunction:

1. Windows will cease functioning, and the system will display a STOP Error screen, also known in more colorful terms as the Blue Screen of Death.

2. Windows will terminate an open application and display a dialog box informing you of this action, and (if configured to do so) will offer you the opportunity to send an error report to Microsoft.

3. Windows will stop and restart the EXPLORER.EXE service, also known as Windows Explorer. A dialog box (essentially the same dialog box that is displayed with symptom #2) informs the user of this event.

4. The computer will suddenly reboot while it is in operation.

5. The system will lock up entirely, and can only be unlocked by pressing the reset button on the computer.

These five symptoms can occur during different stages of Windows operation, including during installation, during startup, and during normal operation. Table 12.1 lists when each symptom may occur:

Table 12.1 Windows Error Symptoms

Windows Status	Symptoms That Can Occur
During installation	1, 4, 5
During startup	1, 4, 5
During normal operation	1, 2, 3, 4, 5

If any of these symptoms occur, they indicate that there is a hardware or software problem that is interfering with the normal functioning of Windows. The troubleshooting methods and tools you use to discover and correct the problem will often be determined by what stage Windows is in when symptom occurs.

Windows Installation Troubleshooting

If you encounter a problem while trying to install Windows XP, there are a few specific things you should look at in order to try to fix the problem and perform a successful installation.

Legacy/Unsupported Hardware Devices

A large number of problems encountered when installing Windows are due to incompatible hardware. This doesn't mean that the hardware device in question is defective, only that the Windows OS does not support it. Although Windows XP supports an impressive number of hardware devices, it would be impractical (if not impossible) to support every third-party PC hardware product that exists (or has ever existed) on the market.

Legacy/unsupported hardware can cause Windows Setup to fail, resulting in a STOP error screen, a frozen computer, or a computer that continually reboots at the same point during the installation process.

Before beginning an installation of Windows XP, you should compile a list of your computer's hardware components and check this list against Microsoft's Windows Hardware Compatibility List (HCL). As of this writing, the Windows HCL is presented on the Microsoft website as a selection of catalogs. You can check hardware components against the appropriate Windows catalog to see whether the device is supported by the operating system. Microsoft is constantly updating these catalogs to include new components as they are tested and approved for Windows XP.

The Windows HCL Catalogs are located at

> http://www.microsoft.com/whdc/hcl/default.mspx

Also, if you are unsure of the compatibility of a hardware device, you should check the support website of the company that produced it. Hardware manufacturers will often release updated driver software and/or information concerning their products' compatibility with Windows XP on their support sites.

Finally, I recommend that you remove nonessential hardware from your system before performing a Windows XP installation. This will minimize the chances of encountering an incompatible hardware device during setup, allowing you to later search for and install functional third-party drivers once the Windows installation is complete.

Windows XP Upgrade Advisor

If you are performing an upgrade installation of Windows XP (that is, installing it on a system that already has a previous version of Windows on it), there may be software programs or device drivers present on the system that are incompatible with Windows XP. These programs and drivers can cause the Windows upgrade procedure to fail, or can result in nonfunctioning devices or programs once Windows XP is installed. This is why I recommend that most users install Windows XP from scratch rather than perform an upgrade installation. However, should you need to perform an upgrade installation Windows XP provides some help.

In order to check the existing files and devices on a machine before you upgrade it to Windows XP, you can use the Windows XP Upgrade Advisor. This program is located on the Windows XP installation CD. To run this program, log on to the system you intend to upgrade, and place the installation

CD into the CD-ROM drive. When the CD startup menu appears, select Check System Compatibility, and then select Check My System Automatically.

The Upgrade Advisor will scan your system, and then create a report that lists all potential software compatibility issues. It will also perform a scan of your hardware devices, and inform you of any possible upgrade issues with them. Use the created report as a guideline and a resource to check into possible problems before you perform an upgrade installation of Windows XP.

For more information on performing an upgrade installation of Windows XP refer to Chapter 3, "Upgrading Windows."

Updating Computer Firmware

One commonly overlooked aspect of a computer's internal "makeup" that can cause a Windows installation to fail is outdated firmware. As I discuss extensively in *Upgrading and Repairing PCs*, firmware is software that is written onto read-only memory (ROM) chips, which are then integrated into a piece of hardware. Every motherboard has a ROM chip that contains the basic input/output system, also known as the ROM BIOS. The ROM BIOS chip holds the startup programs and drivers that are used to get the computer running before the operating system is loaded. Think of the ROM BIOS as the starter engine for your PC; it gets your system firing so that it can start up the big engine—the operating system.

There are a number of different BIOS manufacturers. Companies that build motherboards collaborate with BIOS manufacturers to create a customized version of BIOS for specific models of motherboards. Currently, the most popular BIOS manufacturers are Award Software, Phoenix Technologies, and American Megatrends, Inc. (commonly abbreviated as AMI).

Most modern motherboards store the BIOS on a type of chip known as a flash ROM. The flash ROM gets its name from its ability to be erased and reprogrammed with a flash BIOS upgrade utility program. This procedure is known as flashing the BIOS. When BIOS manufacturers make improvements to their software, they release these updates as flash ROM upgrades. Motherboard manufacturers usually offer these upgrades as downloadable files from their websites. BIOS upgrades are primarily used to add functionality to your system's motherboard, or to fix a bug that was in the earlier version of the BIOS.

Before doing a new installation of Windows XP, you should check the version of the BIOS firmware on your motherboard. The BIOS version information is normally displayed when you first power on your computer. On most systems, you can press the Pause key on your keyboard to freeze the screen when the BIOS version is being shown, so that you have time to write down the information. After you have the information recorded, press any key to resume startup. If this method doesn't work on your computer, enter the BIOS setup and locate the BIOS version in the setup screen. This is done by pressing a certain key (usually the Delete key) after you have switched the power on.

To check whether you have the most recent version of your system BIOS, contact the tech support of the manufacturer of your motherboard, or look up the make and model of your motherboard on the manufacturer's website. Many motherboard companies have lists or tables that match up motherboard models with the most recent firmware version available for them. If necessary, update to the latest version of the firmware before installing Windows XP.

You should also note that the motherboard is not the only system hardware component that has a flash ROM. Video cards, sound cards, and optical drives also have flash ROMs integrated into them, and manufacturers of these components often create and release firmware upgrades for these devices. As with BIOS firmware, check for new versions by visiting the manufacturer's website.

Other Common Windows Installation Issues

If your system hardware is compatible with Windows XP, but the installation process cannot be completed successfully, there is a good chance that there is a fault with either a system component, or with the installation media itself.

Here are some of the more common causes of Windows Setup failures (that aren't related to hardware device incompatibilities):

- *Faulty RAM modules*. A malfunctioning RAM module will create havoc with Windows Setup. RAM chips can malfunction because they are defective, or if you have overclocked your PC's processor in the system BIOS, causing it to run faster than its design specifications. There are third-party memory diagnostic programs available that will run from a bootable floppy or CD that you can use to test the integrity of the system's RAM. Microsoft has a free program called the Windows Memory Diagnostic, which you can download at http://oca.microsoft.com/en/windiag.asp.

- *Defective hard drive*. If the system hard drive has errors on it, it's possible that Windows Setup will be unable to copy critical operating system files to it in order to complete the installation. Again, there are a number of utilities you can use to test a hard drive's integrity; the website of the manufacturer of the drive is a good starting point to look for such a utility.

- *Overheating system*. One common environmental issue that will cause a system to either freeze up or to reboot repeatedly is if the inside of the system is not being adequately cooled. This is of particular concern if you have overclocked any of your system's components (the CPU and GPU in particular). An overheated processor, RAM module, or hard drive can all lead to a locked up system or one that spontaneously reboots. Ensure that all case fans and the CPU cooling fan are installed correctly and are operational.

- *Defective installation media*. Installation problems can be caused by something as simple as a damaged or otherwise defective Windows XP installation CD. Check the surface of the CD for scratches and other marks.

- *Improper power supply load*. If your system hardware requires more power than the power supply is rated to provide, it can cause instability both during and after the installation process. The best short-term solution is to remove any unnecessary hardware from your PC, thus easing the load on the power supply. From there it's time to get yourself a more powerful, high-quality power supply unit, like those available from PC Power and Cooling.

Note

The Windows XP installation process will sometimes result in the creation of a STOP error screen, or Blue Screen of Death. You will take a look at how to interpret STOP errors later in this chapter.

Pre-Windows Startup Troubleshooting

Possibly the most frustrating situation to troubleshoot is when you are unable to successfully start Windows. If something is malfunctioning while Windows XP is up and running, you can use the tools provided by the operating system to try and solve the problem. But, how do you troubleshoot a Windows problem when you can't even get into Windows?

Thankfully, there are also a number of methods and tools available for you to fix a non-starting Windows installation. Some of these options are accessed by using a scaled-down startup version of Windows known as *Safe mode*. Although, before you try to boot Windows in Safe mode, I do recommend that you try to use the Last Known Good Configuration option discussed later in this section.

Before you begin to familiarize yourself with Windows-specific troubleshooting tools and methods, however, you need to be able to recognize and fix errors that can occur before the Windows operating system begins to load.

Common Boot Error Messages and Solutions

The chain of events that takes place when a computer is turned on is known as the *boot process*. There are a number of steps that take place during the boot process that are entirely independent of the operating system installed on the computer. If an error occurs on a Windows-based PC during any of these steps, the boot process freezes and Windows does not begin to load.

The first step in troubleshooting a non–Windows-related boot error message is to determine which software component is responsible for generating the error message. There are four primary software components that come into play during the boot process:

- *Motherboard ROM BIOS*. The Motherboard ROM BIOS is the initial software program that runs upon powering up the computer. It is responsible for testing your system's hardware components, and then initiating the chain of events that leads to the loading of an operating system, such as Windows.

- *Adapter Card ROM BIOS Extensions*. Adapter card ROM BIOS extensions are ROM BIOS chips integrated into hardware components such as video cards and SCSI disk controllers. The motherboard ROM BIOS scans for adapter card ROM BIOS extensions, and initializes these devices accordingly.

- *Master Boot Record (MBR)*. The Master Boot Record (MBR), as discussed in Chapter 10, "Windows File Systems," is a small program located in the very first physical sector of a hard disk (cylinder 0, head 0, sector 1). The MBR contains the master partition table, which lists all of the partitions on a hard disk. Each partition entry in the master partition table includes information on what type of partition it is (primary or extended), whether the partition is bootable or not, where the partition physically exists on the hard disk, and how many sectors it takes up. In addition to the master partition table, the MBR also contains the instructions used to discover and load the volume boot record from the active (bootable) partition, and a two-byte signature (55AAh) used by the Motherboard ROM BIOS to validate the sector occupied by the MBR.

- *Volume Boot Record*. The Volume Boot Record is located in the first sector of the bootable partition on a hard disk. The Volume Boot Record contains information about the volume it resides on, as well as instructions that are used to locate and load the operating system (with Windows XP, the Volume Boot Record is used to find and load the NTLDR file). The Volume Boot Record also contains a two-byte signature (55AAh), similar to the MBR, that is used to validate the sector it occupies.

With this information in mind, here are some common boot error messages and solutions.

Missing Operating System

During the boot process, the Volume Boot Record on the hard disk is tested for a specific two-byte signature (55AAh). If this signature is not found, the error message `Missing Operating System` is shown, and the boot process freezes.

This error is commonly caused by invalid BIOS settings, usually attributable to a dead or dying CMOS battery. CMOS stands for *complimentary metal oxide semiconductor*, and refers to a type of RAM chip that is located on the motherboard. The system BIOS reads and writes settings to and from the onboard CMOS chip, which is powered by a small battery so that the settings aren't wiped out when the computer is powered down. One of the settings that the system BIOS reads from the CMOS chip on startup is the hard disk configuration data.

If the CMOS battery is dead or dying, the hard disk settings in the CMOS chip can become corrupted or disappear entirely. Subsequently, when the system BIOS queries the CMOS chip on startup, it receives invalid hard disk settings, which causes the boot process to fail.

Tip

One dead giveaway that you have a failing CMOS battery is if the date and time information in the BIOS setup screen is constantly resetting itself when you power down your computer.

CMOS batteries can usually be replaced. Many computer and electronics stores carry CMOS batteries; you can also check with the manufacturer of your motherboard to see whether they sell them.

NO ROM BASIC—SYSTEM HALTED

If the two-byte signature of the Master Boot Record is not 55AAh, the Motherboard BIOS displays an error message. These error messages differ between various BIOS manufacturers. The NO ROM BASIC - SYSTEM HALTED error message is displayed by BIOS ROMs created by American Megatrends, Inc. (AMI).

This error message can be caused by missing boot files, a corrupt boot record, a hard disk failure, or a virus. To repair this issue, boot the system from the Windows XP installation CD, choose to open the Recovery Console, and run the fixmbr command. This will rebuild the Master Boot Record. After completing the operation, eject the Windows XP installation CD and reboot the system.

▶▶ For more information concerning the Windows XP Recovery Console, see "Recovery Console," p. 556.

If this solution doesn't work, the problem may be attributable to a boot-sector virus. A boot-sector virus copies code onto the partition table of a hard disk. The virus is loaded into memory on startup, which means that in order to attempt to remove it, you need to use a bootable antivirus program disk. If the program successfully locates and removes the virus, you should restore the MBR using the fixmbr command in Recovery Console, and reboot the system.

Boot Error Press F1 to Retry

This error message is generated by the Phoenix Bios when the Master Boot Record is corrupt or missing, or if the system is unable to access the boot drive. This message is the same as the NO ROM BASIC - SYSTEM HALTED message generated by AMI BIOS. See the previous section for details on how to fix this problem.

Invalid Drive Specification

This error is most commonly caused by trying to access a hard disk that hasn't been properly partitioned and formatted yet, or if the master partition table located in the Master Boot Record has been damaged. If you are certain that the hard disk is properly formatted and partitioned, try to restore the MBR using the fixmbr command from the Recovery Console.

Invalid Media Type

This message is generated if the volume boot sector, directory, or file allocation tables are damaged or not yet initialized. One likely cause of this error is if you attempt to access a hard disk that hasn't been formatted yet. Formatting is what creates the Volume Boot Record, file allocation tables, and directories on the hard disk.

If there is data on the disk that you don't want destroyed, you can try to solve this problem by performing a high-level format (also known as an OS format) on the disk. You will then need to unformat the disk using an appropriate utility such as DiskInternals FAT Recovery (which also works on NTFS volumes) or Norton UnFormat.

Hard Disk Controller Failure

This message indicates that the hard disk controller has failed, or that the controller is unable to communicate with the attached hard disk. Check the drive cables to see if they are properly connected. Also, check if the hard disk is receiving power, and is spinning up when the system is powered on. If these factors are all accounted for, there may be physical damage to the hard disk, the controller, or the data and/or power cables. Try replacing the data cable first, and if that doesn't solve the problem, try replacing the hard disk. If the error still occurs, it's likely that the disk controller on the motherboard is defective.

Windows Startup Troubleshooting

This section deals with errors that occur after the non-Windows portion of the boot process is complete, and the Windows startup process begins. Windows XP offers several tools you can use to identify and solve startup problems. Before digging too deep into how to solve problems with Windows startup, it's important that you have a basic understanding of the steps that a Windows XP–based PC follows during startup. This information can be found in Chapter 4, "Windows Startup."

The method you use to solve a Windows startup problem is generally based on one of three criteria:

- If the problem occurs immediately after you have installed a new device driver, updated an existing driver, or installed a new software application
- Whether or not you are able to start Windows in Safe mode
- How valuable the data is on your system

The third bullet point should not be dismissed lightly. Of course, everything you have on your computer's hard disk counts as valuable data. However, in my experience, there comes a time during an extended troubleshooting session where I ask myself, "Is it worth it to continue working on this problem, or would it be better to just wipe the hard disk clean and reinstall everything?"

If you have reliable backups of your critical data, you should not reject the idea of repartitioning, reformatting, and reinstalling Windows just because it seems like too much work, or because it seems like the coward's way out. Rebuilding a nonfunctioning Windows PC is often the best, most time-effective way to bring a system back to a working condition.

Note

The Microsoft System Configuration Utility is a troubleshooting tool that can be used to configure a number of Windows startup options. You will find more information on this utility in the section "Windows XP Troubleshooting Tools" later in this chapter.

Before proceeding, it's worth noting that many of the tools discussed here, the Recovery Console and System Restore in particular, have applications to troubleshooting Windows that go above and beyond pure startup problems.

Windows Advanced Options Menu

If you are unable to start Windows normally, you need to access the Windows Advanced Options menu. As discussed in Chapter 4, this menu is accessed by pressing the F8 key on your keyboard once the POST is completed, and before the Windows splash screen appears.

Once the Windows Advanced Options menu opens, you can choose from the following actions:

Safe Mode

Safe Mode with Networking

Safe Mode with Command Prompt

Last Known Good Configuration

Start Windows Normally

Last Known Good Configuration

Last Known Good Configuration is not the first option listed in the Windows Advanced Options menu, but it is usually the first method you should use to try to repair a Windows startup problem. Specifically, Last Known Good Configuration should be used as the first method of repair if the Windows startup problem began immediately after

- A new device driver was installed
- An update to an existing driver was made
- A new software program was installed

The Last Known Good Configuration option causes Windows to reverse all driver and Registry changes made since the last time you successfully logged on to Windows. This means that if the problem is related to a newly installed driver or program (and you haven't successfully logged on to Windows since the driver or program was installed), you can use Last Known Good Configuration to revert to the original driver or remove the offending program's entries from the Windows Registry.

To initiate Last Known Good Configuration, access the Windows Advanced Options menu, use the arrow keys on your keyboard to scroll down to the Last Known Good Configuration menu item, and press the Enter key. If you are running more than one operating system on your computer, you will need to select the Windows XP installation from the menu that appears next. Windows will then attempt to revert to the previous settings, and will automatically restart.

Using Last Known Good Configuration will reverse every driver and Registry change made since your last successful logon. If you installed more than one driver or program in the last session before Windows startup failed, all of these changes will be wiped out. In this situation, you may end up with software programs that appear in the Start menu that will not run properly because their Registry entries have been removed. To correct this, manually uninstall the program by deleting the appropriate folder(s) in the Program Files directory, and delete the program shortcut located in the `<systemdrive:>\Documents and Settings\<username>\Start Menu\Programs` folder. Then, reinstall the program.

Tip

If you are positive that you know which driver or program is causing Windows startup to fail, you may want to bypass the Last Known Good Configuration and go straight to trying to start Windows in Safe mode. That way, you can deal with the specific piece of offending software using Device Manager, or through Add/Remove Programs in Control Panel. This allows you to deal directly with the rogue driver or software, instead of reversing all of the driver and Registry changes made since your last logon.

Starting Windows in Safe Mode

If using Last Known Good Configuration does not solve the Windows startup issue, you should try starting Windows in Safe mode. Using Safe mode gives you the ability to load Windows with only the minimal drivers required to start the core operating system. Starting Windows in Safe mode is sometimes the only way to gain access to a system when the problem is related to a software driver or program.

Note

Microsoft recommends that you try using Last Known Good Configuration before you try booting into Safe mode. However, starting Windows in Safe mode does not overwrite the Last Known Good Configuration information; this means that you can still go back and try Last Known Good Configuration even after you have started Windows in Safe mode.

To start Windows in Safe mode, restart the computer and press and hold the F8 key on the keyboard. This will open the Windows Advanced Options menu. From this menu, you can choose to start Windows in Safe mode, with three different options:

- *Safe mode* is the standard mode for starting Windows with only the necessary drivers. This is usually the option to choose when you want to start Windows in Safe mode.

- *Safe Mode with Networking* starts Windows in Safe mode, but includes the drivers necessary for Windows to load its networking components. This can be useful if you want to access online help, but don't have access to another Internet-enabled computer.

- *Safe Mode with Command Prompt* loads the minimum driver set, and then takes you directly to a command prompt rather than loading the Windows GUI interface.

Starting Windows in Safe mode circumvents a number of drivers and settings. For instance, audio drivers aren't loaded, so you will not have sound when in Safe mode. Also, you will usually not be able to access USB or FireWire devices such as external hard drives. However, you can use USB-based keyboards and mice as long as your computer's firmware supports these devices. For more information about using Safe mode, refer to Chapter 4.

If you are able to start Windows in Safe mode, there are a number of tools you can use to diagnose and solve the problem that is preventing Windows from starting normally.

Device Driver Rollback

If the Windows startup problem is related to a new or updated device driver (and you are aware of which driver is causing the problem), you can use the Device Driver Roll Back option to revert to the previous version of the driver.

Every time you install an updated driver, Windows XP stores a copy of the previous driver on your system. When you use the Driver Roll Back function, it looks for the previous version of the driver, and replaces the new driver with the last-used version.

After you have started Windows in Safe mode, open the Control Panel. If you do not have Control Panel configured to appear in Classic view, choose this option in the left-hand sidebar menu, and then double-click on the System applet. Select the Hardware tab and click on the Device Manager button. Expand the hardware category that the device with the offending driver is contained in, and then double-click on the device. Select the Driver tab, and then click Roll Back Driver (see Figure 12.1).

Figure 12.1   Click on the Roll Back Driver button to revert to the previous version of the driver.

You will be asked if you want to overwrite the existing driver. Select Yes to roll back to the previous version. Windows will locate the previous version of the driver, and automatically install it on your system (at the same time it removes the existing driver). In same cases Windows will inform you that the system must be restarted in order for the change to take effect.

There are a few limitations to the Device Driver Roll Back option. You can only revert one iteration of the driver, meaning that if you have used more than two versions, you cannot choose any other version than the one that was installed most recently. Also, due to a quirk with Windows XP, you cannot roll back printer drivers. Installing printers is done through the Printers and Faxes applet in Control Panel, and this applet does not support the Device Driver Roll Back function. Finally, you cannot use the Device Driver Roll Back option to completely uninstall a driver. If you want to uninstall a driver, click Uninstall on the device's property dialog instead of Roll Back Driver (refer to Figure 12.1).

Uninstalling Software Through the Windows Control Panel

If the Windows startup problem is related to a recently installed software program, you can remove the offending program after you have started Windows in Safe mode. To do so, open Control Panel in Classic view and double-click on the Add/Remove Programs applet. Select the program you want to uninstall from the list of installed software that appears, and select Remove.

Although the Add/Remove Programs applet in Control Panel is supposed to remove all traces of a program, this is not always the case. If you remove a program in this fashion and the same problem continues to occur, there is a chance that the program still has data left in the Windows Registry.

In this case, you will need to open the Windows Registry and remove any entries pertaining to the offending program. For more information on how to edit the Windows Registry, refer to Chapter 6, "Tweaking and Tuning Windows," in this book.

Case Study

Here is a real-life example of how a software program can prevent Windows from starting properly, and how the problem was solved.

I was once troubleshooting a corporate laptop that kept crashing during Windows startup. After talking to the employee, I discovered that the problem began immediately after he had loaded a new antivirus program onto the laptop.

I was able to start Windows in Safe mode, and get access to the GUI. I found the antivirus program, and ran its uninstall program. The software uninstalled without a hitch, and I rebooted the laptop, only to discover that it was still crashing during Windows startup.

After puzzling over this for a minute or two, I restarted Windows in Safe mode, went to the Start menu, chose Run, and typed in **REGEDIT** to open the Windows Registry Editor. I opened up the **HKEY_LOCAL_MACHINE** key, opened the **SOFTWARE** item, and looked for the name of the antivirus software's manufacturer. Sure enough, I found a Registry entry for the software that the uninstall program had failed to remove. I deleted this entry, saved the Registry, closed Registry Editor, and restarted the laptop. The Windows splash screen came up, and Windows started without any problems.

In my experience, a large number of Windows-related problems are related to poorly written software. Thankfully, Windows includes a number of tools you can use to remove buggy programs and device drivers.

Using the System Restore Tool

The System Restore tool, as discussed in Chapter 5, "Managing Windows," is included in both the Home and Professional versions of Windows XP. The System Restore service monitors the status of certain key files and settings. Every so often, this service takes a "snapshot" of certain aspects of your computer's current status. These "snapshots" are referred to as restore points. You can use the System Restore tool to roll back your machine to one of the recorded restore points.

Caution

The System Restore tool is not a substitute for an antivirus or spyware solution, nor is it a data backup strategy. System Restore does not save your documents, email, or other such files. It can, however, be used to restore a Windows installation to a previous point in time when it was working properly.

This section takes a look at using System Restore with a system that fails to boot normally.

◀◀ For more generally information on how System Restore works and how it's configured, see "System Restore," p. 220.

If your Windows XP-based PC will not start normally, there are two alternative methods you can use to access the System Restore tool. One method is used if you are able to start Windows in normal Safe mode, the other should be used if you can only start Windows in Safe Mode with Command Prompt.

System Restore in Safe Mode

If you are able to start Windows in Safe mode and get to the Windows GUI, you can initiate the System Restore tool from the Help and Support option in the Start menu. To do this, follow these steps:

1. From the Start menu, select Help And Support.

2. In the Help And Support Center, under Pick a Task, click on Undo Changes to Your Computer with System Restore.

3. You will now see the Welcome To System Restore screen. Select Restore My Computer to an Earlier Time, and click Next (see Figure 12.2).

4. You will be asked to choose the restore point you want to use: Restore points are listed with a date and description. Select the restore point you want, and click Next.

5. This takes you to the Confirm Restore Point Selection page. Ensure that the settings you've chosen are correct and click Next.

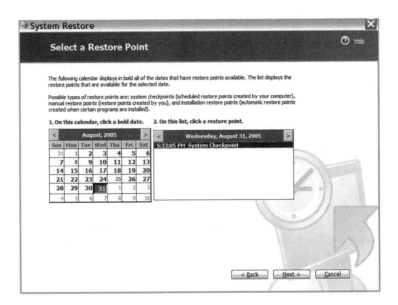

Figure 12.2 Select the desired restore point from the calendar and click Next.

The System Restore tool will reinstate the settings and key system files from the restore point you selected, and will then restart the computer. If you decide for whatever reason that the restore did not accomplish what you wanted it to, you can reverse the process by going back into the System Restore tool and selecting the Undo My Last Restoration option.

System Restore in Safe Mode with Command Prompt

If you are unable to start Windows in Safe mode, you can still access the System Restore tool if you are able to start Windows with the Safe Mode with Command Prompt option. The System Restore tool can be launched from the command prompt by using the following syntax:

```
%systemroot%\system32\restore\rstrui.exe
```

In this instance, `%systemroot%` is the directory where the Windows installation exists. With Windows XP, this directory is named WINDOWS unless the default selection was changed during the installation process.

After you have launched the rstrui.exe file, the command-line version of the System Restore tool starts. If there is an administrative password for the Windows installation, you will be asked to enter it before you can proceed with the restore. You will then be asked to choose a specific restore point to start the restore process. The restore process begins by passing the command to the System Restore service, which accesses the System Restore change logs. The System Restore service uses the change logs to create a restore map, which enables the service to re-create the specific system state you have selected. The restore map is then processed, the system restarts, and the new registry and dynamic data stores are loaded.

Note

For more information on using environment variables, refer to Chapter 9, "Windows Commands and Scripting."

Caution

In order for the System Restore tool to function, the System Restore service must be enabled in Windows. By default, this service is enabled when Windows is installed. However, the service can be disabled either through the System applet in Control Panel, or via the Services option in the Administrative Tools applet in Control Panel.

The System Restore tool can be the best procedure to use if you are unsure which driver or program may be causing the problem, or if uninstalling the driver or program doesn't solve the problem.

Recovery Console

One of the lesser-known maintenance features of Windows XP and Windows 2000 that's very useful in fixing a Windows system that won't fully boot is the Recovery Console. It's an interesting animal— rather than a management tool that you run from Windows, the Recovery Console is a completely independent, standalone, utterly minimal installation of Windows with "plain vanilla" device drivers, a very limited command-line interface, and no GUI. The idea is that no matter how badly messed up your main Windows installation might get, due to bad or incorrect drivers, weird hardware, missing files, or incorrect Registry entries, the Recovery Console should still be able to boot up and work.

Although Microsoft recommends that you try Safe mode first, the Recovery Console gives you a command prompt window from which you may be able to bring a non-bootable system back to life. You can use it to disable a device driver that crashes Windows before it can start up, delete a virus or spyware program, install fresh copies of system files that have become corrupted, and manage disk partitions. Under certain circumstances you can also use the Recovery Console to extract urgently needed files from a nonbootable system without going to the trouble of moving the hard disk to another computer or reinstalling Windows. However, this takes advance preparation.

Recovery Console Access Restrictions

By default, Recovery Console commands can only be used to read, write, and modify files in selected folders of your hard drives:

- The Windows folder (the `%systemroot%` folder) and its subfolders
- The root folders of your hard drives
- The folder from which the Recovery Console booted (`c:\cmdcons` if it was installed on your hard drive)
- Removable media such as CDs, DVDs, and floppy disks

Thus, using default settings, you cannot use Recovery Console to view, modify, or copy in user profile folders or any other folders; attempts to do so will result in an Access Denied error message.

Furthermore, by default, you can copy files from one hard drive to another (subject to the limitations just mentioned), and from removable media to hard drives, but you cannot copy files from a hard disk to a floppy disk, so you cannot use Recovery Console to salvage user files from a nonbootable computer.

You can configure Recovery Console so that it *can* access any folder, and *can* copy files out of the computer to removable media. But the set command, which is used to relax access restrictions, is available only if you make an adjustment to your computer's Security Policy before you boot the Recovery Console, and thus this has to be done before you run into trouble.

If you think you will ever want to be able to use the Recovery Console to copy files out of an unbootable computer to a floppy disk, you should enable the set command *now*. It's best if you also install the Recovery Console on your hard disk at the same time. You can also make the Security Policy changes without installing to disk—the procedure is described in steps 5 through 11 in the next section—but I recommend preinstallation.

Installing Recovery Console on Your Hard Disk

If you plan ahead, you can install Recovery Console on your hard disk, and it will appear as a boot-time option. The advantage of doing this is that you won't have to hunt for your Setup CD when you need to use Recovery Console. At the same time, you can choose to enable the set command that relaxes Recovery Console's access restrictions, or you can make it possible to use the Console without having the Administrator password.

Caution

You should not both enable the set command *and* remove the requirement for the Administrator password. With both of these options enabled, anyone with physical access to your computer would be able to access and view, delete, or take a copy of any file, without having to know any password at all.

Note

If your computer is a member of a domain network, Group Policy settings may be used to override Local Security policy, so your network administrator may prevent your use of the Recovery Console, or your attempt to relax its security restrictions. Likewise, Group Policy can also be used to enable access.

Note

If you have set up software mirrored or RAID disks using the Windows Disk Management console, you must break the mirror before installing the Recovery Console, and you cannot re-create the mirror unless your disks have been converted from Basic to Dynamic disks. See Microsoft Knowledge article support.microsoft.com/kb/229077 for details.

To install the Recovery Console on your hard disk, follow this procedure:

1. Log on as a Computer Administrator and insert your Windows Setup CD.

   On Windows XP, if your Setup CD has the original or Service Pack 1 version of XP, and you have subsequently installed Service Pack 2, you cannot use your original Setup CD. You must find and use an XP Setup CD that has SP2 preinstalled. You might be able to borrow a Setup CD from a friend with a newer computer.

2. Wait for the Windows Setup window to appear, and close it.

3. Open a Command Prompt window, and type the following command:

   `d:\i386\winnt32 /cmdcons`

   but type the letter corresponding to your CD drive in place of *d*.

4. Let Windows Setup complete the installation, and then remove the CD. Close the Command Prompt window.

5. If you want to enable the set command, which will let you bypass Recovery Console's access restrictions, proceed with step 6. Otherwise, skip ahead to step 8.

6. To enable the set command, open the Control Panel, select Performance and Maintenance, open Administrative Tools, and then open Local Security Policy.

7. In the left pane, open Security Settings, Local Policies, and select Security Options. In the right pane, double-click Recovery Console: Allow Floppy Copy. Select Enabled, and then click OK. Repeat with Recovery Console: Access to All Drives and All Folders. Now, skip ahead to step 11.

8. To eliminate the requirement that you enter the Administrator Password to manage this Windows installation using the Recovery Console, proceed with step 9. Otherwise, skip ahead to step 12.

9. To disable the Administrator password requirement, open the Control Panel, select Performance and Maintenance, open Administrative Tools, and then open Local Security Policy.

10. In the left-hand pane, open Security Settings, Local Policies, and select Security Options. In the right pane, double-click Recovery Console: Allow Automatic Administrative Logon. Select Enabled, and then click OK.

11. Close the Local Security Settings window and the Control Panel.

12. Click Start, right-click My Computer, and select Properties. Select the Advanced tab, and under Startup and Recovery, click Settings.

13. Be sure that the default operating system is *not* Microsoft Windows Recovery Console; if it is, select an appropriate default operating system option.

14. Ensure that Time to Display List of Operating Systems is checked, and set the number of seconds to 5. Finally, click OK to close the dialog.

Now, the next time you restart your computer, the Windows loader will display a boot menu, as shown in Figure 12.3. If you make no choice, after five seconds Windows will go ahead and start up as usual. If you need to use the Recovery Console, immediately press the down-arrow key to stop the clock, and then highlight Microsoft Windows Recovery Console and press Enter.

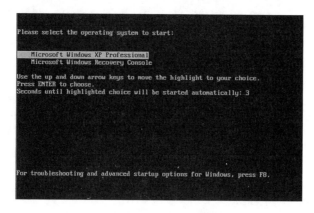

Figure 12.3   After installation, the Recovery Console appears as a boot option.

Note

The `boot.ini` entry for the recovery console is

`C:\CMDCONS\BOOTSECT.DAT="Microsoft Windows Recovery Console" /cmdcons`

although the drive letter may be different on your installation. This is handy to know in case you accidentally remove it from your `boot.ini` file or if you delete and have to replace `boot.ini`.

Caution

If you install Recovery Console on your hard disk and later convert the hard disk from FAT to NTFS format, you must reinstall Recovery Console. Until you do, the bootable version will not work, and you will only be able to start Recovery Console from your Setup CD.

Starting Recovery Console from your Setup CD

If you need to use the Recovery Console to repair a broken Windows installation but you did not preinstall it on your hard disk, you can start it by booting from your Windows Setup CD, using this procedure:

1. Insert your Windows Setup CD into your CD or DVD drive, and restart your computer. You may need to enter your BIOS Setup program to change the Boot Order setting so that booting from the CD drive is enabled, and the CD drive is checked before the hard drive.

2. When the Welcome to Setup screen appears, select R to Repair, and if prompted to do so, C to run the Recovery Console.

3. While the Recovery Console is starting, you will see the prompt Press F6 if you need to install a third party SCSI or RAID driver. If your disk drive interface requires a nonstandard driver, press F6 and follow the same procedure you used during Windows Setup to select an alternate driver.

4. The Recovery console will ask you to select a Windows installation.

Now, proceed as described in the next section.

Note

If your computer is set up for network booting and your organization uses Remote Installation Services, you can also boot Recovery Console through RIS. See Microsoft Knowledgebase article support.microsoft.com/kb/222478 for instructions.

Using the Recovery Console

To start the Recovery Console, if you have installed the Recovery Console on your hard disk, restart your computer and select Microsoft Windows Recovery Console from the boot options menu. Otherwise, boot from your Windows XP Setup CD as described in the previous section.

When the Recovery Console has loaded, there will be a five-second window in which you can press Enter to select an alternative keyboard layout. The default is US English Qwerty.

The Recovery Console will then examine your hard disks for any Windows installations it can find, and it will display them in a numbered list, even if only one is found, as shown in Figure 12.4. Enter the number corresponding to the Windows installation you want to repair and press Enter.

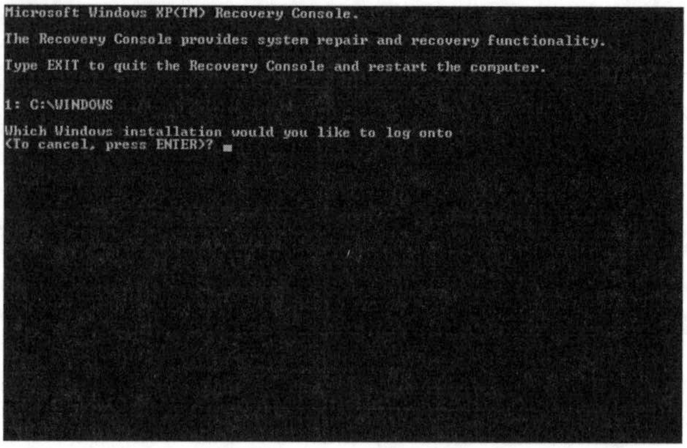

```
Microsoft Windows XP(TM) Recovery Console.

The Recovery Console provides system repair and recovery functionality.

Type EXIT to quit the Recovery Console and restart the computer.

1: C:\WINDOWS

Which Windows installation would you like to log onto
(To cancel, press ENTER)? ▮
```

Figure 12.4   When it starts, Recovery Console lets you select from any detected Windows installations.

If your Windows folder is not displayed, either its disk is inaccessible, or the installation is too corrupted to continue; in this case you need to fix the hardware, or reinstall Windows. You can press Enter to exit the Recovery Console and restart the computer.

Note

If your computer is set up for multibooting into Windows XP, 2000, or NT, be careful. You could damage your Windows installation if you try to use the Windows XP Recovery console on a Windows 2000 installation, or vice versa. Although all Windows installations are listed, work only with installations that match the version of the Recovery Console you're using. Boot from the other OS setup CD to get the right version, if necessary.

If a password is set for your Administrator account, and if you haven't disabled the need for the Administrator logon by modifying Security Policy, as discussed earlier, you will be prompted for the Administrator password.

◀◀   If you cannot remember the password to the Administrator account, see "Dealing with a Lost Password," p. 191.

The Recovery Console window works almost exactly like the Command Prompt window. You can use the cd command to change directories and dir to list directory contents; many of the usual commands like copy and del are available to let you manage files; and as usual, uppercase and lowercase do not matter when entering commands or options. However, there are also some distinct differences:

- Command-line editing functions are minimal. Filename completion is not available. You can use the up- and down-arrow keys to recall previously typed commands, but you cannot use the left- and right-arrow keys to move the cursor around in a command line for editing. To make changes, you must use the backspace key to erase characters and then retype the rest of the line.

- The Recovery Console supports only a small list of built-in commands. No other programs (.EXE files) can be run.

- The input and output redirection operations > and < and the pipeline operator | are not supported.

- Output never scrolls off the screen. If a listing fills the screen it automatically pauses; you can press the spacebar to display the next screen, or Esc to cancel the listing.

- Most commands that accept a filename argument will not accept wildcard specification using ? or *, unless you use the set command to enable the AllowWildCards option.

- Spaces are required between arguments. Although the normal command prompt accepts `cd\windows` as a valid command, Recovery Console doesn't—you must type `cd \windows` instead.

- As mentioned previously, the Recovery Console's default settings prohibit access to folders other than the Windows folder and root folders, and prohibit copying files to floppy disk. If you need to relax these restrictions, use the `set` command to enable the `AllowAllPaths` option.

The next sections show some useful examples. After the examples is a reference of all Recovery Console commands.

Repair the Boot Loader

If you install another operating system such as Linux, MS-DOS, or Windows 98 or Me, the OS setup program will overwrite the boot sector and master boot record boot code and you will not be able to load Windows XP. If you want to dual-boot with Linux, you can use LILO, GRUB, or other Linux loaders as the primary loader, so this may be okay, but in most cases, you will want to reinstall the Windows XP loader. To do this, start the Recovery Console and issue the commands **fixboot** and **fixmbr**. Then type **quit** to restart the computer.

Disable a Buggy Driver or Service

If a buggy device driver (or less likely, a service) is preventing Windows from booting, you may be able to boot after disabling it using the Recovery Console. In some cases, the Blue Screen of Death (BSOD), which displays information about the CPU's state at the time of a Windows crash, lists the name of the device driver that caused the problem, and you will know which driver to disable or roll back. Sometimes, however, the BSOD doesn't display the driver name. In this case, you should start by disabling the driver for any newly installed devices first, before proceeding to try disabling nonessential devices one at a time.

Tip

If Windows automatically reboots after a crash so quickly that you can't see what the Blue Screen of Death says, or it reboots over and over, and you have Windows XP Service Pack 2 or later, you're in luck. Press F8 while Windows is starting to display the Advanced Options Startup menu. Select Disable Automatic Restart on System Failure, and then select Start Windows Normally. This should let you see the crash report. You'll need to power the computer off and back on to restart it if the BSOD is displayed. Ctrl+Alt+Del won't budge it.

Before using the Recovery Console, try booting in VGA mode, and then in Safe mode, and then in Last Known Good mode, in that order, using the F8 boot options menu discussed earlier in the chapter. If Windows starts with one of these selections, you can probably disable the problematic device or update its driver using the GUI Device Manager.

If this doesn't help, use the Recovery Console `listsvc` command to get a listing of all installed device drivers and services. The listing starts like this:

```
drivername       startupmode
    descriptive name
6to4             Auto
    IPv6 Helper Service
Abiosdsk         Disabled

abp480n5         Disabled
```

```
ACPI            Boot
    Microsoft ACPI Driver
ACPIEC          Disabled

adpu160m        Disabled

aec             Manual
    Microsoft Kernel Acoustic Echo Canceller
```

Look for device drivers with the Boot or System startup mode. Use the `disable` startup selection to disable one or two at a time, and *write down the name and original startup mode of each driver you disable*, so you can later re-enable them if you determine that they are not the ones causing the problem.

Disable Spyware, Adware, or Viruses

Most virus spyware and adware programs go to great lengths to prevent you from uninstalling them. Some of the measures include detecting your attempt to install antivirus or antispyware software and blocking the installation program, keeping executable files open and locked so that they cannot be deleted, monitoring the Registry so that startup entries can be immediately replaced if you delete them, renaming their own executable files to make them more difficult to find, and more.

Usually, if you boot your computer in Safe mode these programs do not start up, and you can then delete them manually, or install antispyware software to delete them.

If these programs continue to thwart you even in Safe mode, boot up the Recovery Console. Locate the executable files for these programs and delete them or rename them so that they will not be started. The commands to use are `cd`, to change directories, and `ren`, to rename the executable file. For example, if you found that a program named `malware.exe` was starting up with Windows, and that it was located in folder `\windows\system32`, you could use these commands to thwart it:

```
cd \windows\system32
rename malware.exe malware.bad
quit
```

When Windows restarts, the commands used to run `malware.exe` will not find this file, so it will not start.

Replace a Missing `boot.ini`

If you inadvertently delete the `boot.ini` file from the root folder of your first hard drive, Windows will scan through your drives looking for the first Windows installation it can find. If this is not the right folder, Windows will not boot, and you will need to re-create `boot.ini` before you can start Windows. You can do this with the Recovery console.

Because you have no `boot.ini` file, you will need start the Recovery Console by booting from your Windows XP Setup CD, as described earlier. On Windows XP, you can type the command

```
bootcfg /rebuild
```

`bootcfg` will scan your hard drives for Windows installations. For each located installation, `bootcfg` will prompt:

- **Add installation to boot list? (Yes/No/All):** Press Y to add the Windows folder as a startup selection, N to skip it, or A to add it and all other identified installations. If you press N, `bootcfg` will search for another installation.

- ■ `Enter Load Identifier`: Enter a name for this Windows installation. Whatever you type will appear as a selection in the boot menu. Something like `Windows XP Professional on C Drive` might be appropriate.

- ■ `Enter OS Load Options`: It's safest to simply press Enter and not enter any load options. You can, however, add any of the options listed earlier in the discussion of `boot.ini`. If you add more than one, put a space between each option. Some useful possibilities include the following:

`/fastdetect`	Speeds up detection of COM ports, helpful for normal home or office workstations, where you are not using the headless-server option.
`/noexecute=optin`	Sets Windows Data Execution Protection to monitor Windows plus explicitly listed applications.
`/SOS`	Makes `ntldr` print out the name of each device driver it loads, to help identify a failed driver.

After setting up all desired Windows installations, remove your Windows Setup CD and enter the `quit` command to restart your computer.

On Windows 2000, `bootcfg` is not available. You will have to use the `map` command to see a list of all disk drives in ARC format, using the command

```
map arc
```

Then construct a `boot.ini` file manually on another computer using the examples shown earlier in this chapter in the discussion of `boot.ini`, copy it to a floppy disk, and then copy it to the disabled computer using the Recovery Console. First, if the disabled computer has an existing `boot.ini` file, you can delete it with the commands

```
c:
cd \
copy boot.ini boot.ini.bak
attrib -r boot.ini
del boot.ini
```

Then copy the new version from the floppy disk:

```
copy a:boot.ini c:\
attrib +s boot.ini
attrib +h boot.ini
attrib +r boot.ini
```

Back Up *boot.ini*

If you are going to use Recovery Console to modify your `boot.ini` file, you should first make a backup copy by typing these commands:

```
c:
cd \
copy boot.ini boot.ini.bak
```

Then, if you have to revert to the original version, use these commands:

```
c:
cd \
copy boot.ini.bak boot.ini
Overwrite boot.ini (Yes/No/All): y
```

```
attrib +s boot.ini
attrib +h boot.ini
attrib +r boot.ini
```

Recovery Console Command Summary

This section lists the Recovery Console commands. Each entry includes a syntax description. In the syntax description, several characters are used to indicate optional parts of the command line and are *not* meant to be typed literally:

[ ]	Brackets surround optional arguments
		A vertical bar separates alternate choices
italics	Indicate placeholder names that are to be replaced with actual names appropriate for your system
boldface	Indicates text to be typed literally

attrib—Change Attributes on a File or Directory

Syntax: **attrib +r|-r|+s|-s|+h|-h|+c|-c** *filename*

The attrib command is used to set or clear file attributes. The *+x* arguments set attributes, and the *-x* arguments clear them, where *x* can be any of the following letters:

r	read only
s	system
h	hidden
c	compressed

You can only specify one *+x* or *-x* argument. If you have to change several attributes, you have to issue separate commands for each. Typing the attrib command without a *+x* or *-x* argument doesn't display the file's current attributes as you might expect, but results in an error message. To view a file's attributes, use the dir command.

batch—Execute Commands from a Text File

Syntax: **batch** *inputfile* [*outputfile*]

The batch command instructs the Recovery Console to read the specified file named *inputfile* and interpret its contents as Recovery Console commands. Because there is no edit command in the Recovery Console, to be useful, you must have prepared a batch input file in advance, or must place it on a floppy disk. The output of the commands will be written to the screen unless the optional *outputfile* argument is specified. This command is not available in the Windows 2000 Recovery Console.

bootcfg—Modify *boot.ini* Startup and Recovery Options

Syntax: **bootcfg /add**
       bootcfg /rebuild
       bootcfg /scan
       bootcfg /list
       bootcfg /disableredirect
       bootcfg /redirect [*port baudrate*] | [**usebiossettings**]

bootcfg modifies file boot.ini on the boot drive, which contains the list of operating system choices. It's especially helpful with the /rebuild option to replace your boot.ini file if it was inadvertently deleted. This command is not available in the Windows 2000 Recovery Console.

There are six different versions of the command:

/add	Scans all hard disks for Windows installations and prompts for one to be added to boot.ini. Prompts for a Load Identifier (name to display on the boot menu) and OS Load Options, which are arguments like /SOS as described earlier in this chapter; can be left blank.
/rebuild	Scans all hard disks for Windows installations, and prompts for those to be added to boot.ini. The selected installations are added to any already in boot.ini, so this option is best used only to replace a missing boot.ini. Also, see the discussion on backing up boot.ini earlier in this section.
/scan	Displays a list of Windows installations found on your hard disks; does not modify boot.ini.
/list	Lists the boot entries already in your boot.ini file.
/default	Prompts for a boot.ini boot choice to be set as the default boot choice.
/redirect	The /redirect and /disableredirect options apply only to Windows 2003 Server, and are used to manage boot monitoring over a serial port for "headless" servers with no display adapter.

cd and chdir—Display or Change Current Directory
Syntax: **cd** [[*drive:*]*path*]

The cd command changes the default directory on the current or specified drive. The path may be specified as an absolute path (starting with \) or a relative path. The name .. stands for the parent directory.

(To change the default drive, enter a command line consisting of just a drive letter followed by a colon, as in d:.)

Without any arguments, cd displays the current drive and directory. With a drive letter but no path, cd displays the default directory for the specified drive.

Use quotation marks around any path name containing spaces. For example, cd "\windows\ profiles\username\programs\start menu".

By default, cd only operates the restricted set of folders listed earlier in this chapter. To permit access to other folders, the set command must have been enabled, and you must have used the set command to enable the AllowAllAPaths option.

chkdsk—Check Disk Format for Errors
Syntax: **chkdsk** [*drive:*] [/**P**|/**R**]

The chkdsk command checks the boot drive or the specified drive for errors and prints a report of unlinked sectors and so on. By default, chkdsk will not run unless a drive is marked as "dirty"; that is, if Windows was shut down without properly dismounting the drive. The /P option forces chkdsk to check the drive even it was correctly dismounted. The /R option makes chkdsk read every sector on the disk and check for errors; this can take quite a long time. The /R option implies /P.

cls—*Clear the Screen*
Syntax: **cls**

Clears the screen.

copy—*Copy a File*
Syntax: **copy** *sourcefile* [*destinationfile*]

The copy command copies a file. The file to be copied, the *sourcefile*, can be specified using a path and filename, or just a filename, in which case it is located in the current directory.

The destination file can be specified as a full path, a folder name, a filename, or it can be omitted, in which case the file is copied to the current directory using its original name.

The copy command option has some restrictions unless you have used the set command to remove them. The default restrictions are as follows:

- The source and destination folders must be in the limited list (Windows folder and subfolders, root folders, cmdcons folder, removable media) unless the AllowAllPaths option is enabled.
- The destination cannot be on removable media, unless the AllowRemovableMedia option has been enabled.
- The filename must be fully spelled out, unless the AllowWildcards option has been set.
- If the destination file exists, you will be asked if you want to overwrite it, unless the NoCopyPrompt option is enabled.

Compressed files on the Windows installation CD usually have an underscore as the last character of their filename extension, for example, .EX_ or .DL_. When copying a compressed file to the hard disk to replace a corrupted file, the recovery console will automatically decompress it as it is copied, but you must specify the desired extension in the destination filename, for example, .EXE or .DLL.

del and *delete*—*Delete a File*
Syntax: **del** [*drive:*][*path*]*filename*

The del or delete command is used to delete a file. You can specify the filename with or without a path. If the path is omitted, the file is deleted from the current directory.

The filename must be fully spelled out, unless the AllowWildcards option has been set. See the set command for more details.

Caution

There is no undelete option and no Recycle Bin available in the Recovery Console—if you delete a file, it's gone forever. If you want to disable a bad driver or suspected virus program, it might be safer to use the disable command, or rename the file to something like badprogram.exe.xxx, before taking the more drastic step of deleting it.

dir—*List Files and Subdirectories*
Syntax: **dir** [*drive:*][*path*][*filename*]

The dir command lists all files, including hidden and system files, in the current or specified directory. The listing has five columns, which list the file's modification date, modification time, attributes, size in bytes, and name.

The attributes column uses the following letters:

d	directory
a	archive (changed since backup)
r	read-only
h	hidden
s	system file
c	compressed
e	encrypted
p	reparse point

You can specify wildcards in the filename specification for the dir command. If the list fills the screen, the Recovery Console automatically pauses the listing. Press the spacebar to display the next page or Esc to cancel the listing.

disable—*Disable a Service or Device Driver*
Syntax: **disable** *servicename*

The disable command disables a device driver or service by setting its startup mode to SERVICE_ DISABLED. Disable prints the driver or service's previous startup mode before changing it. You should make a note of the old mode, in case you need to enable the drive or service again.

The listsvc command lists the names of all installed drivers and services. Use listsvc to find the correct spelling of the driver or service's name and type it on the disable command line.

diskpart—*Manage Hard Disk Partitions*
Syntax: **diskpart** [/**add**|/**delete**] [*device*|*drive*|*partition*] [*size*]

diskpart adds partitions to or deletes partitions from a hard disk. You can add or delete partitions based on the disk's device name, drive letter, or partition name (the map command can be used to list device names).

However, unless you need to use diskpart in a Recovery Console batch file, the easiest way to manage partitions in Recovery Console is to type diskpart with no arguments. This displays the interactive partition editor used during Windows Setup, as shown in Figure 12.5.

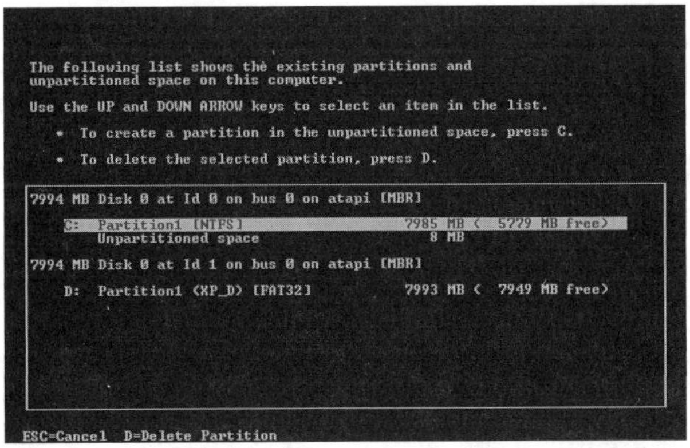

Figure 12.5   The diskpart command with no arguments displays a simple partition editor.

Caution

Do not use the `diskpart` command to manage a disk that you have upgraded from a basic disk to a dynamic disk. `diskpart` could destroy your partition table and make your data inaccessible. To manage the partitions on a dynamic disk, boot Windows and use the Disk Manager.

enable—Enable a Service or Device Driver

Syntax: **enable** *servicename* [*mode*]

The `enable` command changes the boot mode of a specified device driver or service. Service and device driver names can be listed using the `listsvc` command.

With no *mode* specified, `enable` displays the service or driver's current startup mode. The mode can be changed by specifying one of the following keywords: SERVICE_BOOT_START, SERVICE_SYSTEM_START, SERVICE_AUTO_START (corresponds to Automatic in the Services Management console), or SERVICE_DEMAND_START (corresponds to Manual).

Be very careful when changing driver or service boot modes. Disable services and drivers with the `disable` command, and record the original setting in case you must enable it again.

exit—Quit the Recovery Console and Reboot

Syntax: **exit**

The `exit` command closes the Recovery Console and restarts the computer.

expand—Expand or List a Compressed *.CAB* File

Syntax: **expand** *sourcefile* [*/F:filename*] [*destination*] [*/Y*]
       expand *sourcefile* [*/F:filename*] /**D**

The `expand` command is used to extract files from .CAB files (Microsoft's version of the .ZIP file, used mainly on installation disks and in the \windows\system32 folder to hold large numbers of installable device drivers).

The *sourcefile* argument specifies a .CAB file. The command operates on all files in the .CAB file unless the /F option is used to name a specific file. Wildcards can be used in the /F filename specification.

With the /D option, the command lists the files in the .CAB file (or the specified file(s) specified with /F).

Without /D, the command expands the .CAB file(s) and copies them to the destination folder or file specified in the *destination* argument. If the *destination* argument is omitted, the file(s) are copied to the current directory.

If the destination file(s) already exist, `expand` asks you if it should overwrite them. You can respond with the letter N for no, Y for yes, or A to overwrite all files. Alternatively you can add /Y to the command line, in which case `expand` will be allowed to overwrite existing files without asking.

The destination path must be in the Windows folder or a root folder unless the AllowAllPaths option has been enabled with the `set` command. The destination path cannot be on removable media unless the AllowRemovableMedia option has been enabled.

The destination file cannot be read-only. Use the `attrib` command to remove the read-only attribute before using `expand` to overwrite a read-only file.

fixboot—*Rewrite the Boot Sector of the Boot Drive*

Syntax: **fixboot** [*drive:*]

The **fixboot** command writes the Windows boot loader into first sector on the boot (active) partition, as specified by its drive letter. This is the program that locates and starts **ntldr.exe**. You can use **fixboot** if the boot loader gets overwritten by another operating system's installation procedure. If you don't specify a drive letter, the current boot drive is used.

Caution

Damage to your boot sector *could* have been caused by a virus or hardware problem. Microsoft recommends running an antivirus check before using the **fixboot** command.

fixmbr—*Rewrite the Master Boot Record of the Boot Drive*

Syntax: **fixmbr** [*devicename*]

The **fixmbr** command replaces the boot loader contained in the boot partition's first block, called the Master Boot Record. The boot loader precedes the partition table, which is also stored in the Master Boot Record.

The boot drive can be specified using one of the device names displayed by the **map** command. If omitted, the current boot drive is used.

If **fixmbr** detects an invalid or non-standard partition table signature, it will prompt you before rewriting the master boot record (MBR).

Caution

Damage to your Master Boot Record *could* have been caused by a virus or hardware problem. Microsoft recommends running an antivirus check before using the **fixmbr** command.

format—*Format a Disk Volume*

Syntax: **format** [*drive:*] [/**Q**] [/**FS:***filesystem*]

The Recovery Console's **format** command can format hard disk volumes (partitions) but not removable media. You should specify the partition's drive letter and the desired /**FS** value explicitly. The *filesystem* value can be FAT (for FAT-16), FAT32, or NTFS. The /**Q** option specifies a quick format, which creates an empty file system but does not test every block. It can be used to speed the format process but should be used only on a drive that is known not to have any defects.

Caution

Do not use the **format** command on a volume on a disk that you have upgraded from a basic disk to a dynamic disk. To manage the partitions on a dynamic disk, boot Windows and use the Disk Manager.

help—*Print Help Information*

Syntax: **help** [*command*]

Help by itself lists all of the Recovery Console commands (except **set!**) To print the syntax and description of a specific command type **help** followed by the command name.

listsvc—List All Device Drivers and Services
Syntax: **listsvc**

The listsvc command lists all available services and device drivers. The listing will pause when it fills the screen. Press the spacebar to display the next screen or Esc to cancel the listing. You can use the names listed in the left-hand column with the enable and disable commands.

logon—Select a Windows Installation
Syntax: **logon**

The logon command lets you select a different Windows installation to administer. As when the Recovery Console starts, logon lists the detected installations and lets you select one by entering a number. You will be prompted for the Administrator password, if one is set, unless Security Policy for the installation does not require the Administrator password. See the instructions for installing Recovery Console on the hard disk for a mention of this policy setting.

map—Display Disk Devices and Drive Letter Mappings
Syntax: **map [arc]**

map lists the drive letter to physical device mappings that are currently active. This is a typical output printout from map:

```
C: NTFS      7986MB      \Device\Harddisk0\Partition1
D: FAT32     7993MB      \Device\Harddisk1\Partition1
A:                       \Device\Floppy0
E:                       \Device\CdRom0
```

The optional parameter arc tells map to display ARC paths instead of Windows device paths. The output from map arc shows the drive names as they are specified in boot.ini, as in this example:

```
C: NTFS      7986MB      multi(0)disk(0)rdisk(0)partition(1)
D: FAT32     7993MB      multi(0)disk(0)rdisk(1)partition(1)
A:                       \Device\Floppy0
E:                       \Device\CdRom0
```

md and mkdir—Create a Directory
Syntax: **mkdir** *[drive:]path*

The mkdir command creates a new folder. By default, mkdir can create folders only within the Windows folder or its subfolders, the root directory of any hard disk partition, or removable media. You can remove this restriction by enabling the AllowAllPaths option with the set command.

more and type—Display a Text File on the Screen
Syntax: **more** *filename*
        type *filename*

The more and type commands are equivalent in the Recovery Console. Both display a text file on the screen. If the listing fills the screen, the display pauses. Press the spacebar to display the next screen, or Esc to cancel the listing.

net—Torment Users with False Hopes

The Windows XP Recovery Console's net use command is described in the help listing and in numerous Microsoft support documents, and like its regular Command Prompt counterpart it is supposed to be able to let you access a network shared folder. However, it doesn't work—no network adapter or protocol drivers are loaded with the Recovery Console.

rd and rmdir—Delete a Directory
Syntax: **rmdir** [*drive:*]*path*

rmdir deletes the specified folder. The folder must be empty. It works only on folders in the system directories of the current Windows installation, the root directory of hard disks, and removable media, unless you have used the set command to enable the AllowAllPaths option.

ren and rename—Rename a File
Syntax: **rename** [*drive:*][*path*]*filename newname*

You cannot specify a drive or folder path as part of the destination filename.

rename works only on files in the system directories of the current Windows installation, the root directory of hard disks, and removable media, unless you have used the set command to enable the AllowAllPaths option.

set—Enable or Disable a Recovery Console Option
Syntax: **set AllowWildCards = true|false**
      set AllowAllPaths = true|false
      set AllowRemovableMedia = true|false
      set NoCopyPrompt = true|false

The set command is only available if you edited Local Security Policy or Group Policy for the selected Windows installation prior to booting the Recovery Console, and enabled Recovery Console: Allow floppy copy and access to all drives and all folders, as described earlier in the section "Installing Recovery Console on your Hard Disk."

When enabled, the set command can be used to relax Recovery Console's access restrictions. The default settings for the four options is false. To gain increased access you can set any or all of these values to true:

AllowWildCards	If set to true, you can specify wildcards (* and ?) in Recovery Console copy and delete commands.
AllowAllPaths	If set to true, you can access all folders on all drives, rather than just the root and Windows folders.
AllowRemovableMedia	If set to true, you can copy files from the hard drives to floppy disks and other removable media.
NoCopyPrompt	If set to true, Recovery Console will not prompt before overwriting an existing file.

You must separate the words and the equal sign with spaces, otherwise Windows will print "The parameter is not valid," which is a fairly unhelpful remark. A correctly entered command looks like this:

```
set allowallpaths = true
```

Caution

These options compromise Windows security, so you should be sure you want to make this possible before you enable access to the **set** command by editing the Registry. You should not enable the **set** command *and* allow Recovery Console to open Windows without the Administrator password; otherwise, anyone with physical access to your computer will be able access any file without knowing any passwords.

systemroot—Change to the Windows Folder
Syntax: **systemroot**

Sets the current directory to the Windows folder of the currently selected Windows installation, for example, C:\windows. This is handy if you've changed to another directory and want to get back to the original drive and folder.

Automated System Recovery

If you have exhausted all of the options discussed in the previous sections, there is one final, last resort, a "Break Glass in Case of Emergency" tool you can use to attempt to access a Windows installation that won't start up. Windows XP Professional offers a feature in its Backup tool (NTBACKUP.EXE) that can be used to create Windows startup emergency disks that can be used when all other methods have failed. This feature of Windows Backup is known as the *Automated System Recovery (ASR)* tool. Microsoft created the ASR tool to replace the Emergency Repair Disk that was a part of Windows NT and Windows 2000—although Microsoft also recommends that the ASR tool should only be used if there are no other disaster recovery options available to you.

The Automated System Recovery tool is accessed as a wizard within Windows Backup. From the Start menu, go to All Programs, Accessories, System Tools, and then click Backup. Once the Backup program launches, click Advanced Mode, and then click the Automated System Recovery Wizard. The wizard prompts you to provide a floppy disk and removable media, which it uses to create an ASR floppy and ASR backup media set. The ASR media set can consist of backup tapes, recordable CDs or DVDs, or other IDE or SCSI hard disks. You cannot restore an ASR backup set from a network share.

To restore a system by using an ASR backup set, boot your computer from the Windows XP installation CD. You will be presented with an option to select the ASR tool by pressing the F2 key on your keyboard. The tool will ask you to insert the ASR floppy disk, and then prompt you for the backup media set. The tool will then request that you select a destination directory for the restore. You should choose the same directory name you used when you created the ASR backup set; in most instances, this will be C:\Windows. The ASR tool will then proceed to restore the data on the backup set.

Because the ASR tool only backs up and restores the files that are necessary to restore the system state of a Windows installation, it is not a true disaster recovery strategy. It is also important to note that while using the ASR tool may repair a Windows installation to the point that you can start Windows, it can actually overwrite or destroy your personal files on the hard disk during the restore process. It is for that reason that the ASR tool is the last option you should consider when trying to recover a system on which Windows won't start.

Parallel Windows Installation

As I mentioned earlier in this chapter, there are times when you may want to give up on a malfunctioning Windows XP installation, and rebuild the machine from scratch. However, if the hard disk contains valuable data that you want to back up before you rebuild the machine, you won't want to remove the existing partitions and reformat the hard disk. In this instance, you should consider doing a parallel Windows installation.

A parallel Windows installation is sometimes the only way to recover data from a machine that you can't repair through Last Known Good Configuration, Safe mode, or Recovery Console. The goal of performing a parallel Windows installation isn't to repair a system, but it does provide a way for you to access your crucial data and back it up before rebuilding the system from scratch.

To do a parallel Windows installation, reboot the computer with the Windows XP installation disk in the CD-ROM drive. Boot the machine from the CD, and begin the Windows Setup installation process. If there is more than one usable partition on the hard disk, Windows Setup will show you a list of the existing partitions. You can use the same partition that the current Windows installation resides on, or choose a different partition. When Windows Setup presents you with formatting options, you should choose Leave the Current File System Intact (No Changes). This will prevent your existing data from being lost during the installation process. For more information on the Windows installation process, see Chapter 2, "Installing Windows."

After Windows Setup is complete, boot the computer into the new installation of Windows. You should then be able to access the contents of the hard drive and back up the desired data before for-matting and rebuilding the machine.

The Blue Screen of Death: Interpreting STOP Error Messages

At the beginning of this chapter, we split Windows problems into three primary classifications. You've looked at how to solve problems encountered during Windows installation, and problems related to Windows startup; let's turn our attention to dealing with problems that occur when Windows is already up and running.

Although there are a number of different errors that can occur after Windows XP has started up, the most damaging and frustrating is the dreaded STOP error, or Blue Screen of Death (BSOD), which is the first symptom listed in Table 12.1 earlier in this chapter.

Note

The specific shade of blue in the BSOD is the subject of some debate. I have one friend who insists that it is a shade of *periwinkle*. Far be it from me to cast aspersions on her color sense, but we'll just leave it at basic blue for the purposes of brevity.

The appearance of a STOP error screen is always an unwelcome sight (see Figure 12.6). It indicates that the operating system encountered something so catastrophic or destabilizing that it was unable to continue running. As noted earlier, a STOP error screen can appear during Windows installation, during Windows startup, while you are in the Windows GUI, or even during Windows shutdown. Given that it is one of the more common symptoms of a Windows problem, it is important to know more about what information a STOP error screen contains, and how to interpret it.

Let's go through the content of the BSOD shown here, and see what information you can glean from it.

The top line of the screen contains what Microsoft refers to as *bugcheck information*. This includes a hexadecimal code for the STOP error, followed by a number of error parameters. The parameters (which appear in parentheses) are also written in hexadecimal.

This line is followed by a friendly message informing you, in case you hadn't noticed, that Windows has been shut down. Under this message is additional bugcheck information in the form of a *symbolic name*. The symbolic name is often what you will use to look up more information on the error, including possible solutions.

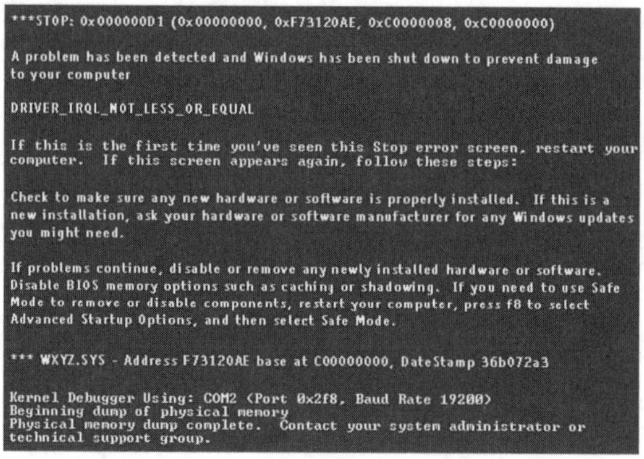

```
***STOP: 0x000000D1 (0x00000000, 0xF73120AE, 0xC0000008, 0xC0000000)

A problem has been detected and Windows has been shut down to prevent damage
to your computer

DRIVER_IRQL_NOT_LESS_OR_EQUAL

If this is the first time you've seen this Stop error screen, restart your
computer. If this screen appears again, follow these steps:

Check to make sure any new hardware or software is properly installed. If this is a
new installation, ask your hardware or software manufacturer for any Windows updates
you might need.

If problems continue, disable or remove any newly installed hardware or software.
Disable BIOS memory options such as caching or shadowing. If you need to use Safe
Mode to remove or disable components, restart your computer, press f8 to select
Advanced Startup Options, and then select Safe Mode.

*** WXYZ.SYS - Address F73120AE base at C00000000, DateStamp 36b072a3

Kernel Debugger Using: COM2 (Port 0x2f8, Baud Rate 19200)
Beginning dump of physical memory
Physical memory dump complete.  Contact your system administrator or
technical support group.
```

Figure 12.6   A Blue Screen of Death.

Under the symbolic name is a suggested course of action for you to take. Microsoft refers to this information as the *recommended user action*. Depending on the nature of the STOP error, the recommended user action can sometimes actually be useful. However, it is fairly generic information, and you will often need to do more investigation in order to isolate the cause of the problem.

After the recommended user action, you will find (if applicable) the name of the driver or program that's associated with the STOP error. This information can be very valuable when trying to determine the source of the error, although in some cases it could be a red herring.

Finally, the last section of the STOP error screen shows information pertaining to debugging tools and memory dump files. If you have a computer running a kernel debugger hooked up to the malfunctioning system via a COM port, this information will be noted in the last section of the error screen. Also, if Windows was configured to create a memory dump file in the event of a system crash (an option that's configured using the Advanced tab in the System applet in Control Panel), the success or failure of this action will be reported here.

Tip

There is a very important setting that affects the behavior of STOP errors that's configured through the System applet in Control Panel. On the Advanced tab, in the section labeled System Failure, you will see an option that reads Automatically Restart. If this check box is filled, the system will only display the STOP error screen for as long as it takes to write the memory dump file, after which it will automatically restart the computer. If you want STOP error screens to stay in place until you manually restart the system (this is almost always the case), you should clear the check box for this option.

Make a Record of STOP Errors

When a STOP error screen appears, before you do anything—before you touch a single key on the keyboard or button on the front of the PC—grab a piece of paper and a pen and write down the contents of the STOP error screen in its entirety.

This cannot be stressed enough: If you fail to write down the information from the STOP error screen before rebooting, you may lose a valuable clue that indicates the source of the problem. Don't be in a hurry to press the Reset button; take the time to start documenting the problem so that you have all the information available at your disposal.

Common STOP Errors

As is often the case with computer-related issues, there are certain problems that are more common to Windows XP than others. This means that there are certain messages that appear on STOP error screens with greater frequency than others.

In this section, you will find a list of the most common STOP error messages (and their probable causes) that appear in the event of a system crash. Each STOP error is listed with its bugcheck information and symbolic name, one or more associated explanations for the STOP error, and a number of possible resolutions.

STOP: 0x0000000A

IRQL_NOT_LESS_OR_EQUAL

This STOP error message is often caused by a flawed device driver or system firmware. If the device driver is listed in the STOP error message, try disabling it or rolling back to the previous version.

If this STOP error occurs while you are doing an upgrade installation of Windows XP, you should do a compatibility check of the system by using the Windows XP Upgrade Advisor. This error can also occur if there is antivirus or antispyware software running on the system you are trying to upgrade. Be sure to shut down any instances of these types of software before upgrading a previous version of Windows.

STOP: 0x0000001E

KMODE_EXCEPTION_NOT_HANDLED

This STOP error is related to unknown or illegal processor instructions. This error can be caused by a flawed device driver, or by memory or IRQ conflicts. If a driver is mentioned in the error message, disable it or roll back to a previous version.

This particular error can also be caused by a third-party "remote control" software program. This is usually indicated by the mention of the file WIN32K.SYS. If this is the case, try to disable the software in question by restarting Windows in Safe mode.

STOP: 0x00000024

NTFS_FILE_SYSTEM

This message indicates a problem with the NTFS.SYS driver file that is responsible for reading and writing to NTFS file systems. Possible causes for this error are malfunctioning SCSI and/or ATA hard drives or the drivers for such devices.

Another possible cause of this error is if you are using certain utilities that access the hard drive in a specific manner, and if these utilities are incompatible with Windows XP. Examples of such programs include antivirus, antispyware, backup, and disk defragmenting software. Check the compatibility of any such programs by looking them up online in the Windows Catalog on the Microsoft website.

STOP: 0x0000002E

DATA_BUS_ERROR

This STOP error message is related to problems with system memory. Types of memory that can cause this error include RAM modules, the Level 2 cache on the CPU, and video memory on a display adapter. Use a third-party utility to test the system RAM, processor, and display adapter memory. Earlier, I mentioned the Windows Memory Diagnostic from Microsoft, which you can use to check system RAM. Another great hardware diagnostic utility is Sandra (**S**ystem **AN**alyser, **D**iagnostic, and

Reporting Assistant) from SiSoftware. You can download the free Sandra Lite version of this tool at http://www.sisoftware.net/.

This error can also indicate that there is a damaged or defective component on the systemboard. If all of the memory checks out as okay, visually inspect the systemboard for any cracks, scratches, or burn marks.

STOP: 0x0000003F

NO_MORE_SYSTEM_PTES

This error message is related to Page Table Entries (PTEs). Specifically, it indicates that the system's PTEs are either depleted or damaged. This can be caused by a flawed device driver, or by an application that is allocating too much kernel memory.

If a device driver is listed, try disabling it, rolling it back to a previous version, or replacing it with a newer version. Other possible suspects include recently installed backup programs, multimedia applications, antivirus software, and CD mastering utilities.

STOP: 0x00000050

PAGE_FAULT_IN_NONPAGED_AREA

Faulty memory, including RAM, processor L2 cache, and video card RAM, are often the culprits behind this STOP error. Test your memory if possible, or if you suspect that a recently installed piece of hardware is the issue, try removing it and see if that solves the problem.

STOP: 0x00000077

KERNEL_STACK_INPAGE_ERROR

This error is caused when Windows kernel data that's located in the virtual memory page file cannot be found. Possible causes include defective memory modules, bad sectors within the page file on the hard drive, or a disk controller error.

More information on this error can be found in the first parameter that appears in parentheses at the top of the STOP error message. Possible entries include:

0xC000009A	Lack of nonpaged pool resources.
0xC000009C	Bad sectors in the page file (hard drive).
0xC00009D	Damaged power or data cables or connections; faulty SCSI termination; problem with hard drive or hard drive controller.
0xC000016A	Bad sectors in the page file (hard drive).
0xC0000185	This code can mean a number of things, including a defective hard drive controller, faulty SCSI termination, damaged cables or loose connections, or it may indicate that two devices attempted to use the same system resources.

STOP: 0x00000079

MISMATCHED_HAL

This STOP error is displayed when the system tries to use out-of-date versions of the NTOSKRNL.EXE or HAL.DLL files. (HAL stands for *Hardware Abstraction Layer*.) This error can occur after you have made repairs using Recovery Console.

There are two versions of the NTOSKRNL.EXE and HAL.DLL files on the Windows XP installation CD; one version is for single-processor systems, the other is for multiprocessor systems. If you copy the wrong version of either of these files to your system, the MISMATCHED_HAL STOP error will occur.

The multi-processor versions of these files are NTKRNLMP.EXE and HALMPS.DLL.

STOP: 0x0000007A

KERNEL_DATA_INPAGE_ERROR

This STOP error is extremely similar to the KERNEL_STACK_INPAGE_ERROR message listed previously in this section. It relates to Windows kernel data that is supposed to be in the page file, but cannot be found or written into memory. Treat this error the same as a KERNEL_STACK_INPAGE_ERROR message.

STOP: 0x0000007B

INACCESSIBLE_BOOT_DEVICE

This error is specific to Windows startup. It indicates that Windows was unable to initialize the file system. This could be caused by a hard drive failure, a damaged hard drive controller, or incorrect settings in the BOOT.INI startup file.

If all of the hardware is functioning normally, it is still possible that the startup files have become corrupted, or that the Master Boot Record has become damaged. Follow the instructions in the "Using Recovery Console" section of this chapter to restore these files.

STOP: 0x0000007F

UNEXPECTED_KERNEL_MODE_TRAP

The most common cause of this STOP error is defective memory such as RAM modules, L2 processor cache, or video card memory. It can also be caused by an overheating system; make sure that all cooling fans, particularly CPU heatsink fans, are working properly.

STOP: 0x0000009F

DRIVER_POWER_STATE_FAILURE

This error is based on power-related activities such as shutting down the system, or suspending/resuming from standby or hibernation mode. Check the driver that's named in the error message, and try replacing it or rolling back to a previous version.

STOP: 0xBE

ATTEMPTED_WRITE_TO_READONLY_MEMORY

This is another "bad driver" error. It occurs when a software driver attempts to write to a section of read-only memory. Replace, roll back, or delete.

STOP: 0xC2

BAD_POOL_CALLER

No, this error has nothing to do with a snarky lifeguard. It has everything to do with a flawed piece of software or device driver trying to do memory operations in ways that it's not supposed to. If it is a software program causing the error, remove it. If it is a device driver, replace, roll back, or delete.

Stop: 0x000000CE

DRIVER_UNLOADED_WITHOUT_CANCELLING_PENDING_OPERATIONS

Another issue related to a misbehaving driver. In this instance, a driver exited without canceling pending operations. Replace, roll back, or delete.

STOP: 0x000000D1

DRIVER_IRQL_NOT_LESS_OR_EQUAL

This error is commonly caused by a flawed driver trying to access pageable memory using an improper IRQL. Replace, roll back, or delete.

STOP: 0x000000D8

DRIVER_USED_EXCESSIVE_PTES

This error is essentially identical to the NO_MORE_SYSTEM_PTES error listed earlier in this section. Follow the same steps that were given for that STOP error message.

STOP: 0x000000EA

THREAD_STUCK_IN_DEVICE_DRIVER

Driver trouble again...although this error is almost always linked specifically to the video card display driver. Check with the manufacturer for a Windows XP compatible driver.

STOP: 0x000000ED

UNMOUNTABLE_BOOT_VOLUME

This STOP error occurs when the input/output subsystem fails to mount the boot volume. This can be due to a damaged file system, but in certain instances can also be caused by a conflict between the disk controller and the hard drive cable.

If the system uses an Ultra Direct Memory Access (UDMA) controller, and the hard drive is plugged in with a standard 40-wire cable rather than the necessary 80-wire UDMA cable, the end result can be the 0x000000ED UNMOUNTABLE_BOOT_VOLUME STOP error.

However, if the first parameter to appear in parentheses at the top of the STOP error is 0xC0000032, the problem is being caused by a damaged file system. Try using the CHKDSK /R command from Recovery Console; if this doesn't solve the problem, try using the FIXBOOT command. (You will take a closer look at the CHKDSK tool later in this chapter.)

STOP: 0x000000F2

HARDWARE_INTERRUPT_STORM

This error is related to interrupt requests (IRQs); specifically, this error occurs when a hardware device fails to comply with an interrupt release signal sent by a device driver. It can also occur if a flawed device driver doesn't send an interrupt release signal to a device, or if the flawed driver claims an IRQ that's assigned to a different device.

The HARDWARE_INTERRUPT_STORM error most commonly occurs just after installing a new piece of hardware. Remove the new device, and see if that solves the problem. If it does, check and see if the device appears in the Windows Catalog as a compatible device. You can also look at the manufacturer's website to see if they have any information concerning Windows XP compatibility issues, or if there are newer drivers available for the device.

STOP: 0xC000021A

STATUS_SYSTEM_PROCESS_TERMINATED

This STOP error is usually caused by a recently installed device driver or software program. If the STOP error lists a driver or program file, try removing the driver or program in order to solve the issue.

This error can also be caused by restoring system data from a backup set, but the backup program doesn't restore certain files that it believes are currently in use on the system. This can be avoided by ensuring that your backup software is compatible with Windows XP.

STOP: 0xC0000221

STATUS_IMAGE_CHECKSUM_MISMATCH

This error message is usually attributable to a damaged system file or device driver. The name of the file causing the error will usually appear as part of the STOP message. Try using Safe mode or Recovery Console to replace the file with a new copy from the Windows XP installation CD.

Windows XP Troubleshooting Tools

Not every problem encountered within Windows XP will bring the entire system to a crashing halt. There are a number of minor problems that can occur that range from the inability to use a peripheral device such as a printer or a gamepad, to a software program that is unable to run without crashing, to a malfunctioning system device such as a modem or an audio card.

Windows XP includes a number of built-in tools and resources for troubleshooting minor errors that occur within the operating system. Some of these troubleshooting tools and resources are

- CHKDSK (also referred to as CheckDisk)
- DirectX Diagnostic Tool
- Dr. Watson (debugging program)
- Program Compatibility Wizard
- System Configuration Utility
- Windows Troubleshooters

CHKDSK

CHKDSK is a tool you can use to check the integrity of a Windows XP file system, and possibly repair any errors that the tool finds. CHKDSK can be used as a command-line tool, or is available through the Windows GUI (although the GUI version doesn't include all of the functionality of the command-line version).

There are a number of switches you can use to determine how CHKDSK will function. If you just type CHKDSK at the command prompt and press Enter without any switches, the program will run as a read-only diagnostic. It will report any errors it finds, but it will not attempt to repair them.

Here is a list of the switches you can use with CHKDSK:

/f	CHKDSK attempts to fix any errors that it finds.
/v	On a FAT or FAT32 file system volume, CHKDSK will display the name and full path of every file on the disk. On an NTFS volume, this switch displays relevant information on any actions CHKDSK performs.

/r CHKDSK attempts to locate bad sectors and recover any readable data from them.

/x Attempts to dismount the volume you want CHKDSK to scan. This switch will not work on the boot volume (the volume that contains the Windows operating files).

/i Forces CHKDSK to use a less complex scan of index entries, which reduces the amount of time CHKDSK takes to run. This switch is relevant for NTFS volumes only.

/c Similar to the /i switch; it forces CHKDSK to skip over verifying the cycles in the folder structure of the volume being scanned.

Before you use CHKDSK to try to correct a problem with a Windows file system volume, you should make an attempt to back up the data on the volume. Also, if the volume you are scanning is fairly large and contains a lot of data, you may want to have a cup of coffee and a magazine handy; CHKDSK can take a very long time to complete when dealing with large volumes. Using the /i and /c switches can help to reduce the time it takes for CHKDSK to complete its scan of NTFS-based volumes.

There is a version of CHKDSK you can run from within the Windows GUI. Double-click My Computer or select it from the Start Menu, and right-click on the volume you want to scan. Click Properties, select the Tools tab, and click Check Now (see Figure 12.7).

Figure 12.7 Running the GUI version of CHKDSK while Windows is running.

From here, you can select three options:

1. Run CHKDSK in read-only mode (finds errors but doesn't repair them) by clicking Start.

2. Run CHKDSK with the Automatically Fix File System Errors check box selected. This is the equivalent of running CHKDSK with the /f switch.

3. Run CHKDSK with the Scan For And Attempt Recovery Of Bad Sectors check box selected. This is the equivalent of running CHKDSK with the /r switch.

◄◄ For more information on CHKDSK and other disk utilities, see "File System Utilities," p. 513.

Interestingly enough, the CHKDSK utility dates all the way back to the days of MS-DOS. CHKDSK was introduced with the release of MS-DOS 2.0—back in 1983! Imagine that—a utility that's been around for over 20 years that still exists in today's most popular desktop operating system.

DirectX Diagnostic Tool (*DXDIAG.EXE*)

DirectX is a suite of multimedia-related application programming interfaces (APIs) built into the Windows operating system. Microsoft first created DirectX for the release of Windows 95. DirectX provides software developers with a standardized platform for multimedia application development, which enables them to create software that can access specialized hardware features, without having to write hardware-specific code. DirectX provides improved communication between software and hardware devices, and interacts with practically everything on a Windows PC that involves video, audio, and input devices. As of this writing, the most current version of DirectX is 9.0c, which was released in August 2004. DirectX 9.0c is compatible with Windows 9x/Me/2000/XP.

Windows XP includes a diagnostic tool that you can use to troubleshoot issues related to DirectX (see Figure 12.8). The DirectX Diagnostic Tool tells you which version of DirectX is installed on your system. It also displays information regarding the various DirectX-related drivers, and provides a series of user-initiated diagnostic tests you can use to determine if DirectX and the hardware devices it interacts with are functioning normally. This can be a valuable tool for troubleshooting Windows problems related to audio and video problems, and input devices such as gamepads.

The DirectX Diagnostic Tool does not appear in the Start menu. To launch it, go to the Start menu, select Run, and type **DXDIAG.EXE**.

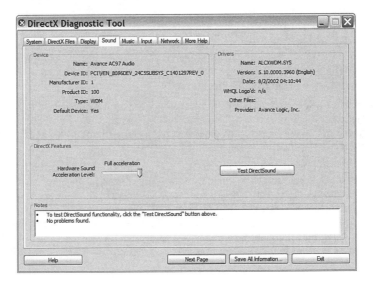

Figure 12.8 Testing DirectSound with the DirectX Diagnostic Tool.

You can navigate through the DirectX Diagnostic Tool using the tabs at the top of the screen, or by using the Next Page button at the bottom of the screen to go through each tab sequentially. The list of tabs includes the following:

- The System tab displays a list of information related to your system configuration. This information includes the current date and time, your computer's name and operating system version, the language setting, the system manufacturer and model, your system BIOS version, the type of processor you have installed, the amount of system RAM, page file statistics, and the version of DirectX that's currently installed on your system.

- The DirectX files tab shows you all of the installed files that are related to DirectX. Also displayed are the version numbers for each file, the date they were created, and the size of each file on the hard disk. Below the file list is a Notes box that displays any error messages that the diagnostic tool generates concerning any of the files.

- The Display tab gives you detailed information on your video adapter, including its name and manufacturer, the chip and digital-to-analog (DAC) type, the amount of onboard video memory, your current display mode, and the type of monitor you have installed. This screen also lists the driver files being used for your video adapter. Below this information, you'll find three diagnostic tests you can run on your system. The first diagnostic tests DirectDraw acceleration, which controls display memory management. The second test checks Direct3D acceleration, which provides 3D graphics support via the video adapter hardware. The third diagnostic checks the AGP texture acceleration, which is a graphics feature that only exists on certain video cards. Below these three diagnostic tests is a dialog box that displays any warning messages generated by the tests.

- The Sound tab contains information on your system's audio components. This includes the name and device ID of your sound card, a manufacturer and product ID, and the drivers associated with the device. This screen offers one diagnostic that's used to test DirectSound, a DirectX component that controls how audio is presented on your system. Again, error messages are displayed in a dialog box near the bottom of the screen.

- The Music tab is similar to the Sound tab, but is more specialized in that it focuses on a DirectX component called DirectMusic. On this screen, you'll find information on any Musical Instrument Digital Interface (MIDI) devices you have configured on your system, and a diagnostic that tests the functionality of DirectMusic.

- The Input tab shows a list of all of the input devices you have attached to your system, including keyboards, mice, and other input devices such as gamepads, joysticks, and trackballs. There are no diagnostics you can perform on this screen, but a dialog box displays any error messages that the DirectX Diagnostic Tool detects.

- The Network tab offers information on DirectPlay components. DirectPlay is a networking API that controls networking services at the transport and session protocol levels. DirectPlay is responsible for moderating the function of network-based games such as massive multiplayer role-playing games (MMPORGs). The Network tab displays a list of registered DirectPlay service providers, a list of registered DirectPlay applications, and two diagnostic tests. The first test checks the DirectPlay Voice functionality, which is used with games that offer players the ability to speak to each other using headsets. The second diagnostic tests the DirectPlay function of DirectX.

- The More Help tab offers four options that are accessed by clicking onscreen buttons. The first option launches the DirectX Windows Troubleshooter. The second button launches the Audio Windows Troubleshooter. (You'll take a closer look at Windows Troubleshooters later in this chapter.) The third button loads the Microsoft System Information Tool, which provides an extremely detailed look at your system's overall hardware, software, and Internet configurations. The fourth button is used to override the default refresh rate used by DirectDraw. Generally speaking, you should leave this button alone, unless you are absolutely sure of what you're doing.

Dr. Watson

Dr. Watson is a software debugging program that, in the event of an application crash, writes debugging information to a log file that can be used by a programmer or software technical support expert to troubleshoot the application. To view the Dr. Watson setup dialog box from the Start menu, select Run, type **DRWTSN32**, and press Enter (see Figure 12.9).

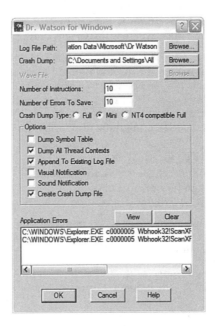

Figure 12.9 Use the Dr. Watson dialog box to configure how debugging data is generated.

There are a number of options you can configure in the Dr. Watson dialog box. The changes that you make using this interface are saved in the Windows Registry key HKEY_LOCAL_MACHINE\SOFTWARE\ Microsoft\DrWatson.

The first time you open the Dr. Watson dialog box, the program automatically creates a folder that it uses to store any log files it creates. By default, the path to this folder is Documents and Settings\All Users\Application Data\Microsoft\Dr Watson. You can select a different location for this folder by using the Log File Path setting at the top of the Dr. Watson dialog box.

In addition to the log files, Dr. Watson is capable of creating a binary dump file that a programmer can load into a software debugger program in order to troubleshoot the error. Activate this option by checking the Create Crash Dump File check box in the Options section of the Dr. Watson dialog box. As with the log files, you can indicate a different default path for the crash dump file by entering it into the Crash Dump line near the top of the Dr. Watson screen.

The Number of Instructions entry tells Dr. Watson how many instructions it should disassemble before and after the program counter for each thread state dump. (A *program counter* is a register that holds the memory location for a thread's point of execution.) The Number of Errors to Save entry sets a limit on the number of errors Dr. Watson will save in a log file.

In the Options section of the Dr. Watson dialog box, there are six variables that you can check or uncheck to switch on or off. Dump Symbol Table configures Dr. Watson to include the symbol table for each software module. Activating this option can cause your dump files to become very large. Activating Dump all Thread Contexts will cause Dr. Watson to log a state dump for every thread in the program that is crashing. If this option is left unchecked, Dr. Watson will only create a state dump for the thread that is causing the error in the program. The Append to Existing Log File option decides whether Dr. Watson should add error data to the end of the existing DRWTSN32.LOG file, or if it should create a new log file for each program error. If you check this option, you should monitor the size of the DRWTSN32.LOG file, as it can grow to a cumbersome size. You can check the Visual Notification and Sound Notification options if you want to receive visual or audible cues when Dr. Watson detects a program error. Finally, there is the Create Crash Dump File option that I mentioned earlier in this section.

Unless you are a software programmer, the log and dump files created by Dr. Watson will be of limited personal use. However, these files can be sent to a Microsoft support specialist or to the creator of the software that is experiencing errors. Usually, a programmer will use the information in these files to determine the exact point in the program's lines of code where the error is taking place, and examine the specific variables in the code that might be responsible for causing the problem.

Program Compatibility Wizard

The Program Compatibility Wizard, which is also discussed in Chapter 9, "Windows Commands and Scripting," is used as a workaround for compatibility issues with a program that was released for an earlier version of Windows that has trouble functioning under Windows XP.

The Program Compatibility Wizard can be launched from the Start menu by choosing All Programs, Accessories. Alternatively, you can right-click on a program's launch file or shortcut, select Properties, and then click on the Compatibility tab.

You can choose to run a program in one of the following Windows compatibility modes for Windows 95, 98, Me, NT4.0 (SP5), and 2000. The Program Compatibility Wizard also offers three display options for older programs:

- Run in 256 Colors
- Run in 640×480 Screen Resolution
- Disable Visual Themes

Tip

If you are running an application in a Windows Compatibility mode, you should close any active antivirus and antispyware programs. These programs can cause problems when running an application in Windows Compatibility mode.

System Configuration Utility

The System Configuration Utility is a powerful troubleshooting tool that allows you to configure a number of Windows startup variables (see Figure 12.10). To access the System Configuration Utility from the Start menu, select Run, and enter **MSCONFIG**.

From the General tab, you can choose to alter the startup method that Windows will use the next time you reboot the machine. Diagnostic Startup is essentially the same as Safe mode; you can further configure this option by selecting which services you want to start by clicking on the Services tab. Selective Startup allows you to further customize startup on a more granular level.

The SYSTEM.INI and WIN.INI tabs contain services and programs that are primarily meant to provide backwards compatibility for programs designed for earlier versions of Windows. The SYSTEM.INI and WIN.INI files are not necessary to run Windows XP, but may be required by older drivers and programs.

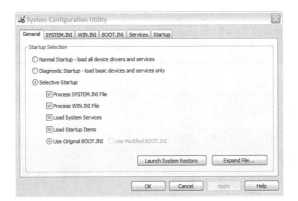

Figure 12.10 Using the Microsoft System Configuration Utility to manually set startup variables.

The BOOT.INI tab gives you convenient access to the BOOT.INI file. This file normally contains information on any other operating systems installed on the computer. You can also use the BOOT.INI tab to add certain switches to the Windows startup process. These switches are

- /SAFEBOOT—Sets the computer to always boot into Safe mode. You can choose additional switches for this option, including MINIMAL (normal Safe mode), NETWORK (Safe mode with Networking), DSREPAIR (Directory Services Repair, normally only used on servers in an Active Directory environment), and MINIMAL/ALTERNATE SHELL (Safe mode using an alternate pre-configured Windows GUI—this option is normally not used)

- /NOGUIBOOT—Same as Safe Mode with Command Prompt

- /BOOTLOG—Writes a detailed log of the boot process to a file named NTBTLOG.TXT

- /BASEVIDEO—Windows will start up using a generic VGA driver rather than the installed video driver (useful if the installed video driver isn't working)

- /SOS—Displays the driver filenames as each driver is loaded during startup (can help to pinpoint where Windows startup is bogging down)

At the bottom of the Boot Options section of the BOOT.INI tab is a button labeled Advanced Options. There are four additional switches that can be added to the Windows startup process via this button:

- /MAXMEM—Allows you to set a limit on how much RAM Windows is able to access (can be used to test if a RAM module is faulty)

- /NUMPROC—Lets you limit the number of processors Windows has access to on a multiprocessor system

- /PCILOCK—Prohibits Windows from assigning IRQ resources to PCI-based hardware; the devices remain as configured by the BIOS settings

- /DEBUG—Starts Windows in debugging mode (this is used when you have a second system hooked up to debug the malfunctioning system)

The Services tab can be used to enable or disable specific services. This can be very useful if you are troubleshooting a Windows startup problem, and want to disable services without uninstalling the associated software. You can view only the third-party services in the list by clicking on the Hide All Microsoft Services check box.

The Startup tab allows you to enable or disable software programs that are started when Windows is started. Common examples of such programs include antivirus software, instant message clients, and third-party control panels for display adapters and audio cards. Again, disabling all unnecessary programs and enabling them one at a time can help to isolate and identify the cause of a Windows startup problem.

If you would like to know what some of the more cryptically named startup items are, you can try looking them up at www.sysinfo.org.

Windows Troubleshooters

Windows Troubleshooters are mini-programs that are used to troubleshoot a minor problem with normal Windows operations. The Windows Troubleshooters are similar in design and function to expert systems. An expert system is a software program that contains knowledge gathered from one or more human experts. When the program is run, it asks a series of questions to collect information from the user, and then uses this information in concert with its internal knowledge to diagnose a problem or analyze a given situation. An expert system possesses an internal logic structure that enables it to follow a deductive process much like someone who is troubleshooting a Windows problem.

Windows XP will offer to open a Windows Troubleshooter when you encounter certain specific problems. However, you can always access the full list of Troubleshooters by selecting the Help and Support option from the Start menu.

In the Help and Support Center, type **List of Troubleshooters** into the Search box located in the top-left corner of the screen, and press Enter. In the Search Results box, click on the List of Troubleshooters link that appears.

Table 12.2 lists all of the Windows Troubleshooters and what each one should be used for.

Table 12.2   Windows Troubleshooters

Windows Troubleshooter Name	Subject Area Covered
Digital Video Discs (DVDs)	DVD-ROM drives and decoders
Display	Display adapters, monitors, and drivers
Drives and Network Adapters	Hard drives, floppy drives, CD and DVD drives, network adapters, tape drives
File and Print Sharing	Workgroups and networks, sharing files and print devices, logon issues
Hardware	Covers a wide variety of hardware, including input devices, USB devices, modems, audio cards, and so on
Home Networking	Home network setup, file and print sharing, Internet connections
Input Devices	Mice, keyboards, trackballs, cameras, and scanners
Internet Connection Sharing (ICS)	Sharing an Internet connection between two or more computers
Internet Explorer	Using Internet Explorer as your web browser
Modem	Internal and external modem connections and operation
Multimedia and Games	Games, multimedia programs, DirectX, audio, and controllers
Outlook Express	Using Outlook Express as your email client
Printing	Installing and operating print devices
Sound	Audio and audio adapters

Table 12.2   Continued

Windows Troubleshooter Name	Subject Area Covered
Startup/Shutdown	Starting and shutting down a system, standby mode, and hibernation mode
System Setup	Installing and configuring Windows
USB	All USB hubs and peripherals

Note

There is a fair amount of crossover between the various Windows Troubleshooters in terms of what subject area each Troubleshooter covers. You should always try to use the Troubleshooter that is most specific for the problem you are working on. For example, if you are dealing with a malfunctioning modem, you should choose the Modem Troubleshooter over the Hardware Troubleshooter, as the first troubleshooter is more relevant to the issue.

With certain Windows Troubleshooters, you may be asked to restart the computer or to exit out of the Troubleshooter before completing a step. Because of this, it is recommended that you manually track your progress through the Troubleshooter on a piece of paper, making a note of the questions asked and your responses to each question. By doing this, you can restart the Troubleshooter after closing it, and get back to where you were.

Installing Additional Windows Support Tools

As you have seen, there are a number of troubleshooting tools and resources available in a normal Windows XP installation. However, Microsoft has also provided a large collection of additional programs known as the Windows Support Tools. These tools are meant for use by Microsoft support specialists and experienced Windows users to help diagnose and solve Windows issues. The Windows Support Tools are not installed by default when you install Windows XP, but they can be installed at a later time from the Windows XP installation CD.

To install Windows Support Tools, place the Windows XP installation CD into your system while Windows is running. Open the contents of the CD in My Computer or Windows Explorer and browse to the Support\Tools folder. Double-click the SETUP.EXE file to install the Windows Support Tools.

Note

If you are running Windows XP Service Pack 2, you should not install the Windows Support Tools from the Windows XP installation disk. Microsoft has an updated version of this package, *Windows XP Service Pack 2 Support Tools*, available as a free download on its website. To download this newer version, visit http://www.microsoft.com/downloads/details.aspx?FamilyID=49ae8576-9bb9-4126-9761-ba8011fabf38&displaylang=en.

There are nearly fifty different command-line programs available in the Windows Support Tools. Thankfully, a help file that describes each tool in depth is placed in the Windows Support Tools item created in the Start menu after installation. Each entry in the help file includes an overview of the support tool, notes on how to use the tool from the command line, the syntax you should use when typing the command as well as all of the available switches, one or more examples of the tool's functionality, and a list of related support tools that may be applicable to the issue you are troubleshooting.

Here are some examples of the types of tools included in the Windows Support Tools:

- **Dependency Walker (`DEPENDS.EXE`).** Dependency Walker displays a hierarchical diagram showing all of the child modules that a parent module (such as an `.EXE`, `.DLL`, or `.SYS` file) is dependent on in order to function properly. This tool can be used to troubleshoot Windows errors that are based on module load issues. When Dependency Walker scans a parent module such as an `.EXE` file, it automatically detects and reports several common application errors such as missing modules, invalid modules, and circular dependency errors.

- **Disk Manager Diagnostics (`DMDIAG.EXE`).** Disk Manager Diagnostics displays the system state and configuration data related to disk storage. This information includes the computer name and the operating system installed, the physical disk type, any existing hard disk mount points, drive letter usage, and disk partition configuration. You can write all of the information produced by this diagnostic to a text file by including a directory path and filename as part of the command (for example, type `dmdiag > C:\diskinfo\diskinfo.txt` at the command line, and the tool will write the information to a file named `diskinfo.txt` in the `C:\diskinfo` directory).

- **Pool Byte Monitor (`POOLMON.EXE`).** Pool Byte Monitor is used to monitor memory tags such as total paged and non-paged pool bytes. This tool is most commonly used to attempt to detect possible memory leaks. Memory leaks occur when a program or service reserves memory for itself, but doesn't relinquish it once it is finished running. Eventually, a memory leak will result in inadequate memory being available for the operating system to function properly, resulting in system errors or lockups. Pool Byte Monitor can be used to track which memory tag's byte levels are increasing over time without being released, which is a common symptom of a memory leak.

Using the Microsoft Knowledge Base (MSKB)

At the beginning of this chapter, I mentioned that part of being a good troubleshooter is knowing where to look for relevant knowledge and information. There are a number of online resources you can (and should) access when you are troubleshooting a Windows problem. One of the most relevant online resources comes from the makers of Windows itself: the Microsoft Help and Support site, home of the Microsoft Knowledge Base (MSKB). The MSKB contains more than 150,000 articles offering technical support for every available Microsoft product, including Windows XP. These articles include troubleshooting tips, how-to articles, coverage of new security updates and Service Packs, and columns that are geared towards software developers.

To visit the Microsoft Help and Support site, point your browser to

http://support.microsoft.com/

From this page, you can access a number of different Windows XP information resources. You can do a search of the Knowledge Base, visit one of the product-specific solution centers, or browse to the Microsoft newsgroups, an online community of users who share their knowledge of Microsoft products.

Every article that appears in the Knowledge Base is assigned an Article ID number (see Figure 12.11). This number serves as the primary reference point for each article. For example, it's possible that you have encountered a sentence like this before:

"For more information, see KB article 314073."

Alternatively, this reference is sometimes abbreviated to simply read "KB314073." In this example, this is the Article ID of the Knowledge Base article #314073, "How to Troubleshoot Network Printing Problems in Windows XP."

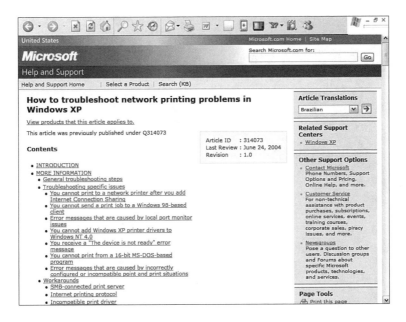

Figure 12.11   Viewing an article in the Microsoft Knowledge Base.

Knowledge Base articles follow a common section structure. Each article opens with a high-level summary of the material it contains. This is followed by an introduction, the main body of the article (usually titled More Information), a list of software products or services that the article applies to, and finally, a list of keywords associated with the article.

If you want to read a specific article in the Knowledge Base and you know its article ID, you can browse directly to it by typing the following URL in the Address bar of Internet Explorer:

`http://support.microsoft.com/?kbid=(Article ID #)`

Alternatively, you can also use Help and Support in the Windows Start menu to open a Knowledge Base article. Open Help and Support, and type the letters **KB** followed by the number of the article into the Search box near the top of the screen (see Figure 12.12).

The Microsoft Knowledge Base also offers a Basic Search, as well as an Advanced Search functionality.

If you would like to keep up with new articles as they are added to the Knowledge Base, Microsoft now offers (as of this writing) *Really Simple Syndication* or *RSS feeds* that you can use to receive notification of new articles. Each RSS feed is based on a specific product, so you can pick and choose which Microsoft products you want to monitor for new Knowledge Base articles.

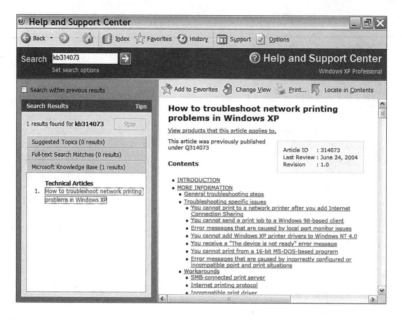

Figure 12.12 You can use the Help and Support feature in Windows XP to view Knowledge Base articles.

APPENDIX A

Windows Tool Reference

Windows Management Tools

This appendix lists sets of Windows management, maintenance, configuration, and monitoring tools that you may not be familiar with. Most of them are not installed by Windows Setup but instead are hidden away in obscure folders on your Windows Setup CD-ROM. Others must be downloaded or purchased from Microsoft. They can be a great help in using, updating, and managing Windows.

We'll discuss the following tool kits:

- *Standard Tools*—Our pick of handy programs installed by Windows Setup that we think are unappreciated and not well-enough known.

- *Support Tools*—A set of useful command-line and GUI programs that can be installed from your Windows Setup CD-ROM.

- *Value-Added Tools*—Several more sets of utilities hidden away on the Windows Setup CD-ROM.

- *PowerToys*—A set of accessories that can be downloaded for free from microsoft.com. The PowerToys include TweakUI, a program that lets you make adjustments to more Windows settings than you knew existed.

- *Resource Kits*—A set of books published by Microsoft for each version of Windows that includes a CD-ROM containing hundreds of utility programs. What you may not have known is that in some cases you can get the Resource Kit program toolkits without purchasing the books.

- *Services For UNIX (SFU)*—A package of network services and command-line tools that provide a nearly complete UNIX environment on Windows XP Professional, Windows 2000, or Windows Server. SFU can be downloaded for free from microsoft.com.

We'll go over each of these toolkits in order in the following sections. Although we don't have room to cover all of the tools in detail, we'll give you listings of the available tools.

Standard Commands

A standard installation of Windows includes a number of command-line tools that are extremely useful. Table A.1 describes a few of them. For a complete list of all command-line programs provided with Windows, scan through the programs listed with type CMD in Appendix B, "Windows Command Reference."

Table A.1 Important Standard Command-Line Commands

Command	Description
control	Opens and runs a control panel from the command line. For details, see the section named, "control," in Chapter 9, "Windows Commands and Scripting."
findstr	Searches through text files for specified strings. (If you're familiar with UNIX or Linux, findstr is like grep.) For more information, see "findstr," in Chapter 9.
ftp	Copies files to and from other computers using the Internet's File Transfer Protocol. You can use the FTP command-line program to post files to a web server, retrieve files from a UNIX host, or perform other file-copying tasks. Type **ftp** and press Enter, and the program will prompt you to enter commands. The most important commands are:
	open *hostname* Establishes a connection to the specified computer
	binary Indicates that the files to be transferred are binary (data) files; use for images and programs

Table A.1   Continued

Command	Description
	`ascii` Indicates that the files to be transferred are text files; use for text and HTML files
	`cd dirname` Changes directories on the remote computer
	`lcd dirname` Changes directories on the local (your) computer
	`dir [filename]` Lists the directory on the remote computer
	`!dir [filename]` Lists the directory on *your* computer
	`send filename` Transfers the specified file from your computer to the other computer
	`get filename` Retrieves the specified file from the other computer to your computer
	`mput filename` Sends multiple files; use wildcards in the filename
	`mget filename` Gets multiple files; use wildcards in the filename
	`prompt` `mget` and `mput` normally prompt you for a yes/no response before transferring each file; `prompt` toggles this prompting on or off
	`quit` Terminates the connection
iexpress	`IExpress` is a wizard that builds a simple setup program for software you've developed yourself. You have to provide the one or more files that comprise your application, and a configuration file that describes where these files are to be copied on the target computer. Additionally you can define Registry entries that are to be made, and you can designate a program or script that is to be run after the files are copied onto a target computer to complete the installation. `IExpress` then compresses all of this into a single executable (`.EXE`) file that you can distribute and run on other computers.
ipconfig	`Ipconfig` displays IP address configuration information for your computer's network adapters. Additionally it can release or renew the adapter's DHCP lease, although the GUI "repair" option on the Network Connections control panel is more thorough. Type **ipconfig /help** for syntax information.
net	The `net` command can perform quite a number of chores, from creating local user accounts, to mapping network drives, to viewing the resources shared on a remote computer, to sharing folders. For more information about `net`, see the section named, "net," in Chapter 9.
netsh	`netsh` is a complex, interactive program that can configure and display just about every aspect of Windows networking. You can work with `netsh` interactively or give it commands from a batch file or script. For syntax information, type **netsh** then **help**. Exit with `quit`.

nslookup	`nslookup` is an interactive program that lets you query Domain Name Service (DNS) servers. `nslookup` is particularly useful for finding information about the ownership of IP addresses. The syntax is the same as the UNIX versions from which it came. To find out the hostname of a given IP address, type
	nslookup *xxx.yyy.zzz.qqq*
	replacing *xxx*, *yyy*, *zzz*, and *qqq* with the corresponding parts of the IP number in question. If this does not produce an answer, type the following commands:
	`nslookup`
	`set type=ANY`
	`zzz.yyy.xxx.in-addr.arpa.`
	`yyy.xxx.in-addr.arpa.`
	`exit`

(continues)

Table A.1 Continued

Command	Description
runas	runas runs a command under another user's credentials. It's like the UNIX utility su, and is most often used to run a management tool as Administrator. The program run can be GUI or command-line, and if you specify cmd as the command, you get a command prompt window from which you can run any other programs. The syntax is runas /user:*xxx* "*command*" where *xxx* is the login name of the user whose credentials you want to use. The three ways I use it most often are runas /user:Administrator "control firewall.cpl" runas /user:Administrator cmd and runas /user:Administrator mmc (For setup and installation programs, it's usually easier to locate the program in Explorer, right-click, and select Run As.)
ping	ping tests network connectivity by sending data packets to another computer on your network or on the Internet, and reports whether the data got through or not. It's a valuable diagnostic tool. For syntax information type **ping /?**. Perhaps the most useful command-line switch is -t. This will keep ping pinging until you interrupt it with Ctrl+C, a very handy thing if you're trying to fix network cabling or find a problem with your network setup.
tasklist	Lists running applications and services. Available on XP Pro and Media Center Edition only*. tasklist can provide detailed information about the services provided by running applications, and can list tasks running under other logins (due to Fast User Switching). Type **tasklist** alone on the command line for a list of programs or **tasklist /?** for syntax help.
taskkill	taskkill kills the program(s) specified on the command line, and it can often kill errant programs that the Windows Task Manager cannot. Available on XP Pro and Media Center Edition only*. Type **taskkill /f /pid ###** to forcibly terminate a program with process ID number ###; or type taskkill /? for a list of all options.
tracert	tracert probes the path between your computer and another computer on your network or the Internet, listing each intermediate network router in between the two. It's an important diagnostic tool. Type **tracert /?** for a syntax description.

For some reason, Microsoft chose not to install tasklist.exe *and* taskkill.exe *on Windows XP Home Edition. If you use XP Home, you might want to grab copies of these two useful tools from the* \windows\system32 *folder of an XP Pro or XP Media Center Edition installation.*

Support Tools

The Windows Setup CD-ROM contains a set of *very* useful diagnostic and maintenance tools that is not installed by default when you install Windows. I recommend that you install these tools on any computer that you personally maintain; or, at least install them on a shared network folder so that you can access them from any computer in your organization or home.

To install the Support Tools, insert your Windows Setup CD-ROM, wait for the menu window to appear, click Perform Additional Tasks if this option appears, then select Browse This CD. (If Autorun is not enabled, open Windows Explorer and browse the CD drive manually.) Open the folder \SUPPORT\TOOLS. If you are logged on as a Computer Administrator, double-click suptools.msi or setup.exe. If you are not currently logged on as an Administrator, right-click suptools.msi or setup.exe, select Run As, and select Administrator as the alternate account.

The installer will copy programs to \Program Files\Support tools, add a Start menu item that opens the Support Tools Help file (suptools.chm), and also add \Program Files\Support Tools to the PATH environment variable, so that the tools may be run from the command line.

When the installation is complete, browse the folder \program files\support tools. Documentation is sparse. There are a few .doc files describing a few of the applications (double-click these to open them in WordPad or Microsoft Word). There are .hlp files for a few more applications (double-click to open these in Windows Help). Several more applications are documented in the Support Tools Help File (click Start, All Programs, Support Tools). Others have no online documentation. For these, open a command prompt window and type the name of the program followed by /?; for example,

xcacls /?

For more information about some of the Windows XP support tools, see http://support.microsoft.com/kb/838079. This article assumes you've installed Windows XP Service Pack 2.

The set of Support Tools provided with Windows varies from one version of Windows to another. Table A.2 lists all of the tool programs and the operating systems which with each is supplied. The letters used in the OS column are

2	Windows 2000 Professional
H	Windows XP Home Edition
P	Windows XP Professional
M	Windows XP Media Center Edition

For example, tools with no "H" in the OS column are not provided with Windows XP Home edition.

The Type column indicates the program type:

CMD Command-line program

GUI Graphical User Interface program

MMC Microsoft Management Console snap-in. Run by typing **start xxx.msc**, replacing *xxx.msc* with the actual filename of the snap-in.

SCR Windows Script Host Script, mostly meant to serve as an example for writing your own scripts. Issue the command
cscript //H:cscript

(just once) to make these work properly from a command-line prompt.

Table A.2 Support Tool Programs

Filename	OS	Type	Description
acldiag.exe	2HPM	CMD	Detects and reports discrepancies in Active Directory Access Control Lists.
activate.exe	HPM	CMD	Activates Windows XP from the command line.
addiag.exe	HPM	CMD	Displays information on published (advertised) applications.
adsiedit.msc	2HPM	MMC	Active Directory LDAP Browse/Edit tool.

(continues)

Table A.2 Continued

Filename	OS	Type	Description
apcompat.exe	2	GUI	Application Compatibility tool, runs applications in an environment that simulates earlier versions of Windows.
apimon.exe	HPM	GUI	Profiles Windows API usage and page faults to tune applications.
apmstat.exe	2HPM	CMD	Displays motherboard APM (power management) availability.
bindiff.exe	HPM	CMD	Compares binary files.
bitsadmin.exe	HPM	CMD	Background Intelligent Transfer Service exerciser.
browstat.exe	2HPM	CMD	Displays Browser server status.
cabarc.exe	HPM	CMD	Creates, lists, or extracts Cabinet files.
clonegg.vbs	2HPM	SCR	Sample script, copies global groups from NT domain to Windows 200x.
cloneggu.vbs	2HPM	SCR	Sample script, copies global groups and users from NT domain to Windows 200x.
clonelg.vbs	2HPM	SCR	Sample script, copies local groups from NT domain to Windows 200x.
clonepr.vbs	2HPM	SCR	Sample script, copies users from NT domain to Windows 200x.
dcdiag.exe	2	CMD	Domain Controller diagnostic utility, checks connectivity and replication in a forest of Windows domain controllers.
depends.exe	2HPM	GUI	Dependency Walker, identifies all of the DLLs used by a given program or module.
dfsutil.exe	2HPM	CMD	Queries Distributed File System configuration.
dhcploc.exe	HPM	CMD	Detects authorized and unauthorized DHCP servers.
diruse.exe	HPM	CMD	Displays disk space usage by directory.
dmdiag.exe	HPM	CMD	Displays information about mounted file systems.
dnscmd.exe	2HPM	CMD	Displays and changes data in Windows Server DNS Server.
dsacls.exe	2HPM	CMD	Displays and changes Active Directory Access Control Lists.
dsastat.exe	2HPM	CMD	Verifies correct AD replication.
dskprobe.exe	2HPM	GUI	Disk contents viewer, displays data by file or sector.
dumpchk.exe	2HPM	CMD	Validates format of a system memory dump file.
dupfinder.exe	HPM	GUI	Duplicate file finder, locates identical files stored in different folders.
efsinfo.exe	HPM	CMD	Displays information about Encrypting File System.
exctrlst.exe	HPM	CMD	Lists application services that have registered performance counters.
extract.exe	8EHPM	CMD	Extracts files from Microsoft .CAB files.
filever.exe	2HPM	CMD	Prints version information stored in executable and DLL files.
ftonline.exe	HPM	CMD	Mounts and recovers files from Windows NT 4 RAID volumes.
getsid.exe	HPM	CMD	Displays Security ID associated with a user account.
gflags.exe	2HPM	GUI	Edits Global Flags to enable operating system debug options.

Table A.2   Continued

Filename	OS	Type	Description
ipseccmd.exe	HPM	CMD	Configures and displays IPSec Security policies.
kill.exe	2	CMD	Kills tasks from the command line (like taskkill).
ksetup.exe	2HPM	CMD	Sets Windows to use MIT Kerberos authentication server.
ktpass.exe	2HPM	CMD	Creates Kerberos keytab file for UNIX hosts.
ldp.exe	2HPM	GUI	Graphical LDAP browser/query viewer.
memsnap.exe	2HPM	CMD	Displays memory usage of all active processes.
movetree.exe	2HPM	CMD	Moves AD objects between domains.
msicuu.exe	2HPM	GUI	Windows Installer cleanup utility.
msizap.exe	2HPM	CMD	Windows Installer cleanup utility, called by msicuu.
netcap.exe	HPM	CMD	Logs network traffic to a file.
netdiag.exe	2HPM	CMD	Comprehensive Windows networking diagnostic tool.
netdom.exe	2HPM	CMD	Manages domain membership and user accounts.
netset.exe	HPM	CMD	Lists, installs, and configures networking components.
nltest.exe	2HPM	CMD	Queries and updates Domain Controller status.
ntfrsutl.exe	HPM	CMD	Displays internal status of File Replication Service.
pfmon.exe	HPM	CMD	Page Fault Monitor, displays memory activity in an application.
pmon.exe	2HPM	CMD	Process Resource Monitor, displays CPU and memory usage.
poolmon.exe	2HPM	CMD	Memory Pool Monitor, displays paged and non-paged pool usage.
pptpclnt.exe	2HPM	CMD	Point-to-Point Tunneling Protocol tester, client side.
pptpsrv.exe	2HPM	CMD	Point-to-Point Tunneling Protocol tester, server side.
pstat.exe	HPM	CMD	Process Status snapshot utility.
pviewer.exe	2HPM	GUI	Process Viewer, displays the status of active processes on your computer or other networked computers. Lists active threads, memory usage, priority level.
rasdiag.exe	HPM	CMD	Dial-Up Networking diagnostic gathering tool.
reg.exe	2PM	CMD	Edits or displays Registry data.
remote.exe	2HPM	CMD	Remote debugging client/server communication program.
repadmin.exe	2	CMD	Replication diagnostic tool, displays replication topology for Windows 2000 Server domain controllers.
replmon.exe	2HPM	GUI	Monitors and queries AD replication.
rsdiag.exe	2HPM	CMD	Remote Storage diagnostic, displays information in Remote Storage (HSM) databases.
rsdir.exe	2HPM	CMD	Remote Storage file information tool.
sdcheck.exe	2HPM	CMD	Displays Security Descriptors for AD objects.
search.vbs	2HPM	SCR	LDAP directory search tool.
setspn.exe	HPM	CMD	Sets Service Principal Name, repairs certain directory authentication problems.

(continues)

Table A.2   Continued

Filename	OS	Type	Description
setx.exe	HPM	CMD	Sets environment variables from the command line.
showaccs.exe	2HPM	CMD	Server Migration tool, lists SIDs found in file system or Registry.
showperf.exe	HPM	GUI	Displays performance counter raw data.
sidhist.vbs	2HPM	SCR	Sample script, demonstrates use of ICloneSecurityPrincipal::AddSidHistory.
sidwalk.exe	2HPM	CMD	Server Migration tool, updates mapped SIDS in file system or Registry.
sidwalk.msc	2HPM	MMC	Security Migration Editor, edits old to new SID mapping.
snmputilg.exe	2HPM	GUI	Browses network data returned by SNMP-enabled devices.
spcheck.exe	HPM	CMD	Service Pack Checker, verifies installation of hotfixes and service packs.
timezone.exe	HPM	CMD	Sets the time zone and daylight savings time start/end dates from the command line.
tlist.exe	2	CMD	Lists tasks running on the system (like tasklist).
tracefmt.exe	HPM	CMD	Formats and displays trace information gathered by tracelog.
tracelog.exe	HPM	CMD	Enables and disables tracing of system components during debugging.
tracepdb.exe	HPM	CMD	Creates trace message database used by tracefmt.
vfi.exe	HPM	GUI	Records snapshot information about files to help detect changes.
whoami.exe	HPM	CMD	Displays current username, security groups, and privileges.
windiff.exe	2	GUI	Compares text files and/or entire folders, highlighting additions, changes and deletions.
wsremote.exe	2HPM	CMD	Remote debugging client/server communication program.
xcacls.exe	HPM	CMD	Edits and displays file Access Control Lists.

Application Compatibility Toolkit

The 32-bit Windows Application Programming Interface (Win32 API) through which Windows provides service and support to application programs has been evolving since its debut with Windows 95. Certain system functions behave slightly differently from one version of Windows to the next, and these differences can trip up an application that depends on a specific behavior. Windows XP lets you set gross compatibility settings through the Compatibility tab on each program's Properties page, but the Application Compatibility Toolkit lets you make extremely fine-grained adjustments to the behavior of specific API functions. This toolkit is meant primarily for software developers, but in some cases end users might find it useful as well—if the company that produced the application is of no help, it can't hurt to mess with these settings before giving up entirely.

The version provided on the Windows XP Setup CD-ROM is version 2.0, via the setup program \SUPPORT\TOOLS\ACT20.EXE, but this is now obsolete. You should download the current version from www.microsoft.com/downloads (search for Application Compatibility Toolkit). The toolkit programs are installed on your hard disk in \Program Files\Application Compatibility Toolkit. Documentation is provided in the default.htm file in that folder; it opens in Internet Explorer. The programs are listed in Table A.3.

Table A.3   Application Compatibility Toolkit Programs

Program	Type	Description
appverif.exe	GUI	This tool watches a designated application while it runs, and reports any attempts the program makes to use the Windows API incorrectly.
CompatAdmin.exe	GUI	Edits the systemwide database of application compatibility settings set for specific applications.
gflags.exe	CMD	Enables and disables debugging options built into the Windows kernel.
GrabMI.exe	CMD	Extracts name and version information from files that is useful for constructing compatibility rule sets.
PageHeap.exe	EXE	Monitors the Windows page heap (allocatable memory) for heap-related bugs.
QFixApp.exe	EXE	Lets you test combinations of compatibility fix settings on an errant applications, by applying "layers" (sets of related fixes), by making adjustments to specific API behaviors.
demoapp.exe	EXE	A sample application that has known problems with specific API functions can be used to test and demonstrate process of compatibility adjusting and testing.

Deployment Toolkit

If you are in the business of (legally) installing identical Windows configurations on large numbers of computers, you may be able to save a lot of time by using the Windows Deployment Toolkit. The toolkit lets you configure a fresh, clean installation of Windows to your liking—you can install applications, add user accounts, make Windows settings, and so on. Then, you run a special Deployment Toolkit program that prepares Windows for duplication. It ensures that the copies will have unique security databases, don't all share a single product ID code, and don't look like illegal copies to Windows Activation. After this preparation step, you can copy the "master" computer's hard disk as many times as necessary. When installed into a new computer, "cloned" disk copies will contain your preinstalled settings and applications.

You should know that Microsoft doesn't provide a disk duplication tool with the Deployment Toolkit—you have to use a third-party disk cloning program or hardware device for that—but once duplicated, each copy will boot up fully configured, customized, with whatever applications and settings you put into the original.

The deployment kit may be installed from the Windows 2000 Professional or Windows XP Setup disc, from \SUPPORT\TOOLS\DEPLOY.CAB. However, the version on the CD-ROM is tied to the service pack level of that CD-ROM. If you intend to apply service packs to the computer before cloning it, you should download and use the deployment toolkit version that applies to the final service pack level. Updated deployment toolkits (new versions of DEPLOY.CAB) are provided on Microsoft-issued Windows Service Pack CD-ROMs, or you may download the correct version from www.microsoft.com/downloads. Search for Deployment Tools, and select the correct Windows operating system version and service pack level.

The toolkit arrives as a .CAB compressed file. To view the instructions for installing and using the toolkit, follow these steps:

1. Use Windows Explorer to locate the DEPLOY.CAB file, and double-click DEPLOY.CAB to view the files within. Or, from the command line, type **start deploy.chm**.

2. Drag the help file DEPLOY.CHM into your desktop.

3. Double-click DEPLOY.CHM on your desktop to view the help file.

The deployment toolkit includes the programs listed in Table A.4.

Table A.4   Deployment Toolkit Programs

File	Description
deploy.chm	Help file describing the deployment process.
ref.chm	Help file documenting deployment configuration files.
cvtarea.exe	Allows specific placement of files in a FAT disk partition. Useful when your disk duplication system requires that disks be distributed in FAT format for later conversion to NTFS. cvtarea lets you reserve empty spaces on the disk to make the NTFS conversion more efficient.
factory.exe	A component program used by sysprep.exe.
oformat.com	Formats a FAT-32 partition in such a way that later conversion to NTFS will be more efficient.
setupcl.exe	A component program used by sysprep.exe.
setupmgr.exe	A Wizard program that helps create configuration files needed for the cloning process.
sysprep.exe	A command-line tool that prepares a freshly installed and configured copy of Windows for duplication.

Value-Added Tools

The Windows Setup CD-ROM may contain additional program suites that are not installed through Windows Setup. These include some programs provided by Microsoft and some third-party tools. We won't list all of the tools, but we will list the general categories. Table A.5 lists the Value-Added Tool folders found on current versions of the Windows 2000 and Windows XP setup CD-ROMs, with a brief description of the tools found inside each folder. The tools provided on your Windows XP setup CD-ROM may be different, depending on your version of Windows and your computer vendor.

To install a given tool set, view the folder in Windows Explorer, and double-click whatever setup program you find: setup.exe or (*something*).msi. Alternatively double-click any .CHM (help), .HTM (HTML), or .TXT (text) files you find; these may contain installation instructions.

Updated third-party tools may be provided on Windows Service Pack CD-ROMs. If you install any third-party tools, be sure to check for updates when you install subsequent service packs. The service pack installer itself may not update these tools.

Table A.5   Value-Added Tool Categories

Folder	Toolkit
\VALUEADD\3RDPARTY\MGMT\CITRIX	Client software for Citrix Terminal Services (a specialized multi-user server version of Windows Terminal Services, similar to Remote Desktop).
\VALUEADD\MGMT\PBA	Phone Book Administrator, used by corporate networks and ISPs to deploy Dial-Up Networking Point of Presence databases. Also called Connection Point Services, Phone Book Service, and Connection Manager Administration Kit.
\VALUEADD\MSFT\FONTS	Arial Alternative fonts for the Minitel/Prestel terminal emulator.
\VALUEADD\MSFT\MGMT\CIMV2R5	Strictly compliant CIM version 2.5 schema file for Windows Management Instrumentation.

Table A.5   Continued

Folder	Toolkit
\VALUEADD\MSFT\MGMT\IAS	Windows NT 4.0 Internet Authentication Service snap-in.
\VALUEADD\MSFT\MGMT\MSTSC_HPC	Terminal Server Client for the Handheld PC.
\VALUEADD\MSFT\MGMT\WBEMODBC	ODBC Driver for WMI.
\VALUEADD\MSFT\NET\NETBEUI	NetBEUI Protocol driver for XP.
\VALUEADD\MSFT\NET\TOOLS	TCP/UDP Test Utility.
\VALUEADD\MSFT\NTBACKUP	The standard backup program for Windows 2000 and XP is not installed by default on Windows XP Home Edition. XP Home users can find it here.
\VALUEADD\USMT\ANSI	User State Migration Tool—Administrator's version of the Files and Settings Transfer Wizard.

PowerToys

Microsoft has an odd habit of making you download some useful tools that really should have been on the Setup CD-ROM to begin with. TweakUI, in particular, is an indispensable tool. It's a sort of Windows Swiss army knife, and gives access to several dozen adjustments and settings that should have been on the control panel.

The PowerToys vary from one version of Windows to another. Check carefully before trying to use "toys" from one version on another. In particular, don't use the XP TweakUI tool on Windows 2000 or 9x, or vice versa.

PowerToys for Windows XP

To download PowerToys for Windows XP, visit www.microsoft.com/windowsxp, and at the left click Downloads, then PowerToys and Add-Ins for Windows XP. Each of the PowerToys is a downloadable installation program (.EXE file). To install them,

1. Select and download a PowerToy from the Microsoft website, and save the .EXE file on your desktop.

2. If you're logged on as a Computer Administrator, just double-click the installer's icon. If you're not a Computer Administrator, right-click the icon, select Run As, check The Following User, and enter an Administrator's username and password.

3. Follow any additional instructions that appear.

4. When the installation is complete, drag the downloaded installer to the Recycle Bin, or move it to a shared network folder for installation on other computers.

5. Click Start, All Programs, Powertoys For Window XP to use the new tool, or select the Readme entry for a description of the tools.

The Windows XP PowerToys available at the time of this writing are listed in Table A.6.

Table A.6   PowerToys for Windows XP

PowerToy	Description
ClearType Tuner	For LCD monitor users only, adjusts Clear-Type to your preferences, letting you make your own trade-off between jagginess and blurriness.
HTML Slide Show Wizard	Creates a nice set of web pages from a folder of pictures, with thumbnails, fo ward and back navigation buttons, and so on.
Open Command Window Here	Adds a handy right-click menu choice for folders selected in Windows Explorer. Clicking Open Command Window Here opens a command prompt window with the selected directory as the current directory. Indispensable if you do a lot of work on the command line.
Alt-Tab Replacement	When this tool is installed, Alt-Tab displays not only the name and icon of each open application, but also lets you view thumbnail views of the associated windows, so that you can more easily select the desired instance of an open application.
TweakUI	A must-have tool, makes adjustments to the XP user interface including menus, the mouse, Windows Explorer, the taskbar, desktop icons, the location of special folders, Control Panel applets, and more. For more details, see "TweakUI," in Chapter 6, "Tweaking and Tuning Windows."
Power Calculator	A peculiar tool—a Reverse Polish calculator with a graphing feature. If you know what Reverse Polish means, you'll love this. Otherwise, hmmmm.
Image Resizer	Resizes one or more images to a selected size, handy for making web pages or thumbnails.
CD Slide Show Generator	Adds a slide-show display wizard to a set of pictures to be burned on to a CD. The CD will then "auto-run" the slide-show display when inserted into a computer running Windows 95 through XP.
Virtual Desktop Manager	Allows you to set up and switch between four separate desktops.
Taskbar Magnifier	Displays in the taskbar a magnified version of the area under the mouse. After installing, right-click the taskbar, select Toolbars, and check Taskbar Magnifier.
Webcam Timershot	Lets you automatically take and save pictures from a webcam or attached camera; the pictures are saved in a designated folder. If the folder is part of a website, this can let you create an automatically updating webcam page.

TweakUI for Windows 9x, NT, and 2000

For Windows 95, 98, Me, NT, or 2000, you can obtain TweakUI version 1.33 from www.microsoft.com. Search for "TweakUI download Windows NT." The download page contains download and installation instructions. The Windows 95-98-NT-2000 TweakUI tool is a control panel applet (tweakui.cpl), meaning that it will appear as an icon in your Control Panel.

Resource Kits

Microsoft sells Resource Kits for its various operating systems, which usually consist of a box containing advanced documentation in printed form and management and diagnostic tools on an accompanying CD-ROM. Some of the Resource Kits' text is available online; for example, the XP Pro Resource Kit text is at www.microsoft.com/resources/documentation/Windows/XP/all/reskit/en-us.

Resource Kits are available for Windows 98, Windows 2000 Professional, Windows 2000 Server, Window XP Professional, and Windows Server 2003. The Resource Kit for Windows XP Professional is a book only and does *not* include software tools. However, you can use tools from the Windows 2000

Professional, Windows 2000 Server, or Windows Server 2003 Resource Kits on Windows XP Professional or Home Edition.

The tools number about 300 and many are quite useful. It's worth obtaining a copy of them for use in your organization. If you subscribe to the Microsoft Developer's Network, you may find that the Resource Kit tools are already included as part of your subscription, and are downloadable or are provided on your library CD- or DVD-ROMs. You can also download the Windows Server 2003 Resource Kit Tools from www.microsoft.com/downloads for free—search for Windows Server 2003 Resource Kit Tools.

For more information, see http://www.microsoft.com/technet/itsolutions/reskits/rktmain.mspx.

Tip

To help you familiarize yourself with the tools, you might want to put shortcuts to their help files on your desktop for easy access. These help files are part of the Windows Help system so the actual command line to open them is complex. It's best to create the shortcut by copying an existing one. To do this, find the Resource Kit help entry in the Start menu under, for example, All Programs, Windows Resource Kit Tools. Right-click the Help entry and drag the help icon to your desktop. When windows prompts you, choose Copy Here.

Table A.7 lists the Resource Kit tools. The Kit column lists the Resource Kit(s) in which the tool is included: 2 for the Windows 2000 Professional and Server kits, and 3 for the Windows Server 2003 Resource Kit.

The Type column indicates the program type:

BF	Batch file (.BAT or .CMD file)
CMD	Command-line program (.EXE file)
GUI	Graphical User Interface program (.EXE file)
MMC	Microsoft Management Console snap-in (.MSC file)
SAV	Screen Saver (.SCR file)
SCR	Windows Script Host Script (.VBS or .JS file)
SVC	Windows Service (.EXE file)

Table A.7   Resource Kit Tools

Command	Kit	Type	Description
addiag	2	CMD	Displays information on published (advertised) applications.
addusers	2	CMD	Adds and removes user accounts from data listed in a text file.
adlb	3	CMD	Active Directory Load Balancing Tool, tunes sharing of workload in multiple-server Active Directory networks (server tool only).
apimon	2	GUI	Profiles Windows API usage and page faults to tune applications.
appsec	2	GUI	Citrix terminal server application security configuration utility.
associate	2	CMD	Registers or deletes Explorer links between filename extensions and application programs; like "assoc."

(continues)

Table A.7   **Continued**

Command	Kit	Type	Description
atanlyzr	2	GUI	Appletalk network device analyzer, scans and lists devices.
atmarp	23	CMD	ATM network diagnostic tool.
atmlane	23	CMD	ATM network diagnostic tool.
auditpol	2	CMD	Modifies local computer audit policy.
autoexnt	23	svc	Service to run a batch file on computer startup (not needed for Windows XP).
bootconfig	2	SCR	Prints "boot configuration", not actually useful (WMI).
browmon	2	GUI	Browser (network neighborhood) monitor, displays info on active workgroups/domains and browser masters.
bus	2	SCR	Lists busses, such as ISA and PCI in local computer (WMI).
cacheinfo	2	SCR	Lists CPU cache information (WMI).
cachemov	2	GUI	Moves offline files and offline content cache to a different drive or folder.
cat	2	CMD	Concatenates named file(s) to standard output, like "type."
cdburn	3	CMD	Burns a CD-R or CD-RW disk from an ISO image file.
cdromdrives	2	SCR	Lists CD-ROM drives present on local computer (WMI).
cepsetup	3	GUI	Installs SCEP add-on for Certificate Services.
checkbios	2	SCR	Lists BIOS information reported by WMI.
checkrepl	3	SCR	Check Replication; monitors domain controller replication (server tool only).
chklnks	23	GUI	Locates shortcuts that point to programs that no longer exist, offers to delete them.
chknic	3	CMD	Checks the computer's network adapters to see whether they are compatible with Network Load Balancing (server tool only).
chkusers	2	SCR	Scans active directory for users meeting specified criteria (ADSI).
choice	2	CMD	Batch file tool that prompts for input and lets user make selection from a list of choices.
classifymembers	2	SCR	Lists members of a specified AD container or group (ADSI).
clean	23	SCR	Deletes all printers from a system (Printer admin demo).
cleanspl	3	GUI	Erases print jobs, spooled files, printers, and print drivers on a remote computer.
clearmem	23	CMD	Flushes the file cache, minimizes working set size of running applications.
clip	2	CMD	Copies standard input to the clipboard so it can be pasted into any GUI application.
clippool	2	GUI	Network shared Clipboard.
cliptray	2	GUI	Notification area tool that lets you create named blocks of text that can be selected and copied into the Clipboard via a pop-up menu.
clone	23	SCR	Generates scripts to clone a computer's printer setup (Printer admin demo).

Table A.7   Continued

Command	Kit	Type	Description
clusrest	2	CMD	Restores cluster quorum data after restoring disks from backup.
clusterrecovery	3	GUI	Server Cluster Recovery Utility; reconfigures cluster disk information after a bus or disk failure (server tool only).
clustsim	2	CMD	Cluster Verification Utility management program.
codecfile	2	SCR	Displays info on installed audio and video codecs (WMI).
compress	23	CMD	Tool to pack one or more files into a compressed file. Can create ZIP and other compression formats.
compsys	2	SCR	Displays information about the computer and its owner (WMI).
con2prt	2	CMD	Establishes and deletes network printer connections (icons).
conall	23	SCR	Establishes connections to (icons for) all printers on a specified server.
confdisk	3	CMD	Stores Server Cluster configuration data in the Automated System Recovery database to help after a failure (server tool only).
consume	3	CMD	Stresses CPU by consuming memory, page file memory, disk space, CPU time, or kernel pool. Used to test the ability of applications and services to deal with marginal conditions.
cpustres	2	GUI	Stresses CPU by consuming CPU cycles.
createusers	2	SCR	Creates user accounts on a domain.
creatfil	23	CMD	Creates a file of a specified name and size.
csccmd	3	CMD	Manages client-side caching (offline files) database (Pro and Server only).
ctrlist	2	CMD	Lists installed Performance Monitor counters.
cusrmgr	2	CMD	Adds or deletes users or groups, sets account parameters, can assign random passwords.
custreasonedit	3	CMD	Adds/edits predefined reasons for logging Windows shutdowns and restarts.
defprn	23	SCR	Sets or displays default printer.
defptr	2	GUI	Task tray tool to change default printer.
delprof	23	CMD	Deletes user profiles; can delete profiles not used with a specified number of days.
delrp	2	CMD	Deletes a file and any associated NTFS reparse points.
delsrv	2	CMD	Unregisters a service.
depends	2	GUI	Dependency Walker: displays modules used by applications.
desktop	2	CMD	Lists desktops and their properties (WMI).
device	2	SCR	Lists and/or controls device drivers.
devicemem	2	SCR	Lists hardware device memory address ranges (WMI).
dh	23	CMD	Displays global and user-mode heap debugging information.
dhcmp	2	CMD	Formats and compares heap dumps created by dh.exe.
dhcploc	2	CMD	Detects authorized and unauthorized DHCP servers.

(continues)

Table A.7   Continued

Command	Kit	Type	Description
dhcpobjs	2	GUI	Installs COM library to remotely administer DHCP server on Windows Server.
diruse	2	CMD	Displays disk space usage by directory.
diskmap	2	CMD	Displays disk drive geometry information.
diskpar	2	CMD	Adjusts disk partition information for large disks to improve access speed under some circumstances.
diskpartition	2	SCR	Lists disk partition information for a computer (WMI).
diskraid	3	CMD	Manages and configures RAID disk configurations (server tool only).
diskuse	23	CMD	Counts disk space usage on a per-user basis.
dmachan	2	SCR	Lists Direct Memory Access (DMA) channels on a computer (WMI).
dmdiag	2	CMD	Displays information about mounted file systems.
dnsdiag	3	CMD	Displays DNS data used by SMTP service to help diagnose mail delivery problems.
dommon	2	GUI	Displays status of domain controller and secure connections between domain controllers.
drivers	2	CMD	Lists installed device drivers.
drives	2	SCR	Lists disk drive information (WMI).
drmapsrv	2	CMD	Maps local drives to host computer when using Terminal Services or Remote Desktop Connection.
drvmgr	23	SCR	Displays, installs, and manages printer drivers.
dsstore	2	CMD	Manages public-key certificates.
dumpcfg	2	CMD	Displays and changes disk signatures (helpful in recovering from mirror failure).
dumpel	2	CMD	Dumps Event log from local or remote computer to a tab-delimited text file.
dumpfsmos	23	CMD	Dumps Flexible Single Master Operation (FMSO) domain controller information.
dupfinder	2	GUI	Locates duplicate files.
dureg	2	CMD	Calculates Registry content size and can search Registry for text strings.
dvdburn	3	CMD	Burns DVD/R or DVD/RW discs from an ISO image file.
efsinfo	2	CMD	Displays information about Encrypting File System.
elogdmp	2	CMD	Dumps Event log from local or remote computer to the standard output.
empty	23	CMD	Frees all working set pages for a specified process (that is, pushes task from memory into page file).
enabledhcp	2	SCR	Lists or sets DHCP settings on network adapters (WMI).
enumclasses	2	SCR	Lists available WMI classes (WMI).
enuminstances	2	SCR	Lists instances of WMI class objects (WMI).

Table A.7   Continued

Command	Kit	Type	Description
enumnamespaces	2	SCR	Lists WMI namespaces—broad categories of WMI classes (WMI).
enumprop	2	CMD	Lists all properties of a given Active Directory object given its LDAP descriptor.
eventcombmt	3	GUI	Searches the Event logs on multiple computers for specified events.
eventlogmon	2	SCR	Monitors Event log and prints new entries as they occur.
exctrlst	2	CMD	Lists application services that have registered performance counters
exec	2	CMD	Runs a command on a remote computer using WMI.
exetype	2	CMD	Displays information about an executable file: expected operating system, and so on.
expand	2	CMD	Expands files from packed files created by compress.exe or from .CAB files.
extract	2	CMD	Extracts files from Microsoft .CAB files.
fcsetup	23	GUI	Installs a file-copy utility that uses Message Queueing Service to copy files over a slow or unreliable network link.
fileinfo	2	CMD	Displays version information stored in system files.
fileman	2	SCR	Deletes, renames, or changes ownership of files on local or remote computers.
filespy	2	CMD	Monitors local and network file I/O activity. Requires FileSpy service (see fspyinst.exe).
filever	2	CMD	Displays version information stored in system files. The Services for UNIX version works only on the Interix system files.
findgrp	2	CMD	Lists all groups of which a user is a direct or indirect member.
findstr	2	CMD	Finds text in files, advanced.
floplock	2	SVC	Service that secures floppy disk drives so they can be used only by Administrators.
forfiles	2	CMD	Scans for files based on name and date, and issues a specified command on each matching file.
forms	23	SCR	Lists, adds, and deletes forms associated with printers (Printer admin demo).
freedisk	2	CMD	Batch file tool, verifies that there is at least a specified amount of free disk space.
frsflags	3	SCR	Enables and disables the Install Override feature of the File Replication Service (Server tool only).
fspyinst	2	GUI	Installs the File Spy service (see filespy.exe).
fspyunin	2	CMD	Uninstalls the FileSpy service (see filespy.exe).
ftedit	2	GUI	Edits Fault Tolerant Disk (software RAID) setup information in Registry.
fxfrinst	2	CMD	Installs File Copy functionality for Terminal Services Client (rdpclip.exe).

(continues)

Table A.7 Continued

Command	Kit	Type	Description
getcm	3	CMD	Downloads and installs a Connection Manager profile, part of the Connection Manager Administration Kit.
getmac	2	CMD	Displays network adapter MAC addresses.
getsid	2	CMD	Displays Security ID associated with a user account.
gettype	2	CMD	Determines current Windows version; useful in batch files when different operating systems require different procedures.
global	2	CMD	Lists members of global groups on remote servers or domains.
gpmonitor	3	GUI	Monitors Group Policy updates/refreshes and displays a report indicating changes (server tool only).
gpolmig	2	CMD	Migration tool—copies Windows NT version 4 policy file settings to Windows Server Group Policy.
gpotool	23	CMD	Checks consistency of Group Policy objects on domain controllers; can also modify preferred controller list.
gpresult	2	CMD	Computes and displays Group Policy Resultant Set of Policy.
group	2	SCR	Lists groups for a given domain or server (WMI).
groupdescription	2	SCR	Lists the descriptive title for a domain or server's groups (WMI).
grpcpy	2	GUI	Copies usernames between groups in a domain, or between domains.
guid2obj	2	CMD	Looks up distinguished (human readable) name for a given GUID identifier.
heapmon	2	CMD	Displays information about the global heap.
hlscan	3	CMD	Scans for and lists all hard links on an NTFS disk partition.
htmlfltr	2	CMD	Removes comments and extra whitespace from HTML files.
httpcmd	2	CMD	Command-line HTTP client, sends a query to an HTTP server and displays response.
iasparse	2	CMD	Formats IAS and RAS server log files into a human-readable text format.
ifilttst	23	CMD	Validates user-built IFilter COM implementations (add-ons to Microsoft Index Server).
ifmember	23	CMD	Tests whether a user is a member of a group; useful in batch files.
iishostsvc	2	SVC	IIS Host Helper Service; registers IIS host header strings (hostnames) with WINS.
iniman	3	CMD	Adds, deletes, modifies, or displays entries in an .INF or .INI file; helpful if you want to use a batch file to create or customize .INI files.
instaler	2	CMD	Installation monitor, creates a log of file, Registry, and .INI file changes made by a setup program (see also showinst.exe, undoinst.exe).
installd	2	BF	Installs a debugging version of NTDETECT.COM on the boot drive (probably works only on Windows 2000, may disable Windows XP).
instcm	3	CMD	Installs a connection manager profile that was obtained by getcm.

Table A.7 Continued

Command	Kit	Type	Description
instexnt	23	svc	Service that runs a specified batch file when computer boots up (not needed on Windows XP as it has a boot-script policy setting)
instsrv	23	CMD	Installs a specified .EXE file as a Windows Service.
intfiltr	23	CMD	Configures a multiprocessor system to handle interrupts on a specific processor.
inuse	2	CMD	File copy utility for files in use by the operating system; if the destination file is locked, the copy will take place at the next reboot.
ipsecpol	2	CMD	Command-line ipsec policy tool; lets you co figure (and document) ipsec policy setup in a batch file.
irqres	2	SCR	Lists hardware interrupt levels in use (WMI).
javareg	2	CMD	Registers Java classes as COM components (servers).
kerbtray	23	GUI	Tasktray tool to display Kerberos ticket information.
kernprof	2	CMD	Gathers and displays Windows kernel statistics.
kernrate	3	CMD	Kernel profiling tool reports CPU usage by location in the Windows Kernel or user-mode processes.
keyboard	2	SCR	Lists information about the installed keyboard (WMI).
kill	2	CMD	Terminates task(s) based on name of the executable file.
kix32	2	CMD	Enhanced logon script processor and batch programming language interpreter. More or less made obsolete by Windows Script Host.
kixplay	2	GUI	Plays KIX "music" files. Appalling.
klist	23	CMD	Lists and deletes Kerberos tickets.
krt	3	GUI	Key Recovery Tool; lets a Key Recovery Agent recover private keys from the Windows 2003 Server Certification Authority (server tool only).
kxrpc	2	GUI	RPC client program.
lbridge	23	BF	Copies logon scripts from a Windows 2000 server to the replication folders of a Windows NT 4 server (demo).
ldordergrp	2	SCR	Lists dependency groups for Windows services.
leakyapp	2	GUI	Allocates and holds memory to test system performance under memory stress.
linkd	23	CMD	Creates links in an NTFS file system. A links is an alternative directory entry for a file or folder.
linkspeed	3	CMD	Displays the speed of the network connection between specified computers.
list	23	CMD	Text file browsing utility. Very useful. Much like "less" on UNIX.
listadapters	2	SCR	Lists information about each network adapter and some network interface layers (WMI).
listdcs	2	SCR	Lists domain controllers for a specified domain.

(continues)

Table A.7 Continued

Command	Kit	Type	Description
listdisplayconfig	2	SCR	Lists display (monitor) settings (WMI).
listdomains	2	SCR	Lists all domains within a namespace (ADSI).
listfreespace	2	SCR	Lists amount of free space on all disk drivers (WMI).
listmembers	2	SCR	Lists all members of an AD container or group (ADSI).
listos	2	SCR	Lists properties of a computer's operating system (WMI).
listprinters	2	SCR	Lists properties of all printers installed on a computer (WMI).
listproperties	2	SCR	Lists properties of a specified Active Directory object (ADSI).
listspace	2	SCR	Lists amount of disk space on all drives on a specified computer (WMI).
local	2	CMD	Lists the members of the specified local security group.
lockoutstatus	3	GUI/CMD	Displays or lists locked-out user accounts in selected domains.
logevent	2	CMD	Adds an entry to the Event log on a local or networked computer.
logmeminfo	2	SCR	Lists physical and virtual memory sizes (WMI).
logoff	2	CMD	Logs off from Windows.
logtime	23	CMD	Batch file utility; creates a log file with timestamps and progress messages.
ls	2	CMD	Directory listing utility, a port of the UNIX "ls" command.
lsreport	23	CMD	Lists Terminal Server license data from a domain's license server(s).
lstdpconinfo	2	SCR	Lists display adapter settings (WMI).
lsview	23	GUI	Displays the status of your domain's license server(s).
mcast	23	CMD	Sends or listens for multicast packets (diagnostic tool).
mcopy	2	CMD	Copies files like "copy" but creates a log file recording progress and problems.
memmonitor	3	CMD	Monitors a task's memory consumption, and triggers a debugger if a set threshold is reached.
memtriage	3	CMD	Monitors memory usage and leakage, and issues a report suggesting ways to save a running system.
mibcc	23	CMD	Compiles SNMP MIB files into binary format used by Windows SNMP service.
modifyldap	2	SCR	Modifies LDAP object properties (ADSI).
modifyusers	2	SCR	Modifies properties of User objects in Active Directory (ADSI).
motherboard	2	SCR	Lists information about a computer's motherboard (WMI).
moveuser	23	CMD	Renames and changes security of a user profile.
mqcast	3	CMD	File replication tool send-side client; uses TCP/IP multicasting.
mqcatch	3	CMD	File replication tool receive-side server.
mtc	2	CMD	Copies files like "xcopy" but creates a log file recording progress and problems.
mtfcheck	2	CMD	Checks that a tape contains a valid Microsoft Tape Format (MTF) backup set; can also erase tapes and restore data.

Table A.7   Continued

Command	Kit	Type	Description
mv	2	CMD	Like "move" or "rename."
netclip	2	GUI	Displays and copies content to and from Clipboard on another computer.
netconnections	2	SCR	Lists network connections (mapped drives).
netcons	2	GUI	Displays current network connections; GUI version of "net use."
netset	2	CMD	Lists, installs, and configures networking components.
netsvc	2	CMD	Start, stop, pause, and query status of services running on remote computers.
networkprotocol	2	SCR	Displays installed network protocol information (WMI).
nlmon	2	CMD	Displays received Browser Service advertisements.
nlsinfo	3	CMD	Displays locale information (national language settings) for a computer.
now	23	CMD	Batch file utility, displays a time stamp and comment text. Can be redirected to a log file if desired.
ntfrsutl	2	CMD	Displays internal status of File Replication Service.
ntimer	23	CMD	Computes time elapsed and CPU time consumed by a specified command line.
ntrights	23	CMD	Adds or removes a Windows 2000 privilege (right) to a user or group on a specified computer.
oh	23	CMD	Displays information about open handles to files, synchronization objects, Registry keys, or threads.
oidgen	2	CMD	Generates a pair of random class and attribute OIDs that you can use when extending the Active Directory schema.
oleview	23	GUI	OLE/COM Object viewer, lets you browse installed OLE/COM objects, view properties and methods, and test interfaces.
osreconfig	2	SCR	Displays the OS recovery settings for a specified computer (WMI).
pagefile	2	SCR	Configures the Windows page file from the command line.
parallelport	2	SCR	Lists parallel port information (WMI).
pathman	23	CMD	Adds or removes folders from the systemwide or per-user PATH environment variable settings.
perfmon4	2	GUI	Updated version of Performance Monitor tool; probably obsolete under Windows XP.
perfmtr	2	CMD	Command-line performance monitor, prints CPU or memory statistics at intervals.
permcopy	23	CMD	Copies the share and file permission settings from one shared folder to another.
perms	23	CMD	Displays a given user's user-level permission settings for a file or files. Does not compute the user's actual net permissions because group rights are not factored in.
persist	23	SCR	Saves or restores user's printer configuration settings (printer admin demo).

(continues)

Table A.7   Continued

Command	Kit	Type	Description
pfmon	23	CMD	Page Fault Monitor, displays memory activity in an application.
playback	2	CMD	Records a sequence of requests received by IIS and can "play back" the requests to the same or another IIS server.
pmon	3	CMD	Displays CPU and memory usage by running tasks. Sort of a text-mode graphical display.
pointdev	2	SCR	List pointing device (mouse) information (WMI).
portconv	23	SCR	Adds TCP ports to a server for printers configured to use the "lpr" protocol.
portmgr	23	SCR	Modifies port settings for local or TCP network-attached printers.
printdriverinfo	3	CMD	Lists information about installed printer drivers.
prncfg	23	SCR	View or set printer's spooling configuration settings.
prnctrl	23	SCR	Manages printer queues from the command line.
prndata	23	SCR	Manipulates or displays printer configuration settings stored in the Registry.
prndemo	2	SCR	Demonstrates use of printer administration object in JavaScript.
prnmgr	23	SCR	Adds, deletes, or lists printers. Can install drivers if necessary.
processor	2	SCR	Lists information about a computer's CPU (WMI).
programgroups	2	SCR	Displays the "program groups" (Start menu subfolders) on a given computer (WMI).
protocolbinding	2	SCR	Lists protocol and adapter bindings (WMI).
ps	2	SCR	Lists the programs running on a specified computer.
pstop	2	SCR	Lists the programs running in order of descending CPU usage (this makes more sense if you pronounce the script's name as "ps top" rather than "p stop").
pulist	2	CMD	Lists the programs running on a specified computer, along with the username associated with each task.
qgrep	23	CMD	Fast file search utility, can use regular expressions like UNIX "grep" and Windows "findstr."
qidle	2	CMD	Identifies idle Terminal Server sessions; used with robosim for Terminal Server capacity planning simulations.
qslice	2	GUI	Displays a histogram of CPU usage for all active processes.
qtcp	23	CMD	Utility to test end-to-end network performance.
query	2	SCR	Performs a general WBEM query and displays the results (WMI).
queryad	3	SCR	Submits queries to Active Directory from the command line; displays results.
quickres	2	GUI	Creates a notification-area icon that lets you select screen resolutions from a pop-up menu.
quiktray	2	GUI	Adds a clunky "quick launch" tool icon to the notification area. The Windows desktop's Quick Launch bar is better.
raslist	2	CMD	Displays RAS server announcements received over the network.

Table A.7 Continued

Command	Kit	Type	Description
rassrvmon	23	GUI	Displays RAS server status and statistics, and can run commands when unusual conditions are detected.
rasusers	2	CMD	Lists user accounts that have RAS access permissions.
rclient	2	CMD	Remote character-mode remote control system; more robust than rcmd. Gives text-mode remote console window.
rcmd	2	CMD	Remote Command shell; lets you run command-line programs on a remote computer running the rcmdsvc service. More secure than telnet, less secure than ssh.
rcmd	2	CMD	Issue command on remote computer running rcmdsvc service.
rcmdsvc	2	SVC	Service component of rcmd.exe.
rcmdsvc	2	SVC	Remote command service.
rconmode	2	CMD	Sets buffer and window size for rclient console window.
rconstat	2	CMD	Lists active rclient connections.
rconsvc	2	SVC	Service component of rclient.exe.
rcontrolad	3	GUI	Adds "Remote Control" to the context menu of Active Directory MMC tools; lets you right click a computer in the AD display and establish a Remote Desktop connection to it.
reducer	2	CMD	Extracts information from log files created by tracelog.exe.
regback	2	CMD	Creates a backup of the system portions of the Windows Registry in a disk file.
regconfig	2	SCR	Displays or sets the Registry maximum size settings (WMI).
regdmp	2	CMD	Dumps Registry contents to a text file.
regfind	2	CMD	Locates and optionally replaces arbitrary values in the Registry.
regini	23	CMD	Creates Registry entries and sets permissions.
regrest	2	CMD	Restores the Registry by installing Registry file backup created by regback.exe. Note—This is not as good or as safe a tool as you would hope.
regview	3	CMD	Displays contents of Group Policy .POL files.
remapkey	23	CMD	Remaps the scan codes of keys on the keyboard; for example, to swap the Caps Lock and Ctrl keys (some programmers of a Certain Age prefer this).
restart	2	SCR	Initiates a shutdown and restart of a remote computer.
rkill	2	CMD	Lists and optionally terminates processes on a remote computer. Requires rkillsrv.exe.
rkillsrv	2	SVC	Service to permit remote use of rkill.exe (remote process kill).
rm	2	CMD	File remove tool like "delete."
robocli	2	CMD	Executes commands sent by robosrv, used for Terminal Server capacity planning simulations.
robocopy	23	CMD	Robust file copy; copies files and folders across a network connection. Very useful.
robosrv	2	GUI	Sends commands to robocli; used for Terminal Server capacity planning simulations.

(continues)

Table A.7 Continued

Command	Kit	Type	Description
rpccfg	3	CMD	Configures the network ports used by Remote Procedure Calls.
rpcdump	23	CMD	Lists Remote Procedure Call (RPC) endpoints on specified computer.
rpcping	3	CMD	Tests RPC connectivity by echoing packets between two computers.
rpingc	23	CMD	Remote Procedure Call (RPC) service test tool, 32-bit Windows client-side test program.
rpingc16	2	GUI	Remote Procedure Call (RPC) service test tool, 16-bit Windows client-side test program.
rpingdos	2		Remote Procedure Call (RPC) service test tool, DOS client-side test program.
rpings	23	CMD	Remote Procedure Call (RPC) service test tool, server-side program.
rqc	3	CMD	Remote Access Quarantine Client tool; used on client side to verify that a computer connecting to the network meets security requirements and can be granted full network access.
rqs	3	SVC	Remote Access Quarantine Service; runs on Windows 2003 server to manage quarantined/full connection of remote hosts.
rqs_setup	3	BF	Installs Remote Access Quarantine Service (Server tool only).
rsetup	2	CMD	Installs and activates rconsvc on local or remote computer.
rshsvc	2	BF	Installs UNIX rsh host service.
rshsvc	2	SVC	Remote Shell (UNIX rsh) host service.
rsm_dbic	2	CMD	Validates the integrity of the Removable Storage Manager (RSM) media database.
rsm_dbutil	2	GUI	Validates the integrity of, backs up, and restores the Removable Storage Manager (RSM) media database.
rsmconfg	2	GUI	Removable Storage Manager (RSM) robotic tape changer configuration wizard.
runapp	2	GUI	Runs an application and reruns it whenever the application exits.
sc	2	CMD	Displays and manages installed services.
scanreg	2	CMD	Searches Windows Registry for specified keys or values.
schemadiff	2	SCR	Compares the Active Directory scheme of two different enterprises.
sclist	2	CMD	Displays stopped and/or active services on a specified computer.
scsicontroller	2	SCR	Lists information about installed SCSI controllers (WMI).
sectemplates.msc	2	MMC	Security Template editor.
serialport	2	SCR	Lists information about a computer's serial ports (WMI).
service	2	SCR	Lists and manages services (WMI).
setedit	2	GUI	Edits chart configuration files for perform4.exe.
setprinter	3	CMD	Manages network shared printers.

Table A.7 Continued

Command	Kit	Type	Description
setspn	2	CMD	Sets Service Principal Name; repairs certain directory authentication problems.
setupmgr	2	GUI	Wizard to help construct answer files for automated installation of Windows.
setx	2	CMD	Sets environment variables.
share	2	SCR	Lists, creates, or deletes shared folders (WMI).
showacls	23	CMD	Displays net access control list (ACL) rights for a file or folder.
showgrps	2	CMD	Lists the security groups of which a specified user is a member.
showinst	2	CMD	Displays file, Registry, and .INI file changes made by a setup program (see instaler.exe).
showmbrs	2	CMD	Lists the users in a specified security group.
showperf	23	GUI	Displays performance counter raw data.
showpriv	23	CMD	Lists users and groups that have a specified privilege.
shutdown	2	CMD	Shuts down, logs off, or restarts a local or networked computer. (Note: Shutdown mode is the default; you must specify /R to cause a restart.)
sipanel	2	GUI	Displays instructions on configuring Windows 2000 to use pen input only with no keyboard.
sleep	23	CMD	Batch file utility, silently pauses for a specified number of seconds. Timeout.exe is an alternative tool.
smclient	2	CMD	Simulation component used in Terminal Server capacity planning simulations.
smconfig	2	GUI	Configures the Windows 2000 service monitor to send email notification when specified services start or stop.
snmputil	2	CMD	Lists data under specified SNMP object IDs. (Support Tools install provides a GUI version of this.)
sonar	3	CMD	Displays File Replication Service statistics and status (server tool only).
soon	2	CMD	Schedules a command to run "soon," much easier than trying to use the "at" command for this purpose.
sounddevice	2	SCR	Lists information about a computer's sound devices (WMI).
splinfo	3	CMD	Displays statistics and status of the print spooling service on a local or networked computer.
srvany	23	SVC	Runs any Windows program as a Windows service. srvany handles interaction with the service manager and runs a specified program.
srvcheck	23	CMD	Lists file shares on a specified computer along with per-user share read/write permissions.
srvinfo	23	CMD	Lists for a specified server the OS version, installed hotfixes, disk space on all drives, and status of all services.
srvinstw	2	GUI	Installs or removes a Windows service on local or remote computer.

(continues)

Table A.7 Continued

Command	Kit	Type	Description
srvmgr	23	GUI	Displays computers in a domain or workgroup; lets you view on each the use of network resources. You may disconnect users if necessary.
ssdformat	3	CMD	Creates an XML file that displays the contents of the System State Data log file (server tool only).
startup	2	SCR	Lists startup programs for a given computer; lists only programs specified in the Run Registry keys. (WMI).
su	2	CMD	Runs a command from an alternate user account. For Windows 2000 only; use runas on Windows XP.
subinacl	23	CMD	Replaces usernames and/or domain names in access control lists for files, Registry keys, and so on.
subnet_op	2	SCR	Lists, adds, and deletes subnet information in Active Directory.
suss	2	svc	Service component of su.exe; use on Windows 2000 only.
svcmon	2	svc	Service that monitors the state of other services; used with smconfig.exe.
sysdiff	2	CMD	Automated installation tool. Takes a snapshot of a computer's files and Registry settings before and after installing stuff; then creates a script to replicate the changes on target computers.
systemaccount	2	SCR	Displays information about standard system accounts like NETWORK.
tail	3	CMD	Displays the last several lines (the tail end) of a text file, for example, a log file.
takeown	2	CMD	Lets you delete old Windows installations from a multiboot system by resetting ownership of some very well hidden files and folders.
tapedrive	2	SCR	Lists information about a computer's tape drives (WMI).
tcmon	3	BF	Runs tcmon.exe when the 'tcmon' command is typed in a random directory.
tcmon	23	GUI	Traffic Control Monitor; monitors Quality of Service (QoS) networking functions.
textview	2	GUI	Text viewing and editing tool, has an Explorer folder view in the left pane and a Notepad-like text editor in the right.
thread	2	SCR	Lists all threads running on a computer (WMI).
timeit	3	CMD	Records time it takes to run a specified command.
timeout	2	CMD	Pauses execution of a batch file for a specified number of seconds. Like sleep.exe but displays a countdown, and allows user to interrupt the delay.
timethis	2	CMD	Prints time elapsed running a specified command.
timezone	23	CMD	Displays and sets current time zone.
tlist	2	CMD	Lists active tasks, tasks using a given DLL, and Windows services associated with tasks.
tlocmgr	2	GUI	Telephony Location Manager, provides task-tray icon to pop up Dialing properties and activate Phone Dialer.

Table A.7   Continued

Command	Kit	Type	Description
top	2	CMD	Console program that displays running applications in descending order of CPU usage. A text-mode GUI; makes one nostalgic for the 1980s.
totlproc	2	GUI	Program that computes total usage of all CPUs and makes the value available to Performance Monitor. Useful? Hmmm. Appears not to work anyway.
touch	2	CMD	Sets file timestamp to specified time or current time.
tpc	2	CMD	Utility to test RSVP services.
tracedmp	2	CMD	Extracts and formats Trace Log data from performance monitor or `tracelog.exe`.
traceenable	2	GUI	Enables RAS and Radius tracing.
tracelog	2	CMD	Enables and disables tracing of system components during debugging.
tsctst	3	CMD	Terminal Services Client License dump; display info on license being used by a Terminal Services Client computer.
tsinstl	2	CMD	Installs a QoS Timestamping service.
tsreg	2	GUI	Edits Terminal Service Client Registry settings (sort of a TweakUI for the TSC).
tsscalling	3	GUI	Installer for Terminal Services Scalability Planning Tools, tools for automated gathering of load information, and capacity planning analysis.
tsver	2	GUI	Tool to let Terminal Server restrict connecting Terminal Service Clients based on client version number.
typeperf	2	CMD	Displays performance data.
tzedit	2	GUI	Time Zone editor; lets you create and modify the time zones that can be selected from the Date/Time control panel.
uddicatschemeeditor	3	GUI	UDDI Services Categorization Scheme Editor; defines categorization schemes for automated gathering of Web Services resources.
uddiconfig	3	CMD	Sets UDDI Service configuration.
uddidataexport	3	GUI	Exports data from the UDDI Registry as XML.
undoinst	2	CMD	Undoes changes made by a setup program (see `instaler.exe`).
uptime	2	CMD	Displays time since a computer's last boot in (optimistically) days, hours, minutes, seconds. Optionally lists boot events, application failure events.
useraccount	2	SCR	Displays information about computer accounts: names, descriptions, password settings, and so on.
usergroup	2	SCR	Adds or deletes users from Active Directory groups; can add lists of names stored in a file.
usrmgr	23	GUI	Manages user accounts for Windows NT 4 workstations and domains.
usrstat	2	CMD	Displays user accounts and last logon date/time for each user in a specified domain.

(continues)

Table A.7 Continued

Command	Kit	Type	Description
usrtogrp	2	CMD	Adds or deletes users from domain local or domain global groups, operates on lists of names entered in a text file.
vadump	23	CMD	Describes the virtual memory space of a specified task, in great detail.
vfi	23	GUI	Records snapshot information about files to help detect changes.
vi	2	GUI	Text-based screen editor from UNIX. Quirky and very powerful.
volperf	3	CMD	Installs or uninstalls Shadow Copy performance counters.
volrest	3	CMD	Displays and restores files from shared folders protected by Shadow Copies for Shared Folders.
vrfydsk	3	CMD	Checks consistency of a FAT or NTFS disk volume. Like chkdsk but uses Shadow Copy so it can check a running system; cannot repair problems.
waitfor	2	CMD	Batch file utility, pauses until a named "signal" is received via the network. Can be used to synchronize multiple computers collaborating on some task.
wc	2	CMD	Counts characters, words, and lines in a text file or read from standard input.
where	2	CMD	Searches for files on the hard disk.
whoami	2	CMD	Displays current username, security groups, and privileges.
windiff	2	GUI	File comparison utility, displays differences between text files.
winexit	2	SAV	Logout (logs user out when system is left idle).
winhttpcertcfg	3	CMD	Imports and installs certificates and private keys.
winhttptracecfg	3	CMD	Enables or disables tracing (debugging) of the WinHTTP service.
winpolicies	3	GUI	Views and refreshes Group Policy settings for the current user and local computer.
winschk	2	CMD	Validates WINS database; can also monitor WINS replication.
winscl	2	CMD	WINS command-line shell, performs limited WINS database management.
winsta	2	GUI	Monitors users logged into Terminal Server.
wpcvp	2	GUI	Cluster Verification Utility main program.
wperf	2	GUI	Spiffy little graphical display of Performance Monitor statistics, very compact. Double-click window to show/hide menu.
wrkill	2	GUI	Displays and kills processes on a selected computer; target computer must be running rkillsrv service (see rkill.exe).
xcacls	2	CMD	Edits and displays file Access Control Lists.
xinst	2	BF	Installs RPC client on another computer over the network; may work only on Win9x clients.
xnet	2	CMD	Utility program to install and start RPC service on remote computer, used by xinst.cmd.

Services for UNIX

In the world of corporate networking and Internet Service Provider operations, the UNIX and Linux operating systems are widely used. To help Windows compete in this market arena, and to help make Windows more palatable to users and managers in a heterogeneous network environment, Microsoft has developed a set of UNIX-compatible programs and network services called Services for UNIX (SFU). The Services for UNIX package includes

- More than 350 command-line programs that UNIX users take for granted, including the Perl scripting language.
- Network services to let UNIX clients access Windows resources and vice versa.
- The Interix (Posix) subsystem, which lets native UNIX applications run on a Windows computer (remember that the Windows NT kernel can support more than one operating system interface). You can also develop your own UNIX applications, using the included gcc compiler suite.
- The X11 Windowing system.

Individuals can use SFU for free; however, it works only on Windows XP Professional, Windows XP Media Center Edition, Windows 2000 Professional, and the various Server versions. It will not install on Windows XP Home Edition.

SFU can be downloaded from www.microsoft.com/windows/sfu, and it is also distributed on the Microsoft Developers Network CDs and DVDs.

The toolkit includes command-line tools that can be run from the Windows command prompt, Windows services, and native UNIX command-line programs that must be run from a UNIX shell (the Korn and C shells are provided). Table A.8 lists the programs included with SFU version 3.5, the current version at the time this was written. The Type column indicates the type of program:

BAT	Batch file (.BAT or .CMD file).
CMD	Windows command-line program (.EXE file).
IX	Interix (UNIX) command-line program, can be run only from an Interix shell.
B/I	Program provided in both Windows batch file (.BAT file) and Interix command-line versions, so that the command can be used in either environment. The Interix version has no filename extension.
C/I	Program provided in both Windows command-line (.EXE file) and Interix command-line versions.
SCR	Script file, usually a sample illustrating a script programming technique, less often a command-line tool.
X11	X-Windows graphical application.

Table A.8   Services for UNIX 3.5 Programs

Program	Type	Description
[	IX	Evaluates an expression on the command line and sets the exit status to the resulting value.
a2p	C/I	Compiles a Perl script from an AWK script. (Even if you don't know what that means, doesn't it sound cool?)

(continues)

Table A.8 Continued

Program	Type	Description
addr	IX	Formats and displays IP addresses and network numbers.
addr2line	IX	Converts executable program address to source code line number.
alias	IX	Lists or sets command aliases.
appres	X11	Displays application resources.
ar	IX	Creates, maintains, and extracts files from 'ar' archive files.
args.wsf	SCR	Windows Script Host Perl script demo.
as	IX	GNU Assembler.
asa	IX	Interprets first character of every input line as FORTRAN carriage control and outputs ASCII control codes.
at	IX	Runs a command at a specified time.
atobm	X11	Converts ASCII text format to X11 bitmap format.
atq	IX	Lists commands scheduled to run with the 'at' command.
atrm	IX	Removes commands scheduled to be run with the 'at' command.
autodfs	CMD	Creates Windows Distributed File System links from UNIX automount map files.
awk	IX	A peculiar but powerful pattern-matching and text-manipulation scripting language.
banner	IX	Prints large block-letter banners from text specified on the command line.
basename	C/I	Returns just the filename portion of a path/filename passed on the command line.
batch	IX	Schedules a command to be run when the system is not busy.
Bc	IX	Text-input calculator; can compute numbers to arbitrary precision.
bdftopcf	X11	Converts font from Bitmap Distribution Format to Portable Compiled Format.
Bg	IX	Lets a suspended program continue running in the background (disconnected from console window).
bgjob	CMD	For users connecting via Telnet, runs a command in the background that can continue to run after your telnet session ends.
bitmap	X11	Creates simple bitmap images.
bmtoa	X11	Converts X11 bitmap format to ASCII text representation.
bp	IX	Generates new text files from boilerplate templates: scripts, source code with a cop right notice, and so on.
c++	IX	GNU C++ compiler.
c++filt	IX	Demangles C++ or Java symbol names; displays original name.
c2ph	B/I	Generates equivalent Perl structure definitions from C structure definitions.
c89	IX	Runs the gcc C compiler in C89 mode.
cal	IX	Displays a calendar.
calendar	IX	Reminder service; displays lines matching today's date; usually run upon logon.
captoinfo	IX	Displays terminfo listing for a specified termcap terminal description file.
cat	IX	Concatenates specified input file(s) to the standard output.
cat32	C/I	Like cat, but circumvents problems when mixing Interix and Windows commands on one command line.
cc	IX	C compiler and linker (gcc).
cd	IX	Changes the current working directory.

Table A.8 Continued

Program	Type	Description
chgpath	IX	Converts pathnames specified on the command line between Windows and UNIX formats.
chgrp	C/I	Changes a file's group ownership.
chmod	C/I	Changes a files read/write/execute permissions.
chown	C/I	Changes a file's user ownership.
chroot	IX	Runs a command or shell that will see a specified directory as the root directory.
chsh	IX	Changes your default (logon) shell.
ci	IX	Checks a source file into the Revision Control System (RCS).
cksum	IX	Computes and displays file checksum and size.
clear	IX	Clears the terminal window (like DOS cls).
cmp	IX	Compares files, reports differences.
co	IX	Checks a source file out of RCS.
col	IX	Removes reverse line feeds and tabs from input; used to filter output of nroff or tbl.
column	IX	Formats input text lines into columns.
comm	IX	Displays or removes lines common to two files.
command	IX	Runs specified command, or determines what program a command would run.
compress	IX	Compresses files. On Interix, compress and gzip are the same program.
config.pl	SCR	Updates the perl interpreter `config.pm` file.
configPPM.pl	SCR	Updates the Perl Package Manager configuration file.
cp	C/I	Copies files.
cpio	IX	Copies files to or from cpio or ar format archives files on disk or tape.
cpp	IX	C preprocessor, interprets `#include`, `#ifdef`, and other directives.
cron	C/I	Manages the Interix task scheduler service (daemon).
crontab	C/I	Manages a user's crontab (Interix task scheduler) table entries.
csh	IX	The standard UNIX C shell command-line interpreter.
csh.bat	BAT	Runs the Interix C shell.
csplit	IX	Splits input file(s) into smaller pieces based on embedded text delimiters or line numbers.
ctags	IX	Extracts the location of functions defined in C, Pascal, FORTRAN, yacc, lex, or LISP source code; output is used by vi editor.
cut	C/I	Extracts parts of each line of input files, writes results to standard output.
date	C/I	Sets or displays the system time and date.
dc	IX	Reverse Polish arbitrary-precision calculator.
dd	IX	File copy utility primarily used to block or deblock files to or from magnetic tape; can perform EBCDIC conversion.
df	IX	Displays amount of free disk space.
diff	C/I	Compares two text files, displays the differences.
diff3	IX	Compares three versions of a file and reports differences.
dig	IX	Domain Name System (DNS) diagnostic tool, queries DNS servers directly.

(continues)

Table A.8 Continued

Program	Type	Description
dircmp	IX	Compares two directories.
dirname	C/I	Displays just the directory portion of a filename specified on the command line.
dnsquery	IX	Domain Name System (DNS) diagnostic tool, uses local resolver.
dos2unix	CMD	Converts line separators in text files from Windows format (CR+LF) to UNIX format (LF only).
dprofpp	B/I	Displays profile data collected from a Perl program's execution.
du	C/I	Displays disk usage statistics.
echo	IX	Echoes command-line arguments.
ed	IX	Simple line-oriented text editor. Not very user-friendly but can be useful in scripts.
editres	X11	X11 Toolkit resource editor.
egrep	C/I	Extended version of the grep text pattern matching utility.
elvis	IX	Variant of vi, can be used instead of nvi.
elvrec	IX	Recovers file edited by elvis after a system or editor crash.
env	IX	Sets or displays environment variables.
ex	IX	Powerful text editor, same as vi but defaults to line-oriented mode.
exetype.bat	BAT	Sets a given program for command-line or Windows execution mode.
expand	IX	Converts tabs to spaces.
expr	IX	Evaluates expressions on command line and displays result.
FALSE	IX	Returns exit status 0.
fc	IX	Lists, edits, or reissues previously entered commands (Korn shell).
fg	IX	Resumes a suspended program in foreground mode (connected to console window).
fgrep	C/I	Fixed-string version of the grep text pattern matching utility.
file	IX	Determines the type of a specified file.
fileinfo	IX	Displays information about executable files.
find	IX	Scans a directory and its subdirectories for specified files.
find2perl	B/I	Compiles UNIX "Find" utility command lines into Perl scripts.
finger	IX	Looks up information about a specified user via a finger server.
flip	IX	Converts text file line endings between DOS (CR-LF), UNIX (LF), and Apple (CR) formats.
fmt	IX	Formats input text by collecting words into lines of about 65–75 characters.
fold	IX	Folds long text lines into shorter lines for easier reading.
fsinfo	X11	Displays X11 server information.
fslsfonts	X11	Lists X11 fonts.
fstobdf	X11	Reads a font and creates a Bitmap Distribution Format file.
ftp	IX	File Transfer Protocol (FTP) utility. Supports passive mode.
g++	IX	GNU C++ compiler.
g77	IX	GNU Fortran-77 compiler.
gawk	IX	GNU implementation of the AWK pattern matching and text-processing interpreter.
gcc	IX	GNU C/C++ compiler.

Table A.8   Continued

Program	Type	Description
gccbug	IX	Tool to help report compiler bugs to the gcc developers.
gcov	IX	GNU C coverage tool; identifies what sections of a program are never executed.
gdb	IX	GNU debugger.
gencat	IX	Compiles national language catalogs into binary format.
GET	IX	Fetches a file from a web server.
getconf	IX	Displays system parameters such as maximum file path length.
getopt	IX	Parses a command line into individual components, validates syntax.
getopts	IX	Parses a command line into individual components, validates syntax.
grep	C/I	Text pattern matching utility.
gunzip	IX	Uncompresses files packed with gzip, zip, or pack.
gzip	IX	Compresses files. Gzip, pack, and zip use different algorithms.
h2ph	B/I	Generates equivalent Perl structure definitions from C structure definitions.
h2xs	B/I	Generates Perl extensions to access C structures.
head	C/I	Displays the first few lines of a text file.
helloworld.wsf	SCR	Windows Script Host Perl script demo.
hexdump	IX	Displays binary data in ascii, decimal, or hex format.
host	IX	Looks up hostnames in the Domain Name Service (DNS).
hostname	IX	Displays the name of the local computer.
hoststat	IX	Displays status information about the sendmail mail server.
iceauth	X11	Edits and displays Inter-Client Exchange (ICE) authentication records.
ico	X11	Displays an animated icosahedron or other polyhedron.
iconv	C/I	Converts text files from one code page to another.
id	IX	Displays the user and group names and numbers.
ident	IX	Displays identification information placed in files by the Revision Control System (RCS).
igetty	IX	Configures serial ports and if specified, starts login shells on them.
IISScriptMap.pl	SCR	Adds file extension mappings to the IIS web server.
imake	X11	Creates a makefile for an X11 application from a template file.
inetd	IX	Internet service daemon, starts host services when incoming requests are received and validated.
infocmp	IX	Compares or prints terminfo descriptions.
infotocap	IX	Converts a terminfo terminal capability description into termcap format.
init	IX	Runs Interix services upon startup.
insight	IX	GNU debugger.
install	IX	Copies files to a target directory.
instclus.cmd	BAT	Installs NFS share resources on a Windows Server Cluster.
ipcrm	IX	Deletes an Interprocess Communications (IPC) resource.
ipcs	IX	Reports status of IPC objects.
ispell	IX	Interactive spell checker for text files.

(continues)

Table A.8   Continued

Program	Type	Description
jobs	IX	Lists active tasks associated with a given Interix shell command window or telnet session.
join	IX	Combines lines from input files based on matching fields, as a relational database's join function would.
kill	IX	Terminates programs.
ksh	IX	Korn command-line interpreter (shell).
ksh.bat	BAT	Runs the Interix Korn shell.
last	IX	List last logon time for users or last user of a given terminal.
lbxproxy	X11	Low bandwidth X proxy.
ld	IX	GNU linker, produces executable files from object and library files.
less	IX	Displays text one screen at a time. Has more features than more utility.
lessecho	IX	Expands wildcards on command line as "echo" would but puts quotes around fil names that contain spaces.
lesskey	IX	Modifies mapping of keys to file manipulation commands for the less utility.
lex	IX	Generates C source code for a lexical analyzer from a specification file.
liblock	IX	Marks a library module as deprecated; warnings are issued if a user attempts to link against it.
line	IX	Reads and echoes one input line from the standard input to the standard output, see read.
listres	X11	Lists resources in widgets.
ln	C/I	Create hard links—multiple directory entries for a single file, with different names or in different folders.
lndir	X11	Creates a directory tree of links to a directory tree of "real" files.
locale	IX	Displays national language locale information.
localedef	IX	Adds locale mappings to the system.
logger	IX	Adds entries to log file `/var/adm/log/logger`.
login	IX	Initializes a user session.
loginenv	IX	Creates a new logon session.
logname	IX	Displays your logon name.
lp	IX	Sends a text file to a printer; like the Windows `print.exe` command.
ls	IX	Displays and formats directory listings (like the DOS `dir` command).
lwp-download	B/I	Downloads large files using HTTP given the file's URL.
lwp-mirror	B/I	Updates a mirror copy of a file or entire website via HTTP.
lwp-request	B/I	Simple HTTP command-line tool; can fetch or post files.
lwp-rget	B/I	Fetches files from a website recursively via HTTP.
m4	IX	A macro language preprocessor.
mail	IX	A simple text-based email program.
mailq	IX	Lists mail messages waiting for delivery.
mailx	IX	A simple text-based email program.
make	IX	Builds programs based on dependency specifications.

Table A.8   Continued

Program	Type	Description
makedepend	X11	Generates dependency lists from C source files, writing results to a makefile.
makedev	IX	Creates special (device) files.
makeg	X11	Runs make with options to create a debugging version of the application.
man	IX	Displays online documentation for Interix programs, library routines, services, and file formats.
mapadmin	C/I	Manages Windows/UNIX username mapping.
maze	X11	Creates and solves mazes.
merge	IX	Merges two sets of file changes into a single file.
mergelib	X11	Merges object libraries.
mkdir	C/I	Creates a directory (folder).
mkdirhier	X11	Creates directories from path specifications, creating parent directories if necessary.
mkfifo	IX	Creates a FIFO special file (named pipe).
mkfontdir	X11	Indexes X fonts.
mknod	IX	Creates regular files, special files, or directories.
more	C/I	Displays text files one screen at a time.
mount	CMD	Mounts (attaches to) NFS network shares.
mpack	IX	Packs one or more files into a MIME mail message format.
mt	IX	Manipulates a magnetic tape drive (usually SCSI-attached).
munpack	IX	Unpacks a MIME mail message file into its component files.
mv	IX	Moves or renames files.
mvwtmpx	IX	Renames the wtmpx (user logon record) file and starts a new one.
newaliases	IX	Rebuilds the mail alias file.
newgrp	IX	Changes your effective user group.
nfsadmin	C/I	Manages Server for NFS, Client for NFS, and Gateway for NFS network services.
nfsmount	IX	Version of mount, supports NFS file mounts.
nfsonly	CMD	Enables/disables NFS-only mode for NFS shares.
nfsshare	C/I	Manages NFS shared folders.
nfsstat	C/I	Displays or resets NFS server statistics.
nfsumount	IX	Version of umount, supports NFS file mounts.
nice	C/I	Runs a program at a specified priority level.
nis2ad	C/I	Imports Network Information Service (NIS) maps into Active Directory.
nisadmin	C/I	Manages the Network Information Service (NIS) service.
nismap	C/I	Manages Network Information Service (NIS) maps.
nl	IX	Prepends line numbers to the input text file(s).
nm	IX	Lists symbol names from compiled object files.
nohup	IX	Runs a program so that it will not be terminated if the shell is closed.
notepad.wsf	SCR	Windows Script Host Perl script demo.
nslookup	IX	Domain Name System (DNS) diagnostic tool, queries DNS servers directly, a predecessor to dig.

(continues)

Table A.8 Continued

Program	Type	Description
nsupdate	IX	Updates DNS servers supporting dynamic update.
ntpath2posix	IX	Converts pathname specified on the command line from Windows to UNIX format.
nvi	IX	A variant of the vi text editor.
objcopy	IX	Copies compiled object files, making alterations along the way.
objdump	IX	Displays information about compiled object files.
oclock	X11	Analog clock.
od	C/I	Dumps binary files in octal, decimal, hex, or ascii format.
pack	IX	Compresses files. Gzip, pack, and zip use different algorithms.
passwd	IX	Changes your Interix password.
paste	C/I	Joins lines from each specified input file creating a tab-delimited file.
patch	IX	Applies diff changes to a text file, creating an updated version.
pathchk	IX	Verifies that a path name is portable and legal.
pax	IX	Enhanced version of the tar file archiving tool.
pcat	IX	Displays files stored in a pack compressed file.
pdomain	IX	Displays the computer's principal domain.
perl	C/I	Perl scripting language interpreter.
perl5.6.0	CMD	Runs this specific version of the Perl interpreter.
perlbug	B/I	Used to report bugs in the Perl core modules to the modules' developers.
perlcc	B/I	Compiles Perl scripts into executable programs.
perldoc	B/I	Extracts documentation from the Perl program library.
perlglob.bat	BAT	Expands wildcards into lists of filenames; used when running Perl scripts from the Windows command line.
pg	IX	Displays text one screen at a time. Has fewer features than "less."
ping	IX	Sends ICMP packets to a network host; diagnoses network connectivity.
pl2bat.bat	BAT	Wraps a Perl script in a Windows .BAT batch file so it can be conveniently run from the command line. Most of the .BAT files in this table were created using this tool.
pl2pm	B/I	Converts Perl scripts to Perl module files.
pod2html	B/I	Converts Perl .POD documentation files into HTML.
pod2latex	B/I	Converts Perl .POD documentation files into LaTeX, a non-WYSIWYG typesetting language.
pod2man	B/I	Converts Perl .POD documentation files into UNIX .MAN documentation format.
pod2text	B/I	Converts Perl .POD documentation files into plain ASCII text.
pod2usage	B/I	Prints the Usage information from Perl .POD documentation format.
podchecker	B/I	Validates the syntax of Perl .POD documentation.
podselect	B/I	Prints selected portions of a Perl .POD document.
popper	IX	Post Office Protocol (POP3) server.
posixpath2nt	IX	Converts pathname specified on the command line from UNIX to Windows format.
POST	IX	Posts a file to a web server.
ppm.bat	BAT	Runs the Perl Package Manager.

Table A.8   Continued

Program	Type	Description
ppm.pl	SCR	Perl Package Manager; downloads and manages Perl add-on modules.
pr	IX	Paginates text files for printing.
printenv	CMD	Displays the values of environment variables.
printf	C/I	Formats command-line arguments.
protoize	IX	Converts C source function prototypes from K&R format to ANSI format.
proxymngr	X11	Manages X proxy services.
ps	C/I	Displays information about running processes.
pstat	IX	Displays process status.
pstruct	B/I	Displays structure offset data extracted from C source code.
psxoffset	IX	Lists or sets POSIX domain offsets.
psxrun	C/I	Runs an Interix program without a connected terminal or console window; for example, X11 programs or Interix-based services.
purgestat	IX	Purges expired messages from sendmail's queues.
puzzle	X11	Tile-shifting game.
pwd	C/I	Displays the current working directory.
ranlib	IX	Provides compatibility with old UNIX make files; does nothing.
rcp	IX	Copies files to a remote system.
rcs	IX	Creates and manages files for the Revision Control System (RCS).
rcsdiff	IX	Displays differences between versions of files in the RCS.
rcsmerge	IX	Applies changes made to an earlier version of an RCS-managed file into a newer modified version.
rdist	IX	Distributes files to multiple remote systems.
rdistd	IX	A component program used by rdist.
read	IX	Reads a line of input from the standard output; used in shell scripts to get user input.
regpwd	IX	Stores a protected copy of your password for use by cron, rlogin, and rsh.
regread.wsf	SCR	Example showing use of Perl under Windows Script Host.
renice	C/I	Modifies the priority of running processes.
reset	IX	Resets your terminal window if, for example, echo gets turned off.
resize	X11	Sets termcap entries to reflect current window size.
rlog	IX	Displays log messages about RCS-managed files.
rlogin	IX	Opens a terminal session on a remote computer.
rm	IX	Deletes files.
rmdir	C/I	Removes a subdirectory.
rpcgen	IX	Generates C linkage source code from a Remote Procedure Call specification.
rpcinfo	C/I	Displays information about and tests Remote Procedure Call services.
rsh	IX	Opens a terminal session on a remote computer.
rshpswd	CMD	Sets your remote shell service password.
rstart	X11	Sample remote start application for rsh protocol.

(continues)

Table A.8   Continued

Program	Type	Description
rstartd	IX	Sample implementation of an rsh remote start helper.
runperl.bat	BAT	Used to run Perl scripts from the command line; read the file for details.
runwin32	IX	Runs a Windows (Win32) program. The Interix shells can run Win32 programs directly, but runwin32 automatically searches the Windows PATH.
s2p	B/I	Compiles a Perl script from a sed (stream editor) script.
script	IX	Creates a transcript of an interactive terminal session.
sdiff	C/I	Compares two text files or directories; displays the differences side-by-side.
search.bat	BAT	Enhanced grep utility.
sed	C/I	Stream editor; applies changes to text line by line, from a file or pipeline.
sendmail	IX	Mail delivery server.
service	IX	Manages an Interix application running as a Windows service.
sessreg	X11	Manages user logon auditing records.
sfuadmin	CMD	Displays SFU version, can also set User Name Mapping server.
sfumgmt.msc	MSC	Services for UNIX Management MMC snap-in.
sh	IX	Default command interpreter shell (same as ksh).
showenv.wsf	SCR	Windows Script Host Perl script demo.
showfont	X11	Lists X fonts.
showmount	C/I	Displays file systems exported by an NFS server.
size	IX	Displaysv information about program section sizes from compiled object files.
sleep	IX	Pauses for a specified number of seconds; used in scripts.
smproxy	X11	X session manager proxy.
sort	IX	Sorts or merges text files line by line.
specialfolder.wsf	SCR	Windows Script Host Perl script demo.
spell	IX	Lists unrecognized (potentially misspelled) words found in a text file.
splain	B/I	Expands upon diagnostics issued by the Perl compiler and interpreter (from the phrase "'Splain it to me, Lucy").
split	C/I	Breaks a large text file into smaller files of at most 1,000 lines.
sqlserver.wsf	SCR	Windows Script Host Perl script demo.
sqlserverevents.wsf	SCR	Windows Script Host Perl script demo.
ssimda	IX	Delivers a mail message to a local mailbox (file on the local computer).
startx	X11	Starts the X window system.
strerror	IX	Displays text description of an Interix (UNIX) error code.
strings	C/I	Displays any printable character strings found in a binary file.
strip	IX	Deletes symbols from compiled object code files.
strsignal	IX	Displays text description of an Interix (UNIX) signal number.
stty	IX	Changes terminal window characteristics.
su	IX	Switches user identity (like Windows runas).
sum	IX	Obsolete version of cksum.
syslogd	IX	Logging service, receives messages from network devices and services and records messages in a log file.

Table A.8   Continued

Program	Type	Description
tail	C/I	Displays the last few lines of a file. The -f option prints additional lines as they are added, very useful for monitoring log files.
talk	IX	Inter-user text chat utility.
tar	IX	Archiving utility; packs files into or extracts files from a single file; a subset of pax.
tcsh	IX	The C shell command-line interpreter with filename completion and command-line editing enhancements.
tee	C/I	Inserted into a command pipeline, saves a copy of the data passing through the pipeline.
telnet	IX	Establishes an interactive session on a remote computer, device or network service.
test	IX	Evaluates an expression on the command line and sets the exit status to the resulting value.
test.wsf	SCR	Windows Script Host Perl script demo.
tftp	IX	Trivial file transfer protocol client.
tic	IX	Compiles terminfo source files into a binary format.
time	IX	Runs a command and displays elapsed and effective CPU time.
tip	IX	Connects to a remote system through a serial adapter.
tnadmin	CMD	Manages the Telnet server.
toe	IX	Displays the terminfo database.
touch	IX	Updates or sets file access or modification times.
tput	IX	Displays or sets terminal capability values.
tr	C/I	Used in a command pipeline; substitutes or deletes specified characters.
TRUE	IX	Returns exit status 1.
truss	IX	Runs a command and displays its system calls and signals.
tset	IX	Sets terminal characteristics upon logon.
tsort	IX	Sorts and formats text describing a directed graph.
tty	IX	Displays the name of the current terminal device.
twm	X11	Window manager for X.
tzselect	IX	Sets the local time zone.
umask	IX	Displays or sets the default file creation mask (read/write/execute attributes given to new files).
umount	CMD	Deletes NFS network mount points.
unalias	IX	Removes aliases defined in the command-line shell.
uname	C/I	Displays information about the local computer's hardware and software environment.
uncompress	IX	Uncompresses files packed with compress.
unexpand	IX	Replaces strings of spaces in a text file with tabs.
unifdef	IX	Interprets and removes #ifdef sections from source code files.
uniq	C/I	Filters out repeated lines in its input file(s).
unix2dos	CMD	Converts line separators in text files from UNIX format (LF only) to Windows format (CR+LF).
unixpath2win	IX	Converts the UNIX file path specified on the command line to Windows format.

(continues)

Table A.8 Continued

Program	Type	Description
unpack	IX	Uncompresses files packed with pack.
unprotoize	IX	Converts C source function prototypes from ANSI format to K&R format.
unvis	IX	Converts visible text representation back to original format; see "vis."
unzip	IX	Uncompresses files packed with zip (use this on .ZIP files from Windows and DOS).
uudecode	C/I	Decodes a uuencoded text file into its original binary representation.
uuencode	C/I	Encodes a binary file into a text format suitable for emailing or other forms of transmission.
vi	IX	Full-screen character-mode editor; same as ex in screen mode.
view	IX	Same as vi but read-only mode is enabled by default; used to peruse files with less risk of saving changes.
viewres	X11	Athena Widget class browser.
vis	IX	Displays a text file with non-printing characters displayed in a visible text format.
wait	C/I	Pauses until a specified program has completed; useful for batch files.
wat	IX	Runs the Windows at command from an Interix shell. (Generally, any Windows command can be run from an Interix shell. These 'wxxx' commands are provided for the cases where there is an Interix command with the same name as a Windows command.)
wc	IX	Displays count of words, lines, and characters in text files.
wdate	IX	Runs the Windows date command from an Interix shell.
wecho	IX	Runs the Windows echo command.
wexit	IX	Runs the Windows exit command.
wexpand	IX	Runs the Windows expand command.
wfc	IX	Runs the Windows fc command.
wfind	IX	Runs the Windows find command.
wfinger	IX	Runs the Windows finger command.
wftp	IX	Runs the Windows ftp command.
which	CMD	Scans the PATH to identify which .EXE file will be run when its name is typed on the command line.
who	IX	Displays a list of logged-on users.
whoami	IX	Displays your logon name.
whostname	IX	Runs the Windows hostname command from an Interix shell.
winpath2unix	IX	Converts the Windows file path specified on the command line to UNIX format.
wmkdir	IX	Runs the Windows mkdir command from an Interix shell.
wmore	IX	Runs the Windows more command.
wnslookup	IX	Runs the Windows nslookup command.
wperl	GUI	Runs a Perl script as a Windows application, not as a console mode program.
wping	IX	Runs the Windows ping command.
wprint	IX	Runs the Windows print command.
wrcp	IX	Runs the Windows rcp command.
wrmdir	IX	Runs the Windows rmdir command.
wrsh	IX	Runs the Windows rsh command.

Table A.8 Continued

Program	Type	Description
wset	IX	Runs the Windows `set` command.
wsort	IX	Runs the Windows `sort` command.
wtelnet	IX	Runs the Windows `telnet` command.
wtftp	IX	Runs the Windows `tftp` command.
wtime	IX	Runs the Windows `time` command.
wtype	IX	Runs the Windows `type` command.
wvisible	IX	Tests whether the current window station is visible (it would not be if the current process was running as a service, or was hidden due to Fast user Switching).
wwrite	IX	Runs the Windows `write` command from an Interix shell.
x11perf	X11	X server performance test program.
x11perfcomp	X11	Compares results of x11perf test runs.
xargs	C/I	Runs a specified command with command-line arguments read from the standard input.
xauth	X11	Manages authentication database for X server.
xbiff	X11	Notifies you of incoming mail.
xcalc	X11	Calculator.
xclipboard	X11	Shared Clipboard tool for X11 applications.
xclock	X11	Analog/digital clock.
xcmsdb	X11	Xlib Screen Color Characterization Data utility.
xcmstest	X11	XCMS application tester.
xconsole	X11	Displays X11 system console messages.
xcutsel	X11	Tool to help manage cut and paste operations between X11 applications.
xditview	X11	Displays formatted output from ditroff.
xdm	X11	X11 display manager.
xdpyinfo	X11	Displays X11 server capabilities.
xedit	X11	Text editor.
xev	X11	Debugging tool, displays events for a given window.
xeyes	X11	Displays a pair of eyes that follow the mouse cursor.
xfd	X11	Displays all characters in an X font.
xfindproxy	X11	Locates X11 proxy services.
xfontsel	X11	Displays and selects fonts.
xfs	X11	X11 font server; usually started automatically.
xfwp	X11	X11 firewall proxy.
xgc	X11	Demonstrates X11 graphical capabilities.
xhost	X11	Manages list of hosts allowed to connect to X11 server.
xieperf	X11	Exercises XIE protocol.
xinit	X11	Initializes and starts X11 server when not started by init.
xkbbell	X11	Manages beep and keyboard feedback.
xkbcomp	X11	Compiles keyboard layout descriptions for X Windows.

(continues)

Table A.8   Continued

Program	Type	Description
xkbevd	X11	X11 keyboard event daemon (service).
xkbprint	X11	Prints a description of an X11 keyboard layout file.
xkbvleds	X11	Virtual LED indicators for keyboard.
xkbwatch	X11	Unknown.
xkill	X11	Kills an X11 client program.
xlogo	X11	Displays the X11 Windows logo.
xlsatoms	X11	Lists X11 protocol atoms (defined strings).
xlsclients	X11	Lists active X11 client applications.
xlsfonts	X11	Lists X11 fonts.
xmag	X11	Magnifies selected part of X11 screen.
xman	X11	Displays manual pages.
Xmark	X11	Summarizes "x11perf" results.
xmkmf	X11	Creates a makefile for an X11 application from an imakefile.
xmodmap	X11	Modifies X11 server keyboard maps.
xon	X11	Starts the X11 window system on a remote computer.
xprop	X11	Displays properties of a selected window or font.
xrdb	X11	X11 server resource database managers; sets user preferences at startup.
xrefresh	X11	Refreshes X11 screen.
xset	X11	Sets user preferences for X11.
xsetroot	X11	Sets X11 window background design.
xsm	X11	X11 window session manager.
xstdcmap	X11	Defines color mapping for X11.
xterm	X11	X11 terminal emulator and command prompt window.
xuctblgen	X11	Sets X11 locale.
xwd	X11	Captures image of X11 window.
xwininfo	X11	Displays information about X11 windows.
xwud	X11	Displays images captured by "xwd".
yacc	IX	Generates C source code for an LR parser from a grammar specification file.
yearistype	IX	Tests whether the current year is leap, even, odd, or a US presidential election year.
ypcat	CMD	Dumps a Network Information Service (NIS) map database.
ypclear	CMD	Clears the NIS map cache.
ypmatch	CMD	Displays NIS data for specified keys.
yppush	CMD	Forces updating of slave NIS servers following an update to the master.
zcat	IX	Displays files stored in a zip compressed file.
zdump	IX	Lists information from the time zone database.
zic	IX	Compiles time zone definitions.
zip	IX	Compresses files. Gzip, pack, and zip use different algorithms. This is the one commonly used on DOS and Windows systems.

APPENDIX B

Windows Command Reference

Programs Provided with Windows

This appendix lists all of the programs installed by Windows Setup on Windows 98, Windows Me, Windows 2000, Windows XP Home Edition, Windows XP Professional, and Windows XP Media Center Edition. It also lists programs installed by Windows Update and Automatic Updates.

The purpose of this appendix is to help you identify programs that you find running in your Task Manager window, and to let you browse for interesting standard programs that you might not be aware of. The programs fall into several categories:

- Graphical User Interface (GUI) programs, such as Notepad and Internet Explorer. GUI programs are delivered as executable files with an .EXE filename extension.

- Command-line (console) utilities such as ping and dir. Most command-line programs are delivered as executable (.EXE and .COM) files, with the exception of a few script files (.VBS and .JS), and some "built-in" commands that are handled directly by the Windows command prompt processor (cmd.exe on Windows 2000 and XP, command.com on Windows 98 and ME).

- Control Panel applets, screensavers, and Microsoft Management Console (MMC) snap-ins. The files have corresponding filename extensions: .SCR for screensavers, .MSC for MMC snap-ins, and .CPL for Control Panel applets.

- Components such as device drivers, Windows services, and programs used solely as "helper" components of other programs. These programs may have a filename extension that makes them look like standard programs, but they are not useful on their own.

This appendix does *not* list the optional programs installed from the \TOOLS folder on the Windows Setup CD-ROM, although it does lists a few subcomponents of these tools that end up under your \windows folder. The tools themselves are listed in Appendix A, "Windows Tool Reference."

Running Applications and Components

Applications can be started in the following ways:

- GUI and command-line programs can be run from shortcuts, from Windows Explorer, or, if they are in a folder listed in the PATH environment variable, by typing their name at the prompt in a Command Prompt window.

- Script files can be run from the command line by name, or can be forced to run in GUI or command-line mode with the wscript or cscript commands, respectively. For more information on scripting, see Chapter 9, "Windows Commands and Scripting."

- MMC snap-ins can be run using the start command, for example

```
start compmgmt.msc
```

or by installing them into an MMC panel. On Windows XP and 2000, you can run an MMC snap-in with Administrator privileges by typing the command

```
runas /user:Administrator "cmd /c xxxx.msc"
```

- Control Panels applets can be run from the Control Panel or from the command line, as in this example:

```
control timedate.cpl
```

On Windows 2000 and XP, you can run a Control Panel applet with Administrator privileges by typing the command

```
runas /user:Administrator "control xxxx.cpl"
```

This technique does not work with `ncpa.cpl`, however.

- Screensavers can be configured and previewed (respectively) using the following commands:

```
start xxxx.scr /c
start xxxx.scr /s
```

- Device drivers and services cannot be run directly, but are managed by tools such as the Services MMC snap-in (`services.msc`) or the `net start` command-line utility. Some Windows services are packaged as `.DLL` files and are executed by the `svchost.exe` program. Services are discussed in Chapter 4.

Command-Line Syntax

To use a command-line utility, you have to know its particular command-line syntax; that is, you have to know how to add options, filenames, and other control information to the command line. To get help for a given command—let's call it *xxx*—there are four things to try, in this order:

- Search for *xxx* in the Windows Help and Support Center.
- Type **xxx -? | more** in a command prompt window.
- Type **help xxx | more** in a command prompt window.
- Perform a Google search for `Windows command xxx`.

Note

The **more** command is used to keep text from scrolling out of view if there's more than one screen. If some text is displayed and then the printout stops, press the spacebar to display the next screen.

There's no way to tell beforehand which one or more of these methods will work, so you should try all four. For more information on using command-line programs, see Chapter 9.

Legend

In the listings that follow, the Program column lists the names of program files installed in the various standard Windows folders. The filename's extension indicates the type of program file:

Extension	Description
.BAT	Batch file (a text file containing a sequence of commands)
.COM	MS-DOS executable program
.CPL	Control Panel applet (actually a dynamic link library loaded and used by `control.exe`)
.DLL	Dynamic link library (not directly executable, these are used by `.EXE` programs to gain added functionality)
.EXE	Windows GUI program, Windows command-line program, or MS-DOS program
.JS	JavaScript script (a text file containing a program written in the JavaScript language)
.MSC	MMC snap-in (actually a dynamic link library or XML file meant to be loaded and used by `mmc.exe`)
.SCR	Screensaver (actually a standard Windows executable file)
.SYS	MS-DOS device driver
.VBS	VBScript script (a text file containing a program written in the VBScript language)

The OS column indicates the operating system(s) with which the program comes:

OS	Operating System Versions
8	Windows 98
E	Windows ME
2	Windows 2000 Professional
H	Windows XP Home Edition
P	Windows XP Professional
M	Windows XP Media Center Edition

The "Type" column indicates the general category into which the program falls:

Type	Description	Directly executable by the user?
BF	Batch file	Yes
CMD	Command-line (console) program	Yes
DOS	MS-DOS application or driver	Yes
GUI	Graphical User Interface (windowed) application	Yes
SCR	Script file, handled by Windows Script Host (cscript or wscript)	Yes
cmp	Component of some other application	No
drv	Windows device driver	No
ndu	Not directly usable, meant to assist some other application	No
svc	Windows service (Services are discussed in Chapter 4)	No

In the Description column, Source indicates the source of a program if it is not installed by Windows Setup. Some programs can have several alternative sources. For example, the .NET Framework may be installed by a Service Pack, Windows Update, a download from microsoft.com, or as part of a third-party application.

Filename	OS	Type	Description
401comupd.exe	E	CMD	Installs Common Controls library (comctl32.dll) version 4.01; probably left over from setup or Windows Update
accstat.exe	8E	ndu	Accessibility status indicator
accwiz.exe	8E2HPM	GUI	Accessibility Wizard
actmovie.exe	8E2HPM	cmp	Direct Show setup tool
addreg.exe	8E	ndu	Sets Internationalization parameters
admin.exe	2HPM	cmp	FrontPage Server Extensions component
adsutil.vbs	2P	SCR	Manages IIS server through ADSI (sample script)
agentsvr.exe	E2HPM	cmp	Microsoft Agent (animated assistant) component
agtcore.js	EHPM	cmp	Component of "Out-of-box" experience, initial setup wizard
agtscrp2.js	HPM	cmp	Windows help script component
agtscrpt.js	EHPM	cmp	Component of "Out-of-box" experience, initial setup wizard
ahui.exe	HPM	cmp	Application Compatibility Wizard component

Filename	OS	Type	Description
`alg.exe`	HPM	svc	Application Layer Gateway Service—Provides support for third-party protocol plug-ins for ICS and ICF
`annclist.exe`	8E	ndu	Component of TV Viewer
`annui.exe`	8E	GUI	Announcement manager—configures filters for data being broadcast through the TV system
`ansi.sys`	8E2HPM	DOS	ANSI Screen driver for MS-DOS subsystem
`aolsetup.exe`	8E	GUI	Launches AOL software installer located on Windows 98 setup CD
`append.exe`	2HPM	DOS	Makes directories appear "local" (archaic)
`arcldr.exe`	2	ndu	Used by Windows boot process
`arcsetup.exe`	2	ndu	Used by Windows boot process
`arp.exe`	8E2HPM	CMD	Displays and edits ARP cache (TCP/IP)
`asd.exe`	8E	ndu	Automatic Skip Driver Agent tool, inhibits device drivers causing Windows boot to fail (see Microsoft Knowledge Base article #186588)
`aspnet_regiis.exe`	2PM	CMD	Used to maintain correct linkage between different installed versions of .NET Framework and ASP.NET applications installed under IIS (source: .NET Framework)
`aspnet_state.exe`	2HPM	svc	Holds session state data for ASP.NET web-based applications (source: .NET Framework)
`aspnet_wp.exe`	2PM	cmp	ASP.NET runtime process—CGI application that runs ASP.NET web-based applications on behalf of IIS (source: .NET Framework)
`asr_fmt.exe`	PM	CMD	Automated System Recovery backup and restore
`asr_ldm.exe`	PM	CMD	Automated System Recovery Logical Disk manager
`asr_pfu.exe`	PM	cmp	Automated System Recovery component
`at.exe`	2HPM	CMD	Schedules program to run automatically (obsolete)
`atmadm.exe`	E2HPM	CMD	Displays ATM Call Manager statistics
`attrib.exe`	8E2HPM	CMD	Displays and sets file/folder attributes
`attsetup.exe`	8E	GUI	Launches AT&T Worldnet Internet access software located on Windows 98 setup CD
`audioconverter.exe`	M	GUI	Windows Audio Converter, converts music files between different encoding formats (source: Standard on MCE, otherwise Plus! for Windows XP)
`auditusr.exe`	HPM	CMD	Manages per-user audit policy settings
`author.exe`	2HPM	cmp	FrontPage Server Extensions component (CGI application)
`autochk.exe`	E2HPM	cmp	Checks and repairs Windows File Systems
`autoconv.exe`	2HPM	cmp	Automates the file system conversion during reboots
`autoexec.bat`	8EP	DOS	Batch file executed upon Windows startup
`autofmt.exe`	2HPM	cmp	Automates the file format process during reboots
`autolfn.exe`	2HPM	cmp	Used for formatting long filenames
`awadpr32.exe`	8E	CMD	Fax Printer icon installer (source: TOOLS\OLDWIN95 Windows Messaging & Fax)

(continues)

Filename	OS	Type	Description
awfxex32.exe	8E	cmp	Microsoft Fax component
awsnto32.exe	8E	cmp	Microsoft Fax component (source: TOOLS\OLDWIN95 Windows Messaging & Fax)
basicfunctions.js	M	cmp	Media Center Edition help component
bckgzm.exe	EHPM	GUI	Internet Backgammon
blastcln.exe	HPM	CMD	MSBLAST virus removal utility (installed by Windows Update)
bootcfg.exe	PM	CMD	Modifies the BOOT.INI configuration file
bootdisk.bat	8E	BF	Creates a Windows 98 Startup boot disk (boots DOS)
bootok.exe	2HPM	CMD	Boot acceptance application for Registry
bootvrfy.exe	2HPM	CMD	Notifies the system that startup was successful
bpcpost.exe	8E	cmp	TV Viewer component
bpcunpak.exe	8E	ndu	Component of TV Viewer
cabbit.exe	E	cmp	System Restore component
cacls.exe	2HPM	CMD	Clears the command prompt window
cafixweb.exe	2	ndu	Service pack installation component, probably targeted at Windows 2000 Server rather than Pro
calc.exe	8E2HPM	GUI	Calculator accessory
caspol.exe	8E2PM	CMD	ASP.NET Code Access Security Policy tool; sets security policy for ASP.NET applications (assemblies) (source: .NET Framework)
cb32.exe	8E2HPM	GUI	NetMeeting component, invokes Chat window
cchat.exe	8E	GUI	Microsoft Chat (no longer useable)
cdlm.exe	M	GUI	CD Label Maker (source: Standard on MCE, otherwise Plus! for Windows XP)
cdplayer.exe	8E2	GUI	CD music player utility
cfgwiz.exe	2HPM	cmp	Front Page Server Extensions configuration component
cfgwiz32.exe	8E	GUI	ISDN Configuration Wizard
chaccess.vbs	2P	SCR	Changes access on website folders (ADSI)
change.exe	HPM	ndu	Used on Windows server only, terminal server management tool
charmap.exe	8E2HPM	GUI	Character map
chart.js	8E	SCR	Windows Script Host demo—creates an Excel chart
chart.vbs	8E	SCR	Windows Script Host demo—creates an Excel chart
chcp.com	2HPM	CMD	Changes console code page
checkconnection.js	E	cmp	Component of Windows Help center
checksr.bat	E	cmp	Component of System Restore procedure on Emergency Backup Disk
chglogon.exe	HPM	ndu	Used on Windows server only; terminal server management tool
chgport.exe	HPM	ndu	Used on Windows server only; terminal server management tool

Filename	OS	Type	Description
chgusr.exe	HPM	ndu	Used on Windows server only; terminal server management tool
chkdsk.exe	8E2HPM	CMD	Checks and repairs file system integrity
chkntfs.exe	2HPM	CMD	Schedules automatic chkdsk at boot time
chkrzm.exe	EHPM	GUI	Internet Checkers
choice.com	8E	CMD	Batch file utility, prompts user to make a choice and communicates selection to batch file through errorlevel
cidaemon.exe	2HPM	svc	Indexing service
cintsetp.exe	2HPM	ndu	Input Method Editor (e.g., Asian language input system) setup component (source: Windows Update)
cipher.exe	2PM	CMD	Encrypts and decrypts files and folders
cisvc.exe	2HPM	svc	Indexing Service—Indexes contents and properties of files on local and remote computers; provides rapid access to files through flexible querying language.
cjime.exe	2	ndu	Appears to be involved in installing or updating national language drivers
ckcnv.exe	8E2HPM	cmp	Cookie converter; Internet Explorer software update component (source: Windows Update)
cleanmgr.exe	8E2HPM	GUI	Disk Cleanup program
cliconfg.exe	8E2HPM	GUI	SQL Server Client Network Utility
clipbrd.exe	8E2HPM	GUI	Clipboard viewer—multiuser
clipsrv.exe	2HPM	svc	ClipBook Service, shares Clipboard across a network
clspack.exe	8E2	CMD	Lists Java system packages
cluster.exe	2	CMD	Windows Cluster configuration tool
cmd.exe	2HPM	CMD	Command shell. Processes commands in batch files or typed into the Command Prompt window. This is the 32-bit Windows replacement for DOS's command.com, and it is a significant improvement. See Chapter 9 for more information.
cmdinit.bat	E	BF	Default batch file run upon opening command prompt windows
cmdl32.exe	8E2HPM	cmp	Connection Manager Auto-Download
cmdninst.exe	E	cmp	Configuration Manager Device Installer Launcher; involved in detecting devices and installing drivers at bootup
cmmgr32.exe	8E2	cmp	Windows Connection Manager component
cmmon32.exe	8E2HPM	cmp	Connection Manager Monitor
cmpagent.exe	8E	GUI	Compression agent; recompresses drives with DriveSpace 3 after changing compression mode
cmstp.exe	8E2HPM	CMD	Connection Manager profile installer
comclust.exe	2	GUI	Cluster configuration wizard for MS DTC
command.com	8E2HPM	DOS	MS-DOS command shell
common.js	E2HPM	SCR	Component of several JS applications (source: Services for UNIX 3.5)

(continues)

Filename	OS	Type	Description
commonfunc.js	HPM	SCR	Component of help center
comp.exe	2HPM	CMD	Compares files
compact.exe	2HPM	CMD	Enables and disables file and folder compression
comrepl.exe	2HPM	CMD	COMREPL replicates one computer's COM+ applications to one or more target computers
comrereg.exe	2HPM	CMD	Appears to repair COM object registry database
comsdupd.exe	P	ndu	Service pack update component
conagent.exe	8E	cmp	Windows component involved in running console programs
conf.exe	8E2HPM	GUI	NetMeeting application
configwizards.exe	8E2HPM	GUI	Lets you adjust .NET security, select trusted assemblies, or repair a managed application (source: .NET Framework)
conime.exe	2HPM	GUI	Input method editor
constants.js	HPM	cmp	Component of Remote Assistance
contftp.vbs	2P	SCR	Restarts paused FTP server
control.exe	8E2HPM	GUI	Starts the Control Panel
controls.js	EHPM	SCR	Component of Windows tour
contsrv.vbs	2P	SCR	Restarts paused IIS server
contweb.vbs	2P	SCR	Restarts paused web server
convert.exe	2HPM	CMD	Schedules conversion of volume from FAT to NTFS
convlog.exe	2PM	CMD	Converts IIS log files to various standard formats
copy2gac.exe	HPM	CMD	Copies .NET assemblies to the Global Assembly Cache to repair damaged installations (see Microsoft Knowledge Base article #827073)
copymar.exe	HP	cmp	MSN Explorer component
country.sys	8E2HPM	DOS	Locale driver for MS-DOS subsystem
cplexe.exe	2HPM	cmp	Japanese Input Method Editor component
cprofile.exe	HPM	ndu	Used on Windows server only; terminal server management tool
csc.exe	8E2PM	CMD	.NET Visual C# command-line compiler (source: .NET Framework)
cscript.exe	8E2HPM	CMD	Windows Scripts Host—command-line version
csrss.exe	2HPM	svc	Client Server Runtime Process
cssetup.exe	8	GUI	Compuserve 2000 installer
ctfmon.exe	HPM	svc	Alternative User Input Services service
cvt.exe	8E	DOS	DOS side of program to convert disk drive format to FAT32
cvt1.exe	8E	GUI	Drive Converter; converts hard disk format to FAT32
cvtaplog.exe	8E	ndu	Disk Defragmenter component
cvtres.exe	8E2HPM	CMD	Converts Resource file data to COFF objects (source: .NET Framework)
dancer.exe	M	GUI	Displays one or two persons dancing on the desktop, optionally to music (source: Standard on MCE, otherwise Plus! for Windows XP)

Filename	OS	Type	Description
davcdata.exe	PM	cmp	Front Page Server Extensions component
dcomcnfg.exe	2HPM	GUI	Displays and manages DCOM configuration
ddeshare.exe	2HPM	GUI	Displays DDE shares on local or remote computer
ddhelp.exe	8E	cmp	DirectX component
ddmprxy.exe	2	cmp	Some sort of networking component
debug.exe	8E2HPM	DOS	Debugs programs (archaic)
defrag.exe	8EHPM	CMD	Defragments a disk volume
deltemp.com	E	cmp	Component of Windows Setup
deltree.exe	8E	DOS	Deletes a directory and all files and subdirectories in it
delttsul.exe	2	ndu	Text-to-speech component
dfrgfat.exe	2HPM	cmp	Disk defragmenter component for FAT file system
dfrgntfs.exe	2HPM	cmp	Disk defragmenter component for NTFS file system
dialer.exe	8E2HPM	GUI	Phone dialer for TAPI/Internet telephony
dialmgr.js	EHPM	SCR	Component of "Out-of-box" experience, initial setup wizard
diantz.exe	2HPM	CMD	Cabinet file maker, same as makecab
digcore.exe	M	GUI	MSN photo email component installer
directcc.exe	8E	GUI	Direct Cable Connection (file transfer) application
discover.exe	2	GUI	Launcher for CD-based "Discover Windows 2000" tour
diskcomp.com	2HPM	DOS	Compares two floppy disks
diskcopy.com	8E2HPM	DOS	Copies a floppy disk
diskpart.exe	HPM	CMD	Manages disk partitions
diskperf.exe	2HPM	CMD	Starts physical disk performance counters (obsolete)
dispnode.vbs	2P	SCR	Displays properties of IIS objects (ADSI)
disptree.vbs	2P	SCR	Displays IIS information objects (ADSI)
dlglib.js	HPM	SCR	Component of help center
dlimport.exe	EHP	cmp	Windows Media Player component
dllhost.exe	8E2HPM	svc	Runs a COM object as a service. Used to run the DCOM/COM+ System Application service and other services.
dllhst3g.exe	2HPM	svc	DCOM/COM+ Server Host with 3GB support
dmadmin.exe	2HPM	svc	Logical Disk Manager Administrative Service—Configures hard disk drives and volumes. The service only runs for configuration processes and then stops.
dmremote.exe	2HPM	cmp	Part of disk management system
doskey.com	8E	DOS	Keyboard editing enhancement driver, permits easier command-line editing and definition of command aliases
doskey.exe	2HPM	DOS	Provides command-line aliases and editing extensions
dosrep.exe	8E	DOS	MS-DOS Report Tool; sends error information to Microsoft Tech support

(continues)

Filename	OS	Type	Description
dosstart.bat	8E	DOS	Batch file run when you click Start/Shutdown/MS-DOS Mode. If you create a shortcut to a program and specify that it is to run in MS-DOS mode, an alternate file can be specified.
dosx.exe	2HPM	DOS	DOS Extender, loaded in AUTOEXEC.NT
dotnetfx.exe	8E2HPM	GUI	Installation program for .NET Framework (source: Download, Windows Update, or application installer)
dplaysvr.exe	8E2HPM	cmp	Direct Play Helper
dpnsvr.exe	HPM	cmp	Direct Play networking component
dpvhelp.exe	E	cmp	Direct Play Voice component
dpvsetup.exe	EHPM	cmp	Direct Play component
driverquery.exe	PM	CMD	Lists installed device drivers
drvqry.exe	PM	CMD	(Installed as driverquery.exe)
drvspace.exe	8E	GUI	Drive Space (disk compression) configuration utility
drwatson.exe	8E2HPM	GUI	Dr. Watson for Win16 programs
drwtsn32.exe	2HPM	GUI	Dr. Watson viewer and configuration manager
dslmain.js	HPM	SCR	Component of "Out-of-box" experience, initial setup wizard
dsssig.exe	8E	ndu	Digital Signature manager component
dtcsetup.exe	2	GUI	Installs the Microsoft Distributed Transaction Coordinator (MS DTC)
dumprep.exe	HPM	GUI	Wizard that offers to submit crash (blue screen) dumps to Microsoft
dvdplay.exe	E2HPM	GUI	Windows DVD player
dvdrgn.exe	E	ndu	Sets DVD region; run indirectly by DVD players
dvdupgrd.exe	HPM	GUI	Detects and installs updated DVD decoders
dvdupgrd.js	HPM	SCR	Component of help center
dw.exe	HP	cmp	MSN Explorer component
dw15.exe	8E2	GUI	Error reporter; run when IE crashes (source: Windows Update)
dwwin.exe	HPM	GUI	Dr. Watson for Windows
dxdiag.exe	8E2HPM	GUI	Direct-X Diagnostics
ebdundo.exe	E	cmp	Component of System Restore procedure on Emergency Backup Disk
edit.com	8E2HPM	DOS	Edits text files
edlin.exe	2HPM	DOS	Edits text files (primeval)
ehmsas.exe	M	cmp	Windows Media Center component; notifies other components of media center events
ehrec.exe	M	cmp	Windows Media Center component
ehrecvr.exe	M	cmp	Windows Media Center component
ehsched.exe	M	cmp	Windows Media Center component
ehshell.exe	M	GUI	Media Center main screen display ("Start" screen)
ehtray.exe	M	GUI	Media Center task tray applet

Filename	OS	Type	Description
emm386.exe	8E	DOS	Expanded Memory Manager driver and configuration utility
encinst.exe	2	cmp	Windows Installer component
enhload.exe	8E	ndu	Enhancement database loader—component of TV Viewer
error.js	EHPM	SCR	Component of "Out-of-box" experience, initial setup wizard
esentutl.exe	2HPM	CMD	MS Database Utility
esserver.exe	8E	ndu	Event System COM component
eudcedit.exe	2HPM	GUI	Private character editor
euroconv.exe	8E	GUI	Euro update tool; changes Windows fonts to include the Euro symbol for users whose Locale setting is in the Euro zone (source: Windows Update)
evcreate.exe	PM	CMD	Writes an event to the event log from the command line
eventcreate.exe	PM	CMD	Adds an event to the event log
eventquery.vbs	PM	SCR	Lists events from the event log
events.js	EHPM	SCR	Component of Windows tour
eventtriggers.exe	PM	CMD	Displays and configures event triggers
eventvwr.exe	2HPM	GUI	Launches Event Viewer (opens eventvwr.msc)
evntcmd.exe	2HPM	CMD	Translates events into SNMP traps
evntwin.exe	2HPM	GUI	Configures event to SNMP trap mapping
evtquery.vbs	PM	SCR	(Installed as eventquery.vbs)
evtrig.exe	PM	CMD	(Installed as eventtriggers.exe)
excel.js	8E	SCR	Windows Script Host demo—stuffs data into an Excel sheet
excel.vbs	8E	SCR	Windows Script Host demo—stuffs data into an Excel sheet
exch_regtrace.exe	HPM	ndu	Used on Windows server only; server management tool
exe2bin.exe	2HPM	DOS	Converts .EXE to .COM file (archaic)
expinst.exe	8E2	cmp	Internet Explorer update component used only on Windows 2000 (source: Windows Update)
explorer.exe	8E2HPM	GUI	Windows Explorer
extrac32.exe	8E2HPM	GUI	CAB File extraction utility; not very user friendly
extract.exe	8E2HPM	CMD	Extracts files from Microsoft .CAB files (source: Win2000 reskit, support\tools)
fastopen.exe	2HPM	DOS	Speeds directory searching (does nothing on Windows XP/2000)
faxpatch.exe	HP	cmp	Fax service component
faxqueue.exe	2	GUI	Fax queue manager
faxsend.exe	2	GUI	Send Fax wizard
faxsvc.exe	2	svc	Fax service
faxview.exe	8E	GUI	Fax viewer utility (source: TOOLS\OLDWIN95 Windows Messaging & Fax)
fc.exe	8E2HPM	CMD	Compares files
fdisk.exe	8E	DOS	Disk partition manager

(continues)

Filename	OS	Type	Description
filecoll.exe	HP	CMD	Install data collector; may be installed with beta releases of Microsoft software
find.exe	8E2HPM	CMD	Finds text in files
findramd.exe	8E	DOS	Part of Windows 98/ME Emergency boot disk startup
findweb.vbs	2P	SCR	Locates virtual websites on IIS computers
finger.exe	2HPM	CMD	Displays information about a user (UNIX)
fixit.bat	E	cmp	Component of System Restore procedure on Emergency Backup Disk
fixmapi.exe	8E2HPM	cmp	Part of Windows/IE/Outlook installation
flattemp.exe	HPM	ndu	Used on Windows server only; terminal server management tool
fltmc.exe	HPM	CMD	Displays, adds, removes file system minifilter drivers (source: Windows XP SP2)
fontreg.exe	8E	CMD	Repairs Registry entries for TrueType fonts (see Microsoft Knowledge Base article #133732)
fontview.exe	8E2HPM	GUI	Displays fonts in a font file
forcedos.exe	2HPM	DOS	Runs a program in the MS-DOS environment
format.com	8E2HPM	CMD	Formats fixed or removable disk
fortutil.exe	2	CMD	Fortezza security setup utility
fp98sadm.exe	2HPM	GUI	Obsolete
fp98swin.exe	2HPM	GUI	Obsolete
fpadmcgi.exe	2HPM	cmp	FrontPage Server Extensions component
fpcount.exe	2HPM	cmp	FrontPage Server Extensions component
fpremadm.exe	2HPM	CMD	FrontPage Server remote administration
fpsrvadm.exe	2HP	CMD	Configures FrontPage Server extensions ver. 4.0
fpsrvwin.exe	2P	GUI	Obsolete
framectrl.js	E	cmp	Component of Windows Help center
freecell.exe	8E2HPM	GUI	Popular Windows Game
fsquirt.exe	HPM	GUI	Bluetooth file transfer utility
fsutil.exe	HPM	CMD	Manages the Windows file system
ftp.exe	8E2HPM	CMD	File transfer protocol
ftpqfe.exe	2	ndu	Not sure; probably involved in installation of Windows patches
fxsclnt.exe	HPM	GUI	Fax Console
fxscover.exe	HPM	GUI	Fax cover page editor
fxssend.exe	HPM	GUI	Send Fax wizard
fxssvc.exe	HPM	svc	Fax—Enables you to send and receive faxes, utilizing fax resources available on this computer or on the network.
gacutil.exe	8E	CMD	Displays and manipulates the contents of the global assembly cache (source: .NET Framework)
gameenum.exe	2	CMD	Appears to trick Windows into installing a game controller (joystick) without the hardware present

Filename	OS	Type	Description
gdi.exe	8E2HPM	cmp	Graphic Device Interface (a fundamental part of Windows)
gprslt.exe	PM	CMD	Computes Resulting Set of Policy
gpupdate.exe	PM	CMD	Forces update of local and Group Policy settings
graftabl.com	2HPM	DOS	Enables display of graphics characters in MS-DOS environment
graphics.com	2HPM	DOS	Loads graphics printer driver (obsolete)
grpconv.exe	8E2HPM	GUI	Program Manager Group converter
gsupdate.exe	8	GUI	WebTV for Windows updater
hcupdate.exe	E	cmp	Component of Windows Help center
help.exe	2HPM	CMD	Displays command-line program usage information
helpctr.exe	EHPM	GUI	Help and Support center GUI
helphost.exe	HPM	cmp	Help and Support center component
helpsvc.exe	HPM	cmp	Help and Support center component
hh.exe	8E2HPM	GUI	HTML Help
hibinv.exe	E	cmp	Component of System Restore procedure on Emergency Backup Disk
hidserv.exe	E2	cmp	USB audio device support service
hilite.js	M	cmp	Media Center Edition help component
himem.sys	8E2HPM	DOS	Memory driver for MS-DOS subsystem
homepage__desktop.js	HPM	SCR	Component of help center
homepage__server.js	HPM	SCR	Component of help center
homepage__shared.js	HPM	SCR	Component of help center
hostname.exe	2HPM	CMD	Displays the local computer's TCP/IP hostname
hotfix.exe	8E	cmp	Windows Update downloaded component (source: Windows Update)
hrtzzm.exe	EHPM	GUI	Internet Hearts
hscupd.exe	HPM	cmp	Help and Support center component
htimage.exe	2	cmp	FrontPage Extensions component—CERN format image map processor
htmlgen.exe	HPM	GUI	HTML Slide Show Wizard power toy (source: Powertoys for XP download)
hwinfo.exe	8E	CMD	Microsoft Hardware Diagnostic Tool (see Microsoft Knowledge Base article #185956)
hypertrm.exe	8E2HPM	GUI	Serial/Telnet terminal emulator
iconnect.js	HPM	SCR	Component of "Out-of-box" experience; initial setup wizard
icsclset.exe	8E	GUI	Browser Connection Manager Setup Wizard—creates wizard disk to run on other computers when setting up Internet Connection Sharing
icsmgr.exe	8E	cmp	Internet Connection Sharing component; monitors need to establish outgoing connection
icsmgr.js	EHPM	SCR	Component of "Out-of-box" experience; initial setup wizard

(continues)

Filename	OS	Type	Description
icssetup.exe	8E	GUI	Internet Connection Sharing Wizard—enables Internet Connection Sharing
icwconn1.exe	8E2HPM	cmp	Internet Connection Wizard component
icwconn2.exe	8E2HPM	cmp	Internet Connection Wizard component
icwoobe.exe	8E	GUI	Internet Connection Wizard component
icwrmind.exe	8E2HPM	cmp	Internet Connection Wizard component
icwscrpt.exe	8E	GUI	Installs or updates Windows Dial-up Scripting
icwtutor.exe	8E2HPM	cmp	Internet Connection Wizard tutorial
idriver.exe	8E2HPM	cmp	Installshield application installer component
idriver2.exe	8E2HPM	cmp	Installshield application installer component
ie4uinit.exe	8E2HPM	cmp	IE5 User Install tool
ie6setup.exe	8E2	GUI	Internet Explorer update, setup, and configuration tool (source: Windows Update)
iebatch.exe	8E	cmp	Internet Explorer updating component
iedw.exe	HPM	ndu	Internet Explorer crash-detection component
ieexec.exe	8E2PM	cmp	.NET Application launcher; responsible for downloading and running .NET applications started from Internet Explorer or Windows Explorer (source: .NET Framework)
ieshwiz.exe	8E2	GUI	Customize This Folder Wizard; lets user specify display options for Active Desktop view of a folder
ieuninst.exe	8E	cmp	Internet Explorer uninstall component
iexplore.exe	8E2HPM	GUI	Internet Explorer
iexpress.exe	2HPM	GUI	Creates simple Installer applications
iextract.exe	8E	CMD	Internet Explorer backup information extractor tool
iframecontentfocus.js	M	cmp	Media Center Edition help component
iframescrolling.js	M	cmp	Media Center Edition help component
iisreset.exe	2PM	CMD	Manages IIS server
iisrstas.exe	2PM	cmp	IIS component
iissync.exe	2PM	CMD	Replicates IIS configuration across a server cluster
ilasm.exe	8E2PM	CMD	.NET Intermediate Language command-line assembler (source: .NET Framework)
imagemap.exe	2	cmp	Front Page Extensions component—NCSA format mage map processor
imapi.exe	HPM	svc	IMAPI CD-Burning COM service and Image Mastering API (CD-Burning COM component)
imejpmgr.exe	2	drv	Japanese Input Method Editor component
imejpmig.exe	2	cmp	Japanese Input Method Editor updating utility
imejpuex.exe	2	drv	Japanese Input Method Editor component
imekrmig.exe	HPM	cmp	Korean Input Method Editor installation component
imepadsv.exe	HPM	cmp	Korean Input Method Editor component
imgstart.exe	8E	GUI	Launcher for Windows 98 Interactive Demo CD
imjpdadm.exe	HPM	cmp	Korean Input Method Editor component

Filename	OS	Type	Description
imjpdct.exe	HPM	GUI	Japanese Input Method Editor dictionary tool
imjpdsvr.exe	HPM	cmp	Japanese Input Method Editor component
imjpinst.exe	HPM	cmp	Japanese Input Method Editor installation component
imjpmig.exe	HPM	cmp	Japanese Input Method Editor installation component
imjprw.exe	HPM	cmp	Japanese Input Method Editor component
imjpuex.exe	HPM	cmp	Korean Input Method Editor component
imjputy.exe	HPM	cmp	Japanese Input Method Editor component
imkrinst.exe	HPM	cmp	Korean Input Method Editor installation component
imscinst.exe	HPM	cmp	Chinese Input Method editor installation component
inetin51.exe	PM	svc	(Installed as inetinfo.exe, see next entry)
inetinfo.exe	2P	svc	IIS services component; provides the IIS Admin, FTP Publishing, Simple Mail Transfer Protocol (SMTP), and World Wide Web Publishing services.
inetmgr.exe	2PM	GUI	Launches Internet Information Services MMC management panel
inetwiz.exe	8E2HPM	GUI	Internet Connection Wizard
installutil.exe	8E2PM	CMD	.NET Framework Installer tool, runs installer components in .NET assemblies (source: .NET Framework)
internat.exe	8E2	GUI	Locale-selection tasktray tool
ipconfig.exe	8E2HPM	CMD	Displays TCP/IP configuration and manage DHCP leases
ipsec6.exe	HPM	CMD	IPSec over IPv6 Security Configuration
ipsecmon.exe	2	GUI	IPSec status monitor
ipv6.exe	HPM	CMD	IPv6 Installer/configuration tool
ipxroute.exe	2HPM	CMD	Displays and edits TCP/IP routing table
irftp.exe	2HP	GUI	Wireless Link (IRDA infrared) file transfer wizard
irmon.exe		svc	Infrared Port Monitor service
isignup.exe	8E2HPM	cmp	Internet Connection Wizard component
isptype.js	HPM	SCR	Component of "Out-of-box" experience, initial setup wizard
isuninst.exe	E	cmp	Uninstaller (source: various)
iun507.exe	E	cmp	Used to uninstall various programs
iun6002.exe	E	cmp	Used to uninstall various programs
jdbgmgr.exe	8E2	GUI	Microsoft debugger for Java 4 (not a virus!)
jsc.exe	8E2PM	CMD	.NET JScript command-line compiler (source: .NET Framework)
jview.exe	8E2	CMD	Command-line loader for Java
kb16.com	2HPM	DOS	Keyboard code set configuration (formerly KEYB.COM)
kb891711.exe	8E	ndu	Security hotfix; runs as background service (source: Windows Update)
key.js	E	cmp	Component of Windows Tour
keyb.com	8E	DOS	DOS keyboard device driver
keyboard.sys	8E2HPM	DOS	Locale driver for MS-DOS subsystem

(continues)

Filename	OS	Type	Description
keyex32.exe		cmp	Personal Key exchange form
kodakimg.exe	8E2	GUI	Imaging for Windows graphics file view/scan/scale utility
kodakprv.exe	8E2	GUI	Imaging for Windows graphics file preview utility
krnl386.exe	8E2HPM	cmp	Windows Kernel API
label.exe	8E2HPM	CMD	Sets the volume label on a disk or mount point
lights.exe	8E2HPM	cmp	Connection status light display
lmscript.exe	8E	cmp	Dial-up networking scripting component
lnkstub.exe	2HPM	cmp	Stands in for obsolete Win 98/Me component and warns of incompatibility
loadfix.com	2HPM	DOS	Runs a program above the first 64KB of memory
loadstub.exe	8E	ndu	Component of TV Viewer
loadwc.exe	8E	cmp	Internet Explorer Web Check (content advisor) component
loc.js	E	ndu	Component of Movie Maker tour
locator.exe	2HPM	svc	Remote Procedure Call (RPC) Locator—Manages the RPC name service database.
locproxy.exe	8E	cmp	TCP/IP networking component; appears to locate proxy servers via DHCP
locprxy2.exe	8E	cmp	TCP/IP networking component; appears to locate proxy servers via DHCP
lodctr.exe	2HPM	CMD	Installs, backs up, or restores performance counter definitions
logagent.exe	8E2HPM	cmp	Windows Media Player component
logenum.js	2P	SCR	Sample IIS management script
logenum.vbs	2P	SCR	Sample IIS management script
login.cmd	2PM	CMD	Telnet server login script
logman.exe	HPM	CMD	Schedules automatic collection of performance information
logoff.exe	2HPM	CMD	Logs off from Windows (source: Win2000 reskit, standard on XP)
logonui.exe	HPM	cmp	Part of logon screen
lpq.exe	2HPM	CMD	Displays printer queue (UNIX)
lpr.exe	2HPM	CMD	Prints a file (UNIX)
lsass.exe	2HPM	svc	Local and Network Security service. Provides IPSEC, NetLogon, NTLM, Protected Storage and Security Accounts Manager (SAM) services
m5drvr32.exe	8E	cmp	Macromedia Shockwave plug-in component for IE
magnify.exe	8E2HPM	GUI	Magnifies the current screen
makapt15.bat	8E2	CMD	Configures ADO.NET to use apartment threading model
makecab.exe	2HPM	CMD	Makes cabinet files from files specified on the command line
makfre15.bat	8E2	CMD	Configures ADO.NET to use free threading model
mapisp32.exe	8E	cmp	Windows messaging component—message spooling service (source: TOOLS\OLDWIN95 Windows Messaging & Fax)

Filename	OS	Type	Description
mapisrvr.exe	8E	cmp	Windows messaging component—MAPI service (source: TOOLS\OLDWIN95 Windows Messaging & Fax)
mcrmgr.exe	M	cmp	Windows Media Center component
mdisp32.exe	8E	cmp	Windows messaging component (source: TOOLS\OLDWIN95 Windows Messaging & Fax)
mdm.exe	2	cmp	Machine Debug Manager
medctrro.cmd	HP	ndu	Empty file in Home, Pro installations
medctrro.exe	M	cmp	Windows Media Center component
mem.exe	8E2HPM	DOS	Displays free memory in MS-DOS subsystem
memmaker.exe	8E	GUI	Restarts Windows in DOS mode and runs DOS portion of memmaker memory optimization utility
metaback.js	2P	SCR	Sample IIS management script
metaback.vbs	2P	SCR	Sample IIS management script
metabackrest.js	2P	SCR	Sample IIS management script
metabackrest.vbs	2P	SCR	Sample IIS management script
migisol.exe	2HPM	ndu	Part of Windows 9x-to-Windows 2000 upgrade process
migload.exe	HPM	cmp	Files and Settings Transfer Wizard subcomponent
migpol.exe	8E2	cmp	.NET Framework updating component (source: Windows Update)
migpolwin.exe	8E2	cmp	.NET Framework updating component (source: Windows Update)
migpwd.exe	2HPM	cmp	Files and Settings Transfer Wizard component
migrate.exe	HPM	ndu	Part of Windows Media Player installer, updates settings from older versions
migrate.js	EHPM	SCR	Component of "Out-of-box" experience, initial setup wizard
migregdb.exe	2HPM	ndu	Windows install/update component
migwiz.exe	HPM	GUI	Files and Settings Transfer Wizard
migwiz_a.exe	HPM	cmp	Files and Settings Transfer Wizard component
mkcompat.exe	8E	GUI	Sets compatibility options for running 16-bit Windows programs (see Microsoft Knowledge Base article #173086)
mkftpdir.vbs	P	SCR	Sample IIS management script
mkw3site.vbs	2	SCR	Creates a new IIS virtual web server, but doesn't let you avoid one server limit on Windows 2000 Pro
mkwebdir.vbs	2P	SCR	Creates a virtual directory in a website
mkwebsrv.js	2	SCR	See mkw3site.vbs
mkwebsrv.vbs	2	SCR	See mkw3site.vbs
ml3xec16.exe	8E	cmp	Windows messaging component (source: TOOLS\OLDWIN95 Windows Messaging & Fax)
mm2ent.exe	8E	?	Unknown
mmc.exe	8E2HPM	GUI	Microsoft Management Console (source: Win98 reskit)
mnmsrvc.exe	8E2HPM	svc	NetMeeting Remote Desktop Sharing Service

(continues)

Filename	OS	Type	Description
mobsync.exe	8E2HPM	GUI	Synchronization manager/wizard
mode.com	8E2HPM	DOS	Configures port, display, and keyboard settings
mofcomp.exe	8E2HPM	CMD	Web Based Enterprise Management (WBEM) database MOF compiler
more.com	8E2HPM	CMD	Displays text a page at a time
mountvol.exe	2HPM	CMD	Creates, deletes, and lists volume mount points
mousetut.js	EHPM	SCR	Component of "Out-of-box" experience, initial setup wizard
move.exe	8E	DOS	Renames and/or moves files between volumes
movefocus.js	M	cmp	Media Center Edition help component
moviemk.exe	EHPM	GUI	Windows Movie Maker
mplay32.exe	2HPM	GUI	MS Media Player
mplayer.exe	8E	GUI	Windows Media Player version 2
mplayer2.exe	8E2HPM	GUI	Windows Media Player version 6
mpnotify.exe	2HPM	cmp	Multiple Provider Notification application
mprexe.exe	8E	cmp	Windows networking component
mq1sync.exe	2	cmp	Microsoft Message Queue Service component
mqbkup.exe	2PM	CMD	MS Message Queue Backup and Restore Utility
mqexchng.exe	2	ndu	MSMQ setup tool for Windows 2000 Server only
mqmig.exe	2	ndu	Used by Windows upgrade process to migrate Microsoft Message Queue (MSMQ) data
mqsvc.exe	2PM	svc	MS Message Queueing Service
mqtgsvc.exe	PM	svc	Message Queuing Service Triggers Service component
mrinfo.exe	2HPM	CMD	Multicast routing using SNMP
mscdex.exe	8E	DOS	CD-ROM extensions driver, loaded after CD-ROM device specific driver
mscdexnt.exe	2HPM	DOS	MS CD Extensions, loaded in AUTOEXEC.NT
msconfig.exe	8EHPM	cmp	Help and Support center component
msdtc.exe	2HPM	svc	Distributed Transaction Coordinator Service
msdtcvtr.bat	HPM	CMD	Distributed Transaction Coordinator debugging script
msg.exe	HPM	CMD	Sends a message to another user
msgsrv32.exe	8E	cmp	Windows 32-bit message server, involved in coordinating logon process, desktop management, installation problems, and interactions between Windows and applications (see KB article #138708)
mshearts.exe	8EHPM	GUI	Hearts game
mshta.exe	8E2HPM	cmp	HTML Application HOST
msiexec.exe	8E2HPM	svc	Windows Installer service
msimn.exe	8E2HPM	GUI	Outlook Express
msinfo32.exe	8E2HPM	GUI	System Information utility—GUI version
msiregmv.exe	2HPM	ndu	Used to update Microsoft Installer data for applications installed under MSI version 1.1

Filename	OS	Type	Description
msmqprop.exe	2	ndu	Used by Windows 2000 SP3 installer to update MSMQ registry values
msmsgs.exe	EHPM	GUI	Windows Messenger
msmsgsin.exe	EHP	cmp	MS Messenger component
msn6.exe	HP	GUI	MSN Explorer
msnboot.exe	8E	GUI	Launches MSN Internet access software
msncli.exe	M	GUI	MSN browser installer
msncreat.exe	8E	ndu	Installs MSN icon
msnmgsr1.exe	8E	ndu	MSN setup component
msnsusii.exe	M	GUI	MSN browser installer wizard
msnunin.exe	HP	cmp	MSN Explorer uninstaller
msoobe.exe	8EHPM	GUI	Windows Activation Wizard
mspaint.exe	8E2HPM	GUI	Paint accessory
mspmspsv.exe		svc	Windows Media Player 7 component (WMDM PMSP service)
msscrdbg.exe	2HPM	GUI	Microsoft Script Debugger (source: Windows Update or download)
msswchx.exe	E2HPM	cmp	Subcomponent of On-Screen Keyboard
mstask.exe	8E2	svc	Windows task scheduler service
mstinit.exe	8E2HPM	cmp	Task scheduler setup, installs scheduled maintenance items
mstsc.exe	EHPM	GUI	Terminal Services Client (Remote Desktop) (source: \add-ons\tsclient\mstsc)
mtstocom.exe	2HPM	ndu	Used by Windows upgrade process to migrate Microsoft Transaction Server (MTS) data to COM+
muisetup.exe	HPM	cmp	Multilingual User Interface Pack installer
muninst.exe	8E2	cmp	Internet Explorer update/uninstall component (source: Windows Update)
mwcload.exe	2	CMD	IBM Mwave modem driver management utility
mwcloadw.exe	2	CMD	IBM Mwave modem driver management utility
mwcpyrt.exe	2	GUI	Displays copyright notice for IBM Mwave modem driver
mwcsw32.exe	2	GUI	IBM Mwave modem driver configuration utility
mwmdmsvc.exe	2	svc	IBM Mwave modem service
mwrcov16.exe	2	ndu	IBM Mwave modem driver installer for Windows 9x
mwremind.exe	2	GUI	IBM mwave modem utility
mwssw32.exe	2	ndu	IBM mwave modem utility
narrator.exe	2HPM	GUI	Onscreen narrator
nbtstat.exe	8E2HPM	CMD	Displays NetBIOS-over-TCP/IP statistics and name tables
nddeapir.exe	2HPM	cmp	NDDE API Server side
net.exe	8E2HPM	CMD	Networking management utility
net1.exe	2HPM	cmp	Part of NET command

(continues)

Filename	OS	Type	Description
netconn.exe	E	GUI	Home Networking Wizard
netdde.exe	8E2HPM	svc	Network DDE and Network DDE DSDM services
netfxsbs10.exe	8E2	cmp	.NET Framework software update component (source: Windows Update)
netfxupdate.exe	8EP	cmp	.NET Framework software update component (source: .NET Framework)
netsetup.exe	HPM	GUI	Network setup wizard
netsh.exe	2HPM	CMD	Network configuration utility
netstat.exe	8E2HPM	CMD	Displays current TCP/IP connections and open sockets
netwatch.exe	8E	GUI	Monitors connections to shared files and folders
network.js	8E	SCR	Windows Script Host demo—reads network information
network.vbs	8E	SCR	Windows Script Host demo—reads network information
ngen.exe	8E2PM	CMD	.NET Native Image Generator; creates and caches native-code versions of .NET assemblies (source: .NET Framework)
nlsfunc.exe	8E2HPM	DOS	Loads country/region information
nocomp.exe	8E	GUI	Startup Disk Wizard—makes a boot floppy disk that doesn't include DriveSpace, to gain additional memory at the expense of access to compressed drives
notepad.exe	8E2HPM	GUI	Notepad accessory
notiflag.exe	HPM	cmp	Help and Support Center component
nppagent.exe	2HPM	cmp	Network Monitor data gathering agent
nslookup.exe	2HPM	CMD	Query DNS servers
ntbackup.exe	2PM	GUI	Backs up and restores files
ntdetect.com	2HP	ndu	Used by Windows boot process
ntdsutil.exe	2	CMD	Active Directory database maintenance utility
ntkrnlmp.exe	2HPM	cmp	Windows NT kernel component
ntkrnlpa.exe	2HPM	cmp	Kernel patch
ntkrpamp.exe	2HPM	cmp	Windows NT kernel component
ntoskrnl.exe	2HPM	cmp	Core NT Kernel
ntsd.exe	2HPM	CMD	System-level debugger
ntvdm.exe	2HPM	cmp	MS-DOS Virtual Machine environment
nw16.exe	2PM	DOS	Netware 16-bit Redirector, loaded in AUTOEXEC.NT
nwlscon.exe	8E	cmp	Logon script processor component for Client for Netware
nwlsproc.exe	8E	cmp	Logon script processor component for Client for Netware
nwscript.exe	2PM	CMD	Runs NetWare logon scripts
odbcad32.exe	8E2HPM	GUI	Data sources (ODBC 32-bit Administrator)
odbcconf.exe	8E2HPM	CMD	ODBC database driver and data source configuration
oemig50.exe	8E2HPM	cmp	Outlook Express component
oemsetup.exe	E	cmp	Component of Windows Setup
oeuninst.exe	8E2	cmp	Outlook Express uninstaller component (source: Windows Update)
oobebaln.exe	HPM	cmp	Component of "Out-of-box" experience; initial setup wizard

Filename	OS	Type	Description
oobeutil.js	HPM	SCR	Component of "Out-of-box" experience; initial setup wizard
openfiles.exe	PM	CMD	Displays files in use by local processes or network users
opnfiles.exe	PM	CMD	(Installed as openfiles.exe, see)
os2.exe	2	cmp	OS/2 subsystem component
os2srv.exe	2	cmp	OS/2 subsystem component
os2ss.exe	2	cmp	OS/2 subsystem component
oschoice.exe	HP	cmp	Boot loader version; may be installed instead of ntldr on boot drive
ose.exe	—	svc	Office source Engine, processes updates and repairs for Microsoft Office, if installed
osk.exe	E2HPM	GUI	Onscreen keyboard
osloader.exe	2HP	ndu	Used by Windows boot process
osuninst.exe	HPM	GUI	Uninstalls Windows XP
packager.exe	8E2HPM	GUI	Object Packager; lets you embed objects into documents
pagefileconfig.vbs	PM	SCR	Manages the system virtual memory page file
partymode.exe	M	GUI	Turns computer into a jukebox that can access music content but not other files (source: Standard on MCE, otherwise Plus! for Windows XP)
pathping.exe	2HPM	CMD	Tests TCP/IP connectivity
pauseftp.vbs	2P	SCR	Pauses FTP service
pausesrv.vbs	2P	SCR	Pauses IIS server
pauseweb.vbs	2P	SCR	Pauses web server
pax.exe	2	CMD	UNIX file archiving utility
pbrush.exe	8E	GUI	Windows Paintbrush accessory
pchschd.exe	E	cmp	Component of Windows Help center
pchsetup.exe	E	cmp	Component of Windows Help center
pentnt.exe	2HPM	CMD	Check CPU for the Pentium math bug
perfmon.exe	2HPM	GUI	Performance console with a Windows NT 4 settings file
perfvd.exe	2	ndu	IIS performance counter update installer
phime.exe	2	CMD	Installs Chinese phonetic Input Method Editor
pidset.exe	8E	?	Unknown
pinball.exe	E2HPM	GUI	Pinball game
ping.exe	8E2HPM	CMD	Ping utility
ping6.exe	HPM	CMD	IPV6 Ping utility
pingname.bat	8E	BF	Not useful; pings some Microsoft servers to test Internet connectivity, the Microsoft servers used no longer respond to pings
pingnum.bat	8E	BF	Not useful; pings some Microsoft servers by IP number, but the servers are no longer in service
pintlphr.exe	HPM	cmp	Chinese Input Method editor component
pmres.exe	E	GUI	Resume troubleshooter; tries to tell you which device driver prevented Windows from resuming after it was suspended

(continues)

Filename	OS	Type	Description
pmts.exe	E	ndu	Power Management troubleshooter component
posix.exe	2	cmp	Posix subsystem component
powercalc.exe	HPM	GUI	Calculator power toy (source: Powertoys for XP download)
powercfg.exe	HPM	CMD	Manages power management schemes from the command line
print.exe	2HPM	DOS	Copies a file to a local LPT-port printer
printimg.exe	E	CMD	Prints image specified on command line; used by Explorer when you right-click an image and select Print
prncnfg.vbs	PM	SCR	Configures printers
prndrvr.vbs	PM	SCR	Installs and lists print drivers
prnjobs.vbs	PM	SCR	Manages print jobs
prnmngr.vbs	PM	SCR	Manages local and network printer connections
prnport.vbs	PM	SCR	Manages TCP/IP printers
prnqctl.vbs	PM	SCR	Prints test pages, starts and stops printer queue
progman.exe	8E2HPM	GUI	Windows 3.1/NT 4-style Program Manager
proquota.exe	2HPM	cmp	Profile quota manager for Windows NT4 domains
protman.exe	8E	DOS	DOS networking component, protocol binding manager
proxycfg.exe	HPM	CMD	Sets HTTP Proxy server
pstores.exe	8E	cmp	Protected Storage system component
psxss.exe	2	cmp	Interix subsystem component
pubprn.vbs	2HPM	SCR	Publishes printers to Active Directory
pws.exe	2	GUI	Personal Web Server (IIS) management utility
pwstray.exe	2	GUI	Personal Web Server (IIS) manager (tasktray tool)
pxhpinst.exe	M	cmp	Windows Media Center Create DVD setup component
pxshare.exe	M	cmp	Windows Media Center Create DVD component
pyime.exe	2	CMD	Installs Chinese Input Method Editor
qappsrv.exe	HPM	CMD	Displays the available application terminal servers on the network
qfecheck.exe	8E	GUI	Displays installed hotfixes and files updated by hotfixes (source: Windows Update)
qprocess.exe	HPM	CMD	Displays information about processes local or remote
qtest32.exe	2	GUI	IBM Mwave modem diagnostic tool
query.exe	HPM	CMD	Displays information about logged-on users, desktop sessions and processes
quikview.exe	8E	GUI	Quick View multiple file-type viewer
quser.exe	HPM	CMD	Same as "query user;" displays list of logged-on users
qwinsta.exe	HPM	CMD	Displays information about Terminal Sessions
raclient.js	HPM	SCR	Component of Remote Assistance
racontrol.js	HPM	SCR	Component of Remote Assistance
rasadmin.exe	2	GUI	Remote Access Services (RAS) status/management utility
rasautou.exe	2HPM	CMD	Creates a RAS connection

Filename	OS	Type	Description
rasdial.exe	2HPM	CMD	Starts and ends dial-up networking connections
raserver.js	HPM	SCR	Component of Remote Assistance
rasphone.exe	2HPM	GUI	Pop-up dial-up networking manager
rcimlby.exe	HPM	GUI	Remote Assistance
rcp.exe	2HPM	CMD	Copies files to another computer (UNIX)
rdsaddin.exe	HPM	cmp	Remote Desktop component
rdshost.exe	HPM	cmp	Remote Desktop component
recover.exe	2HPM	CMD	Extracts data from a damaged disk
redir.exe	2HPM	DOS	Networking redirector, loaded in AUTOEXEC.NT
redir32.exe	8E	cmp	Windows network redirector (provides access to network file resources)
regasm.exe	8E2PM	CMD	.NET Framework registry assembly registration utility; makes .NET classes available as standard COM classes (source: .NET Framework)
regedit.exe	8E2HPM	GUI	Edits Registry
regedt32.exe	2HPM	GUI	Registry editor, old version
regenv32.exe	E	CMD	Copies environment variable set commands between the Registry and autoexec.bat (see Microsoft Knowledge Base article #265835)
register.exe	HPM	ndu	Used on Windows server only; terminal server management tool
registermceapp.exe	M	CMD	Registers Media Center plug-in
registry.js	8E	SCR	Windows Script Host demo—reads/writes Registry data
registry.vbs	8E	SCR	Windows Script Host demo—reads/writes Registry data
regsvc.exe	2	svc	Remote registry service
regsvcs.exe	8E2PM	CMD	Adds .NET assemblies to COM+ 1.0 applications (source: .NET Framework)
regsvr32.exe	8E2HPM	CMD	Registers .DLL file as a COM component
regtlib.exe	8E2	CMD	Registers COM component type libraries (source: Windows Update)
regtrace.exe	2P	GUI	System debugging tool
regwiz.exe	8E2HPM	cmp	Registration Wizard
relog.exe	PM	CMD	Changes format or rate for performance log files
replace.exe	2HPM	CMD	Replaces files
reset.exe	HPM	CMD	Deletes a Terminal Services session
rexec.exe	2HPM	CMD	UNIX remote execute
rg2catdb.exe	8E	?	Unknown
rnaapp.exe	8E	cmp	Remote Networking (Dial-up Networking) component
route.exe	8E2HPM	CMD	Displays or edits the current routing tables.
routemon.exe	2HPM	CMD	(Obsolete, use netsh)
rpcss.exe	8E	svc	Remote Procedure Call service component
rsh.exe	2HPM	CMD	Remote shell (UNIX)

(continues)

Filename	OS	Type	Description
rsm.exe	2HPM	CMD	Manages Removable Storage media pools
rsmsink.exe	HPM	cmp	Removable Storage Manager component
rsmui.exe	HPM	cmp	Removable Storage Manager component
rsnotify.exe	2PM	cmp	Removable Storage Manager component
rsop.js	HPM	SCR	Component of help center system info display
rsopprov.exe	PM	cmp	Resultant Set of Policy provider component
rsrcmtr.exe	8E	GUI	Resource Meter tasktray icon
rstrlfn.exe	E	cmp	System Restore component
rstrui.exe	EHPM	GUI	System Restore
rsvp.exe	8E2HPM	svc	QoS RSVP—Provides network signaling and local traffic control setup functionality for QoS-aware programs and control applets
rtcshare.exe	HPM	GUI	NetMeeting Desktop Sharing
runas.exe	2HPM	CMD	Runs program with another user's credentials
rundll.exe	8E	GUI	Calls an arbitrary function in an arbitrary Dynamic Link Library (DLL)
rundll32.exe	8E2HPM	CMD	Launches a 32-bit DLL program
runonce.exe	8E2HPM	CMD	Causes a program to run during startup
rvsezm.exe	EHPM	GUI	Internet Reversi
rwinsta.exe	HPM	CMD	Resets the session subsystem hardware and software to known initial values
sage.exe	8E	ndu	Windows 95 System Agent to Windows 98 Task Scheduler compatibility/migration component
sapisvr.exe	HPM	cmp	Speech API component
save32.com	E	cmp	Component of Windows Setup
savedump.exe	2HPM	CMD	Saves system dump upon reboot after BSOD
sbeserver.exe	M	cmp	Windows Media Center Create DVD component
scandisk.exe	8E	GUI	Disk corruption check and repair utility
scandskw.exe	8E	GUI	Graphical version of SCANDISK disk check utility
scanprog.exe	E	cmp	Component of Windows Setup
scanreg.exe	8E2HPM	CMD	Searches Windows Registry for specified keys or values (source: Win2000 reskit)
scanregw.exe	8E	GUI	Scans Registry for corruption and backs up Registry, usually run upon startup. If found in a folder other than \windows, may be a virus.
scardsvr.exe	2HPM	svc	Smart Card Helper
schtasks.exe	PM	CMD	Displays and manages scheduled tasks
sconnect.js	HPM	SCR	Component of "Out-of-box" experience; initial setup wizard
scrcons.exe	2HPM	cmp	Scripting system component
script.js	E	ndu	Component of Movie Maker tour
scripts.js	HPM	SCR	Component of Windows tour
scrolling.js	M	cmp	Media Center Edition help component

Filename	OS	Type	Description
sctasks.exe	PM	CMD	(Installed as schtasks.exe)
sdbinst.exe	HPM	CMD	Application compatibility database installer
secedit.exe	2PM	GUI	Manages and analyzes system security policies
separator.js	E	cmp	Component of Windows Help center
services.exe	2HPM	svc	Windows Service manager, also provides event log and Plug and Play services
sessmgr.exe	HPM	svc	Remote Desktop Help Session Manager—Manages and controls Remote Assistance. If this service is stopped, Remote Assistance will be unavailable. Before stopping this service, see the Dependencies tab of the Properties dialog box.
setdebug.exe	8E2	GUI	Enables and disables ActiveX debugging for Java (source: Windows Update)
sethc.exe	2HPM	CMD	Sets High Contrast display
setramd.bat	8E	DOS	Part of Windows 98/ME Emergency boot disk startup
setreg.exe	2	CMD	Displays or modifies Registry settings pertaining to Certificate trust and validation behavior
setregni.exe	P	cmp	.NET Framework software update component
setup50.exe	8E2HPM	cmp	Outlook Express component
setup_wm.exe	EHPM	GUI	Windows Media Player updating tool
setver.exe	8E2HPM	DOS	Lies about MS-DOS version to old applications
sfc.exe	8E2HPM	CMD	Verifies system file integrity
shadow.exe	HPM	CMD	Monitors or controls a Terminal Services session
share.exe	2HPM	DOS	(Does nothing on Windows XP)
shelexec.exe	HPM	GUI	Works like the internal command "start"; open the file named on the command line in the associated application (source: support\tools\act20)
shmgrate.exe	2HPM	CMD	Used during upgrade install from Windows NT 4
shortcut.js	8E	SCR	Windows Script Host demo—creates a shortcut
shortcut.vbs	8E	SCR	Windows Script Host demo—creates a shortcut
showvar.vbs	8E	SCR	Windows Script Host demo—lists environment variables
shrpubw.exe	2HPM	GUI	Create and Share Folders Wizard
shtml.exe	2HPM	cmp	Front Page Extensions component—server-side include processor
shvlzm.exe	EHPM	GUI	Internet Spades
sigverif.exe	8E2HPM	GUI	Signature verifier for system files
sizer.exe	8E	DOS	Component of memmaker utility
skeys.exe	2HPM	cmp	SerialKey (accessibility input device) manager
slrundll.exe	HP	ndu	Component used by Smart Link modem drivers or installers
slserv.exe	HP	drv	Smart Link winmodem device driver
smartdrv.exe	8E	DOS	Disk cache driver and configuration utility
smartnav.js	2PM	cmp	Script component used by web-based .NET applications (source: .NET Framework)

(continues)

Filename	OS	Type	Description
smartnavie5.js	PM	cmp	Script component used by web-based .NET applications (source: .NET Framework)
smbdpmi.exe	E	cmp	Web Base Enterprise Management component; extracts extended BIOS data
smbinst.exe	HPM	CMD	Installs or uninstalls System Management BIOS driver (WMI interface to the system BIOS)
smi2smir.exe	HPM	CMD	SNMP MIB compiler
smlogsvc.exe	2HPM	svc	Performance Logs and Alerts service
smss.exe	2HPM	cmp	Session Manager Subsystem
smtidy.exe	8E	GUI	Start Menu cleanup tool; removes entries for missing programs (source: Plus! for Windows 98)
smtp_regtrace.exe	2	GUI	Enables diagnostic tracing for the IIS SMTP service
snchk.exe	M	cmp	Windows Media Center component
sndrec32.exe	8E2HPM	GUI	Sound Recorder
sndvol32.exe	8E2HPM	GUI	Volume Control
snmp.exe	2HPM	svc	Simple Network Monitoring Protocol Agent service
snmptrap.exe	2HPM	svc	SNMP Trap Service—Receives trap messages generated by local or remote SNMP agents and forwards the messages to SNMP management programs running on this computer
sol.exe	8E2HPM	GUI	Solitaire Game
sonicmmburnengine.exe	M	cmp	Windows Media Center Create DVD component
sort.exe	8E2HPM	CMD	Sorts text files alphabetically (filter)
sp4iis.exe	2	ndu	IIS updater, part of Service Pack 4 installer
spdwnw2k.exe	2	ndu	Service pack installation component
spdwnwxp.exe	HP	ndu	Service pack installer component
spiisupd.exe	2PM	cmp	IIS component
spnpinst.exe	HPM	ndu	Windows Peer-to-Peer service installer; likely used by SP2 installation process (source: Windows XP Service Pack 2 or download)
spool32.exe	8E	cmp	Print spooling component
spoolsv.exe	2HPM	svc	Print Spooler—Loads files to memory for later printing.
sprecovr.exe	HPM	ndu	Part of service pack setup; used to automatically clean up after a failed partial install
sprestrt.exe	2HPM	cmp	Used during install upon failure and reboot
sptsupd.exe	2	ndu	Service pack installation component; updates Terminal Services
spuninst.exe	HPM	ndu	Used to uninstall software updates/hotfixes/ services packs
spupdsvc.exe	2HPM	cmp	Software update installer service; handles post-reboot update tasks
spupdw2k.exe	2	ndu	Service pack installation component
spupdwxp.exe	HP	ndu	Windows XP Service Pack installer component
srdiag.exe	HPM	CMD	Extracts debug info on System Restore

Filename	OS	Type	Description
srw.exe	8E	ndu	Windows System Recovery Wizard, runs during system recover process
ssdpsrv.exe	E	cmp	Simple Service Discovery Protocol (SSDP) server; detects network devices like routers
sslisten.exe	8	ndu	WebTV for Windows component
ssscan.exe	8	ndu	WebTV for Windows component
start.exe	8E	CMD	Starts a Windows or command-line program given a program filename or filename with a filetype association
startftp.vbs	2P	SCR	Starts FTP server
startsrv.vbs	2P	SCR	Starts IIS server
startweb.vbs	2P	SCR	Starts web server
statemgr.exe	E	cmp	System Restore component
stimon.exe	8E2HPM	cmp	Windows Still Image Monitor
stisvc.exe	2	svc	Still Image (scanning) service component
stmgr.exe	E	cmp	System Restore component
stopftp.vbs	2P	SCR	Stop FTP server
stopsrv.vbs	2P	SCR	Stops IIS server
stopweb.vbs	2P	SCR	Stop web server
stub_fpsrvadm.exe	HP	cmp	Stub (nonfunctional) version of FrontPage Server Extensions administrator
stub_fpsrvwin.exe	HP	cmp	Stub (nonfunctional) version of FrontPage Server Extensions
subst.exe	8E2HPM	DOS	Maps a drive letter to a local folder
sucatreg.exe	8E	cmp	Windows Catalog Registration component—validates certificates for signed drivers
sulfnbk.exe	8E	CMD	Restores long filenames in directory entries if they become corrupted (see Microsoft Knowledge Base article #301316). Was the subject of a hoax; is not a virus.
svchost.exe	2HPM	svc	Runs system service contained in a .DLL file, used to run various services
swinit.exe	E	cmp	Macromedia Shockwave component
syncapp.exe	2HPM	cmp	Creates Windows Briefcase.
synciwam.vbs	2P	SCR	Repairs COM+ authentication for applications running under IWAM account
sys.com	8E	DOS	Copies MS-DOS and its boot loader to a disk drive
sysagent.exe	8E	GUI	Launches Scheduled Task manager; may have other functions
syscomponentinfo.js	HPM	SCR	Component of help center system info display
sysedit.exe	8E2HPM	GUI	Editor for system files
syshealthinfo.js	HPM	SCR	Component of help center system info display
sysinfo.exe	PM	CMD	(Installed as systeminfo.exe; see that entry)
syskey.exe	2HPM	CMD	Encrypts and secures system database

(continues)

Filename	OS	Type	Description
sysmon.exe	8E	GUI	System Monitor utility, like Performance Monitor on Windows 2000/XP
sysocmgr.exe	2HPM	cmp	Part of Windows setup
syssoftwareinfo.js	HPM	SCR	Component of help center system info display
systeminfo.exe	PM	CMD	Displays a system hardware and software summary
systray.exe	8E2HPM	GUI	Manages the taskbar and system tray
tapi16.exe	8E	cmp	Telephony interface for 16-bit applications
tapiini.exe	8E	CMD	Rebuilds the telephony configuration file telephon.ini if it's corrupted or missing (see Microsoft Knowledge Base article #120221)
tapisrv.exe	8E	cmp	Telephony services component
tapiupr.exe	8E	ndu	Telephony configuration file upgrade utility (possibly part of Windows 95 to 98 upgrade process)
taskkill.exe	PM	CMD	Terminates a process
tasklist.exe	PM	CMD	Lists active processes
taskman.exe	8E2HPM	cmp	Task manager (activated by Ctrl+Alt+Del)
taskmgr.exe	2HPM	GUI	Starts the Task Manager (same as Ctrl+Alt+Del)
taskmon.exe	8E	GUI	Task Monitor
taskswitch.exe	HPM	GUI	Alt+Tab replacement power toy (source: Powertoys for XP download)
taxonomy.js	E	cmp	Component of Windows Help center
tcmsetup.exe	8E2HPM	GUI	Manages the TAPI Telephony client
tcpsvcs.exe	2HPM	svc	Simple TCP/IP Services and TCP printing Services service
tcptest.exe	2HPM	GUI	TCP/IP network tester for diagnosing IIS problems
telnet.exe	8E2HPM	CMD	Establishes a command-line session on another computer
tftp.exe	2HPM	CMD	Trivial file transfer protocol
themes.exe	8E2	GUI	Desktop theme configuration and selection tool
timershot.exe	HPM	GUI	Webcam timer power toy (source: Powertoys for XP download)
tintlphr.exe	2HPM	cmp	Chinese Input Method editor component (source: Windows Update)
tintsetp.exe	2HPM	cmp	Chinese Input Method editor component (source: Windows Update)
tlntadmn.exe	2PM	CMD	Telnet Server Administrator
tlntsess.exe	2PM	CMD	Displays the current Telnet Sessions
tlntsvr.exe	2PM	svc	Telnet Server Service
tlocmgr.exe	8E2HPM	GUI	Telephony Location Manager, provides task-tray icon to pop-up Dialing properties and activate Phone Dialler (source: Win2000 reskit)
togac.exe	P	ndu	Unknown; appears to be involved in managing the .NET Framework Global Assembly Cache
tour.exe	HPM	GUI	Windows XP Tour (actually a copy of Macromedia Flash Player)

Filename	OS	Type	Description
tour.js	EHPM	SCR	Component of Windows tour
tour98.exe	8E	ndu	Component of Welcome to Windows 98 tour
tourstart.exe	HPM	GUI	Runs the Windows Experience Tour
tourstrt.exe	HPM	ndu	(Installed as `tourstart.exe`, see previous entry)
tourw.exe	PM	GUI	(Installed as `tour.exe`, see that entry)
tp4mon.exe	HP	cmp	PS/2 Trackpoint device manager
tracerpt.exe	PM	CMD	Gathers or summarizes event trace information
tracert.exe	8E2HPM	CMD	Checks TCP/IP connectivity
tracert6.exe	HPM	CMD	IPv6 Trace Route
tree.com	2HPM	CMD	Displays directory structure
tscon.exe	HPM	CMD	Connects to terminal services session
tscupgrd.exe	HPM	cmp	Terminal Services Client upgrade program
tsdiscon.exe	HPM	CMD	Disconnects windows/terminal services session
tskill.exe	HPM	CMD	Terminates a process in a services session
tsprof.exe	HPM	ndu	Used on Windows server only, terminal server management tool
tsshutdn.exe	HPM	CMD	Shuts down or restarts a Terminal Services server
tuneup.exe	8E	GUI	Maintenance Wizard—performs various cleanup/tuneup tasks
tvwakeup.exe	8E	ndu	Component of TV Viewer; may just be splash screen displayer
tvx.exe	8E	GUI	TV Viewer application (WebTV for Windows)
tweakui.exe	HPM	GUI	TweakUI Powertoy for Windows XP; XP version is not a control panel (source: Powertoys for XP download)
twunk_16.exe	8E2HPM	cmp	Twain 16-bit drivers
twunk_32.exe	8E2HPM	cmp	Twain 32-bit drivers
unam4ie.exe	8E	GUI	DirectShow uninstaller
uninst.exe	8E2HPM	GUI	Generic uninstaller (source: various)
uninusb.exe	E	?	Unknown; may be involved in uninstalling USB-based printers
unlodctr.exe	2HPM	CMD	Removes performance counter definitions
unregmp2.exe	2HPM	ndu	Modifies Registry during update of Windows Media Player
unsecapp.exe	8E2HPM	cmp	Web Based Enterprise Management (WBEM) component
unvise32.exe	8E2HPM	GUI	Generic uninstaller (source: various)
update.exe	HPM	ndu	Installs Windows or service pack updates
updcrl.exe	8E2	cmp	Root certificate revocation list updater (source: Windows Update)
uploadm.exe	EHPM	cmp	Upload manager for application and system crash info
upnpcont.exe	HPM	cmp	Universal Plug-and-Play (UPNP) ActiveX container
ups.exe	2HPM	svc	Uninterruptible Power Supply—Manages an uninterruptible power supply (UPS) connected to the computer

(continues)

Filename	OS	Type	Description
upwizun.exe	8E2	ndu	Update wizard file unpacking utility
user.exe	8E2HPM	cmp	Windows API (fundamental component of Windows)
userinit.exe	2HPM	cmp	Logon processor: runs scripts, makes network connections, starts shell
userstub.exe	8E	cmp	Unknown, likely a component used by Internet Explorer for compatibility with Windows 98/ME
usrlogon.cmd	HPM	CMD	Terminal Services logon script (not actually used)
usrmlnka.exe	HPM	cmp	US Robotics Modem driver component
usrprbda.exe	HPM	cmp	US Robotics Modem driver component
usrshuta.exe	HPM	cmp	US Robotics Modem driver component
utilman.exe	2HPM	GUI	Utility Manager—Designates which accessibility aids to use
uwdf.exe	M	cmp	User Mode Driver framework (Media Player component)
vbc.exe	8E2PM	CMD	.NET Visual Basic command-line compiler (source: .NET Framework)
vcmd.exe	2	cmp	Microsoft Voice COM server
vcmui.exe	8E	GUI	Version Conflict Manager, restores and manages multiple versions of files identified during installation of Windows 98
verifier.exe	2HPM	GUI	Driver Verifier Manager
vidsvr.exe	8E	ndu	Component of TV Viewer
vssadmin.exe	HPM	CMD	Displays shadow copy backups and providers
vssvc.exe	HPM	svc	Volume Shadow Copy Service
vwipxspx.exe	2PM	DOS	NetWare protocol stack, loaded in AUTOEXEC.NT
w2kexcp.exe	2	cmp	Internet Explorer update installer component (source: Windows Update)
w32tm.exe	2HPM	CMD	Manages Windows Time service
wab.exe	8E2HPM	GUI	Address Book editor
wabmig.exe	8E2HPM	cmp	Outlook Express component
walign.exe	8E	CMD	Optimizes loading speed of .DLL and .EXE files; limited version of winalign.exe resource kit tool
wangimg.exe	2	GUI	Imaging for Windows (scanner application)
wb16off.exe	E	cmp	Component of Windows Setup
wb32.exe	8E2HPM	GUI	NetMeeting Whiteboard application
wbemcntl.exe	8E	GUI	Web Based Enterprise Management (WBEM) configuration application
wbemperm.exe	8E2	GUI	WBEM permission editor
wbemstop.exe	8E	CMD	WBEM Service shutdown tool (halts WBEM/WMI)
wbemtest.exe	8E2HPM	GUI	Web Based Enterprise Management (WBEM) tester
wdfmgr.exe	M	srv	User Mode Driver Framework manager service
webptprn.exe	E	cmp	Installation component for web-based printing (source: \add-ons\ipp)
webuivalidation.js	2HPM	cmp	Component of ASP.NET client-side validation control (source: .NET Framework)

Filename	OS	Type	Description
welcome.exe	8E2	GUI	Getting Started with Windows welcome wizard
weldata.exe	8	ndu	Holds data for Welcome to Windows 98 tour
wextract.exe	2HPM	cmp	CAB auto-extractor used by iexpress.exe
wiaacmgr.exe	EHPM	GUI	Scanner and Camera Wizard
win.com	8E2HPM	cmp	Provided so that applications that expect to find or run Windows via win.com will work
winchat.exe	2HPM	GUI	Windows Chat
wincool.exe	E	ndu	Pop-up reminder to watch Windows tour after installation; also the name of a (very helpful) third-party tool that lets the CPU run cooler
windows xp media center edition screen saver.scr	M	SCR	Windows XP Media Center Edition
winfile.exe	8E	GUI	File Manager application from Windows 3.1
winhelp.exe	8E2HPM	GUI	Windows Help (.HLP file) viewer
winhlp32.exe	8E2HPM	GUI	Windows Help application
winhstb.exe	2HPM	ndu	Windows Help component
wininit.exe	8E	ndu	Component of Windows startup process
winipcfg.exe	8E	GUI	Displays IP address information for all network adapters, can be used to repair (release and renew) DHCP leases
winlogon.exe	2HPM	cmp	Logon manager
winmgmt.exe	8E2HPM	svc	Web Based Enterprise Management (WBEM) service
winmine.exe	8E2HPM	GUI	Minesweeper game
winmsd.exe	2HPM	GUI	Windows Diagnostic utility; displays system information
winpopup.exe	8E	GUI	Windows Messenger service utility (not the online chat service, but the NetBIOS peer-to-peer service)
winrep.exe	8E2	GUI	Windows Report Tool; prompts for bug reporting information and creates a .CAB file of the entered text and important sytem config files
winspool.exe	2HPM	cmp	Print spooler system
winver.exe	8E2HPM	GUI	Displays the current version of Windows
wjview.exe	8E2	CMD	Command-line loader for Java
wltmime.exe	8E	ndu	Microsoft Wallet component
wltunins.exe	8E	GUI	Microsoft Wallet uninstaller
wmi_data.js	HPM	SCR	Component of help center system info display
wmiadap.exe	HPM	cmp	WMI component, autodiscovery/autopurge process
wmiapsrv.exe	HPM	svc	WMI Performance Adapter—Provides performance library information from WMI HiPerf providers.
wmic.exe	PM	CMD	Queries and manages Windows XP via Windows Management Instrumentation
wmiexe.exe	8E	svc	Windows Management Instrumentation (WMI) service
wmimofck.exe	8E	CMD	Validates correctness of WMI MOF binary files

(continues)

Filename	OS	Type	Description
wmiprvse.exe	HPM	cmp	WMI component, provider host process
wmlaunch.exe	M	cmp	Windows Media Player launcher
wmpenc.exe	M	cmp	Windows Media Player encoder component
wmplayer.exe	EHPM	GUI	Windows Media Player
wmploc.js	EHPM	SCR	Component of Windows tour
wmpocm.exe	2	ndu	Installs or removes Windows Media Player icons and Start menu entries (ocm stands for "optional component manager")
wmpstub.exe	HP	cmp	Component of Windows Media Player
wordpad.exe	8E2HPM	GUI	Wordpad accessory
wowdeb.exe	2HPM	cmp	Windows 3.1 environment component; debugging API
wowexec.exe	2HPM	cmp	Windows 3.1 emulation environment
wpabaln.exe	HPM	GUI	Windows Product Activation balloon reminder
wpnpinst.exe	E2HPM	cmp	Support for Internet Printing Protocol (IPP) printing (source: \add-ons\ipp)
wpwiz.exe	8E	GUI	Web Publishing Wizard—copies files and folders to a web server with FTP or FrontPage Extensions
wrapperparam.js	HPM	SCR	Component of help center
write.exe	8E2HPM	GUI	Launches WordPad (supplied for compatibility with older versions of Windows)
wsasrv.exe	8E	cmp	Windows Sockets Asynchronous Request Server (networking component)
wscntfy.exe	HPM	ndu	Pop-up those "you are at risk" warnings on the task tray; run by the security center service (source: Windows XP SP2)
wscript.exe	8E2HPM	GUI	Windows Script Host—Windowed version
wuauboot.exe	E	ndu	Automatic Updates component
wuauclt.exe	E2HPM	cmp	Windows Update automatic check/download task
wuauclt1.exe	HPM	ndu	Windows Update Automatic Update component
wucrtupd.exe	8E	GUI	Windows Update Critical Update notification service (source: Windows Update)
wuloader.exe	8E	cmp	Windows Update Critical Update notification service component
wupdmgr.exe	8E2HPM	GUI	Windows Update (launches Internet Explorer)
wzcsetup.exe	2	ndu	Installs Wireless Zero Configuration service, part of Service Pack 4 installer
xcopy.exe	8E2HPM	CMD	Copies multiple files
xcopy32.exe	8E	CMD	Console mode program to copy multiple files. This 32-bit version is faster than DOS xcopy as it has access to more memory and 32-bit disk drivers.
xmsmmgr.exe	E	cmp	Component of Windows Setup
xpsp1hfm.exe	HPM	ndu	Part of service pack installer, determines which SP components are necessary
zclientm.exe	EHPM	cmp	Internet games component

Built-In Commands

Built-in commands are handled directly by the command-line interpreter, which is `cmd.exe` on Windows 2000 and Windows XP, and `command.com` under DOS, Windows 98 and Windows Me. There is no corresponding executable file.

Command	OS	Description
assoc	2HPM	Associates filename extensions with file type
call	8E2HPM	Calls a batch file subroutine
cd	8E2HPM	Changes current working directory; same as chdir
chdir	8E2HPM	Changes current working directory; same as cd
color	2HPM	Changes command prompt window color
del	8E2HPM	Deletes files; same as delete and erase
delete	8E2HPM	Deletes files; same as del and erase
dir	8E2HPM	Displays file directory
echo	8E2HPM	Displays text
endlocal	2HPM	Restores environment variables
erase	8E2HPM	Deletes files; same as del and delete
exit	8E2HPM	Ends program or subroutine, or terminates command-line interpreter.
for	8E2HPM	Repeats command
ftype	2HPM	Associates file types to applications
goto	8E2HPM	Performs "go to label" in a batch file
if	8E2HPM	Executes command conditionally
lh	8E2HPM	Loads an MS-DOS TSR program into high memory; same as loadhigh
loadhigh	8E2HPM	Loads an MS-DOS TSR program into high memory; same as lh
md	8E2HPM	Create directory; same as mkdir
mkdir	8E2HPM	Create directory; same as md
move	8E2HPM	Moves files or folders
path	8E2HPM	Sets command search path
pause	8E2HPM	Stops batch file for user interaction
popd	2HPM	Restores current directory
prompt	8E2HPM	Sets command-line prompt
pushd	2HPM	Saves current directory
rd	8E2HPM	Removes directory; same as rmdir
rem	8E2HPM	Denotes remark or comment text
rename	8E2HPM	Renames files or folders
rmdir	8E2HPM	Removes directory, same as rd
set	8E2HPM	Sets environment variables
setlocal	2HPM	Saves current environment
shift	8E2HPM	Deletes and moves command-line arguments
start	8E2HPM	Runs a command or opens a document in a new window
time	8E2HPM	Displays and sets time of day

Command	OS	Description
`title`	2HPM	Sets window title
`type`	8E2HPM	Copies text file to console window
`verify`	8E2HPM	Controls automatic verify-after-write

Control Panel Applets

Control Panel applets are run by the Control Panel program `control.exe`. For information on running control panels applets from the command line, see heading "Control" on page 410.

Filename	OS	Description
`access.cpl`	8E2HPM	Accessibility Options
`appwiz.cpl`	8E2HPM	Add/Remove Programs
`bthprops.cpl`	HPM	Bluetooth Properties (source: Windows XP SP2)
`cttune.cpl`	HPM	ClearType Tuning (source: Powertoys for XP download)
`desk.cpl`	8E2HPM	Display Properties
`fax.cpl`	2	Fax Properties
`firewall.cpl`	HPM	Windows Firewall (source: Windows XP SP2)
`hdwwiz.cpl`	2HPM	Add Hardware Wizard
`inetcpl.cpl`	8E2HPM	Internet Properties
`intl.cpl`	8E2HPM	Regional and Language Options
`irprops.cpl`	2HPM	Wireless Link (IRDA infrared)
`joy.cpl`	8E2HPM	Game Controllers
`main.cpl`	8E2HPM	Mouse, Keyboard, PC Card Properties
`mlcfg32.cpl`	8E	Windows Messaging profile manager (source: TOOLS\OLDWIN95 Windows Messaging & Fax)
`mmsys.cpl`	8E2HPM	Sounds and Audio Devices
`modem.cpl`	8E	Modem Properties
`msmq.cpl`	2	Microsoft Message Queuing Service
`mwcpa32.cpl`	2	IBM Thinkpad modem configuration
`ncpa.cpl`	2HPM	Network Connections
`netcpl.cpl`	8E	Network configuration
`netsetup.cpl`	HPM	Network Setup Wizard (source: Windows XP SP2)
`nusrmgr.cpl`	HPM	User Accounts
`nwc.cpl`	2PM	Client Services for NetWare
`odbccp32.cpl`	8E2HPM	ODBC Data Source Administrator
`password.cpl`	8E	Change Passwords/Remote Administration/User Profiles
`powercfg.cpl`	8E2HPM	Power Options
`sapi.cpl`	HPM	Speech Properties
`sticpl.cpl`	8E2	Scanners and Cameras
`sysdm.cpl`	8E2HPM	System Properties
`telephon.cpl`	8E2HPM	Phone and Modem Options
`themes.cpl`	8E	Desktop themes

Filename	OS	Description
timedate.cpl	8E2HPM	Date and Time Properties
tweakui.cpl	8E2	Tweak UI (source: Powertoys for Windows NT download)
wgpocpl.cpl	8E	Workgroup Postoffice Admin (source: TOOLS\OLDWIN95 Windows Messaging & Fax)
wscui.cpl	HPM	Security Center (source: Windows XP SP2)
wuaucpl.cpl	E2HPM	Automatic Updates (Service Pack 2 or Windows Update)

MMC Management Snap-Ins

MMC Snap-ins are run by the Microsoft Management Control program mmc.exe.

Filename	OS	Description
certmgr.msc	8E2HPM	Certificate Manager
ciadv.msc	2HPM	Indexing Service Management
comexp.msc	2HPM	Component Services (COM/DCOM/COM+) Configuration
compmgmt.msc	2HPM	Computer Management
devmgmt.msc	2HPM	Device Manager
dfrg.msc	2HPM	Disk Defragmenter
diskmgmt.msc	2HPM	Disk Management
eventvwr.msc	2HPM	Event Viewer
faxserv.msc	2	Fax Management
fpmmc.msc	2P	Server Extensions Administrator
fsmgmt.msc	2HPM	Shared Folders
gpedit.msc	2PM	Group Policy
ias.msc	2	Internet Authentication Service
iis.msc	2P	Internet Information Services Administration
lusrmgr.msc	2HPM	Local Users and Groups
mscorcfg.msc	8E2PM	.NET Framework Configuration; manages and installs NET applications, configures .NET security policy (source: .NET Framework)
msinfo32.msc	2	System Information
ntmsmgr.msc	2HPM	Removable Storage
ntmsoprq.msc	2HPM	Removable Storage Operator Requests
perfmon.msc	2HPM	Performance panel: System Monitor and Performance Logs and Alerts
rsop.msc	PM	Resultant Set of Policy
secpol.msc	2PM	Local Security Policy
services.msc	2HPM	Services
tscmmc.msc		Terminal Services Connections Manager
wmimgmt.msc	2HPM	WMI Configuration

Screensavers

Screensavers are run by Windows when the system has been idle for a designated time, or from the Display Properties Control Panel when selecting and configuring a screensaver.

Filename	OS	Description
3d flower box.scr	8E	3D Flower Box (same as ssflwbox.scr)
3d flying objects.scr	8E	3D Flying Objects (same as ss3dfo.scr)
3d maze.scr	8E	3D Maze (same as ssmaze.scr)
3d pipes.scr	8E	3D Pipes (same as sspipes.scr)
3d text.scr	8E	3D Text (same as sstext3d.scr)
architecture.scr	8	Architecture theme (source: Plus! for Windows 98)
baseball.scr	8E	Baseball theme
blank screen.scr	8E	Blank screen (same as scrnsave.scr)
cathy.scr	8	Cathy cartoon (source: Plus! for Windows 98)
channel screen saver.scr	8E2	Channel (same as actsaver.scr)
cityscape.scr	8	Cityscape theme (source: Plus! for Windows 98)
corbis photography (high color).scr	8	Corbis Photography (source: Plus! for Windows 98)
curves and colors.scr	8E	Beziers (same as bezier.scr)
dangerous creatures.scr	8E	Dangerous Creatures theme
davinci.scr	E	Leonardo da Vinci
doonesbury.scr	8	Doonesbury cartoon (source: Plus! for Windows 98)
falling leaves (high color).scr	8	Falling Leaves (source: Plus! for Windows 98)
fashion (high color).scr	8	Fashion theme (source: Plus! for Windows 98)
flying through space.scr	8E	Starfield (same as ssstars.scr)
flying windows.scr	8E	Flying Windows
foxtrot.scr	8	Foxtrot cartoon (source: Plus! for Windows 98)
garfield.scr	8	Garfield cartoon (source: Plus! for Windows 98)
geometry (high color).scr	8	Geometry (source: Plus! for Windows 98)
horror channel (high color).scr	8	Horror theme (source: Plus! for Windows 98)
inside your computer.scr	8E	Inside Your Computer
jazz.scr	8	Jazz theme (source: Plus! for Windows 98)
jungle.scr	8E	Jungle theme
leonardo da vinci.scr	8E	Leonardo da Vinci
logon.scr	2HPM	Windows
my pictures screen saver.scr	E	My Pictures (same as ssmypics.scr)
mypixdx.scr	M	My Pictures Slideshow (Media Center version)
mystery.scr	8E	Mystery theme
mystify your mind.scr	8E	Mystify Your Mind (ssmyst.scr)

Filename	OS	Description
nature.scr	8EM	Nature theme
organic art (plus! 98).scr	8	Organic Art (source: Plus! for Windows 98)
peanuts.scr	8	Peanuts cartoon (source: Plus! for Windows 98)
photodisc (high color).scr	8	Photodisc (source: Plus! for Windows 98)
rock-n-roll (high color).scr	8	Rock and Roll theme (source: Plus! for Windows 98)
science fiction (high color).scr	8	Science Fiction theme (source: Plus! for Windows 98)
science.scr	8E	Science theme
scrnsave.scr	2HPM	Blank screen
scrolling marquee.scr	8E	Marquee (same as ssmarque.scr)
space.scr	8EM	Space theme
sports.scr	8E	Sports theme
ss3dfo.scr	2HPM	3D Flying Objects
ssbezier.scr	2HPM	Beziers
ssflwbox.scr	2HPM	3D Flower Box
ssmarque.scr	2HPM	Marquee
ssmaze.scr	2	3D Maze
ssmypics.scr	HPM	My Pictures Slideshow
ssmyst.scr	2HPM	Mystify
sspipes.scr	2HPM	3D Pipes
ssstars.scr	2HPM	Starfield
sstext3d.scr	2HPM	3D Text
the 60's usa.scr	8E	The 60s theme
the golden era.scr	8E	The Golden Era theme
travel.scr	8E	Travel theme
underwater.scr	8E	Underwater theme
windows 98 (high color).scr	8	Windows 98 (source: Plus! for Windows 98)
windows 98.scr	8	Windows 98
windows.scr	E	Windows ME
world traveler (high color).scr	8	World Traveler theme (source: Plus! for Windows 98)
wpgldfsh.scr	M	Goldfish

INDEX

SYMBOLS

$, 314

NUMBERS

A

F

G - H

How can we make this index more useful? Email us at indexes@quepublishing.com

N - O

Q - R

How can we make this index more useful? Email us at indexes@quepublishing.com

W - X - Y - Z

winmgmt, 157

winnt.exe, 66-69

Winnt.sif, 80-82

WinOldAP system emulation, 373

wireless networks. *See also* networks

    cost of, 293

    defining, 294

    hotspots, allowing, 294

    joining existing networks, 297-298

    Networking Setup Wizard, 299-301

    security risks, 293-294

    setting-up, 294-297

WmcCds, 157

WmdmPmSN, 157

WMI, 157

workgroups

    overview, 165

    selecting during installation, 57

    Setup Manager Wizard encrypted passwords, 79

Write an Event to the System Log option, 246

Write Debugging Information option, 247

wscsvc, 158

WSUS, 116

wuauserv, 158

WZCSVC, 158

xmlprov, 158